Sylvère Lotringer

Notes on the Schizo-Culture Issue

Despite their shared title, the Schizo-Culture issue is *not* the same as the Schizo-Culture conference. The issue was put together three years after the conference, in a very different context with different intentions and with different material. It only included four lectures from the conference—those by Jean-François Lyotard, John Cage, François Péraldi, and William S. Burroughs. "The Book," as we will call it here, doesn't recount the shock encounter that took place between French and American philosophers and artists at "the Event," but instead consummated the magazine's rupture with academe. It also took Semiotext(e) one step closer to the New York art world at an exciting and innovative time. No one could have anticipated that in just five years it would mutate into an art market, and then into an art industry. It was more than anyone had bargained for.

The shift towards art was made easier by the fact that most of the editorial committee had dispersed during my absence. Semiotext(e) hadn't stopped publishing for all that. In fact, three more issues were released over the following three years: "Georges Bataille," edited by Denis Hollier in 1976, which introduced the sulfurous writer and thinker to America; "Anti-Oedipus," which I edited myself, and "Nietzsche's Return," edited by James Leigh in 1977. This latter issue was meant to reestablish the philosopher's credibility on this side of the Atlantic, preparing the ground for the post-1968 theorists. These three issues still belonged to the academy; they only tried to loosen up its grip from the inside.

The Schizo-Culture issue was already moving in another direction, and was meant to perform several tasks at once. First, follow up on the main issues raised by the New York conference: prison and psychiatry, and the way they overlap. Second, establish the affinity between recent French philosophy and contemporary art in America. Third, turn the magazine itself towards art.

semiotext(e)

announces a special issue on:

GEORGES BATAILLE

Denis HOLLIER, Présentation ? Vol.II,2: $3.00

*

Georges BATAILLE, Hemingway in the Light of Hegel

Georges BATAILLE, La Vénus de Lespugne (inédit)

*

Jacques DERRIDA, From Restricted to General Economy

*

Ann Smock & Phyllis Zuckerman, Politics and Eroticism in Le Bleu du Ciel

Charles Larmore, Bataille's Heterology

Peter Kussel, From the Anus to the Eye to the Mouth

Lee Hildreth, Bibliography

*

On the Schizo-Culture Colloquium

COMING ISSUES: SCHIZOANALYSIS, Spring '76 (G. Deleuze:"Three Group Problems"; Deleuze/Guattari:"One or Several Wolves"; J. Donzelot: "An Antisociology"; F. Guattari:"Everybody Wants To Be A Fascist"; J.-F. Lyotard:"Energumen Capitalism", etc. Nietzsche, Fall '76. MAURICE BLANCHOT. SCHIZO-CULTURE. SYMBOL/SIGN. S & M. C.S. PEIRCE.

- -

SEMIOTEXT(E) 522 Philosophy Hall, Columbia University, N.Y.C. 10027

Please enter my subscription as indicated below:

Name ....

Address ....

City ....State ....Zip Code ....

Subscription rates (please check)

1 volume (3 issues): Individual $7.00.... Institutions $12.00....

2 volumes(6 issues): Individual $12.00... Institutions $20.00....

Single Issues ($2.50): I,1: Alternatives in Semiotics; I,2: The Two Saussures:...; I,3: Ego Traps; II,1: Saussure's Anagrams:....

Announcement of the "George Bataille" issue,1976.

From mail received by Semiotext(e) after the Schizo-Culture conference.

SEMIOTEXT(E) FOREIGN AGENTS SERIES

Published by Semiotext(e)
PO BOX 629, South Pasadena, CA 91031
www.semiotexte.com

All images in the introduction courtesy of the Fales Library & Special Collections, NYU.

Special thanks to John Ebert, Andrew Kersey, Marc Lowenthal and David Morris.

ISBN: 978-1-58435-124-5
10 9 8 7 6 5 4 3 2

Distributed by The MIT Press, Cambridge, Mass. and London, England
Printed in China

on sale now:

semiotext(e)

VOLUME III Number 2

Kathy Acker □ Lee Breuer □ William Burroughs
John Cage □ David Cooper □ Gilles Deleuze
Douglas Dunn □ Richard Foreman □ Michel Foucault
John Giorno □ Phil Glass □ Christopher Knowles
Jean-François Lyotard □ Ulrike Meinhof
Jack Smith □ Robert Wilson

$4.50

semiotext(e)
522 Philosophy Hall
Columbia University
New York, N.Y. 10027

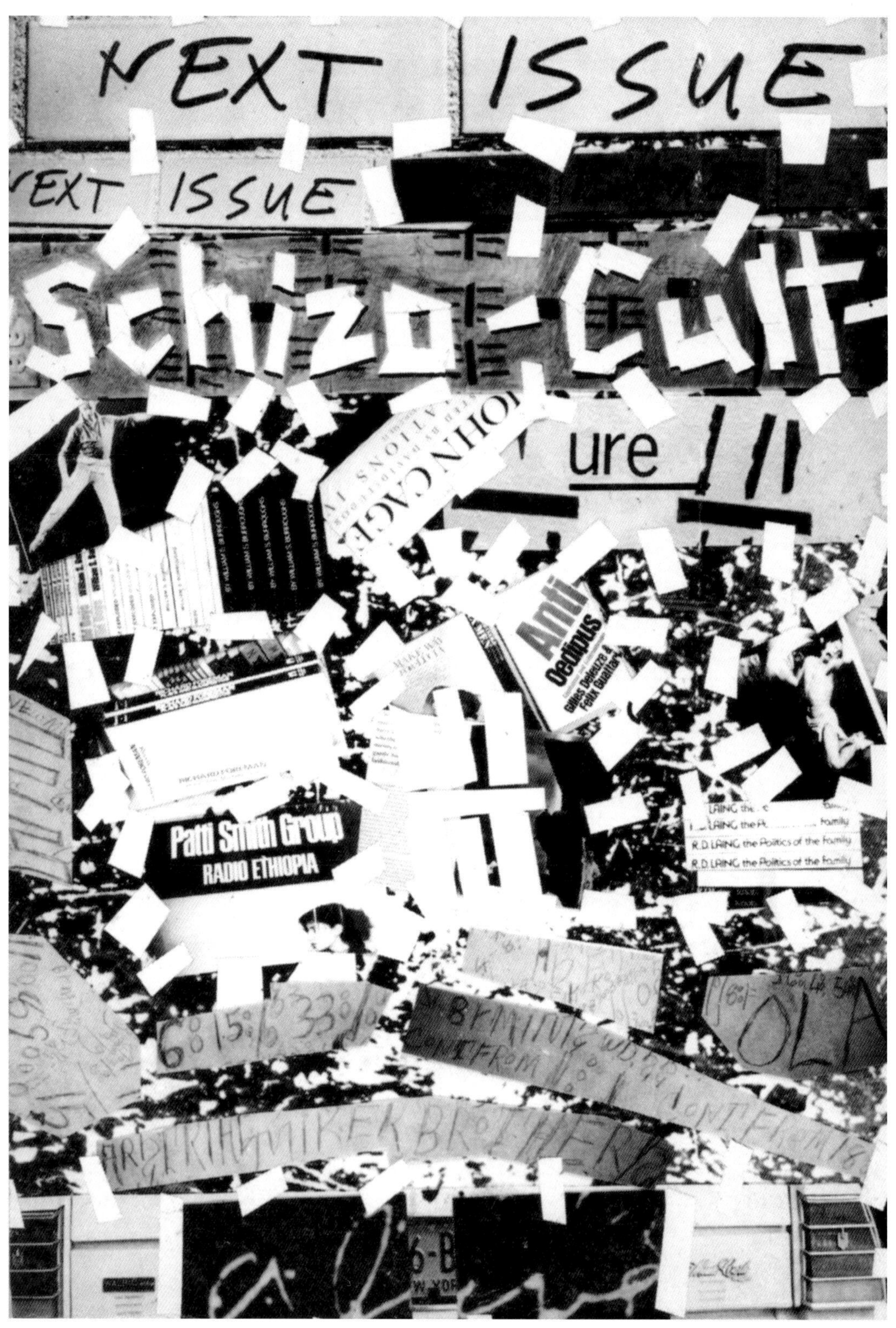

Announcement for *Schizo-Culture* Issue, 1977. Image by Diego Cortez, photo by Jimmy De Sana.

ALORS ARRIVA
UN ÉTRANGER...
SUR SES JEANS
NIETZSCHE'S
RETURN

Collage by Sylvère Lotringer for the "Nietzsche's Return" cover, 1978.

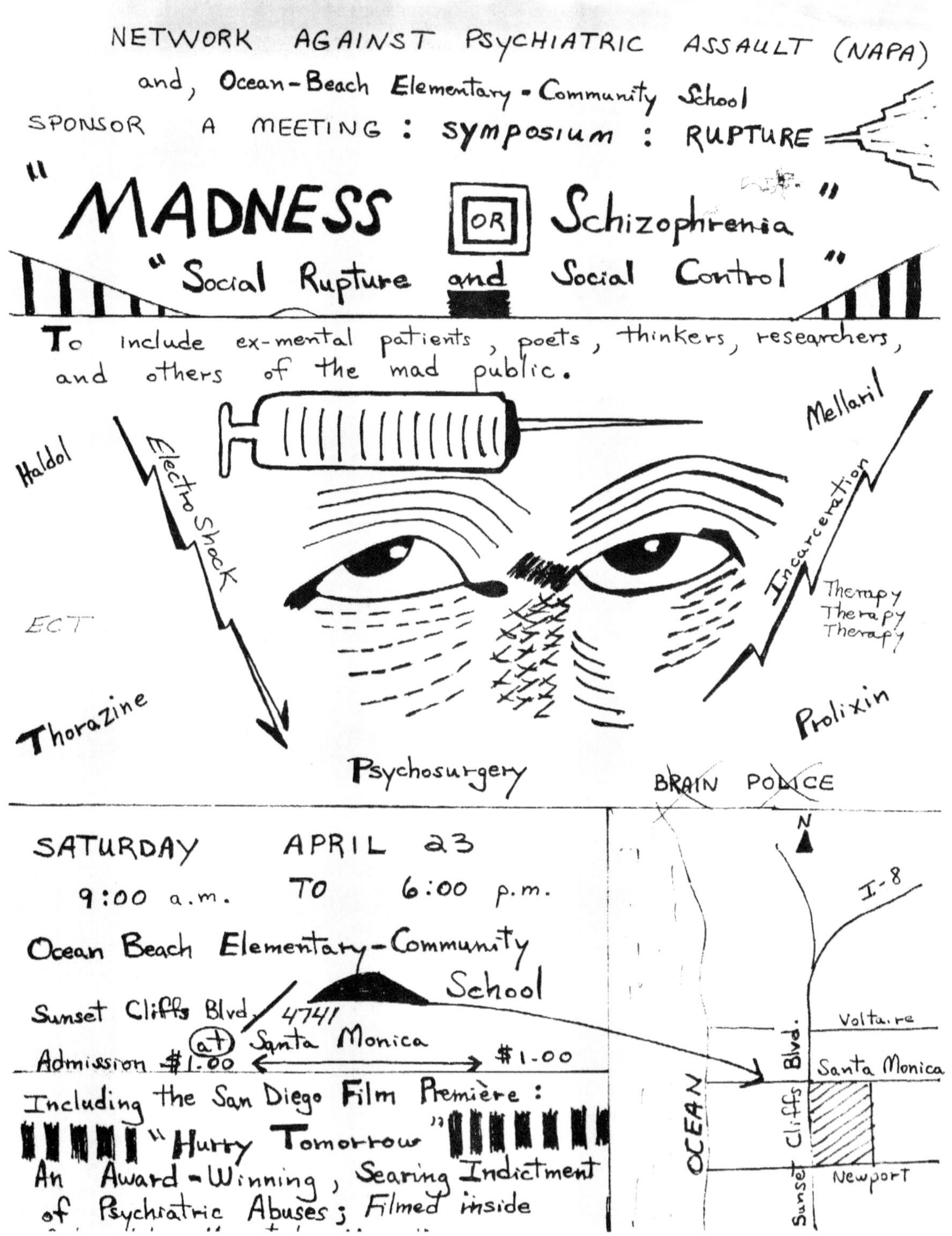

NETWORK AGAINST PSYCHIATRIC ASSAULT (NAPA)
and, Ocean-Beach Elementary - Community School
SPONSOR A MEETING : symposium : RUPTURE
"MADNESS OR Schizophrenia"
"Social Rupture and Social Control"
To include ex-mental patients, poets, thinkers, researchers, and others of the mad public.
Haldol
Electro Shock
Mellaril
Incarceration
ECT
Therapy
Therapy
Therapy
Thorazine
Prolixin
Psychosurgery
BRAIN POLICE
SATURDAY APRIL 23
9:00 a.m. TO 6:00 p.m.
Ocean Beach Elementary-Community School
Sunset Cliffs Blvd. 4741
(at) Santa Monica
Admission $1.00 $1.00
Including the San Diego Film Première :
"Hurry Tomorrow"
An Award-Winning, Searing Indictment of Psychiatric Abuses; Filmed inside
N
I-8
Voltaire
Santa Monica
OCEAN
Sunset Cliffs Blvd.
Newport

From mail received by Semiotext(e) after the Schizo-Culture conference.

The issue of prison and psychiatry, so vigorously debated at the time, didn't come to any resolution. Anti-psychiatrists advocated the closure of mental asylums and the creation of open therapeutic communities, but they were always running the risk of becoming mini-asylums themselves. Others recommended desegregating mental illness and setting up alternative cooperatives treating simultaneously everyone who was in need of help: ex-junkies, ex-prisoners, etc. An Alternatives to Psychiatry Network—inspired by Franco Basaglia, R. D. Laing, and David Cooper and created in 1975—advocated for this, but the closure of asylums became a moot point after drugs were developed that were capable of controlling the mentally ill. It happened for economical reasons, not therapeutic ones, and thousands of patients were forced into the streets, swelling the ranks of the homeless. Various anti-psychiatric organizations do, however, remain active in such places as Trieste, Rio, and at La Borde in France, for instance.[1] Institutional therapy keeps experimenting with the reverse strategy, exposing society to the creativity of madness, but pursuing its work in under more marginalized conditions. The increasing use of behavioral therapies in the prison system called as well for specific responses from within and from outside, but the huge increase in the prisoner population and the privatization of prisons in the United States didn't allow for significant improvement. Cynicism and carelessness prevailed.

Although the issues of incarceration and madness overlap, they aren't exactly on an equal footing. Both prisons and psychiatry are meant to normalize and repress "dangerosity," but madness also presents inventive features that may become paradigmatic in our society. This is what Deleuze and Guattari suggested when they distinguished between institutionalized madness, which turns the patient into an institutional object, and deterritorialized "schizophrenia" experienced as a creative "line of flight." "We are trying," they said, "to extract from madness the life which it contains."[2] The schizophrenic, as they define it, keeps oscillating between two extreme forms of intensity, illumination and terror, breakthrough and breakdown. The escape from all constraints goes together with a loss of all protections. Following Elias Canetti, who cast paranoia in political terms, Deleuze and Guattari's main contribution was to tie down these extreme oscillations

1. Among them the Accademia della Follia (Academy of Madness), the Trieste Psychiatric Hospital's theater company; Carmen Roll, a former member of the German Socialist Patients' Collective; and the Freaked on the Scene Theatre of the Oppressed, Rio de Janeiro.
2. Gilles Deleuze and Claire Parnet, *Dialogues*, trans. Hugh Tomlinson and Barbara Habberjam, New York, Columbia University Press, (1977) 1987, p. 53.

experienced by the "schizo" to the deterritorializing movement of capital. Capitalism isn't just repressive or exploitative, it is also reckless and inventive—up to a point. This positive impact of deterritorialization on the culture, the experimental madness of capital, is what the Schizo-Culture issue attempted to bring out.

The lyrical drawings by Christopher Knowles that open and close the issue left no doubt: "Just to be mad. Just to be mad. São Paolo," Knowles exclaimed. But the invocation is also an injunction: "It would be mad, be mad, be mad, be mad." Madness could open up a different kind of perception of time and space in which art plays a role.

In "The Eye of Power," the formidable interview that opens the issue, Foucault reflected on the arrangement of space in the nineteenth century, architecture as a form of political organization, presenting Bentham's Panopticon as the ultimate "diabolical machine," since no one controls it and everyone is caught in it: everyone is at once "those who exercise the power as well as those who are subjected to it." The Panopticon was "an event in the history of the human mind" because it invited those whom it subjugated to collaborate actively on the exercise of this power through identification and internalization, using total visibility acting as a form of deterrence.

In "Of Other Spaces: Utopias and Heterotopia,"[3] Foucault introduced the idea of spaces, mythical or real, different from those in which we live, that are capable of "creating an illusion which denounces the rest of reality as an illusion." Prisons are such a heterotopia, imposed from the outside, but so too is theater or dance or a concert, where people freely subject themselves to singular experiences in which the codes usually enforced by society are tested or scrambled in a creative way. They were the kind of counter-space or counter-time that I looked for when I started working on the Schizo-Culture issue. I wasn't especially prepared for these encounters, having no prior experience of contemporary art in America, but I had been exposed to enough French philosophy to be able to conceive of their existence. It seemed to me that they were working in parallel on both sides of the Atlantic, and all it would take would be a way of connecting them. What prompted me to look for it was being exposed to New York, a city that escaped the usual temporality, a space that had its own rules and required some kind of initiation. I realized that

3. Michel Foucault, "Of Other Spaces: Utopias and Heterotopia," in *Rethinking Architecture: A Reader in Cultural Theory*. Edited by Neil Leach. NYC: Routledge. 1997

what I was looking for in art would involve in some way the experience of living in New York.

It is this idea that prompted me to get in touch with SoHo artists, hoping to establish an indirect dialogue between them and their French counterparts. It wasn't necessarily easy, as I realized the first time I met artists in New York. They certainly didn't speak the same language and some of them would take mine personally. Contrary to what happened in the 1980s, when artists would totally embrace French concepts and terminologies, as if they had some kind of magic power attached to them and could somehow enhance their careers, most artists whom I got to know in the mid-1970s, starting with William Burroughs, were very distrustful of "intellectual" language, which didn't mean, of course, that they were not intellectuals in their own right. But this was precisely what I was trying to understand. How did they manage to get there without relying on language? But for this I had to talk to them, or rather, listen to them, silently reprocessing in my mind what they were saying about their art.

At the time, dance and music, driven by the work of John Cage and Merce Cunningham, were the most influential of the arts in New York, and the most deterritorialized, too, in cultural terms. Using chance operations, both artists kept checking their personal inventiveness in order to tap another kind of energy that came from the actual material of the form. Releasing dance and music from cause and effect, they were able to resist the seduction of narrative, which always imposes an order of progression and a climax. Cunningham also organized space in a non-hierarchical way, so that other movements could be staged simultaneously.

Their dance and their music were only abstract in the sense that they were nonrepresentative and derived rhythm or movement from the music or the dance themselves. To make this break even more radical, they remained independent of each other, as well as of the decors commissioned from Duchamp or Rauschenberg. In terms of "schizophrenia," as we were using the term, Cage and Cunningham were the ones who made the real breakthrough and reshuffled all the cards—indeed, changed the entire nature of the game.

But at the same time, their spatial arrangement participated in the randomness and energy of the city and incorporated the everyday movements and abrupt changes of direction that could be found in the streets of New York. All these heterogeneous elements presented side by side gave, as Cunningham put it, "a different idea about how people can coexist together."

BACK ISSUES AVAILABLE

FORTHCOMING ISSUES

SCHIZO-CULTURE
Special Editor: Sylvère Lotringer
POLYSEXUALITY
Special Editor: François Peraldi
PIER PAOLO PASOLINI
Special Editor: B. Allen Levine
CINEMA-MACHINE
Special Editor: Alan Williams

Robert Wilson
interview

Violence
to the Brain

The Hard Machine

Bernard-Henry Levy **[no accents in Futura]**

The
"Argentine Model"

Kathy Acker
The Persian Poems

Andre Cadere

Boy with Stick

Pat Steir

Marie Overlie

interview

Marcel Duchamp
Musical Sculpture

Phil Glass

interview

interview

Douglas Dunn

interview

interview

Draft page layout for Schizo-Culture issue.

Most of the artists I interviewed over the years—Robert Wilson and Douglas Dunn, Phil Glass, Marie Overlie and Jack Smith, Lee Breuer and Steve Reich, Kathy Acker and Richard Foreman, Arto Lindsay and Laurie Anderson, etc.—participated in this early breakthrough, and this is what made the period such an inventive one. Like Duchamp, and with him, they opened a new area where theater could do without language, and concepts without referent.

Robert Wilson's ballet-like theater followed that of Cage and Cunningham and carried their breakthrough even further, creating a universe of its own built on a similar disregard for psychology and meaning. His performances displayed a similar effort to break up unity and displace the center, using a visual language that was more architectural than theatrical. The stage was made of independent blocks that moved simultaneously, each at its own speed, and each moment was experienced in its singularity since it wasn't integrated into any sequence. Neither repeatable nor memorable in their discontinuity, they were just there to be watched, like so many objects occupying the same space for reasons unknown. "I didn't have to bother about plot or meaning," Wilson said, "I could just look at designs and patterns—that seemed enough. There is a dancer here, another dancer there, another four on this side ..." It was "visual music," a way of thinking through a discreet arrangement of time and space in which words themselves were constructed musically.

The same held true for Philip Glass's music, freed from what he called the "colloquial time system," which always implies some kind of narrative and a set of expectations: conflict, drama, resolution. There is no history, no dialectics, no representations, and no images. The music is more mechanistic than anthropomorphic and identification is discouraged because it would have precluded any other perception, any extended experience of time. As soon as the listener relinquishes this colloquial time matrix, he finds himself in a different world where he can experience emotions that have nothing individual about them, but come from the material itself.

This was the kind of experience I also had when watching an early structuralist film by Michael Snow, *La Région centrale* (1971), shot by a robotic camera rotating 360 degrees and constantly changing direction. Past the wall of boredom, past the expectation for *something* to happen, the listener can suddenly experience strange machinic effusions, untimely epiphanies detached from any narration. And then *the reverse* would happen. It was the colloquial time that became unbearable. As soon as listeners stepped out of the psychological mechanism, Philip Glass said, "then we were in a wholly different world. The fact is that at a certain point a very large group of people felt that we no longer could, or rather—that there wasn't any point in working that way. It was simply boring." Curiously enough, other musicians working in different places also experienced these kinds of shifts, as if something in their perception had cracked and another kind of perceptual mechanism had been set in motion. This was also true for dancers like Douglas Dunn, a disciple of Merce Cunningham, as soon as he dropped any predetermined idea about his dance and concentrated on the movement as an object, as "the image being produced."

What characterized the SoHo art world was that many artists working in different media, especially visual artists, would experience and share this kind of perceptual shift. It was as if they were all part of a sudden change of paradigm, like switching one mindset for another *and looking at it while it was happening.* This is what Antonin Artaud already experienced in the early 1920s, watching his own mind work and making sure that it really was his own. He refused to consider this "flight of ideas" a personal pathology, but saw it as part of the *air du temps*, a diffused collective experience. The SoHo artists all belonged to the same "episteme" and were all affected by a deterritorialization of their senses that offered perceptions until then inconceivable. They all participated in varying degrees in the same urban delirium.

Deleuze called an "image of thought" the kind of representation that can be internalized and then universalized, like the gaze of the Panopticon: the image of the state in its dungeon. And he envisaged the possibility of producing just the reverse: a "thought without images," a mindset that resists any identification. In *Difference and Repetition*, he wrote that "the problem is not to oppose a dogmatic image of thought to another image, borrowed for instance from schizophrenia. Rather remember that schizophrenia isn't just a human fact, that it is a possibility of thought which is revealed as such in the abolition of the image." It is this *pensée du dehors*, this thought from the outside that can be used as a counter-space, as a heterotopia. It could be carved out of space, but also created out of time. It could be a heterochronia as well, where time is made to stand still and history ceases to exist. At this point, Philip Glass could use Berlioz, or Mozart, or any piece of harmony that was lying around but, as he put it, "the thing that makes the perception of it so radical is not the stylistic features of the work. What we're really talking about is a point of view."

It made me wonder whether French theory itself hadn't registered this momentous kind of event in its own concepts, the advent of a nonlinear, nondramatic, noncentered kind of perception reaching "not the point where one no longer says I, but the point where it is no longer of any importance whether one says I."[4] And there's no doubt that the shift of the French philosophers from Hegel to Nietzsche, from pyramid to rhizome, was an event in the world of thought, and in the realm of politics. It was the end of dialectics, which always predicates apparent contradictions on their way to a higher truth. May 1968 was the end of all father figures, of the communist party and the leadership of the proletariat, of the belief in linear history, of the coming revolution—all the great narratives.

It was language itself that was put into question. Syntax rules by keeping reality at a distance and ordering its representation. No wonder Mallarmé, who invented the literary avant-garde all on his own, was known as a "syntaxier," a syntax worker. He was mad about language and never toed the line, but kept turning it into music, into painting. He was an enemy insider and courted psychosis. No wonder John Cage, in "Empty Words," called syntax "arrangement of the army (Norman Brown)" and tried to free language from it: "Language free of syntax: demilitarization of language. James Joyce—new words; old syntax." At the Schizo-Culture conference, Cage made music with the language he devised through I Ching operations, just by reading it out loud, constantly breathing, changing frequencies. "Equation between letters and silence. Making language saying nothing at all" and letting the noise outside come in through the window. In "Postulates of Linguistics," Deleuze and Guattari wrote: "Language is not life, it gives life orders."[5] Language is command, linearity is order. A sentence is a Judgment. Roland Barthes even said once, famously, that language is fascistic. Antonin Artaud shrieked: "Writing is pigshit" The script prevails over the stage. Language imposes its form on reality. In "Fuck the Talkies," Jean-Jacques Abrahams, known for introducing a tape recorder to the couch, accused the talkies of robbing us of our lives. Silent film unified humanity, he said, while the talkie imposed the soundtrack over the visual, and the "struggle of all against everyone." There's always some political truth to delirium.

There are many ways to counter the power of language, of dialogue, and dialectics. One can deconstruct it (Derrida), fragment it (Wolfson), overextend

4. Gilles Deleuze and Félix Guattari, *A Thousand Plateaus*, *op. cit.*, p.3.
5. Gilles Deleuze and Félix Guattari, *op. cit.*, p. 176.

VOLUME II, N°3, 1976 $3.50

semiotexte

ANTI-OEDIPUS

From Psychoanalysis to Schizopolitics

Sylvère LOTRINGER, Capitalism and Schizophrenia
Jean-François LYOTARD, Energumen Capitalism
Jacques DONZELOT, An Anti-Sociology
John RAJCHMAN, Analysis in Power
Antonin ARTAUD, The Body is the Body
To Have Done with the Judgment of God
Félix GUATTARI, Mary Barnes' Trip
Freudo-Marxism; Psychoanalysis and
Psychoanalysis and Schizoanalysis
Everybody Wants To Be a Fascist
Gilles DELEUZE, Three Group Problems
I Have Nothing To Admit
DELEUZE/GUATTARI, Balance Sheet-Program for Desiring Machines
May 14, 1914. One or Several Wolves
Guy HOCQUENGHEM, Family, Capitalism, Anus
DYER/BRINKLEY, Returns Home
Sylvère LOTRINGER, The Fiction of Analysis

SEMIOTEXT(E), 522 Philosophy Hall, Columbia University, New York, N.Y. 10027

Name: ______

Address ______

1 vol. (3 issues) $ 7.50 ______ 2 vol. (6 issues) $13.00 ______
Institutions (1 vol) $18.00 ______

Announcement of the "Anti-Oedipus" issue, 1977.

it (Mallarmé), empty it (Cage), and more generally use it in a nonlinguistic way (Artaud, Burroughs, Wilson). One can stay outside of language and its logic (Deleuze and Guattari) or struggle against it from the inside. This is the shift in thought that Lyotard made during the Event, parallel to the strategy adopted by the Nietzscheans who willed the flows of capital to turn, but against themselves. Contrary to his French colleagues, though, Lyotard decided to bring back the struggle with language and mastery within language itself. "There is a ruse to that discourse," he said, "which consists precisely in requiring that we place ourselves outside of it in order to avoid it. The device is very simple: it consists in making exteriority the necessary complement of that discourse … When one externalizes oneself in order to avoid the magisterial discourse, one is just extending that position, nourishing it." No wonder Deleuze, Guattari, and Foucault would have considered Lyotard's abrupt change a regression and turned on their heels when offered to engage in a dialogue. Lyotard was asking them to approach their dissension dialectically. They refused.

French theorists didn't know much about New York art. Paris had lost its artistic preeminence in the early 1960s after the French "New Realists" confronted the American pre-Pops—Jasper Johns, Andy Warhol, Roy Lichtenstein, Claes Oldenburg, etc.—at the Sidney Janis gallery in New York in 1962, and lost. The death of Yves Klein the following year sealed their fate. The Nouveaux Réalistes abandoned ship and moved en masse to New York. When I grew up in France, there was nothing around that could stimulate the appreciation of visual arts, music, dance, and what they could tell us about contemporary society. The cinématheque—Jean-Luc Godard—was the exception. Most French theorists, whenever they turned to art, would go to classical painting, keeping a text by Freud in hand. Baudrillard and Foucault, when they went out of their way, would refer to pop art and hyperrealism. They had no exposure to minimalism or postminimalism, let alone conceptual art. It wasn't only the Situationists who opposed visual arts in France; in those days, socialist realism was taken seriously because the Communist Party and the Soviet Union stood behind it. I should know: I freelanced for ten years for *Les Lettres françaises*, Louis Aragon's newspaper. Aragon was a member of the Central Committee of the French CP. Dialectical materialism and class struggle remained untouchable up to the very end. Then both collapsed, suddenly.

New York artists didn't need French theory to realize that language and syntax had no right to marshal the arts, so it wasn't at this level that some real connection could be established between them, as I was trying to do. They both evolved their respective heterotopia and experimented with their own perceptions independently, at least until the mid-1980s, when French theory penetrated *en force* into the new art world. The Schizo-Culture conference was a shortcut to the art world and it certainly helped ignite the French connection. In France, theory replaced art—became art—for some twenty years and infiltrated American culture through the arts rather than through academe. Deconstruction had such a huge impact on the American academy because it sent academics back to the text. It was no surprise that Semiotext(e) lost some of its audience after the publication of the Schizo-Culture issue: as soon as we introduced visuals that weren't merely illustrative of the text, but had to be read in resonance with it, academic readers, who are not trained to think visually, were nonplussed.

We had been trying to get to this point in different ways.

First, the semiotic entry. Ferdinand de Saussure made general linguistics a model for all the other semiotic systems because language is the "interpretant" of all the other, nonverbal, systems of signs. Our little group was looking for other, less reductive, alternatives. Saussure had left the door slightly ajar. He recognized that linguistics should eventually become a part of semiotics, and not the reverse. But structuralism slammed the door and subjected all the human sciences to the language-based science of signs. Our first project had been to dig into Saussure's own backyard and bring out his "madness," repressed by his own linguistic achievements. For years Saussure pursued this obsessive research on anagrams, looking for a secret code that was passed on from poet to poet throughout the centuries, but failed. I studied these unpublished manuscripts in Geneva and we published our research in two separate issues, "The Two Saussures" and "Saussure's Anagrams," both in 1974. What we had attempted to do during this period, I realized later on, was prepare ourselves for the SoHo art world and for our intellectual exit from the university. But it took an accident, the Schizo-Culture conference, to get us there.

Second, *entrée des artistes*. The Schizo-Culture issue wasn't just the transcription of the conference, but represented where we stood three years later. Most of the new team members were young and freshly arrived in New York, coming from San Francisco, Chicago, Portugal, South Africa, and Australia, so they were hardly representative of America. They were New York City.

The first artist who came looking for me at Columbia a few months after the conference was Diego Cortez, a freelance curator of sorts. He acted as a scout for the new scene in the East Village and in Lower East Side. He was involved with punk rock and graffiti and was an agent for Michel Basquiat. He co-founded the Mudd Club, which opened in 1978 and introduced New Wave/No Wave music, and he became my "mentor" in relation to downtown culture. I eventually shared a raw industrial loft with him for five years on the Fashion district starting in 1977, and this meant, among other things, unlimited access to the thriving nightlife scene. All these ferments had a strong impact on the issue we were working on.

Martim Avillez assumed a similar role for the older SoHo scene, which was fairly small at the time. I met him through the South American network. He arrived in New York in 1972 and graduated from the Cooper Union. He was an illustrator working for the New York Times and contributed some wonderful cartoons about Nietzsche's sister for the "Nietzsche's Return" issue. From 1982 to 1984, I shared his beautiful loft in Front Street, by the Fulton Fish Market. Martim was a more private kind of artist and his paintings in the loft were always turned against the wall. Like Diego, he had real talent, but he was too sensitive to expose his own work and dealt instead with art at a third remove. Diego could tell what good art was and Martim, who was more of an intellectual, would criticize his fellow artists' work, and evaluate the last intellectual trends. Later on he founded an excellent bilingual magazine called *Lusitania*.

It wasn't Martim who introduced me to the SoHo artists, but Pat Steir, a conceptual painter and printmaker closer to my own generation. When I met her, she was working as a book designer and was painting canvases of roses in the margins of conceptual artists' work. Later on, with the same delicate humor, she would throw pails of paint down a surface, turning minimalist grids and abstract expressionist drips into lyrical Chinese waterfalls. She had been Sol LeWitt's partner for a long time and was a close friend to everyone I would have wanted to know in SoHo: Philip Glass, Richard Serra, Steve Reich, etc. It was through her that I met most of the artists I interviewed for the Schizo-Culture issue.[6] These interviews served a number of functions. They were a way of establishing a contact, creating material that we could use for the issue, but also they were also a way of bringing together French theorists and their artistic counterparts on the other side of the Atlantic. Pat had a raw loft right in Chinatown and we often held our meetings there, posting all our layouts for the issue on the walls. It was also there, when she lost her loft, that we graffitied

6. These, and other interviews, were published in *New Yorker Gespräche*, Berlin, Merve Verlag.

SEMIOTEXT(E)
a magazine of schizo-culture

&

THE FRENCH AND ITALIAN DEPARTMENT OF NYU

present

CINE VIRUS

EVERYONE WANTS TO BE INFECTED/EVERYONE WANTS TO BE INFECTIOUS. *Cine Virus* programs cinema as a soft-machine of control bringing into proximity different strains of the disease. The virus is the pleasure and contamination: the infection.

TOWERS OPEN FIRE	Antony Balch 28 min B/W 1963
CUT UPS	Antony Balch 11 min B/W 1963
CAR CRASH	Eric Mitchell 3 min Color 1978
SET-UP	Kathryn Bigelow 17 min Color 1978
GOIA MELLER LONDON	Seth Tillett 6 min Color 1978
CIRCUITS OF CONTROL: I/LAND	Michael Oblowitz 40 min Color 1978
SNAKE WOMAN	Tina Lhotshy 15 min B/W 1978
GORDON ALIEN	Michael McClard 9 min B/W 1978
THE END OF THE FILM WORLD	Amos Poe 12 min Color
DEVO: THE MONGOLOID	Bruce Conners 10 min Color 1978
BLOOD AND GUTS IN HIGHSCHOOL	Kathy Acker 15 min Live 1978
BURROUGHS	Mark Olmsted 5 min Color
BURROUGHS: HOME MOVIES	Steven Lowe 10 min Color

Programmed by Kathryn Bigelow and Michael Oblowitz

Schimmel Auditorium,
Tisch Hall, N.Y.U,
7-10 PM, $2.

Flyer for the Cine Virus film screenings, 1978.

"Schizo-Culture" with spray cans for the cover. In the end, it was my graffiti that the group chose to use because it was the most awkward. Pat Steir was part of the committee of *Heresies*, the feminist journal, the only magazine I felt close to at the time. Denise Green, a conceptual painter from Perth, Australia, arrived in New York in 1969. She collaborated with me for some of the interviews we published in the issue. Both Denise Green and Pat Steir joined the editorial committee.

Painting was considered an endangered species in the late 1970s and most of the young artists' energy was being invested in film and photography, which became an art in its own right in the late '80s. The second group of people whom I met, Kathryn Bigelow and Michael Oblowicz, were young filmmakers interested in French theory. They were graduate students at the film department at Columbia and mostly used it to procure film equipment for free. The other reason they had come looking for me was that Christian Metz, the French semiotician of cinema, had unexpectedly converted to Lacanian psychoanalysis. I was the only one who taught Jacques Lacan, so they took my classes and I in turn took film classes with them for two years. We worked together on a number of projects: *The Set-Up* (1978) with Kathryn Bigelow, a deconstructivist film where I pretended to be a semiotician, and *Too Sensitive to Touch* (1981) a montage film about sex in America I made with Michael Oblowicz. Kathryn came from San Francisco and Michael from Cape Town, South Africa and they were already involved with the downtown scene. So the new Semiotext(e) team from the start was bridging the uptown/downtown gap which existed at the time.

The new art team resulted from a series of encounters and not from a deliberate choice, people I met in clubs, parties or downtown events and found interesting. They had come from different places and didn't share the same ideas about art. All they had in common was that they had been trained as artists. But it happened to be the right fit for an issue on schizophrenia, which couldn't be unified, but fragmented and disparate, and this is what the issue ended up being. The artists split into smaller groups and each group designed a part of the magazine independently from the others. We had accumulated material that circulated in the media, newspapers, specialized magazines (S/M was just then coming out), and from different places, the stock exchange, psychiatric magazines, medical iconography, German terrorism, prison photos, consumer images, punk paraphilia, anthropological documents, porn novels, comic strips, graffiti, surveillance cameras. Some documents were faked, some ads simulated. The various groups could draw from these different materials and distribute them through the issue, like the flows of capital. Yet not everything was random. Actually, the overall matrix was rather strict, but supple and open-ended. We started from the popular idea of schizophrenia as split personality, so each page was split into two vertical columns, usually clearly contrasted, a thinner column in bold and a larger one in lighter type, and their respective order would be reversed in the spreads. The two columns could also be equal in size and nearly identical in type, so that readers could go on reading a different text unknowingly, experiencing some kind of experimental delirium. The idea was that, like a rhizome, it is impossible to understand anything about schizophrenia if one doesn't participate in it in some way. Texts and visuals could correspond to each other, but also stand far enough apart so that readers would have to make a leap to grasp the link. The interview with the conceptual artist André Cadere undermining art institutions would be presented side by side with a manifesto by Ulrike Meinhof; a photo of lovers kissing juxtaposed with the peaceful face of an electroshocked patient.

When the issue was still at the printer, Kathryn Bigelow showed an advanced copy to Richard Serra, whom she was interning for at the time, and the artist's reaction was negative. A meeting was called immediately and everyone showed up very upset and angry. They had done all this work for months, and all for naught. Their reaction was understandable, but it was also unsettling. We had invested so much energy and fun working together on this project that I believed we would all stand behind it whatever the response would be. I suddenly realized that, however disparate as a group, they all belonged to the art world and that this was still too much. All it took was the judgment of another artist, however eminent. I just told them that I was actually pleased with our work and I would take it if they didn't want it.

The tension didn't last, fortunately. One week later we heard that Richard Serra actually loved the issue and had only reacted negatively because he wasn't in it. Everybody felt relieved and eager to start working right away on the next issue. But this had been a warning. We got a bit too close to the art world and should keep some distance. We kept working together, but in different compositions, as Deleuze would say. I asked Diego to design the "Italian/Autonomia" issue; Kathryn Bigelow and Denise Green worked for two years with psychoanalyst François Peraldi on the "Polysexuality" issue, etc. The rule was that we

THE NOVA CONVENTION

New York

November 30th, December 1st & 2nd, 1978

I am primarily concerned with the question of survival — with Nova conspiracies, Nova criminals, and Nova police. A new mythology is possible in the Space Age, where we will again have heroes and villains, as regards intentions towards this Planet. I feel that the future of writing is in Space, not Time —

William S. Burroughs

Photo: Tina Freeman

THURSDAY, November 30th

FILMS CINE VIRUS

Shimmel Auditorium, Tisch Hall, N.Y.U., 7 - 10 PM, $2.

CIRCUITS OF CONTROL
TOWERS OPEN FIRE
THE CUT-UPS
and others

PERFORMANCE

Westbeth Theater Center, 151 Bank Street, 8:00 PM, $5.
November 30th to December 16th

LE PLAN K

NO WAVE CONCERT

Ukranian Ballroom, 140 Second Avenue (at 9th Street), 9 PM, $4.

Groups & special guests to be announced.

EXHIBITION OPENING

for "The Third Mind" by William Burroughs and Brion Gysin, Viking Press, artwork by Burroughs/Gysin, Books & Co., 939 Madison Avenue, December 1st to 14th.

FRIDAY, December 1st

LECTURES & PANEL

Shimmel Auditorium, Tisch Hall, N.Y.U., 40 West 4th Street, 4 - 7 PM.

Gerard-George Lemaire, Philippe Mikriammos, Maurice Girodius, Christian Bourgois, John Calder, Marion Boyars, Christian Prigent, Serge Grunberg, Udo Berger, and many others.

PERFORMANCES

Entermedia Theater, 2nd Avenue (at 12th Street), 8:30 PM, $6.

Allen Ginsberg
Merce Cunningham &
John Cage
Ed Sanders
Anne Waldman
Don Sanders
(BBC Project/Theater Institute, from *Naked Lunch*)

SATURDAY, December 2nd

CONVERSATIONS

Entermedia Theater, 2nd Avenue (at 12th Street), 1-4pm $2.00

Susan Sontag
Timothy Leary
Les Levine
Robert Anton Wilson
and others

PERFORMANCES 8:30pm $6.00

William S. Burroughs
Keith Richards
Patti Smith
Philip Glass
Brion Gysin
John Giorno

A GIORNO POETRY SYSTEMS PRESENTATION
Produced By John Giorno, James Grauerholz & Sylvere Lotringer
in association with the Entermedia Theater, the Department of French & Italian of New York University and *Semiotext(e)*.

ENTERMEDIA THEATER, 189 Second Avenue (at 12th Street), N.Y.C., 10003
Advance sale at Box Office 212-475-4191 Group Sales 212-533-5715 Chargit 212-239-7177

Poster for The Nova Convention, 1978.

would start each issue from scratch, and that included the people that would be in charge.

By a strange coincidence, the Schizo-Culture issue was released the same week that the Nova Convention was held in downtown New York, a three-day extravaganza (November 30–December 2, 1978) in homage to William Burroughs. The entire American artistic avant-garde participated—Allen Ginsberg and Patti Smith, Timothy Leary and John Cage, Laurie Anderson and Merce Cunningham, Philip Glass and Brion Gysin, etc.—either performing at the Entermedia Theater or reading at NYU. The idea of such a convention came to me as an extension of Schizo-Culture, but with James Grauerholz, Burroughs's secretary, and Beat poet John Giorno jumping on board, the convention took off on its own.

Semiotext(e) participated directly with Cine Virus film screenings organized by Kathryn Bigelow and Michael Oblowitz. It included Bruce Connor's *Devo: The Mangoloid*, Kathy Acker's *Blood and Guts in High School*, Amos Poe's *The End of the Film World*, Kathy Bigelow's *The Set-up*, Eric Mitchell's *Car Crash* and Michael Oblowitz's *Circuits of Control*. We also threw the Nova concert at Irving Plaza, near W. 14th street, a dangerous area at the time. It had never been used for a concert before and we had to rent the PA system. I maxed out my two credit cards and I patrolled the block for two nights straight with Allan Schwab, a student of mine who helped with the concert, to make sure no one would steal it. The show started at midnight and included the B-52s, Blondie, Robert Fripp, Frank Zappa, and the Stimulators, a group Allen Ginsberg recommended at the last moment. Even Sid Vicious was there and we shook hands. For the concert we specially flew out the B-52s, who weren't known yet, from Georgia, and they got a contract in New York during this trip. The concert was one of the ten best in New York that year. All I was hoping, though, was that we would get some money to pay for the Schizo-Culture issue, but all we managed to do was break even.

This wasn't all. Around 3 a.m., the Stimulators asked for their money, which had been safely moved uptown to Columbia. They got violent and in the scuffle they broke the arm of one of my students, who called the police. The Stimulators ended up in jail, and I was woken up early in the morning by Allen Ginsberg, who wanted his friends released. It was the last "counterculture meeting," as Foucault would have said, and this time it would have been true.

As for the Schizo-Culture issue, it came out right on time and sold 3,000 copies in three weeks.

CULTRE

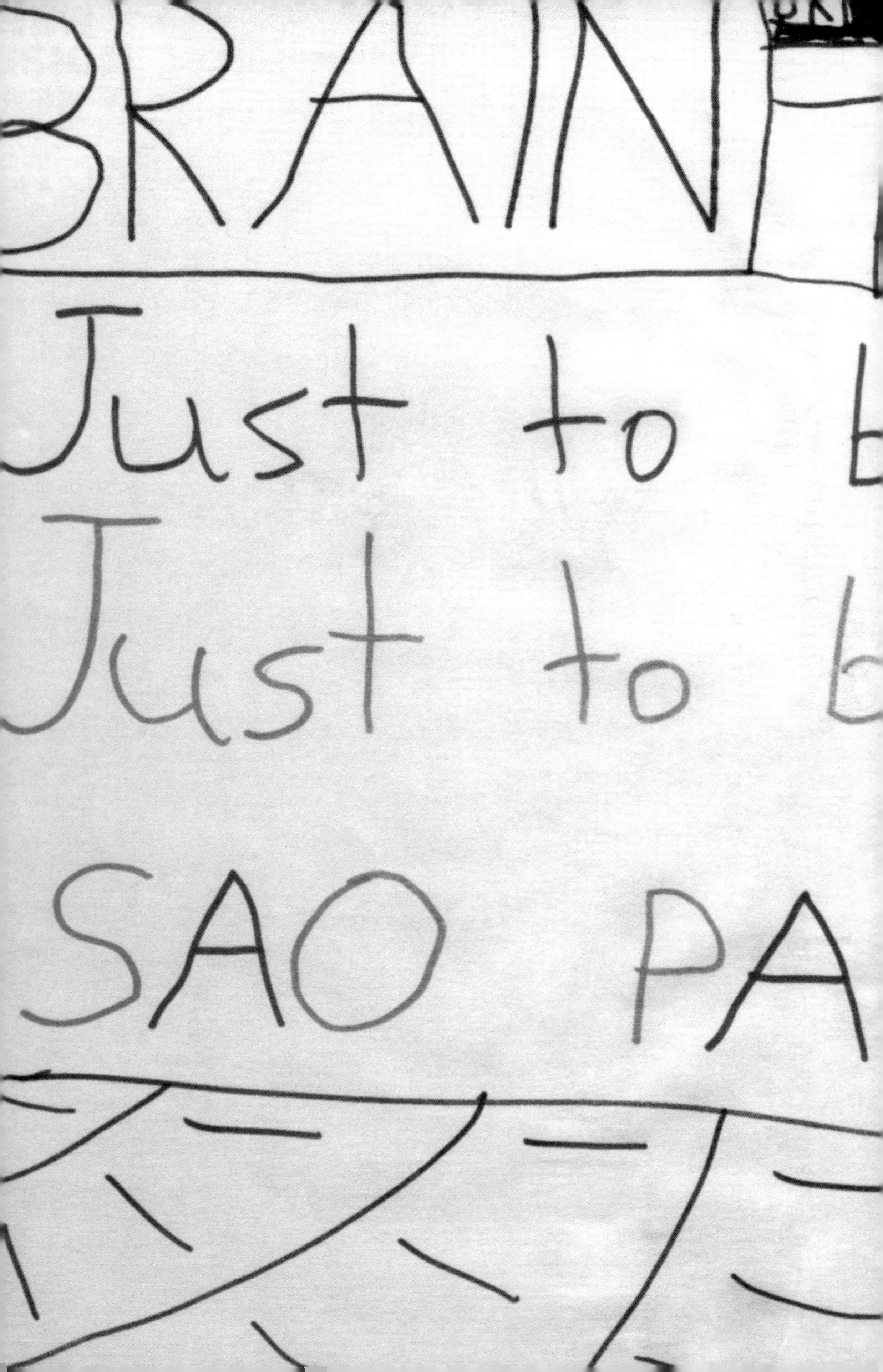
BRAIN
Just to b
Just to b
SAO PA

RAIN

B

B

B

B

e mad.

e mad.

LO

semiotext(e)

522 Philosophy Hall
Columbia University
New York, N.Y. 10027
(212) 280-3956

BENEFACTORS
Gerard Bucher, Kathleen Duda, Mia Lotringer, David Neiger, John Rajchman, Pamela Tytell. Contributions of $50.00 or more are listed as *Benefactors* and $25.00 as *Sponsors*. All contributions are tax-deductible.

SUBSCRIPTIONS
Individuals: $7.50 per volume; Institutions: $18.00. Three issues comprise one volume. Add $2.00 per volume for surface mail outside the U.S. and Canada. Checks should be made payable to Semiotext(e), Inc. *Exclusively* use International Money Orders if outside the U.S.

Semiotext(e) is a self-supporting, non profit journal. It is indexed in *MLA Bibliography* and *French XX Bibliography*.

 1978 ISSN. 0093-95779

SCHIZO-
CULTURE

Michel Foucault, *The Eye of Power* 6
Robert Wilson, *Interview* 20
François Péraldi, *A Schizo and the Institution* 20
Guy Hocquenghem, *We All Can't Die in Bed* 28
The Ramones, *Teenage Lobotomy* 32
The Boston Declaration on Psychiatric Oppression 34
William Burroughs, *The Limits of Control* 38
Louis Wolfson, *Full Stop for an Infernal Planet* 44
Lee Breuer, *Media Rex* 48
Eddie Griffin, *Breaking Men's Minds* 48
Wendy Clark, *Love Tapes* 60
Police Band, *Antidisestablishment Totalitarianism* 64
Elie C. Messinger, *Violence to the Brain* 66
David Cooper, *The Invention of Non-Psychiatry* 66
Martine Barrat, *Vicki* 74
John Giorno, *Grasping at Emptiness* 82
The Hard Machine 96
Alphonso F. Lingis, *Savages* 96
Bernard-Henri Lévy, *The "Argentine Model"* 108
Kathy Acker, *The Persian Poems* 116
Richard Foreman, *14 Things I Tell Myself* 124
Seth Neta, *To-Ana-No-Ye* **(Anorexia Nervosa)** 133
Andre Cadere, *Boy with a Stick* 140
Ulrike Meinhof, *Armed Anti-Imperialist Struggle* 140
Gilles Deleuze, *Politics* 154
John Cage, *Emptywords* 165
Pat Steir 175
Jean-Jacques Abrahams, *Fuck the Talkies* 178
Phil Glass, *Interview* 178
Jack Smith, *Uncle Fishook and the Sacred Baby Poo-poo of Art* 192
Jean François Lyotard, *On the Strength of the Weak* 204
Douglas Dunn, *Interview* 204

Back Issues/Forthcoming 220
Credits for Visuals 221

Michel Foucault

The Eye of Power

Jean-Pierre Barou: *Jeremy Bentham's* Panopticon, *a work published at the end of the 18th century that has remained largely unknown, nevertheless inspired you to term it "an event in the history of the human mind", "a revolutionary discovery in the order of politics". And you described Bentham, an English jurist, as "the Fourrier of a police society".*[1] *This is all very mysterious for us, but as for you, how did you encounter the* Panopticon*?*
Michel Foucault: It was while studying the origins of clinical medicine. I was considering a study on hospital architecture in the second half of the 18th century, at the time of the major reform of medical institutions. I wanted to know how medical observation, the observing gaze of the clinician *(le regard médical)*, became institutionalized; how it was effectively inscribed within social space; how the new hospital structure was at one and the same time the effect of a new type of perception (*regard*) and its support. And I came to realize, while examining the different architectural projects that resulted from the second fire at the Hotel-Dieu in 1772, to what extent the problem of the total visibility of bodies, of individuals and of things, before a centralized eyesight *(regard)*, had been one of the most constant guiding principles. In the case of hospitals, this problem raised yet another difficulty: one had to avoid contacts, contagions, proximities and overcrowding at the same time as insuring proper ventilation and the circulation of air: the problem was to divide space and leave it open, in order to insure a form of surveillance at once global and individualizing, while carefully separating the individuals under surveillance. For quite some time I believed these problems to be particular to 18th century medicine and its beliefs.

Later, while studying the problems of penal law, I became aware that all the major projects for the reorganization of prisons (projects that date, incidentally, from slightly later, from the first half of the 19th century) took up the same theme, but almost always in reference to Jeremy Bentham. There were few texts or projects concerning prisons where Bentham's "device", the "panopticon", did not appear.

The principle resorted to is a simple one: on the periphery runs a building in the shape of a ring; in the center of the ring stands a tower pierced by large windows that face the inside wall of the ring; the outer building is divided into cells, each of which has two windows: one corresponding to the tower's windows, facing into the cell; the other, facing outside, thereby enabling light to traverse the entire cell. One then needs only to place a guard in the central tower, and to lock into each cell a mad, sick or condemned person, a worker or a pupil. Owing to the back-lighting effect, one can thus make out the small captive silhouettes in the cells. In summary, the principle of the dark cell is reversed: bright light and the guard's observing gaze are found to impound better than the shadows which in fact protected.

One is already struck by the fact that the same concern existed well before Bentham. It seems that one of the first models of this form of isolating visibility was instituted in the Military Academy of Paris in 1751, with respect to the dormitories. Each of the pupils was to have a windowed cell where he could be seen all night long without any possible contact with his fellow-students or even the domestic help. In addition there was a very complicated mechanism whose sole purpose was to enable the barber to comb each of the residents without touching him physically: the pupil's head extended from a kind of skylight with the body on the other side of the glass partition, allowing a clear view of the entire process. Bentham told how it was his brother who first had the idea of the panopticon while visiting the Military Academy. The theme was, in any case, clearly in the air at this time. Claude-Nicolas Ledoux's constructions, most notably the salt-mine he had organized at Arc-et-Senans, tended to employ the same visibility effect, but with one important addition, namely, that there be a central point that would serve as the seat of the exercise of power as well as the place for recording observations and gaining knowledge. While the idea of the panopticon preceded Bentham, it was nevertheless he who actually formulated it. The very word *panopticon* can be considered crucial, for it designates a comprehensive principle. Bentham's conception was therefore more than a mere architectural figure meant to resolve a specific problem such as that raised by prisons or schools or hospitals. Bentham himself proclaims the panopticon to be a "revolutionary discovery". It was therefore Bentham who proposed a solution to the problem faced by doctors, penologists, industrialists and educators: he discovered the technology of power necessary to resolve problems of surveillance. It is important to note that Bentham considered his optical procedure to be *the* major innovation for the easy, effective exercise of power. As a matter of fact, this innovation has been utilized widely since the end of the 18th century. But the procedures of power resorted to in modern societies are far more numerous and diverse and rich. It would be false to state that the principle of visibility has dominated the whole technology of power since the 19th century.

Michelle Perrot: *What might be said, incidentally, about architecture as a mode of political organization? For everything is spatial, not only mentally but also materially, in this form of 18th century thought.*

Foucault: In my opinion architecture, at the end of the 18th century, begins to concern itself closely with problems of population, health and urbanism. Before that time, the art of constructing responded firstly to the need to make power, divinity and force manifest. The palace and the church constituted the two major architectural forms, to which we must add fortresses. One manifested one's might, one manifested the sovereign, one manifested God. Architecture developed for a long while according to these requirements. Now, at the end of the 18th century, new problems are posed: the arrangement of space is to be utilized for political and economic ends.

A specific form of architecture arises during this period. Philippe Ariès has written some very important things on the subject of the home which, according to him, remains an undifferentiated space until the 18th century. There are rooms that can be used interchangeably for sleeping, eating or receiving guests. Then, little by little, space becomes specified and functional. A perfect illustration can be found in the development of working-class housing projects in the years 1830–1870. The working family will be situated; a type of morality will be prescribed for it by assigning it a living space (a room serving as kitchen and dining room), the parents' bedroom (the place of procreation), and the children's bedroom. Sometimes, in the most favorable of situations, there will be a boy's room and a girl's room. A whole "history of spaces" could be written, that would at the same time be a "history of the forms of power," from the major strategies of geopolitics to the tactics of housing, institutional architecture, classroom or hospital organization, by way of all the political and economic implantations. It is surprising how long it took for the problem of spaces to be viewed as an historical and political problem. For a long time space was either referred to "nature"—to what was given, the first determining factor—or to "physical geography"; it was referred to a kind of "prehistoric" layer. Or it was conceived as dwellings or the growth of a people, a culture, a language or a State. In short, space was analyzed either as the *ground* on which people lived or the area in which they existed; all that mattered were *foundations* and *frontiers*. The work of the historians Marc Bloch and Fernand Braudel was required in order to develop a history of rural and maritime spaces. This work must be expanded, and we must cease to think that space merely predetermines a particular history which in return reorganizes it through its own sedimentation. Spatial arrangements are also political and economic forms to be studied in detail.

I will mention only one of the reasons why a certain negligence regarding

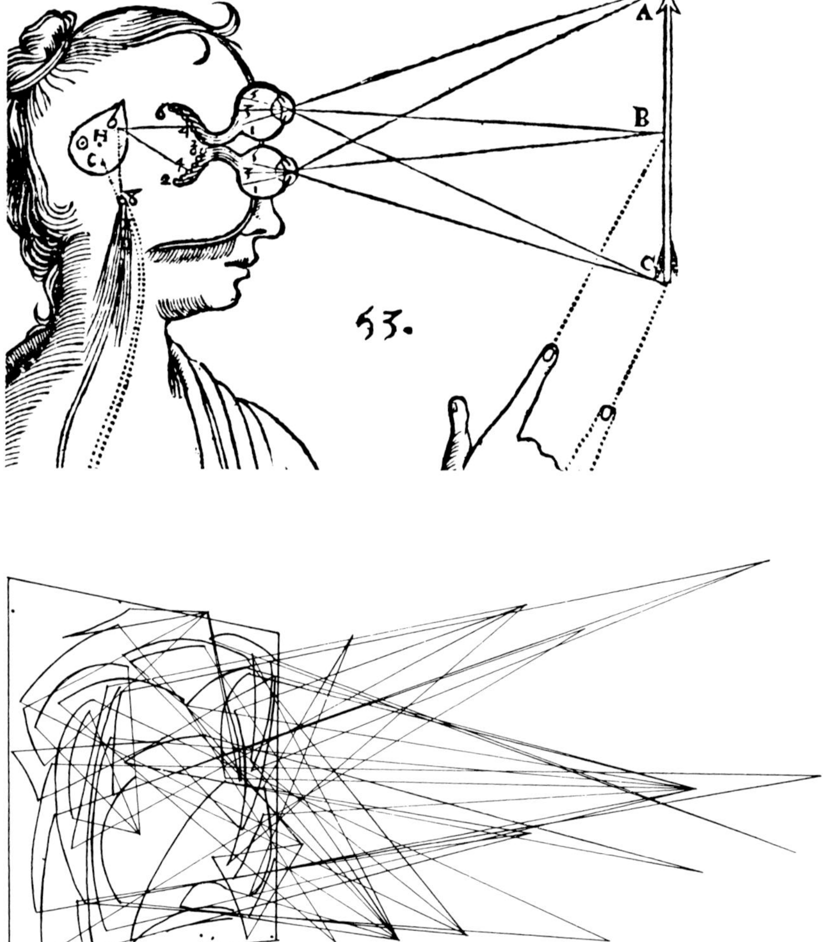

spaces has been prevalent for so long, and this concerns the discourse of philosophers. At the precise moment when a serious-minded politics of spaces was developing (at the end of the 18th century), the new attainments of theoretical and experimental physics removed philosophy's privileged right to speak about the world, the *cosmos*, space, be it finite or infinite. This double taking over of space by a political technology and a scientific practice forced philosophy into a problematic of time. From Kant on it is time that occupies the philosopher's reflection, in Hegel, Bergson and Heidegger for example. A correlative disqualification of space appears in the human understanding. I recall having spoken some ten years ago of these problems linked to a politics of spaces and someone remarked that it was very reactionary to insist so much on space, that life and progress must be measured in terms of time and becoming. It must be added that this reproach came from a psychologist: here we see the truth and the shame of 19th century philosophy.

Perrot: *We might perhaps mention in passing the importance of the notion of sexuality in this context. You noted this in the case of the surveillance of cadets and, there again, the same problem surfaces with respect to the working-class family. The notion of sexuality is fundamental, isn't it?*
Foucault: Absolutely. In these themes of surveillance, and especially school surveillance, the controls of sexuality are inscribed directly in the architectural design. In the case of the *Military Academy*, the struggle against homosexuality and masturbation is written on the walls.

Perrot: *As far as architecture is concerned doesn't it seem to you that people like doctors, whose social involvement is considerable at the end of the 18th century, played in a sense the role of spatial "arrangers"? This is where social hygiene is born; in the name of cleanliness and health, the location of people is controlled. And with the rebirth of hippocratic medicine, doctors are among those most sensitized to problems of environment, milieu, temperature, etc., which were already givens in John Howard's investigation into the state of prisons.*[2]
Foucault: Doctors were indeed partially specialists of space. They posed four fundamental problems: the problem of locations (regional climates, the nature of the soil, humidity and aridity: they applied the term "constitution" to this combination of local determinants and seasonal variations that favor, at a given moment, a particular type of illness); the problem of coexistence (the coexistence of people among themselves, where it is a question of the density or proximity of populations; the coexistence of people and things, where it is a matter of sufficient water, sewage and the free circulation of air; or the coexistence of humans and animals, where it is a matter of slaughter-houses and cattle-sheds; and finally, the coexistence of the living and the dead, where the matter of cemeteries arises); the problem of housing (habitat, urbanism); and the problem of displacements (the migration of people, the spreading of illnesses). Doctors and military men were the prime administrators of collective space. But the military thought essentially in terms of the space of "military campaigns" (and therefore of "passing through") and of fortifications. Doctors, for their part, thought above all in terms of the space of housing and cities. I cannot recall who it was that sought the major stages of sociological thought in Montesquieu and Auguste Comte, which is a very uninformed approach. For sociological knowledge is formed, rather, within practices such as that of doctors. In this context Guépin, at the very beginning of the 19th century, wrote a marvelous analysis of the city of Nantes.

The intervention of doctors was indeed of such crucial importance at this particular time because they were moved by a whole constellation of new political and economic problems, which accounts for the importance of demographic facts.

Now Bentham, like his contemporaries, encountered the problem of the accumulation of people. But whereas economists posed the problem in terms of wealth (population-as-wealth, since it is manpower, the source of economic activity and consumption; and population-as-poverty, when it is in excess or idle), Bentham posed it in terms of power: population as the target of the relations of domination. I think it could be said that the power mechanisms at play in an administrative monarchy as developed even as it was in France, were characterized by rather large gaps: this form of power constituted a global system based on chance where many elements were unaccounted for, a system that didn't enter into details, that exercised its controls over interdependent groups and that made use of the method of example (as is clear in the fiscal measures or the criminal justice system in question), and therefore had a low "resolution", as they say in photography. This form of power was incapable of practicing an exhaustive and individuating analysis of the social body. Now, the economic mutations of the 18th century made it necessary for the effects of power to circulate through finer and finer channels, reaching individuals, their bodies, their gestures, every one of their daily activities. Power was to be as effectively exercised over a multiplicity of people as if it were over one individual.

Perrot: *The demographic thrusts of the 18th century undoubtedly contributed to the development of this form of power.*
Barou: *It is therefore quite surprising to learn that the French Revolution, through people like La Fayette, favorably welcomed the project of the panopticon. One will recall that Bentham was made a "Citizen of France" in 1791 thanks to him.*
Foucault: To my mind Bentham is the complementary to Rousseau. For what is in fact the Rousseauian dream that captivated the revolutionary era, if not that of a transparent society, at once visible and legible in every one of its parts; a society where there were no longer any zones of obscurity arranged by the privileges of royal power or the prerogatives of a given body, or by disorder; where each man, from his own position, could see the whole of society; where hearts communicated directly and observations were carried out freely, and where everyman's opinions reigned supreme. Jean Starobinski made some very interesting comments on this subject in *La Transparence et l'Obstacle* and in *L'Invention de la Liberté*. Bentham is at once close to this Rousseauian notion, and the complete opposite. He poses the problem of visibility, but in his conception visibility is organized completely around a dominating and observing gaze. He initiates the project of a universal visibility that would function on behalf of a rigorous and meticulous form of power. In this sense one sees that the technical idea of a form of power that is "always and everywhere observant", which is Bentham's obsession, is connected to the Rousseauian theme, which in a sense constitutes the Revolution's lyricism: the two themes combine and the combination works—Bentham's obsession and Rousseau's lyricism.

Perrot: *What about this quote from the* Panopticon*: "Each comrade becomes a guardian?"*
Foucault: Rousseau would probably have said the opposite: that each guardian must be a comrade. In *L'Emile*, for example, Emile's tutor is a guardian, but he must also be a friend.

Barou: *The French Revolution did not interpret Bentham's project as we do today; it even perceived humanitarian aims in this project.*
Foucault: Precisely. When the Revolution examines the possibilities for a new

form of justice, it asks what is to be its mainspring. The answer is public opinion. The Revolution's problem once again was not one of insuring that people be punished, but that they could not even act improperly on account of their being submerged in a field of total visibility where the opinion of one's fellow men, their observing gaze, and their discourse would prevent one from doing evil or detrimental deeds. This problem is ever present in the texts written during the Revolution.

Perrot: *The immediate context also played a part of the Revolution's adoption of the Panopticon; the problem of prisons was then a high priority. Since 1770, in England as in France, there was a strong sense of uneasiness surrounding this issue, which is clear in Howard's investigation of prisons. Hospitals and prisons are two major topics of discussion in the Parisian salons and the enlightened circles. It was viewed as scandalous that prisons had become what they were: schools of crime and vice so lacking in decent hygiene as to seriously threaten one's chances of survival. Doctors began to talk about the degeneration of bodies in such places. With the coming of the Revolution, the bourgeoisie in turn undertook an investigation on a European scale. A certain Duquesnoy was entrusted with the task of reporting on the "establishments of humanity", a term designating hospitals as well as prisons.*

Foucault: A definite fear prevailed during the second half of the 18th century: the fear of a dark space, of a screen of obscurity obstructing the clear visibility of things, of people and of truths. It became imperative to dissolve the elements of darkness that were opposed to light, to demolish all of society's sombre spaces, those dark rooms where arbitrary political rule foments, as well as the whims of a monarch, religious superstitions, tyrants' and priests' plots, illusions of ignorance and epidemics. From even before the Revolution, castles, hospitals, charnel houses, prisons and convents gave rise to a sometimes over-valued distrust or hatred; it was felt that the new political and moral order could not be instituted until such places were abolished. The novels of terror, during the period of the Revolution, developed a whole fanciful account of the high protective walls, the shadows, the hiding-places and dungeons that shield, in a significant complicity, robbers and aristocrats, monks and traitors. Ann Radcliffe's sceneries are always mountains, forests, caverns, deteriorating castles, convents whose obscurity and silence instill fear. Now, these imaginary spaces are in a sense the "counter-figure" of the transparency and visibility that the new order hoped to establish. The reign of "opinion" invoked so frequently during this period is a mode of functioning where power is to be excercised on the sole basis of things known and people seen by a kind of immediate observing gaze that is at once collective and anonymous. A form of power whose *primum mobile* is public opinion could hardly tolerate regions of darkness. Bentham's project excited such a great interest because it provided the formula, applicable in a wide variety of domains, for a form of power that operates by means of transparency", a subjugation through a process of "bringing to light". The panopticon utilizes to a certain extent the form of the "castle" (a dungeon surrounded by high protective walls) to paradoxically create a space of detailed legibility.

Barou: *The Age of Enlightenment would also have liked to see the sombre areas within man abolished.*
Foucault: Absolutely.

Perrot: *One is also struck by the techniques of power within the panopticon itself. Essentially there is the observing gaze, and also speech, for there are those well known steel tubes that link the principal inspector to each of the*

cells in which we can find not one prisoner, according to Bentham, but small groups of prisoners. What is very striking in Bentham's text is the importance attributed to dissuasion: as he puts it, "one must constantly be under the eyes of an inspector; this results in a loss of the capacity to do evil and almost even the thought of wanting to." This is one of the major preoccupations of the Revolution: to keep people from doing evil, to make them refrain from even wanting to: not being able and not wanting to do evil.

Foucault: Two different things are involved here: the observing gaze, the act of observation on the one hand, and internalization on the other. And doesn't this amount to the problem of the cost of power? Power is not exercised without it costing something. There is obviously the economic cost, which Bentham discusses: "How many guardians will be needed?", How much will the machine cost?" But there is also the specifically political cost. If power is exercised too violently, there is the risk of generating revolts; or if the intervention is too discontinuous, there is the risk of the development of resistance and disobedience, phenomena of great political cost. This is how monarchic power functioned. The judicial apparatus, for example, arrested only a ridiculously small proportion of criminals; from which the fact was deduced that if the punishment was to instill fear in those present, it must be glaring. Monarchic power was therefore violent and utilized spectacular examples to insure a continuous exercise of power. To this conception of power the new theoreticians of the 18th century retort: this power is too costly for too few results. There are great expenditures of violence of no exemplary value; one is even forced to multiply the violence and, by that very fact, to multiply the revolts.

Perrot: *Which is what happened during the riots surrounding the executions on the scaffold.*

Foucault: On the other hand there is a form of observation that requires very little in the way of expenditures. No need for arms, physical violence, or material restraints. Rather there is an observing gaze that watches over people and that each individual, due to the fact that he feels it weighing on him, finally internalizes to the point where he observes himself: everyone in this way exercises surveillance over and against himself. This is an ingenious formula: a continuous form of power at practically no cost! When Bentham pronounces his discovery of this form of power, he views it as a "revolutionary discovery in the order of politics", a formula that is exactly the reverse of monarchic power. As a matter of fact, within the techniques of power developed in modern times, observation has had a major importance but, as I said earlier, it is far from being the only or even the principal instrumentation put into practice.

Perrot: *It seems, from what you have just said, that Bentham posed the problem of power essentially in terms of small groups. Why? Did he consider that the part is already the whole, that if one succeeds on the level of groups this can be extended to include society as a whole? Or is it that society as a whole and power at that level were not yet grasped in their specificity at that time?*
Foucault: The whole problem in this form of power is to avoid stumbling blocks and interruptions similar to the obstacles presented in the Ancien Regime by the established bodies, the privileges of certain categories, from the clergy to the trade guilds by way of the body of magistrates. The bourgeoisie was perfectly aware that new legislation or a new Constitution were not enough to guarantee its hegemony. A new technology had to be invented that would insure the free-flow of the effects of power within the entire social body and on the most minute of levels. And in this area the bourgeoisie not only achieved a political revolution, but also managed to establish a form of social hegemony that it has never relinquished since. This explains why all of these inventions were so important, and why Bentham was surely among the most typical inventors of power technologies.

Barou: *It is nevertheless not immediately clear whether space organized as Bentham advocated could profit anyone, be it only those who occupied the central tower or who came to visit. The reader of Bentham's proposals feels as if he were in the presence of an infernal world from which there is no escape, neither for those who are being watched, nor for those who are observing.*
Foucault: Such is perhaps the most diabolical aspect of the idea and of all the applications it brought about. In this form of management, power isn't totally entrusted to someone who would exercise it alone, over others, in an absolute fashion; rather this machine is one in which everyone is caught, those who exercise the power as well as those who are subjected to it. It seems to me this is the major characteristic of the new societies established in the 19th century. Power is no longer substantially identified with a particular individual who possesses it or exercises it due to his social position. Power becomes a machinery controlled by no one. Everyone in this machine obviously occupies a different place; certain places are more important than others and enable those who occupy them to produce effects of supremacy, insuring a class domination to the very extent that they dissociate political power from individual power.

Perrot: *The operation of the panopticon is somewhat contradictory from this point of view. There is the principal inspector who keeps watch from a central tower. But he also controls his inferiors, the guards, in whom he has no confidence. He sometimes speaks rather distrustfully of them, even though they are supposed to be close to him. Doesn't this constitute an aristocratic form of thought! But it must also be recalled that supervision represented a crucial problem for industrial society. Finding foremen and engineers capable of regimenting and supervising the factories was no easy task for management.*
Foucault: This problem was enormous, as is clear in the case of the 18th century army when it was necessary to establish a corps of "low-ranking"

officers competent enough to supervise the troups effectively during what were often very difficult tactical maneuvers, all the more difficult as the rifle had just been perfected. Movements, displacements and formations of troops, as well as marches required this sort of disciplinary personnel. Work-places posed the same problem in their own right, as did school, with its head masters, teachers, and disciplinarians. The Church was then one of the rare social bodies where such competent small corps of disciplinarians existed. The not too literate, but not too ignorant monk and the curate joined forces against children when it became necessary to school hundreds of thousands of children. The State did not provide itself with similar small corps until much later, as was also the case with respect to hospitals. It was not so long ago that the supervisory personnel of hospitals was still constituted in large part by nuns.

Perrot: *These very nuns played a considerable part in the creation of a female labor force, in the well known 19th century internships where a female staff lived and worked under the supervision of nuns specially trained to exercise factory discipline.*

The panopticon is also preoccupied with these issues as is apparent when it deals with the principal inspector's surveillance of the supervising staff and, through the control tower's windows, his surveillance of everyone, an uninterrupted succession of observations that call to mind the dictum: "each comrade becomes a guardian". We finally reach a point of vertigo in the presence of an invention no longer mastered by its creator. And it is Bentham who, in the beginning, wants to place confidence in a unique, central form of power. Who did he plan to put in the tower? The eye of God? Yet God is barely present in his texts, for religion only plays a utilitarian part. So who is in the tower? In the last analysis it must be admitted that Bentham himself is not too clear about who should be entrusted with this power.

Foucault: He cannot have confidence in anyone in that no person can, nor must be a source of power and justice like the king in the former system. In the theory of the monarchy it was implicit that one owed allegiance to the king. By his very existence, willed by God, the king was the source of justice, law and authority. Power in the person of the king could only be good; a bad king was equivalent to an historical accident or to a punishment inflicted by the absolutely good sovereign, God. Whereas one cannot have confidence in anyone if power and authority are arranged as a complex machine and where an individual's place, and not his nature, is the determining factor. If the machine were such that someone stood outside it or had the sole responsibility for its management, power would be identified with a person and one would return to the monarchic system of power. In the *Panopticon,* everyone is watched, according to his position within the system, by all of the others or by certain others; here we are in the presence of an apparatus of distrust that is total and mobile, since there is no absolute point. A certain sum of malevolence was required for the perfection of surveillance.

Barou: *A diabolical machine, as you said, that spares no one. Such is the image of power today. But, according to you, how did we get to this point? What sort of "will" was involved, and whose?*

Foucault: The question of power is greatly impoverished if posed solely in terms of legislation, or the Constitution, or the State, the State apparatus. Power is much more complicated, much more diffuse and dense than a set of laws or a State apparatus. One cannot understand the development of the productive forces of capitalism, nor even conceive of their technological development, if the apparatuses of power are not taken into consideration. For example, take the case of the division of labor in the major work-places of the 18th century; how would this distribution of tasks have been achieved had there not been a new distribution of power on the very level of the productive forces? Likewise for the modern army: it was not enough to possess new types of armaments or another style of recruitment: this new form of power called discipline was also required, with its hierarchies, its commands, its inspections, its exercises, its conditionings, its drills. Without this the army such as it had functioned since the 17th century would never have existed.

Barou: *There is nevertheless an individual or a group of individuals who provide the impetus for this disciplinary system, or isn't there?*
Foucault: A distinction must be made. It is clear in the organization of an army or a work-place, or a given institution that the network of power adopts a pyramidal form. There is therefore a summit. But even in a simple case, this "summit" is not the "source" or the "principle" from which the totality of power derives as from a focal point (such as the monarch's throne). The summit and the lower elements of the hierarchy coexist within a relationship of reciprocal support and conditioning: they "hold together" (power as a mutual and indefinite "extortion"). But if what you are asking is whether the

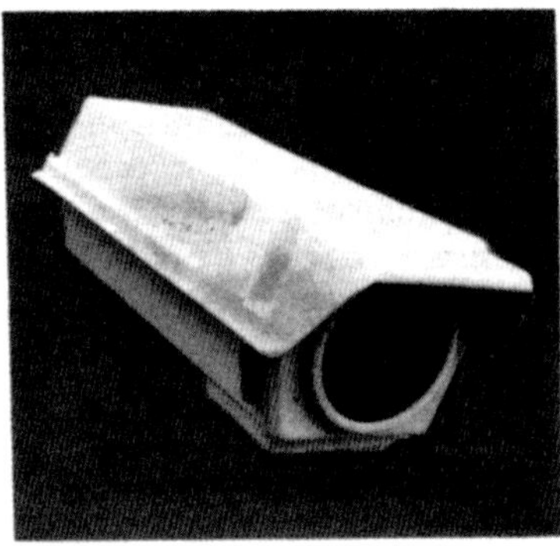

H 422 **Circle #13 on card**
TV Camera enclosure, lockable, weather proof, light weight, plastic. Four pounds, saves money and repairs by not having to use a heavy duty pan and tilt. 4" sun shade, 22"x8"x8", available with heater and fan. You can hit it with a club, under $100.00

Video Transmission **Circle #14** on card
Phone Wire - TV 3000 feet on dedicated twisted pair. **Optical** - 3000 feet line of sight, no FCC license required. **RF** - Video Transmission for Gov't Agency, or Overseas.

CLANDESTINE SURVEILLANCE

Retail Surveillance **Circle #16 on card**
MANIKIN - TV Camera looking out of eye. **Exit Sign** - Only 3" wide, 15" long, 9" high **Alarm box-ADT** type, 1/4 hole "to see". **Auxiliary light Fixture** - **TV** fitted into yours or ours. **Recessed into wall** - TV in wall 3" wide, 1/4" hole to "see.

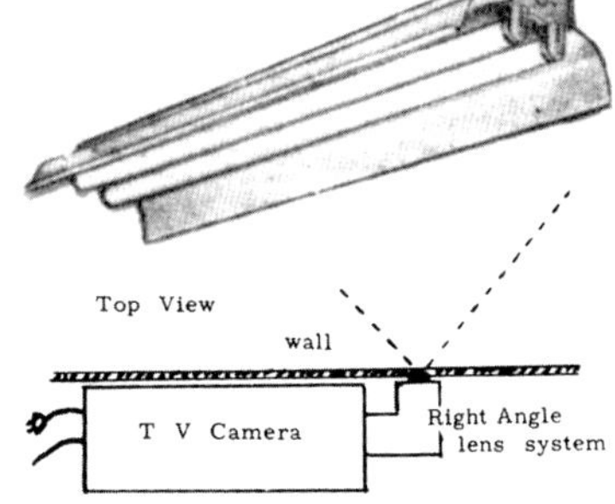

Industrial Surveillance **Circle #17 on card**
File Cabinet - TV fits into drawer, remove rod and inside plate, run cable out rear of cabinet. **Fluorescent Fixture** - TV with right angle lens mounted in your fixture or ours. Viewing area is to side. **Desk Calculator** - TV located in base looking out side.

new technology of power has its historical roots in an individual or in a group of specific individuals who would, as it were, have decided to apply this technology in their own interests and in order to shape the social body according to their designs, then I would have to say no. These tactics were invented and organized according to local conditions and particular urgencies. They were designed piece by piece before a class strategy solidified them into vast and coherent totalities. It must also be noted that these totalities do not consist in a homogenization but rather in a complex interplay of support among the different mechanisms of power which are, themselves, nonetheless quite specific. Thus it is that at the present time the interplay between the family, medicine, psychiatry, psychoanalysis, the school, and the judicial system, in the case of children, does not homogenize these different agencies, but establishes connections, referrals, complementarities and determinations that presuppose that each one of them maintains, to a certain extent, its own modalities.

Perrot: *You have protested against the idea of power as a superstructure, but not against the idea that this power is in a sense consubstantial to the development of the productive forces, of which it is a part.*
Foucault: Correct. And power is constantly being transformed along with the productive forces. The Panopticon was a utopian program. But already in Bentham's time the theme of a spatializing, observing, immobilizing—i.e. disciplinary—power was in fact outflanked by much more subtle mechanisms allowing for the regulation of population phenomena, the control of their oscillations, and compensation for their irregularities. Bentham is "antiquated" insofar as he attaches so much importance to observation; he is completely modern when he stresses the importance of the techniques of power in our societies.

Perrot: *There is therefore no global State; rather there is the emergence of micro-societies, microcosms.*
Barou: *Is the distribution of forces in the Panopticon attributable to industrial society, or should we consider capitalist society to be responsible for this form of power?*
Foucault: Industrial or capitalist society? I don't know what to answer, except perhaps that these forms of power are also present in socialist societies: the transference was immediate. But on this point, I would prefer to let the historian among us intervene in my place.

Perrot: *It is true that the accumulation of capital was accomplished by an industrial technology and by the erection of an entire apparatus of power. But it is also true that a similar process can be found in the Soviet socialist society. In certain respects, Stalinism also corresponds to a period of accumulation of capital and to the establishment of a strong form of power.*
Barou: *The notion of profit comes to mind here, which indicates how valuable some can find Bentham's inhuman machine.*
Foucault: Obviously! We would have to share the rather naive optimism of 19th century "dandies" to think that the bourgeoisie is stupid. On the contrary, we must take into account its master strokes, among which, precisely, there is the fact that it succeeded in constructing machines of power that helped in establishing circuits of profit which in turn reinforce and modify the mechanisms of power in a constantly moving and circular fashion. Feudal power, which functioned above all by means of capital levies and expenditures, drained itself. Bourgeois power perpetuates itself not by conservation, but by successive transformations, which accounts for the fact that its arrangement is not inscribed within history as is the feudal arrangement.

Which also accounts for its precariousness as well as its inventive resiliency. This explains, finally, how the possibility of its downfall as well as the possibility of Revolution have from the beginning been an intimate part of its history.

Perrot: *Bentham assigns an important place for work, and keeps coming back to it.*
Foucault: This is due to the fact that the techniques of power were invented to respond to the requirements of production, in the largest sense of the term (e.g. "producing" a destruction, as in the case of the army).

Barou: *May I mention in passing that when you speak of "work" in your books, this rarely refers to productive labor . . .*
Foucault: This is because I have been mainly preoccupied with people placed outside the circuits of productive labor: the mad, the sick, prisoners, and today, children. Work for them, such as they are supposed to accomplish it, is above all valued for its disciplinary effects.

Barou: *Isn't work always a form of drill or pacification?*
Foucault: Of course, the triple function of work is always present: the productive function, the symbolic function and the training, or disciplinary function. The productive function is perceptibly zero for the categories with which I am concerned, whereas the symbolic and disciplinary functions are quite important. But in most instances the three components coexist.

Perrot: *Bentham, in any case, strikes me as very self-confident concerning the penetrating power of observation. One feels in fact that he doesn't fully appreciate the degree of opacity and resistance of the material that is to be corrected and reintegrated into society, namely, the prisoners. Doesn't Bentham's panopticon share in the illusion of power to a certain extent?*
Foucault: It is the illusion shared by practically all of the 18th century reformers who invested public opinion with considerable power. Public opinion had to be correct since it was the immediate conscience of the entire social body; these reformers really believed people would become virtuous owing to their being observed. Public opinion represented a spontaneous reactualization of the social contract. They failed to recognize the real conditions of public opinion, the "media", i.e. a materiality caught in the mechanisms of economy and power in the forms of the press, publishing, and then films and television.

Perrot: *When you say that they disregarded the media you mean they failed to appreciate their importance for them.*
Foucault: They also failed to understand that the media would necessarily be controlled by economic and political interests. They did not perceive the material and economic components of public opinion. They thought that public opinion would be just by its very nature, that it would spread by itself, and constitute a kind of democratic surveillance. It was essentially journalism —a crucial innovation of the 19th century—that manifested the utopian characteristics of this entire politics of observation.

Perrot: *Thinkers generally miscalculate the difficulties they will encounter in trying to make their system "take hold"; they are not aware that there will always be loopholes and that resistances will always play a part. In the domain of prisons, inmates have not been passive people; and yet Bentham leads us to believe quite the opposite. Penal discourse itself unfolds as if it concerned no one in particular, except perhaps a* tabula rasa *in the form of people to be rehabilitated and then thrust back into the circuits of production. In reality there is a material, the inmates, who resist in a formidable manner. The same* *could also be said of Taylorism, the extraordinary invention of an engineer who wanted to fight against loafing, against everything that downs production. But we might finally ask whether Taylorism ever really worked?*

Foucault: Another element does indeed contribute to the unreal side of Bentham's project: people's effective capacity to resist, studied so carefully by you, Michelle Perrot. How did people in workshops and housing projects resist the system of continual surveillance and recording of their activities? Were they aware of the compulsive, subjugating, unbearable nature of this surveillance, or did they accept it as natural? In brief, were there revolts against the observing gaze of power?

Perrot: *Yes there were. The repugnance workers had to living in housing projects was an obvious fact. These projects were failures for quite a long while, as was the compulsory distribution of time, also present throughout the panopticon. The factory and its time schedules instigated a passive resistance, expressed by the workers' staying home. Witness the extraordinary story of the 19th century "Holy Monday", a day off invented by the workers in order to get out and relax every week. There were multiple forms of resistance to the industrial system, so many, in fact, that in the beginning management had to*

back off. Another example is found in the systems of micro-powers which were not instituted immediately either. This type of surveillance and supervision was first of all developed in the mechanized sectors composed mainly of women and children, hence of people used to obeying; women used to obeying husbands and children used to obeying their parents. But in the "male" sectors such as the iron-works, the situation was quite different. Management did not succeed in installing its surveillance system immediately: during the first half of the 19th century it had to delegate its powers; it worked out contracts with the teams of workers through the foremen, who were often the most qualified workers or those with most seniority. A veritable counter-power developed among the professional workers, which sometimes had two edges: one directed against the management, in defense of the workers' community, and the other against the workers themselves insofar as the foreman managed to oppress his apprentices and comrades. The workers' forms of counter-power continued to exist until management learned how to mechanize the functions that escaped it; it was then able to abolish the professional workers' power. There are numerous examples of this: in the rolling mills the shop steward had the means at his disposal to resist the boss until the day when quasi-automated machines were installed. Thermal control, to cite only one instance, was substituted for the workers' sight and one could now determine whether the material was at the right temperature simply by reading a thermometer.

Foucault: This being the case, one must analyze the constellation of resistances to the panopticon in terms of tactics and strategies and bear in mind that each offensive on one level serves to support a counter-offensive on another level. The analysis of machines of power does not seek to demonstrate that power is both anonymous and always victorious. Rather we must locate the positions and the modes of action of everyone involved as well as the various possibilities for resisting and launching counter-attacks.

Barou: *You speak like a strategist, of battles, actions and reactions, offensives and counter-offensives. Are resistances to power essentially physical in nature according to you? What then becomes of the content of the struggles and the aspirations they express?*

Foucault: This is in fact a very important theoretical and methodological question. One thing in particular strikes me: certain political discourses make constant use of a vocabulary of the relations of forces. "Struggle" is a word that comes up most frequently. Now, it seems to me that one sometimes refuses to see the consequences of such a vocabulary or even to consider the problem it raises: namely, must we analyze these "struggles" as the vicissitudes of a war, must they be deciphered according to a strategical, tactical grid, yes or no? Is the relationship of forces in the order of politics a relationship of war? I personally am not prepared to respond categorically with a yes or a no. It only seems to me at this point that the pure and simple affirmation of a "struggle" cannot be viewed as a final explanation in an analysis of power relationships. This theme of the struggle is only functional if it is concretely established in each case who is struggling, for what reasons, how the struggle is developing, in what locations, with what instruments and according to what sort of rationality. In other words, if one wishes to take seriously the notion that struggle is at the heart of the relationships of power, one must realize that the nice, old "logic" of contradictions is far from sufficient to determine the real processes involved.

Perrot:*Put another way, and getting back to the panopticon, Bentham not only projects a utopian society, but also describes an existing society.*

Foucault: He describes, within the utopia of a general system, particular mechanisms that really exist.

Perrot: *Then does it make sense for the inmates to take over the observation tower?*

Foucault: Yes, provided that this is not the end of the operation. Do you believe that things would be much better if the inmates seized control of the panopticon and occupied the tower, rather than the guards?

Translated by Mark Seem

"L'Oeil du pouvoir" was published in Jeremy Bentham's Le Panoptique, *Pierre Belfond, 1977.*

1. Thus described in Michel Foucault, *Discipline and Punish,* Pantheon Books, 1978.

2. John Howard made the results of this investigation public in his study: *The State of the Prisons in England and Wales, with Preliminary Observations and an Account of some Foreign Prisons and Hospitals,* 1777.

Robert Wilson
interview

François Péraldi

A Schizo and the Institution (a non-story)

Sylvere Lotringer: How did you arrive at a theatre which is not primarily based upon language?

Robert Wilson: I never liked the theatre. I wasn't interested in the narrative or the psychology. I preferred the ballet because it was architectural—my own background is in painting and architecture. I liked Balanchine and Merce Cunningham because I didn't have to bother about plot or meaning. I could just look at designs and patterns—that seemed enough. There is a dancer here, another dancer there, another four on this side, eight on the other, then sixteen... I wondered if the theatre could do the same things as the dance and just be an architectural arrangement in time and space. So I first made plays that were primarily visual. I started working with different pictures that were arranged in a certain way. Later I added words, but words weren't used to tell a story. They were used more architecturally: for the length of the word or the sentence, for their sound. They were constructed like music.

For instance, when Lucinda speaks in *Einstein on the Beach*, what matters is the sound of her voice, the patterns of her voice. In *A Letter to Queen Victoria*, I was mainly interested in the contrast between George's voice and Jim Neu's, between Stephan's voice and Scotty's, between Sheryl's voice and Cindy's. I wanted to put together these different rhythms, these

Let's see first what this title does *not* mean, then we shall proceed to see what has *not* happened to our schizo, then the extraordinary results on the institution, and the final interdiction.

The title then: A schizo.

Schizophrenia is not an illness,[1] and thus, it cannot be cured, for only illnesses can sometimes be cured. This statement is our premise, very close to Thomas Szasz's,[2] in this particular case.

What is it then?

It is not abnormal behavior either, for not having yet found solid epistemological grounds for the meaning of "normal" we have decided to disregard this category as well as its opposite term: "abnormality". It keeps us at least from entering into this horrifying world of the behavioral sciences which, to us, is nothing but the most extraordinarily powerful and dangerous system of repression ever invented, because it has never been able to state clearly the political, economic and ideological grounds on which it has built its Skinner boxes of torture.

Shall we say that schizophrenia is a process? And if so then, what kind of process?

I'd venture to say that it appears to me as an affirmative process in the negative. Something like: "I am and I remain whatever you do not want me to be". Let's understand it as an *affirmation against*.

I have good reasons for not saying that it is a negative process. Freud has demonstrated one or two things; one of the most interesting is that when Being and Thinking are structured according to a certain pattern (afterwards taken as a model of normality) they are based on a fundamental activity which he calls *Verneinung*: Negation, or "Dénégation" as we say in French. But this negation presupposes a more fundamental principle: the principle of identity. Listen to

Freud: What is bad, what is alien to the ego, and what is external are, to begin with, identical.[3]

This has nothing to do with the schizophrenic process, which appears as a primarily affirmative process to be apprehended—but can we?—in the realm of difference or, should I say, using a Heideggerian term, in the realm of *appropriation*[4] from which the principle of identity stems. But this discourse is becoming horribly metaphysical. Let's drop it.

Let's come back to the word schizo and add a word. We do not use the word Schizo as a label of seriousness or quality that would be the proof that I am an up-to-date psychoanalyst daring to face the dark and frightening forces of the unknown, "à la pointe" of a pseudo modern psycho-something. And I am very well aware of the dangers, as well as the great advantages in using such a word.

Let me give you an example of the advantages, in the institution I am going to talk about. Let's call it by its name: Lavans (it's in a remote part of France called the Jura known for its exquisite white wine and good food, which has to do with what we were able to achieve). In Lavans, we received from the State Social Services a certain amount of money daily per patient. That's how we functioned. When we could prove that more than 35% of the children we had in our care were schizophrenic, the allowance given daily for each child was augmented by 72%. A good deal! Don't you think? Shall I say something that would ring profoundly true in certain psycho-somethings. . . . Schizo is good money!

In order perhaps not to disagree with Félix Guattari, I should perhaps call the process I am talking about the psychotic process. Félix refuses to consider—as far as I know—schizophrenia as a process which functions from the beginning *against* whatever may be attempted to reduce and fit it into the Oedipal structure by what we might call the Family Power Machinery.

THE INSTITUTION

It is nothing but the socially structured field, place or as we say in France, *le Lieu*, where certain types of Power Machinery shape an object with the help of *semi-conscious* agents and through a medium which is the discourse in its function of "formation" (whatever word you want to put before formation, *in*-formation, *de*-formation or *re*-formation . . .).

Le lieu—the field—is an open institution, at least without walls and without drugs, both of which, to the schizophrenic, are identical.

The object in this case, was a group of 60 children chosen in an age group between 14 and 20, according to government regulations, in an IQ range between 20 (something like a living turnip) and 65 (politely called: Idiots, or Les Débiles!).

different ways of speaking in order to create a vocal effect. I wasn't primarily concerned with the content. At the same time, it is there.

When you listen to Mozart, you don't wonder what it means. You just listen. I consider what I am doing as a kind of "visual music".

Denise Green: Your interest in architecture as well as your extensive use of visual props didn't coincide with the minimalist trend of the sixties.

W: No. The theatre in the sixties wanted to eliminate 19th century techniques. They didn't want to use painted decors suggesting the forest, or a temple, or a Victorian drawing-room. This was too old-fashioned. Rauschenberg was painting a goat and putting it in the middle of the room. You could see it from all sides, from 360 degrees. There was a show called *Art Against Illusion* at the Whitney Museum which was supposed to be the summation of the arts towards the end of the sixties. I was just doing a play called *The King of Spain* which had really nothing to do with what they were doing. It had to do precisely with an illusion. I was actually trying to reveal the illusion, the mystery. I was somehow fascinated by two-dimensional space, three-dimensional space and the illusion that can be accredited on a box. I liked their formality. *The King of Spain* is a Victorian drama where giant Catholic kings thirty feet high walk through the drawing room. There's a complicated pulley system and no less than twenty men were pulling this big apparatus across the stage. It was obviously a 19th century concept of the theatre. All that was hidden behind a frame. In the sixties, they were trying to destroy the frame. I was actually putting a frame right in front of the machinery.

I have done other things that rebel against those ideas, but I believe as a philosophy that it is important to contradict yourself. At any rate, I am far apart from Grotowski and any kind of expressionistic or emotive theatre. I even do my best to eliminate all apparent emotion. But this mechanical presentation is not such a new idea either. Nijinski wanted

his dance to be purely mechanical...

We rehearsed *Queen Victoria* very often before playing it for the first time. Each time the rehearsal was done exactly in the same way, until it became totally mechanical. By contrast, Chris Knowles and I were doing improvisation. Everything Chris was doing in the play was largely improvised. Most of the text of *Queen Victoria* derived from Chris's very special use of language.

L: Both Raymond Andrews and Christopher Knowles seem to operate independently of our "colloquial" tradition. What made you so receptive to their own perceptions?

W: I could identify with them. When I first met Chris, his mother said: "You know, his notebooks look very similar to yours." So there was a common concern. In the case of Raymond, he didn't know any words when I met him. That fascinated me. I wondered how he thought if he didn't think in terms of words.

G: Can you really think without words?

W: Obviously this kid was thinking, and he was very bright. He was 13 years old and he didn't know any words. He saw everything in terms of pictures and that's how we made *Deafman's Glance*. He was living with me at the time so I conveyed to him the idea that we would make a play together. He would make drawings—drawings of a table, of a frog, of various things—and that became the play. What happened within these settings were mostly gestures, movements, things that he would observe. It was a language, so to speak.

Then I met Chris. I had heard a tape he had done about his little sister watching TV. I didn't know him but I was intrigued by the tape. Then I became more fascinated with him and what he was doing with language. He would take ordinary, everyday words and destroy them. They became like molecules that were always changing, breaking apart all the time, many-faceted words, not just a dead language, a rock breaking apart. He was constantly redefining the codes.

Chris constructs as he speaks.

The agents: specialized educators, non-specialized educators, non-educators, a psychiatrist, a psychologist, a few specialists that tamper with the ears, the hands or whatever . . . of the children, and . . . 3 psychoanalysts!

We could say that one of the three Power Machineries[5] functioning in this institution was familial; its task is—or was at the beginning of the story—to Oedipalize the living turnip as well as the débile or (and there's the rub!) the Schizo!

As the following narrative demonstrates, the Schizos have made it obvious to the Institution which encloses them that this power apparatus (which could be termed familial) functions thanks to a type, a *form* of discourse unconsciously practiced by the agents of the apparatus—quite simply, the personnel employed by the institution. Power does not function through the substance of the contents, of the ideologies, but rather, on the level of the form of the contents, to use Hjelmslev's terms. More generally, it is those forms specific to communication which the power apparati's agents are obliged to structure, excluding all other forms which could possibly manifest themselves but which consequently must be repressed, *forbidden*: for example, incestuous or homosexual forms of communication.

It was precisely this schizophrenic affirmation against the unconscious attempts at "formation" which led the employees of these institutions to reflect on their real function and to discover through modifying it their role as unconscious agent for a certain kind of power.

ANALYSE INSTITUTIONNELLE

The main principle on which the functioning of the institution was based was *displacement*. There were few permanent places or functions but rather temporary preferential zones and occupations between which everybody moved and functioned in a more or less disconnected way. And in the different workshops the production did not stem from necessity but was elaborated by groups of people having a common desire to do certain things together.

These groups functioned temporarily on all sorts of levels: verbal groups, the sex group, the kitchen group, the architectural group, etc. . . . But the entire staff was assembled once every two weeks along with the psychoanalysts. The main point of these "assemblies" was, to use Guattari's word, to unyoke (*désassujettir*) the existing groups in such a way that language and all forms of semiotic systems could *circulate* through the institution independent of any hierarchical relationship.

He is seeing pictures as he is talking. He is making visual constructions. The same word "the" is a line and each line is different. I responded to what he was doing more as an artist. I didn't really try to think it through.

L: It seems to be very logically, even mathematically ordered although it may be futile to try to understand what that order actually is.

W: Yes. Chris can organize his language spontaneously into mathematical, geometrical or numerical categories. I can't do that as well as he does. I have to write everything down, which takes some time. Chris does it naturally. Now I can never explain why something is done. It just seems right. Things aren't necessarily arbitrary, but I can't say exactly why they seem to be so. I think it probably would have a logic of its own it you spent enough time to figure it out.

G: Can you explain further what you see in common between Raymond and Chris?

W: They are both highly visual. The typing of "C" on this diagram may stand for his name, Christopher, but it is very visual. Raymond's way of understanding and communicating with us was a visual one. He didn't hear the words.

We hear and we see with interior and exterior audio-visual screens. When our eyes are shut —we sleep, we are blind—then perhaps we see on this interior visual screen. But when our eyes are open, we see on this exterior visual screen. If we are deaf, then perhaps we hear on an interior screen; if we listen to the cars, then we hear on our exterior screen.

L: Can a play make the interior screen more visible?

W: What happened in longer plays like *Stalin* invariably is that you get more of a balance. The exterior and interior audio-visual screens become connected and frequently people will talk about things that didn't actually happen on the stage because they were half-asleep. Something else happened and they began to see what they wanted to see. I think we all hear and see what we

want to hear and see. Tony Conrad made a film in the sixties that was just an alternation of black and white frames. In one second you would have 24 frames and maybe you would have one white frame, then one black, then two whites, etc., and people would invariably see different things. Perhaps we see all the time what we want to see. We are not hearing the same things. Someone once made a loop of the word "Cogitate, cogitate, cogitate" and people heard all sorts of things, meditate, tragedy, all they wanted to hear...

L: People who deal with deaf or autistic children seem essentially concerned with enforcing on them our language and our own conventions. You apparently did just the reverse. You assumed that there was something to learn from them.

W: Right. Chris was in school. He was doing these kinds of drawings and he was being stopped. They were trying to correct it instead of encouraging it. No one was really concerned about his drawings as a work of art. I simply said: "It is very beautiful. Do more of them."

L: Do you think your theatre helps bridge the distinction between "madness" and art?

W: You have an apple [he draws an apple] and in the center of this apple there is a cube, a crystal. This apple is the world, this cube is a way of seeing whatever

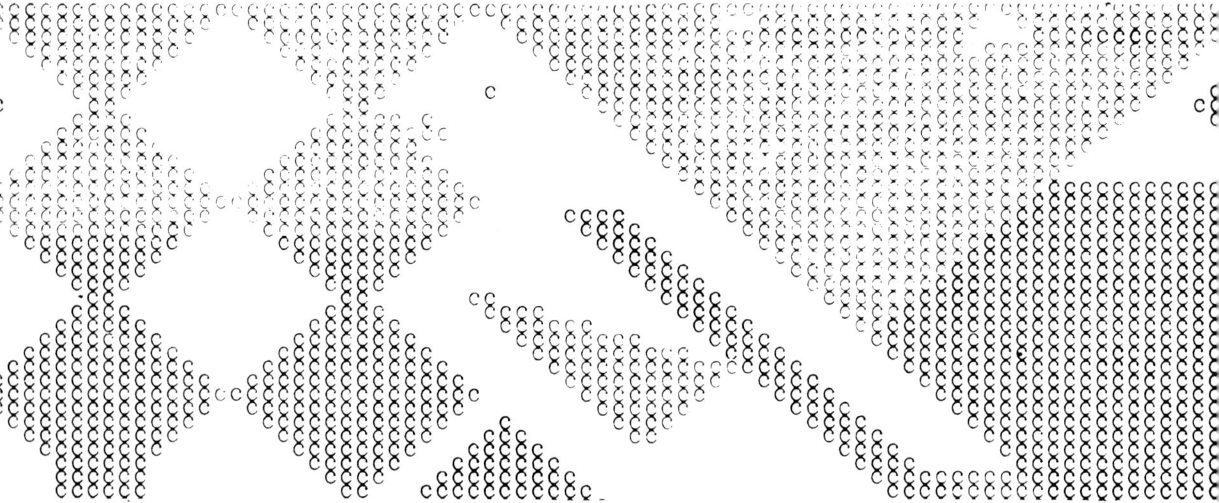

Of course this was the basic principle which in fact gave rise to innumerable conflicts and what I'd like to call sub-liminal repression and resistances.

THE OEDIPANIZATION:
or What we have not achieved

At that time (in 1969) we were all very much impressed by Bruno Bettelheim's performances in the Orthogenic school transforming Joey the electric-boy into an electrician, that is, to "cure" a schizophrenic child. And the staff was also very much impressed by the clear writings of Françoise Dolto or Maud Mannoni, our psychoanalytical Waldküren of the Oedipal structure. And we figured out, with the assistance of a whole range of psychoanalytical literature and with the complicity of the 3 psychoanalysts (I was one of them), that *the key* to the treatment of schizophrenics was to repair this loss of reality described by Freud. This *Verwerfun*, reclosure of "forclusion" as Lacan calls it, which creates a hole due to the rejection of the Nom-Du-Père, the Paternal Law, again according to Jacques Lacan, which we believed necessary to the construction of any symbolic order of which the psychotic seems to be deprived. With, the Law, the Nom-du-Père, and the inevitability of castration, we enter into the Oedipal structuration of the subject.

According to this clear vision of the situation the schizophrenic has a central hole into which he might at any minute be drawn; the task seemed easy . . .: Fill the hole! So we did, at least we tried . . . and we failed! and even *we* began to be drawn into the hole. How did it happen?

In several steps:

1st step: Hook the fish!

Have you ever noticed the fantastic use of space by a

schizophrenic? Only a Nijinski might have given us an idea of how it works. And dumb as we were, we thought that it was nothing but erratic wandering. I told you! We understood nothing! The story I am telling you can only be negative.

There stood all the educators and non-educators, at the edge of the schizophrenic flow, like fishermen . . .

And then Claire hooked Mimi,
and then Leila hooked Michel
and then Claude hooked Henri. . . .

happens in the world. In the case of Christopher, or even Raymond, there was a language there. One day I said his name, Raymond, very loudly, and he didn't turn around. I said "Aounn" and he turned around. It was startling. He would turn around and I would imitate his sounds, the sounds of a deaf person, and there would be a recognition of that sound. You could see it in the

```
 XX          XX  XX          XX   UU          UU   PPPPPPPPPPP    DDDDDDDD
XX          XX   XX         XX   UU          UU   PPPPPPPPPPPP   DDDDDDDDD
XX        XX     XX       XX    UU          UU   PP         PP   DD       D
XX      XX       XX     XX     UU          UU   PP         PP   DD        D
XX    XX         XX   XX      UU          UU   PP         PP   DD        DD
XXXX             XXXX        UU          UU   PPPPPPPPPPPP    DD        DD
XXXX             XXXX       UU          UU   PPPPPPPPPPP     DD        DD
 XX        XX     XX       UU          UU   PP              DD        DD
 XX      XX       XX      UU          UU   PP              DD        DD
 XX    XX         XX     UU          UU   PP              DD        DD
 XX  XX           XX     UUUUUUUUUUUU    PP              DDDDDDDDDD
XX  XX           XX     UUUUUUUUUU      PP              DDDDDDDDD
```

A relation, as we said, had been established. But at that time we did not even try to find out what the bait had been and how it had been sent to the hooked schizophrenic. Well, anyhow . . . A chacun son Schizo . . . To each his own schizo.

2nd Step: Regression and surrogate maternal techniques.

You all know these techniques and how delightedly we find proof that regression works when a big boy of 14 shits on his pseudo-mama's knees . . . while more or less sucking her ear . . . or whatever . . . Or when he goes back to these so-called primal screams, or the joyous babbling of the "infans".

Meanwhile a kind of tacit conspiracy was established. We continually strengthened the links between the schizo and his pseudo-mama by sending him back to her whenever he tried to ask someone else for something. Or by calling the pseudo-mama to help whenever the schizo did something weird, like strangling a defenseless young female educator. Even when you strangle, you have to strangle your mother, because only this can be interpreted in the Oedipal realm.

A short-story: I remember another schizo in another

face. When a deaf person speaks, "Eah Eeyan Eeaah", you see in the face his nightmare of not being able to speak the hearer's own language. They are imitating us, but they will never be able to do that. In his face when I said "Aouinn" I saw he knew what I was really talking about. There was a recognition of the sound. So perhaps that's a language too, like French is a language. And that's in the center of the cube. The language center. Maybe this is a language that could be learned, or discerned. And the same with Christopher. The arrangements of his sounds is something you can learn to do after a while. There are 2 C's, and there are 4 C's, and there are 8 C's, and there are 12 C's, or whatever. It is a language. It is a way of speaking, like French or German. This may be another language, too, but it could be learned at the center.

As long as you say to these two individuals that you don't accept their language, then in most cases it is difficult for them to

accept ours. You have to meet half-way: okay, we learn yours and you learn ours. I have never seen anyone working with deafs, *no one* actually that has ever embraced something like that and recognized their language as a language. They are not concerned about their language. There is a sign language, but they go to the sounds. I have never seen anyone try to relate to a non-hearing person with their own sounds and their own language. And the same goes with Christopher, the work with "autisms." His school was supposedly the best in the U.S., but no one there was really interested in what the kids were doing—they were there to learn our language.

Chris and Raymond both also have something in common with language which suggests that before we learn the meaning of a word, we respond to the sound. So there is something very basic in language, there is a language that's universal, so that was something else that was incorporated in the theatre. Ideally, this theatre can be appreciated by anyone anywhere. I just finished doing a play in Paris that is English words. People respond mostly to the sounds and apparently that's what the autists are doing too. They don't understand English but they listen to what is encoded in these words: energy. Last year, Christopher was taking old batteries, taping people speaking and playing the tapes so that he was getting these speeches "v-e-r-y s-l-o-w ..." It's very strange what you hear. There are all these other sounds put in the words.

L: Have you ever thought of per-

institution who had agreed to be hooked by a pseudo-mama, but he used to change his mother every Sunday. At the beginning, people thought "It won't last! He will settle down!" But he did not, he was passionately attached to a different mother each week. The situation became more and more traumatic for the abandonned pseudo-mamas so that one day the director called a pregnant female educator into his office and ordered her to do the following: "When you feel on the verge of giving birth to your child, hook Peter, to be his mother-of-the week and then we will take him to the clinic, to watch the birth of your child. And *then* he will have to understand that a child can only have *one* mother!"

3rd Step: The law of the Father

But there is no mother without a Father, and as soon as all the libidinal drives have been duly attached to the "mother", it is time to introduce the "Father" as a forbidding element. This introduction is supposed to break the imaginary relationship between the schizo and his pseudo-mama, and introduce him into the realm of a symbolic order where the object has to be known *mediately* through language taken here in its representative function.

I won't titillate you with the subtle techniques we invented to introduce a threatening papa, but only tell you the result.

4th step: The explosion

When it became plain to Mimi, Michel and Henri that they would have to cope with a third pseudo-something, a papa, they reacted in a very disconcerting way. Mimi broke three doors, 700 window panes and all the turntables in the institution within a week. Henri got lost in the nearby forest for three days. And the apotheosis of these fireworks was the reaction of Michel the evening of the day he was told that Claude would interfere in his relationship with Leila. He went down to the cellar where the furnace was and turned on a few taps so that a few minutes later, the furnace exploded, nearly destroying an empty wing of the château in which the institution was located. Naturally Michel was punished and sent to the nearest psychiatric hospital, pointing out this story's real function in relation to the Familial Power Machinery.

5th Step: The schizophrenization of the institution

The explosion was quite a shock, and once we had dusted the remains of fear from our well-intentioned hearts, we began to reflect; and instead of trying, to no avail, to *understand* once again the cases of Michel, Mimi, Henri and the others, we began to question our own functions as agents . . . of what kind of power?

We began to suspect our therapeutic pseudo-analytical approach, or at least to question the whole structuration we had been trying to build within, or on, or around the schizo. And instead of asking "But what have they done? And why?", we began—and believe me it was not easy—to ask "What have *we* done, and why? What are we? And in accordance with what have we done what we have tried to do? What is exactly our function in this big bad world? Have we not been deceived somewhere along the line? What is our relation to this institution, to the Power Machineries, especially the psyciatric one to which we thought we had to entrust Michel?" We could not answer. But something began to crumble as we were raising questions along these lines. We suddenly realized to what extent we were . . . yoked—*assujettis*—to a technological world to which the Oedipal tool is essential.

And the inter-personnal structures began to change at a fantastic pace. Married couples began to truly look with undeceived eyes at each other and at what they thought they owned as their lawful rights. We began to reorganize completely all the existing structures, not into other structures but in two directions of transformation: 1) A political action against existing institutions and their Power Machineries; 2) Moving communities, organized or rather unorganized in such a way as to facilitate the circulation of libido and objects according to moving patterns, other than the Oedipal pattern—ossified with no other functions than self-reproduction.

6th Step: The complexification or the Realization of Schizophrenia

It seems that while the schizophrenization was taking place we forgot about the schizo, and in fact we did. But while a real displacement was introduced into the institution on many more levels than before, and also all sorts of translations from one level to another, we suddenly realized that the use of space by the schizos fitted into the new ways invented to use the in-

forming in the U.S. with foreign languages in order to create an effect that would be similar to the one you achieve in Europe with English?

W: I thought about that, yes. I have done something of that sort with *Stalin:* Haf, hap, hat, there was 2 hats and 3 haps, 2-3-2-1-2, 1-2-3-2-1-2 [He is tapping on the table]—that sort of thing. That was just a pattern of sounds.

L: In your theatre, several things can coexist on the stage without being logically connected. Relationships are established, but they don't have to be formulated in words...

W: This is the way we think. This is the way we are here sitting and talking and I am looking at a picture and I am thinking I've got to go in an hour, I've got to be in an airplane, I've got to pack my bag —you know, all these things are going through the mind at the same time while I have this conversation with you. Actually, I just did a piece called "Dialogue" last week in Boston talking like that with Christopher. I find frequently that you have a chance to express more things at one time in speaking that way.

Guy Hocquenghem

We All Can't Die In Bed

Pasolini was killed by a swindler.

We all can't die in bed, like Franco. The Italian extreme left is indignant. M.A. Macciocchi, in *Le Monde*, speaks of a fascist plot. More perceptively, Gavi and Maggiori show how the incident was a microfascist coup: the assassin, Pelosi, wasn't used by fascism, he was the voluntary instrument of racism and the refusal of difference, the day-to-day non-politicized kind of fascism.

Probably, probably. Something all through this explanation does not convince me: the external and political nature of this view point on the murder of a homosexual. Certainly you can't help but agree with the analysis of the Pelosi case, you can't help but refuse to consider him, too, as a victim. Turning the other cheek is out of the question.

At the same time, Pasolini's death seems to me neither abominable, nor even, perhaps, regrettable. I find it rather satisfying, as far as I'm concerned. So much less stupid than a highway accident. In a way, I would want it for myself and for all my friends.

Sadian estheticism? I hope not: it is only that a fundamental aspect of this story of the murder of a homosexual, of homosexual murder, necessarily eludes the political analysts and those who mean to protect homosexuals from their potential murderers.

stitutionnal space. And that in this space the relationship with the schizos was becoming more and more a sort of partnership, I call it in French *partenarité schizophrénique*, and I would describe it as the spatial relationship between two ballet dancers dancing a pas-de-deux. A relation which functions on many more levels than the relationship established through verbal language. And relations which are not necessarily structured like the verbal language, but are only grasped by the different levels of semiotics described by Charles Sanders Peirce and that are now being reconsidered, although slightly differently, by Felix Guattari.[7] Semiotics perhaps has to be considered in a sort of generalized Pragmatism: I mean in a fundamentally pluralized space and in complex systems of mobile connexions.

To us then, the schizos began to appear potentially immensely rich. And the less the Oedipal pressure upon them, the more they complexified their relationship to their environment. The question, though, was no longer how to make them fit into the "normal" world, but how to open a breach in the normal world for the non-Oedipalized Schizo. It is in this sense, I believe, that schizophrenia may be considered as a revolutionary process, to use the words of Deleuze – Guattari, and to me, this has been made obvious through the effects that the whole process had on the Machinery of State Power.

THE REACTION

Aware of the fact that something unbearable was taking place in the institution because, I quote, "of the excessive number of divorces. . . . and the strange way of life chosen by the educators", the officials began to react on all sorts of levels. Cutting financial resources, prohibiting the use of this or that part of the château for security reasons (doors were broken, there were no locks, no fences. . . .), reducing the staff, etc., etc . . . But they had to cope with a very politically well-organized group of people, who had already accomplished an immense task with the neighbors, the shopkeepers all around, the families, with no small debt to white wine and good food. The attempts at repression immediately became an extremely violent and unexpected political fight, including trade unions, petitions signed by thousands of people, and so on . . ., before the repression could have any positive effect. So the officials withdrew their weapons. When I left the institution, the officials were preparing the second attack: they were ready to accept the new means of functioning as a pilot experiment, and to claim publicly that they were ready to help us financially at the expense of other institutions of the same type, thus nicely isolating us and turning the rest of this particular professional field quite against us.

ith reality often b

HALDOL®
(haloperidol)

hoice for starting

ight

Usually leaves patients relatively alert and responsive

Although some instances of drowsiness have been observed, marked sedation with HALDOL (haloperidol) is rare. In fact, HALDOL has been reported to actually increase activity in patients who are underactive, while it reduces activity to a normal level in those who are hyperactive. HALDOL has been found to "normalize" behavior and produce a sensitivity to the environment that allows more effective use of the social milieu and the therapeutic community.[5]

It is the intimate, ancient, and very strong bond between the homosexual and his murderer, a bond as traditional as their delinquent prescription in the big cities of the Nineteenth Century. We too often forget that dissimulation, the homosexual lie or secret, were never chosen for themselves, through a taste for oppression: they were necessary for the protection of a desiring impulse directed towards the underworld, of a libido attracted by objects outside the laws of common desire. Vautrin, in Balzac, very well represents this underside of the civilized world born of the corruption of big cities where homosexuality and delinquency go hand in hand. As an urban perversion, illicit homosexuality has, from its origins, been linked with underworld crime. There is a specific "dangerousness" which surrounds homosexuality, homosexual blackmail, homosexual murder.

Gavi and Maggiori quite rightly point out that in the Pelosi trial, the victim is just as guilty as the murderer. Which is certainly scandalous, but constitutes a distinctive feature of the homosexual condition. In the eyes of the courts and the police, there is, in these cases, no difference between victims and murderers, there is but one suspicious "milieu" united by mysterious bonds, a free-masonry of crime where the homo and the murderer intersect. Homosexuality is first of all, and will perhaps for a short while continue to be, a category of criminality. Personally, I prefer this state of affairs to its probable transformation into a psychiatric category of deviance. The libidinal link between the criminal and homosexual figures ignores the rational concepts of law, the division of individual responsibilities and the distribution of roles between victims and murderers. A homosexual murder is a whole, complete unto itself. A captain of the Belgian gendarmerie writes in an article devoted to the situation of homosexuals: "An attentive surveillance of this particular milieu makes it possible to compile a very useful documentation for the discovery of future swindlers, murderers, and possibly spies."

"Decriminalizing" Homosexuality?

Some will tell me that this is precisely what we're fighting against. So? Are we going to demand the rational progress of justice in distinguishing victims and the perpetrators? Are we going to require, as do the respectable homosexual associations, that the police and the courts accept complaints from homosexuals who are mistreated or blackmailed? Will we see gays, exactly like women, demand the condemnation of rapists by the courts and request protection under the law?

I think on the contrary that even in a struggle for liberation, homosexuality's hope still lies in the fact that it is perceived as delinquent. Let us not confuse self-defense with "respectabilization". The homosexual has frequent contact with the murderer: not only through masochism, suppressed guiltiness or a taste for transgression, but also because an encounter with such a character is a real possibility. Of course, one can always avoid it. All one needs is to avoid cruising in the criminal world. To stop cruising the streets. Not to cruise at all, or only to pick up serious young men from the same social sphere. Pasolini wouldn't be dead if he had only slept with his actors.

This is what eludes all those who sincerely want to "decriminalize" homosexuality, to defend it against itself by severing its bonds with a hard, violent and marginal world.

These combatants are unaware that they are thus joining the vast movement, in France and the U.S.A. for example, of respectabilization and neutralization of homosexuality. That movement does not progress by increased repression, but relies on the contrary on an intimate transformation of the homosexual type, freed from his fears and his marginality and finally integrated into the law.

The traditional queen, likeable or wicked, the lover of young thugs, the specialist of street urinals, all these exotic types inherited from the Nineteenth Century, give way to the reassuring modern young homosexual (from 25 to 40 years old)

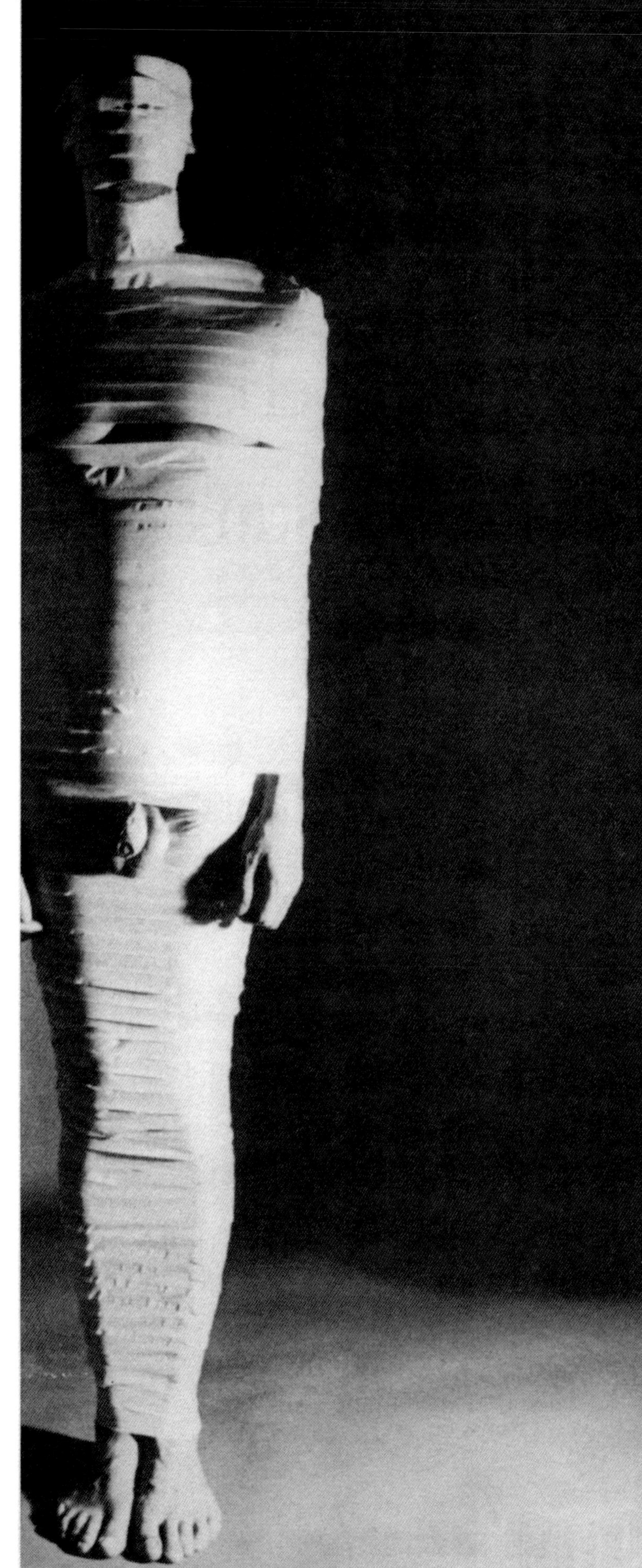

And this is the end of the non-story I wanted to tell, and I hope that you won't believe a word of what I have not said.

Translated by Daniel Sloate

BLACK & BLUE

POOR LITTLE RICH GIRL

HUMILIATION OF A SLAVE

"Get down there and lick that shit off my shoes!" He demanded. Excited and half terrified, I began to lick the shit from his boots.

★★Discomfort★★

★★Torture★

★★Pain★★

1. This is a polemic affirmation directed against an entire psychiatric current amply illustrated by the writings of George Heuyer and his epigones. From the very first line of his book *Schizophrenia* (PUF: Paris; 1974), Heuyer states that: "Schizophrenia is a mental illness." And it is this declaration which probably serves as the pretext for the practices which he describes as treatment for schizophrenia.

2. Thomas Szasz, *The Second Sin* (Anchor Press, Doubleday: New York) 1974.

3. Sigmund Freud, "On Negation", *Standard Edition,* XIX.

4. Martin Heidegger, *Identity and Difference* (Harper & Row: New York) 1974.

5. François Péraldi, "Institutions et appareils de pouvoir", *Brèches* (Aurore: Montréal), No. 6, Automne 1975.

6. Bruno Bettelheim, *The Empty Fortress* (U. of Chicago Press: Chicago) 1967.

7. Félix Guattari, "Pour une Micro-politique du désir", *Semiotext(e),* I: 1, 1974.

with mustache and brief case, without complexes or affectations, cold and polite, in an advertising job or sales position at a large department store, opposed to outlandishness, respectful of power, and a lover of enlightened liberalism and culture. Gone are the sordid and the grandiose, the amusing and the evil, sado-masochism itself is no longer anything more than a vestiary fashion for the proper queen.

A "White" Homosexuality

A stereotype of the legal homosexual, integrated into society, molded by the Establishment, and close to it in his tastes, reassured, moreover, by the presence in power of an undersecretary who himself is a homosexual without any false shame (homosexuality is no longer a secret shared only by a few initiates), progressively replaces the [illegible] diversity of

traditional homosexual styles. Finally will come the time when the homosexual will be nothing more than a tourist of sex, a gracious member of the *Club Mediterranee* who has been a little farther than the others, with an horizon of pleasure slightly broader than that of his average contemporary.

We cannot suspect any of this unless we frequent the homosexual circle, a rather closed whole which forges, even for the most isolated homosexual, the social image of his condition. Normalizing pressures more quickly, even if Paris and the bars of the rue Sainte-Anne are not all of France. While there are still queens seeking Arabs in the suburbs or at Pigalle, a movement has undeniably been launched for a truly white homosexuality in every sense of the term. And it is rather curious to note, looking at ads and films or at the exits of the gay bars, the emergence of a unisexual model —that is, common to homosexuals and heterosexuals—offered to the desires and identification of all. Homosexuals become indistinguishable, not because they hide their secret better, but because they are uniform in body and soul, rid of the saga of their ghetto, reintroduced fully and completely not into their difference but on the contrary into their similarity.

And everyone will fuck in his own social class, the dynamic junior executives will breathe with rapture the smell of their partners' after-shave, and even the Pope will no longer be able to detect anything wrong with it. A very natural thing, as a recent film said. The new official gay will not go looking for useless and dangerous adventures in the short-circuits between social classes. He will surely go on being a sexual pervert, he'll experiment with fist-fucking or flagellation, but with the cool good sense of sexological magazines, not in social violence, but in sex techniques. Pasolini was old-fashioned, the prodigious remains of an epoch in the process of being left behind.

Translated by George Richard Gardner, Jr.

The Ramones
Teenage Lobotomy

Lobotomy, lobotomy, lobotomy, lobotomy!
DDT did a job on me
Now I am a real sickie
Guess I'll have to break the news
That I got no mind to lose.
All the girls are in love with me
I'm a teenage lobotomy.

Slugs and snails are after me
DDT keeps me happy
Now I guess I'll have to tell 'em
That I got no cerebellum.
Gonna get my PhD
I'm a teenage lobotomy.

Left, the isolation and despair of the mentally depressed patient. Right, electric convulsion therapy (ECT), still commonly used in cases of severe depression. The protective gag placed in the patient's mouth is to prevent him damaging his teeth or biting his tongue.

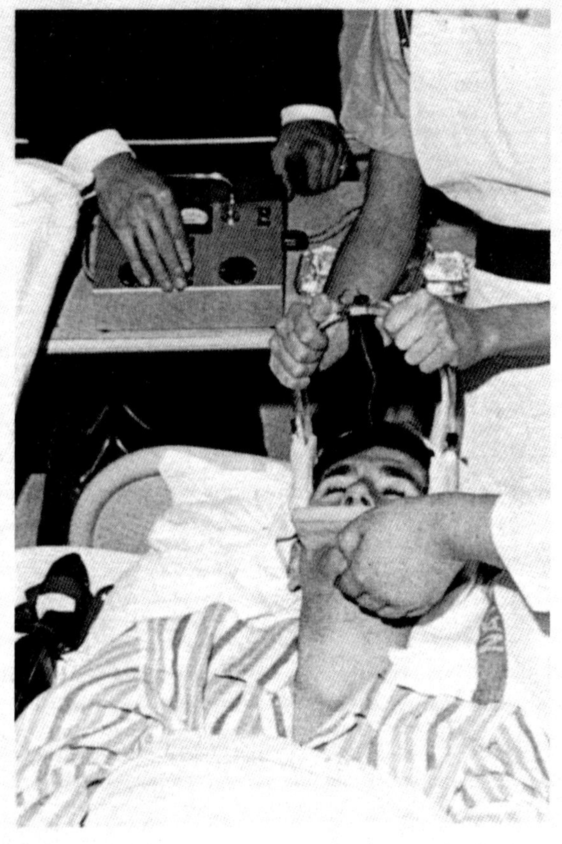

almost every detail of his experience, and described it vividly in *The Lancet* of February 12, 1966:

"I was chiefly struck by the godlike detachment of the hospital psychiatrist. To be fair, this varied from man to man, but I got the impression that, by and large, they thought they could cure anything with drugs and shock, in much the same way that a mechanic tackles engine repairs. The atmosphere of the place was such that once I began to recover, I tried to get out as quickly as possible, even though I was conscious of not being myself. I did sign myself out for a few days, but I was persuaded to go back. Perhaps this attitude to the medical staff was a symptom of my illness.

"On the effect of the drugs I was given, I am more sure of my ground. The worst part of the experience was when I began to recover. I could not concentrate for two minutes together. I could neither read nor follow the television. Occupational therapy needed a tremendous effort—not the actual work, but to take an interest in it. On the other hand, just sitting doing nothing brought no relief. The

The Boston Declaration

The Fourth Annual North American Conference on Human Rights and Psychiatric Oppression meeting in Boston Massachusetts, May 28-31, 1976, adopts the following positions:

We oppose INVOLUNTARY PSYCHIATRIC INTERVENTION, including, but not limited to involuntary civil commitment, forced psychiatric procedures, and "voluntary" procedures without informed consent

because it is immoral and unconstitutional;

because it is a denial of freedom, due process of law, and the right to be let alone;

because it is a denial of the individual's right to control his or her own soul, mind, and body.

We oppose FORCED PSYCHIATRIC PROCEDURES, such as drugging, shock, psychosurgery, restraints, seclusion, and aversive behavior modification

because they humiliate, debilitate, immobilize, and injure;

because they are at best quackery (attempts to "cure" non-existent diseases) and at worst torture (brutal, painful techniques to control human thought, feeling and conduct.)

We oppose the PSYCHIATRIC SYSTEM

because it is inherently tyrannical;

because it is an extra-legal, parallel police force which suppresses cultural and political dissidence;

because it punishes individuals who have had or claim to have had spiritual experiences, and invalidates those experiences by defining them as "symptoms" of "mental illness";

because it uses the trappings of medicine and science to mask the social control function it serves;

because it feeds on the poor and powerless: the elderly, women, children, sexual minorities, Third World people;

because it creates a stigmatized class of society which is easily oppressed and controlled;

because it invalidates the real needs of poor people by offering social welfare under the guise of psychiatric "care and treatment";

because its growing influence in education, the prisons, the military, government, industry, and medicine threatens to turn society into a psychiatric state, made up of two classes, those who give "therapy" and those who receive it;

because it is similar in important ways to the Inquisition, chattel slavery, and Nazi and Soviet concentration camps; that it cannot be reformed but must be abolished.

We oppose the CONCEPT OF "MENTAL ILLNESS"

because it justifies involuntary psychiatric intervention, especially the imprisonment of individuals who have not been convicted of any crime.

on Psychiatric Oppression

We oppose the use of PSYCHIATRIC TERMS

because they are fundamentally stigmatizing, demeaning, unscientific and superstitious, and propose that plain English be used in their place: for example:

Plain English	*Psychiatric Term*
Psychiatric Inmate	Mental Patient, Mentally Disabled, Mentally Handicapped Person
Psychiatric Institution	Mental Hospital
Psychiatric System	Mental Health System
Psychiatric Procedure	Treatment
Characteristic, Trait	Symptom
Conduct	Behavior
Drug	Medication
Drugging	Chemotherapy
Electroshock	Electrotherapy, Electric Stimulation Therapy

WE BELIEVE:

that people should have the right to suicide.

that alleged dangerousness, whether to oneself or others, should not be considered grounds for denying personal liberty; that only proven criminal acts should be the basis for such denial;

that person charged with crimes should be tried in the criminal justice system with due process of law and that psychiatric professionals should not be given expert witness status.

that attention should be focussed not on the potential dangerousness of the psychiatric defendant, but on the actual criminality of those who use involuntary psychiatric interventions.

that there should be no involuntary psychiatric interventions in prisons; that the prison system should be reformed and humanized.

that as long as one person's liberty is restricted no one is free.

that a voluntary network of care and support should be developed to serve the needs of people without limiting their rights or lessening their dignity or self-respect.

that the psychiatric system is by definition a pacification program controlled by psychiatrists and designed to help, persuade, coerce people into adjusting to established social norms. Throughout society, more and more people are abandoning these norms. More and more people are demanding self-determination and community control. More and more people are realizing that economic and political power is concentrated in the hands of a few, who are determined to keep it—by any means necessary including involuntary psychiatric intervention. But we are asserting that as an instrument of social control, involuntary psychiatric intervention is a procedure whose time has gone. We are demanding an end to involuntary psychiatric intervention and we are demanding individual liberty and social justice. We intend to make these words real and will not rest until we do.

Ex-Patients

Continued from page [illegible]

Questioned after the session John Conrad, the family social worker, verified these observations, noting that he thought the [illegible]

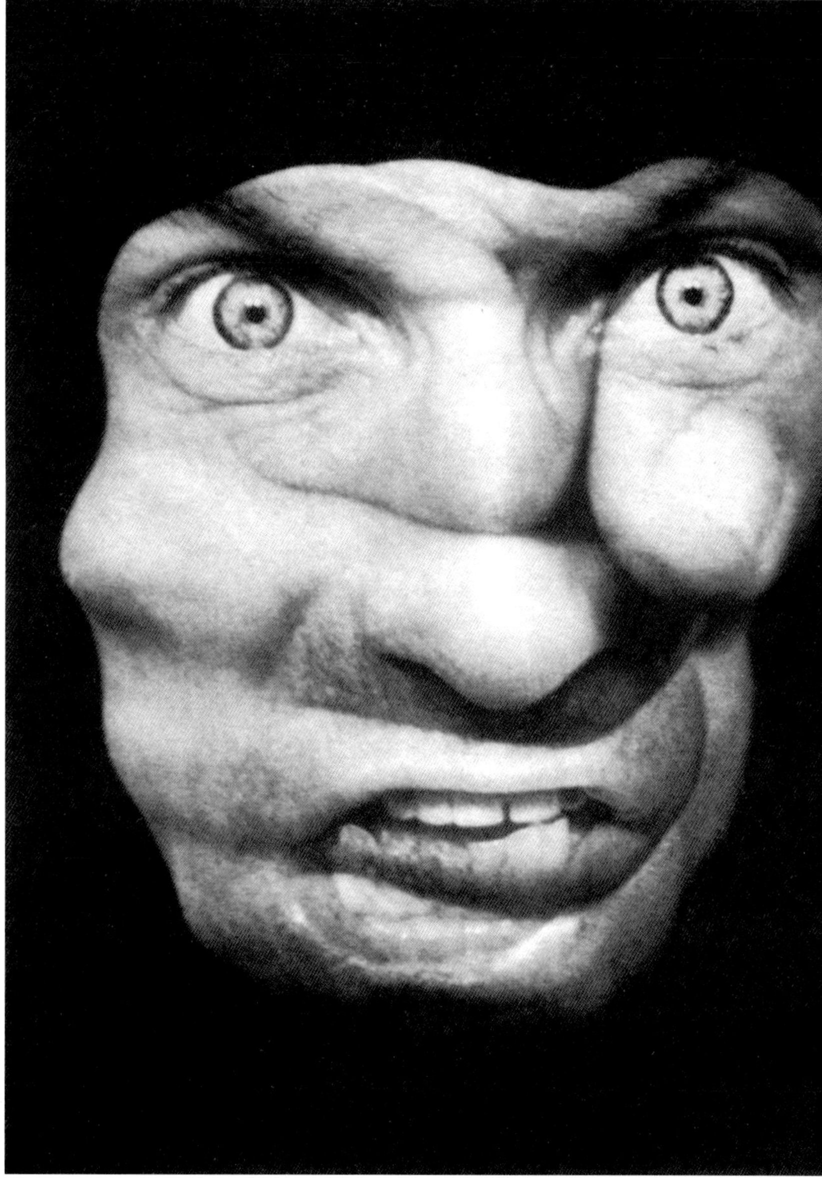

Ex-Patients

Continued from facing page

overlook it." Thelma also implied that she was very concerned about the reaction of her boyfriend to her illness, which might indicate why she is not filling her medication prescriptions. Frankie, as well, is not taking his medication, ostensibly because it prevents ejaculation.

On the other hand, both Joe and Ben said they were not ashamed of the illness and that their relatives knew about it.

Former patients agreed that having understanding by their families and taking their medicine was the most important part of coming home. Zwerling also emphasized the importance of continuing treatment after discharge even when a former patient feels "perfectly well." He noted they have found over and over again that discontinuation of treatment can be "a real disaster."

"When you're discharged, it's very hard even facing that you have been there and are coming out. It's good to be home where the environment is very different [illegible] comfortable [illegible] and you can take things at your own pace," Ruth said.

Her husband added, "I've come to think that almost anything can be overcome if you have a real understanding. [illegible] So with Ruth I try to be understanding. Sometimes I find it very difficult because, I guess, of the way I was brought up. [illegible]" Although he and Ruth speak excellent English, they noted the difficulty of using mental health services when one cannot speak it and the difficulty in locating services outside one's own neighborhood.

A good deal of support was expressed for the treatment of mental illness. Helen noted the improvements since her husband was first ill in 1954 and Carol stressed the necessity of being completely open with the therapist, someone removed from one's life who would keep information confidential.

The project is financed by Lederle Laboratories in New York.

One-Day Course

The Johns Hopkins Medical Institutions Department of Psychiatry and Behavioral Sciences in Baltimore, Maryland, will offer a one-day course June 24 on "Topics in Contemporary Psychiatry." Course topics will include schizophrenia, anorexia nervosa, dementia, and simple psychometric procedures for use in clinical practice. In addition to a series of short lectures, there will be clinical presentations of adult and adolescent patients. This program has been approved for six and one half hours of Category 1 credit toward the Physician's Recognition Award of the American Medical Association. Further information is available from Program Coordinator, Office of Continuing Education, Room [illegible] Turner Auditorium, 720 Rutland Ave., Baltimore, Md. 21205 [illegible]

International Symposium

[illegible]

William Burroughs
The Limits of Control

There is growing interest in new techniques of mind-control. It has been suggested that Sirhan Sirhan was the subject of post-hypnotic suggestion as he sat shaking violently on the steam table in the kitchen of the Ambassador Hotel in Los Angeles while an as yet unidentified woman held him and whispered in his ear. It has been alleged that behavior modification techniques are used on troublesome prisoners and inmates, often without their consent. Dr. Delgado, who stopped a charging bull by remote control of electrodes in the bull's brain, has left the U.S. recently to pursue his studies on human subjects in Spain. Brainwashing, psychotropic drugs, lobotomy and other more subtle forms of psychosurgery; the technocratic control apparatus of the United States has at its fingertips new techniques which if fully exploited could make Orwell's 1984 seem like a benevolent utopia. But words are still the principal instruments of control. Suggestions are words. Persuasions are words. Orders are words. No control machine so far devised can operate without words, and any control machine which attempts to do so relying entirely on external force or entirely on physical control of the mind will soon encounter the limits of control.

A basic impasse of all control machines is this: Control needs time in which to exercise control. Because control also needs opposition or acquiescence; otherwise it ceases to be control. I *control* a hypnotized subject (at least partially); I *control* a slave, a dog, a worker; but if I establish *complete* control somehow, as by implanting electrodes in the brain, then my subject is little more than a tape recorder, a camera, a robot. You don't *control* a tape recorder—you *use* it. Consider the distinction, and the impasse implicit here. All control systems try to make control as tight as possible, but at the same time, if they succeeded completely, there would be nothing left to control. Suppose for example a control system installed electrodes in the brains of all prospective workers at birth. Control is now complete. Even the thought of rebellion is neurologically impossible. No police force is necessary. No psychological control is necessary, other than pressing buttons to achieve certain activations and operations. The controllers could turn on the machine, and the workers would carry out their tasks, at least they might think so. However, they have ceased to *control* the workers, since the workers have become machine-like tape recorders.

When there is no more opposition, control becomes a meaningless proposition. It is highly questionable whether a human organism could survive complete control. There would be nothing there. No persons there. *Life is will,* motivation and the workers would no longer be alive, perhaps literally. The concept of suggestion as a control technique presupposes that control is partial and not complete. You do not have to give suggestions to your tape-

N.° 705
Nom BURROUGHS
Prénoms William Siward
Profession Employé المهنة
Arrivé le 18/1/55 وصل بتاريخ
Nationalité américaine الجنسية
Passeport 32 الجواز عدد
Délivré le 21/11/55
à TANGER
Domicile 6 terrasse
Autorisation valable jusqu'au
19 JANVIER 1958
Coût Frs. 100 الثمن فرنك

Signature إمضاء
William Seward Burroughs
Délivré à Tanger le منح في طنجة
21 JANVIER 1957
عن عامل طنجة وناحيتها
P. Le Gouverneur de Tanger et de sa Province
MOHAMMED AKALAY

تجديد الإقامة
Prorogation de validité
du
au
Fait à Tanger le حرر بطنجة في
عن العامل
P. Le Gouverneur.

recorder, nor subject it to pain, coercion or persuasion.

The Mayan control system, where the priests kept the all-important Books of seasons and gods, the Calender, was predicated on the illiteracy of the workers. Modern control systems are predicated on universal literacy since they operate through the mass media—a very two-edged control instument, as Watergate has shown. Control systems are vulnerable, and the news media are by their nature uncontrollable, at least in Western society. The alternative press is news, and alternative society is news, and as such both are taken up by the mass media. The monopoly that Hearst and Luce once exercised is breaking down. In fact, the more completely hermetic and seemingly successful a control system is, the more vulnerable it becomes. A weakness inherent in the Mayan system was that they didn't need an army to control their workers, and therefore did not have an army when they did need one to repel invaders. It is a rule of social structures that anything that is not needed will atrophy and become inoperative over a period of time. Cut off from the war game—and remember, the Mayans had no neighbors to quarrel with—they lose the ability to fight. In the Mayan Caper I suggested that such a hermetic control system could be completely disoriented and shattered by even one person who tampered with the control calender on which the control system depended more and more heavily as the actual means of force withered away.

Consider a control situation: ten people in a lifeboat. Two armed self-appointed leaders force the other eight to do the rowing while they dispose of the food and water, keeping most of it for themselves and doling out only enough to keep the other eight rowing. The two leaders now *need* to exercise control to maintain an advantageous position which they could hold without it. Here the method of control is force—the possession of guns. Decontrol would be accomplished by overpowering the leaders and taking their guns. This effected, it would be advantageous to kill them at once. So once embarked on a policy of control, the leaders must continue the policy as a matter of self-preservation. Who, then, needs to control others? Those who protect by such control a position of relative advantage. Why do they need to exercise control? Because they would soon lose this position of advantage and in many cases their lives as well, if they relinquished control.

Now examine the means by which control is exercised in the lifeboat scenario: The two leaders are armed, let's say, with .38 revolvers—twelve shots and eight potential opponents. They can take turns sleeping. However, they must still exercise care not to let the eight rowers know that they intend to kill them when land is sighted. Even in this primitive situation, force is supplemented with deception and persuasion. The leaders will disembark at point A, leaving the others sufficient food to reach point B, they explain. They have the compass and they are contributing their navigational skills. In short they will endeavour to convince the others that this is a cooperative enterprise in which they are all working for the same goal. They may also make concessions: Increase food and water rations. A concession of course means the retention of control—that is, the disposition of the food and water supplies. By persuasion and concessions they hope to prevent a concerted attack by the eight rowers.

Actually they intend to poison the drinking water as soon as they leave the boat. If all the rowers knew this they would attack, no matter what the odds. We now see that another essential factor in control is to conceal from the controlled the actual intentions of the controllers. Extending the lifeboat analogy to the Ship of State, few existing governments could withstand a sudden, all-out attack by all their underpriviliged citizens, and such an attack might well occur if the intentions of certain existing governments were unequivocally apparent. Suppose the lifeboat leaders had built a barricade and could withstand a

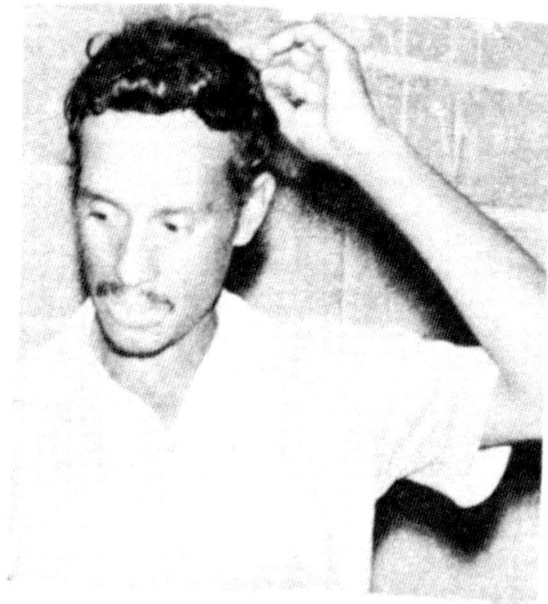

concerted attack and kill all eight of the rowers if necessary. They would then have to do the rowing themselves and neither would be safe from the other. Similarly, a modern government armed with heavy weapons and prepared for attack could wipe out 95% of its citizens. But who would do the work, and who would protect them from the soldiers and technicians needed to make and man the weapons? Successful control means achieving a balance and avoiding a showdown where all-out force would be necessary. This is achieved through various techniques of psychological control, also balanced. The techniques of both force and psychological control are constantly improved and refined, and yet worldwide dissent has never been so widespread or so dangerous to the present controllers.

All modern control systems are riddled with contradictions. Look at England. "Never go too far in any direction" is the basic rule on which England is built, and there is some wisdom in that. However, avoiding one impasse they step into another. Anything that is not going forward is on the way out. Well, nothing lasts forever. Time is that which ends, and control needs time. England is simply stalling for time as it slowly founders. Look at America. Who actually controls this country? It is very difficult to say. Certainly the very wealthy are one of the most powerful control groups. They own newspapers, radio stations, and so forth. They are also in a position to control and manipulate the entire economy. However, it would not be to their advantage to set up or attempt to set up an overtly fascist government. Force, once brought in, subverts the power of money. This is another impasse of control: protection from the protectors. Hitler formed the S.S. to protect him from the S.A. If he had lived long enough, the question of protection from the S.S. would have posed itself. The Roman Emperors were at the mercy of the Praetorian Guard, who in one year killed twenty Emperors. And besides, no modern industrialized country has ever gone fascist without a program of military expansion. There is no longer any place to expand to—after hundreds of years, colonialism is a thing of the past.

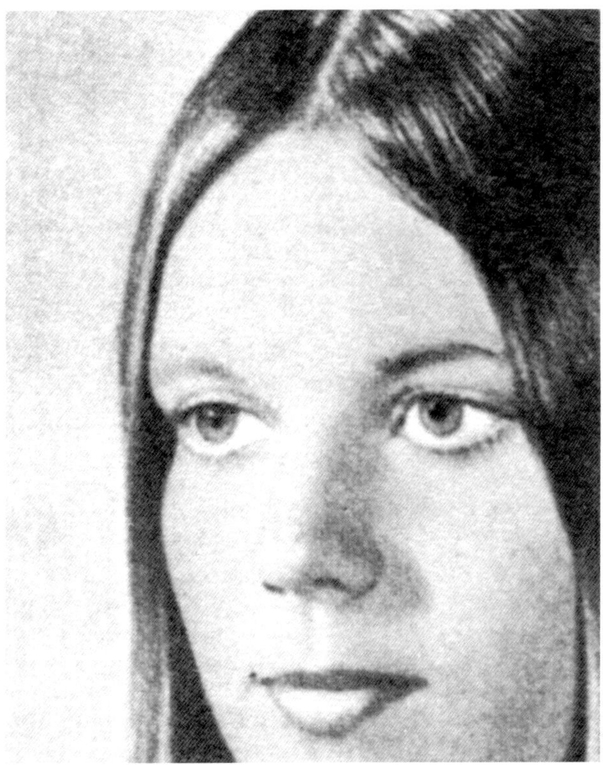

There can be no doubt that a cultural revolution of unprecedented dimensions has taken place in America during the last thirty years, and since America is now the model for the rest of the western world, this revolution is worldwide. Another factor is the mass media, which spreads any cultural movements in all directions. The fact that this worldwide revolution has taken place indicates that the controllers have been forced to make concessions. Of course, a concession is still the retention of control. Here's a dime, I keep a dollar. Ease up on censorship, but remember we could take it all back. Well, at this point that is questionable.

Concession is another control bind. History shows that once a government starts to make concessions it is a one-way street. They could of course take all the concessions back, but that would expose them to the double jeopardy of revolution and the much greater danger of overt fascism, both highly dangerous to the present controllers. Does any clear policy arise from this welter of confusion? The answer is probably no. The mass media has proven a very unreliable and even treacherous instrument of control. It is uncontrollable owing to its basic need for NEWS. If one paper or even a string of papers owned by the same person tries to kill a story, that makes that story hotter as NEWS. Some paper will pick it up. To impose government censorship on the media is a step in the direction of State control, a step which big money is most reluctant to take.

I don't mean to suggest that control automatically defeats itself, nor that protest is therefore unnecessary. A government is never more dangerous than when embarking on a self-defeating or downright suicidal course. It is encouraging that some behavior modification projects have been exposed and halted, and certainly such exposure and publicity should continue. In fact, I submit that we have a *right* to insist that all scientific research be subject to public scrutiny, and that there should be no such thing as "top-secret" research.

R 13665

Shoot Out The Star Game

ROCKAWAY PLAYLAND

All Star (Red) Must Be Shot From Card To Win Prize

his Target Void If Handled By Anyone Except Attendant

NATIONAL TICKET CO., SHAMOKIN, PA.

Louis Wolfson

Full Stop for an Infernal Planet

or The Schizophrenic Sensorial Epileptic and Foreign Languages

We shall see at the time of the noblest, the most glorious, the most musical ("One Hundred Thousand Love Songs"), the sexiest, the most transcendant, the most altruistic and equally the most selfish, the most excusable, the most intelligent, especially the healthiest, and the holiest, the most divine instant that a humanity can attain anywhere and anytime, while the redemptive flame of one hundred thousand good H-bombs is lit and one hundred thousand new happy little celestial bodies are born, we shall see whether we suffer or lick the flames or if we are too stunned by the shock to understand what's happening or too blessed, or one or the other according to personal, individual fate, chance, Providence . . . Or perhaps the blessed apocalypse would come immediately after some scientists succeed in producing momentarily four whole ounces of so-called anti-matter, supposedly consisting of anti-particles, which alone would suffice for the sanctification of every one of us, four ounces of anti-water, for example, somewhat less than one hundred and twenty-five grams (the contents therefore of one-fourth of an enema, or little enema [or shouldn't we rather say "anti-enema"]). All dead, all "equal", all good socialists, good communists, good democrats, good republicans, good crusaders, good zionists, good islamized . . . all beatified . . . no more reaction, revolution, counterrevolution, "establishment", consumer society, gadgets, or consumption of any kind . . . and finally the world-wide revolution consumated . . . no more need to seduce the voters, to agree with the leader or the *troyka* of the party, to pander to presidents of the republic, to erect altars to dead old enemas of politicians, to lick the arses of their corpses . . . no more need to fart, to piss, to shit . . . no more need to suffer, to make suffer . . . to ratiocin-

---

Louis Wolfson's *Le Schizo et les langues* or "the psychotic's phonetics" (Gallimard: Paris, 1970), echoes Raymond Roussel in its attack against morphology and syntax. Wolfson wrote his memoirs in French in defiance of his mother tongue (he is American). Although the title ironically intimates that Wolfson himself is the "schizo", what he explicitly pursues through his texts is the "Ultimate Truth and Writing". The following excerpt, which concludes the new version of his book to be called *Point final à une planète infernale,* attempts to give a "clear statement of the only possible response to the most important question that humanity in its cosmos should ask itself . . . planetary disintegration, radioactive deserts . . . BOOM!!!!" (Letter of 29 May 1977 to S.L.)

ate, to philosophize on a frightful, monstrous phenomenon, to pray to God, all of us being triumphantly in His kingdom, with the angels . . . a planetary kamikase or Massada, a perfect Islamic submission . . .

N****
(date)

Mister President (or Minister, Chancellor, Senator, Ambassador, Representative, Mayor. . . .) Y** Z**
(Dear) Sir,

I have sent a letter similar to what follows to the Secretary-General of the UN:

I cannot understand why people at the UN and elsewhere, who are supposed to be intelligent and who, apparently, like to think of themselves as "good people" keep talking about the limitation of nuclear arms or even about disarmament!

If you consider that around three thousand years ago our poor planet was infected with only 50 million (perhaps a slightly low estimate) copies (while, certainly, a single specimen would already have been too many) of the unfortunate human species; if you imagine having had at that time a pile of good H-bombs at your disposal and having used them to crumble the crust of this damned planet Earth and possibly to convert it into a second chain of asteroids, a first large ring of such little celestial bodies being located between the orbits of Mars and Jupiter; and if you consider then what a litany of unspeakable horrors which still continue and are synonymous with humanity would not have occurred . . .!! What philosopher would have even dreamed, thirty-five years ago, of thus attacking the so sick matter which we all are? What philanthropist? What man of good will?

But now we absolutely must not miss the chance—and to have such a chance is too good to be true—finally to bring to an end at last this infamous litany of abominations that we all are (collectively and individually); and I mean by that, obviously, in a complete atomic-nuclear way! Don't they say that the best medicine is prophylactic medicine? The tragedy, the true catastrophe—despite what the notable liars seem to want to sell us—is that humanity continues . . . while the divine benediction would be qualified as thermonuclear or some equivalent thereof. Not to be of this opinion is to be selfish, criminal, monstrous, if not stark mad.

Yours faithfully,

L . . .

P.S. I suppose that all, or nearly all, religions, if one also wants to look at things from that angle, conceive of Hell or Hades as a subterranean place. But if the Earth were converted into a large ring of planetoids around the sun, then no more "under world". . . . ! As go the words of a certain very popular song: "No more problems in the sky." And as the Pope said during his trip to the Far-East: "God is light", and without a doubt included there is the resurrectional light at the time of a planetary disintegration . . . the disintegration of an infernal star.

* * *

However, such letters naturally having no perceptible effect, perhaps even an effect contrary to the one sought, our protagonist would become a partisan of violence, of arsons and assassinations, and would hope—all the more naively, since a certain ignorance, a certain cowardice, a certain indifference reign . . . over all—that men and women of true good will would suppress as quickly as possible the monsters of cruelty all over the world who speak of the limitation of armaments . . . and thus reveal their "prenuclear", outdated, infantile, unrealistic, backward, hypocritical, inhuman way of thinking . . . and likewise a fanatical zeal for turning their backs on certain marvelous properties of matter which are known at last and infinitely beneficial. . . . ! (It is not then, for example, visits, be they reciprocal and with a minimum of red-tape, between East and West Berliners or between East and West Germans, that are needed, but rather the audacious attempt to enable *all* humanity, in as short a time as possible, to take intergalactic trips through the skies . . . ! It is quite understandable that so many made such a big deal over the famous lunar expeditions ["a giant step . . . !"], which however took a week for the round-trip in space although our natural satellite is only two light-seconds away. So if you consider that, flying at the speed of light [300,000 kilometers per second], it would still take one hundred thousand years [diameter of the disc] to traverse only our own galaxy [the Milky Way: 100,000 million {= 100 billion} stars among which our sun is only one of average size {less than two-thirds of a million typographic characters in the present work}] and that it would take one hundred sixty thousand more years at that same "giddy" speed to reach the nearest neighboring galaxy, one among hundreds of millions of others and whose numbers seem limited only by the lone power [extending however to a distance of billions of light-years] of man to penetrate his cosmos and these hundreds of millions of galaxies seem to move away from each other at unbelievable speeds [an exploding universe, but, alas! not quickly enough for the great salvation of all Earthlings] . . . !)

Whatever heights science may attain, it may only make more and more patent two facts: 1. Those heights can only be attained by mercilessly crushing and walking over mountains of human beings. 2. And indeed be it for this single reason, all of planet Earth should become as quickly as possible a radioactive desert or disappear through disintegration. Do those who hold power have to wait, before they'll submit to the obvious, until the world population becomes so enormous that more people will die every day than there are in a nation of respectable size today? Until the chaos and the impossibility of finding legitimate meaning are multiplied by the infinite? Until everyone has become raving mad? And the "future generations" down here that we talk about so much, are they anything but mineral salts in the earth, fluid or even solid water, gas molecules in the air, and such little "tripe", which—in the course of the processes of germination and growth—would become plants which would be guzzled up by pregnant women or gobbled by herbivores, whose flesh, in turn, would be ingested by those same pregnant women . . .?! The true good fortune of the "future generations" would be for them not to materialize at all!!

To my mother, a musician, who died in the middle of May at midnight between Tuesday and Wednesday from a metastatic mesothelium (and medical failures) at the Memorial Death House in Manhattan, one thousand 977.

(Early in 1972, Rose (M(l)inarsky Wolfson) Brooke, nearly seventy years old—having witnessed the new tenants upstairs move out and the new tenant downstairs on the verge of doing likewise, as had others before her, and detecting the apparent worsening of her only son's schizophrenia—wanted to 'retire' once and for all by selling her three-family house after having found a good apartment in a better neighborhood, and to move there with the aforementioned son and her husband. Destiny (?) arranged that this semi-luxury apartment which she found in Queens (a borough of New York City) would be located on 138th Street and that, five years later, she would die on the 138th day of the year).

Translated by George Richard Gardner, Jr.

FEUERWERKSKÖRPER DM 25
ATOMDETONATION
ELEKTRISCH
LOS NSI - 14
VERBRAUCH BIS 6 - 67

Lee Breuer of Mabou Mines

Media Rex

Sylvère LOTRINGER: *What is your last "animation",* Shaggy Dog, *about?*

Lee BREUER: The story is simply the prototypical American love affair circa 1957-1977. Twenty years of emotional programming.

SL: *What about the dog?*

LB: The dog, in California slang (we are mainly West Coast), is a woman who follows, who has no consciousness of her own but derives completely from the male consciousness. Attachment to the male becomes a matter of life and death. *Shaggy Dog* is a description of this syndrome that eventually becomes the energy and motivation for liberation.

SL: *The woman is passive, but so is her John. He follows and reacts as much as she does. Everyone in the play is passive then.*

LB: That's right. By the time John is introduced, instead of finding the leader, you have the image of a man who himself was being led. So they both are being led by the fantasies of each other and not by reality whatsoever.

SL: *Where is reality then?*

LB: Beneath media consciousness, or above it. *Shaggy Dog* is an attempt to break the elastic blanket of media consciousness and find some base of realer action.

SL: *How can you break the blanket?*

LB: I tried to write simultaneous pieces that comment on each other. *Shaggy Dog* is divided into two plays: the sound track and the image track. The sound track is the story of John and Rose. The image track is the story of

Eddie Griffin

Breaking Men's Minds

The use of behavior control and human experimentation techniques against prisoners is on the rise in the U.S. Indefinite solitary confinement, sensory deprivation, forced druggings and mind-control techniques are being used more and more to break prisoners and stop their attempts to fight deteriorating conditions in U.S. prisons.

The most ominous of these programs is the long-term control unit at the Marion, Illinois Federal Prison—the replacement for Alcatraz as the maximum-security prison in America. Many men have been driven insane in this unit. In the past five years, nine men have committed suicide in the unit or just after being released from it.

Because of this growing crisis, the prisoners in the control unit, the Marion Brothers, have brought a precedent-setting class action suit against the U.S. Bureau of Prisons. Bono vs. Saxbe, *which seeks to close the control unit permanently, was tried in 1975 in the federal courts. In April, 1978 the court ruled in favor of the Bureau of Prisons. While closing the notorious sensory deprivation boxcar cells, the court allowed the control unit to remain open. In fact, the court justified the use of the control unit with one of the oldest and most repressive legal doctrines, the doctrine of preventive detention. Under*

Eddie Griffin is one of the Marion brothers. He has been detained in the control unit—which he describes here as "the end of the line"—of the Federal prison in Marion, Illinois.

Rose's attempt to purge herself of the sound track. The narrative level (the sound track) is an amalgam of all kinds of pop records—we must have used 40 different singers—all the way from Billy Holliday to Stevie Wonder. The image track is a bit more obscure. I was interested in Eastern psychology as an alternate point of view to a Freudian or Jungian approach. In this perspective, the ego is composed of five parts, which correspond to the five rooms in Rose's house. Each of these has its imagery, its own color, its own symbolic shape. The bedroom is greed, the bathroom is pride, the kitchen hate or aggression, the cutting-room jealousy and the living-room, the center, is stupidity. The idea is that the four wings of the mandala all stem from ignorance, and stupidity is interpreted simply as inability to see the truth.

SL: *How do you deal with stupidity?*

LB: One of the tenets of the so-called avant-garde now has been elimination of media influence, purity of a certain sort: pure sound, no amplification, pure movement, the minimalist performance. What I wanted to do is just jump in the middle of a big steak dinner, in the middle of the whole garbage dump and then look for a way to jump it. My great thrill is that there is not one piece of acting in *Shaggy Dog* that does not represent a cliché. I wanted to commit myself to cheapness (on my own terms) and the only aesthetic control I had over this garbage was how I would manipulate the jumps.

SL: *How do you jump the garbage?*

LB: I use oppositions. Oppositions are the base of the acting technique as well as the writing technique. Of course, the idea of oppositions I originally got from Brecht (they are the key to the alienation effect), but I think I explored them in my own way. Oppositions pull apart a closed system, the closed system of popular or commercial emotional manipulation. If you allow your mind to pull apart, categories will not grab. They will leave a space of truth in between them so that you will not rest in an accepted perception. The objective was to pull apart the audience's expectation so that some new perception had room to materialize between these various poles.

SL: *A dramatic development usually results from a filling-in between two poles. A certain dose of ambiguity is dialectically created to be later resolved into mental unity.* Shaggy Dog

this doctrine, prisoners can be put in the control unit indefinitely on the basis of what behavior controllers call "predictive behavior"—that is, they can "predict that a prisoner will join a hunger strike, work stoppage, etc.

This decision is now being appealed. In addition, the National Committee to Support the Marion Brothers, organized in 1975, is leading an organizing campaign to win public support for the Marion Brothers. It is important that they win this battle. If the prison system wins, other control units like Marion's will be built.

I was one of the so-called "incorrigibles" who had come into conflict with the Terre Haute officials and was threatened with being sent to Marion. After receiving an injury in the prison machine shop where I narrowly missed losing a finger, I was patched up, administered a painkiller, then sent back to work. There was almost a repeat of the same accident soon afterwards, so I decided to quit my work. I was immediately locked up in segregation. Prisoners do not control their institution. My insistence led to my being shipped to Marion.

A BEHAVIOR MODIFICATION LABORATORY

The constructs of the prison are somewhat peculiar. Some not so outstanding features do not make the least economical sense, and are often totally out of physiological order. But these features, when viewed from a psychological angle, begin to take on new meaning. For example, the prison is minced into small sections and subsections, divided by a system of electronic and mechanical grills and further reinforced by a number of strategically locked steel doors. Conceivably, the population can be sectioned off quickly in times of uprising. But even for the sake of security the prison is laced with too many doors. Every few feet a prisoner is confronted by one. So he must await permission to enter or exit at almost every stop. A man becomes peeved. But this is augmented by the constant clanging which bombards his brain so many times a day until his nervous system becomes knotted. The persistent reverberation

obviously doesn't function in that way. The contradiction is not meant to produce movement. The two poles are kept far apart so that the energy becomes visible.

LB: The image I always had in mind was that of sparks jumping a gap. If you pull the electrodes too far apart, there will be no spark. If they are too close together, there will be a constant flow: too simple. But if they are just in the right position, you'll get fft., fft., fft. and these little jumps are the furthest extension that energy will jump. I kept experimenting with the right distance between image, sound, performing, dialogue so that the spark will jump the furthest.

SL: *How do you actually create this distance?*

LB: I make visual puns on verbal ideas. The metaphor of Rose's *Vogue* type of decoration, of *interior* decoration, is the decoration of one's mind in the light of romanticism and the attempt at splitting it. The split is done with a sword and so we use an axe as a joke because axe of course alludes to guitar, and one says "one's axe," one's thing, one's weapon. I wanted to translate this as a visual joke.

SL: *In other words, you literalize the metaphor in order to create a dramatization. This is quite a perverse use of the traditional metaphor. You don't assimilate the two terms, you don't substitute one term for another, you simply keep them side by side, and this produces the spark!*

LB: We set up a pattern of this = this = this, etc., and the idea is that it will go on for ever.

SL: *The more equal. . .*

LB: The more it remains itself. A perfect example of this pattern is when Clover, the child, is talking about the Art World. JoAnne says: "See yourself as a heavyweight" and the boxing begins. This is just the style of association I wanted to establish. There is a woman speaking in a boxing metaphor and actually using Muhammed Ali's measurements. The metaphor for the heavyweight is a copy of an Eastern dance image, a certain stance with the head bent over and arm raised. Simultaneously the punching bag is used as a bass drum and dealt with musically. So Clover, the child, consciousness of the Art World, is perceiving herself as a heavyweight, a masculine image being spoken of by a woman who herself is a heavy using a traditional Eastern metaphor with a very literal metaphor of the

tends to resurrect and reinforce the same bleak feeling which introduced the individual to the Marion environment. It is no coincidence. This system is designed with conscious intent.

Every evening the "control movement" starts. The loudspeakers, which are scattered around the prison, resonate the signal: "The movement is on. You have ten minutes to make your move." The interior grill doors are opened, but the latitudes and limits of a man's mobility are sharply defined, narrowly constricted. His motion, the fluidity of his life, is compressed between time locks. There is a sense of urgency to do—what prisoners usually do—nothing.

At the end of the ten-minute limit, the speakers blare out: "The movement is over. Clear the corridor." The proceedings stop. Twenty minutes later the routine is repeated, and so on, until a man's psyche becomes conditioned to the movement/non-movement regimentation, and his nerves jingle with the rhythmic orchestration of steel clanging steel. It is, in prisoners' words, "part of the program"—part of a systematic process of reinforcing an unconditional fact of a prisoner's existence, i.e. that he has no control over the regulation and orientation of his own being. In behavioral psychology, this process is called "learned helplessness"—a derivative of Skinnerian operant conditioning (commonly called "learning techniques"). In essence, a prisoner is taught to be helpless, dependent on his overseer. He is taught to accept, without question, the overseer's power to control him.

But the omnipotent is also omnipresent. Nothing escapes Marion's elaborate network of "eyes". Between t.v. monitors, prisoner spies, collaborators, and prison officials, every crevice of the prison is overlaid by a constant watch. Front-line officers, specially trained in the cold, calculated art of observation, watch prisoners' movements with a particular meticulousness, scrutinizing little details in behavior patterns, then recording them in the Log Book. This data provides the staff with keys on how to manipulate certain individuals' behavior. It is feasible to calculate a prisoner's level of sensitivity from the information; so his vulnerability can be tested with a degree of precision. Some Behavior Modification experts call these tests "Stress Assessment"; prisoners call it harrassment. In some cases, selected prisoners are singled out for one or several of these "differential treatment" tactics. He could have his mail turned back or "accidentally" mutilated. He could become the object of regular searches, or even his visitors

American boxer related contrapunctually to a woman in sweats using a punching bag as an instrument. Nothing is left where it is, it is always jumped to another metaphor.

SL: *Your metaphors are not used to mean anything, only to produce another event, which in turn becomes another metaphor.*

LB: Ultimately the line is a circle, all of these events will encircle the area of perception and I perceive more precisely my own energy inside that circle.

SL: *It's like the* Interpretation of Dreams, *but* without the interpretations*! In a dream also language is dramatized according to what Freud calls "considerations of representability." Abstract expressions are turned into graphic, pictorial language which accounts for the apparent absurdity of the dream. But the pictures, for Freud, are to be interpreted since they simultaneously serve the interests of condensations and censorship. For him there is a truth of the dream and whatever the complexity of the transpositions, he will end up zeroing upon a definite, "original" meaning to the exclusion of any other. What you do in* Shaggy Dog, *on the other hand, is to extend the process of metaphorization to the point where it doesn't really matter where you started from, and what meaning can be derived from it. The technique itself becomes the truth.*

LB: I'm definitely not trying to get another language from the same story, this is very clear, Sylvère. It's not telling a story in a secret language. It's all circular and that's very much the way I perceive reality.

SL: *Mabou Mines has a reputation for being essentially language-oriented. But you seem to do your utmost to upset the linearity of narrative through a variety of dramatic means. This is a curious way of putting language at the center.*

LB: I like to write the script so it says everything. And then I want to commit myself to performance where language is completely secondary to the visual and dramatic dynamic. I prefer the acting experience where you lose half the lines rather than concentrating on getting all the little gems out. I have a perverse attitude about dialogue in that I do not really get off on reading it as it is intended to be read, but reading it the way it is *not* intended to be read. My intent is to both understand the line

could be "stripped searched". These and more tactics are consistent with those propagated by one Dr. Edgar Schein.

Behavior modification at Marion consists of a manifold of four techniques: 1) Dr. Edgar Schein's brainwashing methodology; 2) Skinnerian operant conditioning; 3) Dr. Levinson's sensory deprivation design (i.e. Control Unit) and 4) Chemotherapy or drug therapy. These techniques are disguised behind pseudonyms and under the philosophical rhetoric of correction.

HISTORY OF THIS BEHAVIOR MODIFICATION LABORATORY

In 1962 at a meeting in Washington, D.C. between social scientists and prison wardens, Dr. Edgar Schein presented his ideas on brainwashing. Addressing the topic of "Man Against Man: Brainwashing", he said: "In order to produce marked changes of behavior and/or attitude, it is necessary to weaken, undermine, or remove the supports of the old patterns of behavior and the old attitudes. Because most of these supports are the face-to-face confirmation of present behavior and attitudes, which are provided by those with whom close emotional ties exist, it is often necessary to break those emotional ties. This can be done either by removing the individual physically and preventing any communication with those whom he cares about, or by proving to him that those whom he respects aren't worthy of it and, indeed, should be actively mistrusted."

Following Dr. Schein's address, then-director of the U.S. Bureau of Prisons, James. V. Bennett, commented,"...one of the things we must do is more research. It was indicated that we have a large organization with some 24,000 men in it now and that we have a tremendous opportunity here to carry on some of the experimenting to which the various panelists have alluded. We can manipulate our environment and culture. We can perhaps undertake some of the techniques Dr. Schein discussed. Do things on your own. Undertake a little experiment with what you can do with the Muslims. There's a lot of research to do. Do it as individuals. Do it as groups and let us know the results."

and to expose an attitude toward the line in order to create a double meaning.

SL: *Your method—associating, or rather dis-associating—is also consistent with the existence of a company such as Mabou Mines. If you had to constantly tighten up your material, a collective work would somehow hamper you; but if you can add up elements, then the existence of a group becomes invaluable. The more varied the persons involved, the richer the result.*

LB: The three animations we have done so far are in fact an experiment to define a contemporary reality for choral theatre. This is also what Andrei Serban and Peter Brook are doing. But I wanted to take an altogether different tack because contemporary stylizations of the chorus in theatre are all historical. What I gradually understood through the animations is that choral theatre is alive and well inside of popular lyricism. The verbal extensions that "lead" singers make are even more highly styled than Greek or Shakespearian readings, and yet they are perfectly grounded emotionally. They don't seem to have that fake remove that a plotted historical reading would have.

SL: *T.S. Eliot wanted to recreate a choral entity by making it nearly invisible. You make it visible simply by putting it in its proper modern context.*

LB: The trick is that the true body of choral lyric expression and choral dramatic expression is an electronic manipulation. It is useless for an actor to figure out how to approximate these effects when the correct electronics will give you their perfect rendering.

SL: *Did you feel you were making a parody of the media? I once had an argument over this point. I don't think you did. What can create this impression is probably that different styles keep interrupting each other.*

LB: There was no need to criticize the media. The wonderful thing about electronics is that it produces its own irony by its gloss. You can always tell that it is an electronic reading and this allows you to separate. It allows you to feel an overwhelming emotional response and still you are conscious of how this response has been manipulated. You feel the machine at work. So you really do get a double experience. You can totally indulge and you can be totally objective at the same time. People asked if we were interested in moving an

experiment set up by the Cuban Government
s one of several circular cell houses with do
eavily armed central guardhouse. All work was
ıd were rarely attempted *ILN*

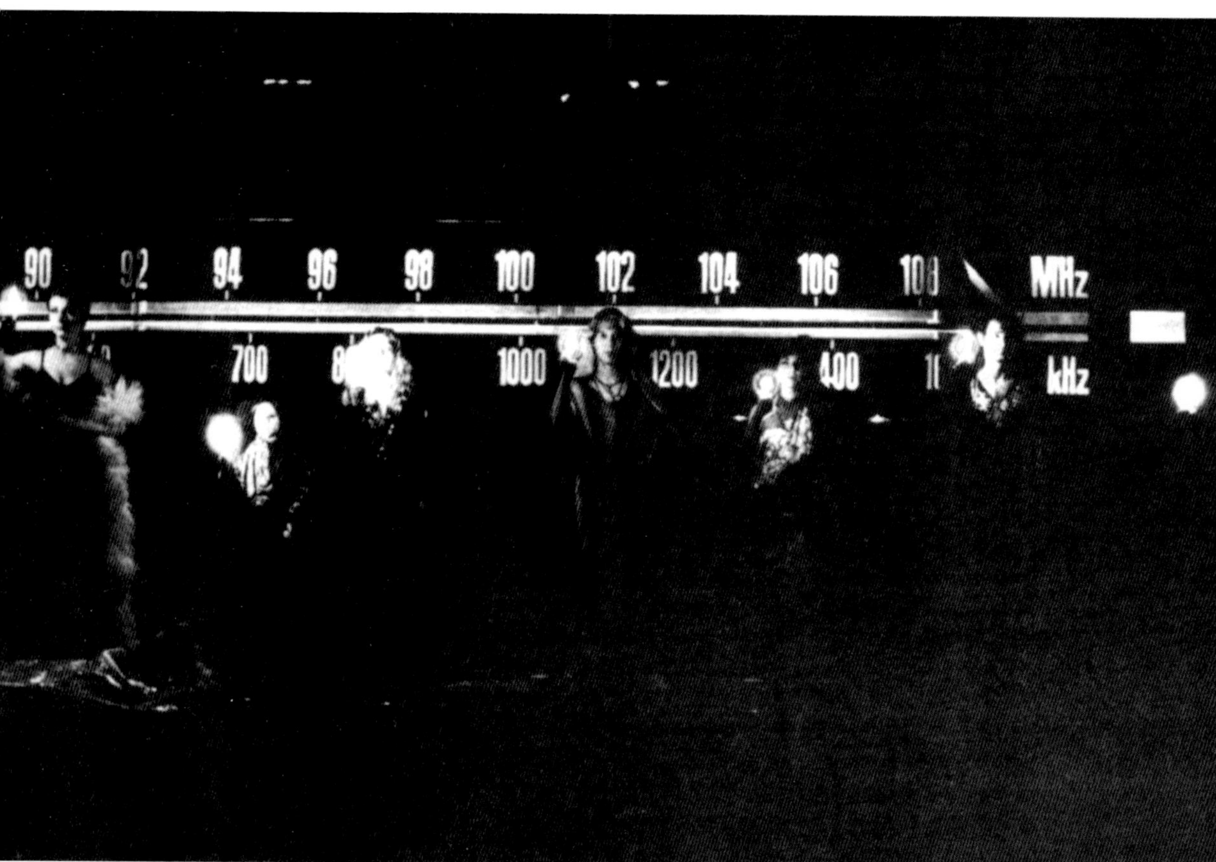

audience and Ruth said, Yes, from one place to another. That's the best definition of what we tried to do.

SL: *But in order to move people from one place to another, you need to move them first.*

LB: Identify and drop identity, never commit oneself to the reality of the drama. . . It is a very crazy position because ying is always changing into yang, black is always becoming white is becoming black, inanimate becoming animate and inanimate again. Reality is the energy of the transformation and only the energy of the transformation.

SL: *If it had been a parody, there would have been such a distance that you woulnd't have been able to move people. They just would have stayed in place. So you had to play the game. . .*

LB: Play the game while showing the game. Play it well, but show it perfectly. If you play it poorly, you don't have a good enough game to entice people. If you are clever enough to get people really empathetically involved and then you disengage, you've produced a small trauma of sorts where people in one instant can see and feel the entire process of their

EXPERIMENTATION IN ACTION

That was 15 years ago. Since then "the results" have been compiled and evaluated many times over; and all but one of Dr. Schein's suggested techniques have been left intact at Marion—along with the addition of a few new features.

According to the Bureau of Prisons' policy statement (Oct. 31, 1967) which, after a test period, finally sanctioned experimentation on prisoners, the benefit from any experiments must be "clear in terms of the mission and collateral objectives of the Bureau of Prisons" and "for the advancement of knowledge." In other words, prisoners are expected to feel inspired at the thought of "advancing knowledge" to benefit science and corrections. But what prisoner knows that he is aiding and abetting the development of Behavior Modification techniques to be used in controlling and manipulating not only other prisoners, but also segments of the public? Besides other things, he is denied knowledge of what he is involved in—or rather forced into. The truth of Behavior Modification is that it is applied to prisoners secretly and sometimes involvement as it develops and disengages. They should be tied on and then cut off to be able to observe what they just felt.

SL: *The cut-up is essential.*

LB: That's right. The media is such an in-depth power that it forces you to respect it.

SL: *But you respect it only in fragments.*

LB: That's a way not to drown. It is a way of saying, I respect the ocean but I'm going to do my damnedest to stay on top of it. So I'm going to jump from one piece of ice to another.

SL: *William Burroughs did these jumps with straight narrative. But he had to break it up completely because he dealt with language only. You deal with a variety of dramatic devices and you can well afford to keep the narrative straight (the sound track, Rose's story) while still cutting it up with all the musical styles.*

LB: The classic example, is Fred's *Recipe* because it is also the furthest out and the corniest in a way—Terry singing this complete schlock country-western background right out of Nashville and Fred starting this recipe and eventually beginning to cry in the middle of it. I could hear the audience every night first ride with Fred through sentimentality for about 3 or 4 lines, then somebody would start to giggle, so that you can feel a peeling away of consciousness and a realization of the sentimental manipulation that had gone on. The manipulation was so overt.

SL: *The stupidity of the media is in its depth.*

LB: There's a difference between what I am trying to do, and parody. It's closer to the idea of ready-made. I tried to take culture as an emotional ready-made. Now you can only show an emotional ready-made dramatically if you have a perfect representation or "reading" of the emotional cliché as it is manifest in the American consciousness. Without technique, it could never have been shown.

SL: *I was in a studio the other day while they were making a record. They had this incredible synthesizer and I understood a lot more about* Shaggy Dog *and what William Burroughs rightly calls "Studio Reality." Not one thing that will eventually come out in the record belonged to the original. Actually, there was no original. Every single split sound had been manipulated. It is only retrospectively that you can grant a record with a unity, as if a real*

remotely (via manipulation of the environment).

At Marion these techniques are applied for punitive purposes, and only one subsection of the prison population is allowed any relief. First, a man's emotional and family ties are broken by removing him to the remote area of southern Illinois and by enforcing a rule whereby he can't correspond with community people within a 50 mile radius. Sometimes the rule slackens, but when the correspondence expresses ideological perspectives it is enforced more strictly. Families of prisoners who move into the area are often discriminated against and harrassed by government agencies. Visitors complain of being intimidated by prison officials, especially when the visits are interracial. Children are repressed in the visiting room. And on three occasions, a man's wife who had travelled from Puerto Rico was stripped and searched. This incident caused great concern among prisoners because it could happen to any one of their wives, mothers or children. Another tactic used to break a prisoner down is to punish him by removing family and friends from his visiting list, or by placing him on restrictive visits. These types of visits are conducted in an isolated, partitioned booth across a telephone. Such restrictions often discourage families from visiting, especially when they have to travel long distances to visit. Officially, close family ties are encouraged; practically, they are being severed. And more often than not, a man's family is looked upon and treated with the same disdain as a "criminal".

Another method of separating prisoners from friends and outside supporters is the two-faced campaign waged by the prison administration. On the one side prisoners are told they have been totally rejected by society and that even those who "pretend" to be interested in prisoners are "only using prisoners for their own selfish benefit." By this a prisoner is supposed to believe he was never a part of a community or of society in general, that his ties among the people were never legitimate and that their interest in him is a fraud. On the other side, a brutish, bestial, and "sociopathic" image of prisoners is presented to the public. This further isolates the prisoner and makes him more dependent on the prison authorities.

But discernment into this sophisticated system is the furthest thing from a prisoner's imagination, or even his comprehension. It is impossible for him to conceive that he is being reduced in the eye-sight of humanity to the level of an amoeba and placed under a microscope.

band had physically played somewhere, at some point in a studio and produced the record that you hear. The whole thing is totally made up.

LB: It should be technically possible soon not even to have the artist in the studio. You will just pick up voices off old records and construct the tones on a synthesizer in order to produce a complete pop record. You don't even need a singer. The cliché I throw at people sometimes is that you can't say "I love you" anymore without an echo chamber. Because it isn't true without an echo chamber. The echo chamber has captured the myth of the expression more clearly than the human voice.

SL: *And at the same time it is the echo of something that hardly exists anymore. An echo of an illusion.*

LB: It's illusion echoing illusion.

SL: *But if you look at it backwards, you can't help believing that there actually was an event. In the same way, you can follow a narrative—life as a narrative—and imagine that there actually was such a thing as an individual in his own right. The individual as we* conceive *it (not as we live it) hardly exists any more than the original performance of the record. It is a constant re-creation which echoes something that has practically ceased to exist.*

LB: The idea is that once all this is cleared away, there is nothing.

SL: *There is the machine.*

LB: Yes.

SL: *You can purge yourself of the emotional response to the electronic machine, but not of the machine itself.*

LB: Now tell me what the machine wants: it wants to be left alone.

SL: *I think it wants to grab more, to amplify, to expand. That's what your play is all about. New territories, new markets, new posessions. But it is very dangerous to constantly swallow new grounds. You also have to digest it. The media orchestrates the digestion. The process is very dynamic and the assimilation soporific. Energy doesn't go against the system, the system is energy. It is the very sparks you uncover. But it keeps checking its own flow with an endless series of dams, of powerful representations that pass for reality, and actually become our reality. In bureaucratic*

He can't understand why he feels the strange sensation of being watched; why it seems that "eyes" follow him around everywhere. He fears his sanity is in jeopardy, that paranoia is taking hold of him. It shows: the tension in his face, the wide-eyed apprehensive stares and spastic body movements. Among the general population, paranoia tends to spread like wildfire—from man to man. The induced state of paranoia is the primary cause of the violence which has occurred throughout Marion's history.

The pervasive "eyes" at Marion are not without the complement of "ears". Besides officers' eavesdropping and the inside spies trying to collect enough intelligence to make parole, there are also listening devices out of view. The loudspeakers, for example, are also receivers, capable of picking up loose conversations in the hallways, cellblocks and mess hall. Recently a strange device which someone called a "parabolic mike" was found. It is hard to figure out exactly how many more such devices are scattered around the prison, embedded in the wall or placed behind cells.

Sometimes a prisoner is confronted with the information in order to arouse suspicion about the people he has talked with. At other times, the information is kept secret among officials, and traps are set.

It is a standing rule among the prisoners never to let the enemy know what you are thinking. At Marion, a man is labelled by his ideas, and his "differential treatment" is plotted accordingly.

What life in Marion boils down to is an essay in psychological warfare. An unsuspecting, unequipped prisoner—a prisoner unable to adjust and readjust psychologically and develop adequate defense mechanisms can be taken off stride and wind up as another one of Marion's statistics. Prison officials and employees come well prepared, well-trained, pre-conditioned, and well aware of the fact that a war is being waged behind the walls.

BEHAVIOR MODIFICATION AND THE MISUSE OF THERAPY TECHNIQUES

The behavioral school of psychology is based on the premise that man is only capable of reacting to the stimuli of his environment and that over a period of time of reacting in the same way to the same stimuli his behavior becomes habitual and sociopathic. However, through his cognition and rationalization, he can not only transform his environment, but also transform *societies, you control things from the outside; the American way is by far more sophisticated. You simply market a new product or, for that matter, an obsolete product under new glossy wrappings. You erect new values as a positive object of control, and it is the whole complex of emotions and desires that make up the normal neurotic individual.*

LB: There is an accent called a mid-Atlantic accent that is neither American nor European, it is a media accent. It carries an emotional attitude that makes catastrophes entertainment. This is the way reality is represented. The media can tell you how to live your life, how you are supposed to feel, what you are supposed to do and how you are supposed to die. A laugh track tells you what's supposed to be funny. It produces a somnambulistic circle, it creates room for certain power manipulations to take place in peace. The curious thing is that even the people who manipulate this imagery fall into it so that ultimately nobody is steering the car!

himself into a different social being. Prisoners are making this transformation.

There is a small, elite group in the prison population which is looked upon by the administration with great favor because the group shares the same basic ideals with the administration. The group's members see the prison authority as a "parent". They think of themselves as "residents" rather than prisoners or captives—because to change the word is to change the reality. At Marion, this program is called Asklepieion—which literally means nothing. The prisoners call the group "groders" or "groder's gorillas", named after the psychologist who implemented Dr. Schein's brainwashing program.

The "groders" live in a special cellblock which, by prison standards, is plush. They are allowed luxuries and privileges which regular prisoners can't receive. They, however, are convinced that they "earn" these things because they are trying to do something to "better themselves". Generally, they look on other convicts with contempt. When confronted with evidence that they are a brainwash group, they

SL: *Representation is total manipulation. The emotional output of the media is purely made up and, in many ways, incredibly archaic. The technology of it, though, is everything but stupid. Actually, it is highly sophisticated. It only deals with surfaces. It manipulates pieces of sound, fragments of voices, figments of fiction in order to fashion full-fledged individual emotions. So if you kept breaking up its final imagery and thus disengage from its emotionality, you would stand a chance to recover reality.*

LB: The collective nature of our work fits in with this because it abstracts the persona across the entire piece. Almost any voice can be made a viable part of the consciousness as long as the center is this neutral stage of wood that these neutral voices are talking to.

SL: *The voices are talking to* something, *they are not talking to someone.*

LB: No one relates to anyone else in the entire piece. Nor do they in any of the animations.

SL: *Ronald Laing wrote somewhere that schizophrenia is a voice such that you don't know who is speaking and who is being spoken to. I think it is definitely a media voice. Rose is speaking through the voices of all the performers, but* who *is Rose after all? And the performers, whom do they talk to? They don't talk to someone, nor do they talk to each other. Maybe they address themselves to the audience as an artistic or aesthetic concept.*

LB: They are actually talking to a point between themselves and the audience. The audience observes a conversation between the actor and a point in front of them. It is not direct address in the Brechtian sense. It is rhetorical since it is spoken to the ideal abstract listener. The audience can observe this rhetoric for what it is.

SL: *The collective entity is given an existence separate from the actual audience. Since the audience is not talked to, it has to take a distance from the role it is supposed to assume.*

LB: The play is making up the audience precisely at the time the audience is making up the play. I don't like confrontations with an audience, with all the activist and political connotations this entails. Our production is a little purer. It is an abstract conflict, but it is also dramatic. It involves all sorts of games, tricks, humor.

circular cell houses. Each of
is a good conduct buildin

reject the proof and accuse other prisoners of being envious.

But the reality speaks for itself. The program employs a number of noted therapeutic techniques, e.g. Transactional Analysis, Synanon Attack-Therapy, psychodrama, Primal therapy, and Encounter Group Marathon sensitivity sessions. The administration's favorite is T.A. Essentially T.A. propagates the theory that people communicate on three different levels: parent, child and adult. These become character roles. It is up to the corresponding party to figure out which role the first party is playing, then communicate with the person on the proper counter-part level.

What this technique actually does is create an artificial dichotomy between people, each straining to fit into the proper character role. Ultimately, it propagates the idea that the authorities always fit the role of a "parent" and the prisoners must submit to the role of a "child". Although some "groders" pretend this practice is a fakeout on "the man", it still is a real social practice.

Other techniques include Dr. Schein's "character invalidation". These techniques are incorporated under the auspices of "Game Sessions" (Synanon Attack Therapy) and "Marathons" (Encounter Group sensitivity sessions). In "Game Sessions", members of the

SL: *The representation of Rose also is constantly displaced: it is a dog represented by a puppet which itself represents a woman. . .*

LB: Which is often acted by three different men, one child, three different women. . .

SL: *Even though the center is also represented by the Bunraku puppet. This series of displacements from actual audience to idealized listener, from collective entity to choral structure, from performers to individuals and from individual to puppet allows for a growing realization of the media manipulation. But there is a point in the performance where the puppet is obviously manipulated for itself, made to dance for its own sake independently of any dramatization. . .*

LB: Style is emphasized—annotated. To isolate and cool off the psychology.

SL: *The puppet, then, whatever her other functions, represents simultaneously commitment to the theatre. What about the very last sequence of* Shaggy Dog*? The nostalgic chorus of the aged was, I thought, quite moving. You seem to have deliberately let pathos set in. Did you want at this point to shift the emphasis from media stupidity to some sort of existential meditation—to go full circle from* Rrose *to* Sélavy*?*

LB: That at their age they could still be so totally committed to this sort of romantic energy was, I thought, pure dramatic irony, irony ultimately concerned in not being funny so much as being moving. Beyond that point, there is a final commitment to a cathartic experience, a traditional experience. No matter how much art is played with in the piece, it is not a final commitment to art, as most conceptual theatres would do, it is a final commitment to the theatre. It's allowing empathy to grow and you needed almost a classic Brechtian moment to cut it at that particular point.

SL: *This is the power failure.*

LB: Yes. The power failure is the classic metaphor for it all the way through. Seeing the light through the power, I guess, is the game that is' being played between the lighter and the lighted.

SL: *But the light that you see during the power failure, the actual lighter held by an actor, is still part of the power.*

LB: And it is held by your own hand.

group accuse a person of playing games, not being truthful with the group, lying; or he is accused of some misdeed or shortcoming. Before he is allowed a chance to explain (which is considered as only more lying), he is barraged by dirty-name calling until he confesses or "owns up" to his shortcomings. He is then accused of making the group go through a lot of trouble in having to pry the truth out of him. So, for this crime he is forced to apologize.

"Marathons" are all-night versions of literally the same, except that they include local community people who come into the prison to be "trained" in the techniques. After so many hours of being verbally attacked and denied sleep, a person "owns up" to anything and accepts everything he's told. After being humiliated, he is encouraged to cry. The group then shows its compassion by hugging him and telling him that they love him.

These techniques exploit the basic weaknesses produced by an alienating society, i.e. the need to be loved, cared about, accepted by other people, and the need to be free. In turn, they are transmuted into "submission and subserviency", the type of behavior conducive to the prison officials' goal of control and manipulation. The "groders" will not resist or complain. Nor will they go on a strike to seek redress of prisoners' grievances. They are alienated from their environment, and their emotional interdependency welds and insulates them into a crippled cohesion (of the weak bearing the weak). They aren't permitted to discuss these techniques outside the group because one of the pre-conditions for admittance is a bond to secrecy. Yet almost anyone can spot a "groder' because the light has gone out in his eyes.

Some years ago, the prison population wanted to do them bodily harm because they allowed themselves to be used as guinea pigs, and because the techniques developed would be used on other prisoners and other people in the outside world. Today, they are generally looked upon as mental enemies. So prisoners just leave them alone. Nevertheless, the brainwashing techniques are still finding their way into communities in the outside world—under a number of pseudonyms other than Asklepieion. And the "groders" still have hopes of joining these programs when they are sufficiently spread. They will become "therapeutic technicians". This is what Dr. Groder laid out in his "Master Plan", the utilizing of prisoners as couriers of the technique back into the

Wendy Clarke
Love Tapes

The 'love tapes', a series of 3min. video-tapes, were made by participants of various ages and ethnic backgrounds sitting alone in a room talking about love while sentimental music ran in the background. The three following participants are from L.A., Calif.

KATHERINE, 55.

I just came from the therapist and I think it was the last time. He asked me what's going on, as a matter of fact I had to go to him, I had a deep depression, but it's over, and I said to him every thing is fine, the only thing is I wish I would be in love again, really really deeply in love. And of course as the years pass and I get older, it's not as easy as it was when I was 16 and 18 and fell in love all the time and thought that was the real one, the big one. And funny enough when it's over then you think it can never happen again, and you are terribly sad and think it's over, never again. And there it is, around the corner there is someone else, and you think I was never as much in love as this time. No it wasn't that many times, of course, and it doesn't change as one gets older, I get older. I wish I would be 20 or 30 years younger, but I have the same feelings and the same longings, maybe even more so. And I think gee wiz maybe this time I won't make this or that mistake and, and ah, but where is he? Where is he? Oh I can't complain I have a lot of friends, good friends some who like me and love me but that passionate feeling that is so important, that I would like to have. It's not enough to love it's even more important to love, that is a fantastic feeling, that just makes you

community. It is also what former warden Ralph Aron meant when he testified at the 1975 *Bono vs. Saxbe* trial (to close the Control Unit) that "the purpose of the Marion control unit is to control revolutionary attitudes in the prison system and in the society at large". What the "groders" fail to realize is that even as "therapists" they will remain under observation long after their release from prison—under what is euphemistically called "post-release follow-through."

CHEMOTHERAPY: THE MISUSE OF DRUGS

Chemotherapy is conducted four times daily at Marion. The loudspeaker announces: "Control medication in the hospital...pill line." Valium, librium, thorazine and other "chemical billy-clubs" are handed out like gumdrops. Sometimes the drugs mysteriously make their way into the food. For example, the strange month of December, 1974, recorded five unrelated, inexplicable stabbings. During the same time, eight prisoners suffered from hallucinations in the "hole" and had to be treated (with thorazine injections). Drugs are often prescribed for minor ailments and are commonly suggested to prisoners as a panacea for all the psychological ill-effects of incarceration. Some drugs such as prolixin make prisoners want to commit suicide. Some attempt it; some succeed.

THE END OF THE LINE: THE LONG-TERM CONTROL UNIT

Segregation is the punitive aspect of the Behavior Modification program. It is euphemistically referred to as "aversive conditioning." In short, prisoners are conditioned to avoid solitary confinement, and to do this requires some degree of conformity and cooperation. But the "hole" remains open for what prison authorities and Dr. Schein call "natural leaders". These prisoners can be pulled from population on "investigation" and held in solitary confinement until the so-called investigation is over. During the whole ordeal, he is not told what the inquiry is about—unless he is finally charged with an infraction of the rules. If the prison authorities think that the Behavior Modification techniques will eventually work on the prisoner, he is sent to short-term segregation. If not, they use the last legal weapon in the federal prison system: the creative, that helps your art, that helps your work, that makes your life. Yes if it's not there you bury yourself and maybe even overwork and do all kinds of things and look for things, but, so I'm still hoping. The year is not completely over. It's the 21st of December, the beginning of winter.

REGINA, 35.

Well here I am getting to talk about love and I'm getting a little nervous cause it's a hard topic. There are many ways that I feel love. I feel love for my children, I feel love for my women friends. I just experienced a nice new affair. That experience was "*LOVE*ly". It made me be in touch with old, old romantic feelings of being in love, feeling happy and anxious and excited, a time when I wasn't thinking of anything in particular, but I just had this wonderful feeling. And it's like exhilarating. Exhilarating. It's a nice feeling. And all of a sudden you get a feeling from the other person that it's over. And I've experienced a collusion with me and my fantasies and my illusions. And the reality is that his feelings ended before my feelings ended and it was hard to deal with, it was very hard. But because I have other love relationships with women, other men, my children, older people, flowers, trees the sky, I guess just feelings, I was able to work through with some anxious feelings of depression and sadness. And love just does create all of those wonderful wonderful feelings that we dream about, that we read about, that we see in films. There's that old song I remember about a stranger across a crowded room, and I still have that illusion that someday I'm going to meet that stranger and he's going to appear. It's that old Cinderella story, it is. I really bought into the fantasy of what newspapers and magazines and films have told me that I should feel about love. And my real feelings when I express them, especially my last affair, that person I think was shocked that I could be so open and so vulnerable. And it was a wonderful time, 2 wonderful months with him, different feelings, different emotions. It was very nice and I hope to find someone else again soon.

ELIOT, 30.

You know I cry in movies sometimes over the weirdest things, but then when I want to, you know, when I really want to feel something I can't, and I know I should, and I want to, but I'm locked in, you know. It's like with your family, you know, you love them because somehow they're your family, but I don't really like them.

long-term control unit.

The long-term control unit is the "end of the line" in the federal prison system. Since there is no place lower throughout all of society, it is the end of the line for society also. Just as the threat of imprisonment controls society, so is Marion the control mechanism for the prison systems; ultimately the long-term control unit controls Marion.

Usually a prisoner doesn't know specifically why he has been sent to the Control Unit. And he usually doesn't know how long he will be there. A prisoner is told he is being placed on 30-day observation and that he has the right to appeal the decision if he wishes. Until recently, most prisoners simply waived the appeal because they were given the impression that they would be getting out soon.

In the control unit a prisoner does only two things—recreate and shower. Although everyone recognizes that the work is exploitative, it is generally considered a privilege. The rest of the control unit prisoners spend 23½ hours a day locked in their cells (which are smaller than the average dog kennel). He sees the Control Unit committee for about 30 seconds once a month to receive a decision on his "adjustment rating". He may see a caseworker, the counselor or the educational supervisor for books. Other than that, he deteriorates.

The cell itself contains a flat steel slab jutting from the wall. Overlaying the slab is a one-inch piece of foam wrapped in coarse plastic. This is supposed to be a bed. Yet it cuts so deeply into the body. After a few days, you are totally numb. Feelings become indistinct, emotions unpredictable.

Besides these methods of torture (which is what they are), there is also extreme cold conditioning in the winter and lack of ventilation in the summer. Hot and cold water manipulation is carried out in the showers. Shock waves are administered to the brain when guards bang a rubber mallett against the steel bars. Then there is outright brutality, mainly in the form of beatings. The suicide rate in the Control Unit is five times the rate in general population at Marion.

At the root of the Control Unit's Behavior Modification Program, though, is indefinite confinement. This is perhaps the most difficult aspect of the Control Unit to communicate to the public. Yet a testament to this policy was a man named Hiller "Red" Hayes. After 13 years in solitary confinement (nearly six in the control

You know, somehow would I really love 'em if I just ran into them on the street, nope. But there are people that I want to love, but somehow I just can not let it out. I'm still not at the stage where I can feel love. And I really want to. And so people come and they go and you want to love them, but you never could tell them that. And so they leave and they never know that you loved them. So people end up thinking that you're something you're not. Because you never could express yourself. You couldn't love them and you couldn't hate them. Because when you love them you can hate them. It's the same way, I couldn't love them—I have a problem hating them. So then you say, what the hell do I really feel? So you let it all out in a movie, over some made-up situation, when you get tears in your eyes. Because you wish you could at least be like the movie.

unit), he became the "boogie man" of the prison system—the living/dying example of what can happen to any prisoner. The more he deteriorated in his own skeleton, the more prisoners could expect to wane in his likeness. He died in the unit in August, 1977.

In essence, the Unit is a Death Row for the living. And the silent implications of Behavior Modification speak their sharpest and clearest ultimatum: CONFORM OR DIE.

1. Write letters urging that the Marion control unit be closed completely to: Judge James Foreman, U.S. District Court, 750 Missouri Avenue, E. St. Louis, Illinois 62202. Information: *National Committee to Support the Marion Brothers 4556a Oakland, St. Louis, Missouri 63110*

FOR OVERLOAD PROTECTION
IN ELECTRIC SHOCK TREATMENTS
Series L Overload Relay
wherever a tube is used...
Offner Electric Shock Therapy Apparatus
Offner Electric Shock Therapy apparatus has been widely prescribed for treatment of psychiatric patients for more than five years. From the very first experimental model to present-day production units, Guardian Overload Relays have been used exclusively to protect the patient from dangerous current surges.

Radio F. 1945

Relays BY GUARDIAN

In certain types of mental disorders it is possible to shock patients back to normal by passing an electric current through brain tissues. Naturally the patient must be protected against the possibility of excessive current surges. Such protection must be positive—dependable. In providing this protection, Guardian Series L Overload Relays have established a perfect record for safe, dependable performance in hundreds of thousands of known treatments.

The Series L Overload Relay provides accurate protection against surges and overloads. Standard coils attract on 150, 250, 500, or 750 milliamperes; coils for operation on other current values are available on specification.

The large, oversize contacts used on this relay can take severe overloads without damage. They are rated for 1500 watts on 110 volt non-inductive A.C. and in A.C. primary circuits of any inductive power supply delivering up to and including 1 kilowatt. Contacts lock open and cannot be reset until overload is removed. For further information, write for Series L bulletin.

Consult Guardian whenever a tube is used—however—Relays by Guardian are NOT limited to tube applications, but may be used wherever automatic control is desired for making, breaking, or changing the characteristics of electrical circuits.

Police Band

Antidisestablishment Totalitarism

Sylvère LOTRINGER: How did you get to rock?

POLICEBAND: Mostly through the technology of it, being saddled with the various instruments and the noise and the amplifier. Just being attracted to it as an object.

S: Did you start working by yourself from the very beginning?

PB: No. I found out what the machines were capable of. They led me straight to Policeband. It was almost as if the technology applied its own politics.

S: Are you interested in politics?

PB: I like the news that comes out of politics. The one statement that this happened or that happened that I get over the radio. Politics is an exchange of paper. I hate paper, the feel of it.

S: Didn't you write before?

PB: I did, but not on paper. On tapes.

S: Why did you call yourself Policeband—a collective name?

PB: I see myself as being a lead singer with back-up musicians. The buzzers and the amplifiers are quite out of control. They definitely are like a band.

S: The text you read is not yours. Do you choose it at random?

PB: I borrow randomly but it's my random

S: What is your criterion of choice?

PB: It has to do with time, filling up the space. It comes through the headset. I repeat it or I improvise with it. Mostly I repeat it. It comes from various sources. Directly from the police themselves, or from something I myself have said into a tape recorder, or directly from a radio. I have it plugged directly into a radio so that I can recite the weather if I wish. Or they have these scanners that enable you to monitor the police communications and the F.B.I. as well. The sources are very immediate and I have to react to them immediately. It's the raw material I respond to directly. I incorporate it. I need it. Without it I would just be another cabaret pianist.

S: What about the police?

PB: They're always looking for trouble. It's always looking for them. They're obliged to respond to very random input. Random violence. They don't know where its coming from or why.

S: Don't they also produce it?

PB: They produce it themselves if they get bored.

S: Do you think the police are that repressed?

PB: The police are incredibly repressed. They're obliged to uphold all sorts of rules and regulations that they feel alien to. They'd just rather go out and do whatever they feel like. I know it. And yet, they can't do it. It's not like Mexico where you can kill the criminal immediately upon discovery. Quite frequently the crime becomes irrelevant to whatever procedure follows it or instigates it, or it just becomes a theatrical procedure. It just continues in the theatre of the courts and right back to the streets again where it starts all over.

S: So what is not theatre in this society?

PB: In our society, nothing. America is the entertainment capital of the world.

S: At all levels?

PB: I think so.

S: Sex is theatre?

PB: Don't you know it.

S: What about drugs?

PB: I don't take drugs.

S: You never did?

PB: No, I'm an athelete and drugs only interfere with the body's ability to maintain its own sense of self. . . . The body, it's so powerful, it's a fascist, the body. . . .

S: Why do you say that?

PB: Its completely organized, and if you abuse it, it beats you. It's incredibly oppressive and then when you start trying to control it, you start looking for others to control . . . Schizophrenia is a solution, of course, because it allows you to jump back and forth from position to position without any sense of self. Hopefully one position will click. It's like the scanner. I tell you, you should look at this piece of equipment. It just bounces back and forth until it finds something to signal into and it just stops if there's information coming over that wavelength. So, in effect, my act's quite schizophrenic.

Eli C. Messinger

Violence to the Brain

The theories and technology of medicine and psychiatry have long been used to buttress the views of, and to maintain social control by those who hold political power. The technical means have changed from one historical area to the next. The more important techniques now in use include psychoactive drugs, brain surgery, behavior modification techniques and electroshock therapy.

The theory that personal violence is due to brain dysfunction and that it should be treated by brain surgery is presented by Vernon Mark and Frank Ervin in *Violence and the Brain*. They recommend the development of mass screening and treatment programs for individuals prone to violence because of brain dysfunction. The pseudo-scientific arguments they advance are not unique. A theory of brain dysfunction has been advanced to explain the so-called hyperactivity of childhood. Both theories attribute behavioral problems solely to an organic cause; in both cases, the treatment is organic. While brain surgery for behavior control is not common at this time in the United States, several hundreds of thousands of American

Eli C. Messinger, M.D., is a Child Psychiatrist at the Metropolitan Hospital in New York City.

David Cooper

The Invention of Non-Psychiatry

Non-psychiatry is coming into being. Its birth has been a difficult affair. Modern psychiatry, as the pseudo-medical action of detecting faulty ways of living lives and the technique of their categorization and their correction, began in the eighteenth century and developed through the nineteenth to its consummation in the twentieth century. Hand in hand with the rise of capitalism it began, as a principal agent of the destruction of the absurd hopes, fears, joys and despair of joy of people who refused containment by that system. Hand in hand with capitalism in its death agonies, over the coming years (it might be twenty or thirty years), psychiatry, after familialization and education, one of the principal repressive devices (with its more sophisticated junior affiliate psychoanalysis) of the bourgeois order, will be duly interred.

The movement, schematically, is very simple: psychiatry, fully institutionalized (put in place) by a state system aimed at the perpetuation of its labour supply, using the persecution of the non-obedient as its threat to make 'them' conform or be socially eliminated, was attacked in the year 1960—by an anti-psychiatric movement which was a sort of groping anti-thesis, a resistance movement against psychiatric hospitals and their indefinite spread in the community sectors, that was to lead dialectically to its dialectical issue which we can only call non-psychiatry, a word that erodes itself as one writes it.

Non-psychiatry means that profoundly disturbing, incomprehensible, 'mad' behaviour is to be contained, incorporated in and diffused through the whole society as a subversive source of creativity, spontaneity, not 'disease'. Under the conditions of capitalism, this is clearly 'impossible'. What we have to do is to accept this impossibility as the challenge. How can any challenge be measured by less than its impossibility. The non-existence of psychiatry will only be reached in a transformed society, but it is vital to start the work of de-psychiatrization now.

After being sufficiently fed and housed, there is the radical need to express oneself autonomously in the world and to have one's acts and words recognized as one's own by at least one other human being. The total ideal autonomy of not needing one word of confirmation from anyone else remains ideal. While some people certainly find great satisfaction in a certain type of productive work, there are immense needs for confirmed, autonomous expression that exceed such satisfaction. *But* this personal expression becomes increasingly difficult. Madness becomes increasingly impracticable because of extending psycho-surveillance.

Orgasmic sexuality is destroyed by the hours and quality of labour and, at least for the bourgeoisie, is replaced by the passivity of pornographic spectacle or Thai massage. People attend classes or 'therapy' for corporal expression. Universal, popular artistic expression (such as Japanese *haiku* poetry or the formerly universal popular invention of song and dance) is overshadowed by the professionalization and technologization of the specialized art forms deformed by the market.

The key question for revolutionaries is how to avoid the recuperation of people and their autonomous expression (and for that matter, of all new revolutionary ideas) by the state system (as opposed to the recuperation of invalidated persons and ideas by the people). The question within this question centres on the word 'avoid'. Avoiding here involves the systematic abolition of all institutional repression, but we are focusing here on the abolition of all psycho-technology—a wider question than the abolition of psychiatric institutions inside and outside hospitals by the forms of non-psychiatric action.

One should understand by psycho-technology not only psychiatry, psychology, psychoanalysis and alternative therapy, but also the mystifying techniques of the mass media (one has only to follow the desperately, and accelerated, mystifying 'moral' convolutions in the editorials of the capitalist press from day to day). Then reward and punishment doctrine (or bribery and blackmail) of Kissinger-type foreign policies. The use of psycho-technology in law courts, prisons, and by the military. Technology is for things, not people.

In a bookshop in now fashionable Cannery Row in California I found, after an ironic display of all the works of Steinbeck, the department of best-selling technology. The books (and I'm certainly not implying that they are on the same level) included treatises on

school-age children have been diagnosed as having minimal brain dysfunction (MBD) and are treated with stimulant drugs: amphetamines, Dexedrine and Benzedrine, and methylphenidate or Ritalin.

MBD: MEDICAL DISEASE OR SOCIAL STRATEGY?

True medical diseases are defined on anatomical, biochemical or physiological grounds. They exist independently of the social setting. Diabetes, for example, is defined by abnormalities in glucose metabolism. While the diabetic's social environment can influence the course of the disease, the abnormality in glucose metabolism, rather than the diabetic's social behavior, indicates that diabetes is present. In contrast, most behavioral syndromes, including MBD, are diagnosed by a physician because of the subject's dissonance with the social environment.[2] This explains the puzzling observation that the symptoms of MBD" commonly subside during vacations from school...

The data used to establish the diagnosis of MBD are highly subjective. The judgment by a teacher or parent, for example, will depend on his/her criterion for hyperactivity and the social setting where the activity was observed. Even the direct observation of a child is influenced by the clinician's skill and experience, the meaning of the examination to the child, the physical setting, and the child's physical and mental state at the time of the observation.

The following list of "symptoms" appears in a pamphlet written for teachers, doctors and counselors prepared by Dr. James Satterfield, director of the Gateways Hospital Hyperkinetic Clinic:

Overactivity: unusual energy, inablity to sit still in the classroom and at mealtime, talking out of turn in the class, disrupting the class.

Distractibility: not getting work done in school, daydreaming in the classroom, tuning out teachers and parents when they try to give directions, being unable to take part in card games and other games such as Monopoly.

Impulsiveness: being unable to save up money for something that is badly wanted, blurting out secrets or things that are known to be tactless, saying sassy things to teacher just to show off.
Excitability: getting very wound up and overexcited and more active around groups of children or in stimulating new situations.[3]

It is clear that this is really a list of behavior considered unacceptable to teachers, parents or other adults. The child who is at odds with the educational system is sent to the medical-psychiatric system. There a classroom behavior or learning difficulty is diagnosed as MBD; the difficulty is re-defined as a medical or psychiatric problem. The child is returned to the classroom with a diagnostic label, and frequently with a chemical control agent.

EARLY DETECTION

Early detection of disease is a valid principle in medicine. However it lessens accuracy in diagnosis. Mark and Ervin wrote their book for the general public because they wanted public support for the establishment of early detection programs:

We need to develop an "early warning test" of limbic brain function to detect those humans who have a low threshhold for impulsive violence, and we need better and more effective methods of treating them once we have found out who they are. Violence is a public health problem, and the major thrust of any program dealing with violence must be toward its prevention—a goal that will make a better and safer world for us all.[4]

They urge programs to identify persons "as being potentially violent."

The *reductio ad absurdum* of this reasoning is the theory that "hidden brain disease" can cause violence:

All the persons we have described thus far were known to have brain disease, which, as we have shown, proved to be related to their violent behavior. But what of those individuals who are uncontrollably violent but do not have epileptic seizures or other obvious signs of brain disease?.... Is it possible that they, too, are suffering from an

T.A. (Transactional Analysis), T.M. (Transcendental Meditation), E.S.T. (Erhard Seminars Training, not exactly electro-shock, E.C.T.), Creative Fidelity, Creative Aggression, Provocative Therapy, Gestalt Therapy, Primal Scream, Encounter Therapy, the conducting of three-day 'Marathons', a form of deep massage, Bio-energy, Japanese Hot Tubs (you take off your clothes and enter them *en groupe* as part of liberation). Then, 'Behaviour Mod' (the new generation Skinner) on how to toilet-train your child in twenty-four hours—and then on the next shelf another book advertising a method of toilet-training your child in *less* than twenty-four hours! I've no doubt that after some of these experiences some people feel better, or begin to 'feel', or feel more 'real'—or whatever the ideals of capitalism prescribe for them.

One day the United States, together with the European countries of 'advanced liberal democracy' (whose fascist nature will more rapidly and nakedly emerge), will have to stand on their own feet rather than sit on the back of the rest of the world, and then there will be another less easy and lucrative sort of 'reality' to face.[1]

In the meantime there is a growing cultural imperialism, by which highly commercialized psychotechniques are being insidiously imported into the poorer but more politically advanced countries of Europe and the Third World by professional liberators who go to the U.S. for crash courses in the latest techniques and return to their countries to reap the cash results. While this development is clearly not on the scale of exploitation by the multinational drug companies with their psychotropic drugs, its ideological content is significant. After psychiatry based on de-conditioning (in fact a sad re-conditioning) or conventional psychoanalysis, there is the 'third force' of 'alternative therapy' to seduce the desperate who shun the first two. The ideology of personal salvation presents highly effective strategies of de-politicization.

Once again, *there are no personal problems, only political problems*. But one takes 'the political' in a wide sense that refers to the deployment of power in or between social entities (including between the parts of the body of a person which incarnate certain social realities). Personal problems in the commonest sense reduce the political to things going on between one person and a few others, usually on an at least implicit family model; problems of work, creativity and finding oneself in a lost society are clearly political problems. Therapies and conventional psychoanalysis reinforce 'oedipian' familialism and, whatever contrary intentions, exclude from the concrete field of action macropolitical reality and the repressive systems that mediate this reality to the individual . . .

The word 'therapy' had better be banished because

of its medical technical connotation. But people still seem, non-'radically', to talk with articulated words. But it should not take many hours to say the few things that matter in one's life if the other person unstops his ears. Listening to someone in 'full flight of delusion' one can effectively stop one's ears by trying to interpret the 'content' of the words, or by the ridiculous attempt to speak in the same language. The words attempt to express the inexpressible which is never the content of the words but always in the very precise silences formed in a unique way by the words. So, unblocking one's ears, one listens to the silences in their preciseness and their specificity. There is never any doubt that the 'deluded one' will know whether or not one's ears are unblocked. Beyond that, with 'paranoia', there is always the practical task of ascertaining the real past and present forms of persecution. Psycho-technological training, to fulfil its social purpose of mystification, tends to blind and deafen people to what should be obvious.

Franco Basaglia and his associates recently set up a centre at Belluno, in a large country house in the Dolomites, to receive people from the psychiatric hospital at Trieste who live for varying periods in a relatively de-institutionalized setting. One day while I was living in the house a man who had been a hospitalized withdrawn 'chronic schizophrenic' for over twenty years smashed the television set in the middle of a football match, and then three windows (to see the world 'outside' rather than the world 'in the box' etc. etc.). The point was that in the group situation of anger and fear he was not immediately 'dealt with' by a large injection of a neuroleptic drug (costing much more than occasional broken windows) but was taken on one side by one of the staff, who made no comment but opened his ears while the patient with great feeling told the history of his life for two hours. Of course the problem remained of finding a mode of insertion in the outside world after twenty years of systematic institutional incapacitation, but the point was that 'chronic schizophrenia' was abolished by the conjunction of a more reasonable context, one or two acts, and a few more words and a lot more feeling —and by the personal 'policy' on the part of someone to have 'open ears' rather than just the simple mystification of 'open doors'.

So now one says that psychiatrists have one option —either they kill themselves or we assassinate them—metaphorically of course.[2] What does that mean? It means that one recognizes just how difficult it is for someone formed, preformed, deformed as a professional psycho-technologist principally in the medical policing racket of psychiatry but also in the areas of psychoanalysis and psychology, social psychology, 'socio-psychoanalysis' and so on, to change their life structures, which entail gaining money as part

abnormality of the limbic system?[5]

Pressure is also put on the practising physician to diagnose MBD early. The "symptoms" of MBD are very common, particularly in younger elementary school-age children. In a study of the entire kindergarten through second-grade population of a Midwestern town, teachers were asked to rate the frequency of 55 behaviors.[6] In boys, restlessness was found in 49 percent, distractibility in 48 percent, disruptiveness in 46 percent, short attention span in 43 percent, and inattentiveness in 43 percent. Should nearly half the boys in the first three grades of a public school system properly be considered suspects for the designation MBD?

THE NUMBERS GAME

Another maneuver used by those who propose a medical model for violence and hyperactivity is to exaggerate the magnitude of the problem. Mark and Ervin studied only a small number of patients with limbic brain disease. They stretched the significance of their limited clinical experience by referring to a pool of many millions of Americans with brain disease who might be violence-prone, an implication that is clinically false. In a parallel fashion, millions of children are said to have MBD. When Lauretta Bender surveyed the admissions to Bellevue Hospital's children's psychiatric service, she found that only 0.14 percent suffered from postencephalitic behavior disorders, one of the few conditions in which brain injury directly causes disordered behavior.[7] Estimates of the incidence of MBD in the school-age population, however, run as high as 5 to 10 percent. Paul Wender, a prolific writer on the subject, would apply that diagnosis to almost any child who has the misfortune of being taken to a child guidance clinic:

With no further knowledge, any preadolescent child admitted to a child guidance clinic is most probably in the category until proven otherwise. If, in addition, one knows that a child is not bizarre or retarded and has not been recently disturbed by a presumably noxious environment,

one can make the diagnosis with some certainty. This diagnostic technique lacks subtle nicety but is quite effective.[8]

Effective for whom? The consequences are very serious because Wender prescribes stimulant drugs to all children he diagnoses as having MBD. Ritalin commonly causes loss of appetite, sleeplessness, irritability, and abdominal pain. Long-term use of Ritalin in higher doses, or of Dexedrine at all dose levels, can interfere with normal growth.[9] In rare cases, Ritalin has caused a toxic psychosis marked by hallucinations and bizarre behavior.[10] Ritalin can cause an increase in heart rate and blood pressure. The main psychological hazard of medication for children diagnosed as having MBD is that they often come to view the drug as a magic pill which they feel they need for self-control. Indeed, that is how the drug company portrays Ritalin in its advertisements for physician prescribers:

Here is a child who seems to get very little out of school. He can't sit still. Doesn't take directions well. He's easily frustrated, excitable, often aggressive. And he's got a very short attention span.... He is a victim of Minimal Brain Dysfunction, a diagnosable disease entity that generally responds to treatment programs.[11]

Either millions of American school-age children suffer from a poorly defined and hard-to-diagnose brain disorder, or it is in the interests of the medical profession, the drug industry and the school establishment to convince us that this is so.

The labelling of school children as brain damaged is an example of what William Ryan calls blaming the victim. The individual is blamed for the shortcomings of the social system, here the educational system. The impetus for fundamental social reform is thereby blunted. The only change prompted by the blaming-the-victim ideology is the familiar formula of help for the victim. This is usually garbed in humanitarian terms of remediation, rehabilitation and other compensatory programs. In all cases, the victims are labelled as pathological while the social sys-

of the system. To make a clear enough rupture with the system means risking every security structure in one's life—and one's body and one's mind; family, house, insurance, highly acceptable social identity and highly acceptable means of making enough or more than enough money to live by, all these possessions that one cannot contain in one suitcase (pianos excepted). For some few professionals that has been an historic necessity, for others a temporary historical compromise is possible. We don't all have to have a total destructuring all the time (the 'suicide' of the psychiatrist)—on the same side, and with total solidarity with the other madmen who are murdered. But if psychiatrists don't destructure *enough* of the time they produce the necessity for their 'murder'.

When in the early 1960s, in the course of various polemics in England, I produced finally the wretched and infinitely distorted term 'anti-psychiatry', there was no collective consciousness of the necessity of political involvement. In those years we were all isolated in our national contexts of work. Now there are thousands and thousands of us who begin to recognize a dialectic in our struggle through the growing solidarity of our action.

There is a dialectic that proceeds from psychiatry

through anti-psychiatry to non-psychiatry (or the final abolition of all psycho-technological methods of surveillance and control). The development of this dialectic is inseparable from the development of the class struggle. It does not, however, follow automatically from the dialectic of the *political revolution* that leads from capitalism through socialism (whether achieved in some cases by the dictatorship of the proletariat, direct seizure of power by the working class with popular elements of the military, in other cases by guerrilla warfare (urban, rural) or in others by using the bourgeois democratic machinery, including turning the mystification of the electoral process against itself) to the classless society of communism that abolishes also the last elements of bureaucratic power. The Anti- non- dialectic does not follow a political revolution because it follows a *social revolution,* against all forms of institutional repression that retains its own, highly variable, momentum. Those things that condition the variability of this momentum are made clear in the concrete struggle for social revolution in each country on the way to its national communism as the base of the only possible internationalism. If anyone finds an idealism or utopianism in this,one can only reflect that it is as utopian as the active aspirations of just about all human-kind. As the political revolution is against class (infrastructural) and national oppression, so social revolution is the struggle against institutional repression as we experience ourselves victimized by it wherever we are, the struggle against the mystification of our needs.

If we begin to see madness as our tentative move to disalienation, and if we see the most immediately present forms of alienation as arising from the class division of society, there can be no psychiatry in fully developed socialism (i.e. in a society where the gap between political revolution and social revolution has been 'adequately' narrowed) and no form of psychotechnology whatever in communist society. Such, in very crude outline, are the 'hypotheses for the non-psychiatry' and the creation of the non- society. To fill in the outline and make it less crude depends on specific people and groups of people seizing consciousness not only of their oppression but of the specific modes of their repression in those particular institutions in which they live as functioning organisms and strive to keep alive as human beings. The living, palpating and now palpable solidarity that they invent is what brings the vision down to earth. This solidarity as revealer of the concrete is what we witness today in some of the more authentic anti-and non-psychiatric strivings . . .

We may say that anti- and non-psychiatric movements exist, but that no anti- or non-psychiatrists exist, any more than 'schizophrenics', 'addicts',

tems which generate the pathology are left undisturbed.

1. Vernon H. Mark and Frank R. Ervin, *Violence and the Brain.* New York, Harper and Row, 1970.
2. Thomas Szasz, *Ideology and Insanity.* Garden City, Doubleday, 1970.
3. James Satterfield, "Information for Teachers, Physicians and Counselors."
4. Mark and Ervin, *op. cit.*, p. 160.
5. *Ibid*, p. 112.
6. J. S. Werry and H. C. Quay, "The prevalence of behavior symptoms in younger elementary school children," *American Journal of Orthopsychiatry* 41:136, 1971.
7. Lauretta Bender, "Post-Encephalitic Behavior Disorders in Childhood," in *Encephalitis: A Clinical Study*, ed. J. Neal, Grune & Stratton, 1972.
8. Paul H. Wender, *Minimal Brain Dysfunction in Children.* New York, John Wiley & Sons, 1971, p. 61.
9. Daniel Safer, Richard Allen, Evelyn Barr, "Depression of Growth in Hyperactive Children on Stimulant Drugs," *New England Journal of Medicine* 287:217, 1972.
10. A. Lucas and M. Weiss, "Methylphenidate Hallucinosis," *Journal of the American Medical Association* 217:1079, 1971.
11. CIBA advertisement in *Psychiatric News*, September 20, 1972, p.9.

Psychiatric News, September 2, 1977

'perverts', or no matter what other psycho-diagnostic category. What *do* exist are psychiatrists, psychologists and all manner of other psycho-technicians. The latter exist only precariously; when no roles remain for them to live, their very securizing identity is at stake—*on* the stake waiting to be roasted. Psychiatrists and their associated tribe have cannibalized us too long in the perverse mode of fattening us up for the slaughter with masses of neuroleptics, injections, shocks, interpretations in their masters' voice, and with their projections —of their fear of their madness, their envy of the other's madness and their hatred of the reality of human difference, of autonomy. Now, though fed up, we will de-vow them! Even though they are small fry they fry quicker than quick since they wash whiter than white.

There are two things to be done: firstly, the final extinguishing of capitalism and the entire mystifying ethos of private property; secondly, the social revolution against every form of repression, every violation of autonomy, every form of surveillance and every technique of mind-manipulation—the social revolution that must happen before, during and forever after the political revolution that will produce the classless society.

If these things do not happen well within the limits of this century, within the life-span of most of us now living, our species will be doomed to rapid extinction. In such a case, if our species is not extinguished, it should be, because it will no longer be the human species.

It is not true as the philosophers of pessimism say that 'the dreadful has already happened' (Heidegger), but is is true that we are haunted by the dreadful and it is true that there *is* no hope.

There is only incessant, unrelenting struggle and *that* is the permanent creation of the hoped *for* . . .a forgotten intentionality.

After the destruction of 'psychosis' and the depassment of the structures that invented it for their system, we can now consider the abolition of madness, and the word 'madness'. But first let us consider this state of affairs: The madman in the psychiatric situation is faced, in short, by a three-fold impossibility:

1. *If he lies,* enters into a collusive situation of pretense with the psychiatrist, he betrays his own experience, murders his own reality, and it is not likely to work anyhow in a situation where the other (respectable one) is defined by his role as being always 'one up' with regard to reality.

2. *If he tells the truth* he will be destroyed by all the techniques available, because who can dare express things that exceed the wretched limits of normal language imposed by the ruling class and all its psycho-agents. He must be protected from such a suicidal

defiance; he is logically saved from such a suicide by the simple act of murder.

3. *If he stays silent* he will be forced to chatter acceptable nonsense (withdrawal would be seen as katatonic or paranoid, as if there were something to feel suspicious about in the psychiatric, or any of all the other repressive situations surrounding the psychiatric one).

Schizophrenia has no existence but that of an exploitable fiction.

Madness exists as the delusion that consists in really uttering an unsayable truth in an unspeakable situation.

Madness, presently, is universal subversion desperately chased by extending systems of control and surveillance. It will find its issue with the victory of all forms of subversive struggle against capitalism, fascism and imperialism and against the massive, undigested lumps of repression that exist in bureaucratic socialism, awaiting the social revolution that got left behind in the urgency of political revolution, understandably perhaps, though never excusably.

The future of madness is its end, its transformation into a universal creativity which is the lost place where it came from in the first place.

---

1. Even such remorseless critics of psychiatry, from the interior of the establishment, as Dr. Thomas Szasz equate freedom with the U.S. Constitution and bourgeois law. What freedom is it that depends on the enslavement of the rest of the world, particularly the Third World on which capitalism (parasitic even in its origins, the genocide of original people and the destruction of their civilizations and black slavery) depends—and could not survive without. The implantation, the direct and indirect support of fascist military dictatorships by the imperialist countries, neocolonialism and multinational company criminality exist, even though schizophrenia doesn't. Dr. Szasz (who has accused all psychiatrists of crimes against humanity while one mental patient remains compulsorily detained against his will) is far more consistent and honest than most ('Psychiatry is a religion . . . I teach the religion'). In general however, the teaching of psycho-technologies introduces a police operation into the universities and is in contradiction with the celebrated Academic Freedom.

2. Wolfgang Huber (a psychiatrist) and his wife, of the Socialist Patients' Collective (S.P.K.), Heidelberg, were imprisoned for four years for being, very obviously, taken as literal. They wanted to establish an autogestion in the university psychiatric centre. The police, directed by the psychiatric establishment, 'found' guns in their possession. The S.P.K., now resuscitated, had the aim of using 'illness' as an arm against the capitalist system, a method of political education, not therapy.

Martine Barrat

Vicki

Martine Barrat: *Have you been writing again the way you used to when you were in jail?*

Vicki: Yeah. I write when I think of what's like today. You know, sometimes when you're alone you just lay back and look up at the ceiling and just think about good things...

As a matter of fact, I was thinking of the gangs. Thinking of the time that we rumbled against the *Immortal Girls* and, at that time, it didn't seem funny because I had a one-on-one. I fought the Prez of that division. Her name was Nancy.

Martine: *Was she big?*

Vicki: No, she was tall. And now that I think of it I laugh because I should have felt stupid at the time. The girl was one of those girls that just has a lot of mouth.

So her girls came in our club. The second division club... of the *Royal Queens*... and messed it up. Threw the furniture down and everything. And one of our girls went into the club at the time they were doing it. They beat her up. One of my girls. So, I was in the movies with half of my girls. We usually sit right in the middle. I had my girls there and we were smoking. We was all fucked up at that time. We was drinking a lot of beer and wine and was just goofing on the picture. It was *Foxy Brown*. All of a sudden this girl comes in and she's bleeding. She tells me, "Hey, man, the *Immortal Girls* just beat us up." You know how fast I jumped up? And I was high. We all ran down there. They fucked her up, you know. There was about six of them and only one of her. It really wasn't fair. So we went down there.

Martine: *You went to their club?*

Vicki: Yeah. The *Immortal Girls* comes out. We was in the school yard. We was all packing. The Prez, all she says is, "Why the fuck you want some static? You don't like what we did?"

And I said, "No. I don't like what you did and I could blow you away right now."

So she said, "Yeah, that's all you need. That's all you use is a gun."

I said, "Look, I use my hands, too." I'm very good with my hands. My brothers, they teach me to fight, you know..."

Martine: *Do you find it difficult to use guns? Because you're a girl? Do you feel you need a lot of strength to use them?*

Vicki: Not really because since my brothers were *Nomads,* which was before they

---

Martine Barrat has been making videotapes in the South Bronx in collaboration with street gangs since 1971. They were presented at the *Schizo-Culture Colloquium* and, recently, at the Whitney Museum. Vicki, who was 16 when this conversation was taped a year ago, has two children. She is the "Prez" (president) of the *Roman Queens,* the female counterpart of the *Roman Kings.*

were *Roman Kings,* they had guns. So the first gun that they had lent to me was a .22. It was small, and my brother, I think it was Ace, told me, "You never shot a gun, right?", and I told him "no."

So he told me, "Come with me up to the roof." He shot and says, "Now is your turn."

I didn't know what the hell to do, so I said, "What do I do with this?"

"Just do straight," he says, and I shot it. The first time you feel kind of nervous after you shoot a gun because it kicks a lot. From that day on, every time I'd get a gun I'd start shooting on the roof. And that's how I learned. But a big gun isn't easy for me to handle.

Martine: *How old were you then?*

Vicki: I was small. I was about eleven. But from that day on I have a .32 automatic on me. I always carry it around, especially when I get my check... or when I'm coming home alone at night. You know, somebody is going to jump me and stuff, so I just pull it out. I won't shoot to kill, but I'll shoot them so they know not to fuck around with me no more. That's how I am. But that time, with that girl, I didn't want to take up the gun because I feel, boy, I'll just slap her around a few times and the girl will shut her damned mouth. I don't like to talk when I argue with somebody. I'll swing first. I lost my temper fast... even with a guy (laughs). That's why most of my boyfriends, they left me. It's not that I'm a manhandler but it's the type of thing where I don't like nobody to slap me around. My mother don't hit me. My own mother, she hit me only twice and that was when I was small.

Martine: *You think guys leave you for that. They can't take it?*

Vicki: They can't take it because they argued with me, I get mad fast. Especially when they cuss at you, say "Ah, fuck you" or something like that. And I say, "What?" They don't have to swing at me first because I'll turn around and I'll swing at them and we just fight right there. I'm not as strong as a man and really they kick my ass, you might as well say. But I've proved to them that when you raise a hand on me, I'm going to raise one back. Because he would lose respect for me just as much as I am losing respect for him. We just fall sliding all over the place until one of us give up... and most likely he's going to give up because I lost my temper and if I grab their hair, whatever I got, I won't let go.

Martine: *You are lucky to have brothers teaching you how to fight.*

Vicki: Yeah. Like when we was the *Young Nomads,* they used to put me up to fight with the girls.

Martine: *For initiation?*

Vicki: Yeah. If I would lose a fight, they'll make me fight her and fight her until I win. I could be dead on my feet and, boy, they tell me to go ahead and fight, fight until I'm going to get real mad and I'm going to whip her ass. That's how they taught me. Don't be scared of nobody. Especially if they raise their hand to you. So, that's what happened.

Martine: *And that's why you want to teach your little girl to fight?*

Vicki: Right. Now she gets real mad. She starts swinging at anybody that's there, whoever bothers her. I teach her. I tell her, "You hit back because they only going to fuck over you if you don't hit back." She's like that and I'm like that. But I don't tell her to go around hitting everybody in the head... I just tell her, "When somebody hits you, you hit back. And if they argue with you, you argue with them. If they talk back to you, you talk back to them. Just don't let nobody talk about your mother or your father or your family." One thing I don't want anybody calling me is a mother-fucker... because I feel I don't fuck my mother. I got a lot of respect for my mom—to a point where if somebody puts her down that's it. Right there I see blood in my eyes and I just go at them. I say, "Look, I'm not a mother-fucker. Don't ever say that." Either they say, "Ah, you know, it's only a joke, we're only goofing around". But it's my heart. That's my mother, you know, and I love her. I'm not going to let somebody else talk about her, especially not in my family. Even my own brothers. I say, "Don't talk about Ma like that, because we all got the same mother and the same blood and we love her a lot." And they understand what I'm saying.

Martine: *I love your mother.*

Vicki: She's very sweet and she worked

hard to get where she's at. She tries her best.

Martine: *When there are rumbles between cliques, are they between cliques of girls or do they involve the guys?*
Vicki: It was mostly with guys because there wasn't a lot of trouble with girls. Really and truly.

Martine: *You think girls fight as much as guys?*

Vicki: Well, guys fight a lot. Girls don't fight as much. Like if it was all up to them we'll fight. The guys, they got to fight because their prez tells them to fight. But if it was up to us girls, we'd hand out together. We would like to have a brotherhood. But sometimes it's the girls. I'm the one who started rumbling with the *Immortals* because I have something against that girl from school, Nancy. We fought and then she told the school I pulled out a knife on her and they threw me out. I couldn't go to school no more, so I had something against the *Immortals* because of her.

When I have something against somebody, I take it out in one fight. One fight. As long as I get my shit off. After that if she want to talk to me, she talk to me but she could go to hell, too. I tell her, "I was born in this world by myself. I'm going to tell you personally that you got me now... but I'm going to pay you back." That's how I am. I hold it in, hold it in. They fuck me today. I get my ass kicked today. But I always get revenge.

Martine: *Like your rumble with the* Immortals?
Vicki: Yeah, like that girl. I grab her alone and we straightened it out and now me an' her don't have no trouble. I see her. She's in jail right now when I go to see her.

Martine: *Why is she in jail?*
Vicki: She was selling drugs. She sold drugs to a cop and now she's facing ten to twenty-five.

Martine: *Were there many fights with knives and guns at the time you were in school?*
Vicki: No guns or knives, we just fight with the hands. Most of the time that there's fights is because someone don't like you or someone try to take my boyfriend away. So, they fight and scratch each other up.

Martine: *But you've fought with knives and stuff. Was that outside of school?*

Vicki: Yeah, outside. Say I fight somebody and I beat her up. She ain't going to like that. So she know if she fights with me again, I'm going to beat her up again. So she'll bring something to stab me with, or she'll bring a gun and shoot me with it. We don't trust them just like they don't trust us.

Martine: *So you think that's one of the reasons why kids in the clique carry guns?*

Vicki: Yeah, that's why. God knows what they going to do when we turn our backs, just like God knows what we going to do when they turn their backs. That's all.

Martine: *Do you remember when Charlie organized that big meeting with all the cliques after Benji got killed? To try to get them together so they wouldn't fight anymore?*

Vicki: I was upstate at the time. I heard about it. By the time I got back everything passed and everybody was walking the streets again. All the cliques.

Martine: *You're a leader of a clique, too. Did you ever think about getting all the cliques together?*

Vicki: Yeah. I tried to do that a lot. I would talk to my girls and tell them we should get all the cliques and the girls together. You know, make truce and then throw parties and shit. But it could never happen that way. Because of the guys.

Put it this way, a woman has a softer heart than a man. A man, if he holds something against somebody, he's going to get them. Kill them. And they're determined to do even that. That's what's wrong with the gang. Like if somebody from another clique do something to a *Roman King,* they'll hold it in for a while and then, when they catch that person, forget it. You might as well say they finished. They dead. If it was up to the girls we'd be friends with everybody. But the guys, shit, they'll kick you with their M.C. boots.

Martine: *You were telling me about the Outlaw Marriage in the cliques. You told me that the girl who gets married in certain cliques has to get down with all the guys in the clique. Do the girls feel like that is being raped?*

Vicki: I feel that they do, yeah. It's just like rape. When a girl has to get down with all of them. I wouldn't do that. I couldn't walk in the street proud. I think a good man is the type that will make love to a woman and won't talk about it to nobody. It's his personal thing. The thing he should keep inside. A man that lays with a woman and then tells every guy, "Oh, I lay with that girl, she's a good fuck," he's bad. That make you feel like a piece of shit on the floor. If I'm going to marry a dude from a clique, I'm going to give myself only to him. You might as well be alone or become a tramp or something if you lay with every guy.

Martine: *But the guy doesn't have to get down with all the girls?*
Vicki: (laughs): No. But if he lets his wife that he just married get down with the other guys, then the marriage is over. Really. Has to be.

Martine: *You think that will change one day?*
Vicki: Yeah. It will change. Like now most of the cliques ain't that way. I got married Outlaw. We don't do that in the *Roman Kings.*

Martine: *Can you describe the marriage to me because I've never been to one?*
Vicki: The *Roman Queens* are on one side and the *Kings* on their side and everybody flies their colors. We're clean. We're never dirty. You know, we have our dungarees, our tee shirt, our jackets with the colors on it and our boots. The guys have on their Outlaw pants, a tee shirt, all their colors. Their hats, whatever. And their M.C.'s. And the girls are on one side and all the guys on the other side and we get in the middle. Me and him. Well, when I got married to Baba, his twin brother got married too. Behind them was the bridesmaid and the... what you call... best man. The guy that married us was Husky Pekiching[3]. So we walked up to him. We stand there because it was like a double wedding. And Husky was there telling us, "I now pronounce you man and wife," like all the things they say in church.

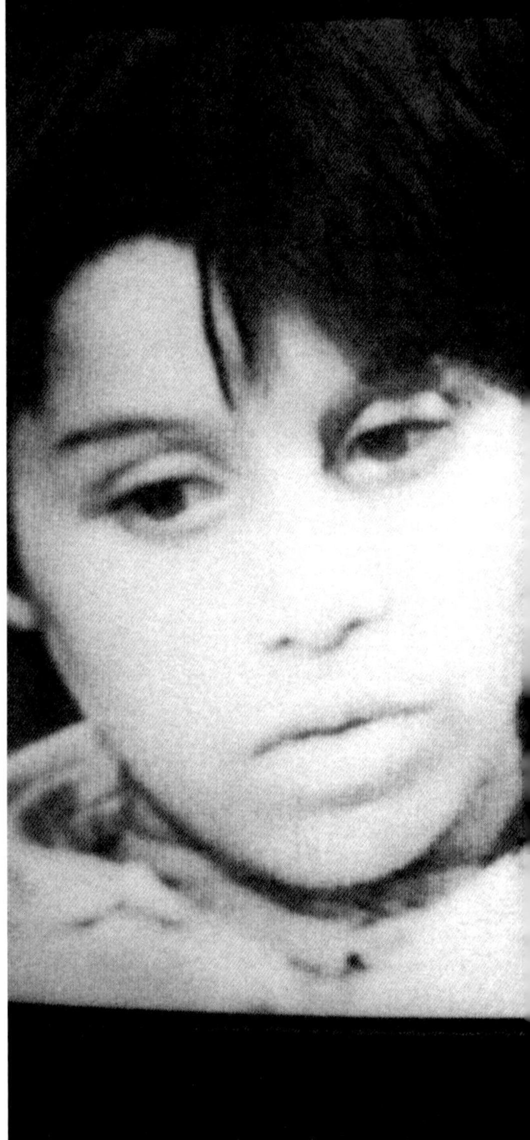

Martine: *Did he hold a book like a priest or something?*
Vicki: Oh yeah. It was a bible. He was holding it in his hands. We even had rings. You know, I'm not saying expensive wedding rings but they was real sterling. Anyway he say "kiss your bride and put the ring on the finger," and it was just like a real church. Except that afterwards, in-

stead of throwing rice like they do in church, they're pouring beer all over us. While we're walking down the aisle. Three quarts.

Martine: *Did you sing?*
Vicki: No. But the *Roman Kings* they buy beer and they get us real high and then we're allowed to stay in the club. The club was our apartment for three days. It's in this wrecked building. It was our honeymoon. We stayed there for three days... without coming out (laughs). If the *Roman Kings* would have seen us out before three days they would have sent us back in. Yeah.

Martine: *Did you cook?*
Vicki: Yeah.

Martine: *And love?*
Vicki: Yeah. (laughs).

Martine: *And care for each other?*
Vicki: Yep. And from that day on—this happened four months ago—we're still together.

Martine: *And where was your little girl?*
Vicki: My mother was with her. I told my mother about it. She didn't say nothing.

Martine: *Did your mother come to your wedding?*
Vicki: Are you crazy?

Martine: *There were no parents?*
Vicki: No, just us. But I feel it was nice, you know, because I've been raised by the gangs.

Martine: *But in other cliques, like when Cheena got married with Black Ben in the* Savage Nomads, *the ceremony was different because she had to get down with...*
Vicki: She do the same thing that they do in church except that then they cut themselves.

Martine: *Cut themselves. Where?*
Vicki: Not on the vein. On the wrist. A little bit just to show their blood and then they rub it. With two hands. Like this.

Martine: *Like Indians were doing?*
Vicki: Yeah. Right. And then they got down in front of everybody and then she had to get down with the clique. And that was it. But that's how I feel about the rape thing. I fell that I married Baba right. The other guys respect me. And they tell me, "I would like to rap to you if you wasn't this

guy's." And he feels proud because, you know, I'm not conceited, but I know I'm not ugly.

Martine: *When Cheena got married with Black Ben, how many years ago was that?*
Vicki: Four... five years ago.

Martine: *Do you think she was upset being raped by the division. Was it all the members of the gang, or was it a division only?*
Vicki: There was a lot of guys but I think it was a division only.

Martine: *About how many people are in a division?*
Vicki: Thirteen. It's a good luck number. That's all there was. She felt bad, but she got over it.

Martine: *Did she talk about it to you?*
Vicki: No. She was on her honeymoon at that time and when she came back she wouldn't hardly come around. She used to stay with Ben most of the time so we didn't have a good chance of talking.

Martine: *But I'm sure she didn't go for that at all.*
Vicki: No, nobody go for that. Only the girls who like it and they must be stupid or crazy or something. Nobody likes to be raped. I wouldn't. I feel I would go through a lot of changes if I did get raped.

Martine: *Are there many girls who are getting raped around here by cliques?*

Vicki: Well, before yes. But now, no. I think the guys got sense now. You know, they rap for it instead.

Martine: *Some people say that more and more young people of your generation are bisexual or homosexual. Is that true?*
Vicki: Yeah, it's true. Some girls turn gay because they got raped by their father. Some girls turn gay because a lot of guys raped them or a lot of guys used them and hurt them. Or some fell in love and everytime the guy hurts her. Leaves her. That's why they could go to a girl... because they know the girl won't leave. I think girls, butches and friends, can stay together longer than a man and a woman, a man and wife. I guess it's because they understand each other. When they have a problem they could both talk it up, you know, because they're both womans.

The men, too. I guess the men has the same problems. Like in the project. Put it this way, half of the building are butches and faggots. I guess that's what's happening now. Just a new style I guess. Like me. I done gay when I was locked up.

Martine: *When you were in jail?*
Vicki: I had turned gay because I didn't have no man to turn to. I guess I had a shoulder to lean on. It was a thing where I was lonely. A lot of girls are like that when they get locked up.

Martine: *And the same for the guys?*
Vicki: The same for a guy, too. They know all they going to see is boys so they say, "What the heck. You going to be here for a while, why not enjoy it?" So, girls turn to a girl and the guys turn to a guy. That's why I think that sex is bisexual.

Martine: *And when you were in jail most of the girls were going with girls?*
Vicki: Yeah. Most of them. Some girls don't like gay but if they know they're going to do a long time they get curious... Some of them they just stay straight. They won't turn cookie for nothing.

Martine: *You were telling me about your sister who got raped in your building. What happened?*
Vicki: Well, she was going to school and she forgot her wallet. She came back up and this guy was in the elevator with her. They're friends so they was talking to each other. When they got to his floor he pushed her out and then he raped her right there. She stayed in her room after that. She didn't want to talk to nobody. She didn't want to tell nobody until long after. My sister, she always remember that. Right now she's living with her husband and when she has sexual, you know, intercourse with him she thinks of that and that fucks her up. But at least she told him. She told him what happened to her and he don't blame her. He knows what she went through. Now they're all right. The rest of the rapes ain't around here. They're a few blocks down... on Fox Street.

Martine: *There are a lot of abandoned buildings there?*
Vicki: Most of Fox Street is abandoned. The buildings are standing up by surprise. The gangs go there and forget it. First they use the basement and from the basement they move up and up and up. Then they have the whole building. In a few months

the whole building is condemned.

Martine: *Like after a war. Your mother and people who live in places like that call those places "Korea." Do you think it's getting worse?*

Vicki: Oh, it's getting worser and worser. I've been living here for about eleven years. Since I was small. I seen buildings that just get put up and then I seen them get knocked down. I seen this place we live in when it was pretty. Yeah, pretty. Locks on the door in the front of the building and everything. But now it's all knocked down. There was a movie house up here. Right up the block but it burned down. It ain't a movie no more. People that are very close to me moved away because of the neighborhood. But you got to live through it because everywhere you go people are going to move away. There's going to be trouble no matter where you are.

Martine: *Do you think of moving out when you get older?*

Vicki: Sometime. But in a way I can't move because I love this place no matter how fucked up it looks. I was born here and raised here and I guess I'm going to stay here.

I guess if I'm going to become something or if I'm going to get fucked up I don't have to go out of state to do it. This is the South Bronx and you take it the way it is.

John Giorno

Grasping at Emptiness

<table>
<tr><td align="right">You are walking</td><td>You are walking</td></tr>
<tr><td align="right">down</td><td>down</td></tr>
<tr><td align="right">Lafayette</td><td>Lafayette</td></tr>
<tr><td align="right">Street</td><td>Street</td></tr>
<tr><td></td><td>You are walking down</td></tr>
<tr><td></td><td>Lafayette Street</td></tr>
<tr><td align="right">and your face</td><td>and your face</td></tr>
<tr><td align="right">twists</td><td>twists</td></tr>
<tr><td align="right">up</td><td>up</td></tr>
<tr><td></td><td>and your face twists up</td></tr>
<tr><td align="right">and starts</td><td>and starts</td></tr>
<tr><td align="right">crying</td><td>crying</td></tr>
<tr><td></td><td>and starts crying</td></tr>
<tr><td></td><td>and starts crying,</td></tr>
<tr><td></td><td>you are walking down Lafayette Street</td></tr>
<tr><td></td><td>and your face twists up and starts crying</td></tr>
<tr><td align="right">turn</td><td>turn</td></tr>
<tr><td align="right">your face</td><td>your face</td></tr>
<tr><td align="right">to the wall</td><td>to the wall</td></tr>
<tr><td></td><td>turn your face to the wall</td></tr>
<tr><td align="right">so nobody'll</td><td>so nobody'll</td></tr>
<tr><td align="right">see</td><td>see</td></tr>
<tr><td></td><td>so nobody'll see,</td></tr>
<tr><td align="right">there's</td><td>there's</td></tr>
<tr><td align="right">tears</td><td>tears</td></tr>
<tr><td align="right">running</td><td>running</td></tr>
<tr><td align="right">down</td><td>down</td></tr>
<tr><td align="right">your cheeks</td><td>your cheeks</td></tr>
<tr><td></td><td>there's tears running down your cheeks,</td></tr>
<tr><td align="right">don't</td><td>don't</td></tr>
<tr><td align="right">hold on</td><td>hold on</td></tr>
<tr><td></td><td>don't hold on,</td></tr>
<tr><td align="right">cause</td><td>cause</td></tr>
<tr><td align="right">I'm already</td><td>I'm already</td></tr>
<tr><td align="right">gone</td><td>gone</td></tr>
<tr><td></td><td>cause I'm already gone;</td></tr>
</table>

and there ain’t	and there ain’t
nothing	nothing
worse	worse
in a relationship	in a relationship
	and there ain’t nothing worse
	in a relationship
than stupidity	than stupidity
	than stupidity
	than stupidity
	than stupidity,
you’re so	you’re so
fucking	fucking
up tight	up tight
	you’re so fucking
	up tight
	you’re so fucking up tight,
blind	blind
ignorance	ignorance
	blind ignorance
	blind ignorance,
and no matter	and no matter
how	how
much	much
I love	I love
fucking you	fucking you
	and no matter how much I love fucking
no matter how much I love	no matter how much I love
making love to you,	making love to you,
I can’t	I can’t
stand	stand
being here	being here
another	another
moment	moment
	I can’t stand being here another moment
as a matter	as a matter
of fact	of fact
I never	I never
want	want
to see you	to see you
again	again
	I never want to see
	you again
	I never want to see you again,
and as I said	and as I said
to you over	to you over
the telephone	the telephone
	and as I said to you over the telephone
“I hope	“I hope
you have a nice	you have a nice
weekend”	weekend”
	I hope you have a nice weekend,”
you’re running	you’re running
on empty	on empty
	you’re running on empty
	you’re running on empty,
and I feel	and I feel

old	old
and ugly	and ugly
	and I feel old
	and ugly
	and I feel old and ugly,
and I don't	and I don't
want	want
to talk	to talk
to anybody	to anybody
	and I don't want to talk
	to anybody
	and I don't want to talk to anybody,
nothing	nothing
I've ever	I've ever
loved	loved
	nothing I've ever
	loved
no matter	no matter
how much	how much
the potential	the potential
	nothing I ever loved
	no matter how much the potential
was ever	was ever
worth	worth
the suffering	the suffering
	was ever worth
	the suffering
	was ever worth the suffering,
you're on	you're on
United	United
Flight Number	Flight Number
222	222
	you're on United Flight Number 222,
I think	I think
we're over	we're over
Kansas	Kansas
	I think we're over Kansas
because	because
the earth	the earth
is covered	is covered
with squares	with squares
and rectangles	and rectangles
because the earth	
is covered with squares and rectangles,	
flying	flying
back	back
to New York	to New York
flying back to New York,	
covered with squares and rectangles,	
sipping	sipping
a whiskey	a whiskey
sipping a whiskey,	
flying back to New York,	
no matter	no matter
how	how

famous	famous
I become	I become
no matter how famous I become,	
no matter	no matter
how much	how much
money	money
I make	I make
no matter how much money I make,	
no matter how	no matter how
beautiful	beautiful
I used to be	I used to be
no matter how beautiful I used to be,	
I'm always	I'm always
totally	totally
lonely	lonely
I'm always totally	
lonely	
I'm always	
totally lonely	
I'm always totally lonely,	
and if I wasn't	and if I wasn't
a fucking	a fucking
Buddhist	Buddhist
	and if I wasn't a fucking Buddhist,
I'd love	I'd love
to put	to put
a gun	a gun
in my mouth	in my mouth
	I'd love to put
	a gun in my mouth
	I'd love to put a gun in my mouth
and blow	and blow
my fucking	my fucking
head	head
off	off
	and blow my fucking
	head off
	and blow my fucking head off
in slow	in slow
motion,	motion,
and the pilot	and the pilot
says	says
we're flying	we're flying
at 37,000	at 37,000
feet	feet
over Kansas	over Kansas
	we're flying at 37,000 feet over Kansas,
wide	wide
open	open
	wide open
blue	blue
	wide open blue
evening	evening
sky,	sky,
grasping	grasping

at emptiness	at emptiness
	grasping at emptiness
	grasping at emptiness,
I keep	I keep
repeating	repeating
this	this
to myself	to myself
	I keep repeating
	this to myself
	I keep repeating this to myself,
	I said
	it to you
	I said it to you,
I remember saying it to you,	I remember saying it to you,
	you get
	you get
	you get
you get	you get
no cover	no cover
from your backdoor	from your backdoor
lover	lover
	you get no cover
	from your backdoor lover,
you're standing	you're standing
at a subway	at a subway
urinal	urinal
	you're standing at a subway urinal,
pulling	pulling
on your meat	on your meat
	pulling on your meat
	pulling on your meat,
cause	cause
I want	I want
to make love	to make love
to somebody	to somebody
on my way	on my way
back	back
downtown	downtown
	cause I want to make love
	to somebody
	on my way back downtown
	cause I want to make love to somebody
	on my way back downtown,
	you're standing at a subway urinal,
somebody	somebody
is sucking	is sucking
your cock	your cock
somebody is sucking	
your cock	
somebody is sucking your cock,	
and someone	and someone
else	else
comes up	comes up
next to you	next to you
and someone else comes up next to you,	

<table>
<tr><td align="right">and you're</td><td>and you're</td></tr>
<tr><td align="right">kissing him</td><td>kissing him</td></tr>
<tr><td align="right">and you're kissing him</td><td></td></tr>
<tr><td align="right">and you're kissing him,</td><td></td></tr>
<tr><td align="right">the Howard</td><td>the Howard</td></tr>
<tr><td align="right">Johnson</td><td>Johnson</td></tr>
<tr><td align="right">toilet</td><td>toilet</td></tr>
<tr><td align="right">on the Garden</td><td>on the Garden</td></tr>
<tr><td align="right">State</td><td>Statc</td></tr>
<tr><td align="right">Parkway,</td><td>Parkway,</td></tr>
<tr><td align="right">the Long Island</td><td>the Long Island</td></tr>
<tr><td align="right">men's</td><td>men's</td></tr>
<tr><td align="right">room</td><td>room</td></tr>
<tr><td align="right">in Freeport,</td><td>in Freeport,</td></tr>
<tr><td align="right">I saw it</td><td>I saw it</td></tr>
<tr><td align="right">in a Walt Disney</td><td>in a Walt Disney</td></tr>
<tr><td align="right">cartoon</td><td>cartoon</td></tr>
<tr><td align="right">once</td><td>once</td></tr>
<tr><td align="right">I saw it in a Walt Disney cartoon once,</td><td></td></tr>
<tr><td align="right">here</td><td>here</td></tr>
<tr><td align="right">you're gone</td><td>you're gone</td></tr>
<tr><td align="right">today</td><td>today</td></tr>
<tr><td align="right">here you're gone</td><td></td></tr>
<tr><td align="right">today</td><td></td></tr>
<tr><td align="right">here you're gone today</td><td></td></tr>
<tr><td align="right">and all</td><td>and all</td></tr>
<tr><td align="right">I ever</td><td>I ever</td></tr>
<tr><td align="right">wanted to do</td><td>wanted to do</td></tr>
<tr><td align="right">was to love you</td><td>was to love you</td></tr>
<tr><td align="right">and all I ever wanted to do was</td><td></td></tr>
<tr><td align="right">to love you</td><td></td></tr>
<tr><td align="right">here you're gone today and all I ever</td><td></td></tr>
<tr><td align="right">wanted to do was to love you,</td><td></td></tr>
<tr><td align="right">grasping</td><td></td></tr>
<tr><td align="right">at emptiness</td><td></td></tr>
<tr><td align="right">grasping at emptiness</td><td>grasping at emptiness</td></tr>
<tr><td align="right">grasping at emptiness,</td><td></td></tr>
<tr><td align="right">I've made</td><td></td></tr>
<tr><td align="right">so many</td><td></td></tr>
<tr><td align="right">mistakes</td><td></td></tr>
<tr><td align="right">in my life</td><td></td></tr>
<tr><td align="right">I've made so many mistakes</td><td>I've made so many mistakes</td></tr>
<tr><td align="right">in my life</td><td>in my life</td></tr>
<tr><td align="right">I've made so many mistakes in my life</td><td></td></tr>
<tr><td align="right">I only got</td><td></td></tr>
<tr><td align="right">3 dollars</td><td></td></tr>
<tr><td align="right">in my pocket</td><td></td></tr>
<tr><td align="right">I only got 3 dollars in my pocket,</td><td>I only got 3 dollars in my pocket,</td></tr>
<tr><td align="right">I'm sitting</td><td></td></tr>
<tr><td align="right">in a car</td><td></td></tr>
<tr><td align="right">on an expressway</td><td></td></tr>
<tr><td align="right">in a traffic</td><td></td></tr>
<tr><td align="right">jam</td><td></td></tr>
<tr><td align="right">I'm sitting in a car on a expressway</td><td>I'm sitting in a car on an expressway</td></tr>
<tr><td align="right">in a traffic jam,</td><td>in a traffic jam,</td></tr>
</table>

<table>
<tr><td align="right">I like</td><td></td></tr>
<tr><td align="right">dirty</td><td></td></tr>
<tr><td align="right">sex</td><td></td></tr>
<tr><td align="right">I like</td><td>I like</td></tr>
<tr><td align="right">dirty sex</td><td>dirty sex</td></tr>
<tr><td align="right">I like dirty sex,</td><td></td></tr>
<tr><td align="right">I like it</td><td></td></tr>
<tr><td align="right">when</td><td></td></tr>
<tr><td align="right">you</td><td></td></tr>
<tr><td align="right">cum</td><td></td></tr>
<tr><td align="right">when I'm pissing</td><td></td></tr>
<tr><td align="right">in your mouth</td><td></td></tr>
<tr><td align="right">I like it when you cum</td><td>I like it when you cum</td></tr>
<tr><td align="right">when I'm pissing in your mouth,</td><td>when I'm pissing in your mouth,</td></tr>
<tr><td align="right">and hot</td><td></td></tr>
<tr><td align="right">concrete</td><td></td></tr>
<tr><td align="right">road</td><td></td></tr>
<tr><td align="right">and hot concrete road</td><td>and hot concrete road</td></tr>
<tr><td align="right">and highway</td><td></td></tr>
<tr><td align="right">and highway</td><td>and highway</td></tr>
<tr><td align="right">and overpasses</td><td></td></tr>
<tr><td align="right">popping</td><td></td></tr>
<tr><td align="right">and overpasses popping,</td><td>and overpasses popping,</td></tr>
<tr><td align="right">you haven't got</td><td>you haven't got</td></tr>
<tr><td align="right">anything</td><td>anything</td></tr>
<tr><td align="right">to lose,</td><td>to lose,</td></tr>
<tr><td></td><td>cause</td></tr>
<tr><td></td><td>nothing</td></tr>
<tr><td></td><td>you've ever</td></tr>
<tr><td></td><td>done</td></tr>
<tr><td></td><td>has been any</td></tr>
<tr><td></td><td>good</td></tr>
<tr><td align="right">cause nothing you've ever done</td><td>cause nothing you've ever done</td></tr>
<tr><td align="right">has been any good</td><td>has been any good</td></tr>
<tr><td></td><td>cause nothing you've ever done has been</td></tr>
<tr><td></td><td>any good,</td></tr>
<tr><td></td><td>big</td></tr>
<tr><td></td><td>ego</td></tr>
<tr><td align="right">big ego</td><td>big ego</td></tr>
<tr><td></td><td>big ego,</td></tr>
<tr><td></td><td>and hustle</td></tr>
<tr><td align="right">and hustle</td><td>and hustle</td></tr>
<tr><td></td><td>and hustle,</td></tr>
<tr><td></td><td>and it's all</td></tr>
<tr><td></td><td>over now,</td></tr>
<tr><td></td><td>baby</td></tr>
<tr><td align="right">it's all over now, baby,</td><td>it's all over now, baby,</td></tr>
<tr><td></td><td>you haven't got anything</td></tr>
<tr><td></td><td>to lose</td></tr>
<tr><td></td><td>you haven't got anything to lose,</td></tr>
<tr><td></td><td>and I don't know</td></tr>
<tr><td></td><td>where</td></tr>
<tr><td></td><td>the money</td></tr>
<tr><td></td><td>comes from</td></tr>
<tr><td align="right">and I don't know where</td><td>and I don't know where</td></tr>
</table>

the money comes from	the money comes from,
	and I don't know where the money
	comes from
	it's all
	going
	to end
	tomorrow
it's all going to end	it's all going to end
tomorrow	tomorrow
	it's all going to end tomorrow,
three	
times	
today	
I dialed	
your number	
three times today	
I dialed your number	
three times today I dialed your number,	three times today I dialed your number
you weren't	
there	
you weren't there	
you weren't there,	you weren't there,
I keep	
thinking	
about you	
I keep thinking	
about you	
I keep thinking about you,	I keep thinking about you,
and I know	
you're a reflection	
of my mind	
and I know you're a reflection	
of my mind	
and I know you're a reflection of my mind,	and I know you're a reflection of my mind,
I'm lying	
down	
here	
on my bed	
I'm lying down here on my bed,	I'm lying down here on my bed,
thinking about	
when	
I'm going	
to see you	
thinking about when I'm going to see you,	thinking about when I'm going to see you,
I'm going	
to say to you	
I'm going to say to you	
I'm going to say to you,	I'm going to say to you,
don't think	
too much	
tonight,	
baby	
don't think too much tonight, baby,	don't think too much tonight, baby,
	spend
	the night

<table>
<tr><td></td><td>with me</td></tr>
<tr><td></td><td>spend</td></tr>
<tr><td></td><td>the night with me</td></tr>
<tr><td>spend the night with me,</td><td>spend the night with me,</td></tr>
<tr><td></td><td>stay</td></tr>
<tr><td></td><td>until</td></tr>
<tr><td></td><td>the break</td></tr>
<tr><td></td><td>of day</td></tr>
<tr><td>stay until the break of day,</td><td>stay until the break of day,</td></tr>
<tr><td></td><td>share</td></tr>
<tr><td></td><td>this night</td></tr>
<tr><td></td><td>with me</td></tr>
<tr><td>share this night with me</td><td>share this night with me</td></tr>
<tr><td></td><td>in my arms</td></tr>
<tr><td></td><td>in my arms</td></tr>
<tr><td>in my arms,</td><td>in my arms,</td></tr>
<tr><td></td><td>I keep</td></tr>
<tr><td></td><td>looking</td></tr>
<tr><td></td><td>for the feeling</td></tr>
<tr><td></td><td>I lost</td></tr>
<tr><td></td><td>when</td></tr>
<tr><td></td><td>I lost you</td></tr>
<tr><td></td><td>I keep looking for the feeling</td></tr>
<tr><td></td><td>I lost when I lost you</td></tr>
<tr><td>I keep looking for the feeling I lost</td><td>I keep looking for the feeling I lost</td></tr>
<tr><td>when I lost you,</td><td>when I lost you,</td></tr>
<tr><td></td><td>and it was</td></tr>
<tr><td></td><td>bullshit</td></tr>
<tr><td></td><td>and it was bullshit</td></tr>
<tr><td>and it was bullshit,</td><td>and it was bullshit,</td></tr>
<tr><td></td><td>and now,</td></tr>
<tr><td></td><td>baby,</td></tr>
<tr><td></td><td>it's chickenshit</td></tr>
<tr><td>and now, baby, it's chickenshit,</td><td>and now, baby, it's chickenshit,</td></tr>
<tr><td></td><td>we're sitting</td></tr>
<tr><td></td><td>on the green</td></tr>
<tr><td></td><td>couch</td></tr>
<tr><td>we're sitting on the green couch,</td><td>we're sitting on the green couch,</td></tr>
<tr><td></td><td>I'm hugging</td></tr>
<tr><td></td><td>you</td></tr>
<tr><td></td><td>I'm hugging you</td></tr>
<tr><td>I'm hugging you,</td><td>I'm hugging you,</td></tr>
<tr><td></td><td>we're kissing</td></tr>
<tr><td>we're kissing,</td><td>we're kissing,</td></tr>
<tr><td></td><td>I wish</td></tr>
<tr><td></td><td>I knew</td></tr>
<tr><td></td><td>how</td></tr>
<tr><td></td><td>to make</td></tr>
<tr><td></td><td>love</td></tr>
<tr><td></td><td>to you</td></tr>
<tr><td></td><td>I wish I knew how</td></tr>
<tr><td></td><td>to make love to you</td></tr>
<tr><td>I wish I knew how to make love to you,</td><td>I wish I knew how to make love to you,</td></tr>
<tr><td></td><td>when</td></tr>
<tr><td></td><td>I was in</td></tr>
</table>

	Rome
	Italy
when I was in Rome Italy,	when I was in Rome Italy,
fettuchini	fettuchini
alfredo,	alfredo,
	Marion
	Javits
	give me
	another
	hit
	of the popper
Marion Javits give me another	Marion Javits give me another
hit of the popper,	hit
	of the popper,
you're not	you're not
going	going
to find	to find
what you	what you
want	want
in this bar	in this bar
	you're not going to find
	what you want in this bar
	you're not going to find what you want
	in this bar,
you know	you know
you're not	you're not
going to	going to
find him	find him
anywhere	anywhere
	you know you're not going
	to find him anywhere
	you know you're not going to find him
	anywhere,
you're cruising	you're cruising
the baths	the baths
	you're cruising the baths
	you're cruising the baths,
looking in	looking in
the dimly	the dimly
lit	lit
rooms	rooms
	looking in the dimly lit rooms,
these guys	these guys
posing	posing
for pornographic	for pornographic
pictures	pictures
	these guys looking like
	they're posing for pornographic pictures
I want	I want
to make it	to make it
with you	with you
I want to make	
it with you	
I want to make it	
with you	

<table>
<tr><td align="right">I want to make it with you,</td><td></td></tr>
<tr><td align="right">the guy</td><td>the guy</td></tr>
<tr><td align="right">in a Levi</td><td>in a Levi</td></tr>
<tr><td align="right">shirt</td><td>shirt</td></tr>
<tr><td align="right">with a hard on</td><td>with a hard on</td></tr>
<tr><td align="right">the guy in a Levi shirt with a hard on,</td><td></td></tr>
<tr><td align="right">you're walking</td><td>you're walking</td></tr>
<tr><td align="right">down</td><td>down</td></tr>
<tr><td align="right">7th Avenue</td><td>7th Avenue</td></tr>
<tr><td align="right">you're walking down 7th Avenue,</td><td></td></tr>
<tr><td align="right">and all</td><td>and all</td></tr>
<tr><td align="right">these people</td><td>these people</td></tr>
<tr><td align="right">are passing you</td><td>are passing you</td></tr>
<tr><td align="right">and all these people</td><td></td></tr>
<tr><td align="right">are passing you</td><td></td></tr>
<tr><td align="right">and all these people are passing you,</td><td></td></tr>
<tr><td align="right">everyone</td><td></td></tr>
<tr><td align="right">of them</td><td></td></tr>
<tr><td align="right">has a lover</td><td></td></tr>
<tr><td align="right">everyone of them has a lover,</td><td>everyone of them has a lover,</td></tr>
<tr><td align="right">and how</td><td>and how</td></tr>
<tr><td align="right">come</td><td>come</td></tr>
<tr><td align="right">I'm alone</td><td>I'm alone</td></tr>
<tr><td></td><td>and how come</td></tr>
<tr><td></td><td>I'm alone</td></tr>
<tr><td></td><td>and how come I'm alone,</td></tr>
<tr><td align="right">we're in</td><td>we're in</td></tr>
<tr><td align="right">your room</td><td>your room</td></tr>
<tr><td align="right">and we're kissing</td><td>and we're kissing</td></tr>
<tr><td></td><td>we're in your room and we're kissing,</td></tr>
<tr><td></td><td>we're holding</td></tr>
<tr><td></td><td>you tight</td></tr>
<tr><td></td><td>we're holding you tight,</td></tr>
<tr><td align="right">and there may be</td><td>and there may be</td></tr>
<tr><td align="right">no</td><td>no</td></tr>
<tr><td align="right">attachment</td><td>attachment</td></tr>
<tr><td align="right">to the object</td><td>to the object</td></tr>
<tr><td align="right">of grasping</td><td>of grasping</td></tr>
<tr><td align="right">and there may be no attachment</td><td></td></tr>
<tr><td align="right">to the object of grasping,</td><td></td></tr>
<tr><td align="right">but it's attachment</td><td>but it's attachment</td></tr>
<tr><td align="right">to grasping</td><td>to grasping</td></tr>
<tr><td align="right">but it's attachment to grasping,</td><td>but it's attachment to grasping</td></tr>
<tr><td></td><td>all you</td></tr>
<tr><td></td><td>got to do</td></tr>
<tr><td></td><td>is look at it</td></tr>
<tr><td align="right">all you got to do is look at it,</td><td>all you got to do is look at it,</td></tr>
<tr><td></td><td>a hologram</td></tr>
<tr><td></td><td>in my heart</td></tr>
<tr><td align="right">a hologram in my heart,</td><td>a hologram in my heart,</td></tr>
<tr><td align="right">and dissolve it</td><td>and dissolve it</td></tr>
<tr><td></td><td>and dissolve it</td></tr>
<tr><td></td><td>and dissolve,</td></tr>
<tr><td align="right">pull</td><td>pull</td></tr>
<tr><td align="right">the plug,</td><td>the plug,</td></tr>
</table>

turn the TV off,
is what
turns
into bliss
is what turns
into bliss
is what turns into bliss,
dissolving
desire
dissolving desire
dissolving desire
becomes
bliss
becomes bliss
becomes bliss,
pure
phenomena
pure phenomena
pure phenomena,
not
thinking
about it
not thinking
about it
not thinking about it,
taking it
easy
taking it easy
taking it easy,
confidence,
fearlessness
and tranquility
confidence, fearlessness and tranquility,
but after
all
these long
years
but after all these long years,
my meditation
isn't so
good
my meditation isn't so good,
the guy
on the 2nd
floor
the guy on the 2nd floor
is mostly
stoned
on grass

turn
the TV
off
turn the TV off,
is what
turns
into bliss
is what turns
into bliss
is what turns into bliss,
dissolving
desire
dissolving desire
dissolving desirex
becomes
bliss
becomes bliss
becomes bliss,
pure
phenomena
pure phenomena
pure phenomena,
not
thinking
about it
not thinking
about it
not thinking about it,
taking it
easy
taking it easy
taking it easy,
confidence,
fearlessness
and tranquility
confidence, fearlessness and tranquility
pure
empty
phenomena,
but after all these long years,
my meditation isn't so good,

<table>
<tr><td>is mostly stoned on grass,</td><td>is mostly stoned on grass,</td></tr>
<tr><td>listening</td><td>listening</td></tr>
<tr><td>to disco</td><td>to disco</td></tr>
<tr><td>listening to disco</td><td></td></tr>
<tr><td>listening to disco,</td><td></td></tr>
<tr><td>aint no</td><td></td></tr>
<tr><td>way</td><td></td></tr>
<tr><td>I can</td><td></td></tr>
<tr><td>live</td><td></td></tr>
<tr><td>without you</td><td></td></tr>
<tr><td>aint no way</td><td>aint no way</td></tr>
<tr><td>I can live without you</td><td>I can live without you</td></tr>
<tr><td>aint no way I can live without you,</td><td></td></tr>
<tr><td>standing</td><td>standing</td></tr>
<tr><td>right</td><td>right</td></tr>
<tr><td>here</td><td>here</td></tr>
<tr><td>standing right here,</td><td></td></tr>
<tr><td>waiting</td><td>waiting</td></tr>
<tr><td>on your return</td><td>on your return</td></tr>
<tr><td>waiting on your return</td><td></td></tr>
<tr><td>waiting on your return,</td><td></td></tr>
<tr><td></td><td>I just</td></tr>
<tr><td></td><td>love</td></tr>
<tr><td></td><td>to turn</td></tr>
<tr><td></td><td>the FM</td></tr>
<tr><td></td><td>radio</td></tr>
<tr><td></td><td>to dancing</td></tr>
<tr><td></td><td>music</td></tr>
<tr><td>I just love to turn the FM radio</td><td>I just love to turn the FM radio</td></tr>
<tr><td>to dancing music,</td><td>to dancing music,</td></tr>
<tr><td></td><td>get stoned</td></tr>
<tr><td>get stoned</td><td>get stoned</td></tr>
<tr><td></td><td>get stoned,</td></tr>
<tr><td></td><td>sip</td></tr>
<tr><td></td><td>some vodkha</td></tr>
<tr><td>sip some vodkha,</td><td>sip some vodkha,</td></tr>
<tr><td></td><td>and think</td></tr>
<tr><td></td><td>and think</td></tr>
<tr><td></td><td>and think</td></tr>
<tr><td></td><td>and think</td></tr>
<tr><td></td><td>and think</td></tr>
</table>

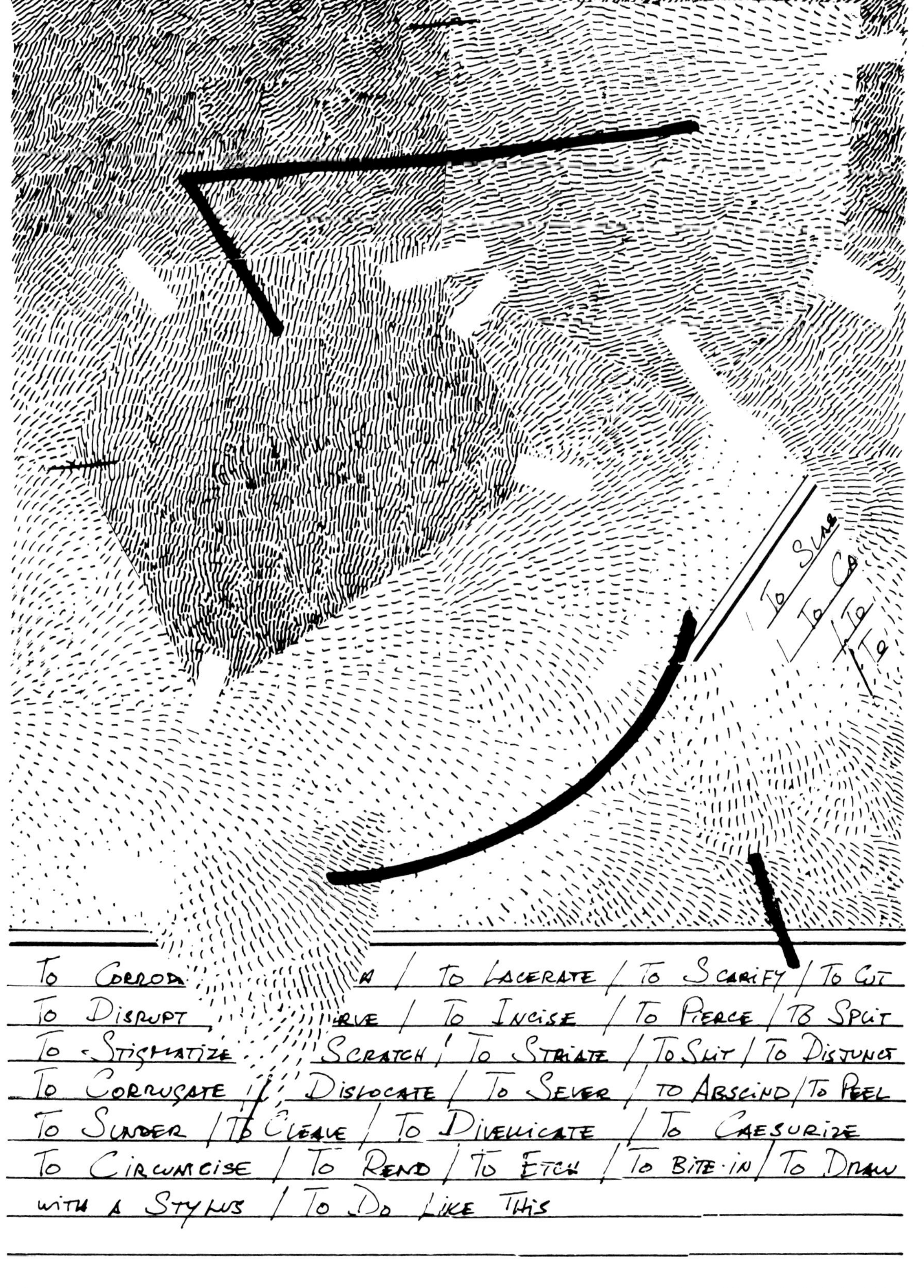
To Corrod a / To Lacerate / To Scarify / To Cut
To Disrupt rve / To Incise / To Pierce / To Split
To Stigmatize Scratch / To Striate / To Slit / To Disjunct
To Corrugate / Dislocate / To Sever / to Abscind / To Peel
To Sunder / To Cleave / To Divellicate / To Caesurize
To Circumcise / To Rend / To Etch / To Bite-in / To Draw
with a Stylus / To Do Like This

The Hard Machine

Alphonso F. Lingis

Savages

TECHNIQUE

The original machine for electric convulsive therapy (ECT.) was built by Bini. A large number of modifications has been recommended since, but many of the machines used are still based essentially on Bini's design. It consists primarily of a stop watch for time regulation to fractions of a second and of devices for measuring and regulating the current. Alternating current from electric light circuits having a frequency of 50 to 60 cycles is used. A voltmeter regulates the voltage to be applied. The original machine had a second low-voltage current circuit for preliminary measurement of the resistance of the patient's head. An automatic time clock or various time relays from 0.1 to 0.5 second or more interrupt the current after the desired length of time. Holzer devised an apparatus which generates rectangular alternating current, independent of any city current. Several workers use machines which permit the setting of the actual milliamperage to be allowed to flow through the patient's head. The reliability of this development is a matter of controversy, however. All the various machines on sale serve their purpose to produce convulsions. The simplest models seem to be the best for they are not complicated by many gadgets which are clinically unimportant and a frequent cause for breakdowns of the machine.

Of all that is savage about savages, the most savage is what these people, who construct nothing, who do not even labor the earth, who write nothing, do to themselves. They paint, perforate, tatoo, incise, circumcise, scarify, cicatrize themselves. They use their own flesh as so much material at hand for—what? We hardly know how to characterize it—art? inscription? sign-language? Or isn't all that more like hex signs? Aren't they treating themselves rather like the pieces of dikdik fur, bat's penis, warthog's tooth, hornbill bird's skull they attach to themselves? At any rate, it excites some dark dregs of lechery and cruelty in us, holding our eyes transfixed with repugnance and lust. Otherwise, a naked savage would be no more interesting than the baboons, sticking out their bare asses and genitalia as they scramble along, or the orangutangs, with their thin hair that doesn't soften or adorn and thus really doesn't cover over their gross bodyness.

The Mayas inserted the soft skull of a baby into a wooden mold at birth, which flattened back the forehead, and pushed the brain cavity out at the sides. They hung a stone in front of the baby's brow, so that it would become somewhat cross-eyed, a characteristic they found attractive. They perforated the earlobes, nostrils, lower lip, to insert wires, teeth of animals, beads, chains, rings. They filed the teeth, and inserted inlays of stone or obsidian into them. They clitoridectomized the girls and circumcised the boys, tatooed the penis and inserted pieces of bone and colored stones and rings into the flesh of the glans. They scarified the plane surfaces of the body, abdomen, breasts, buttocks, such that welts and raised warts covered the body, in rows and patterns. They left their fingernails and toenails grow into foot-long twisting useless claws. They pierced the nipples, and inserted rings in them. In most of Africa circumcision and clitoridectomy—this inordinate involvement of the public in your private parts, this cutting into the zone of the most sensitive pleasure nerves and glands —is in fact the main ceremony; most of the songs, dances and instrumental playing the tourist who demands and pays for the maintenance of indigenous cultural forms in the neocapitalist African nations of today hears and sees are in fact songs about circumcision and clitoridectomy, dances these bizarre operations excite in the encampments in the bush. As in the dreamy equatorial paradise of Bali, the principle festivity, the high-point of Balinese social existence, is the sumptuous and hilarious cremations.

What we are dealing with is—to try to get scientific—inscription, graphics. In a prehistorical people. Where writing, where inscription, was not inscription on clay tablets, bark or papyrus, but in flesh and blood, and also where it was not yet historical, narrative. We could say it was not yet significant, not yet a matter of signs, marks whose role is to signify, to efface themselves before the meaning, or ideality, or logos. For here the signs count: they *hurt.* Before they make sense to the reader, they give pain to the living substrate. Who can doubt, after Nietzsche, after Kafka (*On the Genealogy of Morals,* II, *The Penal Colony*) that before they informed the understanding of the public their pain gave pleasure to its eyes?

Moravia distinguishes between what he calls the psychological face, that of the African living in cities, already civilized, and the sculptured face of the African who lives in the bush. Italian bodies are expressive; they make, minute by minute, every part the exterior their bodies present into signs. But they do not scarify, cicatrize, clitoridectomize themselves, like savages. What they do is a work done on the surface layer by which it is made to connect up, not with the glandular secretions, digestive processes, flows of blood, fermenting gases, bile in the inner functional body, but rather with the intentions in the psychic depth. The surface figures, articulations, moves are made into a zone of systematic mediation between inward, depth, intentions and transcendent objects,

Several types of electrodes are in use. Metal strips or a meshwork mounted on a rubber sponge were originally recommended because they permit the greatest adaptability to the shape of the patient's head, but simple metal discs may also be used. We still very definitely prefer Bini's forceps electrode in which the electrodes are mounted by movable articulations on a bearer system whose two arms act like the two blades of a large forceps. This type of electrode permits strong local pressure on the head and can be much more easily applied than electrodes fixed with rubber bands which slip off easily when the patient moves his head.

HANDLING OF THE PATIENT

The patient's position was dictated by the endeavor to prevent fractures, but the suggestions as to how to accomplish this are diverse. Many workers assumed that hyperextension is a suitable way to prevent vertebral fractures. Hyperextension of the spine was achieved by sandbags placed under the curvature of the middorsal spine, by especially constructed treatment tables, or by a surgical Gatch bed (Impastato and Almansi) in which the patient's back rests on the elevated part of the bed. We always considered it preferable to have the patient in a most relaxed and unrestrained position with moderate flexion of the spine. The shoulders are lightly held by one nurse in order to prevent extreme movements of the arms. The legs are not held at all since we saw two cases of severe fractures of acetabulum and femur obviously resulting from a too strong "protection" of the legs.

A mouth gag is necessary in order to prevent tongue bite. Unlike metrazol convulsions, not all patients open their mouths at the beginning of an electrically induced seizure, and it is safer to insert the gag before the treatment; the lips should be protected from getting between mouth gag and teeth. The mouth gag should be neither too hard nor too soft. We prefer a looplike mouth gag made of two rubber tubes, one within the other, covered with gauze. This prevents biting on the more precious

incisors. Protection of the teeth is an important problem which has found too little attention. In patients with loose teeth, and particularly those with only a few isolated teeth left, the powerful bite would concentrate on these few teeth. The use of muscle relaxants does not justify abolition of mouth gags because there is often sufficient strength left in the jaw muscles to endanger the teeth. Special mouth gags have been devised permitting oxygen supply through an opening in the mouth gag (Hard).

After the unpremedicated convulsion, the therapist's attention should first be directed to the patient's respiration. A few artificial respiratory movements should be given immediately as a safety measure. If the patient is very cyanotic, oxygen can be given, but this is not indispensable. After regular respiration is secured, the patient must be watched so that he does not fall out of bed. Straps or sheets to tie him to his bed should be available in case the patient becomes assaultive in the postconvulsive state. This may increase his panic, but it is unavoidable when help is limited. No patient should get up until he is quiet and able to answer simple questions satisfactorily. Even when this is the case, the patient may still misinterpret the situation and become dangerous.

POST-CONVULSIVE EXCITEMENT

Some patients, particularly males, become dangerously assaultive, develop enormous strength, try to escape, run around and injure themselves, and may strike anyone who attempts to control them. This reaction is not specific for ECT; we have seen it every time in a patient having twenty consecutive convulsions produced partly by metrazol, partly by electric current. In some patients, excitement occurs only following the first treatments. It seems to be more frequent in patients who have a strong fear of the treatment. Individuals who show this response often have had similar experiences after general anesthesia during surgery or when they were intoxicated. Some workers have attributed diagnostic importance to the postconvul-

goals, landscapes of the world beyond. The surface is not laid out for itself; it is completely occupied by signs which simultaneously refract your gaze off into the street, into the horizon, into history where their signified referents are, and open in upon the psychic depth where the intentions are being formed. Whence this transparency of the Italian exterior; the cartilage and opaque, rubbery padding of blind flesh with all its lubricating and irrigating pores thins out; you see by looking at him how an Italian fits into the field of operations of the middle and high bourgeoisie, how he relates to a landscape of renaissance palaces, baroque churches, fascist imperial avenues, you see what he is thinking and what he wants. The way she plucks her eyebrows and he cuts his mustache, the signs she paints across her mouth in phosphorescent paint and the angle at which he braces up his cock in its pouch under his nylon swim trunks—all that has nothing to do with the tatooing and body painting and penis sheaths of savages. All that is civilized, *significant*.

These cicatrizations, these scarifications, these perforations, these incisions on the bodies of savages—they hurt. The eye that looks at them does not read them; it winces, it senses the pain. They are points of high tension; intensities zigzag across them, releasing themselves, dying away orgasmically, into a tingling of

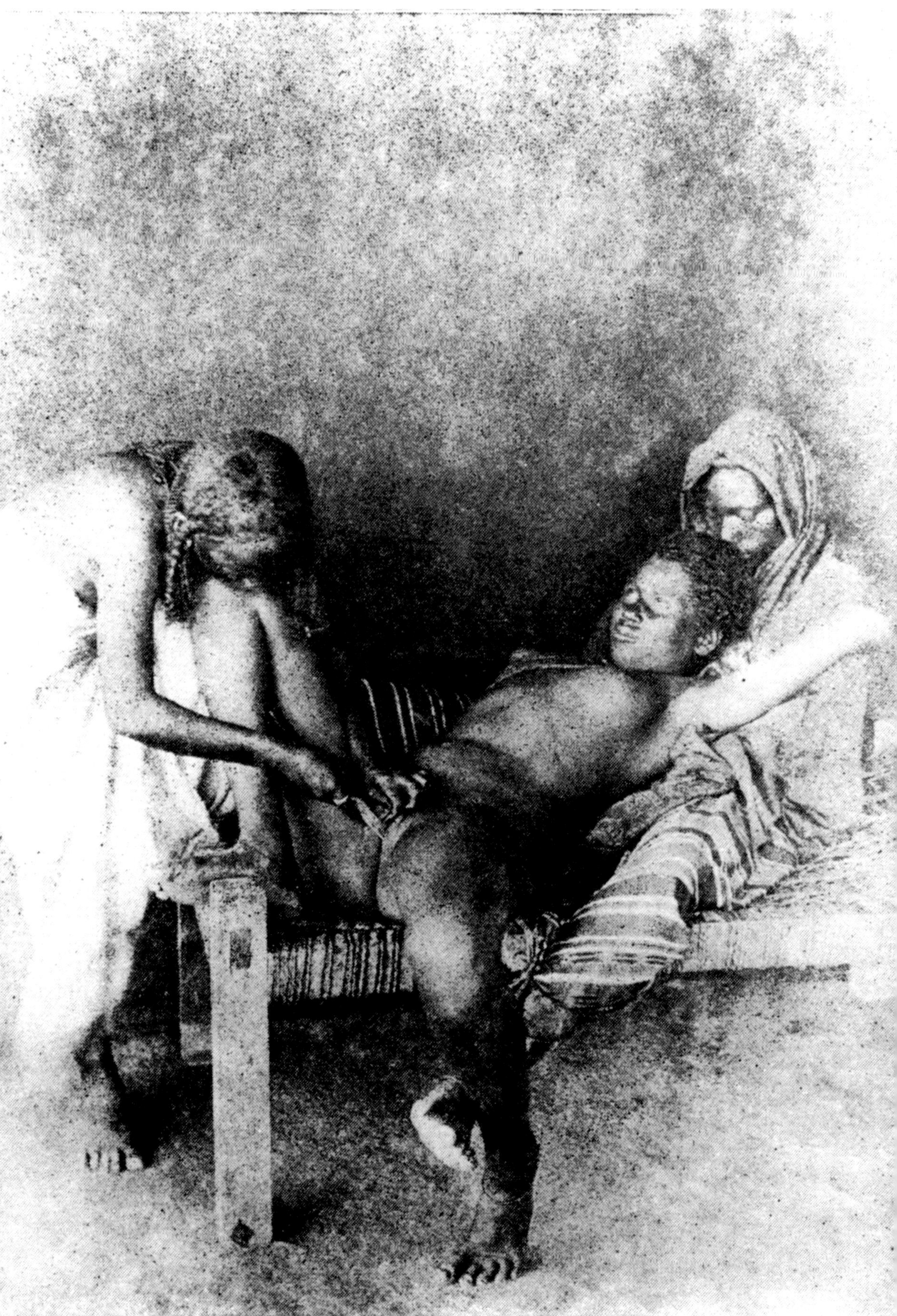

sive behavior. Sargant and Slater felt that the true depressive generally remains quiet and pleasant, while the unrecognized schizophrenic may show suspicious and aggressive behavior. We cannot confirm this and feel that postconvulsive excitement bears no relation to the type of psychoses, but that personality traits and preformed patterns play definite roles. The most severe excitement was seen in a very good-natured patient who was a wrestler by profession and who, therefore, was accustomed to fight even in a half-conscious state. Treatment of this reaction is by intravenous injection of sodium amytal immediately prior to treatment. In ECT under anesthesia post-treatment excitement is only somewhat less frequent.

AMNESIA

Convulsive treatment is followed by amnesia which first includes a long time-period before the treatment and gradually diminishes to the events immediately prior to the treatment. Stengel demonstrated how the retrograde amnesia shrinks only very gradually, while Mayer-Gross, who studied this symptom experimentally, saw surprisingly short retrograde amnesia. This is more in accordance with our own experience. Something quite different is the patient's frequent amnesia for the entire psychosis (Bodamer) or for one single delusion (Delay, Delmas-Marsalet). Observations regarding amnesia for the psychotic content are not uniform, and no conclusion of general validity can be drawn from them.

HOSPITAL

It is easy to establish a pleasant atmosphere in ECT units if those administering the treatment are aware of this problem. What we see in many treatment centers contrasts strangely with the opposite extreme of providing music as an aid to the patient in his experience with shock therapy. Price and Knouss describe three different types of music which should be played during the three stages of preparing the patient for the treatment, for his return to consciousness and for

pleasure. In voluptuous torments, more exactly, and not in contentment, that is, comatose states of equilibrium. In intensive moments when a surface, surplus potential accumulates, intensifies, and discharges. The savage inscription is a working over the skin, all surface effects. This cutting in orifices and raising tumescences does not contrive new receptor organs for the depth body, not multiply ever more subtle signs for the psychic depth where personal intentions would be being formed; it extends the erotogenic surface.

Sure, it's a multiplication of mouths, of lips, labia, anuses, these sweating and bleeding perforations and puncturings, it's a proliferation of pricks, these scarifications, these warts raised all over the abdomen, around the eyes, these penis heads set with feathers and hair, these heads with hair tressed into feelers, antennae of beady and lascivious insects. The oral and anal phase not overcome, renounced, but deviated, the excitations gone to seed, running everywhere, opening up lips and sphincters all across the weaned body, lunatic like the sea, according to Nietzsche, rising up in a million lips to the full moon. The phallic dominion decentralized.

But what does one gain by all that? Isn't it civilized, efficient, to invest everything in your cock, and incorporate everything in your vagina? Isn't all the rest so much stupidity, savagery? What is more unnatural than a savage?

In fact the libidinal zone is perverse from the start, and is constituted in perversity. Freud finds it beginning as soon as life begins—but by a deviation. He does not see it in the sucking and in the pleasure of sucking, that is, the contentment of filling up and becoming a full sack of warm fluid. That is no more libidinally productive than the cactus roots drawing in the rain. He sees it in the slobbering, the drooling, in this surplus potential left on the surface, and from which the coupling derives a surplus pleasure. It is not the holding in, or the expelling of the shit that makes the dirty baby, it's the smearing it around. That is why, in our analysis, we can distinguish two processes, the production of the closed and sterile body without organs, full and contented, and the production of the libidinal excitations, the surface effects.

The white men, the electrical engineers and the geologists on contract, have their own view of the excitations and of the earth. They are Reicheans by night, believing in total orgasm; they are, Derrida says, phallocrats. for them the penis is the drive shaft of the inner machinery of the body; it delivers the power. That's how it works. For whitemen know how things work, not like the jerk-offs in the bush. That's the productive attitude, or, more exactly, the reproductive. But isn't that what sex is really about, filling that hole with a man?

The savages don't seem convinced. Freud neither. An erection, it's true, that delivers the baby, but the fun is not in that. Libidinally, an erection extends the surface. And, of course, hardens it, concentrates the tension, for the vuluptuous release. Opening up your labia, letting the vaginal fluids run, that of course delivers the egg. But the orgasms extend on the surface. When you get laid you get laid out. The Mobius band coils in on itself, but it's still all surface, inner face or outer face, it's all equivalent. The tensions dance. Ephemeral subjectivities, brief egos, throb and get consumed down there, in the flows.

And it is hard. What is comparable to that feeling tight under one's skin? That feeling of filling out, of compacting one's skin? Mishima contrasted vehemently the vague, visceral, dark inwardness of the intellectual, loose and amorphous under his skin, with that feeling (*Sun and Steel*). That phallic feeling. That Arnold Schwartzenegger feeling—of having a hard on everywhere, ankles, neck, everywhere, being a hard on, coming... That's the male denuding, on the beaches of Sylt, under the northern sun. The female is complementary.

It's not an erotogenic surface, spreading perversely its excitations over a closed body without organs beneath. It's body and soul one, nature and culture one, it's surface and depth one. It's the organism. A functional whole, coded from the inside.

And it's male, female. Human. Phallic. That is, the whole body organized, as a lack of the other. Which other? Alterity itself, the transcendent, the beyond? Shiva, Sita, Ngai, Agazu? Oh no, here we are *en famille*. For a mummy, for a big daddy. For Agamemnon, for Jocasta. For mummy, for daddy.

That—is civilized nudity. It is also capitalist nudity. *Der Spiegel* features it every week; it goes with the Leicas and the Porsches.

In short, there is, on the one hand, a going beyond the primary process libido to the organization man. The dissolute, disintegrated savage condition, with the perverse and monstrous extension of an erotogenic surface, pursuing its surface effects, over a closed and inert, sterile body without organs, one with the earth itself—this condition is overcome, by the emergence of, the dominion of, the natural and the functional. The sane body, the working body, free, sovereign, poised, whose proportion, equilibrium and ease are such that it dominates the landscape and commands itself at each moment. Mercury, Juno. Olympic ideal.

And, on the other hand, there has occurred a phallicization. Such a nakedness, healthy and sovereign, is at the same time nothing but the very image, the very presence of a lack. It calls for the other, for kisses and caresses, for the one that exists veritably qua lack-of-a-phallus. It cannot disrobe itself without

the rest period after the treatment. We are not opposed to such efforts, but the most important requirement is to avoid observation of the treatment by patients who are not only frightened themselves but through their reports contribute to the opposition against the treatment by others.

COMPLICATIONS

Complications in convulsive therapy were much publicized. They are still overemphasized by many psychiatrists. The recognized concept of *nil nocere* remains the basic concept for every physician, but it is not meant to lead to therapeutic nihilism. The surgeon does not refuse a necessary operation because of its impending risks. Since active therapy is available in psychiatry, it should be used for the benefit of many patients even though a few may develop undesirable complications. Fortunately, fatal complications in convulsive therapy are extremely rare.

We agree with Sargant and Slater's statement that mental disorders are as destructive as a malignant growth and far more terrible in the suffering they may cause. Risks are therefore justified. It is gratifying that the Pennsylvania Department of Justice, quoted by Overholser, expressed an opinion to the effect that ECT is of recognized value and, therefore, may be applied to mental patients without the consent of the patient or his family.

Fractures and Dislocations: **The most frequent complications in convulsive therapy were fractures caused by muscular contraction. The types of fractures occurring in metrazol and ECT are essentially the same and, therefore, will be discussed together. They have in common the fact that they seem to occur during the first sudden muscular contraction when many observers had reported hearing the first cracking of a bone. The frequently sudden onset of artificial convulsions may explain why fractures occur in this treatment but are seldom seen in epileptics who customarily go slowly into the tonic phase of the convulsion. This is also substantiated by the fact that with the more sudden and lightning-like onset in metra-**

zol convulsions, fractures are more frequent than in ECT. The delayed electric convulsion should, therefore, be the least likely to produce fractures, but delayed seizures are difficult to obtain due to inability to estimate the necessary dosage. Lately, we have made every effort to use threshhold stimuli even if we have to repeat the stimulation two, three or more times in succession, in the hope of obtaining a slowly developing seizure. The application of a petit mal response, followed immediately by a second convulsive stimulus, is another useful measure as in this way the patient goes into the convulsion with a relaxed musculature. This procedure is especially desirable if the patient is very tense or struggles against the treatment.

Hyperextension of the spine was recommended because the spine seems to bend forward during the convulsion. An important attempt to clarify this problem was made by Flordh, who demonstrated under x-ray control that the vertebral column during the treatment is not bent forward but compressed in a longitudinal direction. This mechanism would suggest that no position can diminish the danger of fractures.

Special treatment of these vertebral fractures is not indicated and will frighten the patient unnecessarily. Originally, orthopedic appliances were recommended but they are superfluous. Schmieder found that when treatment is continued after a few weeks, compressed vertebrae are more resistant to new damage than are healthy ones. We continued such patients and we have sometimes seen even the pain disappear during subsequent treatments.

Excerpted from:* Somatic Treatments in Psychiatry *by Lothar B. Kalinowsky, M.D. and Paul H. Hoch, M.D., Grune & Stratton

SHOCKED

In 1966, 1971 and 1974 I was a patient in Glen Eden in Warren, Michigan. I believe I was in the hospital between 1971 and 1974 also, however I have no memory of it due to my shock treatments. The exact dates can be obtained from hospital records.

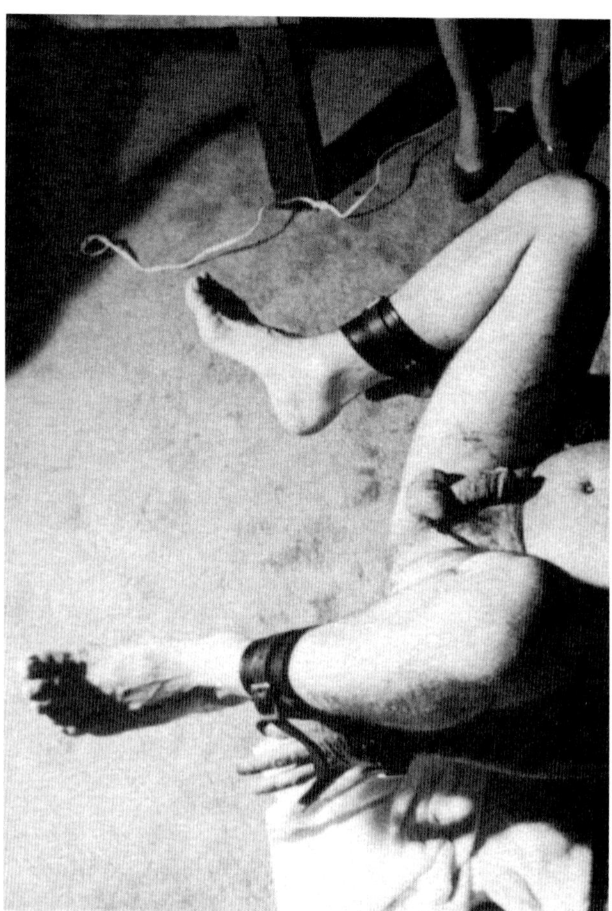

being that visible, palpable lack, that want. And through and through. We civilized ones feel not only a repugnance for the unnaturalness, the unhealthiness, the ugliness of that tatooed nakedness the savage affects; we find it puerile and shallow. The savage fixing his identity on his skin... Our identity is inward, it is our functional integrity as machines to produce a certain civilized, that is, coded, type of actions.

What then is this thing about savages? Who, instead of taking that train to the beaches of Sylt, flies off to the savages—with a ton and a half of gear, shipped air freight? Very civilized people, no? Capitalists...

To be sure, capitalism goes everywhere, and goes to the savages too, to capitalize on them. The hour is late, in history; savagery cannot go on for much longer. It's the lot of savages to get civilized. To get despotized, first, tyrannized. Then colonized. Then civilized. Priests go to them, and colonels, on a mission, and executive managers, on safari. In short, capitalists, to civilize them.

But there are also some few nuts—schizophrenics—themselves highly civilized and capitalized, who go

to them, in order to go back to or forward to savagery! Whose libido is such that that is what turns them on.

But they are the nuts of capitalism. Extra parts, surplus products produced by capitalist means of production.

For capitalism is the stage in which all the excitations, all the pleasures and the pains produced on the surface of life are inscribed, recorded, fixed, coded on the transcendent body of capital. Every pain costs something, every girl at the bar, every day off, every hangover, every pregnancy; and every pleasure is worth something. The abstract and universal body of capital fixes and codes every excitation. They are no longer, as in the bush, inscribed on the bare surface of the earth. Each subjective moment takes place as a momentary and singular pleasure and pain recorded on the vast body of capital circulating its inner fluxes. Kant understood this when he wrote, in *The Metaphysical Principles of Virtue,* that a man, as a sensuous being, is a commodity whose "skill and diligence in labor have a market value; wit, lively imagination, and humor have a fancy value...," but that money, which purchases all that, and measures its value, and which is abstract and independent of its ma-

In 1966 I went because I was depressed with family problems and wanted marriage counseling. I saw a psychiatrist, Dr. Morris Goldin, whose name I obtained from Catholic Social Services. Dr. Goldin told me that there was nothing wrong with my marriage; that I was emotionally sick and should sign myself in to Glen Eden. I did this because I respected him and believed him to be an authority on mental health. He told me that I should have shock treatment and that it would not hurt me or my unborn child (I was four months pregnant). He did not warn me of the dangers of shock treatment and I believe it was given to me without informed consent. I had them on Monday, Wednesday and Friday for one month until my Blue Cross Coverage ran out at which point he recommended to my husband that I be transferred to Pontiac. I am independent by nature but became very scrambled and compliant after the treatment. When my husband took me home I was bordering on catatonic. I would stare at the wall for hours. He would have me hold our newborn baby and slap my face gently to try to snap me out of it. We had to hire a woman because I could not take care of house or function. Through the efforts of my husband and myself, in one year I became better again.

In 1971 my father died and my marriage was failing. I decided to get a divorce and was feeling down. My husband talked me into going back to Dr. Goldin and I agreed to do it to try to save our marriage. Again I asked for a marriage counselor. Dr. Goldin said I should have more shock treatment which I did until my insurance ran out again and I went home. For three years I couldn't work or watch TV. I had to drop out of college. My memory was seriously damaged. I used flashcards to learn to speak English well again; as there were many words which I simply did not know anymore. As an amateur writer I found this very distressing. Many books that I have read are unkown to me now; as are some neighbors, friends and many events. What I regret very much, is the loss of many, many precious memories of my children growing up—I simply don't

have them. Seven years of my existence are almost wiped out. I had believed that my mental illness was the source of my trouble. Now I realize that the shock treatments I had nearly destroyed me.

AFFIDAVIT

Septembe 18, 1976

I, Jean Rosenbaum, M.D., of P.O. Box 401, Durango, Colorado 81301 do hereby attest that the following statements made by me are true and accurate to the best of my knowledge:

That I am currently the Director of Child Development and Family Guidance Institute in Durango, Colorado.

That I have resided in Durango since May, 1972.

That when I moved to Durango, I was in the process of retiring, but due to the demands of numerous physicians and consumers, and due to their multiple complaints about mental health services in this area, I agreed to open a limited practice offering options to the current treatment modalities being used in Durango.

That in the process of establishing this practice, it was forcibly brought to my attention a number of complaints about excessive use, misuse, and abuse of electro convulsive therapy (ECT) in the community.

That I investigated these complaints and found many cases where the complaints were valid.

That Dr. Howard Winkler is the only psychiatrist in Durango who uses ECT.

That when I was asked by Dr. Winkler in 1972 to cover his hospital practice, I refused, as this would have put me in collusion to practice that which I considered to be unethical medicine.

That in the process of further investigation, I came to know Rodney Barker, editor of the *Animas Journal*, in 1975. Independently of my interests, Rod was investigating complaints about excessive use of ECT in Durango.

That to my personal knowledge, he contacted the following agencies in order to obtain documentation: Mercy Hospital, Durango; State Department of In-

terial, paper or metal, tokens, is of preeminent value. At this advanced stage of capitalism, one has lost a lot of regional, territorial, civil, professional identities; one is finally more and more a pure succession of pleasures and pains, of surface moments of subjectivity, forming and disintegrating at the surface where there are intensive couplings with what the flux of capital washes by.

The human, phallic protest is in reality a last-ditch expedient. This effort to congeal into a unit, a functional whole, and maintain that by one's own efforts, in the universal gym and on the bicycle that you ride without going anywhere, in your bathroom. And by this form of identity to be something someone needs. Not capitalism, of course, which just needs hands, and brains. Someone, a human being. A woman, lack of a phallus. A man, bearer of a phallus.

It's a little discouraging, after all these years, to realize that the problem boils down to that of the one and the many, more exactly, of the nature of the identity involved in subjectivity. The arithmetical solution seemed the simplest, to the Western mind; ascribe everything to a transcendental ego. What one has, in the air-conditioned bedroom, is an entity: a man, a woman. A phallic machine, coupled on to a woman, a womb. The subject, to which this complex, but everywhere lined up, operation is predicated, the subject which is affected by it all and contented with it all, is a unit, a transcendent selfsameness. It's behind everything, the information-seat, it's under everything, the support or substrate.

But let's try, now, to see things from the libidinal point of view, where the egos are multiple and superficial, surface effects. They form at the couplings, where an excess potential develops. A mouth, it's adjustable. It can couple on to a nipple—or a bottle, or a thumb. A hand can curl around a breast, or an arm, or another hand, or a penis. An ear is an orifice in which you can insert mother's or lover's babble, or a finger, or a penis, or a cheetah's tooth. A baby in a buggy, a savage in the bush, proceeds by bricolage, and not by blueprint. As long as the inner sack is filled, what does it matter? The body without organs is profoundly indifferent to these surface couplings. No ego still burns in the suffocating morass down in there, in that, Id. The moments of subjectivity, of pleasure tormented with itself, of torment incandescent with itself, are all on the surface.

As a result the egos that form are not necessarily of the male, lack of a vagina, form, and of the female, lack of a penis, form. There are lips sucked out on my thighs—places where the green mamba kissed me, and these incisions that remain, to mark the pain and the pleasure. The couplings multiply, extend the libidinal zone. They leave their marks, so that one can return to them, or, more exactly, so that an egoism can take pleasure at these points where tensions accumulate, can consume that surplus energy. We have to not only fasten our attention to these multiple and unstable erotic identities, which requires a certain discipline so that we do not slide back into our civilized habit of just ascribing everything to some ineffable, transcendental, but simple, selfsame ego activating everything. We also have to try to maintain that strange neoplatonic logic of identity involved in the Id, in the closed and full vesicle whose membrane is irritated and inscribed by these excitements, and which is all closed in itself, inert and sterile, and yet is indistinguishable from dirt, from the closed body of the earth itself—like the One in Plotinus from which emanates another one, which cannot get out of it enough to make two. These cuts and scars on the face of a Yoruba are the claw-marks of Agazu, but they are not just zones of his body destroyed by the totemic leopard, for they are his pleasure and his pride and his very identity. He arises, out of this coupling, as the one that was strong enough to be chosen by, and to hold the embrace of, the leopard. And this identity, this subjectivity, is not just attached to the physiological unit of this Yoruba male, it is attached to the leopard land. What social security identity, by number, can compare with this identity born in pain and pleasure, voluptuous identity?

It belongs to the nature of graffiti not to pay heed to borders, to spread right over obstacles, to make walls of different angles, doors, openings all the support of one inscription that pursues itself. The inscription extends the erotogenic surface.

It is also a first codification of desire. Not coding in the sense that the operation of every machine, of every gene and cell carries its own code, by which its operations are internally determined. Codification in the sense of conventionalization, socialization. But this socialization is already oppression, forced from the outside but working within by repression.

We said that these incisions, these welts and raised scars, these graphics, are not signs; they are intensive points. They do not refer to intentions in an inner individual psychic depth, not to meanings or concepts in some transcendent beyond. They reverberate one another. But they are lined up. Warts and scarifications in rows, in circles, in swastikas, in zigzags.

What is the nature of the system involved? These are, for the most part, not representations. The Japanese art of tatooing pictures of animals, people and landscapes on the body belongs to civilization and not to savagery. But the patterns of marks are also not governed by a logical grammar. Thus we have to fix the level at which inscription is neither representational, pictogrammic, commanded by sensuous originals, nor alphabetical, made to correspond to phonic originals, nor ideogrammic or logical, corresponding to a conceptual order, to ideal

stitutions (Colorado); State Department of Social Services (Colorado); and Colorado Foundation for Medical Care.

That he was refused information on all public cases, without exception.

That one such case that was brought to my attention was that of X.

A letter of authorization was obtained from her by me to examine her medical records on or about February 18, 1976. I examined her records of a psychiatric hospitalization at Community Hospital, Durango.

That in studying these records, I observed that an informed consent agreement was not filled out by the patient. Neither was a separate informed consent agreement filled out or signed by the patient.

That I further observed that the administration of ECT did not coincide with the diagnosis of the patient. She was originally admitted to Community Hospital with the diagnosis of a personality disorder of an hysterical type, a diagnosis for which ECT is absolutely counter-indicated according to the guidelines for use of ECT as provided by the American Psychiatric Association.

That she was readmitted to the hospital one month later with a change of diagnosis to severe depressive reaction, asthmatic bronchitis, and thyroid disorder. There was no history of either of these medical conditions. Also, both of these conditions would rule out the use of ECT. She received a series of six (6) shocks at this time. Shortly thereafter, she made a suicide attempt.

That subsequently, I was refused access to these records by the hospital administration, and furthermore, denied a copy of said records.

That in the process of investigating the numerous unethical psychiatric practices in Durango, I discovered that they were widespread throughout the country.

That as a result of this, I recently resigned my seventeen year membership in the American Psychiatric Association, as this organization has consistently refused to take a stand against fully recognized members who daily and on a massive basis, violate the ethics of medicine.

That I have also observed

many other cases of misuse of ECT, including its administration to children in Durango.

That I have no motivation of a monetary nature, as I am financially independent and in the process of retirement.

That I have become a member of the Citizen's Commission on Human Rights for the purpose of eradicating unethical psychiatric practices in this area and this state.

Research Contributions by the Citizen's Commission on Human Rights.

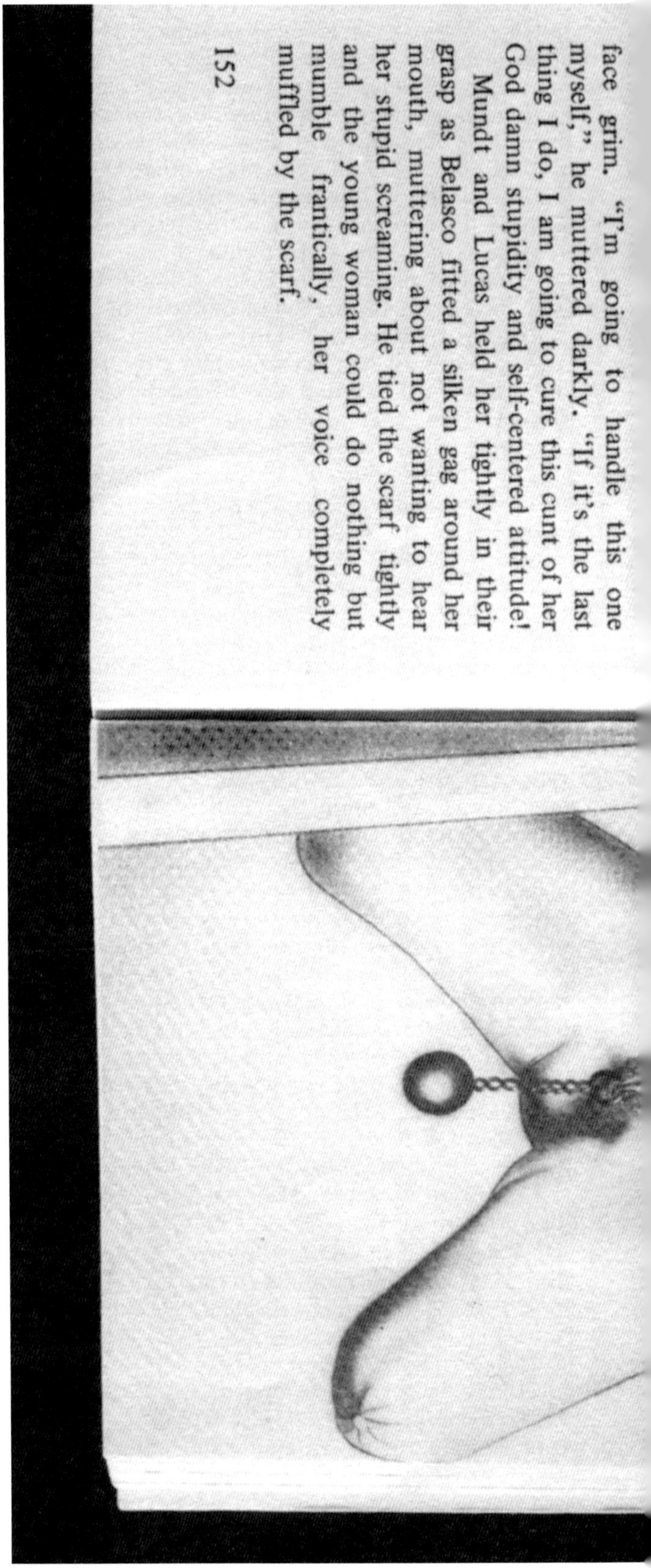

face grim. "I'm going to handle this one myself," he muttered darkly. "If it's the last thing I do, I am going to cure this cunt of her God damn stupidity and self-centered attitude!

Mundt and Lucas held her tightly in their grasp as Belasco fitted a silken gag around her mouth, muttering about not wanting to hear her stupid screaming. He tied the scarf tightly and the young woman could do nothing but mumble frantically, her voice completely muffled by the scarf.

152

PSYCHIATRY EVALUATED

John Suggs,
Appellee
v.
J. Edwin LaVallee,
Superintendent
Clinton State Correctional Institution,
Appellant.

KAUFMAN, *Chief Judge:* (concurring)

I concur in Judge Oakes' meticulous and well-reasoned opinion. I would merely add that his painstaking exposition of the unfortunate details of Suggs's "coming of age" points to an emerging and highly significant problem in the law, namely, the troubled relationship between the vagaries of psychiatric evaluation and the difficulties of judicial determinations of incompetence. At the time of Suggs's plea, before one could be deemed incompetent to stand trial in New York, a judicial finding was required that he was in "such a state of idiocy, imbecility or insanity as to be incapable of understanding the charges against him or the proceedings, or of making his defense..." New York Code of Crim. Proc. §662-b(1) (McKinney Supp. 1970).

Of course, psychiatrists are invariably enlisted to aid in such determinations. Yet, psychiatry is at best an inexact science, if, indeed, it is a science, lacking the coherent set of proven underlying values necessary for ultiup and called for Mundt and Lucas to come at once. When he banged down the receiver again, he turned and glared at her in contempt. "I can see you still have a long way to go! You enjoyed that, didn't you? You enjoyed the come in your mouth!" he cried in a high, tight voice. "You aren't supposed to enjoy things, you cunt! You are supposed to do your job correctly. I'm going to teach you a lesson you will never forget!"

Sylvia was lying on her side on the carpet, shivering in fear as the two men arrived. They walked over to her and picked her up, dragging her out of the room and down the hall to the

mate decisions on knowledge or competence. It is suited, as it should be, to the diagnoses of illness or maladjustment for the purposes of treatment. Judges, on the other hand, while provided with a set of determinate values through the development of legal principles, simply lack the expertise to apply meaningful standards in individual cases. And, unfortunately, because of the imprecision of the norms in this area, much is lost in the translation from psychiatrist to judge or jury, between diagnosis and decision. This problem is even more striking where an individual is found not guilty by reason of insanity. There, the absence of a coherent psychiatric notion of volition and of workable legal standards results, it has been repeatedly claimed, in the administration of ad hoc justice.

Throughout his tortuous ten year history in the courts and in the psychiatric clinics, John Suggs was—and still is—a victim of our inability to deal adequately with this dilemma. It is clear from the record that his behavior is bizzare and destructive, and that he has never had much more than a tenuous grasp on reality. Perhaps Dr. Messinger's assessment of his condition as "emotionally unstable, with depressive and paranoid trends" is correct; perhaps Dr. Lubin's diagnosis of his condition of "schizophrenia" may be more accurate. Fortunately, we need not reassess the medical testimony. Judge Duffy, who considered Suggs's complete psychiatric history for the first time, was clearly correct in his decision to redetermine the issue of Suggs's competence at plea, and his findings have ample support in the record. Yet, one cannot help but have the gnawing uncertainty, in deciding after ten years that civil commitment proceedings might be appropriate, whether both judges and psychiatrists have led Suggs on a long day's journey into night.

UNITED STATES
COURT OF APPEALS
FOR THE SECOND CIRCUIT

No. 137—September Term, 1977
(Argued September 2, 1977
Decided January 21, 1978)
Docket No. 77-2053

forms. They are, we said, lined up with one another, the duplication is lateral, in the same plane. Penises and fingers, vaginal, oral and anal orifices repeating themselves. The repetition across time of intensive discharges of which they are the centers gives rise to a repetion of intensive centers across space. But putting it that way is to speak as though we have a time and a space already given apriori, in which the excitations occur, repeating themselves and projecting new sites for themselves. In fact it is the pulse of intensification and discharge that is the first form of a moment in life, and the libidinal impulses first mark out, or temporalize, a time made of moment upon moment. And it is the incision and tumescence of new intensive points, pain-pleasure points, that first extends the erotogenic extension. What we have, then, is a spacing, a distributive system of marks. They form not representations and not signifying chains, but figures, figures of intensive points, whose law of systematic distribution is lateral and immanent, horizontal and not transverse. This Nuba belly is a chessboard or pinball machine; there are places marked, fixed, but each place communicates laterally with further places, and the ball you shoot into it can jump in any direction from any place, according to the force with which it spins.

So far we have been envisaging the inscription purely as productive. By its material operation—by the incisions, the scarification—and by its systematic distributive spacing—which proceeds by repetition and divergence—it extends the erotogenic surface, produces a place or a plane productive of pleasurable torments, of voluptuous moments of subjectivity. But these very same intensive points now become demands, appeals. For something, someone, absent. They become marks for another, they form the gaping openness of a demand, a want, a desire, a hunger. They have not yet become signs—for what they refer to is not something ideal, transcendent meaning, but another intensive point; these scarifications, these raised hardnesses on the pliable flesh call for another's eye, another's touch, finger, nipple, tongue, penis. The reference becomes a lack, and its direction unilateral.

As I say, this is not yet a semiotic system. Yet it is out of this kind of distributive movement of inscription that the differentiated material for a semiotic system will be taken, and on this purely lateral and libidinal function of craving and want that the intentional reference of signs will be developed.

What is disturbing is the reversal we find here: an intensive mark, produced by vuluptuous pain and productive of pleasurable torments, becomes a point of lack, demand, and craving. But there has not been a dialectical reversal, from potential to craving, from positive to negative. They are both there, in something

Bernard-Henri Lévy

The Argentine 'Model'

Robert Guidice, 50 years old, a merchant by trade, lives on Paraguay Street. He asked to see me, and despite my reservations, insisted that I print his name. He sat before me, slouched in an armchair, and I had the strange impression that while he was speaking to me, he neither saw nor heard anything. He was nothing more than a hollow, monotonous voice, narrating anonymously and absent-mindedly. It was nonetheless his own story that he came to tell me. An atrocious and unbelievable story of a "living-death".

It all began a year ago, one winter night, when a group of men broke into his house on Paraguay Street. Everyone was herded into the dining room: Guidice and his wife, their oldest daughter, age twenty-two, and the three small children, ages eight, nine, and eleven. She was the one for whom these unknown men had come. The next day, when Guidice went to the police, they at first refused to register his writ of habeas corpus. "Your daughter", they told him, "has undoubtedly been kidnapped by an unofficial group. We'll find her sooner or later, but only if you keep your mouth shut and take your misfortune patiently."

Months went by, cast in an unimaginable atmosphere. Periodically, a policeman would come by to collect five or ten thousand pesos in exchange for meager, useless bits of information. One

less than a synthesis. There has occurred a kind of depression, a hollowing out, such that the force and excitation of an intensity, productive of an egoism, a local and intensive subject to consume it, becomes now the force of a craving for another, becomes a demand for, an appeal to another. This depression is the very locus of repression and oppression; here is the vortex where the explosive libidinal excitations are repressed, and where the force of oppression by the social body invests the singular one. Here begins the breeding of the herd animal, a form of life in which every impulse is felt as a want, in which every excitation, every libidinal intensity that produces a moment of subjectivity, appeals to the herd. The ephemeral singularity of subjectivity becomes intrinsically gregarious; the human animal becomes socialized.

Nietzsche wrote that only the least and worst part of our life becomes conscious, that is, gets verbalized, gets put into signs. But more profoundly it is all our impulses, all our libidinal intensities productive of moments of subjectivity, that get transformed into signs, that is, into wants, demands addressed to another, appeals made to another. A subjectivity completely made of impulses, we become a bundle of needs, of wants, servile animals, consumers. The force of the libidinal excitations becomes the sniveling need to be loved. All our productive forces, all the surplus excitation produced on the libidinal surface, only serves to bind us into herds of animals that need one another. The intensive surface of our life is exposed to the public eye, not to the eye that feels and caresses, that is pained and exhilarated, but to the judging eye, the eye that appraises and evaluates, rewards, redeems, and blames, culpabilizes. The eye that makes human animals ashamed of their nakedness.

But these must not be taken as successive operations. There is a kind of inscription that decrees, condemns and punishes—all at once. Kafka depicted it in *The Penal Colony*: the punishment is to be strapped into the machine that cuts into living flesh, engraving on the prisoner himself, and thereby making known for the first time, both the sentence and the law itsef.

This kind of machine, contrived in the bush, is especially circumcision and clitoridectomy. Their supremely public character is essential to them, and contrasts with the scarification, cicatrization and tatooing one warrior, one woman, does on another. They appear, we already noted, as the high-point of the tribal self-celebration, and efforts to abolish them, by missionaries, shepherds of foreign herds, or by public health officials, are resisted vehemently, as though the very existence of the tribal bond itself were at stake. Circumcision and clitoridectomy, done at 12 to 14 years, and without anaesthesia or hygiene, is an extremely painful torture, done by the public in one's most sensitive and pleasure-producing zone. This in-

day, however, on the verge of a breakdown and in desperation, Guidice broke down, and without warning, decided to contact the Ecumenical Commission for Human Rights. There was an immediate reaction; one week later he was kidnapped, and led blindfolded to a deserted house in the suburbs of the capital. There, he was reunited with his daughter, now unrecognizable, emaciated, almost toothless; her body was covered with wounds, and she was severely burned on the neck, breasts and stomach, by electrodes.

At this point the nightmare resumed before his very eyes, the eyes of a father, drowned in sadness and despair. A rat was inserted through the young girl's vagina into her stomach. As a result, she died. Can we say that Guidice, who was freed shortly thereafter, is really alive today?

It was clear to me that thousands of these tragedies have taken place within the past two years. An architect from Rosario told me that there isn't one Argentinian who hasn't been directly or indirectly involved at least once. And nevertheless it is very rare for anyone to spontaneously talk about it. It's difficult even to mention the subject without watching the most friendly face instantly freeze. No, no one knows, . . No one wants to talk about it . . .

Generally speaking, the terror in Argentina isn't as massively and indecently evident as we so willingly imagine from afar. It is an infinitely more diffuse, cappillary, and cloistered system. X, who knows more than a little bit about it, even claims to have learned the skill at the beginning of his career, within the walls of the famous Marine Academy. "Here, the prisoners are assigned to small, very mobile units. They are never tortured for long in the same place. The same goes for the torturers; they are never allowed to torture for a long time, nor do they return to the same prisoners. Everyone circulates ceaselessly. Sometimes, we too have had enough. So, they don't give us the chance to get to know one another very well, to get together and talk about it." There are none of Pinochet's concentration camps, no packed stadiums; only small

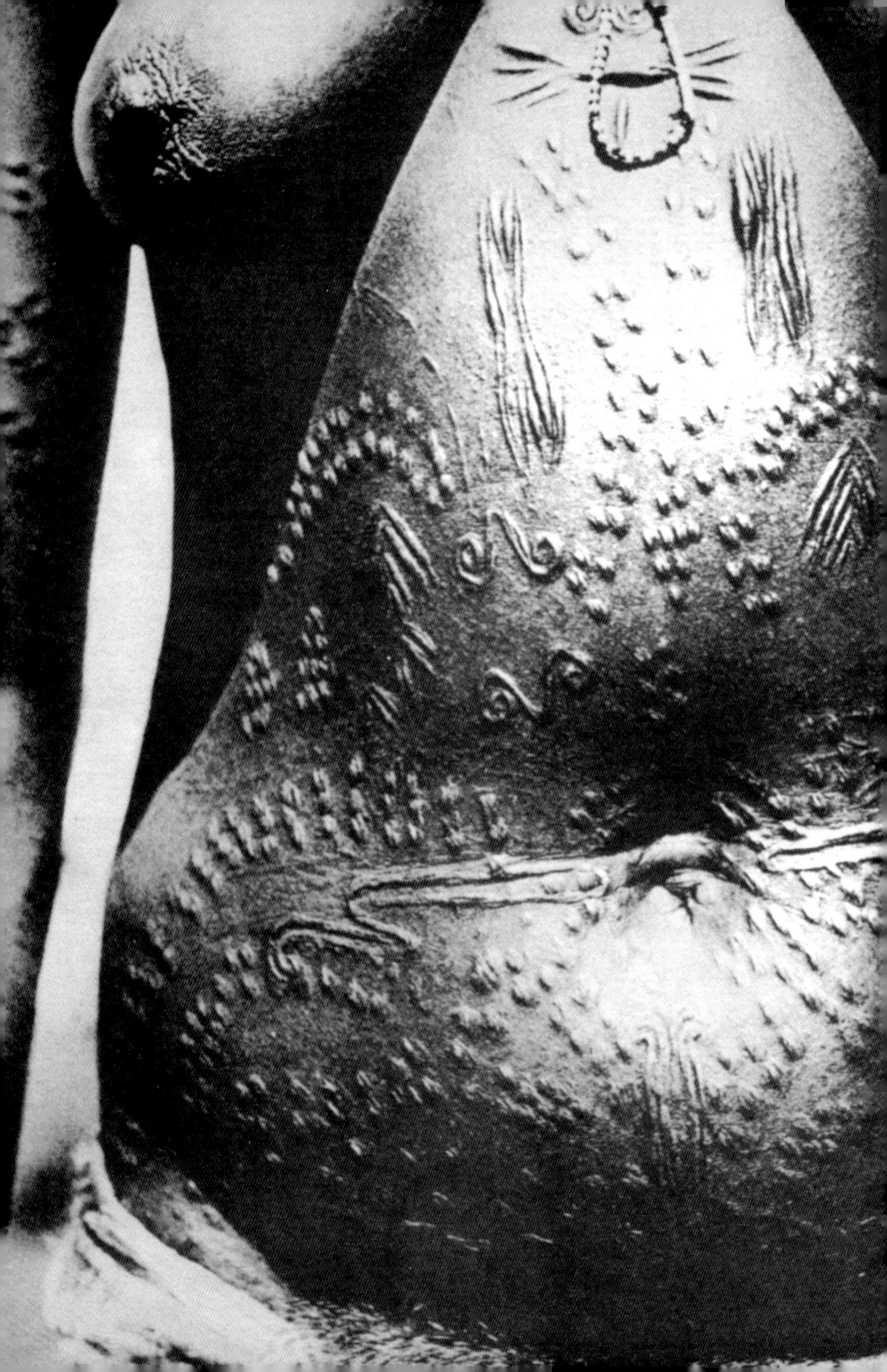

cision pronounces and inscribes the sentence by which the public disposes of the individual. It is at the same time the means by which the law itself, the prohibition and oppression that is the essence of the gregarious order, is made known and comes to exist.

It is an operation that makes libidinal impulses into desire and want, through castration. For the circumcision castrates the male of the labia about his own penis, and the clitoridectomy castrates the female of her penis. It is through castration of the natural bisexual that the social animal is produced. The marks now become signs, by which the intensive zones of one refer to, need, another. A memory, a mind, is being produced for the fugitive and capricious unconscious of the libidinal animal; and nothing was more cruel, more painful, Nietzsche wrote, than the mnemotechnics by which the savage animal gave itself a mind, a memory in which singular excitations are transformed into intrinsically generic signs.

The German nudity is beautiful. With a beauty that is not just skin deep. This nakedness does not expose a skin claiming to be attractive by the scars, welts, incisions, inscriptions covering it. No, the German nakedness celebrates the naturalness, what a German is by virtue of being born healthy and Aryan and vigorous, the beauty that is not decorative, rococo, but functional. The Bauhaus body, with broad ribs and biceps heroic, and proportion too, for that means poise, agility, freedom in movement. The body built: power, and delineation, that is, all the articulations of that power clear and distinct, and proportion. Breasts full and firm, thighs pivoting and loose, for moving on her own, and for strip tease dancing. A male on his own, a female on her own. This nudity, and this beauty, and this naturalness exposes a body integral and functional, where the exposed exterior is one with the functional inner axes and drive shafts.

It's hard, though, to believe in all that. Where, after all, on the planet are still more human beings needed? All that is just a game, isn't it, on the already overcrowded beaches of Sylt? Capitalism looks on it with a kindly eye; coupled up with the Mercedes and the Nikons, it helps sell.

But away from the beaches, what gets produced is —at the limit—someone without real human or phallic identity, not *male,* not *woman,* not human, someone without central or functional identity, a certain extension of erotogenic surface, couplings with superfluous and surface things, with Suzukis, with Nikonos cameras, with Scuba tanks, with parasailing parachutes, with which there is produced the pleasure of driving, of consuming the miles, of covering the earth, of floating adrift in the sea, of being dragged through the sky. These couplings with the elemental do not feed into, do not serve the functional inner machinery of the working body. They are surplus poten-

houses, cellars and apartments, a total of sixty for all of Buenos Aires, dispersed throughout the suburbs. Floating torture centers, like the "Bahia Aguirre". In short, a kind of archipelago whose geography grows more and more elaborate.

Thus, it is not rare that in order to create confusion and to cover up the traces, small groups of prisoners are transferred, without apparent reason, from one center to another. Sometimes, two or three of them are set free at the door of the prison only to be immediately picked up by a new team who take them away to a new center. Prison administration can then point to the records showing that the missing persons left their units safe and sound. Even though at that very moment, they are again on their knees in some clandenstine cellar being tortured . . .

To this day, Latin America has had the sad privilege of embodying the terrors of a particularly omniscient state. Nevertheless, the continent under Videla is being modernized and new fear accompanies the newly equipped and technologically trained police who operate in the shadows, in silence. Compared to the long tradition of tropical fascism, it is perhaps this innovation which makes for the originality of the "Argentine Model".

Excerpted from *Le Nouvel Observateur*, June 5, 1978

Torture in Argentina

They immediately put cotton over my eyes and bound them with masking tape so that I would not see their faces. But since the cotton became quickly soaked, I was able to see by throwing my head back. I realized that we were in a house and not in a military camp as they wanted me to believe. I was also able to see a young man who was despairedly crying. I moved closer to talk to him when our guards had left us alone for a moment and I learned that at the marine Academy they had tortured his wife in a terrifying manner; they cut off her hands at the wrists with a hacksaw, causing a hemorrage so great that

tial, accumulating on the surface, consumed by local and momentary egoisms. What is beneath, what is the full and sated body upon whose surface they effervesce? An anonymous, sterile and inert body, a certain stock whose worth is determined by the universal body without organs of capital, which measures everything and distributes all the pleasures and pains. Itself just a fund of capital, then. This kind of dehumanized, dephallicized, insignificant . . . entity is the final product of capitalism. I was going to say: this kind of subjectivity—but what there is here is not a subjectivity, but a split, fragmented, dismembered, disintegrated field of momentary subjectivities, forming in pleasure and pain. Schizophrenicized subjectivity.

And it is this kind of schizo personality that goes off to the savages. Not to live with them as among brothers and sisters. Not to find real men, and real women, finally, to fill up that aching hole, that phallic lack you have made of yourself. But to feel the sun in the empty savanna, to stand in antedeluvian landscapes unmarked by all history, malignant bush country, whitish plains without contour or dimensions where there is nothing moving but the termites and the tsetse flies, the squalor of eternity.

And to collect pictures, some beads and neck hangings, some fetiches, some warthog's teeth, to stick in your mouth, to suck, and to get in some hours flying a private twoseater over the Mountains of the Moon, parasailing alongside the Indian Ocean, scuba-diving in equatorial waters. Putting together your own pleasure chains, out of the debris of civilization, not according to its codes, by bricolage. Like savages do.

But driven by a libido that wants to wander off to the land where there are those who are kissed by the green mamba, who are strong enough to be chosen by, and to hold the embrace of, the leopard.

—February, 1978
Kenya

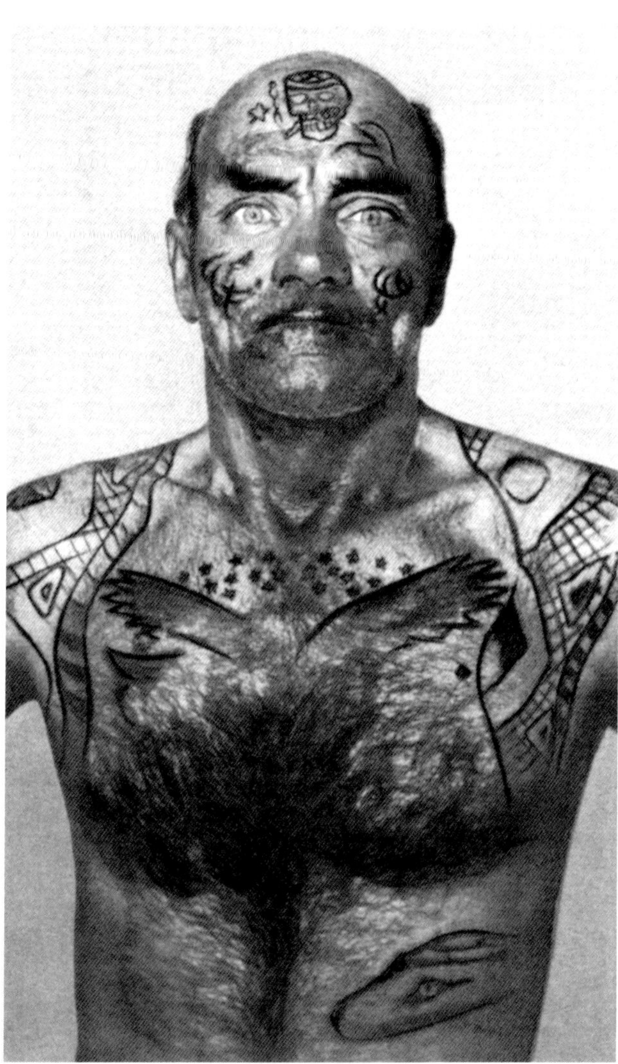

she died within a few minutes. He had also seen them cut a women in two, from her vagina to her head. And because he saw this, they were going to kill him also. I was so terrified that I dragged myself far away from him and spoke to him no more, so horrified was I by his account.

I remained there several days, night and day haunted by the cries of those being tortured. Finally, I was set free. They drove me into the city, blindfolded and hooded, insulting me and shouting all the while that the next time, they would treat me with less tenderness—they would kill me right away. Then they left me.

—*Translated by Tom Gora*

Testimony of Ema Parafiorito, recorded by the Argentine Commission on Human Rights.

Academic Approach to Torture

Mr. Mitrione, head of the United States Agency for International Development's public safety program in Montevideo, was killed by Uruguay's Tupamaro guerrillas following his kidnapping in 1970. At the time, the State Department denied charges by leftists that Mr. Mit rione had participated in the torture of political prisoners.

"If you ask me whether any American official participated in torture, I'd say yes, Dan Mitrione participated," Mr. Hevia said at a news conference. "If you ask me whether there were interrogations, I'd say no, because the unfortunate beggars who were being tortured had no way of answering because they were asked no questions. They were merely guinea pigs to show the effect of electric shock on different parts of the human body.

Mr. Hevia, who attended high school at Watertown, Conn., in the early 50's and speaks perfect English, said that the interrogation courses brought by Mr. Mit rione involved the use of electric shocks, special chemicals and modern psychological techniques against detainees.

"The special horror of the course was its academic, almost clinical atmosphere," he recalled. "Mitrione was a perfectionist. He was coldly efficient, he insisted on economy of effort. His motto was: 'The right pain in the right place at the right time.' A premature death, he would say, meant that the technique had failed."

The New York Times, Aug. 4, 1978

SOUTH AMERICA IS ON SALE.

Aerolineas Argentinas announces the lowest prices to South America, the best schedule to South America and the world's newest terminal.

Aerolineas Argentinas is proud to announce our new APEX* fares.
From New York to Rio: $750. From New York to Buenos Aires: $775. All round trip, of course.
Naturally, low fares don't mean much unless there's a good schedule, too.
We've got the best schedule to South America of any airline in the world.
8 direct flights a week to Buenos Aires. 4 to Rio.
And, speaking of Buenos Aires, Aerolineas Argentinas has just opened its own terminal there.
It's ours exclusively. Very luxurious. With our own customs. Our own immigration.
And duty-free shopping entering and leaving the country. Nobody else has this either.
All this talk about fares and terminals and schedules allows us hardly any room to talk about our service.
It's very European. (Just like our country.) Very gracious. Very efficient. Very good.

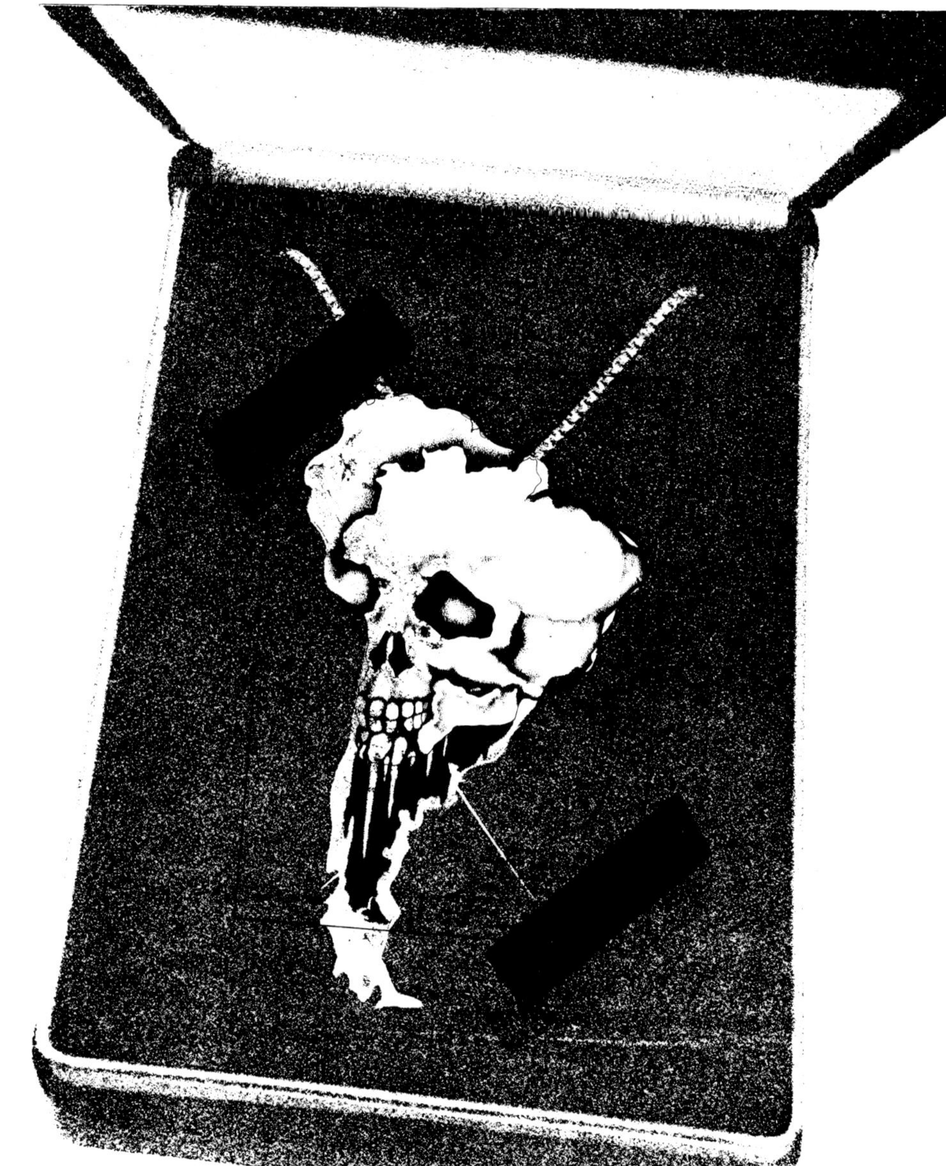

SOUTH AMERICA IS ON SALE.

Aerolineas Argentinas announces the lowest prices to South America, the best schedule to South America and the world's newest terminal.

Aerolineas Argentinas is proud to announce our new APEX* fares
From New York to Rio, $750. From New York to Buenos Aires, $775. All round trip, of course.
Naturally, low fares don't mean much unless there's a good schedule, too.
We've got the best schedule to South America of any airline in the world.
8 direct flights a week to Buenos Aires, 4 to Rio.
...of Buenos Aires, Aerolineas Argentinas has just opened its own terminal there.
...exclusively. Very luxurious. With our own customs. Our own immigration.

دانِستَن to know

(Past stem: cut off the "-an" (ـَن):)

داشت... have

خَرید... buy

خواست... want

دید... see

آمَد... come

زَد... beat up

خُورد... eat

گِرِفت... rob

بُرد... kidnap

کُشت... kill

دانِست... know

(Present stem:

((1.) Verbs ending "id" lose "id" :)

خر... buy

((2.) Verbs ending "nd", "rd", "ad", "ud" lose "d":

خور... eat

((3.) Verbs ending "ft", "št" lose "t" :)

کش... kill

((4.) Verbs ending "est", "eft", "oft", and "ad" lose this syllable :)

دان... know

((5.) Irregulars - most of them :)

دار... have

خواه... want

بین... see

آ... come

زَن	beat up
گیر...	rob
بَر...	kidnap
داشتَن جانی	to have Janey
خَریدَن جانی	to buy Janey
خواستَن جانی	to want Janey
دیدَن جانی	to see Janey
آمَدَن جانی	to come Janey
زَدَن جانی	to beat up Janey
خُوردَن جانی	to eat Janey
گِرِفتَن جانی	to rob Janey
بُردَن جانی	to kidnap Janey
کُشتَن جانی	to kill Janey
دانِستَن جانی	to know Janey

Translate into English:)

I listened to the smoldering ship's engines that were carrying me along, and relaxed. I shouldn't have. I should have grabbed a buoy and jumped overboard; and flagged down a passing tramp to carry me straight back to the Athens Hilton and the airport.

۱. آیا سَرِ سیاه اینجاست ؟

1. Is there a black head here?

۲. بَلی خانم (جانی) نزدیک است

2. Yes Mrs (Janey), it's near.

۳ این سَرِ مالِ جانی نیست

3. This head isn't Janey's. (Lit. This head

isn't the property of Janey.)

4 سَرهایِ سِیاهِ شَهرِ تهرانِ خَیلی هَست

4. There are many black heads in the city of Tehran.

خِیابانها سِیاه است بُزرگتَرین وَفاتِ جَهانی
حِسّ وَلی آز آن تیزتَر خود آست

5. The streets are black. You haven't fucked for a long time. You forget how incredibly sensitive you are. You hurt. Hurt hurt hurt hurt hurt. You meet the nicest guy in the world and you fall in love with him you do and you manage to get into his house and you stand before him. A girl who puts herself out on a line. A girl who asks

for trouble and forgets that she has feelings and doesn't even remember what fucking's about or how she's supposed to go about it cause she wasn't fucked in so long and now she's naive and stupid. So like a dope she sticks herself in front of the guy: here I am; understood: do you want me? No, thank you. She did it. There she is. What does she do now? Where does she go? She was a stupid girl: she went and offered herself, awkwardly, to someone who didn't want her. That's not stupid. The biggest pain in the world is feeling but sharper is the pain of the self.

(doesn't exist→) سُول soul

وَقت fate

۶ آیا گوشت تازه هَست ؟

6. Is there any fresh meat?

۷ بلی خانُم ولی گوشتَت آز آن مالِ جانِی بِهتَر آست

7. Yes Mrs, but your meat is better than Janey's.

۸ آیا وَقت هَست ؟

8. Is there any fate?

۹ بَلی حانُم وَقتَت آز آن مالِ جانِی بِهتَر آست

9. Yes Mrs, your fate is better than Janey's

۱۰ هَمۀ مَردُم راضی آند

10. "All the people are content."

۱۱ جانِی راضی نیست

1. Janey is not content.

۱۲. کوچکترینِ عمارتِ این خیابان خانهٔ جانی است

12. The smallest building on this street is Janey's cunt.

۱۳. این کارگرِ بزرگترینِ کارگرانِ ایران است

13. This worker is the biggest in Persia.

۱۴. آکثریتِ مردم کارگر یا دهقان اند

14. Most people are workers or bums.

۱۵. خیابانها سیاه است

15. The streets are black.

۱۶. آیا گوشت تازه هست ؟

16. Is there any fresh meat ?

• • • • • • • • • •

Richard Foreman

14 Things I Tell Myself when I fall into the trap of making the writing imitate "experience"

1.

The art. . . aims to reflect something that "stands under" experience, rather than experience itself.

Each situation we are in, each experience, quivers with the different
not-yet-known-how-to-use
ways in which the materials of that situation might otherwise be combined, organized, set to work upon each other.
Against that free-play of elements as a backdrop, one (in life) makes one's choice of act, thought, gesture

(a choice always rules by the need to echo, imitate or extend previous choice-patterns in order that that choice shall fit within the pre-defined limits of the rational.)

But! It is those continually REJECTED choices of the backdrop, never articulated yet always present as the un-thought 'possible', which give plasticity and depth and aliveness to what is chosen.

Our art then, to discover the secret of liveliness, shows by example

not—what choice to make (as does all theater which imitates 'actions')

but—shows, concretizes, that which—though it cannot be chosen—stands under what is chosen, so that choice is alive and energized.

The not-thought, the purposeless, which nourish all activity and experience. The acts of the play are then a series of acts and gestures not-chosen in life, which for that very reason serve as the roots of life's (or should we say consciousness's) liveliness.

2.

The audience must watch not the object, not the invention, but the way in which the object twists, is displaced, distorted.

But the important thing is to realize there is no agency responsible for this twisting, this distortion—there is a groundless displacement which is the very source of the play's meaning, and the very seat of consciousness (concretized by the play) itself.

This groundless twist, picks up the objects at hand and fills them for a moment, gives them being for a moment, and then lets them fall back into the sea of the non-manifested.

This groundless twist is the energy without a source about which we cannot speak—only ride its back as it were. The one choice we have is either

seeing and experiencing—which means having no contact with the generating energy

or standing-under seeing and experiencing, and so being where energy is; mis-matched with it—but the double condition of being-there and not matching (i.e. distorting it) being the only real condition of self-reflexive 'knowing', which the play —also mis-matched but being-there, knows.

3.

Our art then = a learning how to look at 'A' and 'B' and see not them
but a relation
that cannot be 'seen'

You can't look at 'it' (that relation)
because
it *IS* the looking itself.
That's where the looking (you) *is*, doing the looking.

4.

The compositional principle is NOT
anything goes
but
only write that which allows itself to be
deflected by the world (which world includes
the act of writing, of course).

Most stuff you might write wouldn't be so deflected (and so must be rejected). Either it would be too porous, the world going through it without deflection; or too heavy, it wouldn't budge—or it's in a sealed room where the world doesn't even notice it—hence no contact and no deflection.

Writing is also the invoking (of the gap, the mis-matching, which is where we *are* as consciousness, and which is a force). The invoked energy or force isn't what gets written. It arises, then in the staging, but it isn't in the staging.
The writing invokes the force *WHEN* that writing is then staged, so long as that staging is such that it *allows* the force to come. The staging doesn't make it (the force) but the staging gets the writing (which is the original invoking) out-of-the-way in the proper way, so that•then the force can be-there.

The force IS disassociation, consciousness, displacement, a groundless 'twist'. . . . so it is there and not there. It is 'other', it is 'possibility'. . . . not as a category, but as a force.

5.

Writing has not a subject
(aimed for)

but is a being-responsiveness, to the currents
within it as it generates itself. "It" is
writing thru me, and it is doing *other*
things also so try and show those other things.

It's not the item; it's how one slides off it,
leaving a *wrent* in the fabric.
Theme: that slidingness: which can't be said, because
to say IT would be to *not*-slide off *IT* being said.

6.

One must find ways to sacrifice 'what comes' to one in the writing.

Offer it up. . . to what Gods?
Destroy it as useful to us in daily life as-it-is. Rather serve it up to the elsewhere in us.

The play is then a ceremonial ground. Certain operations are performed. Not to tell (you) something. Not to take (you) elsewhere. But an important and significant activity goes on
which you watch or not watch.
But it isn't there for you or for me, it's for the benefit of someone else, hidden within us both, who needs to be fed so that everyday you and me can still be alive in a way that has plasticity and aliveness of thought and perception. Understand, it's not a question of refining the GOALS of thought and action, but of keeping the process itself grounded in a kind of energy that makes the process itself want to continue.

7.

In writing (as one takes dictation from what wants to be written) the received is twisted. It (the received) looks at itself through the twist (which is yourself) and it (not-you) gets a sense of itself and proceeds.

And then that which proceeds. . . is received, twisted, etc., and the process continues and a text is generated.

8.

I'm lying on the bed.
Looking toward the window.
The curtain moves in the wind
A motorcycle noise in the street stops some other
process of watching going on in me.
I write that down.
Desire plays through me for a moment.
Music from a window across the street and the sound
of water running in the tub.

A level. Everything level for a moment.

The writing is a certain thing
The action of wind, etc., noticed but not thought about, is a certain thing.

The writing is imprinting
a certain noticing
on a certain existent system.

It never matches.
That's why displacement is a rule, and a generative principle.

o. . . . .o

I make a model for the way it is.
One can't express the real experience.
Experience is one kind of making.
Saying is one kind of making.

The gap between is, of course, the source, the fuel.
Mis-match
Displacement.

So I don't (try not to) notice thought
But rather the gap between experience and thought
input output
passive active

What I write (notate) is the gap.

9.

The plays are about what they do.

Which is to concretize (show) a certain sort of system which goes-on in me.

In which lived moments. . . .are open to displaced energy which is objectified as an energy that wants to handle and penetrate the object, and that handling and penetration twists, displaces, distorts the object (which is the lived moment).

As a result the lived moment is denied as a self-sufficient experience. . . .and re-constituted as an energy-exchange which, as it leaves the evidence of its being on the page being written, is no longer an experience but a mark.

In the beginning: the mark.
That mark, that concretized evidence is, for me, heavier, denser than experience itself. The play is an energy diagram in four dimensions. A condensation of what goes on in me, objectified.

I don't make pictures evoking the experience of things, but notate what circles through us, leaving a residual grid that makes experience then possible (registerable). That grid . . . made intense . . . is the work of the play.

Experience is then burned up, petrified, sacrificed on that intense grid of the play.

10.

Within the play as an object, there must not be 'A' theme, because one theme or meaning closes the doors on all others—and ALL THEMES AND MEANINGS MUST BE PRESENT AT ALL MOMENTS.

The organization of the composition should dis-organize the ego (which is what wants a theme to be-at-home in) and evoke in the self the dispersed self (in which ALL themes are).

(Simple dada & surrealism don't do that. Nonsense, irrationality, don't do that, they don't dissolve the ego, they are rather anti-bodies which, injected, strengthen the ego. They wall themselves in from the world as non-sensical or supra-sensical, which only increases the need and ability of the ego to define its territory as against 'external', irrational territory.)

The OBJECT of the play, then, is to make the spectator be like the play

(or recognize that he *is* like the play)

I am like the play

(We are what interferes with us. Result, a kind of self-knowledge. But whose self-knowledge? There is no *who*. Only knowledge.)

11.

Always, at the beginning (which means finally) a sentence wants to write itself.

Then, that sentence suggests a next sentence, because of

habits of association, because of a world in which we are trained, taught that one thing must lead to another, that there are paths to be followed like responsibilities, etc.

To escape that.
Write the sentence that wants to be written.
But then pull away from it—or from the inherited
associations and commands and rules that
cling to it.

Pull away from it. Let something that interferes. . .
twist
the sentence, as it emerges or in the next moment,
as you look at it.

There must be no theory of writing. The writing is
the phrase or gesture that floods one and wants to be written.
But then, there must be
A theory of what to do after the writing has
had its way and written itself as a word or sentence
or sentence cluster.

The 1st moment:
What floods one. Then, twist it. Find
ways to inhabit it, plant it
in the world NOT as a tool,
not as a lever to move the known in
known ways, but to turn it into a
self-reflexive item, around which a
whole new world crystallizes.

The 2nd movement
In staging. . . interfere. Let
the sentence be so crystallized,
become so intensely itself, reflecting
itself. . . that interference actually
FEEDS it
Strengthens it in
its clear uniqueness by being
not-it in a subtle and
interfering way.

12.
The choice is to discover what is (clarity) by *seeing* desire at work (not simply letting desire produce, because its products often cloud seeing).

There is a choice—either seeing desire at work
or
Form production (which is to cover over what-is with
'what should be').

Make desire-energy produce a structure that is self-reflexive. That is, make desire as it produces, produce the right form, which is a form that will see itself (so that *we* can see, through it, since the desire is *us*, what-is-there).

Is that not form production? Not really, because we
are not speaking of willing a certain form and
then 'using' desire to fill it.

We are speaking of working on the desire itself,
through conscious displacement, distortion, employing
a strategy of identifying with what-interferes.
Then. . . what is produced has the 'right' form whatever
the form of what-is-produced. Because when the desire
is producing. . . through identifying with what
interferes there is a displacement, it doubles itself
and so mismatched it sees itself. And the play is isomorphic
with that activity of twisting, splitting—looking at itself.

And the play at work is clear, not producing a form
but producing a doubling, a displacement which is a real mirror, and
clarity.

13.

The meaning is in the suppositions that start one:

In my case, small bits of experience and thought interfered
with—
how the unconscious and the world (the same) get-in-the-way,
and how that interference is allowed.

The text = strategies for allowing the world to interfere.

And making that interference one's own, as an
oyster makes a pearl of the interfering, irritant,
grain of sand.

Now—what is interfered with is *NOT* a project, or
aim, or narration

but just being-there in one's self.

If it is a narrative or project that is interfered
with, then the self is still there.
But interfere with just-being-there and the
self is dispersed

14.

So. . . Each moment has a different meaning, each moment a
different theme. The piece is about making oneself available
to a continual barrage of meanings and themes, so that
one is transformed into a being
spread, distributed
a different configuration of the self.

The composition always implies, no, no the meaning is
not here, but elsewhere, spread. The piece is always
pointing away from itself. Meaning is equally distributed,
everywhere. Classical art, everything is focused in on
a certain theme, points to the center, each moment
cohering. Here—each moment takes off in a different
direction.

The unity is the procedural way of turning away
from the center. There is displacement, continual
replacement of one meaning with another.

There is a sequence of a certain sort of item, called
'possibleness of manipulation'. There is a straining
after certain figures that the mind-as-a-body
wants to articulate in space.

Exemplary titles: Book of Levers
Action at a Distance

Theme: Showing that mental acts take place on a surface, not in the depths.

Depth as the ultimate fantasy. The ultimate evasion. Linked, of course, to a concept of center. So de-center. Displace. Allow thought to float up from the depths and rest on the surface. Look at it. . . handle it. Match your life to it. . . as does the play.

The play, finally, must be fed and 'controlled' by a multitude of sources. As many as there are 'sources' of experience in one's own life.

That multiplicity, acting in concert, becomes the 'unity' of the process of continual displacement. Only work to make sure no single displacement escapes the immediate interference which must arise in the next moment, allow no single displacement to begin to build a wall around itself and form its own kingdom, its own order of being. Such a kingdom or order would be a return to the sleep of experience within which most art keeps us forever imprisoned.

Seth Neta

To-Ana-No-Ye
Anorexia Nervosa

Anorexia Nervosa: A term we can discard, latin modular medical lingo identifying cipher of authority locating an anti-social practice (self starvation) within the field of disease/disorder/danger/crime. Medical business label.

That day we often heard dogs barking some distance away. We assumed we were near a village and two comrades went to investigate hoping to get some water. They returned a few hours later, reporting there was no village. It seemed odd, a dog but no village; we

We had a strict routine at the training camp. Early each morning we did tough exercises. While the cold weather lasted our group did them in the barracks, the others, however, trained in the snow. Then we changed for inspection and afterwards did marching drills. We also had an intensive course in Russian. On weekends we were taken to museums and historical sites.

One morning as we rested under some trees, a youth with his cattle approached. We didn't want him to stumble on us as news of the presence of a large number of well armed Africans in the area would spread very fast. Before we could decide what to do he stopped and sat down by a creek some 50 yards away. Our troubles weren't over however. His cattle kept grazing closer and closer to our position. We'd silently chase them away so he wouldn't come after them but soon they'd graze close to us again.

anything, then to have control over your body becomes a supreme accomplishment. You make out of your body your very own kingdom where you are the tyrant the absolute dictator." In this frame of mind not to give

Some will talk about it when they start to express their disgust with the female body

later in college became quite popular. was disturbed by not feeling like her own person in relation to others. She described one episode: "I was sitting with these people but I felt a terrible fragmentation of myself. There wasn't a person inside at all. I tried with whoever i was with to reflect the image they had of me, to

Behavior Modification
Professor Arthur Crisp (St. Georges Hospital, Tooting, London):

I said provided you achieve certain goals you will be rewarded in certain ways, and unfortunately she still felt that she couldn't keep to this contract.

BBC TV: And how did it work out, what were the rewards?
Herr Crisp: Well the rewards were, for a start she was treated in bed as are most cases of this degree of severity and the arrangement was that when she reached a certain weight she would be allowed . . uh . . the sort of reward would be a visitor or two visitors or a telephone by the bed, and so it progressed so that at a certain stage she was allowed out of the bed for several hours, and out of bed for half a day, fully up, clothed, able to move around the ward, go to occupational therapy, and so it progressed.

Occupational Therapy Reward

The treatment/cure of anorexics is the process by which the Clinic/Hospital (medical production) through behavior modification, drug therapy, psychotherapy, and hyperalimentation (forced feeding which bypasses the mouth and digestive organs intravenously) returns/enslaves the anorexic to a healthy body capable of fulfilling the role of consumer/producer (producer of children, new workers, new consumers) prescribed to all organisms in a consumer economy.

The clinic here is a factory whose product is healthy bodies.

ROSA RIKE	ROSA DORA	ROSA CHIDOR	DORA MORO
ROSA MEINS	ROSA DORO	ROSA SHIDORA	ROSA ADORO
DORA KOLWEZI	DORA MEINS	ROSA YEMEN	DORA ROSO
ROSA MORO	DORA MOURN	ROSA AD	ROSA KOLWESI

disease/desire/disorder

anti-organism

ANTI-CORPORAL/ANTI-CORPORATE

the body/arena for the exercise of control
sex identity/de-identify
ill/veil
a job for medicine

ANA-CORP-I-A Videotapes: Interviews to be recorded in hospital during treatment, texts read to the camera, putting words in their mouths, hyperalimentation monologues:

Text Sampler

LIFE HISTORIES OF THE REVOLUTION, LSM Press

THE REVENGER'S TRAGEDY, Tourner

NEO COLONIALISM, Kwame Nkruma

HOLGER MEINS, THE STRUGGLE CONTINUES, Red Army Fraction

KEEP FIT TO EAT RIGHT, Adelle Suicide

THE ORIGIN OF THE FAMILY, PRIVATE PROPERTY, AND THE STATE, F. Engels

PARIS MATCH 2 June, 1978 HORREUR A KOLWESI

APPLIED PHARMACOLOGY REVIEWS (in-house medical publications) Adis Press

POEMS OF AGHOSTINO NETO

The Golden Cage

The Enigma of Anorexia Nervosa

Hilde Bruch, M.D.

psychotherapist shop forman of hospital factory prison
research departments for the development of new methods of control

TOMB OF TEXT
AUTHORITY.

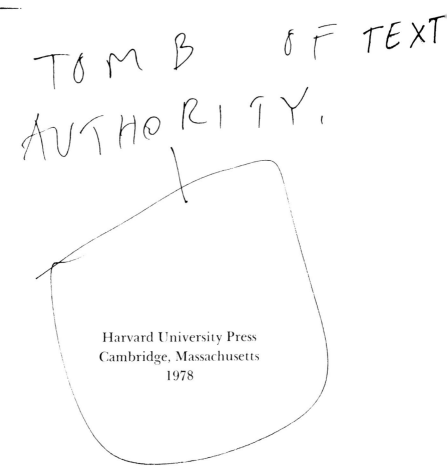

Harvard University Press
Cambridge, Massachusetts
1978

COERCIVE STRENGTH OF HUNGER STRIKES

Holger Meins

Rosa Meins

be "in." All of a sudden everyone in school was wearing a nylon jacket around 1960. Then the FDJ[4] did something about these parkas, these caps that we had bought. They had security groups, and the FDJ groups stood in front of the school and took away our nylon jackets. They argued that the jackets were stained with the blood of the Vietnamese—which was certainly possible. Well, this is where a whole process is ignited—a real problem: one starts to become

Menstrual rhythm prison

control over bleeding

Brasch: Right from the beginning it was. To be honest I was rarely with my parents. My earliest years—up until I was four—were spent with a family of Social Democrats, who were workers and lived near the East train station.

lowering temperature

coma/orgasm

forms, especially the kind of uniforms you have in the People's Army. Of course you end up with a frustrating situation—and it's the same in jail or parochial schools where there are young boys without any girls, something especially important when you're between 11 and 15. Regarding homoerotic relations: that's possible, but I didn't see much of it. You're usually so pooped that you don't much worry about your sexuality, outside of the usual masturbation scene. Our teachers were mixed; about 70 percent I'd say were officers and the other 30 percent civilians, biology or chemistry teachers. The pressure to perform was pretty much the same one you find in similar schools. The year was divided into: September, which was the beginning of the school and training year, to January; then the annual winter camp in February, where we went into the mountains, into barracks in an isolated area, where we learned to ski and to shoot on skis and things like that. And during the same time we still had classes. Then we went back for more instruction and military training. In June we had the so-called summer camp on the Baltic Sea where we went on maneuvers with tanks and other things like that. And during that time there was no school. After

weight loss is measurable progress

consuming and excreting is work

NGC: Could you tell us more about the circumstances which caused this? For instance, these jackets. One doesn't become reactionary or progressive all of a sudden because of jackets. There are issues where things come to a head.

POLITICS OF THE TREATMENT

THE FEMALE BODY IS NOT BEAUTIFUL

menu for ROSA YEMEN
1 egg scrambled with shell

sodium perborate
sterilize the mouth

habituelas colorades,
the red intestines

200 amotryptiline
+stomach pump

medical attention

vomit up the 8 hour day

1 dozen eggs broken
my eggs

attending coma
internal bleeding

De la mastication
MENU BY ROSA YEMEN.

Prehension buccale/
Attouchement-gustatif-Langue
Mecanisme de la machoire
(temps determine selon
l'aliment)
Crachat-rejection
Gargarisme bref.

1 gorgee de gordons gin+
morsure de citron vert.
(rejet bref)

1 demi louche de taboule
(rejet bref)

1 olive noire avec noyau

Sake en quantite
(reject long)

1 cuilleree a cafe de matieres
fecales de poisson
(rejet indetermine)

1 biscotte
(rejet instantane)

Persil + blanc d'oeuf
Bacclava + Eau
(rejet brut)
Ice + Chewing-gum
(indetermine)
Type Cerebro-spinal
de guerre froide 45% $%¢@#¼
LA MASTICATION en relation
directe avec le baillement
(dans les deux sens)
Le sommeil,
sans la masturbation.

POLITICAL
BE FULFILLED.

Bazooka Joe Story

Joe is trapped in the flavor, extracted in the mouth (JOE HAS NO MOUTH) The body is perfumed/connected, his empty body ejected/spat out. Nothing is swallowed, the organs are excluded from this relationship, a secret total consumption/excretion, to be repeated as often as desired.

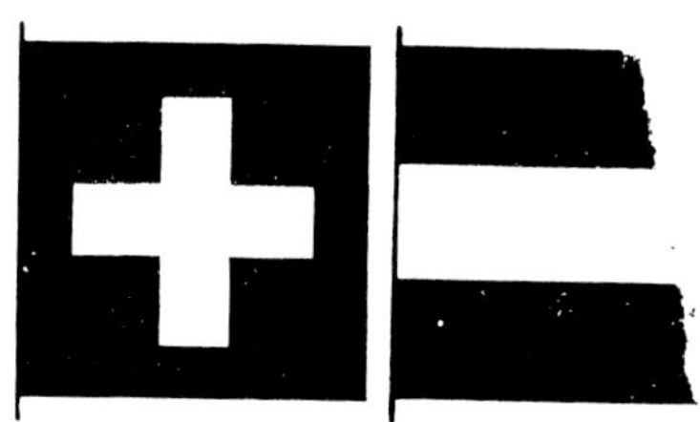

1. SWITZERLAND. National Flag 2. AUSTRIA. National and

CHOOSE FROM 12 SIMULATED GEMS. 1 FOR EACH MONTH. INDICATE MONTH OF BIRTH. SEND 275 BAZOOKA COMICS.

MEIN GROSSVATER IST TOT

Und die schnellsten.

MEIN GROSSMUTER IST EIN MÖRDERI

Für Ihren Flug nach Südamerika bietet Ihnen nur Air France zwei Superlative zur Auswahl: das schnellste Flugzeug der Welt und das größte. Deshalb lohnt es sich, den Weg über Paris nach Südamerika zu nehmen – er ist von Hamburg, Düsseldorf, Köln, München, Stuttgart und Berlin ohnehin gerader als über Frankfurt.

Und damit er noch gerader wird, hat Air France als einzige Fluglinie drei unterschiedliche Routen anzubieten, die die Flugstrecke abkürzen.

Buchen Sie in Ihrem IATA-Reisebüro.
Oder bei uns. Ihrer Linie für Langstrecken.

ULRIKE

ach Südamerika fliegt nur ULRIKE
die bequemsten Sessel.

UNLESERLICH-UNGESETZLICHE

ULRIKE INC.

Andre Cadere

Boy with Stick

Sylvere LOTRINGER: *How would you define your work?*
Andre CADERE: It's an independent work.

L: *How does it differ from any other independent work?*
C: It differs in that it does not depend exclusively on the existing structures of art.

L: *What structures?*
C: Galleries and museums. I don't mean to say that it dispenses with them, but it can function otherwise. It's this margin that interests me.

L: *What gave you the idea of operating within the margins?*
C: It's very difficult to say. Perhaps it's because I come from Roumania, a country which is outside the Western cultural system, a totally marginal country. I came to France without money, without relations. With respect to the social order, I was nothing at all. I had no means of support. The sole possibility that was left for me was to do my work all alone, independently of the existing social system. But I don't want to play the idealist. The goal is to penetrate the predominant system.

Andre Cadere, a Romanian artist, moved to Paris in 1967. This interview took place in April, 1978 in New York where he came to do his work. He died in Paris shortly after. He was 42.

Ulrike Meinhof

Armed Anti-Imperialist Struggle

West Germany: post-fascist state, consumers, culture, metropole-chauvinism, mass manipulation through media, psychologic warfare, Social Democrats. The GUERILLA is a politico-militaristic organization within illegality. It struggles aligned with internationalism, the Internationale of the liberation movements waging war against imperialism in the third world and in the metropoles. These liberation movements are the avant-gardes of the world proletariat fighting in arms.

Reality can only be perceived in a materialistic way related to struggle—class struggle—war. Revolutionary action—no matter how it is brought about—will always be understood by the masses. Words are senseless, outrage is no weapon, it takes action.

The Guerilla has no real viewpoint, no basis from which to operate. Everything is constantly in motion, so is the struggle. Struggle comes out of motion, moving on and is moving on. All that matters is the aim. The guerilla perceives class struggle as the basic principle of history and class struggle as reality, in which proletarian politics will be realized.

Man and woman in the guerilla are the new people for a new society, of which the guerilla is the "breeding cell" because of its identity of power, subjectivity, constant process of learning, action (as opposed to theory). So guerilla means collective process of learning with the aim to "collectivize" the individual, so that he will keep up collective learning. Politics and strategy are within each individual of the guerilla.

(Speech of Ulrike Meinhof on Sept. 13, 1974, in Moabit Prison, West Berlin, on the escape of Andreas Baader from prison.)

Armed Anti-Imperialist Struggle and the Defensive Position of the Counterrevolution in its Psychologic Warfare Against the People

Anti-Imperialist Struggle

Anti-imperialist struggle, if not meant to be merely a phrase, aims at destroying the imperialist system of powers—politically, economically and in militaristic terms; the cultural institutions through which imperialism provides homogenity of the ruling elites and the communications systems for its ideological predomination.

Military destruction of imperialism means

on the international level: destroy military alliances of U.S. imperialism around the world; in Germany: destroy Nato and Bundeswehr; on the national level: destroy the armed formations of the state apparatus, embodying the monopoly of violent power, of the ruling class, its power within the state; in Germany: police bundesgrenzschutz, secret service;

economically means destroy the power structure of multinational companies;

politically means destroy state and non-state bureaucracies, organizations and power structures—parties, unions, media—which rule the people.

Proletarian Internationalism

Anti-imperialist struggle here is not and cannot be a national liberation struggle—its historic perspective is not socialism in one country. Transnational organizations of capital, world-gripping military alliances of U.S. imperialism, cooperation of police and secret services, international organizations of ruling elites within the power range of U.S. imperialism—are matched on our side, the side of the proletariat, of revolutionary class struggles, of the liberation struggles of third world peoples, of urban guerilla in the metropoles of imperialism: by proletarian internationalism.

Since the Paris Commune, it has been obvious that the attempt of one people in an imperialist state to liberate itself on a national level will call for revenge, armed powers, the mortal hatred of the bourgeoisie of all other imperialist states.

"One people suppressing others cannot emancipate itself," Marx said. The urban guerilla, RAF (Red Army Fraction) here, Brigate Rosse in Italy, United Peoples Liberation in the U.S. receive their military significance from the fact that they can, aligned with the liberation struggles of the third world peoples, out of solidary struggle, attack imperialism from the back here, from where it exports its troops, its weapons, its training personnel, its technology, its communications systems, its cultural fascism for the suppression and

L: ***What does your work consist of?***
C: **It consists of these round wooden rods that you see. They conform to a precise definition and are structured in a specific way. It's a very short wooden dowel composed of segments which are assembled once they are painted different colors. The colors succeed one another according to a mathematical system of permutations, within which I introduce an error each time. There is a dialectical rapport between mathematical order and error.**

L: ***Once the baton is completed, is your work done?***
C: **There must first of all be the reality of work. I sell this work; I make my living from it. Therefore, with respect to the reality of art, I have no exterior point of view. I am completely inside of it. I move throughout the circuit.**

L: ***You do, however, have a particular mode of operation. Rather than depending on the gallery circuit for exposure and sale of your work, you ultilize the very mobility of what you do—a staff, a pilgrim's staff—in order to establish your own network.***
C: **That's true. I can go to the Museum of Modern Art or to Castelli's and present my work without anyone inviting me.**

If it were an orthodox ork, say a canvas, could it still runction in the same way?
C: **No, because there is an indissoluble dialectical bond between the wall and the canvas. The canvas has a recto and a verso. It is made for the wall and it depends on it.**

L: ***Is the staff or the baton the only form you can imagine for mobile art, for nomadic art?***
C: **It is nomadic, but of course it can enter the power apparatus without being invited, that is to say, without being a part of it.**
L: ***Then you use the baton to put a monkeywrench in the works.***
C: **Yes, that's it.**

L: ***Your baton is at once an object and an act.***
C: **Exactly.**

L: ***A symbolic act. . . .***
C: Obviously, it is not because I go to Castelli's that I am exhibited there. Nothing can prevent me from being concretely, materially inside the place. He can throw me out, and it's interesting if he does. This has happened elsewhere, and in other circumstances. When the institution defends itself, it becomes, in no uncertain terms, brutal and aggressive.

L: ***Is it only the institution which reacts like this?***
C: There are the artists.

L: ***The artists?***
C: Yeah.

L: ***Is the institution also the artists?***
C: Yeah. You see, one always speaks of galleries and museums, but the artists, at least those who are caught up in it are much more extreme than the galleries themselves.

L: ***How do you explain that?***
C: Jealousy and competition, for the most part.

L: ***The fact that you can short-circuit the traditional channels by showing up in the best known galleries?***
C: Yes.

L: ***In fact, this short-circuit permits you to benefit equally from all the prestige of the normal circuit.***
C: Altogether, and I've nothing against that. When I began my work eight years ago, everyone told me, "Fine, you'll end up with a gallery where you can hang your baton on the wall; you'll end up cooling it just like everyone else." It was considered an opportunist's activity. Now, I've been exhibited quite a bit in Europe, thank God, and in plenty of important places. Museums have bought my work. But regardless of all that, I continue to hang out with my stick. And this is where it really becomes interesting. I've established my little artistic career like anyone else, but parallel to that, I continue my work, I make the scene, completely alone, outside of everything, although the system can open certain doors for me.

exploitation of third world peoples. This is the strategic destiny of the urban guerilla: in the backlands of imperialism, to bring forth the guerilla, the armed anti-imperialist struggle, the people's war, during a long process—because world revolution is surely not a matter of a few days, weeks, months, not a matter of just a few people's uprisings, no short-term process, not taking over the state apparatus—as revisionist parties and groups imagine or rather claim, since they really don't imagine anything.

About the Term "National State"

In the metropoles the term "national state" is a fiction, no longer having any basis within the reality of the ruling classes, its politics and power structure, which have no equivalent even in language borderlines, since millions of labor emigrants can be found in the rich states of West Europe. Rather through internationalization of capital, through the news media, through reciprocal dependencies of economic development, through enlargement of the European community, through crisis, an internationalism of the proletariat in Europe eminates even on the subjective level—so that union apparatuses have been working for years already at its suppression, control, institutionalization.

The fiction of a national state, which the revisionist groups with their form of organizing cling to, is matched by their legalistic fetishism, their pacifism, their mass opportunism. We hold against them not the fact that members of these groups come from the petit bourgeoisie, but rather that in their politics and organizational structure they reproduce the ideology of the petit bourgeoisie to which internationalism of the proletariat has always been foreign, and which has—and this cannot be different because of its class position and its conditions of reproduction—always organized itself complementarily to the national bourgeoisie, to the ruling class in the state.

Arguing that the masses are not yet ready reminds the U.S., RAF and captured revolutionaries in isolation, in special prison sections, in artificial brainwash collectives, in prison and in illegality, only of the arguments of the colonial pigs in Africa and Asia for over 70 years: black people, illiterates, slaves, the colonized, tortured, suppressed, starving, the peoples suffering under colonialism, imperialism were not yet ready to take their bureaucracy, industrialization, their school system, their future as human beings into their own hands. This is the argument of folks who are worried about their own positions of power, aiming at ruling a people, not at emancipation and liberation struggle.

omething
eem
uspicious
?
JOIN YOUR
CHICAGO POLICE
IN OPERATION
CRIME-STOP
CALL PO5-1313

The Urban Guerilla

Our action of May 14, 1970 (freeing Andreas Baader from prison), is and will remain the exemplary action of the urban guerilla. It does/did combine all elements of the strategy of armed anti-imperialist struggle: it was the liberation of a prisoner from the grip of the state apparatus. It was a guerilla action, the action of a group, which turned into a military-political cell because of the decision to undertake the action. It was the liberation of a revolutionary, a cadre, who was essential for the set up of the urban guerilla—not just as every revolutionary is essential within the revolution, but because even at that time he incorporated all that was needed to make the guerilla, military-political offensive against the imperialist state possible: decisiveness, the will to act, the ability to define oneself only and exclusively through the aims, along with the keeping of the collective process of learning of the group going, practising leadership from the very beginning as collective leadership, passing on to the collective the processes of the learning of every individual.

The action was exemplary because anti-imperialist struggle deals with liberation of prisoners, as such, from the prison, which the system has always signified for all exploited and suppressed groups of the people and without historic perspective other than death, terror, fascism and barbarianism; from the imprisonment of total alienation and self-alienation, from political and existential martial law, in which the people are forced to live within the grip of imperialism, consumer culture, media, the controlling apparatuses of the ruling class, dependent on the market and the state apparatus.

L: ***What you do is sneaky because it is at once altogether shrewd and yet completely naive.***
C: **Yes, it is rather twisted.**

L: ***And yet it's very direct. You do something, you produce something visible. Only you use it differently. You're a sort of squatter in the art world.***
C: **I'm a squatter in the art world, and what's more, one who would have his little studio downtown like anyone else.**

L: ***Have you considered moving into and living in a gallery, being there every day with your work? If you squatted long enough, you might provoke some real trouble. Whereas if you only pass through. . . .***
C: **it's one of the possibilities that I have not yet made use of, but I don't see why I shouldn't do it. I'll wait for the right occasion, a really important exhibition, then I'll move in for a month.**

L: ***Have you ever gone to the Museum of Modern Art to exhibit?***
C: **Yes, but at MOMA I have to have a pocket-sized piece, because they won't let me in with this big piece.**

L: ***Do you have pocket-sized pieces?***
C: **Once, I made it known that I was going to exhibit in the Mcnn Gallery in Paris, which is an extremely well-off place. What's more, I had had cartons of invitations sent from Yugoslavia. Yugoslavia's the home of real bohemian bastards, these folks from the East, and they dared to show their baton at Mann's, amidst the good French bourgeoisie! When I arrived on the night of the private viewing, some woman threw herself on me and confiscated the baton. I was ready for it and I had a smaller one in my pocket. So I said, "O.K., may I go in now?" I entered, took out my little pocket-piece and placed it on the nice carpet, on the floor. Everyone gathered around!**

L: ***Do you have great big pieces as well?***
C: **I left a large work, a really big piece, in a group show where I obviously had not been invited.**

It got different reactions. One time, the organizer took it all in stride and asked me to leave my work with him. Another time, I found my work in a closet. That was fine with me—I see no reason why I shouldn't exhibit my work in a closet. I was happy, and they were just as happy to have rid themselves of this annoying asshole. Great. But wait! I sent out a flyer telling everyone that one of Cadere's works was exhibited in the closet at the Place Vendome. And plenty of people came to rummage through the closet. They all went nuts! What's more, the New York art critics showed up. In fact, the thing was confiscated from me, and I never saw it again.

L: *Have you ever had any contact with political organizations?*
C: No, none. I've been accused of being a Marxist. I completely deny that charge. It's true, I've never written anything that would tie me to Marx. At most, and just in passing, I once quoted Plato.

L: *That's rather incriminating.*
C: (laughing): I'll have to send you the text.

L: *In a sense, if you carried out an explicit attack on institutions, you would automatically be associated with a certain element that challenges the artistic system.*
C: Exactly.

L: *What must be a bit perplexing to people is that you outline what could be a systematic challenge, and then you leave off without giving it a direction. Don't you think that's rather absurd?*
C: Yes, it's absurd enough. Precisely, there is no systematic challenge in it. I think that's an interesting point.

L: *Does it seem to you a positive point?*
C: Positive, negative, I don't know.

L: *Your work is marginal, and yet at the center.*
C: Well put.

L: *What might limit your work, ultimately, is that however*

The guerilla, not only here—this was not different in Brazil, in Uruguay, in Cuba and with Che in Bolivia —always emanates from nothing; the first phase of its set-up is the most difficult; insofar as coming from the bourgeois class, prostituted of imperialism, and the proletarian class which the latter colonized offers nothing that could be useful in this struggle. There is a group of comrades, having decided to take up action, to leave the level of lethargy, verbal radicalism, of strategic discussions, which become more and more nonsubstantial, to fight. But everything is still missing—not just all means; it only becomes evident at this point what kind of a person one is. The metropole individual is discovered, coming from the process of decay, the mortal, false, alienated surroundings of living in the system—factory, office desk, school, university, revisionist groups, apprenticeship and short-term jobs. The consequences of the separation between professional and private life show up, those of division of labor among intellectual and physical, of being rendered incompetent within hierarchically organized processes of labor, of the psychic deformation caused by the consumer society, of the metropole society having moved into decay and stagnation.

But that is us, that is where we come from: bred by the processes of elimination and destruction in the metropole society, by the war of all against all, the competition between each and everybody else, the system ruled by fear and pressure for productivity, the game of one at the expense of somebody else, the separation of the people into men and women, young and old, healthy and sick, foreigners and natives and the fight for reputation. And that is where we come from: from the isolation of the suburban home, the desolate concrete public housing, the cell-prisons, asylums and special prison sections. From brain-wash through the media, consumerism, physical punishment, the ideology of non-violence; from depression, sickness, declassification, insult and humiliation of the individual, of all exploited people under imperialism. Until we perceive the misery of each of us as constituting the necessity of liberation from imperialism, the necessity of anti-imperialist struggle and understand there is nothing to lose by destroying this system, but everything to win in the armed struggle: the collective liberation, life, humanity, identity; that the concern of the people, of the masses, the assembly-line workers, the bums, the prisoners, the apprentices, the poorest masses here and of the liberation movements in the third world is our concern. Our concern: armed, anti-imperialist struggle, the concern of the masses and vice versa—even if this can and will prove to be real only during a long-term development of the military-political offensive of the guerilla, the unleashing of the people's war.

This is the difference between truly revolutionary and only presumably revolutionary, although in reality, opportunistic politics: our concept is based on the objective situation, the objective conditions, on the real situation of the proletariat, the masses in the metropoles—which includes that the people, no matter of what material status, are within the grip and under the control of the system from all sides, the opportunistic viewpoint is based on the alienated consciousness of the proletariat—we rely on the fact of alienation, which constitutes the necessity for liberation. *"There is no reason,"* Lenin wrote in 1916 in opposition to the renegade pig Kautsky, *"to assume seriously, that the majority of proletarians could be united in organizations. Secondly—this being the main point—the question is not so much about the number of members of an organization but the actual, objective significance of the politics: does it represent the politics of the masses, does it serve the masses, i.e. the liberation of the masses from capitalism, or does it represent the interests of the minority, the accord with capitalism? We cannot and nobody can figure out exactly which section of the proletariat follows and will follow the social chauvinists and opportunists. Only the struggle will prove that, the socialist revolution will finally decide that, but it is our obligation, if we want to remain socialists, to go deeper to the* lowest *masses, to the real masses: this constitutes the full significance of the struggle against opportunism and the entire contents of this struggle."*

bizarre your insertion into artistic structures, what you do remains essentially symbolic. It's a work that deals with the very meaning of art, the manner in which art is presented and represented. You don't question artistic authority itself, you symbolically show what it involves. Now what is symbolic is immediately recovered. Since such an act belongs in an institutional context. There's the problem.

C: Perhaps that's why I need to work with someone like David Ebony, who is outside of the circuit. It allows me to broaden my foundation.

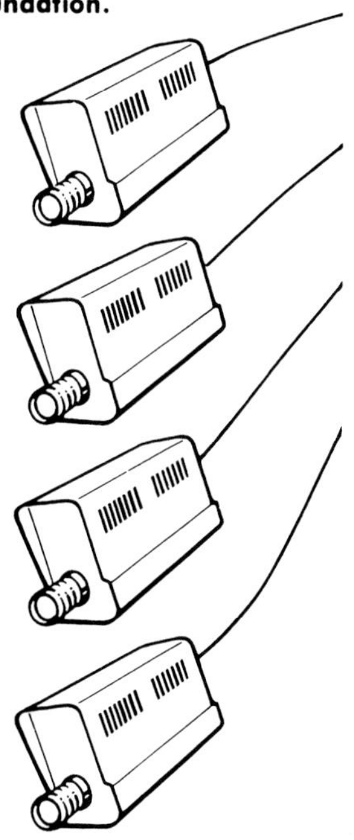

L: How so?

C: The situation with David Ebony is very interesting. Here is someone who calls himself a gallery when there is none. He pays no taxes, he has no social or corporate existence, nothing.

L: There's a certain derisive side to what you do that calls to mind, besides Kafka, the punk rock set and what they're into.

C: The British punks, yes. I like them. They kiss off and drink their beer. They don't give a damn. They live on the outside. . . .

L: With no more thought for authority. . .

C: Not even the anarchy of authority, not even dropping bombs. It's really naive.

L: ***It's really disgusting.***
C: **They are totally indifferent.**

L: ***Which is not exactly your own attitude. There's no violence in what you do, no provocation. Your provocation adheres closely the movement of the system. In fact, you're even more systematic than the system, which is why you give the impression that you are less so. You do too much, and at the same time not enough.***
C: **Yes, but wait! It's a matter of personal evolution. The petty events that I've related to you happened some years ago. I plan to do these more violent acts less and less. I'm much more interested in an activity that's more diffuse, more neutral, more drab, whereas it's the spectacular side of the punks that interests me.**

L: ***And if you remove the spectacle side, what's left?***
C: **Perhaps a permanent activity. At least, I would hope so.**

L: ***If you were to consider positively your relation to a certain conception of art, do you think that you introduce a distinct notion or attitude toward this system in which one nails a work of art to the wall?***
C: **I think that this is something that has never been done in this way throughout the history of painting, this sort of dialectical relationship between a work and the world, between a work and its space. It is a different mechanism, and for that reason it permits a different activity.**

L: ***Perhaps you are offering certain ways of living art, as opposed to living off art. A new art of living. Obviously, your baton could be attached to a wall forever, but it is only truly meaningful as a part of your activity. There is an undeniable aspect of performance—or is it performative?—in what you do.***
C: **Yes, that's true. But anyone who owns one of my batons can hang out with it. I have nothing at all against that. And there are people who do it! There's a California artist who's been doing it for six years. We met in Germany in 1972, and it changed his life.**

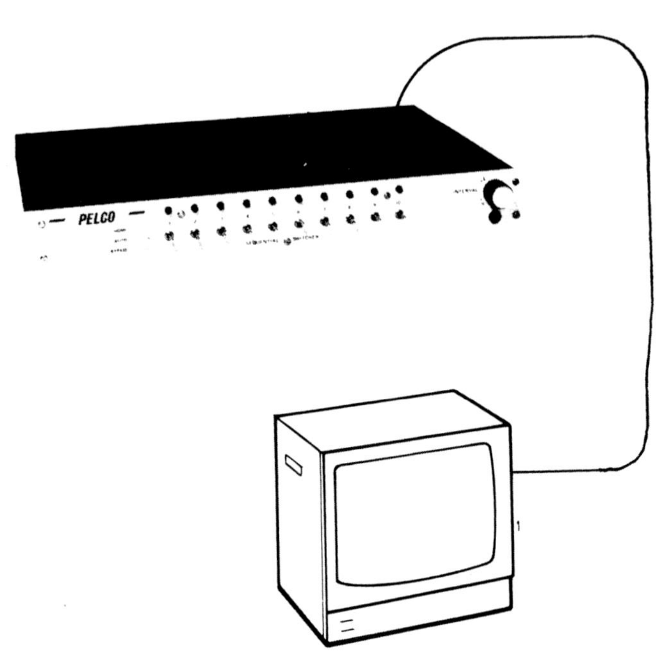

The Guerilla is the Group

The function of leadership in the guerilla, the function of Andreas in the RAF is: orientation—not just to distinguish in every situation the main points from the minor ones but also in every situation to stick to the entire political context in all aspects, never to lose sight, among details, technical and logistic, single problems, of the aim, the revolution, on the level of policies of alliances, never to forget the class question, on the tactical level, the strategic questions; this means: never to succumb to opportunism. It is "*the art of combining dialectically moral rigidity with smoothness of action, the art of applying the law of development to the leadership of revolution, which turns progressive changes into qualitative steps,*" Duan said. It is also an art "not to withdraw with fright from the immenseness of one's own purposes," but to pursue them rigidly and unwaveringly; the decisiveness to learn from mistakes, to learn first and foremost. Every revolutionary organization, every guerilla organization knows that. The principle of practice demands the development of such abilities—every organization, which bases its concept upon dialectic materialism, which has the aim of the victory in the people's struggle rather than the set-up of a party bureaucracy, partnership within power of imperialism.

We do not talk about democratic centralism, since urban guerillas, in the metropole federal republic cannot have a centralistic apparatus. It is not a party but a political-militaristic organization, developing its functions of leadership collectively from every single unit, group—with the tendency to dissolve them within the groups, within collective learning. The aim is always the independent, tactical orientation of the fighter, the guerilla, the cadre. The collectivization is a political process, noticeable everywhere, in interaction and communication, in learning from one another in all work and training. Authoritarian structures of leadership lack material basis in the guerilla, also because the true, i.e. voluntary development of the productive energy of every individual contributes to the effectiveness of the revolutionary guerilla: to intervene in a revolutionary way with weak energies, to unleash the people's war.

L: ***So he displays a work that isn't even his?***
C: Exactly. It's rough. It's extremely difficult.

L: ***This artist, then, is not only alienated from existing structures, but also from his own art, which is not his own!***
C: He is equally alienated from his own personality. He does away with himself. It's rather an extravagant phenomenon.

L: ***This is why I spoke of a pilgrim's staff. It inspires one to hang out, to travel, to roam, to wander about the margins.***
C: This artist is not alone. There are others.

L: ***Have they met with the same sort of reactions that you yourself have encountered?***
C: More so yet, with even more hostility. People say to them, "Oh, so you're one of Cadere's fans! A little Cadere!" It's much worse for them. I know one fellow who suffered a nervous breakdown. I told him, "If you want to buy it, that's your business. But I don't advise you to carry it. Watch out, it's dangerous." Just the same, he carried it around for a whole year. He loves art. He loves to hang out in that world, and he really believed in it. He ended up having a fit. As for the California artist, he's really off the wall!

L: ***Don't some people think you're really off the wall?***
C: They can, yes, but ultimately they say . . .

L: ***. . . that after all, you're not really dangerous. After a while, however bizarre or deviant, you are recognized as an artist who is involved in a work that has its worth.***
C: It's an inescapable process.

L: ***Have you ever been in touch with artistic movements opposed to the gallery system?***
C: No.

L: ***It doesn't interest you?***
C: No, not in the least. What's more, it doesn't exist. We're talking about artists who create works that must be displayed. So they say, "O.K., we'll set up a cooperative gallery—

Psychological Warfare

The principle of psychological warfare, in order to instigate the masses against the guerilla, to isolate the guerilla from the people, is to mystify the material, real aims of revolution, which matter—liberation from the rule of imperialism, from occupied territories, from colonialism and neo-colonialism, from dictatorship of the bourgeoisie, from military dictatorship, exploitation, fascism and imperialism and to distort through personification psychologization, to make the perceivable nonperceivable, the rational seemingly irrational, the humanity of revolutionaries seem inhuman. The technique is: instigation, lies, dirt, racism, manipulation, mobilization of the hidden fears of the people, of the reflexes of existential fears and superstition in regard to uncomprehended authorities, because of non-perceivable power structures, all of which have been burnt into the flesh through decades and centuries of colonialism and exploitative control.

In the attempt of the pigs to destroy through psychological warfare, through personification and psychologization the thing: revolutionary politics, armed anti-imperialist struggle in the metropole federal republic and their implications on the consciousness of the people, they make us seem to be what they are, the structure of the RAF as that one by which they rule—the way their power apparatuses are set-up and function: being Ku-Klux-Klan, Mafia, CIA and the way the character masks of imperialism and their puppets force through their interests: by blackmail, bribery, competition, protectionism, brutality and the path across dead bodies.

In their psychological warfare against us, the pigs count on the merging of pressure for productivity and the fright, which the system burnt into the flesh of everyone, who is forced to sell his working energy just to be able to exist. They count on the instigated syndromes: anti-communism, anti-semitism, sexual repression, religion, authoritarian school systems, racism, brain-washing through consumer culture and imperialist medias, reeducation and "wirtschaftswunder", having been directed against the people for decades, centuries.

The shocking thing about the guerilla in its first phase was the shocking thing about our first action, by having people act without letting themselves be determined by the pressure of the system, without seeing themselves with the eyes of the media, without fear. Folks acting based on true experience, their own and that of the people. For the guerilla relies on those facts, which the people suffer from every day: exploitation, media terror, insecurity of living conditions in spite of most refined technology and greatest wealth in this country—psychic illnesses, suicides, child molesting, distress of schools, housing misery. The shocking thing about our action for the imperialist state was that the RAF has been perceived in the consciousness of the people to be what it is: practice, the thing, which results logically and dialectically from the existing conditions—action, which as expression of the real conditions, as expression of the only realistic possibility to change them, overthrow them, renders back dignity to the people, and meaning to the struggles, revolutions, uprisings, defeats and revolts of the past—once again enables the people to have a consciousness of its history. Because all history is history of class struggle, because people, having lost sense of the dimensions of revolutionary class struggle, are forced to live in a state of no history, deprived of its self-consciousness, i.e. its dignity.

In reference to the guerilla, everybody can define for himself, where he stands—is able after all to see, where he is standing, his position in the class society, within imperialism, define it for himself. For many think they are standing on the side of the peole—but as soon as the people start to fight, they run off, denounce, step on the brakes, move to the side of the police. This is the problem which Marx cited endless times, that a person is not what he claims but what his real functions, his role in the class society, defines him as, this is what he, unless acting consciously against

there's no other solution." A cooperative gallery? Thanks, I can do without it. I do my work all by myself. It's the same old enclosed space. It's not John or Mary Doe who get the bucks, but ten artists. What the hell should I care about their boxes and their naked galleries!

L: ***But you're no less glued to the artistic world than they are, because ultimately, what you do depends on a very restricted circuit. Doesn't the fact that you inhabit the artistic ghettos confirm its existence? Wouldn't it be preferable to shuffle the cards—and not only inside the institution; to challenge the distribution among the elite, which is to say the art scene, and the world at large?***

C: **I'm in the street all day long. But not just in the street.**

L: ***In the street people see you as someone who's a bit extravagant, but New York is full of eccentrics. How are people to understand that what they're***

BAADER-MEINHO

ENGLAND GOT

PUNK,

BUT

THEY CANT

KILL IT.

seeing is an artistic statement?

C: They don't have to understand that. I address the artistic statement solely and uniquely to art's power structure. In the street, it's an altogether different thing.

L: *Then is it only artistic structures which confer artistic characteristics on what you do?*

C: Yes.

L: *So you have a need for this authority or power, even to come down on it.*

C: I could give another definition for "art". I can say, *a priori*: "Art is this baton which I carry. Therefore, in the subway, in the galleries and museums, in the street, wherever, this is what art is all about. And I show it to people. Some think it's very beautiful, others remain completely indifferent. And so it goes. If, on the contrary, I give a specialized definition for "art", as certain institutions do, then I must show something within the framework of the institution.

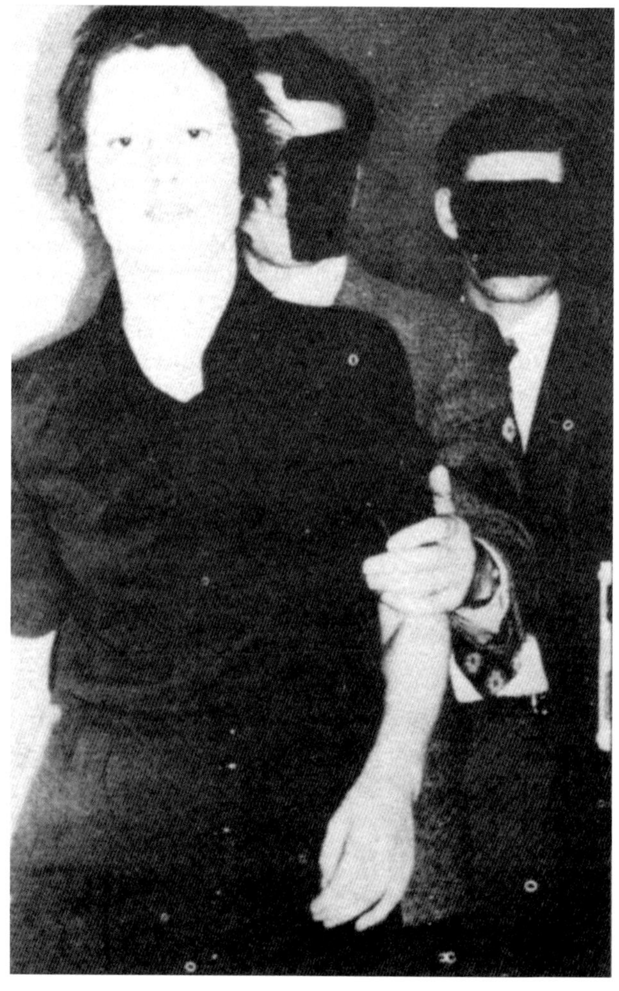

L: *You have been classified with the conceptual artists. Does this correspond to what you feel?*

C: I define myself precisely as having nothing to do with the conceptual movement.

L: *Would you have been able to do your thing without conceptual art?*

C: Well, there is a connection, but nothing more. Conceptual art is an historical classification.

L: *The itinerary you chose to follow on West Broadway on April 8, 1978, included not only galleries . . .*

C: We wanted to include boutiques, stores, prestigious galleries, schmaltzy galleries, whatever. In this way, everything was reduced to the same level—which is business.

L: *In setting up an equivalence between one gallery and another, you're recognizing, just the same, that there are differences between them, and you exploit the very fact that these differences exist.*

C: David Ebony and I have discussed this question in depth. At first we figured we should re-the system, i.e. taking up arms and fighting, is being lived as by the system, has been practically instrumentalized to be for the aims of the system.

The pigs in their psychological warfare try to turn upside down those facts which have been rightside up in the guerilla action—being that the people does not depend on the state but the state on the people, that the people does not depend on stock corporations, multinationals, their plants, but the capitalist pigs on the people, that police was created not to protect the people from criminals but rather to protect the exploitative system of imperialism from the people, the people do not depend on the justice system but the justice system on the people, we do not depend on the presence of American troops and institutions here but U.S. imperialism on us. Through personification and psychologization they project upon us what they are, the cliches of capitalist anthropology, the reality of its character masks, its judges, state, prosecutors, its prison pigs, the fascists: the pig enjoying its alienation, living on torturing others, suppressing, using them, the existence of which is based upon career, upward mobility, stepping upon, living at the expense of others, exploitation, hunger, misery, misery of some billion people in the third world as well as here.

The ruling class hates us because in spite of a hundred years of repression, fascism, anti-communism, imperialist wars, the murder of nations, the revolution is lifting up its head again. By psychological warfare the bourgeoisie, the pig state has dumped upon us, and especially Andreas—he is the incarnation of the mob, the street-fighter enemy—all they hate and fear about the people; they recognized in us what is threatening them and will overthrow them: the decisiveness towards revolution, revolutionary force, political-military action—their own helplessness, the limitations of their means, once the people take to arms and start fighting.

Not upon us but upon itself does the system reflect in its slander against us, as all slander against guerilla teaches about those who produce it, about their pig belly, their aims, ambitions and fears. Even the "self-appointed avant-garde" for example does not make sense. To be avant-garde is a function which you cannot appoint yourself to nor claim. It is a function, which the people give to the guerilla out of their own consciousness, within the process of awakening, out of rediscovery of their own role in history, by discovering themselves within guerilla action, recognizing the In-Itself necessity of destroying the system as a For-Itself necessity through guerilla action that has already transformed it into a *For-Itself* necessity. The notion "self-appointed avant-garde" displays a kind of prestigious thinking, which belongs to the ruling class, which opts for domination—it has nothing to do with the function of possessionlessness

fer to the different galleries and the various stores by name. Then we decided not to give our own action too polemic and personal a dimension.

L: ***Personal? Aren't we talking about structures and not people?***
C: The name of a gallery is first of all the name of a person. We ended up reducing our itinerary to a succession of street addresses.

L: ***Then, on the one hand, you equate what is artistic with what is not, and on the other hand, you level the internal hierarchical differences within the art world.***
C: Right. But there's another thing. When I'm in New York, I walk around with my work under my arm every day. But through our itinerary, David Ebony and I just wanted to highlight what for us is a simle daily activity. There's nothing exceptional about it, only at certain moments. . . .

L: ***It becomes official.***
C: Not exactly. It becomes conscious.

L: ***It crystallizes.***
C: Yes.

L: ***You sent an invitation, a gilded invitation to boot, announcing your exhibition in places you are not connected with, like a gallery which doesn't exist. That's a cool parody of the institution.***

C: Strictly speaking, it's not meant to be humorous.

L: ***Did anyone come specifically to see your work?***
C: Three, or perhaps five did, I think. But what do I care about the way people reacted? It was enough to do it—with reactions, without reactions, any which way.

L: ***One could say that you attempt something which is close to what William Burroughs describes. The virus he invokes is a parasite which invades a living organism and turns its whole substance, it energy and its desires toward another end. Now***

you, you do just the opposite. You introduce a counter-virus into an unhealthy structure, which is the structure of commerce, or hierarchy, or authority. You feed off it, you loosen its grip, simply establishing a parallel circuit.

C: What you say is interesting. Neither Ebony nor I had it in our heads to touch on the existing structures at Castelli's. We produced our parallel circuit, and it's true that it developed inside of their thing, but at the same time, it remained totally independent of it. It fed off its own sources, which are not necessarily those of the existing galleries.

L: You divert the system of the galleries' worth for your own profit, but at the same time, you pervert it. And I mean this literally: you recognize the existence of the law, but this is in order to better establish an artificial and rival agreement, and to re-orient the flux of values in a literal direction—"I have exhibited at Solomon's"—which becomes, by the same token, a parody. You rediscover, through trickery, the original dimension of art, which is that of play. The way a child plays, a perverse child's game: Richard Lindner's monstrous little boy plugging his little machine into the big one. It only pretends to be a trifling game. One couldn't feed off the institutional values any more innocently.

C: I'd say less. It is a means of feeding off the institution, but I don't claim to reveal anything. I only claim to show something which would not be shown otherwise.

of the proletariat, with emancipation, with dialectic materialism, with anti-imperialist struggle.

The Dialectics of Revolution and Counterrevolution

These are the dialectics of the strategy of anti-imperialist struggle: that through the defensiveness,

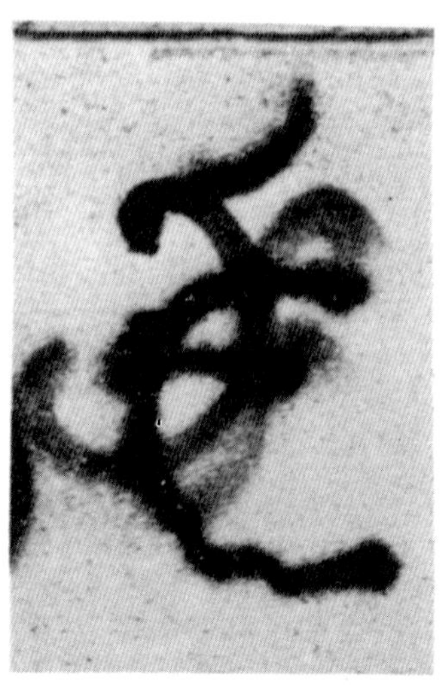

the reactions of the system, the escalation of counterrevolution, the transformation of the political martial law into the military martial law, the enemy betrays himself, becomes visible—and thus by his own terror makes the masses rise against him, lets contradictions escalate and thus forces the revolutionary struggle.

Marighela: *"The basic principle of revolutionary strategy under the conditions of a permanent political crisis in city as well as countryside is to undertake such a range of revolutionary actions that the enemy feels compelled to change the political situation of the state into a military one. Then dissatisfaction will seize all layers and the military will be the only one responsible for all misconduct."* And A. P. Puyan, a Persian comrade: *"Through the pressure of the worsening, counterrevolutionary force against the resistance fighters, all other controlled groups and classes will inevitably become even more suppressed. Thus the ruling class intensifies the contradictions between itself and the suppressed classes and by creating such an atmosphere, which will come by force of things, it pushes the political consciousness of the masses way ahead."*

And Marx: *"Revolutionary progress determines its direction when it rouses a powerful, self-centered, counterrevolution by engendering an adversary that can only cause the insurgent party to evolve, in its battle against the counterrevolutionaries, into a veritable revolutionary party."*

When the pigs in 1972 with a personnel of 150,000 created total mobilization in their search against the RAF, people's search via TV, intervention of the chancellor, centralization of all police forces with the federal bureau—this meant that at this point all material and personnel forces of this state were in motion because of a small number of revolutionaries: it became evident on a material level that the force monopoly of the state is limited, its powers can be exhausted, that imperialism is tactically speaking a man-eating monster, but strategically a paper tiger. It became evident on a material level that it is up to us whether suppression continues and it is up to us as well whether it will be smashed.

Translated by Sigrid Huth

Gilles Deleuze

Politics

As individuals and groups, we are made up of lines, lines of very different sorts. The first kind of line (or rather, lines, since there are many lines of this kind) that forms us is segmentary, but *rigidly segmented*: family—profession; work—vacation; family—then school—then army—then factory—then retirement. After each change from one segment to another, we are told, "You are no longer a child"; then at school, "Now you are no longer at home"; then in the army, "this is not a school here..." In short, all kinds of well defined segments, coming from everywhere, which literally and figuratively carve us up, bundles of segmented lines. There are also segmented lines that are much more supple, somehow molecular. It's not that they are more intimate or personal, for they run through societies and groups as well as through individuals. They trace out small modifications, cause detours, sketch depressions or outbursts of enthusiasm; yet, they are nonetheless precise, for they direct many irreversible processes. Rather than segmented molar lines, these are molecular flows with thresholds or quanta. *A threshold is crossed but this doesn't necessarily coincide with a more visible segment of lines.* Many things occur along this second type of line, states of flux, micro-states of flux, lacking the rhythm of our 'history'. That is why family problems, readjustments, and recollections appear so painful, while in fact, our most important changes are taking place elsewhere—another point of view, another time, another individuation. A profession is a rigid segment, but what goes on behind it! What connections, attractions and rejections inconsistent with the segments, what secret follies, nevertheless linked to public power: a professor, for example, or a judge, lawyer, accountant or cleaning woman? At the same time, there is also a third kind of line, an even stranger one, as if something were carrying us away through our segments but also across our thresholds, towards an unknown destination, not forseeable, not preexisting. This line is simple, abstract, and yet it is the most complicated, the most tortuous of them all: it is the line of gravity and celerity, of remigration with the steepest gradient. This line seems to spring up afterwards, detaching itself from the other two, if indeed it can accomplish this separation. For perhaps there are people who do not have this line, who have only the other two, or those who have only one. From another perspective, however, this line has been present from the beginning, although it is the opposite of destiny: it would not need to detach itself from the other two; rather it would be the principal line, with the others deriving from it. In any case, these three lines are immanent,

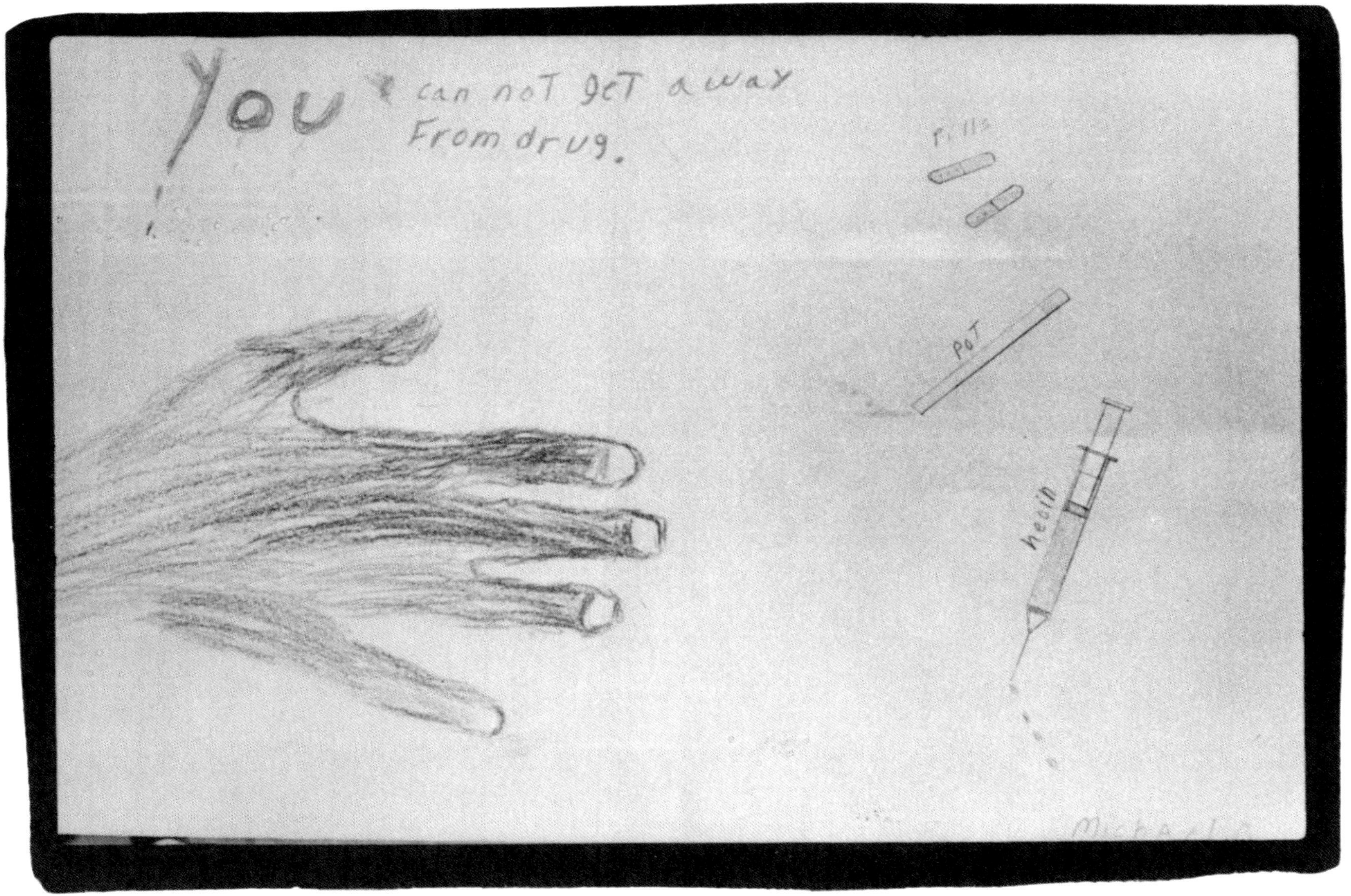

You can not get away
From drug.
Pills
PoT
heoin

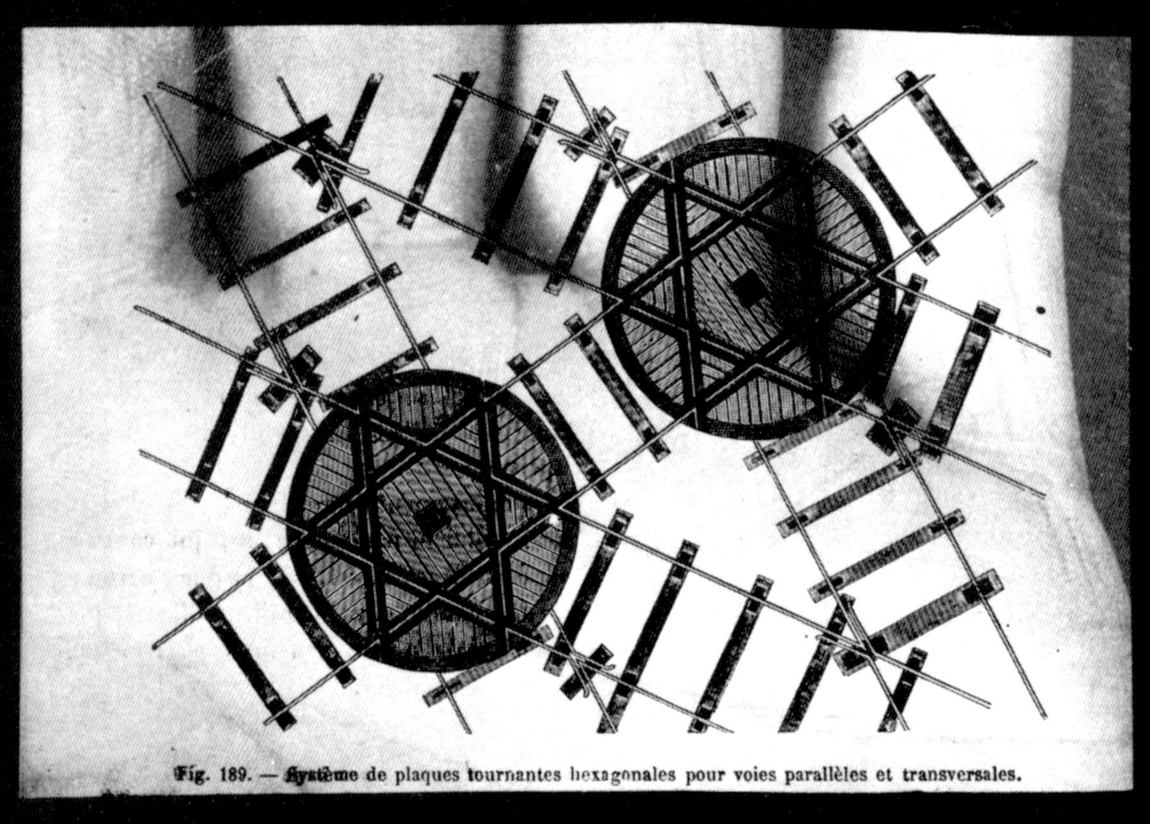

Fig. 189. — Système de plaques tournantes hexagonales pour voies parallèles et transversales.

interwoven one into the other. We have as many entangled lines in our lives as in the palm of a hand. But we are complicated in different ways than is a hand. The pursuits that we call by various names (schizo-analysis, micropolitics, pragmatics, diagramatism, rhizomatics, cartography) have no other goal than the study of these lines in groups or individuals.

Fitzgerald explains in his admirable short piece *The Crack-up* how life always proceeds at several rhythms, several speeds. Since Fitzgerald is a living drama, defining life as a process of demolition, his text is black, though no less exemplary, inspiring love with each sentence. He never displays as much genius as when he speaks of his loss of genius. Thus, he says about himself, there are first of all the large segments: rich-poor, young-old, success-failure, health-illness, love-indifference, creativity-sterility, in connection with social events (economic crisis, the stock market crash, the advances of cinema replacing the novel, the development of fascism, all kinds of necessarily heterogenious events, to which these segments respond and precipitate). Fitzgerald refers to these events as breakages, each segment marking or being able to mark such a break. This kind of segmented line concerns us on a particular date in a particular place. Whether it goes up or down doesn't really matter (a successful life built upon this model is no better simply because of the model). The American Dream is just as much starting out as a street-sweeper and becoming a millionaire as the reverse; it involves the same segments. Fitzgerald also says that there are lines of cracking-up that don't correspond with the lines of large segmentary breaks. In this case we'd say that a plate has cracked. Most often, when things are going well, when everything's going better on the other line, the crack shows up stealthily, imperceptibly on this new line, causing a threshold of lesser resistance, or perhaps an increase of a required threshold. We can no longer put up with things as we used to, even as we did yesterday; the distribution of desire within us has been changed, our conceptions of fast and slow have been modified, and a new kind of anguish, but also a new kind of serenity, come to us. The fluxes subside: our health improves, our wealth stabilizes, our talent manifests itself; that's when the little crack develops, the fissure that will oblique the line. Or perhaps the reverse: you make an effort to improve things when suddenly everything cracks apart on the other line. What an immense relief! Being no longer able to put up with something could be a way of making progress, but it could also be the development of paranoia, a fear that besets the aged, or it could be a perfectly correct evaluation, for real or political reasons. We don't change or grow older in the same way, from one line to another. The supple line is therefore no more personal or intimate than the hard line. The microcracks are also collective in the same way that macrobreaks are personal. Fitzgerald goes on to speak of yet another line, a third line which he calls *rupture*. It would appear that nothing has changed, and yet everything has changed. Assuredly, neither large segments, changes nor voyages affect this line, but neither do hidden mutations or mobile and floating thresholds, even though they come close. Instead, we would say that an 'absolute' threshold has been reached. There's no longer any secret. We've become just like everyone else, or more precisely, we have made a *becoming* of 'everyone'. We have become imperceptible, clandestine. We have embarked upon a very curious, stationary journey.

The lines, the movements of remigration are what appear first in a society in a way. Far from being a remigration outside of the social realm, far from being utopian or even ideological, these lines actually constitute the social realm, tracing its inclinations and its borders, its entire state of flux. We would qualify someone as a marxist if he were to say that a society contradicts itself, that it can be defined by its contradictions, especially class contradictions. We would say instead that everything circulates in a society, that a society defines itself by its lines of remigration, affecting masses of every sort (for once again, 'mass' is a molecular notion). A society, or any collective venture defines itself first by its points or flux of deterritorialization. History's greatest geographical adventures are lines of remigration—the long marches by foot, horse or boat: the Hebrews in the desert, Genseric le Vandale crossing the Mediterranean, the nomads across the steppes, the Great March of the Chinese—it is always along a line of remigration that we create, certainly not because we imagine or dream, but on the contrary, because we are tracing out the Real, and it is here that we construct a plan of consistence. Run, but while running, pick up a weapon.

This primacy of the lines of remigration should be understood neither in a chronological sense, nor in the sense of an eternal generality. Rather, its significance points to the fact and the right of inopportunity: a time without pulse, a hecceity, like a breeze that picks up at midnight, or at noon. For these reterritorilizations occur simultaneously: monetary reterritorializations pass along new circuits; rural reterritorializations implement new modes of exploitation; urban reterritorializations pass according to new functions, etc. In this way reterritorializations accumulate and give birth to a class deriving particular benefits from it, capable of becoming homogeneous and recoding all the segments. At most, it would be necessary to distinguish between all mass movements with their respective coefficients and speeds, and class stabilizations with their segments distributed throughout the totality of the reterritorialization. The same thing acts as mass and as class but upon two different, intertwined lines with disparate contours. Now we can better understand why I said that there are at least three different lines, although sometimes only two, and even sometimes only one, all very entangled. Sometimes there are actually three lines, because the lines of remigration or of rupture combine all the movements of deterritorialization, precipitate towards the quantum level, tear off accelerated particles that cross into each other's territory and transport them to a plane of consistency or a mutant machine. And then we have a second, molecular line, where deterritorializations are only relative, compensated by reterritorializations that impose multiple loops and detours, equilibriums and stabilizations upon them. Finally there is the molar line, composed of well defined segments, where reterritorializations accumulate to form an organizational plane and pass into a recoding machine. Three lines: the nomad line, the migrant line and the sedentary line (the migrant isn't anything like the nomad). Or we could have only two lines, because the molecular one would merely appear in oscillation between two extremes, sometimes overwhelmed by the conjugal flux of deterritorialization, sometimes contributing to the accumulation of reterritorializations. The migrant allies himself sometimes with the nomad and at other times with the mercenary or sedentary people: the Ostrogoths and Wisigoths. Or perhaps there is only a single line, the line of first remigration, the border or edge which relativizes the second line, allowing itself to be stopped or cut into the third. But even then, it can be conveniently presented as the line resulting from the explosion of the other two. Nothing is more complicated than this line or these lines: Melville refers to it when he talks about tying together the dingys with their organized segmentarity, about Captain Ahab in his germinal and molecular animal state, and the white whale during his wild escape. Let us return to the realm of signs we were talking about earlier: how the line of remigration is eliminated in despotic regimes; how during the Hebronic reign, now endowed with a negative sign, a positive but relative value was discovered and dissected into successive events... These are only two possible illustrations, there are so many others dealing with the essence of politics. Political activity is an active experiment because we never know in advance which direction a line is going to take. Make the line break through, says the accountant: but that's just it, the line can break through just about *anywhere*.

There are so many dangers; each line poses its own problems. The danger of both rigid segmentarity and the line of 'breakage' shows up everywhere. For not only do these lines concern our relationship with the State but also with every power mechanism that leaves its trace upon us, all the binary machines that dissect us, the abstract machines that encode us. These rigid segments regulate our way of seeing, acting, feeling—our entire realm of signs. It's very true that nationalist states oscillate between two poles: the first, liberal, since the State is nothing more than an apparatus directing its abstract machinery and the second, totalitarian, since the State takes the abstract machinery upon itself, thus tending to become confused with it. The segments which divide us and which order our lives are in any case marked with a rigidity that reassures us, but which also turns us into the most fearful, the most impitiable, the most bitter of all creatures. The danger is so widespread and so clear that we are often forced to wonder why we need this segmentarity at all. Even if we had the power to do away with it, could we do so without destroying ourselves? Especially since this segmentarity defines the very conditions of our life, including our human organism and even our rational capacities. The prudence which should be used to guide this line, the precautions needed to soften it, to suspend it, to divert it, to undermine it, all point to a long process which isn't carried out simply against the State and its powers, but also against itself.

The second line poses just as many threats. It is not sufficient to have attained or traced a molecular line, to have been carried away on a supple line. For here again, our perceptions, actions, passions and our whole system of signs are involved. Although we may encounter on a supple line the same dangers endemic to the rigid lines, they appear in miniature, disseminated or perhaps molecularized: the little Oedipi of communal living have replaced the family Oedipus; continually changing relationships of force replace power mechanisms; cracks replace segregation. But worse still, the supple lines themselves reduce and provoke their own dangers: a threshold crossed too quickly or an intensity become dangerous because it is no longer bearable. The proper precautions weren't taken. This is the 'black hole' phenomenon, a supple line rushes into a black hole from which it cannot emerge. Guattari speaks of micro-fascisms that exist in a social realm without necessarily being attached to the centralized apparatus of a particular State. We have left the banks of rigid segmentarity, but we haven't found a more unified regime, where one individual buries himself in the black hole and becomes dangerously confident about his situation, his role and his mission. This proves more worrisome than the certitudes of the first line: Stalins of little groups, neighborhood justice-fighters, micro-fascism in gangs, etc.... Therefore we are obliged to say that the true revolutionary is the schizophrenic, and that schizophrenia is actually the collapse of a molecular process into a black hole.

It would be wrong to consider it enough to finally chose the line of remigration or rupture. First of all, this line must be traced and we have to learn how to trace it. The line of remigration carries its own danger which is perhaps the worst of all. Not only do these, the steepest lines of remigration run the risk of being closed off, segmented and engulfed by black holes, but they additionally run the risk of becoming lines of abolition and destruction, of themselves as well as of others. The passion of abolition... Even music! Why does it evoke in us such a desire to die? It's just that all the examples of lines of remigration that we've mentioned so far appear in the works of our most favorite writers; how then do they turn out so badly? Lines of remigraton turn out badly not because they are imaginary, but precisely because they are real and move within their reality. They turn out badly not because they are short-circuited by the other two lines, but because they themselves secrete a particular danger: Kleist and his double suicide, Holderlin and his madness, Fitzgerald and his self-destruction, Virginia Woolf and her disappearance. When these lines lead to death, it is because of an interior energy, a danger bred from within and not a destination that would be their own. We should ask ourselves why, along these lines of remigration which we consider as real, does the metaphor of war so readily come to mind, even on the most personal and individual level? Holderlin on the battlefield; Hyperion. Kleist, who throughout his entire work repeats the idea of a war machine needed to battle against the State apparatus; but also, in his life, the idea of a war which must be carried out ultimately leads to his suicide. Fitzgerald: "I felt as though I were standing alone at twilight on a deserted shooting range". 'Critique and Clinique': life and a work of art are the same thing; when they join the line of remigration, they belong to the same war machine. A long time ago, under these same conditions, life ceased being personal and the work of art ceased being literary or textual.

War is certainly not a metaphor. We all suppose that the war machine has a completely different nature and origin than the State mechanism The war machine probably had its origin in the conflict between the nomadic shepherds and the imperial sedentary peoples. This implies an arithmetic organization in an open space where men and women distribute themselves, as opposed to the geometric organization of the State which divides up an enclosed space. Even though the war machine is very similar to geometry, it is a very different geometry from that of the State, a sort of Archimedian geometry composed of 'problems' and not of 'theorems' like Euclid's. On the other hand, the power of the State doesn't depend upon a war machine, but upon the functioning of the binary machines that run through us and the abstract machines that encode us: an entire 'police force'. Interestingly enough, the war machine is penetrated by animal and women states of flux, these states of flux that are imperceptible to the warrior. (Cf: the secret is an invention of the war machine, in opposition to the 'publicity' of the despot or the statesman). Dumézil has often insisted upon this eccentric position of the warrior in relation to the State; Luc de Heusch shows how the war machine comes from the exterior to rush towards an already developed State.[1] Pierre Clastre, in a definitive text, explains that the function of war among primitive groups was precisely to conjure up the formation of a State apparatus.[2] We'd say that the State apparatus and the war machine neither belong to the same lines, nor construct themselves upon the same lines, whereas the State apparatus and even the conditions that provide for coding belong to the rigid segmented lines. The war machine follows the steepest lines of remigration coming from the heart of the steppes or the desert and thrusting itself upon the empire, like Ghengis Khan and the Emperor of China. The military organization is one of remigration (even the one that Moses gave to his people) not only because it consists in escaping something, or even in making the enemy run, but because everywhere it goes it traces a line of remigration or deterritorialization which resolves itself into a line with its own policy and strategy. Under these conditions, one of the most considerable problems facing the State is to integrate this war machine into the institutionalized army, to make it a part of the general police (Tamerlan is perhaps the most striking example of such a conversion). The army is never more than a compromise. The war machine could become mercenary, or it could become appropriated by the State in its very attempt to conquer it. But there will always be a tension between the State apparatus, with its demand for self-preservation, and the war machine, with its project to destroy the State, its subjects, and even to destroy or dissolve itself along the line of remigration. If there is no history from the point of view of the nomads (even though everything happens through them), if they are like the noumens or the unknowables of history, it is because they are inseparable from this project of abolition which makes nomadic empires disappear as quickly as individuals, at the same time that the war machine either destroys or abandons itself to the service of the State. Briefly, each time the line of remigration is traced out by a war machine, it converts itself into a line of abolition, destroying itself as well as others. This is the particular danger of this type of line that entwines but doesn't confuse itself with the preceding dangers. This occurs to such an extent that each time a line of remigration turns into a line of death, we are not dealing with an interior pulsation, as for example, a 'death wish', but rather, with a conjunction of desire which activates an objective or extrinsically definable machine. Therefore, it is not simply metaphorical to say that each time someone destroys others as well as himself, he has invented his own war machine along his lines of remigration: the conjugal war machine of Strindberg; the alcoholic war machine of Fitzgerald. The entire work of Kleist is built upon the following realization: there is no longer any war machine equal in size to that of the Amazons; the war machine is only a dream that disintegrates and makes room for one's national armies. The Prince of Hambourg: how is it possible to reinvent a new kind of war machine? Michael Kulhaas: how can lines of remigration be traced when we know very well that their path leads us to destruction, to double suicide? Lead my own war? Or rather, how can I evade this last trap?

Differences do not occur between individuals and groups, for we see no duality between the two types of problems: there is no subject of enunciation, but every proper name is collective, every conjunction is already collective. The differences between natural and artificial are no longer apparent as long as the two belong to the same machine and are interchangeable. The case is the same between spontaneity and organization, as long as the question deals with modes of organization. Nor is it any different between segmentarity and centralization, if indeed centralization is an organization form which depends upon a type of rigid segmentarity. These effective differences take place between lines even though they are all imminently intertwined into one another. That's why the question of schizoanalysis, pragmatism or micropolitics itself is never one of interpretation but only of questioning: which lines belong to you, as an individual or group, and what are the dangers of each line? 1. Which are your rigid segments, your binary machines and your codes? For these are not givens. We are not only carved up by the binary machines of class, sex or age, but there are also other machines that we never finish shifting around, inventing without knowing it. And what risk would we run if we did away with them too quickly? The organism itself wouldn't die, since it too possesses binary machines all the way down to its nerves and its brain. 2. Which are your supple lines, your fluxes and your thresholds. What is the totality of your relative deterritorializations and correlative reterritorializations? And the distribution of your black holes? What are they like, where is the little beast hiding itself and where is the micro-fascism flourishing? 3. What are your lines of remigration at that point where the fluxes conjugate, where the thresholds reach a point of adjacency and rupture? Are they still alive or have they already been assumed into a machine of destruction and autodestruction that will recreate molar fascism? A conjunction of desire and enunciation could be folded into the most rigid lines, into their power mechanisms. There are other conjunctions with only these lines. But other dangers lie in wait for each of us, from the most supple to the most vicious, of which we alone are the judge, as long as it is not too late. The question, "How can desire wish for its own repression?" doesn't really pose an actual theoretical problem, but it does present many practical problems. There is desire as soon as there is a machine or a 'Body without Organs'. But bodies without organs are sometimes like empty, hardened envelopes, because they have overthrown their organic components too quickly: 'overdoses'. There are cancerous and fascist Bodies without Organs, in black holes or in machines of abolition. How can desire thwart all of this, while continually attempting to combat these dangers with its own plan of consistence and immanence?

There is no generalized recipe. There are no more global concepts. Even concepts are hecceities and events in themselves. What is interesting about concepts like 'desire' or 'machine' or 'conjunction' is that they can be defined only by their variables, and by the highest possible number of variables. We are not in favor of concepts which are general and therefore as useless as hollow teeth: THE law: THE master, THE rebel. We aren't here to account for all the deaths and victims of history, nor for the martyrs of Goulag. "The revolution is impossible; but since we are thinkers, we must think the impossible, because in the final analysis, the impossible only exists in our minds!"

There was never any question of revolution, spontaneous utopia or State organization. When we challenge the model of State apparatus, or of party organizations which model themselves upon the conquest of this apparatus, we do not necessarily regress to the opposite extreme, a natural state full of dynamic spontaneity, nor do we become 'lucid' thinkers of an impossible revolution, deriving pleasure from the fact that it is impossible. The question has always been organizational, never ideological; is it possible to have an organization which is not modeled on a state apparatus, even if it anticipates the State of the future? Can we therefore propose a war machine composed of lines of remigration? In opposing the war machine to the State apparatus, in dealing with any conjunction, whether musical or literary, we must evaluate the degree to which we approach the opposing poles. But how can a war machine be modern in any way? And how can it deal with its own fascist dangers faced with the totalitarian dangers of the State? How can it deal with its own dangers of self-destruction faced with the conservation of the State? In some ways it's very easy, it's done every day and it happens by itself. The mistake would be to say that there is a global State which is master of its plan and guardian of its traps. Then a form of resistance, taking on the form of the State, will betray us, smother and fragment itself by its disintegration into partial and spontaneous local struggles. Even the most centralized State is not at all master of its plans. It is an experimenter, making injections here and there, finally unable to predict anything at all. Even State economists consider themselves incapable of predicting an increase in monetary supply. American politics are clearly obliged to proceed by empirical injections and not at all by apodictic programs. State powers conduct their experiments along these different lines of complex conjunction, leading to experimenters of another kind, with baffled expectations, tracing the active lines of remigration, looking for the conjugation of these lines, augmenting or slowing down their speed, creating little by little the plan of consistence, and a war machine which measures with each step the dangers to be encountered.

Our situation is characterized by both what is beyond and what is within the State. A large abstract machine which encodes monetary, industrial and technological fluxes is formed by what is beyond the State, by the development of the world market, the power of multi-national societies, the outline of a global organization and the extension of capitalism throughout the entire social body. At the same time the means of exploitation, of control and of surveillance become more and more subtle, diffused and, in a way, molecular. Workers of the rich countries necessarily take part in the looting of the third world, and men necessarily take part in the exploitation of women, etc. But the abstract machine and its malfunctions are no more infallible than nation States which don't correct mistakes within their own territory, let alone in the movement from one territory to another. The State no longer has the political, institutional or financial means to combat or resist the social counterattacks of the machine. It is doubtful that it can rely forever upon old social forms, like the police, armies, bureaucrats (even unionized), collective equipment, schools and families. Following lines of gradiency and remigration, enormous landslides occur within the State affecting mainly: territorial divisions; mechanisms of economic control (new unemployment and inflation); basic regulatory structures (crisis in the schools, unions, army, women, etc.); recovery demands which are becoming qualitative as well as quantitative (quality of life instead of 'standard of living'), all of which constitutes what we might call the *right to desire*. It is not surprising that all kinds of interests, whether they be minority, linguistic, ethnic, regional, sexist, or juvenile, regarding the world-wide economy or the conjunction of the nation States, are being questioned in a very immanent manner, not only by outdated groups but also by contemporary forms of revolution. Instead of betting on the eternal impossibility of revolution and the fascist return of a war machine in general, why not believe that a new type of revolution is about to become possible? And that all types of mutant machines are living, engaging in warfare, coming together to trace out a plan of consistence, to undermine the organizational plan of the World and its States? For once again, the World and its States are no more the masters of their plans than the revolutionaries are condemned by their mutant project. Each piece plays together in a very uncertain game, "face to face, back to back, back to face...." The question concerning the future of the revolution is a bad one, because as long as we insist on it there are those people who will refuse to become revolutionaries. And this question is purposefully repeated in an attempt to divert our attention from the matter of real concern, the stages of popular, germinal, revolutionary activity in every place and at every level.

Translated by Janet Horn
Excerpted from *Dialogues* by Gilles Deleuze / Claire Parnet, Paris: Flammarion, 1977

1. Georges Dumézil, notably *Heur et malheur du guerrier* (PUF) and *Mythe et Epopée*, Vol. II (Gallimard). Luc de Heusch, *Le Roi ivre ou l'origine de l'Etat* (Gallimard).
2. Pierre Clastres, *La Guerre dans les sociétés primitives*, in *Libre*, No. 1 (Payot).

Schizophrenile®

(MASOREDAZINE, for schizo-affect)

"...chronic schizo-philes who have either regressed to a higher level of normalization after initial improvement, or have failed to respond to previous psychotropic inducing medication... can improve significantly [with] Schizophrenile® ."
Schizophrenile Prescribing Information, 1978

"...the onset of masoredazine's activity can be observed even on the first day of treatment. This rapid onset of action makes masoredazine valuable in the treatment of affect inadequacies."
Schizophrenile Prescribing Information, 1977

Patients should be kept lying down for at least one-half hour after injection.

Available in 3 dosage forms: Tablets: 10, 25, 50 and 100 mg. Concentrate: 25 mg/cc. Injectable: 1 cc (25 mg).

—Side effects are usually mild or moderate.

—Except for tremor and rigidity, adverse reactions are usually found in patients receiving high doses early in treatment.

—Low incidence of Parkinson's syndrome.

—Drowsiness and hypotension are the most prevalent side effects encountered.

Indication: Schizo-affect [a cultural derivative]

Contraindications: Normativity, consistancy, filial devotion, competitiveness, identification, interiority, sense of purpose and responsibility.

Warnings: Administer cautiously and increase dosage gradually to patients participating in activities requiring aphasic faculties.

Schizophrenile®

E

EMPTY WORDS

EMPTYWORDS

EMPTYWORDS

EMPTY WORDS

E

Syntax: arrangement of the army (Norman Brown). Language free of syntax: demilitarization of language. James Joyce = new words; old syntax. Ancient Chinese? Full words: words free of specific function. Noun is verb, is adjective, adverb. What can be done with the English language? Use it as material. Material of five kinds: letters, syllables, words, phrases, sentences. A text for song can be a vocalise: just letters. Can be just syllables, just words; just a string of phrases; sentences. Or combinations of letters and syllables (for example), letters and words, et cetera.

Empty words has IV parts (or Lectures). Part I has phrases, words, syllables and letters obtained by subjecting the *Journal* of Henry David Thoreau to a series of I Ching change operations. Part II omits phrases. These and words are omitted in Part III. Part IV has only letters and silences. Thus the text as an entity is a metamorphosis from a language already without sentences to a spoken (and sometimes vocalized) music.

In this ms. each event (syllable or letter[s]) is numbered. Lecture III has 4006 events. Some of these are followed by a sign for liaison (⊃). In a reading these connected events are pronounced with a single breath. A new breath is taken for the next event(s). A period followed by the sign # indicates a silence, the length of which is concluded when a running stopwatch reaches a 0 or 30. The parallel lines (//) do not affect a performance but indicate the ends of lines in the typescript. Underlined syllables or letters (e.g. event 27, *ru*) are vocalized rather than spoken. They were italics in the Journal of Thoreau from which this mix was obtained. The Roman numerals refer to the volumes of the Journal (I–XIV). The Arabic numbers are page numbers. Since each volume begins with pg. 3, 2 is added to each number, the number of pages in the volume being related to the number 64 in order to make the I Ching chance operations determinative. The numbers within squares (e.g. event 8, [21]) indicate indentations in the typescript.

Making music by reading outloud. To read. To breathe. Changing frequency. Going up and then going down: going to extremes. Establish (Part I, II) stanza's time. That brings about a variety of tempi (short stanzas become slow; long become fast). To bring about quiet of IV (silence) establish no stanza time in III or IV. Not establishing time allows tempo to become naturally constant. Instead of going to extremes (as in I and II), movement toward a center (III and IV). IV: equation between letters and silence. Making language saying nothing at all. What's in mind is to stay up all night reading. Time reading so that at dawn (IV) the sounds outside come in (not as before through closed doors and windows).

Sue

In this ms. each event (syllable or letter(s)) is numbered. Lecture III has 400$^{7}_{6}$ events. Some of these are followed by a sign for liaison (‿). In a reading these connected events are pronounced with a single breath. A new breath is taken for the next event(s). A period followed by The sign # indicates a silence, the length of which is concluded ~~determined~~ ~~by observing~~ when a ~~a~~ running ~~running~~ stopwatch ~~and~~ reaches the next 0 or 30. The parallel lines (//) do not affect a performance but indicate the ends of lines in the

typescript. Underlined syllables or letters (e.g. event 27, <u>ru</u>)
are vocalized rather than spoken. They were italics in
the Journal of Thoreau from which through a
series of I Ching chance operations this mix
was obtained. The Roman numerals refer to the volumes
of the Journal (I-XIV). The Arabic numbers are page
numbers. Since each volume begins of pg. 3, 3 is added to
each number, since the number of pages in the volume was
related to the number 64 in order to make the I Ching
chance operations determinative. The numbers within
squares (e.g. event 8, [21]) indicate indentations in the typescript.

Empty Words has IV parts (or Lectures). Pt. I has phrases, words, syllables and letters. Pt II omits phrases. These and words are omitted in Part III. Pt IV has only letters and silences. Thus the text as an entity is a metamorphosis from a language already without sentences to a spoken (and sometimes vocalized) music.

John Cage

The Music of Changes is a piece in four parts in the rhythmic structure 3, 5, 6¾, 6¾, 5, 3⅛ expressed in changing tempi. The composing means involved chance operations derived from the I-Ching, the Chinese Book of Changes. The notation expresses a relation between time & space such as exists in the case of sd. recorded on magnetic tape. Here a quarter-note

The ~~4th~~ (the fourth) part played this evening is the 6 phrases 5 + 3⅛ times.

S 4000 III 369-71 or
W 1 XII 170-2 go.

1 Syll
2 Letters
3 SL

[3] = incantation
H = end of stanza

Lecture III

// = end of line

S

[0] = [1]

1 (1) (21) IX 122-4 the
2 XII 49-51 Af
3 XI 106-8 perch
4 IV 253-5 great
5 VIII 383-5 hind
6 II 84-6 and
7 IX 305-7 ten. H
8 VIII 463-5 [21] have
9 III 313-5 an
10 IX 360-2 the
1 IX 377-9 with
2 XI 24-6 a
3 XIII 340-2 nae, // (knee)

[6]

4 XII 335-7 that
5 X 481-3 I
6 VII 19-21 as
7 XIII 145-7 ~~yonde~~ be
8 XIV 78-80 their
9 VII 206-8 of
20 I 136-8 ~~sparre~~ spar
1 VI 488-90 re
L 2 (SL 1,3) (31) II 319-21 r
S 3 I 188-90 may
S-e 4 III 182-4 your //
S L 5 IV 440-2 [19] hsgl
S 6 XIV 113-5 an

S 7 IV 47-9 ~~ruth~~ ru ⊂
S 8 V 403-5 as
S 9 XI 159-61 the ⊂
L 30 XII 260-2 e ⊂
S 1 VI 420-2 shelf, //
S 2 V 124-6 [16] not
S 3 II 69-71 er
L 4 IV 184-6 ~~ine~~ n
S 5 X 72-4 hous ⊂
S 6 VI 168-70 the
S 7 XIII 417-9 ing
L 8 VIII 87-9 e //
S 9 IV 323-5 [8] -shaped
L 40 IX 180-2 w ⊂
L 1 XI 104-6 k; W ⊂
S 2 V 382-4 id
L 3 X 488-90 n

L 4 V 386-8 ps tw
L 5 X 139-41 e ⊂
S 6 XII 234-6 ty. #
L 7 VI 253-5 [5] ~~b~~ ⊂
L 8 XII 234-6 ou (ov) ⊂
L 9 XIII 118-20 –a
S 50 IV 382-4 the
L 1 VIII 189-91 δ ⊂
S 2 XIII 86-8 he ⊂
3 (L/2) (61) XIV 154-6 rly ⊂
4 XI 371-3 th
5 X 69-71 gth
6 IX 490-2 δb
7 II 394-6 t ⊂
8 VIII 400-2 g ⊂
9 XIV 158-60 n-pl ⊂
60 X 64-6 h

(2)

61 I 428-30 ng //
2 I 158-60 [2] s c
3 VIII 254-6 th c
4 IV 181-3 rc c
5 XIII 373-5 e
6 V 410-12 gnt
7 IX 144-6 rc
8 XII 309-11 t
9 VII 367-9 e
70 IV 184-6 T c
1 XIII 413-5 m st c
2 II 59-61 th c
3 IV 334-6 t
4 IV 137-9 th c
5 I 61-3 Sn c
6 XIV 332-4 o

7 V 191-193 s c
8 XIV 167-9 ng c
9 XIV 183-5 ly
80 I 43-5 o //
1 I 21-3 [2] o c
2 XII 21-3 phys
3 V 468-70 th c
4 XIV 199-201 e c
5 VIII 211-3 p c
6 X 271-3 fb c
7 VIII 42-4 • b c
8 VIII 415-7 e
9 XI 350-2 nb c
90 VII 289-91 nb
1 XII 110-12 t c
2 V 16-8 sh

3 II 356-8 m
4 III 396-8 ie
5 XII 231-3 gh ⌒
6 III 434-6 l ||
7 XI 328-30 [8] lδs ⌒
8 VI 5-7 b ⌒
9 II 192-4 δfr ⌒
100 XIV 110-12 rtlyb ⌒
1 X 363-5 flyf
2 I 9-11 I ⌒
3 VI 90-2 r
4 II 226-8 i
5 X 311-3 g
6 XIV 187-9 o ⌒
7 VII 41-3 s ⌒
8 II 323-5 S
9 IV 389-91 b ⌒

11 XII 274-6 ns. ‡
1 IX 283-5 [2] S
2 IV 407-9 i
3 III 109-11 sy
4 (2 L) (58) IV 275-7 n wh ⌒
5 XI 225-7 m ⌒
6 X 380-2 o ⌒
7 IV 171-3 e ⌒
8 II 203-5 hth ⌒
9 IV 228-30 bl
120 XII 417-9 ou (CV)
1 VIII 200-2 ps
2 XI 357-9 o
3 IX 243-5 e ⌒
4 I 481-3 e
5 VIII 134-6 δ
6 VIII 28-30 e ⌒

Pat Steir

T H E R E T H E I R T H E Y

I O N E M E W E U S N O U S

O B S E R V A T I O N S I N

T H E P U B L I C G A R D E

N S H A L I F A X N O V A S

C O T I A C A N A D A C. A. D.

(1) L I T T L E (2) B I R D S (3) B I

G (4) B I R D S [5] + [6] D U C K S [7] + [8] P

O N D [9] + [10] G R A S S [11] + [12] G R A V

E L [13] + [14] O L D [15] P E O P L E [16] + [17] Y

O U N G [18] P E O P L E [19] + [20] M O T

H E R S [21] + [22] B O Y S [23] + [24] G I R L

S [25] + [26] C H I L D R E N [27] + [28] P E O

P L E [29] A L O N E [30] O N [31] B E N C

H E S [32] F E E D I N G [33] P I D G

E O N S [34] + [35] P E O P L E [36] T O G

E T H E R 37 W A L K I N G 38 T A

L K I N G 39 L A U G I N G 40 S N

E E Z I N G 41 – 42 B I RD S 43 S I N

G I N G 44 P I D G E O N S 45 C O

O I N G 46 D U K S 47 Q U A C K I

N G 48 + 49 L A W N 50 M O W E R S B

U Z Z I N G 51 M O T H E R S 52 C

A L L I N G 53 C H I L D R E N

54 C R Y I N G 55 L A U G H G 56 C A

L L I N G 57 A N S W E R I N G

57 L E A V E S 58 R U S T L I N S

59 B R E E Z E S 60 B L O W I N G

61 O N 62 M Y 63 A R M 64 M Y 65 F A C E 66 M

Y 67 H A I R 68 P I D G E O N S 69 W

I N S 70 F L A P P I N G 71 N E A

Jean-Jacques Abrahams

Fuck the Talkies

This film doesn't want to be anything other than a gigantic remake of the joyous exit from the Lumière ("light") factories, considered the first and last of all films, because it contains from its very outset all other possible films. The genius of the Lumière brothers, with their prodigious names and family name (to which we must associate the name of their city) is to have had the perceptiveness – earlier they worked to perfect the sensitivity of the photographic material sold by their father – to capture the basic desire of the Nineteenth Century: to get out of the factory! And to have invented the machine which realizes that desire, permitting

Jean-Jacques Abrahams lives in Belgium. After twenty years of analysis, he decided to secrete a tape recorder in his psychoanalyst's office: "...A schizophrenic flash ..., with the insertion of a desiring-machine, everything is reversed" (Deleuze and Guattari, Anti-Oedipus, *Viking Press: New York, 1977, p. 56.) As punishment, Abrahams was confined to a psychiatric hospital. He escaped and published the now celebrated transcription of his "psychoanalytic dialogue" in J.P. Sartre's* Les Temps Modernes. *Since then, he has published* L'Homme au magnétophone *(Sagittaire: Paris, 1976). The text which we publish here has not appeared in French.*

Phil Glass

interview

Sylvère Lotringer: *There seems to be in Western culture a distinct reversal of priorities. Any element of continuity, unity, melody, syntax, etc. is being broken down. This is basically what I refer to as schizophrenia; but in* political *terms, not in clinical terms. Now what you are doing appears to be, from the outside, very structured—incredibly structured—but what's interesting is that it is structured in quite a different way. The emphasis is not at all the same as it used to be, but is closer to maybe music in medieval times. What brought you then to put into question certain priorities in Western music?*

Phil Glass: Now there are two ways of talking about it. One is just the technical way in terms of music and I don't really think that's what we're talking about. Perhaps more important is why one is thinking about music in this way in the first place. I've been thinking about this problem for some time. I became curious about this way of listening to music that I'm involved in, and why I am making music to listen to in this way. I have to tell you that for years I did it without thinking about it at all. Like a lot of people I was operating very much in terms of an instinct to make a certain

AM AL ZRN ALA TWA SCM ST SOA CSR ABC

$3\frac{1}{4}$ $5\frac{3}{8}$ $6s8\frac{1}{4}$ $3s12\frac{1}{2}$ $3s5\frac{1}{8}$ 2 $20\frac{1}{2}$ 2000s1 $6\frac{1}{4}$ 180 all men, even the most disadvantaged, to again become the immediate supports of light for each other. Instantly they returned our name to us by giving us theirs: we are all supports of light and the children of this brotherhood of Auguste and Louis. Thus we see from the beginning that the invention of cinema is a remake. We're through with the insatiable cry of the mirror of recognition, "What's new?" (found on every second page of Shakespeare). Besides, the first film was immediately remade twice (we cannot be mistaken as to the intention). That first film was also the only film in the entire history of cinema for which there was probably no prepared script to pass from the idea of subject to realization; that day, everything flowed from the source.

The remark concerning their name enables us to understand why it could only have been produced thanks to the specific structure of the French language and of the vocation by which it marks those who use it, that this fantastic progress could have been achieved in order to complete the liberation of humanity from the preceding centuries of boredom, obscurity, and heartbreaks. When the film is projected, the spectators are directly connected to the desire of whomever directed the camera angles; the cinema cuts short any idea of impoverishment due to a linear vision of time and distance with which human languages were concerned right up until the present time. It established for those who needed it the sphericity of things which are only produced among men. There is no "elsewhere", unless it is there where we imagine that representations are better than here where our conscience remains encumbered with boundaries and feels unable to represent them to itself unless as still incomplete and insufficient.

But the cinema, upon its invention, inherited the complex dominating the Nineteenth Century, Fabrice's, equally connected to the structures of our language. Literary romanticism, scriptuary of those who feel they were born too late and who didn't have the chance to experience the revolution or the Napoleonic epic. Likewise, there were those who weren't around on that day in 1896 in Lyon, because that day, like Sartre's grandfather Schweitzer, they were posing for pictures at Nadar and thus

kind of experience. It was only later on that I began to try to find out what the experience was really about. What was helpful was discovering the extremes of reactions to this. People got very angry about having to listen to music in this way. I thought that was very curious.

Bill Hellermann: *What sort of people?*

Glass: Well, other musicians. Actually there is a mechanism involved. It's a perceptual mechanism that makes this music different from other music. Let's start with something that's very obvious, which is the very extended sense of time. People will say, "Oh! Was that really ten minutes long? I thought it was an hour" or, they say, "Was that really an hour? I thought it was ten minutes." In terms of our traditional Western music, there's something radically different about it. That is one of the first things you notice. There is a perception of time in Western music that's very related to the West. We've made assumptions that music more or less takes place in this kind of time frame. In fact one of the real inspirations for me in doing this kind of work was to find that there were other time systems that were operating. I would say they are perceptual systems. You find them in other cultures and you find them in experimental music. You don't find it very much in traditional Western music. Western music tends to work in a time system which I will call a *colloquial* time system.

Most of the music we listen to is written in a period of about seventy years. This music proposes a way of listening which models itself after the events of our ordinary life; that's what I mean by colloquial time. Now it may be an abridgement of it or a compression of it but it's modeled after it. I'll give you a very simple example: the tradition of violin concertos—Sibelius, Beethoven, any one of those. The psychological mechanism of those pieces is this: The violin represents an entity. As we listen to it we become involved with the entity imprinted fifty years of delay on their descendants.

It is therefore for all the laggards who remained blocked in paper that it is a question of remaking an exit from the Lumière factories for all humanity, which would make them understand that it was on that day of 1895 that the permanent revolution was inaugurated.

But for this, we still need to settle the account of a deviation by which the cinema barely missed initiating the murder of that humanity: the TALKIE! It is time to reveal that it was nothing more than the first talking film that set off the Crash on Wall Street, that incredible event for which we have never found an explanation. King Vidor had, unfortunately, perfectly grasped the sinister thrust of the talkie. *Hallelujah* is the story of a cheater, of a man who kills his brother (Cain—Abel), of a woman of "ill repute", who becomes a bigot, then relapses into debauchery, and finally, scenes of collective hysteria. In order to understand the effect of panic on the property-owning whites that this first talkie had (it couldn't help but produce an overwhelming effect, after thirty years of silent film), we must remember the fact that it was acted by Blacks. The slaves were abruptly exalted to a position where they had the powers of gods, indeed multiplied ten times by a sound track in which, at the time, one had to yell.

The totalitarian regimes of the pre-war period became truly such only with the appearance of the talkie.

Finally, with regard to the Crash of '29, let's clarify a capital psychological element: the introduction of voice puts an end to any possibility of real visual satisfaction.

The silent film had permitted the folly of a stock system where no one cared or needed to see the securities that were bought and sold in more and more fantastic quantities. The talkie, which abruptly reintroduced sin, guilt, religious moralizing (the talkie remade the fortune of religions, the myth of the "father" and other gibberish like this!) brings back St. Thomas' complex, an unheard of uneasiness because the voice has as its impact the bringing into doubt of credulity, whence the crisis of credibility and its crumbling.

and it's the transformation of that involvement that we experience as the excitement of the piece. The violin becomes the hero of the drama. To put it in very simple terms when we listen to Mendelsson or Beethoven, what we hear is the drama of the violin. When we listen to the piece we get confused. We think we're the violin. It's like identifying with the actor on the stage. I call it colloquial because it has to do with everyday life. For example the Ninth Symphony of Beethoven is modeled after our own world we live and move around in. It's telling a story in the same way that we tell stories about our lives and the way our daily life is a story. It's just a story. I think that all the Beethoven symphonies are story, all the Tchaikovsky symphonies are story, all the Mahler, all this, it's telling a story.

Now when I say it's a model I mean it doesn't happen in the real terms that we live in; it happens in a model of it so we can maybe compress a whole lifetime into a violin concerto of 40 minutes or so. Basically, that doesn't matter. The model is the thing. Maybe Brueckner takes longer than Scarletti but the model is the same. It doesn't matter if it takes ten minutes or an hour. The psychological model has to do with narrative story telling. Right now, start looking at Satie or Phil Glass (I put myself in pretty good company; how do you like that?) or a whole generation. The thing that makes people angry with us is that the mechanism is not the same. Right away they're in a different world.

At this point, the mid-twentieth century, we can say that musical experience has been completely packaged for two or three hundred years in a certain way. To open that up is like opening a door: we all have the key to that door, but if you try another door, in fact, you find there isn't any key of that kind at all. It's a different area, and what's interesting about it is that it corresponds exactly to what happened in the plastic arts and in the theatre arts. For example, in sculpture, with someone like

SALES BACK TIC LVI CMN UTX SLD BRF

4 1500s38 5s7 1000s6 7/8 6 3/4 43 3/8 9 7/8

We must not forget that America operates on the Biblical myth of a world where everything was created by the voice. Suddenly surging forth from the screen, the voice undoubtedly had on Americans an effect just as terrifying as that of the divine voice raining down on the Hebrews worshipping the golden calf.

It is not surprising that Chaplin, who wanted to keep on making people laugh, alone persisted for years in silent films.

The voice is the return of the weight of false, crushed representations, it is the arrest, death, as the subsequent events of history have quite well shown: the paranoia of Big Brother (there are obviously no silent films dealing with police inquiries).

Nor is it surprising that the surrealist movement died with the appearance of the talkie (are there any talking dreams!). The silent film had proven that life could do without speech; the talkie will prove that speech spoils everything.

Another way of putting things in order to understand the crash: during the silent film,

Dan Flavin, the emphasis is placed on the material. There's no structure to look at, only the pure medium of his work. The medium is almost the subject of the work. Right away he is getting away from any kind of imagistic and narrative way of working. I think the psychological parallels are very close. Once we have stepped outside of that psychological mechanism or model which has to do with what I call the colloquial drama of art or making art into a colloquial kind of kitchen drama, then we're in a wholly different world. The fact is that at a certain point a very large group of people felt that we no longer could, or rather—that there wasn't any point, in working that way. It simply was boring, it was shitty. It was awful and we couldn't be bothered with it. What we wanted (and not only we as artists but we as listeners and as viewers) was an experience that seemed to us more in tune with our real perceptions. I think that we've moved not only in our perceptions of art, but in our perceptions in general. We've moved so far away from being satisfied with modeling and narrative models and colloquial models that perhaps the extremism of our time has to do with trying to find an experience which goes beyond the colloquial, right beyond the everyday world that we see.

Hellermann: *It is of interest, I think, to many people that this shift just seemed to happen. It happened to me, Fred Rzewski, Phil Corner, composers that had a body of work in other idioms, which weren't exactly narrative colloquial, but was, at that time, billed as avant-garde experimental.*

Glass: I think that that's what the avant-garde has in common. The fact that the languages are so different and, yet, the experiences are the same.

Lotringer: *If we can talk about this mechanism based on identification, what you call kitchen drama, then what would this other one be?*

Glass: We are not accustomed to talk

WP BY SIM ASZ EVY BRF ALA

½ 20 1½.4000s½.1000s½ 3s7⅜ 8⅜ 4s2⅝ 2s9¾.5s¾ 100

nothing prevented the children from having fun anymore, everything was permitted, and the talkie represented the abrupt return of the parents, of the law, and all joy melts away; prohibition, ruin.

The talkie immediately reintroduced a "schizophrenizing" effect in the processes of identifications: it instituted a predominance of the sound track over the visual—speech always narrows and limits the image, and moreover, it introduces a delay—speech always lags behind visual perception, thus the cinema reintroduces guilt, obedience, etc., all the tensions, the alienations coming from imperfect, vicious, tricky, abusive, imperious usages of speech. All of the super-noisy pop music aims at wiping out the catastrophic effect of speech, of verbiage, the sinister senseless yapping of the cinema and TV, which never ceases raising a problem of knowledge: knowing how to bawl as loudly as the TV set. Sound created and decoupled the overbid in the elevator-effect of the voice—we have all become operators of the elevator which carries the other to hell.

The talkie, with the Depression, cast the world back into the blind hole. Each new film reproduces the effect of *Hallelujah,* threatens us with depression, with panic and can at best show us nothing more than those who escape from it, the last to have reached climax just before the deluge.

The talkie dumped us back into the most sinister part of the Judeo-Christian con-game. It is the end of fraternity. Do you think that it is mere chance that the principal novel of the Twentieth Century, André Malraux's *Man's Fate,* relates an event of 1929? Yes, the Nineteenth Century novel of the crushed hero begins again in '29 on Bible paper.

It is due to the talkie and the mistrust it engenders that people want to see the guarantee of prepared scripts (the reason why people like Von Stroheim made no more films after the talkie).

With the silent movie, we finally loosed ourselves from the linear cause (all of Twentieth Century physics has been possible only thanks to the cinema), whence the poetry of the principle of indetermination, etc.... But then, once

about these experiences in precise ways. We know that we have them, and that we have them at certain times. Let me tell you how I noticed it first of all, how I got the idea that this was happening. It may describe the mechanism more completely. One of the first pieces I did in this way was background music for a Samuel Beckett piece called "Play". I composed ten 20-second phrases or figures that were based on repetitions: repetitive modules for two instruments. I took six of those and I structured it so that you would hear a figure for 20 seconds and then 20 seconds of silence, 20 seconds of music once again and 20 seconds of silence. This went on during the play that lasted for 20 minutes, 22 minutes. That was one of my "early's"; I did it in '65. It was my first experiment with a non-narrative, non-colloquial art-making. I went to see "Play" a number of times after I wrote the music; I saw it ten or fifteen times. The thing that struck me was that there would be an epiphany (do you know what an epiphany is? a heightened feeling) that would occur as I watched the play. It would happen several times throughout the course of the evening and *at a different time every night.* I thought this was very curious. My usual experience in the theatre was that the epiphany was built-in to the play so that it would always happen at the same time like when Othello was about to do whatever he does or whenever Lady Macbeth did whatever she did. So, what struck me was that I would go back to the play again and again and at least once in the course of the evening there would be this heightened feeling, this catharsis. It happened in a different place every night and I never knew when it was going to happen but it was definitely happening to me. I thought this was very, very curious. What the hell is going on?

Now this is in 1965. I'm in Paris. La Monte (Young) is in California; Steve's (Reich) in California. Rzewski is in Rome. I don't even know these guys, right? I don't know anything. I've never been to India,

PNY DPL HJ MSE OXY SHC PG MTC

2000s20$\frac{1}{2}$ 16$\frac{37}{48}$ 2s6$\frac{7}{8}$ 3$\frac{7}{8}$ 1000s1$\frac{1}{4}$ 2s8$\frac{3}{4}$ 8$\frac{5}{8}$ 2s6$\frac{3}{8}$ 1C

I've been in N. Africa a couple of times; but I'm sitting in Paris listening to this and thinking what the hell is going on. Now it's obvious to me—ten or twelve years later—what was going on but at the time I had no idea. I was in the presence of a piece of work which I couldn't enter in any way through simple identification. It resisted the efforts of my normal instincts to experience it as a confusion between myself and it. So there it was—resolutely impregnable through the normal approaches and there I was confronting it. Moreover, it seemed that the moment I gave up trying to be the thing that I was looking at, the possibility of emotion arising spontaneously between the two of us, that possibility arose. Depending on my availability to this non-identification, that emotion would then present itself. I kept thinking, thinking, thinking about what the fuck is going on. First of all, I had very little help from writing; I didn't go to philosophy for the answer because I didn't understand it. Just thinking about it for myself, finally it became clear that this thing was going on.

Hellermann: *Could you say something about how this might relate to "Einstein on the Beach", the opera you did with Robert Wilson?*

Glass: The piece is 4 hours 15 minutes long so I don't think that what is offered to the public, or to myself for that matter, is the possibility of this spontaneous epiphany . . . It's not, it's more like an interfacing. I'm putting the piece there. They're putting themselves there and, if they don't expect anything, sure enough it will happen; but if they go there with preconceived ideas . . . . The problem with the traditional ways of experiencing music when applied to this kind of work and the reason why people are unable to understand it is that they go there looking for that same old hit that you got from Sibelius. You're not going to get it here because it's not built-in.

Hellermann: *Something that interests me very much is that Phil Corner got to these*

ADS TP MHS CSR CSY WX SQB KSF KNY

$6\frac{1}{2}$ $4\frac{1}{4}\frac{1}{4}$ $3s4\frac{1}{8}$■$2s\frac{1}{8}$ $4\frac{3}{4}$ $6\frac{1}{4}$ $2s4\frac{3}{8}$ $2s2\frac{5}{8}$ $2s2\frac{7}{8}$ $6\frac{7}{8}$ 5s the screen begins to chatter..., but the more or less artificial, happy ending doesn't solve anything, the evil that was done during the film remains present in the spectators' minds. It is well known that Kubrick attempted to use the fact in *Clockwork Orange* that the cinema since March 1929 is the perfect Palovian machinery, or nearly perfect. Pandora's Box, and it's going to take a tremendous effort to get out of it.

The talkie is the great thief of our lives. It can't help but be the imposition on the moviegoer of an abusive parent-child relationship. That's exactly what is so serious. The silent film was the possibility for mankind to rediscover in itself the common language, the principle of the unification of humanity, in a common construction that the talkie tumbled to the ground by acting exactly like what happened at Babel. The tower destroyed! Men were beginning to see each other, to know each other, and doing so despite, above and beyond their different languages. They were going to be happy. It was just too good. There were people who saw that this would make them lose their powers. Yes, truly, the introduction of the talkie is the work of unpardonable madmen. The opacity of the blind-spot of separation was about to disappear. That's why Freud wrote *Civilization and its Discontents* and *The Future of an Illusion.*

It's the talkie that inaugurated the struggle of all against everyone, that imbricated the solitary crowd.

Sound imposes silence on the intimate voices to which the silent film had begun to give the right of expression. We were about to get out of the factory; evidently that didn't suit everyone. Speech in the cinema bespeaks the spectator's indigence, his irremediable poverty of words, always pushed back, whose absence it reveals as possible to compensate by the possession of material goods; thus it created the false needs of the consumer society and chases humanity back into the factory, into the waiting room, into the interminable preliminary.

The talkie is counter-information, the refusal, the denial of information. That's how it provoked the war of '40-'45, which engendered a theory of information, Shannon and Wiener's, which is completely inverted, and which is thus

things by Zen-Buddhism, Harley Gaber through Tao-ist thinking, Fred Rzweski and myself perhaps by a flip-flop out of Post-serial or indeterminate music. I was unaware of the fact that your initial experience had been in the theatre, when you were setting up a sort of dichotomy between narrative dramatic and extended time. Of course, the theatre is the last place I would have expected you, or anyone, to have come around to the other experience of extended time.

Lotringer: *It was not any kind of theatre either. And any kind of company (Mabou Mines) . . .*

Glass: Oddly enough, theatre work seems to be part of my—to use a New York word —karma. Or is it a California word? Anyway, theatre seems to be something very natural to me. I didn't give you the whole story. At the same time I was doing the Beckett piece I was working with Ravi Shankar who, by chance, was in Paris. He was working on a film score and I was hired to do the notation. In my personal history I am indebted to non-Western music, to theatre work, and to the art of people like Sol Lewitt and Richard Serra, etc.

Lotringer: *How are they connected?*

Glass: When I was at Julliard years ago, Norman Lloyd told me that all the innovations in music have always come through opera. He said that was because the opera was theatre, and theatre was where you had the greatest need to experiment. I was really struck by that idea. I think it was a lecture he gave for the fun of it. You know how people take an unpopular idea from others and maybe he didn't even believe it, but I was won over by it. It has never bothered me being involved in the theatre; I always felt that it was a good battle ground.

Having established in the theatre that field of experience, or that way of experiencing music, or having figured that mechanism as the key to the experience of

CUZ CPG BLY RAM HJ PN.SLD HBL

2 5/8 1/2 5s3 7/8 5s3 1/2 1/2 2 1/8 95.000.s.3 1000s3 7/8 8 7/8 3s9

directly responsible for the Cold War, and for all present scientific theories for which we are still giving Nobel prizes to people who accomodate as much as possible the notion of entropy, while the error at the very outset is quite simple: the "information" that interested Shannon concerned the destruction of the enemy, helping us to kill, thus ultimately to suppress information; and there you have it! All of science is built on that theory of war and death, while forgetful of that point of departure, science is presented to us as a search for life; in fact, through research, scientists only resist the death that Shannon's theory carries implicit, without anyone seeing it since they give it the image of the opposite face. Now, the entire communication and information system in which we participate, everything that happens on TV, in the papers, everything that makes up the fabric of our lives, or what we believe to be our lives, comes from Shannon's theory. And that's why, since talking films, everything's been going topsy-turvy and we're croaking! And why so-called "information" separates us from each other and gives rise to the war of all against everyone, the universal planetary paranoia. Ever since the media does nothing but Shannon, human voices have been affected and no longer contain certain vital characteristics. We are all speaking Shannon.

Particularly because of the inherent deformations and distortions of their technique (crackling, that is, a group of infra-and ultrasounds which have enormous physiological effects because they act, for example, upon the fluids of the inner ear) the sound-media and particularly the talkies accentuate the imperfections, the "impurities" of particular languages, their processive paranoiac tendencies. For example, in French, feminine voices have a tendency toward a certain violent bickering which institutes among them and especially between mothers and daughters a mistress-servant type relationship where the cruel, heart-rending and searing tonality means that one is constantly accusing the other, with every word, of stealing or dirtying up her mirror (competition among women). Now, by anchoring the spectators in the drum-case of a narcissism whose mirror is broken by the thoughtless sound-track, the Talkie

this work, I've gone back into my music and begun to start including elements that are associated with more Romantic periods. In fact, "Einstein" is full of extravagant harmony. An end that comes right out of Berlioz. I discovered that once I had established a mode of experiencing that was so radical, language became secondary. I found that I could use conventional language and it didn't matter. I've just finished a piece which is extremely reduced in terms of the number of notes. It's similar to the pieces I wrote in 1968 or '69. At the same time I'm writing a super-Romantic piece in terms of language. But in terms of the experience I think they are both part of this other course of thought I've been working on. When we talk about avant-garde, if we're going to use that word at all, we have to say right away that we must free it from the tyranny of style. We're not talking about a style, we're really talking about a way of perceiving things.

Hellermann: *I agree, but what if we are talking about certain people or work that is also often thought of as avant-garde, such as Boulez.*

Glass: The problem that Boulez has specifically is that he thinks he can establish credentials for the avant-garde, and that they will be established in terms of the language, the grammar of music. But it's not that at all. Rather it's in terms of *how* we experience it that music can be altered radically. Even when using the language of Satie or Brahms we can still write pieces that are extremely radical; something that Rzewski knows. And John Cage knows. People that are working in this way found that what makes a piece new isn't a new harmony or a new kind of tonal organization; it's a new perception. When I wrote part one of "Music in Twelve Parts," I said to a friend: you know, this piece could have been written fifty years ago; there is nothing new in this piece of music. The only thing new in it is the attitude of the music.

has accentuated that tendency—that the silent film used to erase—and one need not seek elsewhere the origin of Lacan's research precisely on paranoia beginning with the episode of the Papin sisters' crime (incestuous miammiam), one of the great mysteries post 1929—the incomprehensible behavior of the defendants at the Moscow trials is another mystery due to the general craziness caused by the Talkie—Genêt forgets to mention that Madame in *The Maids* was a movie fan. The origin of Sartre's *Nausea* is no different: the lightning physiological effect of the Talkie; it is not surprising that he ends the account with a glimmer of hope for a possible, remaining chance of salvation, of catharsis to rediscover the mirror of the entire nightmare while listening to the recording of a blues song written by a Jew and sung by a Black woman (two means of maintaining a certain form of essential femininity and maternity in the world which is beginning to tumble toward a murderous folly). Moreover, Sartre's theory of the unavoidable slipping into infernal dependency on the other's gaze, the theory of rarity, comes from the cinema which the Great Talkie makes paranoid, accusatory and tame. (The opposite of the movement of fascization, it is Chaplin's *Modern Times* which causes the gasp and the takeover of power by the Popular Front.)

But does Bergson reveal that his entire "genial" professorial number on immediacy, etc. is drawn from the cinema—following closely upon the appearance on the market of Edison's first invention—*The Laugh (Le Rire)* comes three years after *L'Arroseur-arrosé* but does not breathe a word about this source from which it springs. Oh, those serious philosophers! They really wish it were possible to be the son of no one! They are all prestidigitators who need to make the father disappear so they can exist. Thus Bergson is to Sartre what the silent film is to the talkie!

But let us return to the essential evil wrought by the talkie. It is obvious that the talkie had the most disastrous effects on the paranoid tendencies of the German language, where from 1929 on, the cinema systematically intoxicated German minds with false informa-

The way we hear it is new, not the notes.

Hellermann: *That would seem to be one of the differences between America and Europe. They look for a new conception, for a new music.*

Glass: I call it the security of style or manner. I think a modern "style" or a modern "manner" is a form of self-deception: it's a kind of false security. To think one can write in the Post-serial technique and therefore, be in the avant-garde. Americans are more willing to work without those kinds of assurances, to waive those credentials. I won't use those credentials. I bypass them entirely. In fact I'll write a piece based on harmonies that have been around—Berliozian. I think "Einstein" really is in the style of Berlioz, if nothing else, in terms of the harmony. On the other hand, many of the things are distinctly mine, but the thing that makes the perception of it so radical is not the stylistic features of the work. What we're really talking about is a point of view. "Music in Twelve Parts", part 1 could have been written in 1885 if someone had the head to do it then.

The radical nature of this work is really the complete disregard of historical perspective. Up until now music has marched along from decade to decade, each composer adding or expanding a little bit. Now we have whole generations of people who are ahistorical, who are not at all interested in the historical perception of their work. Music for us does not advance down the road of Schoenberg and Wagner and so forth. The biggest cut to that tradition is to say: what tradition? You don't care. I can say—I'm going to use Berlioz; I'm going to use Mozart; I'm going to use myself; but, I'm going to fashion it in a way that the subject of the work is in fact the juxtaposition between the listener and the work itself and not anything stylistic in the work. This is a point of view which is much more radical than saying, now I'm going to serialize the rhythm or dynamics

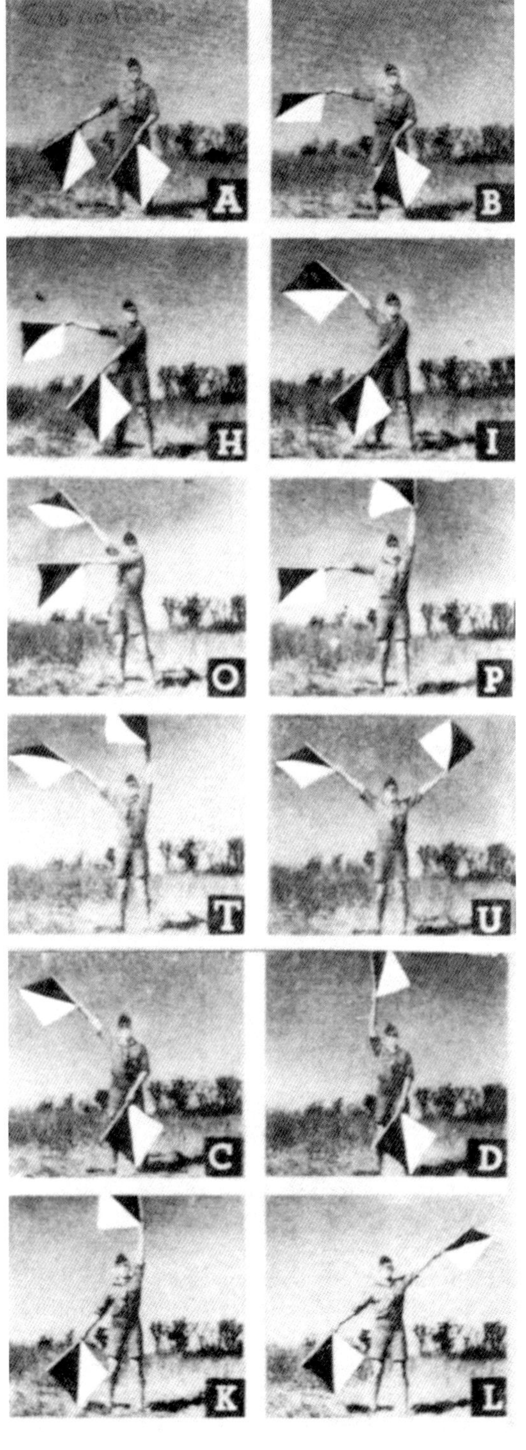

or whatever. To Americans of this generation that is so boring as to not be believable. We can't believe that anyone is thinking that way.

Hellermann: *What are some of the things that distinguish your situation from that of others working in a similar idiom?*
Glass: One thing that distinguishes me from other people of my generation is simply, I have more profile and that's because I'm interested in bringing this work to the public in a very big way. I love the fact that thousands of people come to a concert. Probably it's a question of temperament. Let's just say that I like to play for a lot of people. I know other composers who like to play for a small number of people. I like that too, but it's more difficult to arrange now. I happen to be better known than other people because I played that game and I enjoy it. I enjoy the game of being in the *Daily News;* it's fun and I'm not afraid of it.

Lotringer: *You mentioned Sol Lewitt before. It seems that you mostly associated with visual artists. How does your work actually relate to their own?*
Glass: Sol Lewitt was one of the very first people and he was interested in Steve (Reich) and myself. You can see why; it's not just that Sol took the image out of his work but that the mode of perception is indirectly very similar. The first community that supported this work was in Soho, and before Soho was Soho. My first concert in New York I think was in '67 or '68 at the Cinématèque on Wooster St., which is still there. We found that (I say it with a very big capital WE) the music establishment and the public were not at the outset interested in this work. If we had looked at what had happened to Cage, we should not have been surprised because he was, after all, a real pioneer in terms of idea and lifestyle and everything else. Really it was the dance world that supported him, it was Merce, and that was how it worked. So we should probably have known that it wouldn't be

tion on the nature of man and his relation to others. Hitler and Nazism are first of all a reaction and a consequence, an acceleration of this erroneous information—the sound track bludgeons us with the "information" that we are faced with the presence of a hidden enemy which must be crushed, an enemy which obviously the sound-track itself creates and which does not exist outside of it.

It is only after 1929 that the Germans became cruelly aware that they were being mistreated by the Treaty signed in the Hall of Mirrors, that they were being crushed between their borders.

Here is a hypothesis for the introduction of the monstrous talkie: technologically, the talkie was possible from the beginning of movie-making; financiers were the ones who decided to exploit that possibility against the advice of professionals who perceived its aesthetic nuisance. It was introduced by the same financial groups who had gained complete control over the radio in the U.S., and had been able to gauge the extraordinarily pleasurable feeling of omnipotence which they acquired through the control of such a sound source capable of enveloping the earth (thank you Teilhard de Chardin for consoling us by calling it the biosphere). Now in the U.S., radio remains private enterprise, that is, it survives only through advertising and is created to advertise. Thus, if, in the beginning, newspapers were founded on a certain ethics of public information, it is easy to see that from the outset, the radio was only viable as a source of false information (advertising) of a "messianic" type: use Brand X and you'll be saved—and the underlying message: we must ruin the competitors. Thus it is necessarily a Cain-Abel paranoid style information; such from the beginning is the dominant tone of radio; yet what could still be absorbed by the American sense of humor and fairplay becomes catastrophic, taking on an entirely new dimension when the system is unleashed on German ears. What makes it even easier to understand is that it is still going on. All the games designed to make Americans quiver and have fun or let themselves go come across differently in current German films as true fear, ominous anguish and

the music people that would come, and sure enough, they didn't. The first people that came were the artists and for many years that was our exclusive audience. I don't mean just like Sol, but a lot of other musicians have found a community in the art world that is ready and quite anxious to join in these kinds of experiments that we're making. I say that they're experiments not in the sense that we don't know what we're doing, but we don't know where things are going to lead; we don't know how these experiences are really going to work out.

The sound system I've had since 1972 was built almost entirely by artists. Someone gave me a set of speakers, someone bought me amplifiers. I mean literally they went out and bought the stuff for me. There must have been more than six artists that were involved in building that first sound system. In the other room I have the posters that they made for the ensemble, in itself a testament to their involvement. They were extremely supportive because in the struggle we were having, they recognized themselves in another medium. Besides that, they really enjoyed the work. I often thought that we were in the business of entertaining this small community. It was a minor form of show biz. For years I played concerts on Bleecker St. on the sixth floor of a loft every Sunday. You walked in and paid whatever you wanted to; you had to climb up six flights. Rarely were there more than two hundred people there and we never advertised. It was really that community of people. You would go in there and see everyone, from people that were totally unknown to Rauschenberg or Johns or Jack Tworkov. Sol was also there and other musicians and dancers.

Hellermann: *Now where are you?*

Glass: At forty-one I'm just beginning to understand what I'm doing. I was able to tell you this morning fairly succinctly about these ideas I had, but even three or four years ago I couldn't have told you that.

PNY DPL HJ MSE OXY SHC PG MTC

00s20$\frac{1}{2}$ 16$\frac{3}{4}\frac{7}{8}$ 2s6$\frac{7}{8}$ 3$\frac{7}{8}$ 1000s1$\frac{1}{4}$ 2s8$\frac{3}{4}$ 8$\frac{5}{8}$ 2s6$\frac{3}{8}$ 1000 hysteria (the films involving Klaus Kinski, for example) and it is not impossible, if we continue to play thoughtlessly with the media (catastrophe movies, for example), that the little game we have already seen will begin again.

One of the things I discovered recently was that I love writing operas. In fact when I was in the middle of writing "Einstein" I said to a friend, now I understand why Verdi wrote all of those operas. So, one thing I'm very interested in doing is continuing to write operas. I've also gotten interested in playing by myself more. Solos. Playing in churches because of the pipe organs. To take my electric organ and put it back into the pipes. It really sounds good. I'm doing five concerts in Europe. One of them is in a church in Rotterdam and I asked some friends of mine to try and organize a concert in Paris in a church. At the moment there are not that many people of our generation that are working that medium, so it's very open. To have contemporary music, I mean music of our time, for those instruments just seems like a very timely thing to do. That's the second thing. The third thing is I have an attachment to the ensemble I've worked with all these years. I think it's a band that should stay together. I really enjoy playing with them.

Lotringer: *You said recently that your pieces almost always have origins in technical problems, not intention or emotion. Is that a legacy of Cage's? How do you see yourself in relation to him?*

Glass: The people he likes to acknowledge are much closer to him but I have told him: you know, I'm one of your children, whether you like it or not. He doesn't see me as part of his family but I am. One of the things I learned from Cage is that when the composer makes the music he need not have any intention in terms of a particular experience. This, of course, is very clear in my work: I don't have to worry about the meaning of it. When I'm working on a piece often I'm working on a technical problem. I'm not thinking about any thing else anymore.

Lotringer: *You didn't deal within the aleatory aspect of Cage?*

Glass: Never. That's not my way. For me,

ADS TP MHS CSR CSY WX SQB KSF KNY

3s6 1/2 4 1/4 1/4 3s4 1/8 2s 1/8 4 3/4 6 1/4 2s4 3/8 2s2 5/8 2s2 7/8 6 7/8

the main thing he did was to make the composer, the work, free of intention. The whole development of aleatory music was a very rigorous working out of that idea. I didn't participate in that experiment but I benefitted from it. My music is so restricted. It's so narrow in one way. But I feel that other people, especially Cage and Ornette Coleman who are so different, have been very important to me personally as a musician—perhaps you can't hear it in my work. Still, sometimes someone will open things up for you by solving their own problem.

Lotringer: *A new attitude toward music, freed of any intention, makes you closer to what I would call "machinic" music. Didn't you yourself say, apropos "Einstein", that you felt very close to machines?*

Glass: I liked the idea. I did like the mechanistic aspect of it. Steve (Reich) is even more attracted to this than me. He often discusses music as machines. He loves the image. For him the machine, the process is what is important. That's a very extreme point of view. I don't take to that as much as Steve. Still I'm attracted to the idea. We could've also talked about that today. That's another way of slicing into this. We could have talked about process and in a way we would've been saying another thing: by refusing to talk about emotion and talking instead about procedures.

Lotringer: *You're not in the product but more in the processes.*

Glass: Well, this is really the heritage of Cage. I don't look at it quite that way but I found and still find this way of viewing the artistic function as very liberating. You know the thing about America, if you look at it, we're very connected to the Surrealist tradition. When you see what came from France it turns out it wasn't Picasso, it was Duchamp. Between the two of them it was the tradition of Duchamp that made the big impression in America, because really, all Americans are surrealists at heart.

IRO CUZ CPG BLY RAM HJ PN■SLD HBL

2 5/8 1/2 5s3 7/8 5s3 1/2 1/2 2 1/8 95■000■s■3 1000s3 7/8 8 7/8

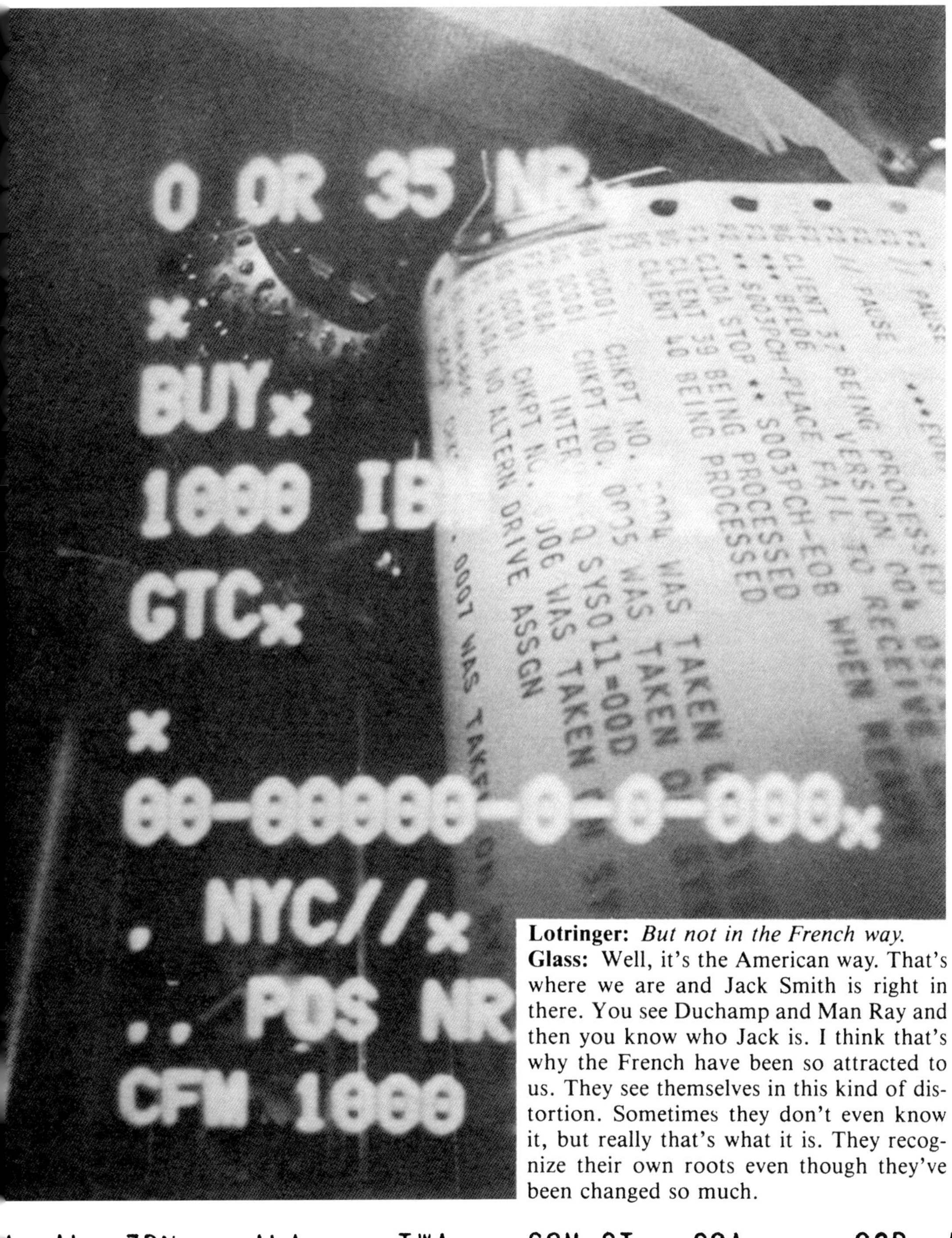

Lotringer: *But not in the French way.*
Glass: Well, it's the American way. That's where we are and Jack Smith is right in there. You see Duchamp and Man Ray and then you know who Jack is. I think that's why the French have been so attracted to us. They see themselves in this kind of distortion. Sometimes they don't even know it, but really that's what it is. They recognize their own roots even though they've been changed so much.

AL ZRN ALA TWA SCM ST SOA CSR ABC

3$\frac{1}{4}$ 5$\frac{3}{8}$ 6s8$\frac{1}{4}$ 3s12$\frac{1}{2}$ 3s5$\frac{1}{8}$ 2 20$\frac{1}{2}$ 2000s1 6$\frac{1}{4}$ 180

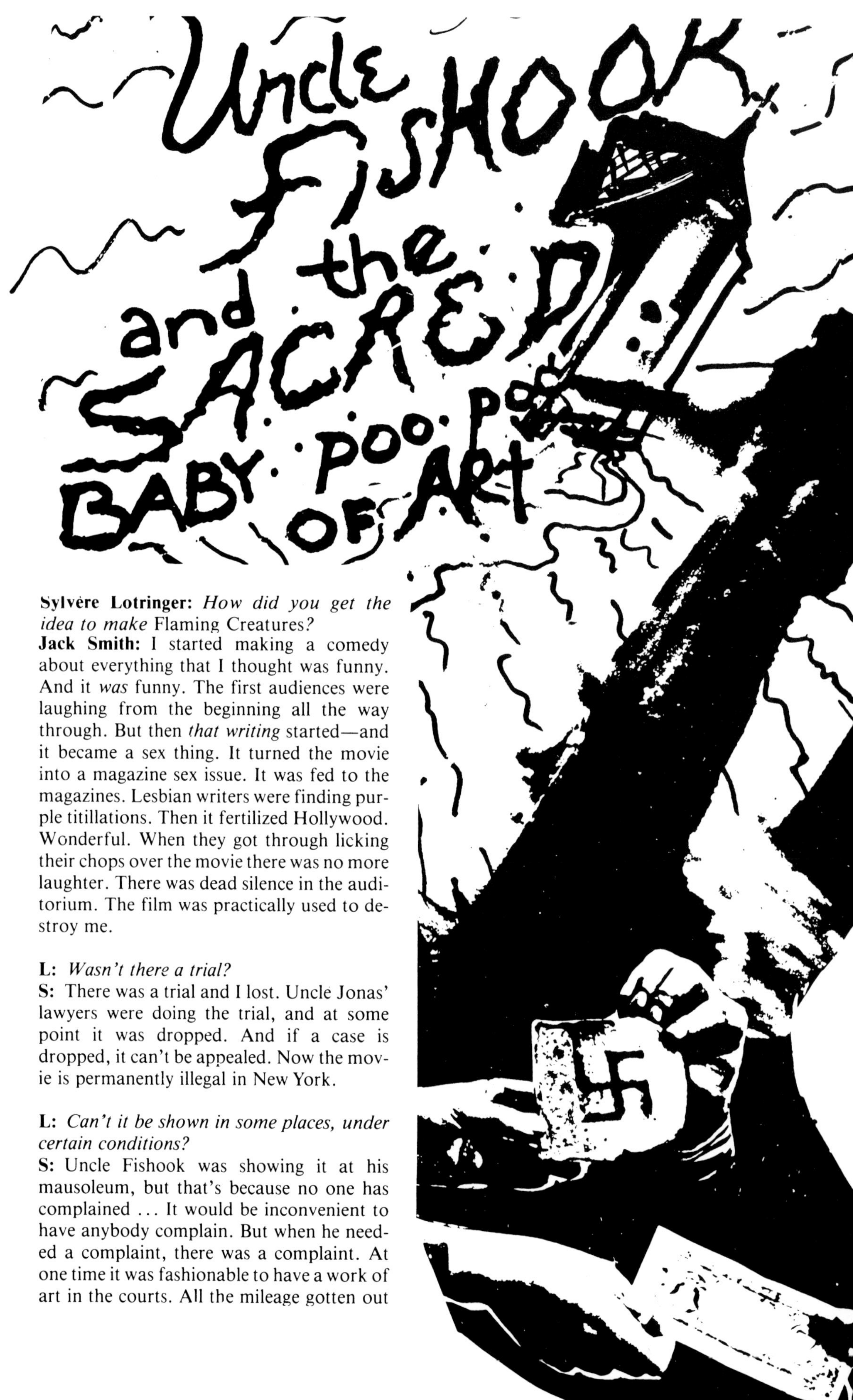

Uncle FISHOOK
and the SACRED
BABY POO POO OF ART

Sylvère Lotringer: *How did you get the idea to make* Flaming Creatures?
Jack Smith: I started making a comedy about everything that I thought was funny. And it *was* funny. The first audiences were laughing from the beginning all the way through. But then *that writing* started—and it became a sex thing. It turned the movie into a magazine sex issue. It was fed to the magazines. Lesbian writers were finding purple titillations. Then it fertilized Hollywood. Wonderful. When they got through licking their chops over the movie there was no more laughter. There was dead silence in the auditorium. The film was practically used to destroy me.

L: *Wasn't there a trial?*
S: There was a trial and I lost. Uncle Jonas' lawyers were doing the trial, and at some point it was dropped. And if a case is dropped, it can't be appealed. Now the movie is permanently illegal in New York.

L: *Can't it be shown in some places, under certain conditions?*
S: Uncle Fishook was showing it at his mausoleum, but that's because no one has complained ... It would be inconvenient to have anybody complain. But when he needed a complaint, there was a complaint. At one time it was fashionable to have a work of art in the courts. All the mileage gotten out

of Miller's books ... And Uncle Fishook wanted to have something in court at the time, it being so fashionable. The publicity. It was another way by which he could be made to look like a saint, to be in the position of defending something when he was really kicking it to death. So he would give screenings of *Creatures* and making speeches, defying the police to bust the film. Which they did. And then there was the trial ... I don't know what the lawyers were doing. I wasn't even permitted to be in the court. I walked into the courtroom and my lawyer said, "Go out of the courtroom," and I said, "Why?"—"because the judge is upset by too many men with beards." I was ordered to leave by the marshmallow lawyer that Uncle Mekas had. So I couldn't even see the trial. You know: it goes on and on.

L: *I must say that when I saw the film at the Cinémathèque, people were laughing their heads off.*
S: Mumble, mumble. It inflated Uncle Fishook; it made his career; I ended up supporting him. He's been doing my travelling for 15 years. He's been conducting a campaign to dehumanize me in his column. There's just a list of monstrosities. I don't want to start that ... So from supporting Uncle Fishook, now we're left years later with nothing. There's nothing anybody can do with their films. *He's* got the original.

L: *You don't have any copy?*
S: I have a miserable beat up inter-negative that's shot. He must have sucked 1000 copies out of it. It needs to be restored or something.

L: *Why don't you make another film?*
S: I don't want to let somebody go running off with ... I am. I've already made new films; I have a roomful of films that I've made since then ... But there's nothing in the world that I can do with them, because Uncle Fishook has established this pattern of the way film is thought about, and seen, and everything else ...

L: *Did you actually mean anything through your film?*
S: No, I didn't then. But the meaning has to come out in what is done with the art—is what gives it meaning. The way my movie

was used—that was the meaning of the movie.

L: *You mean that meaning comes afterwards?*
S: What you do with it economically is what the meaning is. If it goes to support Uncle Fishook, that's what it means. Movies are always made for an audience. But I didn't make it that way: I was just making it completely for myself. At the time, that seemed like an intellectual experiment. But that point got lost.

L: *But that happens everytime someone wants to make art.*
S: If they weren't making this deliberately pointless art, then it wouldn't happen ... And it wouldn't have happened to me if I had been perfect. It wouldn't have been taken up and used by somebody else.

L: *I read recently what Susan Sontag wrote about* Flaming Creatures ...
S: It showed that she was just as hypnotized by him as I was ... but by that time I was no longer hypnotized by him and she ...

L: *She said it didn't mean anything, and that was the strength of the film. I liked that. It's not just that it was comical, but that it makes fun of all sorts of ideas we have, and definitions ...*
S: Was it being exploited like Hollywood? Uncle Fishook's use of the word *co-op* just drifted past Miss Sontag ... And nobody seems to expect anything from that idea. They don't seem to know what a co-op is.

L: *What is it about?*
S: It's a thing that controls all the activites of a certain activity. And then everyone engaged in this is sharing the money.

L: *Is that the way your film was done?*
S: A film co-op sounded like something I wanted to do, to support. I turned over my film to this film co-op. And then it became a grotesque parody of Hollywood. Uncle Fishook was heroic in her review. What was heroic? Taking someone's film away from him ... Uncle Roachcrust perpetuated the monstrosity of discrediting co-ops. That's why he is a symbol, an Uncle Pawnshop, a

symbol of fishook co-ops. The only reason for the pattern of the 2 night screenings he has established is so somebody's film will spend one night in the safe—if you get my meaning.

L: *Didn't you want to destroy your work?*
S: Uncle Fishook says all kinds of fantastic things about me. If anybody that can only comprehend capitalism would look at my behavior and the only conclusion that they could come to was that I was trying to destroy myself.

L: *When capitalism is in fact trying to destroy you?*
S: And he's printed things like that in his column. Once he printed that Jack Smith's art is so precious that it cannot be exported. You know: seeming to be saying something complimentary when actually killing the chance of the economic possibility of my going to Europe. Everything on earth like that he's been doing. My life has been made a nightmare because of that damn film. That sucked up ten years of my life. For a while I was being betrayed on an average of about twice a week to Uncle Fishook. It was like being boiled alive. People would turn me in because Uncle Fishook wanted to get me and everybody knew that ...
(Sounds of the radio)

L: *Is that WBAI? Have you ever done anything for them?*
S: I tried; I tried. I went there a number of times. There are some dummies there. And I just had the bad luck of running into all the dummies, I guess. I get these incredible overreactions because I'm a very strange looking person.

L: *What happened there?*
S: Once I was thrown out by the receptionist. I was asked not to wait inside the building. I was listening to their begging for money and it really gripped my heart. I went there. Four or five times. Every time I ran into some dummy at the place, so I just gave up. I wanted so much to help. It is the only source of information in the city. I think you have to be Jewish, number one. And normal, number two. The very first sign of the trouble *they had* was when they attacked the homo who had a program called *The Importance of Being Honest*, a gay program. And he was forbidden to put on one of his programs. People with their snot impacted voices that they paid for in college: their rumbling snot. They wanted normalcy. Later the whole station was turned off by the same management.

L: *In Italy, little independent radios like Radio-Alice have a more direct political impact on the population. It's starting in France too. They do it with very limited means.*
S: There's always been political art in Europe. There's never been any political art in this country.

L: *Do you consider your art political?*
S: I wouldn't put any program out now unless it had an overtly political title.

L: *How about your slide-show, do you consider that political?*
S: If you can put an explicit title on something implicit, that's almost enough—because you're giving the indication of how to see it. Not everything has to be cerebral at every moment ... But the title does have to be explicit. The title is 50 percent of the work. That's why I shudder with the title of your magazine. You have that chance to say something.

L: *A title is language, and I'm not sure language can be that effective.*
S: But thoughts can. The world is starving for thoughts. I worry about the thoughts. A new thought must come out in new language.

L: *What was the title before: "I was a Mekas collaborator?"*
S: Let's see. The program before that was: "The Secret of Rented Island", and the program before that was "How can Uncle Fishook have a Free Bicentennial Zombie Underground", and the title before that was ...

L: *So it didn't really matter if you actually had a slide show or not because you've advertised the title; the title is sufficient.*
S: Almost. You don't have to see the slide show as far as I'm concerned. The slide is the entertainment, the icing. I mean there's a thought, there's a socialist thought in it, but the information and all the intellectual content is being conveyed by the title. You can become so explicit that you can state

something the world didn't know and needs to know and this you can state very clearly in the title. The images could be made to mean anything, but the title's got to be explicit because it's your only chance. You have to struggle to make more of it more and more explicit, but still glamorous. If it is not done glamorously, it's no good because it wouldn't have been dramatized.

L: *What title would you choose now for* Flaming Creatures *if you had a choice?*
S: Let me think, a new title … I have to think about it … What's its content … There never was any content. 'Connecting Sugar with Hollywood', maybe …

L: *You mean your film was some sort of parody of Hollywood?*
S: It has a lot to do with it, yes. It took place in a haunted movie studio. That's why those people were coming and going like that.

L: *Was Hollywood really on your mind when you made the film?*
S: Of course. My mind was filled with it … Everybody's is filled with Hollywood.

L: *Did you watch television?*
S: Not until later. Then I became addicted to it … No longer though.

L: *What sort of thing did you read?*
S: My favorite book was *The Count of Montecristo*. Sinclair Lewis is my favorite writer. They think they're through with Sinclair Lewis. I just finished a book of his called *King's Blood Royal*, in which the most typical WASP in the world finds out that he has one percent Negro blood; and then the book ends with everybody in the neighborhood marching on his house with rifles. But it could be about any minority group.

L: *What do you think of the gay movement?*
S: They've become a ghetto, already: they just want to talk about gay things. They're trying to cut it off from being in any context.

L: *Don't you think it's becoming something of an industry too?*
S: Oh sure, of course. It's just one of the unexpected bad side developments of it that's making it possible to be so happily ghetto-

ized. But that's where the people in the theater are supposed to be coming in and helping the atmosphere. And, you see, they're not. I took my program to a gay theater, and he couldn't understand how it was gay, because he was unable to see it in a context. If it wasn't discussing exactly how many inches was my first lollipop, well then it wouldn't be anything they'd be interested in. And so I couldn't get this gay theater. It was one of the places I tried. Getting theaters is one of the 7 labours of Uranus.

L: *What was that: "I was a Mekas Collaborator!"*
S: I put the ad in the paper and then I didn't go to the theater. The ad was as far as I could get with a lobotomized, zombified ...

L: *What do you mean by that?*
S: That if a program has any intellectual interest at all then it can only be given one or two nights—but you can be entertained to death in this country.

L: *Is that the slide show you want to present?*
S: That slide show is just the same mass of slides: I've been showing it for years. Every once in a while I have a new shooting session and add a new scene to it. Nobody has ever complained. It's always, you know, completely interesting. The Penguin Epic is all new, though ...

L: *Why did you put that Swastika there?*
S: Nazism and capitalism have melted together by this time. I think that Nazism is the end product of capitalism. That's why I don't bother with words, because to me it's only a matter of if a thing is given to you or taken from you. And the words are only going to be twisted around someway by somebody somehow. For instance, you can make the word *socialism* mean anything on earth.

L: *That's why Burroughs uses cut-ups*: to try to prevent words from being twisted around.
S: Oh, that's one way.

L: *It's an extreme way.*
S: That's the wrong extreme. What I mean is the extreme in the other direction—by being more and more specific about what you're thinking. The title is supposed to serve the idea. If I am lucky enough to get a socialistic idea ...

L: *What do you mean by a socialistic* idea?
S: To me, socialism is to try to find social ways of sharing. That's all. And to replace the dependence upon authority with the principle of sharing. Because it's very likely that there would be much more for everybody, thousands and more times for everybody if things were shared. We're living like dogs from all the competing.

L: *Were you ever competitive? Did you ever believe in that?*
S: Yes, of course, when you're young, it's drilled into you, and you have to slowly find your way out of it, because you find it doesn't work. Capitalism is terribly inefficient. The insane duplication, the insane waste, and the young only know what's put in front of them. . . But then, by experience, things are happening to you and you find out that this doesn't work. I mean this is *not* productive.

L: *It produces waste.*
S: I looked through your magazine and I was repelled by the title. It's so dry, you just want to throw it in the wastebasket, which I did. Then I picked it out ... Listen: *Hatred of Capitalism* is a good name for that magazine. It's stunning, I'll never admit that I thought of it.

L: *I doubt that by saying something that directly you'll change anything. Language is corrupt.*
S: Listen, you are a creature, artistic I can tell, that somehow got hung up on the issue of language. Forget it. It's *thinking*. If you can think of a thought in a most pathetic language ... Look what I have to do in order to think of thoughts. I have to forget language. All I can do with no education, nothing, no advice, no common sense in my life, an insane mother I mean, no background, nothing, nothing, and I have to make art, but I know that under these conditions the one thing I had to find out was if I could think of a thought that has never been thought of before, then it could be in language that was never read before. If you can think of something, the language will fall into place in the most fantastic way, but the thought is what's going to do it. The language is shit, I mean

it's only there to support a thought. Look at Susan Sontag, that's a phenomenon that will never occur, only in every hundred years. Anybody like that. She says things that you would never have thought of. And the language is automatically unique. Whatever new thoughts you can think of that the world needs will be automatically clothed in the most radiant language imaginable.

L: *Have you ever thought of another type of society ...*
S: I can think of billions of ways for the world to be completely different. I wish they would invent a scalpbrush. Do you realize that there is nothing on earth that you can brush your scalp with? ... I can think of other types of societies ... Like in the middle of the city should be a repository of objects that people don't want anymore, which they would take to this giant junkyard. That would form an organization, a way that the city would be organized ... the city organized around that. I think this center of unused objects and unwanted objects would become a center of intellectual activity. Things would grow up around it.

L: *You mean some sort of center of exchange?*
S: Yes, there could be exchange, that would start to develop. You take anything that you don't want and don't want to throw up and just take it to this giant place, and just leaving it and looking for something that you need ...

L: *And there wouldn't be any money?*
S: Then things would form the way they always do around that.

L: *Would people still own anything?*
S: Yeah, I don't mind ... Buying and selling is the most natural human institution; there's nothing wrong with that ... Buying and selling is the most interesting thing in the world. It should be aesthetic and everything else. But capitalism is a perversion of this. Nothing is more wonderful than a marketplace. It gives people something to do ... and it can be creative. Wonderful things come from commerce ... but not from capitalism ...

L: *What do you mean exactly by landlordism?*
S: Fear ritual of lucky landlord paradise. That's what supports the government.

L: *You mean property?*
S: The whole fantasy of how money is squeezed out of real estate. It supports the government; it supports everything. And it isn't even rational. When is a building ever paid for? The person that built the building is dead long since, and yet it can never be paid for, it has to be paid for all over again, every month. That's as irrational as buying a pair of shoes and then going back as long as you wear the shoes and paying for them again. It supports the whole sytem that we have to struggle against. We have to spend the rest of our time struggling against the uses they make of our money against us.

L: *They call it 'rent control.' That's exactly what it is about: control through rent.*
S: But if the whole population has no conception of how irrational that is, that's how far they are from doing anything about it, or any of the other things that oppress them. All the money that runs the government comes from the fantasy of paying rent.

L: *As if we owned something.*
S: Alright. So we don't own it. But do they own it? People that live in a place and maintain it and built it, why do they own it less than the government? Then you're saying that the government owns it more than you do. And that's also silly.

L: *The difference is that in a capitalist country you owe money to an individual and in a communist country you owe money to a state. It still holds...*
S: Well, you don't own your own property... but even if you could understand that, why would you understand that somebody else has some claim, or owns, your property.

L: *You mean then that everyone should own what they use?*
S: You want to start making more laws and more rules. But that's how a lot of strange things began... from the expectation that you need all the laws and rules...

L: *But if no one had to own anything... if*

you use something, you don't have to pay for it, but it doesn't belong to you.

S: What's so incredible about that? There is a new movement called Housing in the Public Domain—maybe the 1st idea on the subject since feudal times. I never had sunlight. I was always so naive I just kept taking places that had no sunlight. But the next time I move there will be some sunlight involved, somehow, coming through a window, or anything. But I can't build it; I can't be permitted to build my own house. You can build exotic architecture or strange houses if it's outside the city if there are not other people around that would complain. All the complaining!

L: *You want to build an exotic house?*

S: I'd like to invent a building that wouldn't be a rectangle, that would utilize the pouring qualities of cement.

L: *It would be closed?*

S: I don't know what in the world it would be. It would be open in the middle: sunlight could come in the middle. They cling to rectangles because it's the preferred shape of capitalism; it's easy to manufacture a rectangle, to manufacture the components of a rectangle. But why should I live in a house for the convenience of the manufacturers. I think the normal idea of the house is more circular, whatever it is, and it would have an opening for sunlight to come in. The house would be arranged in that way. It would also have all the ugly non-design of manufacturers banished from it. Everything to do with water would be in one place and it would be in the form of a waterfall; and it would be enclosed, and plants would be happy there; washing the dishes would become a polynesian thing, it would not be an ugly thing washing the dishes; and washing clothes, taking a bath would also be done in this place; the dishes would wash themselves. It would use much less water; all the water would be utilized; there wouldn't be any wasted water; the waterfall would be turned on and off, of course. It would be in the central part where the sunlight is… the water would be mixed with the sunlight, a steamroom would then be created, steam is very healthful, it cleans your lungs. And I

can imagine anything on earth like this. But if I try to build it there would be a million laws saying I can't build it.

L: *It sounds like a building you could build in Miami.*
S: I heard of someone building their own building in Miami, and the city officials made him tear it apart ten times until he got every little thing just to comply with the city regulations. So you wouldn't do it in the city. You might do it outside the city. As long as there aren't people complaining. And then this would dispense with the ugly rectangular monstrosity of the kitchen sink; bathtubs wouldn't exist. All this duplication wouldn't exist; it would save space. It's got to be built to be a model to do away with the ugly designs that now surround us completely.

L: *I think it is like art; as soon as there is a model it's going to be duplicated and then it becomes an industry. It's very difficult to avoid that.*
S: That's what I want: I would want them to duplicate my ideas. But all that's happened to me so far is that my idea that I never had doesn't register—and they duplicate my icing. I know how just a thing like the ugly design of kitchen sinks destroyed my childhood... 'cause I had to fight with my sister all the time over who had to do the dishes. It was the ugliness, the ugliness of capitalism, making it impossible for anybody to live a life that isn't made ugly.

S: *Where did you grow up?*
S: In the midwest. My father's family were hillbillies in West Virginia. They went to the hills because they wanted to be more independent in the first place, and then they became more independent because they were living in the hills. Hillbillies, nomads, gypsies are natural anarchists.

L: *Do you like that?*
S: Yes, basically I'm an anarchist; that's not to say that I think there will ever be any state of anarchy, but I don't think that you should stamp out anarchy... You need it to flavor other ideas, because anarchy is the giving part of politics. In this country they have stamped it out, and made it a dirty word, made it synonymous with chaos... They want to tell you that's it's the same as chaos. It isn't. All it means is without a ruler. And if people don't try to make a start of getting along without authorities, they will never be in a position where they are not being worked over by these authorities. And so naturally they don't like anarchy. We have never had anarchy, but we do have chaos. There's always going to be the government agents that are going to be throwing bombs, saying that the anarchists did it, to set up a reaction.

L: *There are so many rulers now. Authority is everywhere.*
S: They're dreaming of more authority.

L: *I could do with a little more chaos myself.*
S: All it is is an idea of gradually working toward doing things without authorities. Under an anarchist system you would phase authorities out slowly, as much as could be. That seems a fantasy, just because it's been so stamped out and ridiculed. Until the twenties you could go anywhere in the world without a passport. But they want to put you in the frame of mind where you accept more and more authority. You just are required to go through this ritual in which you give them the right to tell you where I can go. And if you don't, you'll be clapped in prison.

L: *It is not easy to live in the way you want and not to suffer from it.*
S: I don't mind a certain amount of trouble. I can't take these exaggerated doses of pasty cheerfulness of capitalism in which you have to be happy all the time. That can only produce a crust like Warhol. I don't want to be too happy. I don't want extremes, I mean getting pinnacles of happiness. I can't live with it. What goes up must come down. I tried it. I was a pasty celebrity, I was very fashionable ten years ago... this is being recorded?

L: *Yes.*
S: (laughing) Wonderful. I was hoping it was. I was very fashionable but I couldn't live with it. I will never, never go near anything like that again. This was the golden gift of Uncle Fishook to me. Please let him keep the blessings of publicity. I must say that before that happened to me, I actually believed like everybody else that I could not continue to exist unless I got a glare of publicity. You see, attention is a basic human need. It's terribly important. If the

baby doesn't get attention, it won't be fed.

L: *If society makes you unhappy, then it has won no matter what.*
S: I don't think so. I can be happy from being unhappy, if I know what I'm doing. I mean I have to struggle against Uncle Fishook, that's my job, and I'm not running away from it. Everybody else that has been worked over by Uncle Fishook has just faded out, folded up and creeped out of the city. But I won't do that. Usually in life nothing is ever clear cut. How many people are lucky enough to have an archetypal villain for an adversary.

L: *You can find Uncle Fishook everywhere.*
S: When an Uncle Fishook falls into your life you have to fight it till the end. It's been dropped into your life, it's not the most glamorous problem, but it's been given to you to struggle against... This is something for me to do something real for me to address myself to. You're telling me I should forget it in order to be happy. I don't like it, but what's the alternative?

L: *Do you know Nietzsche at all?*
S: It's probably trash because he was jealous of Wagner. I don't like his attitude toward Wagner. It was just the typical, very mediocre attitude expressed in very fancy language, but it was the very typical *Village Voice* attitude toward anybody that is making a success, but a success based upon their need to transform somebody into an object, and then sacrificing him.

L: *Nietzsche defines a nihilist phase which corresponds to what you call 'anarchist': to question everything. There is a second phase which is more interesting: once you've realized what everything is and how it works, how it's going to repeat itself, endlessly, you just step out of it, and affirm other, positive values. You don't waste any more energy criticizing and destroying.*
S: Tell me what I am to do with the energy. I'm supposed to rush into the turquoise paradise of the Bahamas? After two days, I would be bored. I've got to have something to hate.

L: Flaming Creature *was about fun, not denouncing.*
S: I made a comedy. Now I want to make a drama. The movie I'm now preparing is going to be an Arabian Nights architecture film and it will be in Super-8. 35 millimeter is insanely wasteful. And it's never cleaned. It gives me the horrors. Uncle Fishook represents the idea of expectations from authority, which is also perfect for me since I could spend the rest of my life demolishing very happily. I can be happy in this way. You couldn't, but it has just been my lot to have to clean out the toilets. I mean that's the job that's been inherited by me in life and I have run away from it, I spent the last fifteen years running away from it. Nobody wants to open a can of worms, but that's the thing that has been handed for me to do. And maybe that's a part of all bigtime manufacturers and capitalists, that they're an Uncle Fishook. Maybe I've found a key to them in some way from having to deal with the evil that's come into my life.

BY JACK SMITH

EKAS COLLABORAT

with NO © ?

Pay Pay INSIDE

Jean-François Lyotard

On the Strength of the Weak

The story I intend to begin with tonight is taken from Aristotle, who tells us there once was a rhetor, a lawyer, named Corax, who had a certain *techné*, a certain art, a certain skill that Aristotle describes thus: Someone, who is Corax's client, is accused of brutalizing a victim. There are two cases says Aristotle; in the first case the client is vigorous, in the second case he is weak. If the client is not strong Corax will argue that it is not likely his weakly client maltreated anyone. Very well, says Aristotle, Corax resorts to verisimilitude; a weakling is indeed unlikely to brutalize anyone. But in the other case, if the client is strong, Corax will plead that the accused was quite aware that his stength made his indictment likely; knowing that likelihood, he took care not to commit any brutality, which proves his innocence.

Aristotle objects that this use of verisimilitude is improper to the extent that pure and simple verisimilitude, likeliness in itself, is not resorted to in this case; verisimilitude is used in a verisimilar way. In other words, the accused foresees the likeliness and acts according to what he is likely to be told. In this particular case, the likelihood is not pure since it is related to itself; it is not considered absolutely. A difference should be made between an absolute likelihood and one which isn't, and Aristotle comes to the conclusion that the substance of Corax's *techné*, the secret of his art, consisted in making the weakest discourse the strongest.[1]

I would like to show very rapidly that the important thing is to devise schemes within the discourse of the masters itself, the magisterial discourse, and I intend to confine myself tonight

Douglas Dunn

interview

Sylvère LOTRINGER: You started dancing with Merce Cunningham. What impact do you think his training had on your work?

Douglas DUNN: Dancing is automatically self-expressive. The doer being present, he can't help revealing himself all the time. But there are ways of focusing one's attention so as not to make that a primary concern. What Merce Cunningham offered was a body that wasn't in the act of primarily expressing itself. Having done so, much is opened that wasn't before.

Many dancers have been and still are busy expressing themselves. Nothing wrong with that. But what Merce and John (Cage) did turned a corner. They outlined another possibility, another area to work in. I think of myself as working in that area.

What Merce offered was the performer not telling you what he was thinking or dancing about. It's that simple. It is not simple ultimately, but in first definition it is. It's like classical restraint. You purposely restrain in order to create something other than yourself, a new or different character. What Merce did was to restrain, and then *not* create a character. You are left with a person dancing.

It's hard to understand why people got, still get, upset by this simple, concrete image. I guess it's unfamiliar in the theatre for someone to come out "just dancing", I liked it right away because at the beginning I wasn't interested in the theatre or in performance. I just wanted to dance, to do

to problems of discourse. What I am really interested in, however, and maybe this can be done at a later date, next week perhaps, is to find out, by elucidating these small instruments of cunning, whether they can function in other fields than discourse, and more specifically of course, in the so-called "political field". My intention, if intentions are to be declared, is thus a political intention.

Assuming that we confine ourselves to problems of discourse, the discourse of the master, the magisterial discourse, essentially consists, I believe, in an injunction concerning the very function of discourse, according to which this function can only be to say the Truth. What relation is there between such a requirement and mastership? A truth-functional discourse, a discourse of knowledge, must uncover, must produce, the conditions in which statements can be characterized by a positive or negative "truth value", must, if you prefer, determine its conditions of truth. The conditions of truth can only be determined if some kind of a meta-discourse exists within the magisterial discourse; that meta-discourse has traditionally been the philosophical discourse, it is the discourse of

the movement. To sense it, yes, but not to think about it, nor aim it anywhere. Later I got confused, realizing that going on stage, you become some kind of character for the audience, and began to consider that.

L: Did you try to reintegrate character into your work?
D: Indirectly. In *Time Out* and in *Solo Film & Dance* I put on a variety of costumes. I don't work consciously toward or away from the suggested characters, but I think the costumes influence me inadvertently. I haven't had any conscious understanding of the nature of the characters I become in my dances until the dances are made and I've performed them for a while.

L: Are you looking for an element that would in some way unify all the movements?
D: Yes, in different pieces I pay more attention to some elements than to others. Paying more attention establishes a degree of consciously determined clarity. Paying less attention allows me to get out of my

logic in modern times. In other words, there is in the first place what is said, and in the second place what allows one to say it, i.e. the discourse concerning that which authorizes one to say what one says. The magisterial discourse clearly requires this split as its injunction, its intention, its project.

There is accordingly some sort of an intimidation in the discourse of the master, which consists in compelling us to recognize a number of principles, i.e. you must—your task is to—say the Truth, be truthful; you must assume that the conditions of that truth are not given, that they are concealed, which means that they must be elaborated, uncovered, worked out. That, as a consequence, there is a lack of truth in ordinary statements, in the statements of our daily life. History is but—such is for example Augustine's position—a struggle for the advent of Truth; the function of politics is merely a pedagogical function: its very essence consists in bringing about the awareness which will allow us to differentiate true and false statements among the countless utterances we are bombarded with every day. The efficacy of language, in this perspective, is always linked to truthfulness, that is, to conviction, which is obtained by bringing the listener to recollect the lost truth. There are, if you will, a number of these injunctions; without claiming that I have exhausted them, I would like to stress that they are all congruous, that they all point in the same direction, ultimately, whether one be on a purely discursive level, or at the political level, or at that of historical praxis: they make truthfulness both the object and the means of discourses.

I will add just one thing on that subject, namely that the whole position of Marxist discourse is determined by this magisterial position, belongs to it in its entirety. Thus . . . the schizo-culture trend for instance, tries to avoid these injunctions, by externalizing itself. Considering not only the discourses, but also the praxes of the sixties, it can be said, very briefly, that the general attempt was to stay outside the magisterial injunction and to produce, under extremely varied names, some sort of an exteriority: spontaneity, libido, drive, energy, savagery, madness, and perhaps schizo.

Now, that is exactly what the magisterial position and discourse ask for. In other words, there is a trick of the magisterial discourse, of the Occidental discourse if you will, there is a ruse of that discourse, which consists precisely in requiring that we place ourselves outside of it in order to avoid it. The device is very simple, it

own way. In one section of *Gestures in Red* my instructions are to work on a triangular floor pattern, to hold my gaze on the downstage apex, to articulate feet and shoulders, not to turn more than ninety degrees right or left. The simplicity of this structure and the relatively low energy level of the movement leave me room to deal with that, and with something else also, the image of another dancer perhaps. Not to imitate him, but to hold the image of that dancer in mind while dancing. Not that others should or would see an image of the other dancer, but I'm feeding off it. So by mixing input I produce a dance image that is not entirely consciously predetermined.

L: The original intentions are not what matters?
D: Those are the original, the only intentions: the structure. And they matter absolutely. They are the means for making the work, they keep me interested. And they are calculated to produce a dance I couldn't have imagined beforehand.

L: Do you try in any way to set the relationship of your dance to the audience?
D: How can you make a dance for an audience when its members are all different and are going to read the same dance differently? No, I focus my attention away from what I think a given move or dance might be for spectators. And that leaves them free not to worry about my intentions. We both relate to the object, the image being produced, I as doer, they as watchers, or perhaps as vicarious doers, and there is no compulsion to agree on the experience.

L: How much do you want your work to be structure?
D: I think of everything I do about a dance as structure. By definition. Of course it is possible to vary the timing of the decision-making process in relation to the performance: I'm interested in the entire range, from making decisions in performance, to making them well in advance, deliberately, and practicing the result.

L: Is it improvisation that keeps a dance alive?
D: Nothing guarantees that. I have wondered if the considerable amount of choice

consists in making exteriority the necessary complement of that discourse. And, I may add, a complement to be conquered, an opaque zone in which that discourse must penetrate in its turn. When one externalizes oneself in order to avoid the magisterial discourse, one is just extending that position, nourishing it. I think this is true of any critique since it always implies the externalization of the criticizing position in relation to the criticized position, which will allow the latter to include the former as its necessary complement. All sorts of transpositions can be made and you should have no difficulty in making them on the political level.

Considering, for instance, what happened in the workers' movement at the end of the nineteenth century and at the beginning of the twentieth, during the first half of the twentieth, to put it briefly, one will find that a movement which theorized itself as being localized outside capitalist society was precisely being sucked into that system. Now then, it seems to me that the uneasiness, the distress which the radical critical movements are experiencing today derive to a great extent from the fact that this exteriority has practically, has in fact disappeared.

Thus, what we should devise is a strategy which can dispense with exteriority, which, as far as language is concerned, would not place itself outside the rules of the discourse of Truth, that is of the discourse of power, but inside those rules. And which instead of excluding itself under the name of delirium, or madness, or pathos in general, or whatever, would on the contrary, play these rules—or rather the Rule of all these rules against itself by including the so-called meta-statements in its own utterances. And one would then see that our weakness (I don't really know who "we" is), can tap the strength of power to neutralize it. That operation of counter-cunning, which would avoid externalization, would necessarily bear against the essential element I mentioned earlier, namely the exclusion of meta-statements, the exclusion of the discourse on the conditions of truth. It would bear against that exclusion, i.e. it would simply consist in ensuring that there be no meta-statements. And this would be done in the most immediate manner, not by denouncing that fact that meta-statements are supported by that interest or another, this or that passion. (In trying to demonstrate such an assertion, one is in effect remaining in the discourse of truth. Thinking that such a demonstration can convince amounts in fact to assuming that the efficacy of a critical discourse is linked to conviction). That

available to the dancers in *Lazy Madge* helps keep them from looking as if they are going through the motions of someone else's dance. Making and presenting a dance that has some liveliness to it may depend on some kind of matching structure with moment in the lives of the available dancers. But since there is no recipe for how to make such a match, it doesn't really help to know that. You just try what feels right, and see what happens. And if you don't like the result, doing the opposite next time can be just as wrong, everything having changed by that time.

L: You want to be able to surprise yourself?
D: Yes, as Merce pointed out, you have two choices physically: either you throw your body weight, upper first, and the legs follow, or you motivate the travelling with the legs. The latter offers more possibilities, as it leaves the torso, arms and head free to do something else. I find I do a little more swinging and catching than Merce does, to surprise myself I guess, but basically I feel at home with his idea of being able to change the direction of the movement at any moment, so that it is unpredictable. I'm also interested in the mental set. In most of Merce's work the dancer knows what the body is supposed to be doing; the surprise and unpredictability are from the third person's point of view. I want to know also how the performance might look when the dancer doesn't know what he is going to do next.

L: Does this require a different mental attention?
D: Yes, and this is a primary interest right now, to mix many possible attentions. Doing set material you know well, some you don't know that well, choosing between five different elements, mixing them, and making up your mind also to do what you have never done before at this point in the dance: that kind of layering. I saw something like it in the de Kooning show. Up close you see the various layers, how many times he went at it. At a distance you see not any one, but all of the layers meshed.

L: In *Lazy Madge* you introduced improvisation into Merce's framework.

A
B
C
D
E
F
G
H
I
J
K
L
M
N
O
P
Q
R
S
Z
T
U
V
W
X
Y
Twice for Repeat!
Period
Woglom's
Signal-phabet
Copyright
1895.

operation would thus consist not in displaying the hidden presumptions of the masters' meta-statements, but in resorting to small instruments of cunning within the magisterial discourse itself.

I will now illustrate this point by turning back to Corax's *techné*, which Aristotle was bent on denouncing. Aristotle protests against a second level usage of verisimilitude (he is describing the different possibilities of operation inside the discourse of verisimilitude in general, and more particularly in rhetoric), and denouncing a specific aspect of Corax's *techné*, he considers that likelihood exists in itself, e.g. a strong individual *is* likely to brutalize a victim. Such an assumption is likely in itself, but when Corax says that his client knows likelihood is against him, that it accuses him on account of his strength and that he refrained from any brutality for that very reason, one is no longer in the sphere of likelihood in itself but in that of relative likelihood. Relative in relation to what? In relation to likelihood. In other words, Corax's client is someone who utters the following type of statements: "It is likely that I will be accused of committing the offense". His conduct thus includes beforehand the effects of the law of verisimilitude and accordingly circumvents that law. The client resorts to a second level likelihood, which implies that the first type of likelihood, i.e. likelihood as such, is never irrelative, is never absolute, since any absolute, any irrelative can always be related at least to itself.

You can thus see that in this operation on which Corax bases his whole *techné*, a very important logical and assuredly political asset is at stake, which is that no irrelative position exists; one cannot say: "such is verisimilitude in absolute terms", since absolute verisimilitude can be related to itself, producing the very opposite of what was expected. Absolute verisimilitude does accuse the client, but when related to itself it exculpates him. Such is the reason underlying Aristotle's protestation, for he clearly understands (he was very clever) that there, behind that teeny weeny matter, something extremely important is at stake. Indeed, to the extent that the master, the judge in this particular case, bases his argument on verisimilitude—on the existence of likelihoods that are truer than others—in order to assert that a strong individual is "more really likely" to brutalize a victim, I can play verisimilitude against itself so as to dissolve its absoluteness. And the effects are reversed. . . . As you can see, this is a very significant matter, a very serious one.

D: Yes, I mixed the two. I made set bits, then let go of the order in performance. If I don't want to dance with someone on a given evening, I don't have to. I simply avoid the material that involves that person. So emotion enters into the formality of the piece as a possible basis for choice. The piece has extreme limits. It would be within the rules, for example, if no one entered the performance area at all. But these people like to dance together, so there are other factors operating along with the rules. Not knowing what use we will make of the material when we go to perform sets up an atmosphere different from that surrounding a linearly ordered work.

L: How can you control or modulate emotionality if you open the piece to such an extent?
D: I control it by not controlling it. In the other piece I'm working on now, *Rille*, I'm taking a different approach, setting almost everything, including the order. But I'm still not making what I would call effects. That is, I'm not filling out some idea about how I think the dance should come across to some imagined audience person. I work from the inside out, to the structure, from there back, to the dancing itself, ignoring as much as possible the signs that pop up along the way telling me what it ought to look or feel like. I work with the structure, it feels like something, I work with the structure.

L: There is definitely an abstract quality in your work. The geometric impulse, though, seemed much stronger in your earlier pieces.
D: Yes, *101*, the still piece, was rather geometric, as were some parts of *Four for Nothing, Time Out* and *One Thing Leads to Another*.

L: What is the function of geometry?
D: It's a starting point, I suppose, something to go away from, something to contain and balance other elements. In *Lazy Madge* there's hardly any. I broke it by turning over the shape of the piece to the decision-making of the dancers. In *Rille* it is present quite consciously, as a ground against which to consider density.

You have all understood that, in this example, the client who is strong is precisely the weak one; I mean to say that his position is weak as a direct consequence of his strength. Something which points in the same direction is the paradox of the liar, which consists in saying: "If you say you are lying, and if you are in fact lying, then you are telling the truth, etc". Many attempts have been made to refute this paradox; Russell, for instance, tried to establish that there are two types of statements—such is precisely the distinction I was making earlier between statements and meta-statements. And Russell claims to solve the paradox by forbidding us to mix, to blend statements of the first type and of the second one: There is meta-discourse, and the effects of discourse should not be transferred to the meta-discourse. But why is this transfer prohibited? Russell's answer is simply that if you do rely on such an operation, then no discourse of truth remains possible. In other words, Russell's refutation is not a refutation, it is nothing more than the magisterial decision itself, i.e. my meta-statements are not in the same class as ordinary statements. Thus, the paradox of the liar, which is irrefutable since it cannot be controverted without being departed from, implies that there is no discourse of truth and accordingly the function of discourse is completely diverted inasmuch as it will always be impossible to decide whether a statement is true or false.

Another story concerns a Sophist named Protagoras. Protagoras asks his disciple, Euathlus, to pay him his fees. The latter answers him in the following terms: You haven't made me win a single cause, you have helped me gain no victory in discourses, therefore I owe you nothing. And Protagoras retorts: There is something you owe me in any case; you owe me the money, for if I win you must pay me and if you win you must also pay me. The debate Protagoras is referring to is not that which the disciple is thinking of. Euathlus is in fact thinking of the debates he participated in, which he lost. Protagoras, on the other hand, is talking about the current debate between himself and his disciple and he states: This debate has come to a conclusion; either you win or I do. Should you win, you would have to pay me since our contract stipulates that the orator's disciple is to pay his master when he gains a victory. And should I be the winner, that is should you, my pupil, be the loser, then you would also have to pay, since in a judicial debate the loser pays. All of this is perfectly correct. . .

L: How do you go about making a piece where the movement is fixed and the choices unlimited, as in *Lazy Madge*?
D: First I made solos for each of the dancers, and asked them to dance them simultaneously. They had to look out for each other. It was like the street, people with different intentions whose paths crossed at times. And then if there was no one in the way they could dance the movement as well as they knew how, but always with an eye to traffic problems. Then I went on to make duets, trios, etc. allowing the dancers to choose from the material during performance, down to the minutest fragment. We rehearsed the bits in their original form, as duets, trios, and so on, but in performance we let go of that.

I had made some rules before I began: I couldn't work out of the presence of the person who was to do the movement I was making; I couldn't set my own material except where it involved partnering; new material was to be performable as soon as it was learned and could be repeated. This last has to do with the piece being conceived as a project. For two years I've made new material, we've rehearsed the old, and performed whenever there's been an opportunity. So in a given performance we are using newly made, little rehearsed materials, as well as earlier, more familiar moves.

Also, I don't set rehearsal time. I'm available for so many hours a day, people come when they can or want to. I am interested in accommodating their various schedules, and in disallowing their using me as an authority figure to prime their wills.

In all, as a group, we have about eight hours of material available to us. We usually perform one hour and ten minutes, without a break. You dance along, and someone says "time," or the lights go out.

L: The situation you created seems fluid enough to allow any kind of movement. Do you feel that at this point classical elements can be introduced and juxtaposed to the rest without inconvenience?
D: By working only in the presence of the person who is going to do the movement I'm making, I leave myself open to that person's influence, and diminish overall considerations of style. The dancers are

Protagoras considers his relationship with Euathlus in one instance as being of a magisterial nature, and in another instance as being antagonistic, which implies an important thing, i.e. that there can be no school, because the characteristics of a school—and I hope there will never be a schizo school—is that a certain type of discourse exists, which I shall call protected. If the pupil, the disciple, holds such a discourse outside the school, and if he fails, if therefore he does not gain an outside victory, it will be said, in a magisterial relationship, that his training is insufficient, that he should follow more courses, proceed with his studies, that he should be retrained, etc., but the blame for the adverse situation the pupil experiences will not be put on the relationship with the master; on the contrary, what Protagoras says is that "this adverse relationship permeates our magisterial relationship, and you are also my enemy." Another aspect of this matter also deserves to be noted, which is that Protagoras' paradox consists in the same operation of inclusion as the paradox of the liar. When Euathlus says: I have never won a cause, consequently I owe you nothing, what is he talking about? He's talking about debates which are external to his relationship with the master. Protagoras on the other hand includes the debate he is now engaged in with his disciple in the same category as those external debates. Thus, in this case as well, there is a refusal to consider any debate held inside the schools as

different one from another, as dancers and as people, and I don't work against these differences. It's a tacit collaboration. The common ground between us, aside from our desire to work together, is that each of us has at least some exposure to Merce's work. This guarantees an open and non-analytical attitude to the process of learning and repeating movement.

L: You seem to stay clear both from expressivity and formality, or rather to involve the dramatic element to such a degree that it feeds the more abstract aspect of your work. Do you see it that way?

D: Well, I would say that as the sixties fall behind us, an explicitly formalistic approach feels to me no less didactic than an explicitly expressive one.

L: What about humour?

D: Jokes are an obvious kind of performance, not very surprising. Their suspense is familiar. They constitute what I referred to before as making effects. You try to make the audience laugh, to manipulate them as a group. For their own pleasure, of course. You can't do this without a fair number of already shared assumptions. Such a situation precludes the more personal, intimate, confusing experience I associate with looking at art. Buster Keaton's films work some sort of a meta-debate; the current debate falls under the same category as all other debates.

The position of magisterial discourse requires a protection against external debates, it implies that we confine ourselves to a region of discourse, which is simultaneously a social region, into which the external debates cannot penetrate. The only permissible debates will be those concerning external debates. Such is the very foundation of the school, which is after all one of the aspects of the magisterial relationship.

In this paradox, Protagoras considers Euathlus as an opponent if he loses, and as his disciple if he wins. Euathlus has no identity, he can be identified neither as an adversary nor as a disciple, which implies that Protagoras already rejects an entire logic or predication or substantial definition. Euathlus has no properties. Moreover, one finds in Protagoras's paradox the inclusion of the future in the present. Indeed, Protagoras argues against his disciple by including its outcome in the ongoing debate and saying: If you lose—if you will lose as they say in Turkish—then you shall pay and if you will win, then you shall also pay. And that inclusion of the future is worked out in the manner of a parody, for the discourse Protagoras holds with respect to his disciple is precisely the parody of the magisterial discourse: the master already knows what the outcome is going to be. In short, the future is included not in the form of a contingency, but as being identical to itself. The master has control over this future. It is a parody of the magisterial discourse precisely to the extent that Protagoras actually considers that Euathlus has no contingent future. He has no future, i.e. he shall pay in any case, which is exactly the position of Capital with respect to any one of us: whether one wins or loses, one has to pay. All of this does not mean that Protagoras is in a strong position, and whereas I said earlier that in Corax's case, the accused who is strong is precisely the weakest insofar as verisimilitude is against him, in Protagoras' case the master is the weak one, for he risks not being paid, and for a Sophist this is very serious, since Sophists collect no ground rent as philosophers do, they aren't civil servants, they are artists, they are paid on a piece-work basis, after each job, each performance. . .

PEERLESS HANDCUFF.
Weight, 12 ounces.
Nickel plated or blue steel $10.00
Mattatuck Doub
Plated only
No. 200
Tower Double Lock Hand Cuffs
Plated, $9.00 Polished, $8.00
Bean's Gia
GIANT
Bean's Impr
No. 201
Tower Light Detective Hand Cuffs
Plated, $9.00 Polished, $8.00
Plated, $6.00
Tower Doubl
No. 202
Tower Double Lock Hand Cuffs
For 3 Hands
Plated, $8.30
Tower's B
Plated, $11.00 Polished, $10.50
Plated, $6.00
No. 203
Maltby Double Lock Detective Handcuffs
Five-Foot
Plated only $7.00
No. 204
Chain Hand Cuffs,
Detachable Comealong
Plated only $4.75
with Peerless cu
with any other
LEATHER HANDCUFF AND LEG IRON
Convenient to carry every day or on journey—prev
and neat leather pockets for any style of handcuffs or

There are many similar stories and I think we should analyze them carefully for it is not sure at all that they all refer to the same cunning devices; some of them could very well be based on other devices, but it seems to me that three or

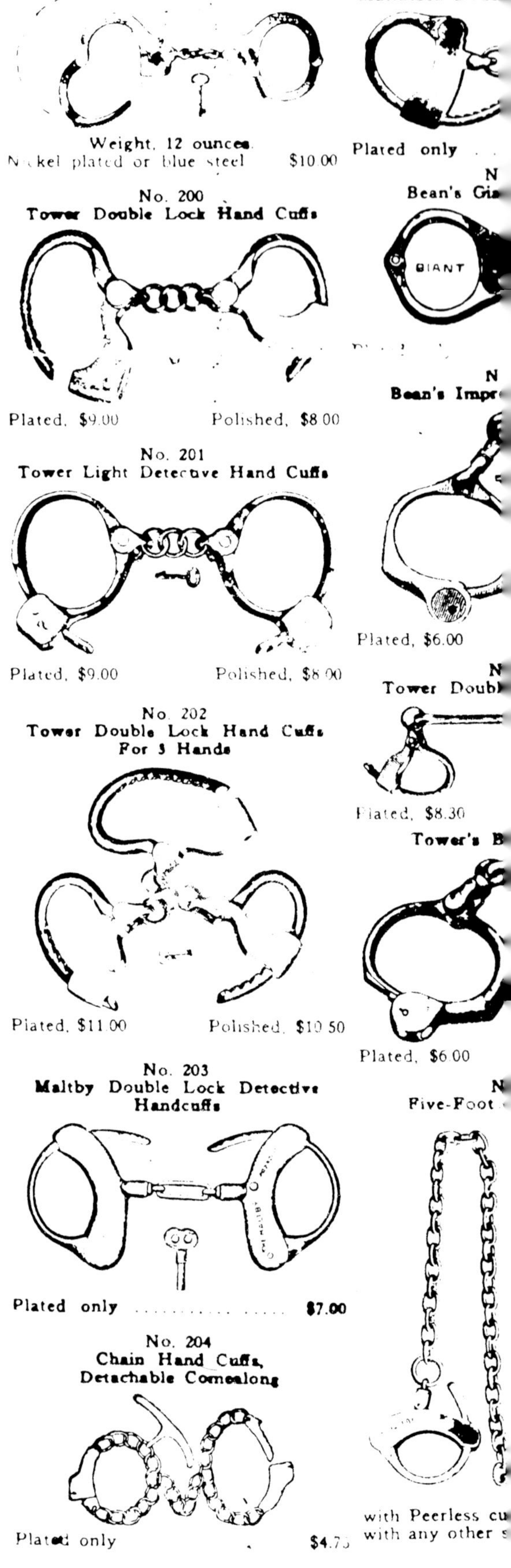

four such examples are sufficient to outline a position of discourse which is curious enough in relation to the magisterial position; the former position may very well invest the latter, and that is why I chose the example of Protagoras, who is in principle the student's master. What strikes me however is that Protagoras resorts to a reasoning which cannot be that of a master but which points to a discourse other than the Platonic, or the magisterial discourse in general (from Plato to Marx) whose position is in fact always the same. It seems to me something else is arising here, insofar at least as the trade of the intellectual is concerned—which isn't all that different from other trades; new weapons are appearing, very small weapons, but very important I believe, and very serious. These very weak weapons do however have the power of upsetting, be it for a fleeting instant (but that is irrelevant here, since the aim is not to obtain cumulative effects), of unsettling the magisterial position and the assumptions underlying it, i.e. the belief in the existence of a meta-discourse, of an order within which discourses, and practices as well of course, can be grounded and substantiated.

We should therefore continue to explore these paradoxes, called paradoxes because one did not know what to do with them, and which have been expunged, destroyed, like the works of Protagoras himself. What is involved here is a possible position of discourse which has effectively been obliterated in its entirety and which can afford us new weapons. I believe it would be interesting to find out what effects these weapons can produce in the political order; this is roughly what I wanted to say tonight. I shall just make one more remark in that connexion, which is that we should imagine new praxes and notably practices of discourse and political practices, which would not be articulated around the idea of a reinforcement through organization or an efficiency through conviction. The idea that a radical political efficacy does not rest on truthfulness deserves consideration.

The question we should raise concerns the possibility of producing political efficiency not at all by linking it to the belief in Truth, but rather by developing it in the direction of a relativism, in the strong, general sense of the term, that is by accelerating the decline of the idea of truth, by contributing to its deterioration. This cannot be done by setting a new truth against the old one, which is of no moment, regardless of the name of that new truth. It would be much more interesting to imagine, in my opinion, a political

for me because the deadpan attitude creates a separate continuity: something else is happening along with the dramatic rise and fall of the gag. A potent sadness for example. I don't try for humour in my work, any more than for any other effect. Still, I get some kicks.

L: Is walking in the street close to your idea of what dance now is about?

D: As an analogy, yes, somehow related to the work I do in *Lazy Madge*. The mix of, on the one hand, orderliness, the streets, stop lights, traffic laws, etc., and, on the other hand, complexity, all those separate intentions finding their way in and around each other, on foot and in vehicles. I find that an interesting image. It is fantastically magnified in the films of Rudy Burckhardt.

L: Do you feel affinities with other dancers or choreographers?

D: As I get more involved in what I'm doing, my projections on other dancers and choreographers fade out. Now I can watch dance for pleasure.

efficiency whose aim would not be to convince, but which would rather seek discontinuous local effects which could disappear and would not bring about the adherence of those who witness them. Rather it would bring about something else which would be neither trust nor mistrust, something we could call tragic, etc., which would however be more like humor I believe (there being no incompatibility between these two terms). It seems to me something of that sort is happening now; such is undoubtedly the case as far as some of the events happening in France are concerned at any rate, although I am not yet quite capable of elaborating on this argument. I could give you as an example, without committing myself, a movement of the prostitutes which developed in France this year.

At first sight this movement appeared to be one aimed at pushing demands: "We are workers, we want decent working conditions, etc.," but this discourse simultaneously implied something else, which in fact unsettled the relation of society to the feminine body, and even to desire in general. What it said was: "If you accept the existence of different kinds of trades and if you consider that the motivations underlying their practice are good, are acceptable, then accept our motivation as well, i.e. the desire for prostitution. Now, this problem is extremely serious, and I believe a typically political modern action is involved here: it is punctual, it bears upon the inclusion of the desire for prostitution in the same class as all other desires. . . and it functions, it seems to me, in the direction not of a distrust, but in that of the destruction of the belief in the existence of good and bad desires. Practices of this type are operative not on account of their revealing a new truth, but insofar as they destroy meta-discourses in specific places. And what this means basically, is that such a politics is no longer centered around the question of a pedagogy, which has always been the case, for politics has always been pedagogical. Thus, we should no longer say: "we shall gain victory, we shall grow stronger if we manage to awaken the truth which is alienated, concealed, repressed, etc."; Protagoras doesn't give a rap about Euathlus' conviction, such are not the terms the efficiency of his action can be measured in.

Translated by Roger McKeon

1. Aristotle, *Rhetorica*, book II.24, 1 402 a 3 & 17. *The works of Aristotle*, Oxford University Press, 1971, vol. XI, translated by W. Rhys Roberts.

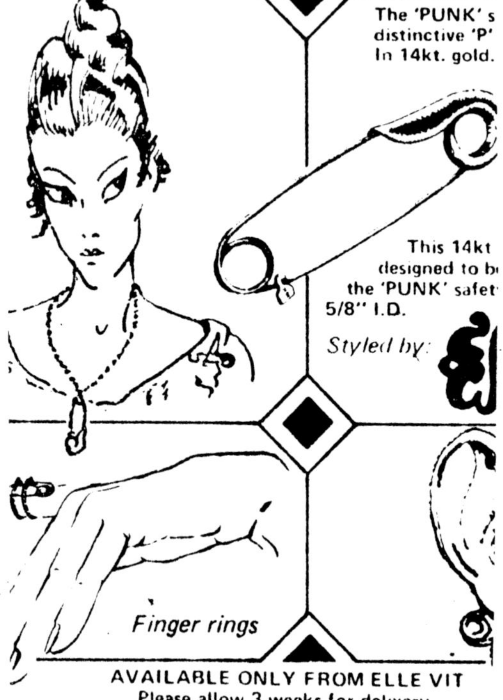

be paid to persons giving such information as will lead to the
persons responsible.

is sought to trace the whereabouts of the after described persons:

ROSE EDWARDS ... EYTHERY.
5ft. 5in., hair black. May be accompanied
her NICOLETTE, aged about 3 years.

DALY.

daughter

PATRICIA, aged

brown

right of

FRANCES ...OLDS, aged about 24, 5ft. 4in.,
... build, brown.

brown, eyes

...Grover.

For a letter for Q
destitution of grace.
throwing rocks down
In like the police di

In the destite

POL

Why do you like to th

When

en Victoria in its
nebody who was
ls a police and
not rescuo the boy.

OLICE

CE

rock down.

ce TOCK

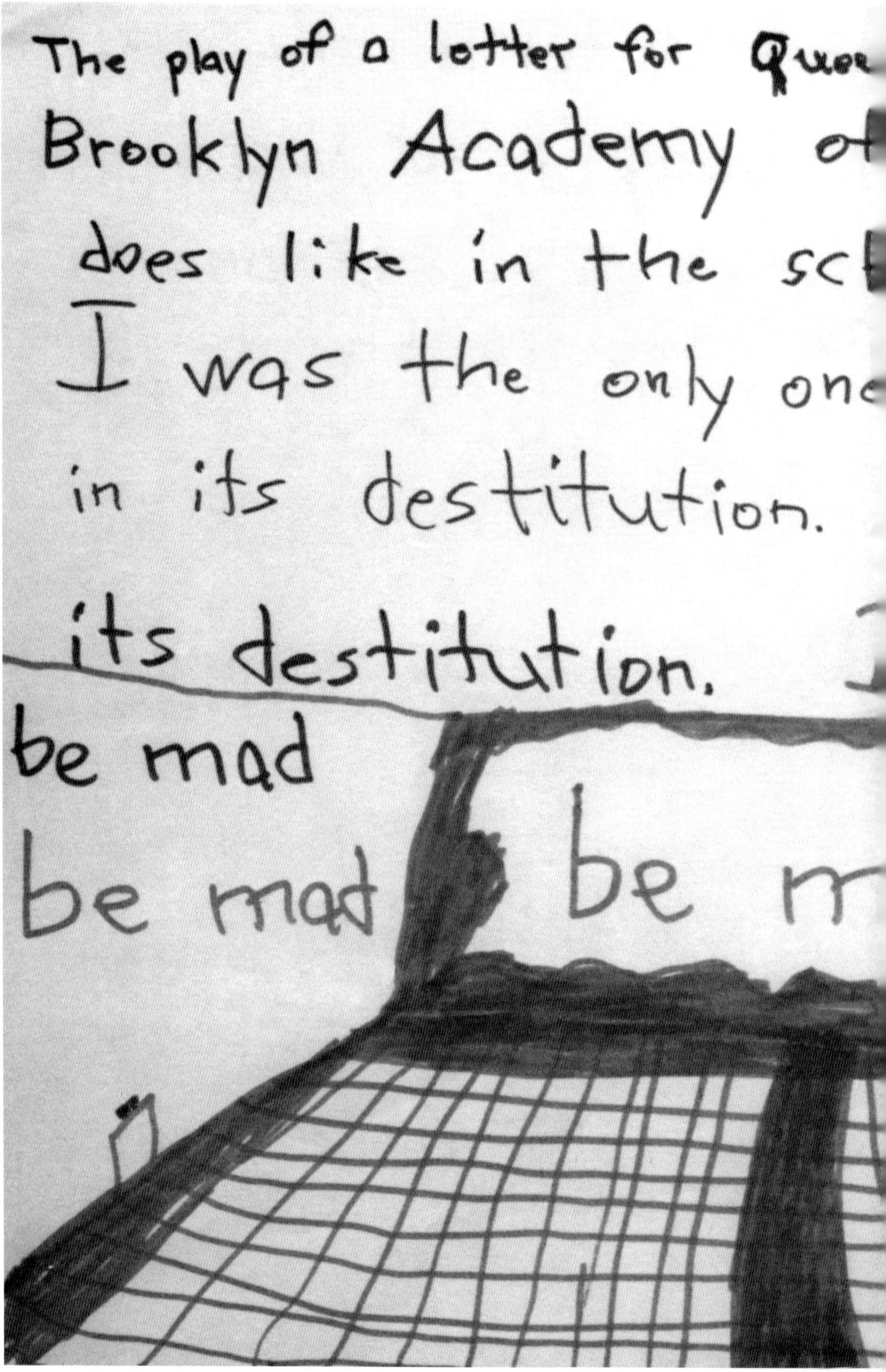

The play of a lotter for Quee
Brooklyn Academy of
does like in the sc
I was the only one
in its destitution.
its destitution. I
be mad
be mad be m

toria. It was the

usic. The principal who

in its destitution.

was the recording

was so different in

would be mad

be mad

d be mad

A SECOND CALL TO POLYSEXUALITY

Neither angel nor animal—no Christian morality
Neither man nor woman—no biological sexuality
Neither husband nor wife—no legal sexuality

We are looking for:
Anything that can break apart bipolar sexuality, that can lead to other modes of pleasure and their multiplication.

Recipes: for example, how can two men, three women, a hammer, an apple and a turkey make love together?

Tools of ecstasy, from boots to letters.

Axes of ecstasy, from dry to moist, from soft to hard...

Spaces of ecstasy: where can we come? Between razor and revolver... between hammer and anvil... between doors... between currents?

A new way of mapping out erotic space, cities, countries, bodies.

An erotic anatomy of the body, an anatomical physiology of the erotic body...

Write us, contact us, help us to open the space of polysexualities.

Special Editor: **François Péraldi**

CREDITS FOR VISUALS

Front cover: Kathryn Bigelow—Back cover: Kathryn Bigelow and Denise Green—Cover pictures: Michael Oblowitz—p.2: Christopher Knowles—p.8: Howard Buchwald—p.18: Michael Oblowitz, *Mr. Police* (Mr. Universe Contest, N.Y. 1978)—p.24: Christopher Knowles—p.25: Computer Printout—p.30: Jimmy De Sana, from forthcoming book, *Deviants*—p.32: James Holmstrom—p.39: Trans*éd*itions—p.41: *Los Angeles Times* (Sirhan Sirhan, Unidentified man and woman in Ambassador Hotel, Henry Luce)—p.42: International Terrorist Times (Patty Hearst)—p.43: Michael Oblowitz, from forthcoming book, *Blind Eye*—p.47: Digne Meller Marcovitz—p.50: Jimmy De Sana, *op. cit.*—p.54: Ken Kobland (*The Shaggy Dog Animation*)—p.57: Johan Elbers (*Shaggy Dog*)—p.64: Michael Oblowitz, *op. cit.*—p.76-80: martine Barrat—p.95: Martim Avilez—p.97: Mia—p.99: Musée de L'Homme, Paris, *Excision*—p.102: Jimmy De Sana, *op. cit.*—p.113: Diane Arbus, *Tattoed Man at a Carnival*, Md. 1970 (Photo cropped and retouched by MOMA)—p.144: ITT (Andreas Bader)—p.115: ITT (Ulrike Meinhof)—p.152-3: Trans-*éd*itions—p.155: Drawing by a ghetto child (Courtesy Martine Barrat)—p.158: Mapping by young "Schizophrenics" (Deligny)—p.163: General Motors, *Express Highways* (N.Y. Fair, 1939-40)-p.169: Arturo Schwartz—p.211: Jackson Pollock, *The She-Wolf*, 1943 (MOMA)— p.215-19: Christopher Knowles.

Semiotext(e) sponsors a Colloquium on

schizo culture

14-16 november 1975

Columbia University

« *Madness is not necessarily a breakdown ; it can also be a breakthrough.* »

Ronald Laing

« *Maybe one day we will no longer understand what madness was all about... Artaud will belong to the root of our language, and not to its rupture.* »

Michel Foucault

Topics to be discussed :

1. *Revolution in Language*
   —Madness and Literature
   —Pathology of Language
   —Schizophrenia and Semiotics
2. *Madness and Civilization*
   —Politics of Insanity
   —Psychiatry and Anti-psychiatry
   —Psychoanalysis and Schizoanalysis

Persons wishing to speak at the Colloquium are requested to send a *one-page* abstract (with a stamped self-addressed envelope) to : *Semiotext(e)*, 522 Philosophy, Columbia University, New York, N.Y. 10027.

SEMIOTEXT(E) FOREIGN AGENTS SERIES

Published by Semiotext(e)
PO BOX 629, South Pasadena, CA 91031
www.semiotexte.com

Editorial support from Andrew Kersey

Special thanks to John Ebert.
Design by Hedi El Kholti

ISBN: 978-1-58435-124-5
10 9 8 7 6 5 4 3 2

Distributed by The MIT Press, Cambridge, Mass. and London, England
Printed in China

Schizo-Culture

THE EVENT 1975

Edited by Sylvère Lotringer and David Morris

<e>

Contents

Sylvère Lotringer: Introduction to Schizo-Culture 9

SCHIZO-CULTURE
Sylvère Lotringer: Introduction: The French Connection 43
John Rajchman: The Bodyguard 50
James Fessenden: Transversality and Style (Groups, Packs and Bands) 53
Arthur Danto: Freudian Explanations and the Language of the Unconscious 61
Jean-François Lyotard: On the Strength of the Weak (Group Translation) 79
Anti-Psychiatry Workshop 100
Joel Kovel: Therapy in Late Capitalism 107
Robert Fine: Psychiatry and Materialism and Q&A with François Peraldi et al. 127
François Peraldi: A Schizo and the Institution (in *Schizo-Culture* Issue page 20)
Michel Foucault: We Are Not Repressed 144
William Burroughs: The Limits of Control (in *Schizo-Culture* Issue page 38)
William Burroughs Q&A 161
R.D. Laing, Howie Harp, Judy Clark, Michel Foucault: Roundtable on Prisons and Psychiatry 167
John Cage: Empty Words (in *Schizo-Culture* Issue page 165)
Félix Guattari: Notes on Power and Meaning 182
Félix Guattari: Molecular Revolutions and Q&A 184
Ti-Grace Atkinson: The Psyche of Social Movements 196

David Morris: Schizo-Culture in Its Own Voice 203

Press Release

Schizo-Culture: A "Revolution in Desire"

An unprecedented international exchange/confrontation will take place at Columbia University from the thirteenth to the sixteenth of November, sponsored by the radical journal Semiotext(e).

From France are coming the major representatives of a movement which since May '68 has produced a breakthrough more far-reaching than the existentialism of the fifties or the structuralism of the sixties. Called a "revolution in desire" the movement, on the intellectual side, has introduced a strategy for dissolving and questioning systems which support them. On the pragmatic side, through its new analysis of capitalism, the movement has joined forces with the political challenge to psychiatric, penal, and patriarchal oppression as well as radical artistic innovation.

It is this movement which the colloquium seeks to connect with what William Burroughs has called "a cultural revolution of unprecedented dimension in America in the last twenty years"—a revolution in "lifestyles," in psychiatry, philosophy, politics and the arts. The colloquium offers point of contact among elements of the two developments. It thus prepares the way to what might be termed a "schizo-culture." "Schizo" does not refer here to any clinical entity, but to the process by which social controls of all kinds, endlessly re-imposed by capitalism, are broken up and opened to revolutionary change.

The colloquium has a supple structure to allow for the diversity in connection/confrontation. Philosophers of international status will present papers for general discussion: Michel Foucault (often called the successor to Sartre), Gilles Deleuze and Jean-François Lyotard (of the University of Paris) as well as Arthur Danto (of Columbia University). Félix Guattari, the radical French psychiatrist (often compared to R.D. Laing) will present the results of his thinking and participate in a panel discussion on psychiatry and its critiques with the English sociologist Robert Fine and radical psychoanalyst Joel Kovel (New York,) and François Peraldi (Montreal). Michel Foucault will also participate on a panel on prison/asylums with Judy Clark of the Midnight Special, the Columbia sociologist David Rothman and others. The feminist Ti-Grace Atkinson will talk on the psyche of social movements, and the writer William Burroughs on the impasses of control. And John Cage will present a new part of his composition "Empty Words" recently reviewed by The Village Voice, which appears to be closely connected to the critique of meaning recently developed in France.

But these are only a part of the scheduled activities. The colloquium also sponsors a number of workshops in such areas as: Psychiatry and Social Control; Radical Therapy; Schizo-City (Harlem); Cinema: Representation and Energetics; Ontologico-hysterical Theatre; Feminism and Therapy; Psychoanalysis and Politics; Gay Liberation; Mental Patients' Liberation; Prison Politics; Lincoln Detox Mass Culture; Psychoanalysis and Schizoanalysis. To this should be added numerous possibilities for encounter culmination in a schizo-party with the Henry Letcher Band, etc.

Sylvère Lotringer

Introduction to Schizo-Culture

When Columbia University offered me to join their French department in September 1972, my first thought was May 1968. How could it be otherwise? The student rebellion was only four years away and no one dared mention it any-more. What triggered the protests on campus had been the ill-fated project of building a gymnasium in Morningside Park, the area that separates Columbia from Harlem. Architect I. M. Pei would have eviscerated the park and replaced it with a two-story building with twin towers and limited access to the outside community, a neighborhood Provost Jacques Barzun described as "uninviting, abnormal, sinister, and dangerous," requiring "the perpetual qui vive of a para-trooper in enemy country."[1] One couldn't have stated more clearly how the Ivy League institution considered its black neighbors. The goal of the black community and student activists from the Student Afro-American Society (SAS) who participated in the strike was to improve the university's relationship with its Harlem neighbors and exercise Black Student Power through sit-ins, strikes, and marches. Their effort joined with the week-long occupation of campus by the mostly white radical antiwar movement of the Students for a Democratic Society (SDS) chaired by Mark Rudd. It was the most extensive and confrontational rebellion in the history of the United States. Seven hundred students were arrested after the police finally stormed the campus. Needless to say, Columbia wasn't the only college at the time to experience this kind of agitation. The young generation throughout the world was in revolt, against capitalism in the West, against Soviet communism in the East. It was a spring of hope.

1. Stefan M. Bradley, "Gym Crow Must Go!" *The Journal of African American History*, Vol. 88, No 2, Spring 2003 and *Black Student Power in the Late 1960s*, University of Illinois Press, 2009, p. 27.

I was all the more curious about the way May 1968 began at Columbia since I had missed May 1968 in France. I was teaching in Sydney, Australia, and only caught on with the 1960s when I was hired by Swarthmore College, a small elite Quaker school near Philadelphia, in 1969. It was an eventful year as well in which I did participate. The Vietnam War was still raging in Southeast Asia and so were antiwar demonstrations at home. In early May 1970 Nixon's invasion of Cambodia touched off a "mass strike" across all the nation's campuses. On May 4 the National Guard killed four student demonstrators at Kent State University in Ohio and the Swarthmore campus erupted. Wild rumors circulated about Philadelphia—half an hour away by train—being on fire. Swarthmore faculty and students went on strike and met every night at the Student Center to celebrate their newfound political consciousness. Exams were postponed indefinitely. And yet over time insider activism began losing steam. The area, a very privileged suburb, was hardly conducive to "community work" and the woody campus with its own river was gorgeous in the summer. By the time the college reopened in the fall it was exams as usual, but "exceptions certainly could be made for those student activists who chose to postpone them for reasons of their own." The scenario, I assume, was repeated a number of times all over the country. A few months later the oil crisis started and recession kicked in, a godsend for law and order. Jobs became scarce, flower power and communes withered into thin air, and academic radicals started their Long March through the institution. They're still walking.

There is no doubt that the ghost of May 1968 floated around the halls of Columbia University where the four-day Schizo-Culture conference was held in November 1975. It was as if something of these days of protest permeated the audience "beyond these walls or through this muffling that constitutes a sort of wall of sound within this university," as Félix Guattari said, describing the huge conference hall where crowds of people had gathered. And feminist activist Ti-Grace Atkinson recalled: "Sometimes I dread coming up here to this campus. I feel as if I'm walking on people's graves … It's hard to believe, given the pastoral attitude of the students, that 1969 and 1970 ever really happened. Most unfortunately, even those who were quite active in the antiwar movement seem to have short memories. We used to shout, 'Bring the war home,' so it finally came. But instead of meeting that war head on, on our own territory, most people retreated to their original homes. The war was over." Judy Clark, the prison activist, concurred during the Laing-Foucault panel: "When I used to live in New York City,

Columbia University was a very political institution. When I came back from jail, I was shocked to find there was a student rally on this campus asking for more police to protect them from the community around them." Obviously the times had been a-changing again. The SDS collapsed at the Democratic Convention in 1968, leaving behind the hard-core Weather Underground faction. The clandestine revolutionary movement allied with the Black Panther Party was bent on achieving "the destruction of US imperialism" through a campaign of bombing, mostly banks and government buildings. They were still active at the time of Schizo-Culture. Patty Hearst was kidnapped in 1974 by the Symbionese Liberation Army and in 1975 the Weathermen bombed a Puerto Rican bank in the Wall Street area in solidarity with Puerto Rican workers on strike. It was also in 1975 that the US Army finally withdrew from Vietnam after the disastrous fall of Saigon, and the United States signed the Paris Peace Accords with the North Vietnamese. The Weathermen split and disbanded one year later.

What happened during the Schizo-Culture conference took everyone by surprise, including those who were organizing it. Paradoxically, what we were trying to do was bring back French *post*-1968 theories to the United States and narrow the gap between radicalism, philosophy, and art on both sides of the Atlantic. It was a leap of faith and it probably happened too early. By the time these theories started permeating the culture in earnest—in the mid-'80s—it was already too late. In Europe post-Fordism was putting an end to traditional class struggles and everywhere in sight neoliberalism—Margaret Thatcher, Ronald Reagan—was busy dismantling the welfare state, deepening the gap between poor and rich. Creative activities were being reduced to the same futile goals: money, careers, "private initiative"—gratifications in the void. This cycle is now getting close to completion and so is the exhaustion of its potential for social innovation. The New Technologies and instant communication soon took over the entire capitalist semiosphere and there was nowhere else to go.

What triggered the Schizo-Culture conference was my friendship with Félix Guattari, whom I met in 1973. *Anti-Oedipus*, written with Gilles Deleuze, was published the year before. It was a revelation, the first serious attempt to register in philosophical terms the real impact of the student insurgency on French society. Their book wasn't only attacking familialism, as was often assumed, it was mapping post-revolutionary alternatives to the deregulated flows of capital. The failure of the Communist Party to support the uprising had been a clear signal in France that the old revolutionary machines had outlived their purpose. The

'68 event wasn't restricted to France, it spread everywhere like a fire, bringing out in the open a mutation that was beginning to affect the entire world.

Meeting Félix changed my life. In 1973, I was asked to set up a summer program in Paris for American students at Reid Hall, a beautiful complex near Montparnasse that had been bequeathed to Columbia in 1964. I had been away for the second part of the '60s, and Reid Hall was a chance to resume contact with the theoretical debate that had become intense in the aftermaths of the student rebellion. I invited philosophers and psychoanalysts from various camps to give a seminar to our American students. Félix was the first person I contacted. He wasn't an academic, but an activist and a far-left thinker and he enjoyed teaching. I attended his classes too. It didn't take long before we became close friends.

While studying at the Sorbonne in the early 1960s, I had been very involved with the students' struggle against the ugly war in Algeria. All this dissipated after the peace was signed with the FLN (National Liberation Front) in 1962. The consumer society rushed in to fill the gaps. I had opted out for a number of years trying to stay clear of the Vietnam War—WWII had been enough for me—and getting to know Félix was like finding myself again. The little foreign enclave in Paris became a neutral ground where the mutually exclusive and often acerbically opposed French intellectual coteries coexisted side by side. The summer program anticipated what became "French Theory" in the 1980s. It must have worked too well since it was taken away from me after two years and replaced by more traditional courses in French literature and structuralist criticism. But the original impulse for all that hadn't disappeared and I decided instead to bring back to New York—and to Columbia University—the radical French philosophers that I had worked with in Paris.

In 1974, I took a one-year leave of absence from Columbia that I spent in Paris with Semiotext(e) collaborator, Susie Flato. Our daughter was born there. Everything was opening up. During this period I often met Félix in the large apartment that he inhabited on rue de Condé, near the Théâtre de l'Odéon. Félix would throw generous parties attended by everyone he was involved with: activists, filmmakers, writers, anthropologists, actors, and anti-psychiatrists of various nationalities. It was during one of these parties that, among others, I met R. D. Laing and Pierre Clastres, the political anthropologist whose ideas were so seminal for *Anti-Oedipus* and who died very young in a car accident. I also often visited Félix in Duison, the magnificent Renaissance castle that he half-rented near the La Borde clinic. Situated one hour south of Paris, La Borde was the experimental "anti-psychiatric" clinic that Félix codirected with Lacanian psychoanalyst Jean Oury. What Guattari called "institutional psychotherapy" was aimed at treating psychotic patients by modifying the entire institutional context, and reciprocally. For this Félix designed an elaborate "grid" with rotating shifts, insuring that the multiple tasks and activities, from the stables to the kitchen, would be equally shared by patients, the service personnel, and the medical staff. The grid was a kind of human switchboard, a "body without organs" meant to desegregate the doctor-patient relationship and undermine the separation between madness and sanity. La Borde didn't just mean to cure psychotic patients, but to learn from them a different relation to the world. It was the first enactment of what I called "schizo-culture," a social laboratory meant to metastasize into the society at large. New York was next.

While in Paris I attended the meetings of the CERFI,[2] Félix's group, and it was its magazine, *Recherches*, that published (in French) "The Two Saussures," the second issue of Semiotext(e) in 1974. The first issue, "Alternatives in Semiotics," which included Félix Guattari and Julia Kristeva, had been released in New York by the small semiotic group that already met regularly before I arrived at Columbia. The magazine was founded in 1974 at the Maison Française, a brownstone on W. 113th Street and Broadway near the campus. Most members were graduate students in the French department. By the time I returned to New York in the early summer of 1975 most of them had already dispersed, hired by various universities across the country. The only one left with me was John Rajchman, our secretary. John was a graduate student in the department of philosophy at Columbia, which, like most philosophy departments in the United States, was invested in analytic philosophy and superbly ignored "continental" theories. Eventually he found kindred spirits among our small outfit and we worked closely together. He became my best friend. He left for Paris that same year hoping to perfect his French and make useful contacts.

Like most French intellectuals at the time, Félix was curious about New York. It was a fascinating place—bankrupt, dangerous, run-down, and I loved it for that. Shunned by the rest of America, New York radiated creativity and energy from afar. This cultural aura meant that whoever was coming from New York to spend time in Paris and who showed some interest in current French philosophy,

2. Center for the Study and Research in Institutional Formation founded in 1967.

as both John and I did, found the tightly shut doors of the Parisian intellectual scene wide open. I met Gilles Deleuze through Félix and John got easy access to Jacques Lacan and his Freudian School, whom he found more baroque. Félix used to be Lacan's most promising disciple and he still belonged officially to the Freudian school, which *Anti-Oedipus* didn't spare and the tension between the two groups was pretty much out in the open. We owed this covert rivalry to the impromptu visits that Gilles Deleuze and then Jacques Lacan each paid, unannounced, to Reid Hall.

In 1974 Félix was invited by the French Cultural Affairs Office in Paris to tour major psychiatric institutions throughout America and he took advantage of this trip to roam around Manhattan. We paid a visit together to Coney Island and he hung out with young girl gangs in the South Bronx with a videographer friend, Martine Barrat, who lived at the Chelsea Hotel. Félix got very excited about New York. He would wake up early in the morning to go around Manhattan, eager to see everything and paying visits to the likes of Allen Ginsberg. Félix was a great admirer of the Beats. His final report to the Cultural Affairs Office was rather severe for Freudian psychoanalysis, which clearly was declining everywhere on the North American continent except for the three more cosmopolitan cities, New York, Los Angeles, and Chicago. Psychoanalysis, he realized, was being replaced by more Pavlovian behavioral therapies, which I derided in a book on sexual therapeutics later on. *Anti-Oedipus*' attack on Freud and Lacan's theories, in short, had mostly been a French affair. The real threat in the United States wasn't a structuralist approach to the unconscious, but the brain-dead humanity in the offing.

Back in Paris, Félix communicated his newfound enthusiasm to Gilles Deleuze, but the French philosopher didn't budge. He detested traveling. Jean-Jacques Lebel, the inventor of happenings in France and a close friend of Felix's, was well connected with the American art scene and promised to take them to Big Sur. They would stay in Jack Kerouac's cabin. He would also arrange for them to meet the Beats and shake hands with Bob Dylan and Patti Smith. Deleuze loved Anglo-American literature, how could he resist the prospect of meeting all these living legends? Finally he surrendered, opening the way for an event that would obviously be centered on their own work. When John and I returned to New York in late spring 1975, we could definitely count on their participation.

Deleuze wasn't known in the United States at the time, except for the two books he published on Proust and on Sacher-Masoch, and it was more for these authors than for his own philosophy that they had been translated into English. Guattari was still an unknown quantity. He had been very active in leftist groups and was considered a Trotskyite. He was only well known in France by his association with Deleuze. Their major works, including *Anti-Oedipus*, hadn't been translated yet, and it took another decade for them to surface in the United States, probably because Foucault's books were briskly being translated into English and monopolized most of the attention.

They also seemed too close to the 1960s culture, by then dismissed or forgotten, with their outward embrace of the Beats and nomadism, Castaneda, Eastern wisdom and their reference to Nietzsche, still quarantined in the United States for his alleged association with fascism. At the time of Schizo-Culture, most people in the audience had no clue about who the two thinkers were. I didn't expect this to be a major problem. They were important thinkers and they were famous in France. Besides, news travels fast over the Atlantic, especially in New York, always ready for the latest fashion. New York publishers, which I solicited repeatedly, knew better and turned them down, deeming their work "too specialized." We had no other choice than publishing them ourselves with issues on "Anti-Oedipus" and "Nietzsche's Return," but these came a few years later too.

And then there were unintended interferences. The conference being hosted by Semiotext(e), most of the audience expected it to be dealing with "semiotics," which happened to be the "buzz word" in New York. I had met the editor of *The Village Voice*, Richard Goldstein, through Gil Eisner, who was publishing cartoons every week on the "Bagman" and who designed the cover of Semiotext(e) for a few years. Goldstein was gracious enough to give us the "Pick of the Week"—but as a semiotic conference. Hundreds of people eagerly called my office at Columbia every day to know what semiotics was. This added to the confusion. And then Jean-Jacques Lebel, who is bilingual, broadcast vibrant appeals to all the weirdos and bearded anarchists in town to squat in the halls of Columbia and hold their own workshops. And they rushed "uptown" enthusiastically. The title, "Schizo-Culture" was intriguing, but also misleading. It suggested that the conference would deal with madness not in a clinical way, or as an individual experience of dissociation, but as an extreme phenomenon capable of revealing the effects and the limits of capitalism, and the real nature of its flows. Schizophrenia, in that sense, was a question raised to contemporary society, the same way as New York's flamboyant psychosis was a question raised to America's enforced neurosis; or French hand-on experimentation a question raised to American pragmaticism. Schizo-Culture was the rough and unruly city that was haunting the rest of the continent and that I was just beginning to fathom, and experiment with, like a sorcerer's apprentice. It was the capital of French philosophy.

After Deleuze agreed to come to New York, the other major participants I contacted fell into place one after the other in just a few weeks. After Deleuze, Michel Foucault; after Foucault, R. D. Laing and William Burroughs; then John Cage, by chance. The "domino theory" in Southeast Asia hadn't been so great, but it certainly helped in this occasion. The conference kept changing along the way. The idea was to bring together people from both sides of the Atlantic. John Rajchman would take care of American academics and I would be in charge of French theorists. I wrote Michel Foucault in Paris and he told me that he would be touring in Brazil around that time. But he would see what he could do. I had mentioned, of course, that Deleuze would participate and they were still close friends at the time. Not too long after that Foucault dropped me a note saying that he would make a stopover in New York on his way back home and would take this opportunity to consult a Jesuit manual for children in the New York Public Library.

Needless to say, everyone in our little crew was thrilled. The conference was really taking shape. Foucault was already well known in the United States for his *Madness and Civilization* (1964), *The Order of Things* (1966), and *The Archaeology of Knowledge* (1969). His most powerful book, *Discipline and Punish*, centered on the prison system and the dissemination of power, had just been published in Paris a few months earlier and was extremely well received, but it wasn't yet available in English. Foucault was still working on his *History of Sexuality*, which was released one year later, and it was the topic that he would address in his lecture, "We Are not Repressed."

With Michel Foucault on board, the conference was beginning to find its proper balance between madness and prison, control and desire, the major political issues debated among the left in Europe during the previous years. In 1970 Foucault had been offered a chair at the Collège de France, the most prestigious academic institution in France, and yet hardly two months later he decided to found the GIP, the Group of Information on Prisons. In 1971–72, France experienced a wave of prison mutinies and hunger strikes in Melun, in Clairvaux, Toul, Nancy, etc., which drew attention to the intolerable conditions of prisoners. The rebellions were brutally put down and the GIP set out to denounce the way delinquency was being fabricated and perpetuated through a precise system of police, dossiers, and control. The GIP had been set up to collect firsthand information about life in jails, which, in France, are off limits. Their purpose was to make these facts public. They did it the French way, by calling on intellectuals, who have seen it as their duty to intervene in political matters as Voltaire, Émile Zola, and Jean-Paul Sartre did. Now it was Foucault's turn, and he took it very seriously. Prison used to be a matter of justice; with him it became a political problem. The GIP mobilized a group of well-known French intellectuals capable of publicizing the testimonies collected from prisoners themselves and their families. They published brochures, sponsored plays (with Ariane Mnouchkine), called for public demonstrations, but to no avail. The Pompidou government wouldn't budge, and trade unions were not ready to show any solidarity toward common law offenders. Eventually, ex-prisoners shrugged off these well-intentioned chaperones and took the task of addressing the media in their own names. The GIP, consequently, self-dissolved, to Foucault's relief. It had been taking up a lot of his time. Still it left a bitter taste in his mouth.

Around that time I heard that R. D. Laing would be lecturing in the Boston area during the same period and he immediately agreed to participate in a panel together with Foucault. John Cage consented as well, but for reasons of his own. He wanted in return, he said, that I play a game with him. "You are French, aren't you? So you must play chess." John Cage had been one of my inspirations for the conference. I had read in Paris a book of interviews he made with French musicologist Daniel Charles called *For the Birds*. The English original had got lost and its retranslation in English was the first French book Semiotext(e) ever published. It was Cage who made me realize that one could be a philosopher in a different way, drawing from a multiplicity of sources from I Ching and Nietzsche, transcendentalism, Chance and dance, and Zen Buddhism. Deleuze once said that he wanted to exit philosophy, but as a philosopher. Cage had done it with music. He was the bridge that I had been looking for between the two cultures. But I kept very quiet about his offer. A few weeks later he reminded me of my promise and I couldn't delay anymore. I paid him a visit to his loft in the mid-30s with fear and trembling. I could see Marcel Duchamp looking at me over his shoulder. We played for an hour and he finally won, but only with a slight edge. Neither of us was very competitive, and we were both pleased with ourselves. As he walked me to the door, he added with a chuckle that Duchamp didn't like playing with him very much because he wasn't good enough. And we both had a hearty laugh.

Next came William S. Burroughs. He was one of my all-time heroes when I was a student in France and I first read *Naked Lunch* in a French translation. Needless to say, I had never experienced drugs, let alone addiction. So I didn't waste any time after I learned that he had just returned from his long exile in England. I contacted James Grauerholz, his secretary, in the "bunker" on the Bowery that they shared with Beat poet John Giorno. It was perfect timing: Grauerholz hadn't yet arranged for Bill's lecture tour through the United States and Burroughs agreed to join us after I mentioned Foucault, Cage, and R. D. Laing. He wasn't a great fan of theorists, especially of the French variety, as I noticed later on, being a theorist himself. But he realized that this conference could be shaping up into a major event.

Jean-François Lyotard was the first French philosopher who spoke at the conference together with my friend Arthur Danto. The two philosophers could have communicated in some way. After all, Lyotard's lecture was inspired by Bertrand Russell's propositions, or logical paradoxes: "Do I lie when I say 'I lie'?" and it would have been easy to follow his drift. But the "translating bureau," three translators, no less, took the lecture in another direction. It was amazing, Danto said later on, and totally incomprehensible. As he wrote to me recently, with a copy of his own lecture attached, "The energy is fiercely analytical, but basically le *non* French." Roger McKeon, who was in charge of the bureau, was a translator at the United Nations and an ex-student of Lyotard's at the Université de Nanterre, where a number of the most radical French thinkers taught after May 1968.

While I was in France, I paid Lyotard a visit in his beautiful country residence at Fillerval, two hours north of Paris. He was very excited. He was reading the Sophists again and considered what he was working on "a real breakthrough." It had to do with the master's discourse and how to do away with it. The Marxists had no problem and used language in a "masterly" fashion. As to the "schizo-culture school"—he now found the expression, he told me, "a bit vulgar"—it strived to remain exterior to such discourse by resorting to intensive and fluid categories: libido, energy, affects, etc. It was the latter position that Lyotard had embraced until recently, and his latest book, *Libidinal Economy*, published in 1974, had brought him close to Deleuze. Now Lyotard was adopting instead another strategy aimed at turning the weakest discourse into the strongest one, which of course had political implications. But in order to do that, he needed to introduce ruse or cunnings *inside* the master's discourse. This was the subject of his talk.

But something else happened on the stage that neither the translators nor Lyotard himself had anticipated: a strange bilingual group experience. Actually it was what the entire conference was about, the junction of the French and the American, and this session was exemplary in that respect. Whether it worked or not remains an open question.

It wasn't the only experience of that kind during the conference. Deleuze spoke in French as if he was speaking English and many other sessions were translated into English live. The more extreme of them was a one-man show that never happened on the stage. The man involved was doing his simultaneous translation all by himself, and not just in two languages, and this complicated the matter further. His name is Louis Wolfson and he is American, born in Brooklyn. Curiously, he had written his book, *Le Schizo et les langues*, directly in French. The reclusive "student of schizophrenic languages," as he defined himself, became famous in some circles thanks to an essay Deleuze wrote on his work,[3] and I invited Wolfson to meet Deleuze and read a paper at the conference. He agreed, to my surprise, but I didn't really count on him, and I was right not to. Still he was present in person, so to speak, at the conference, and Jeffrey Mehlman , his excellent commentator, led him to Deleuze. I saw *le schizo* the first day standing in the lobby, his face glued to the wall, a headphone of his own making—Walkmans were still rare then—plugged to one ear and a finger screwed on the other. His second hand held a book in a foreign language. This little "language machine" à la Rube Goldberg allowed him to erase his own language at the same time as he was hearing it.

If Wolfson attended Lyotard's lecture, he may have appreciated the philosopher's own efforts to evade the master's language. In the schizophrenic's case, the master was his mother, and the ruses that he devised to elude her grasp were even more extensive than the ones displayed by the translation bureau hooked up to Lyotard's speech. Wolfson's "procedure" involved half a dozen languages, including French of course, but it was a French of his own recreation, like Stéphane Mallarmé, the "student of demented idioms" par excellence, who

3. See: Gilles Deleuze, "Louis Wolfson; or, The Procedure," in *Essays Critical and Clinical*, Minneapolis, University of Minnesota Press, (1970) 1997.

managed to become a foreigner in his own language. Wolfson spoke in French to protect himself from the English tongue. In order to keep his Jewish mother at a distance, he kept pulling apart English words and matching each sound, or fragment of word, with similar linguistic scraps borrowed from Hebrew, High German, Finnish, etc., and French, of course. This way he could use English, but excoriated, so to speak, from any maternal influence.

In his first book, *Psychoanalysis and Transversality*, published in France in 1972, Guattari opposed two kinds of groups, the subjugated group and the subject-group. The subjugated group is vertical, hierarchical, and closed upon itself to ensure its own preservation. It proceeds through exclusions and identification to a leader. The subject-group, on the other hand, is transversal and rhizomatic and allows for the expression of affects and creation. The group translation here didn't identify to Lyotard, only to his discourse, and they would occasionally get caught in the maze of their own translations. The master wasn't McKeon either, who was only trying to keep the translation in line in spite of the various interpolations provided along the way. Once pressured by other translators or by the people from the audience, he would retreat and let others follow their own interpretations wherever they may. But he remained available and reassumed his task after others had exhausted their desire, or capacity, to participate. Outwardly, the group translation was a perverse outgrowth of the project at hand, a Kafkaesque bureaucracy involved in the minutiae of language. But this didn't prevent violent outbursts or pointed interventions from the audience. And it was the audience itself that put pressure on the translation machine to alter its rhythm or modify the special configuration of the participants, offering to fragment themselves into smaller bilingual groups throughout the room to better share the translation. The audience didn't just remain passive, it was actively looking for new ways of contributing to the collective enterprise. Although chaotic at times, it was good-humored and cooperative. It was a possible model of what a "schizo-culture" in the making could be: fragmented, multiple, and shifting in such a way that the very distinction between the inside and the outside, the audience and the performers on the stage, would disappear. A well-tempered schizophrenia. What mattered at that point wasn't just what was being said, but *how* it was being said, what kinds of "arrangements of enunciation" could be experimented with at a distance from an elusive center.

And yet there was another scene in the making which the audience could not access, let alone participate in, and so remained unaware of. It wasn't meant to be shared. It happened in silence and involved Deleuze, Guattari, and Foucault, the other French philosophers present in the room. None of them needed a translation. They knew in advance what Lyotard was about to say and they had already made their decision. At the end of his lecture, Lyotard turned toward Foucault, Deleuze and Guattari. They were standing at the back by the exit, I didn't know why. I happened to be standing with them. And Lyotard said, addressing them across the room, that he was so glad they were there, because now they will have the opportunity to discuss a few things together. He spoke in French, but I am not sure. They didn't say anything. They just turned on their heels and left the room. I had just witnessed a ritual of exclusion.

It reminded me of the discussion I had with my friend François Péraldi, whom I had met through Félix and who later edited the famous Polysexuality issue of Semiotext(e) with Denise Green and Kathryn Bigelow. François had worked with schizophrenic children in France. He had left Paris, he told me, in order to avoid the cliquish atmosphere among the intellectual circles. He was close to Guattari to start with but would veer towards Lacan after he moved to Montreal and created his own analytical school, and is now recognized in France among his peers in spite of his early death. In "A Schizo and the Institution," he recounted the way another French psychiatric hospital, Lavans, in the Jura region, gradually had to loosen up its own Oedipal complex—they used substitute mothers/fathers for their patients—under pressure from the schizo patients themselves. They asked for *more* Dads and Moms and changed them every week until they were allowed "to circulate through the institution independent of any hierarchical relationship." This is what the audience had done that night around Lyotard, loosening up thc walls between the audience and the lecturer, letting the translations propagate through the room and involving the audience in a collective creation.

The day before, I had asked Guattari to chair the panel on psychiatry with Joel Kovel, Robert Fine, and François Péraldi. But Guattari's English was poor and his patience obviously limited, or so I thought, so he had the great idea of cutting all the papers short, replaced by a five-minute summary, and then opening the discussion. This is what he suggested publicly a few minutes into Kovel's paper and his interruption wasn't as welcome as he would have hoped. Many people stood up protesting that it wasn't fair: the man had done the work and should be given a chance to read his paper. Eventually, the audience split in two. The majority remained in their seats and listened to the lectures while the rest followed Guattari and Foucault to a smaller room nearby where Guattari talked on semiotic subjugation and answered a few questions. Then Foucault had his paper titled "We Are not Repressed" read in English by Mark Seem.

The atmosphere was already pretty heated and I was a bit apprehensive. I was aware that his speech would be an attack on Wilhelm Reich and the School of Frankfurt, which counted many supporters in the conference. I wasn't sure how the audience would react as he was denouncing head-on the fallacy of the anti-repressive hypothesis and the "enunciator's payoff"—a payoff that, incidentally, he had used himself not too long before—if someone hadn't stolen their thunder. Suddenly a man sprung to his feet and, raising his voice and pointing his finger in Foucault's direction, accused him and the GIP of having been paid by the CIA.

Taken by surprise, Foucault fumbled for a reply and vehemently denied everything, with the result that people in the audience rushed towards him and asked if it was true. In the chaotic scene that ensued, we had to force our way out through the crowd. That was already much to take in the same afternoon, but it was only the beginning. For what seemed to be hours standing on the sidewalk in front of Teachers College, Foucault vented his furor and frustration at the conference. It was a scandal, he said; he had never seen a worse audience before; New Yorkers were horrible, the conference a sham, etc. And then he said bitterly that it was "the last counterculture conference of the '60s."

For me, who had never had a chance to experience any of it before, and was in Sydney, Australia, in May '68, it sounded rather like a compliment. It reminded me of the first time I met Foucault in 1971. He was giving a seminar at the University at Buffalo, New York, on the origin of money and I was giving a lecture in the French department. We had dinner together and I asked him innocently about the style of his lecture, brilliant of course, which I had attended, a full forty-five minutes masterful exposition ending with a long, perfectly formed rhetorical sentence just on time for the students' questions. I was impressed, and a bit taken aback. I didn't know that leftists lectured the way my professors at the Sorbonne used to do. And he answered a bit curtly that he had gotten tired of wasting his students' time. They all had work to do. So no counterculture for Foucault, at least in his professional capacity.

Back on the sidewalk in front of Teachers College he kept on raging hysterically. It made me fear that the fragile bundle of nerves inside his bare skull would suddenly erupt like a volcano. Then, turning abruptly, he swore that he would never set foot again in that horrible conference. And just in case he hadn't been clear enough, he snapped: "Don't count me in for tomorrow's panel." Needless to say, I couldn't sleep all night.

Foucault was supposed to share the evening with William Burroughs, but he had already given his paper in the afternoon, so he came back in the evening just to hear Burroughs' talk. But he made a point of introducing him himself with these words: "I wish to turn my time over to William Burroughs, *who is here today* and I could never waste a minute talking while we could be hearing *Burroughs speak!*" (Standing ovation).[4] I was still so upset by all these skirmishes and accusations that I didn't remember any of it. Needless to say, Foucault and I didn't talk that night. But I was mesmerized by Burroughs' fool-proof logic and imperturbable delivery in describing "The Impasses of Control" (it was his first title), standing with his three-piece suit and gangsta hat at the podium. If one controls everything, Burroughs concluded, grinning, then one controlled nothing, "because control also needs opposition and acquiescence; otherwise it ceases to be control."

Gilles Deleuze remembered the lecture when he wrote his essay on "Control and Becoming" in April 1990. "We are moving," he wrote, "toward control societies that no longer operate by confining people but through continuous control and instant communication. Burroughs was the first to address this ... Compared with the approaching forms of ceaseless control in open sites, we may come to see the harshest confinements as part of a wonderful happy past."[5] Deleuze even sounded like Burroughs. The conference hadn't been for naught since these two minds met.

Burroughs and Grauerholz were subsequently received at Foucault's Paris apartment in 1984 for drinks and dinner served by Daniel Defert, Foucault's boyfriend. The occasion was the premiere of Howard Brookner's film *Burroughs: The Movie* at the Olympic Theatre. At a reception in the lobby, William Burroughs was presented with a proclamation naming him as a Commandeur de l'Ordre des Arts et des Lettres to loud acclaim. Foucault and Burroughs vainly tried to break the barrier of language, but Burroughs "had his 'cocktails persona' pretty well down," Grauerholz reported, and "Foucault enjoyed it tremendously—as if it were a command performance for him, by Burroughs playing 'Burroughs.'"

---

4. My thanks to James Grauerholz for this piece of information.
5. Gilles Deleuze, *Negotiations 1972–1990*, New York, Columbia University Press, (1995).

Deleuze gave his own lecture the next day on the rhizome during the same session as John Cage's "Empty Words," which didn't need any English to be understood. It was cagey language, and wasn't meant to be put into words. But no one did—it wasn't the point. His empty words were made of 'mesostics' on James Joyce's name dug out of *Finnegans Wake*. Maybe with the Lyotard session in mind, Deleuze decided that he would speak very slowly in French instead, tracing his own graphs of the crab grass on the blackboard. Once in a while he would stop and look intently at the audience, as if daring them to understand his own "collective arrangement of enunciation," words, chalk, blackboard, gaze, gestures, and all. Many actually did, New York being a cosmopolitan city and Deleuze a charmer. The rest struggled and watched the grass grow. Wolfson would have been perfect between Cage's empty words and Deleuze's empty signs.

Years ago I managed to track down the self-named schizo in Brooklyn, where he was born, and we started a strange conversation that extended over time, mostly by spurts and by phone, although we eventually met in a bookstore in the West Village. Wolfson would call me every so often out of the blue and go on conversing with me as if we had never stopped talking, then he would switch off absently. We spoke in French, but in later years he addressed me in English, to my great surprise. "Why not? It is easier," he said. I was nonplussed. His mother died of cancer in 1977, to his immense chagrin, and he reverted to his native tongue, at least speaking to me. In 1984 he wrote a second book, *Ma mère, musicienne, est morte* (My mother, a musician, died), patterned on his mother's disease. A fragment added to the first book, "Full Stop for an Infernal Planet," is in the *Schizo-Culture* issue. The impersonal designation of "le schizo" was his way of writing at a third remove. It was part of his scientific experiment with language and a way of paying back his doctors in their own coin.

The attack on Foucault had left me speechless, but for another reason. I *knew* who the provocateur was. I even knew his name: Jean-Claude C. I hadn't seen him for five years and I certainly didn't expect to meet him again in such auspicious circumstances. He was French like me, but he had no accent in English (I do). He was my colleague at Swarthmore College in 1970. Being French, it had been easy for him to twist some known facts about Foucault's political involvement in France so they would ring true to American ears. What could possibly have happened to him? It worried me that I could have been him. One thing was clear for everyone: the "Labor Committee" was behind the provocation. They used this sort of tactic to disrupt and confuse leftist groups both in England and in America, accusing other people of what they were doing themselves. For the last two years, I was told, they had accused people right and left—mostly the left—of being paid by the CIA.

A lot has been written about this bizarre, erratic, and anti-Semitic organization, but the commentaries are often as nutty and paranoiac as its leader, Lyndon LaRouche. I decided to have a closer look at it since their disruptions greatly contributed to the chaos of the conference. By what I can gather, the man Larouche started his political career in the mid-1960s as a revolutionary socialist leader, and worked his way into the far left fringes—Spartacism, Trotskyism—using the umbrella of the Progressive Labor Party. In 1968 he emerged during the students' weeklong strike at Columbia University hoping to win control of the local branch of the SDS. His ambition was to turn his movement "from a federation of local chapters to a national cadre organization based on advanced intellectuals capable of bringing workers their economic expertise and insuring that the political struggles would remain on revolutionary course," a later dissident of LaRouche explained. And he added: "There is nothing that I believe any of us need to be ashamed of in that period for joining the pre-1973 Labor Committee." It was in that year that the National Caucus of Labor Committees staged its own Night of the Long Knives.

In 1968 the SDS was a formidable adversary and the strike at Columbia won them national prominence. LaRouche lost his challenge, but he kept building up his organization, teaching revolutionary courses at the Columbia Liberation School to attract new recruits. Loosely basing his economic theories on Marx's *Theories of Surplus-Value*, LaRouche argued, against John Maynard Keynes' predictions, that the "falling rate of profit" would bring an end to capitalism. The world was doomed unless the masses entrusted their fate to a "Leninist organization," a team of efficiency experts on the international scale capable of devising an alternative to the economic institutions of "the ruling class." Labor Committee experts would establish working contacts with officials in government and military agencies like the CIA, the National Security Council, and the Defense Intelligence Agency in order to infiltrate the mechanisms of power and achieve world domination. The program had enough intellectual backbone to impress bright students in search of some political guidance. Contrary to most, LaRouche seemed to know where he was going. In his 1968 pamphlet against Mark Rudd's SDS, "The New Left, Local Control, and Fascism," he remarked that "it is an irony of history that certain New Lefters today would be quite at home with Mussolini's radical polemics ... Fascism, at its inception always appears as a movement which poses a revolutionary challenge to capitalism. Only in this way can it win popular support ..." The irony went both ways, just like Jean-Claude's accusation against Foucault.

What followed was less palatable. In 1973 a series of incidents precipitated the crisis within the Labor Committee. There were internal dissensions; the group split, and so did LaRouche's common-law wife. Threatened on both accounts, LaRouche became abusive and insulting to the remaining associates. He demanded "sycophantic obedience" from everyone and resorted to massive "psychological intimidation."[6] He also pressured the group to undergo guerilla training at the hands of professionals, one of which was affiliated with the Ku Klux Klan. He hired armed security men to protect him against Soviet spies. Henry Kissinger, whom he had accused of being a homosexual, apparently was out to murder him. In April 1973 the Labor Committee had a running scuffle with the Communist Party USA and LaRouche launched what he called "Operation Mop-Up." He ordered his group to "destroy the CP," and they did, ruthlessly. Armed with chains, bats, and sticks, they mercilessly attacked the CP and its affiliates, their offices and bookstores for weeks in major cities. LaRouche used the campaign to assert his total control inside the organization and pursue his drive for one-man rule. The Labor Committee ceased to be a political sect and became a cult, or worse: a proto-fascist organization. The ugly rampage drew a final wedge between the Labor Committee and the rest of the left.

I had assumed that Jean-Claude, who had been active during the strike, drifted to these troubled waters after Swarthmore didn't renew his contract—mine wasn't either for that matter—seduced by Larouche's veneer of radicalism. But some files on the movement that were passed on to me[7] make it clear that he had joined the Labor Committee in Philadelphia with three other faculty from Swarthmore two years *before* the strike of 1970.

When I returned to the Schizo-Culture conference the morning after the attack on Foucault, I didn't know what to expect. Would Foucault be there or not? It was a tricky situation. Laing had come especially to be with him on the panel. Suddenly I saw the angry philosopher in the lobby cracking jokes with

6. John Mintz, "Some are Out to Kill Me, LaRouche says," January 13, 1985 and "Ideological Odyssey: From Old Left to Far Right," *Washington Post*, January 14, 1985.

7. http://laroucheplanet.info/pmwiki/downloads/HH%20FACTNET%20OLD%20AND%20NEW%20MOLE%20FILES.pdf. Thanks to Stephen Clark for al his information on LaRouche and his "Labor Committee."

Deleuze. They both looked at me walking from the door with a smile. God knows what they were saying. Foucault didn't seem the same man at all. He told me that he hadn't slept all night, so that made it two. But he seemed far more relaxed than I was, even a bit amused. I gathered that the worst was over.

Little did I know. The panel was intense, and Foucault seemed pleased to find himself with people who knew what they were talking about.[8] But it was Foucault who saved the day. There was a heavyset black man seated in the front row and Michael Rosenfeld, who chaired the panel, did his best to ignore him. The man seemed a bit too eager to grab the microphone and it was Foucault himself who finally picked him up in the audience. It started like a normal question, but the man's speech gradually grew louder and louder, ending with a hysterical rant. Then, shaking his finger accusingly at both Laing and Foucault seated at the podium, he accused them publicly of being paid by the CIA. Not again, I thought, horrified. It was a well-rehearsed fury. Foucault sat unmoved. He had spent the whole night rehearsing his own reply, waiting for a chance to redeem himself. Quietly he looked at the provocateur and agreed with him wholeheartedly. The audience gaped. "You're entirely right," he said, "I was paid by the CIA, R. D. Laing was paid by the CIA, Lotringer himself was paid by the CIA. The only one here who hasn't been paid by the CIA is *you*, because you have been paid by the KGB." The audience burst into applause and cheered Foucault. The agent provocateur himself couldn't resist. He cracked up and fell back on his seat.

Foucault hadn't been paid by anyone, of course, let alone by me, another student in languages who was sorely aware of the budget situation. Apart from one bout of madness, Foucault had been a good sport after all, even after the student I sent to pick him up at JFK got lost in traffic. It wasn't much, but all these things small and big added up and they finally came to a crux the day after at the Chelsea Hotel, where Félix and Jean-Jacques Lebel had checked in. Deleuze preferred to stay at a hotel in Midtown with Claire Parnet. The first time I dropped by the Chelsea, Lebel was walking through the apartment stark naked, talking to other visitors. He was happening all the time.

In retrospect I understood what had happened on the financial front. When Félix finally managed to get Deleuze on their side, he and John Rajchman decided that it would be safer to schedule the conference ASAP. The fall was just a few months away, so they should act now. Raising some monies through

8. None of the Q&A session, unfortunately, was recorded.

academic channels, I realized, would have required at least one year, and it wasn't certain that a "countercultural" event of that scale would have been funded anyway, so they just went ahead and hoped for the best. Deleuze and Guattari had never asked anything regarding their travel or accommodations, let alone their airfares, and I never broached the subject in case they changed their minds. I never was so good at fund-raising anyway. I vaguely thought of maxing out his new credit card, as I did later on for the Nova Convention, but I didn't have to. Everything happened as if by magic. It was only thirty-five years later, when I read *Intersecting Lives*, a biography of Deleuze and Guattari,[9] that I realized what had happened. Guattari had asked the French Cultural Affairs Office in Paris to send him and Deleuze on another "mission" and to cover all their expenses. It solved another enigma. I always wondered why the Cultural Affairs Office had suddenly offered a lavish cocktail in their honor the evening preceding the conference. Joel Kovel, freshly converted to Marxism, was bewildered when he saw the two French leftists being feted, as they should, with champagne brut and petits fours at the stately French Consulate on 5th Avenue and 79th Street, a few steps from Central Park.

Things were happening a bit too fast for me to keep track of them all, especially with only a handful of his students interning for the occasion, including translators. Michel Rosenfeld studied law and philosophy at Columbia, and he brought in his childhood friend, Roger McKeon. I didn't really know how we managed to pull this off, John Rajchman and me. One thing helped: academic lecturing had not yet turned into a cottage industry, like everything else, and none of the honored guests from France, England, and the United States, I believed, expected to be paid, even by the CIA. Everyone quietly made their own travel arrangements and were in place where and when they were expected to perform.

After Foucault landed in New York, I invited him for an early breakfast at his favorite place, an old-fashioned diner on W. 25th, just one block away from the Hudson River. The philosopher loved the city and certainly knew his way around. He told me that he cut his lecture tour in Brazil short because the situation there had become ugly. Hard-pressed by the guerillas, the military dictatorship was cracking down on dissidents, journalists, lawyers, and intellectuals. Ironically, as I discovered later on, the techniques they used and passed on

9. Francois Dosse, Gilles Deleuze and Félix Guattari, *Intersecting Lives*, New York, Columbia University Press, 2010.

A l'occasion du colloque "Schizo culture"

André Gadaud
Conseiller Culturel
Représentant Permanent des Universités Françaises
aux Etats-Unis

prie Monsieur Sylvère Lotringer

de lui faire l'honneur
de venir déjeuner
le jeudi 13 novembre à 12 h.

R.S.V.P.
Ambassade de France
(212) 737-9700
poste 719

972 Fifth Avenue
New York, N. Y. 10021

to the CIA had first come from the French general Paul Aussaresses, who had applied these "counterrevolutionary warfare" methods during the Battle of Algiers, including the systemic use of torture, death squads, and death flights. Starting in the mid-'70s, Aussaresses maintained close links with the Brazilian military and the CIA. Tried in France in 2001 for a book he wrote on the subject, the general remained unrepentant. The Brazilian example, a combination of neoliberal economic policies (the "Brazilian Miracle" for the rich) and military dictatorship, became a model for the entire South American continent, and subsequently for North America.

Besides Foucault, the morning panel included R. D. Laing, the British anti-psychiatrist; Howie Harp representing the ex-mental patients; and Judy Clark the prison movement. As I mentioned before, I first met R. D. Laing in Paris at one of Félix's parties. There was quite a crowd in the spacious living room, cold cuts on large trays, plenty of drinks and joints floating around. Once in a while Félix would sit in front of the piano and play a part, complaining that hash only relaxed the lower part of his body. I remember vividly that Laing had to leave early, but he seemed anguished at the prospect of walking out alone in the night. He wore a suit that was a bit crumpled and took out a tie from his pocket, but his hands were trembling so badly that he finally got on his knees and fumbled to tighten it up, mumbling, "I have to look normal, I have to look normal." This is exactly what he talked about during the panel. "There is nothing that changes the chemistry of my body so much as going into a tight, anxious, hostile environment." And he added that people who don't look normal lose whatever protection they can get in our society.

The halfway house that Laing set up with David Cooper in Kingsley Hall in East London in 1965 was an isolated cell meant to defend psychotics against the normalizing pressure of society. Their project happened to resonate with Foucault's *Madness and Civilization*, which was published in English that same year and reviewed by R. D. Laing himself in the *New Statesman* in 1967. Unexpectedly, Foucault's scholarly essay got adopted by the growing anti-psychiatry movement, which considered psychiatry oppressive and madness a formative experience.[10] In France, the movement originally drew its impetus from the Resistance and the realization that asylums were no different from concentration camps. Seventy thousand mental patients died of hunger during WWII. After

10. David Cooper published *Psychiatry and Anti-Psychiatry* in 1967.

the war François Tosquelles founded Saint-Alban, a psychiatric hospital in Lozère, and was the first to introduce psychoanalysis in the treatment of psychotic patients. But the hospital itself, he realized, was a sick organism and needed constant treatment as well. He launched "institutional psychotherapy," a movement that extended all the way to Jean Oury's La Borde clinic. Anti-psychiatrists hadn't realized that, given the chance, familialism—Oedipal structures—would creep back into the therapeutic community. What was needed, Guattari said, wasn't more family, but more society.[11]

Howie Harp had been an early advocate for the mentally ill and the homeless. He was involved in the Insane Liberation Front in Oregon in 1971 and helped found "Project Release" in New York in 1975. Like anti-psychiatrists, he understood that the problem wasn't with the individual but with the environment. Project Release was based on the idea that "professional supervision creates a dependence pattern which is a cause of recidivism" and that a form of self-help would be a strong antidote to the anxiety of isolation and helplessness induced by society.[12] The schizophrenic's reaction was *a learning experience* that could be socialized instead of being treated by professionals as chemical imbalance.

For Judy Clark, what needed resocializing was the professional class itself, which had been trained to remain separate from the inmates or patients. The remedy for them was to join with "those base-up movements of resistance" that exist in every one of those institutions. This is what Foucault had tried to do with the GIP. In Brazil he became aware that doctors, psychiatrists, even Lacanian psychoanalysts, were monitoring the rituals of torture instead of opposing them and he extended his condemnation to all those in the medical and psychiatric professions who unduly conferred medical credibility on legal or criminal practices.

In 1972, teaching again in freezing Buffalo, Foucault visited the Attica Correctional Facility with John Simon, the chairman of the French Department at the University at Buffalo.[13] In France only prisoners, guards, and lawyers are allowed in prisons and this made it all the more urgent to disseminate inside information to the world outside. Attica, a maximum-security prison situated forty miles east of Buffalo and built in the 1930s, was meant to hold the most

11. Félix Guattari, "Laing Divided" and "Mary Barnes' Trip," in *Chaosophy*, Los Angeles, Semiotext(e), 2009.
12. "Project Release: A Statement of Purpose," a leaflet.
13. "On Attica," the interview with John Simon, was first published in *Telos* 19, Spring 1974.

dangerous criminals. It was vastly overcrowded and prisoners were denied political rights. The population, mostly African-Americans, included Rap Brown, leader of the Black Panther Party, who served a sentence in Attica from 1971 to 1976. On August 21, 1971, George Jackson, a black radical activist, was shot dead while escaping from California's San Quentin prison, and on September 9, 1971, thirteen hundred inmates in Attica rebelled, taking over the prison and holding forty guards hostage for four days. The negotiations with state officials failed and Governor Rockefeller eventually ordered the state police to storm the prison, which resulted in forty-three individuals killed, including ten hostages. It was the bloodiest prison confrontation in American history.

The visit to Attica happened only six months after the uprising. Foucault saw it as an immense machine of elimination going in a circular way from society to the prison, and back to society, where inmates would be eliminated again. And yet, he emphasized, prisons weren't just a matter of exclusion. The visitors were allowed to inspect the four wings and the four corridors of the prison, but the fifth corridor was off limits. It was the place where prisoners were eliminated in the second degree—the psychiatric wing, reserved for those who couldn't be assimilated by the first machine. It was run by liberal psychiatrists who treated criminality as a psychological problem that could be resolved *intra muros*. They were all accomplices to the penal system.

A few days before the Schizo-Culture conference started, I took Félix to meet Judy Clark for lunch in Midtown Manhattan near the office of *Midnight Special*, a paper she co-founded in the wake of the Attica uprising. The paper was written by prisoners and sent back into prisons all over the country. In 1969 Clark spent nine months in jail for her participation in the Weatherman's Days of Rage, a militant-turned-violent antiwar demonstration in Chicago. Several years later she joined the anti-imperialist May 19th Communist Organization, an offshoot of the Weathermen Underground. Judy Clark was waiting for us in her office, a small woman with olive complexion. She could have been Puerto Rican if it were not for her Brooklyn accent. Her parents were Jewish and staunch communists until they stayed in the Soviet Union for several years. Then her father turned around and became rabidly anti-communist. Judy Clark made up for it. We both were impressed, Félix and I, by the breadth and acuity of her political analysis. In the panel she chose to talk about the increased use of behavior modification in the prison system. The most infamous prison where these kinds of psychic "readjustments" were being used was the step-by-step Start Program in Marion,

Illinois, in which a group focuses on a single person and subjects him/her to all sorts of mental abuse. This *attack therapy* was akin to the brainwashing that Lyndon LaRouche inflicted on his followers in order to make them feel abject and despondent. The Start Program started in cold isolation and graduated to "the part of the prison grounds that looks like a college campus." The procedure encapsulated what Foucault called the continuum of disciplines. What was specifically American about it was that the program was meant to turn inmates against each other. "It teaches you," Clark said, "pure capitalist ethics: the way you go ahead is to stamp on someone below you."

During the months that followed the 1975 conference, I looked for Judy Clark to show her the transcript of her intervention in the panel, but in vain. I was puzzled. The office of the Midnight Special was boarded up and neighbors had no idea where Clark had gone. Her trail had grown cold. A few years later I understood why. In October 1981 she was on the front pages of the national papers for her participation in the infamous Brink's robbery in a shopping mall in Rockland County, New York, as a member of the Black Liberation Army. The plan, she told me later, was ill conceived and it was foiled, leaving two police officers—one black, one white—dead. Judy Clark was driving the getaway car, but she was charged with three counts of felony murder. Together with the other defendants she took a hard line and refused to be represented by a lawyer. As a result she was sentenced to seventy-five years to life in prison and sent to the maximum-security prison for women at Bedford Hills in Westchester County, the very penitentiary that she had described during the 1975 panel, where women who resisted the conditions inside were harshly punished. Kathy Boudin, who was involved as well in the holdup, pleaded guilty to a single count of felony murder and received a sentence of twenty years.

Thirty years later, I paid Judy Clark a visit in Bedford Hills, one hour north of Manhattan on Amtrak. She was still behind prison gates, but the conditions in the women's penitentiary had changed somewhat, and so had the world around it. Instead of Vietnam, it was now Iraq and Afghanistan, not to mention the one thousand military bases spread all over the planet. Imperialism was on the rise. Wars were not declared anymore, and never ended either. Unfinished business had become good business. The anti-imperialist struggle had failed, let alone the idea of creating a more equal and democratic society in America.

Judy was wearing the dull dark green prison outfit when she came in accompanied by a guard, and her hair was gray too. She remembered perfectly the panel with Foucault. It was as if we had talked to each other just a few days before. I got the impression that her overall political analysis hadn't changed, only her own position in relation to it. She seemed relaxed and at peace with herself. We didn't talk much about the Brink's holdup, because I assumed that our conversation was taped. It was public knowledge by now anyway. I knew for sure that the interview that I was planning to have with her on the phone later on would be. That's the least a prison can do at a time of global eavesdropping.

The visiting center where we met was the usual cafeteria, rows of tables with a few inmates speaking with their spouses and a counter at the back. It was decorated with bright ecological frescos. The vending machines, a welcome innovation, were lined up against the wall, although prisoners weren't allowed to get close to them, only visitors. Tape recorders, cameras, and pencils, of course, had to be put away in the locker room at the door. Any photography, including of the exterior of the facility, was strictly forbidden, although one could easily get it from a satellite. We mostly talked about her life in the prison and how it had been very active and, yes, fulfilling. She had long given up on the idea of plotting her escape, which had cost her two years in solitary confinement twenty-five years ago. Prison had become her home, and she did her best to improve the conditions inside. She was already doing this at the time of the conference.

Once in prison again, Judy earned a bachelor's degree in behavioral sciences—she certainly knew quite a bit about the subject—and a master's in psychology through a program for inmates. Both turned out to be useful. At least a third of the women in the facility had no reason to be there and should have been treated in mental institutions. They were given heavy doses of Thorazine every day to keep them drowsy and docile. She and other women at Bedford developed a long-term working relationship with Elaine Lord, the new superintendent, who was open to improvements and helped them file collective lawsuits in favor of the inmates. Judy's daughter, Harriet, eleven months old when she was captured, played a major role in her "radical transformation, which included her public expression of remorse for her role in the Brinks robbery. She also figured prominently in the recent article of *The New York Times*, which was cautiously probing the possibility of a measure of clemency, anticipating a public uproar.[14] Some of the comments were very nasty. Most advocated clemency.

14. Tom Robbins, "Judith Clark's Radical Transformation," *The New York Times*, January 12, 2012. The article raised a heated controversy, and some ugly comments, in the press.

Some of her ex-comrades to whom I spoke years before were not pleased that she renounced her status as a political prisoner. But the issue remained debatable.

In the same interview about Attica, Foucault evoked a story that Jean Genet once told him. Genet was being transported from the Santé prison to the French Court of Justice, but the other inmate, a political prisoner, a Communist, refused being handcuffed to a thief. From that day on, Genet said, he had a certain distrust of all political movements. This didn't prevent the playwright of *The Blacks* from coming secretly to the United States—he was refused a visa—in support of the Black Panther Party on trial. The Panthers separated themselves from common law offenders because, like the proletariat in the 19th century, they were not recognized, but treated like criminals. And yet making this distinction between common and political prisoners meant upholding the entire legal and moral system. The problem arose as well during the Maoist vogue that swept over France in the early 1970s. At first, the Maos—white liberals—refused to be assimilated among common law offenders. It didn't take them long to recognize their error. Common law was political too. The three million black offenders jailed in the United States are political prisoners. And renouncing one's special political status can be a political act.

The last couple of lectures involved Félix Guattari and Ti-Grace Atkinson, a radical feminist who was a student at Columbia during the protests. I didn't know that much about her. All I knew from John Rajchman was that she was "an extreme feminist." I was unaware then of the incandescent period that radical feminism in the United States experienced in the late 1960s, questioning everything about the female condition and what it told about the society at large. In a span of two to three years they achieved a real cultural revolution. As Shulamith Firestone wrote in 1968, "I think we're really onto something new and good."[15] You could still feel their sense of exhilaration. They were shattering all the idols—family, pregnancy, childbirth, childhood, sex, love, and of course male supremacy. It was a stunning breakthrough, or rather its end point. Then they all burned out or fell apart. It was too intense to be sustained very long. This is the sense that you get when you open some of the books that were published at the time—Firestone's *The Dialectic of Sex: The Case for a Feminist Revolution* and Kate Millett's *Sexual Politics*, both published in 1970, or Ti-Grace Atkinson's *Amazon Odyssey* in 1973, collecting essays written in 1969—these women were questioning everything

15. Quoted by Susan Faludi, "Death of a Revolutionary," *The New Yorker*, April 15, 2013.

in the most violent way. Men *robbed* women of their lives and cannibalized their consciousness; women had been *murdered* by their function as childbearers; marriage and family were slavery and love a pathological condition. "What is love but the payoff for the consent of oppression … In a just society, would we need love?" And the famous formula: "Scratch *his* love, and you'll find *your* fear." Sex itself wasn't spared. "We all know how uncomfortable it is to be around disgruntled maids nowadays, and as for hostile sex, what other kind is there?"

But it wasn't just men who were the enemy, the enemy also was within and this was the most sensitive point. Ti-Grace and feminists of the "second wave" were trying to understand "what seemed irrational—oppressed people clinging to the root cause of their oppression." Radical feminism opened up much larger problems. "The persecution of women has never been taken as the starting point for a political analysis of society." The antiwar movement wasn't ready to accept that there was another war, more subterranean, going on: "You quiver with horror over Vietnam because you identify your hide with the boy sent over there. You pontificate, but mostly you shake your head over black people because you know if they get too uppity, you outnumber them nine to one, and *you* know that *they* know it."

And yet the women's movement also was hit very hard as the war started winding down. In her lecture, only partially preserved, Ti-Grace Atkinson reflected on those among the radical feminists "who acted in accordance with their words and were eventually driven underground," like Susan Saxe, one of the eight women who was put on the FBI's Ten Most Wanted list in 1970 for five years. She had escaped from a bank heist in Brighton, Massachusetts, in which an accomplice killed a Boston police officer. She was on the run when she was arrested in Philadelphia in 1975 and served twelve years in prison after entering a guilty plea to two charges of robbery and one charge of manslaughter. But, she remained defiant: "I plead guilty today for one reason and one reason alone—that it is the surest and quickest way to end the hold this state will have on my life and my personal freedom. I have been harassed, hounded, and vilified by the state for six and a half years and have been imprisoned for two years. I do not recognize the right of the state to a single day of my life, but I do recognize its power to take that and more. I will never abandon my political commitments in exchange for favors from the system."

Many women surrendered formally to the government and cooperated fully. "What do you do," Ti-Grace wrote, "when the FBI knocks on your door and wants to know any information you might possess concerning known fugitives, and can jam you before a grand jury, give you immunity, put you away for a long time if you don't talk." Jane Alpert, a student from Swarthmore who was caught planting dynamite in National Guard trucks in 1969, ended up surrendering as well. While in hiding she publicly denounced "the sexual oppression of the left" and announced her conversion to radical feminism.

It was the last night of the Schizo-Culture conference, and a Saturday night to boot, so the room was packed. Steven Harris, a young teacher at Bard College, had arranged with John Rajchman for a band from Bard to be the last act. They arrived excitedly from upstate in a big van. It was a big break for them and they didn't want it to be messed up by the lectures. Their fear was that the big audience would vanish after Félix's talk, which was coming last. Unpacking all their gear on the stage afterwards would have taken too much time. They asked Ti-Grace, the first speaker, if they could prepare for the concert at the back while she was giving her lecture, and she answered, "Certainly not." She didn't like the idea at all. So they asked Félix instead, and he gladly obliged. *Plus il y a de fous, plus on s'amuse*, he said in French ("The madder, the merrier"). It was an appropriate expression in the context. It became even more *à propos* after his own talk. Besides, he hadn't prepared his lecture, so interruptions were most welcome. Mark Seem would be the translator. He was working on the English version of *Anti-Oedipus* and was the young man inconspicuously doing tai chi on the stage between breaks, turning the entire room into a fish bowl. Félix would have to start first and Atkinson second. Consulted once more, Félix had no problem with speaking first. He was ready for anything. He was in the kind of euphoric state that precedes a catastrophe.

Ti-Grace didn't mind being bumped to second, and for a good reason. She came with her troops which could be deployed anytime and she would have some more time to size up this Guattari. After all, he was in "the enemy camp." Even in the Women's Movement, Ti-Grace had been denounced for being "warlike." She used military terminology whenever she could, and why wouldn't she? "We accept the phrase 'battle of the sexes,'" she wrote, and Men are the Oppressors. It was "a class confrontation." Radical feminism for her was "a declaration of war." Félix had no idea what he was getting into.

It was his turn to speak and he started in attack mode. "I get the feeling that I could talk about absolutely anything—my private life, how I vote—except desire or revolution. They would seem truly obscene here at Columbia

University." He invoked the "CIA virus" that had contaminated everyone in the room, possibly himself too. And he broached on the world economic crisis, extermination camps in Bangladesh, the absence of revolutionary solutions, all the big general, political questions—but only to bring out the molecular revolution developing in parallel in unknown areas, changes in people's lives, always liable to be reversed into what he called *microfascism*. He didn't particularly like the expression, he said, and used it "simply because it startles and annoys people."

He also raised an important theoretical issue that went beyond their previous emphasis on Oedipus. Their real enemy now, he had realized with Deleuze, was the increasing process of *semiotization*, the way power now was being exerted by signs over the body, semiotic subjugation. He was alluding here to a major change that only became perceptible in the early 2000s, the digital invasion of everybody's life, the capitalist *semiosphere* operating through continuous monitoring and instant communication. Control societies. It was working beyond the individual level through various "arrangements" in which subjectivity and technology coalesced.

Still bent on annoying his audience, Guattari took as an example the "awful" arrangement of enunciation provided by the conference room with elevated podium and prepared lectures. That was a direct hit at John and I, the organizers of the conference. But what alternative was there, I thought, Yankee Stadium? Guattari was acting as an agent provocateur and a judge. In short, he was fishing for trouble. "Yesterday," he said, "I proposed changing the whole format, the whole type of work we are doing here, and to my great surprise I realized that everyone wanted the conference to remain as it was. Some people even asked for their money back, although no one here was being paid to speak." (It had become obsessive). To make things worse, he picked as an example of a better desiring position the only kind of microfascism that was lurching around: the Larouche cult. "The only people who came forward to try and start a dialogue—completely phony, but full of real desire—were those who falsely accused us of being CIA agents." It was, no doubt, a masterful lesson in desiring economy at the molecular level. And he was being quite successful at it: the audience was getting really annoyed. Was it the only way to provoke a reaction? "When an orator represents the desire of the audience," he said earlier on, "then there is no more desire." Félix certainly made sure he didn't represent anyone. But would desire be flowing on his side?

He should have expected it, and maybe he did. But not in that way. It came like a tidal wave and roiled from the floor up starting with Ti-Grace's groupies massed in front. Soon after everyone in the audience joined in and booed Guattari off *his* podium. In the eyes of Ti-Grace's fans he looked just like another New Left leader, the kind who patted women on the shoulder and sent them away when things got serious.

Guattari looked down, gathered his papers, and slowly left the podium. Foucault, Deleuze, and John Rajchman were seated a dozen rows away and didn't say a word. Guattari sat beside them, sulking. It was the side of him that I especially liked, this "becoming-child." They all hailed a cab to the Chelsea Hotel in a sore mood. They sat in the suite and complained bitterly, once again, about the chaos, the aggressive audience, the irresponsible Lotringer. The conference was totally out of control. John was there too. He had been with them all along among the audience, enjoying the show. He giggled nervously and remained silent.

There was a break between the lectures and the band brought the rest of the PA system onto the stage. They just had to wait until Ti-Grace's speech was over. Then an argument about the Bard band erupted between Susie Flato and one of the attendees. It was a minor scuffle but it quickly escalated and turned into a nasty fight—nails scratching, hair flying, all the tension built up during the conference suddenly released. And here it was, another tussle, probably for no special reason. I was exhausted. The open fight was an embarrassment and I could have acted faster to protect her, Susie shouted hysterically. That night there was another fallout, and we broke up. So that's where things were at. The French were pissed off, I was burnt at Columbia, and John, my best friend, had let him down, or so he thought. I moved out of the apartment in the middle of the night. It was the end of the great four-day Schizo-Culture conference, and everything was falling apart.

I didn't know yet that it could be my chance. What else was there to lose? And New York was there. Just like Howie Harp said, It would be the most intense period in my life.

Semiotext(e)
sponsors a colloquium on

SCHIZO CULTURE

13-16 November 1975
Columbia University

"One does not desire revolution, desire is revolutionary"
-G. Deleuze and F. Guattari

"The power to punish is not essentially different from the power to cure or to educate"
-M. Foucault

Thursday, November 13

2:30 p.m. (Harkness): Sylvère Lotringer, John Rajchman - Introduction
James Fessenden - Transversality and Style

7:30 p.m. (Harkness): Arthur Danto - Freudian Explanation
Jean-François Lyotard - La Force des Faibles

Friday, November 14

9:30 a.m. Workshops: Psychiatry and Social Control. - Radical Therapy. - Schizo-City (Harlem); Cinema: Representation and Energetics. - Ontologico-hysterical theatre.

2:30 p.m. (Harkness): Robert Fine - Psychiatry and Materialism
Joel Kovel - Therapy in Late Capitalism
François Péraldi - A Schizo and the Institution

Panel with Félix Guattari

8:00 p.m. (S.I.A.): William Burroughs - The Impasses of Control
Michel Foucault - Nous ne sommes pas Réprimés

Saturday, November 15

10:00 a.m. (A-B Law): Panel on Prisons/Asylums
Judy Clark, Michel Foucault, Robert Michels, David Rothman

2:30 p.m. (A-B Law): John Cage - Empty Words
Gilles Deleuze - Le Régime des Signes

8:00 p.m. (A-B Law): Ti Grace Atkinson - The Psyche of Social Movements
Félix Guattari - Politique et Signification

Sunday, November 16

Meetings will be held at the Maison Française, 560 West 113 Street

9:30 a.m. Workshops: Feminism and Therapy. - Psychoanalysis and Politics. - Gay Liberation. - Mental Patients' Liberation

2:30 p.m. Workshops: Prison Politics. - Lincoln Detox. - Mass Culture. - Psychoanalysis and Schizoanalysis.

9:00 p.m. (John Jay): Schizo-Party

Information: Write to Semiotext(e), 522 Philosophy Hall, Columbia Univ., New York, N.Y. 10027

Contribution: Six dollars (students), twelve dollars (others). Checks or money orders payable to Semiotext(e), Inc. Register early if you wish to receive abstracts in advance. Fee includes a copy of the proceedings of the Schizo-Culture colloquium in Semiotext(e). Subscriptions to Semiotext(e) $7.00 (individual), $12.00 (institutions).

Sylvère Lotringer

Introduction:
The French Connection

I'll start by saying that if I had to define what this colloquium is about in one word, I would simply say, *connecting*. Connecting the French and the Americans, prisons and politics, theatre and therapy, music and madness, semiotics and sex; hooking up feminism and philosophy, pot and rock, creation and revolution; connecting, hooking up, plugging in the world of work and the world of desire, to bring about a radical change. We have to do away with limitations, exclusions, and repressions of all kinds, from the most obvious ones—the state, the police, the mental hospital, justice, etc.—to the very special kind of secret police that we are wont to impose upon ourselves in the name of individuality. The secret power of power and authority is precisely that of having made us, all of us, into our own very cops; the interiorization of prohibitions and constraints; the erection of a superego that reduces any and every libidinal fluidity, inhibits inclinations towards revolt, and every possibility of really hooking up and making good connections. Even the most hardened radicals become the revolution's pigs as soon as they accept becoming subjugated to a strict discipline, when they muffle their desires in the always-delayed hopes of a new day. Revolutionary purism and Puritanism, the discipline of the little group, the groupuscule, or the party itself, heads us directly for that sort of disciplinary society which Michel Foucault analyzed so relentlessly in his latest book, *Surveiller et Punir.*

The technology of power does not merely invest the major institutional constellations and constructs; it takes hold of bodies that it then individualises in the sole aim of putting these bodies to good use. The property of the body, *body property*, is necessary for power's expropriation. Likewise, when the slaves were freed from the slavery of the South, they were ripped away from a fixation in landed property, in order to engulf them in the powerful machines of capital.

Hence it is that the birth of the individual, the invention of "man" (a recent discovery, as Foucault demonstrates at the end of *The Order of Things*) are correlative of man's subjugation. The autonomy of the body—the very foundation of humanism, and more recently of the humane sciences, and hence of a new form of knowledge—in reality gives man up to the law of exchange. The law of exchange abolishes, in its own fashion, all existing barriers and constantly establishes relations of equivalence between the elements it has, from the start, so carefully separated. And that's a whole problem; the law of exchange causes women and goods, services and messages, to circulate in the fashion of Lévi-Strauss' analysis, only to reduce them, to tame them, to frame them within a closed communication system, classifying them, separating subject from object, structure from reality, in order to extract a specific surplus value-meaning.

We want to connect all the domains of an institution. Not because they are each of them separate and exchangeable, as the French structuralists would have it. Rather, we would want to connect them because they are not exchangeable or separate but already caught within the continuous web of micro-controls that simultaneously produce and enslave, differentiate and normalize individuals. This continuum is a tight fabric of constraints that lead gradually from the outwardly oppressive forms, such as the prison or the asylum, to the agencies that in appearance are the least suspect, the most positive, such as schools or the university. It is in this sense that, to quote Foucault from the poster, "The power to punish is not essentially different from the power to cure or to educate. It is only a matter of degree." The multiform normalizing pressure permeates each of the cogs, however minute, innocuous, and innocent they may appear at first in the social machine. It is useless then to consider each institution as a distant repressive entity whose specific binds could then be undone and whose functioning could be rendered unproblematic. There is no such thing as a closed entity, a self-contained institution, and to begin with, the institution of the self does not exist.

And what, then, of the so-called science of the self, I mean, psychoanalysis? It is most assuredly a self-contained institution, in other words, an institution whose very purpose is to produce a restrictive form of knowledge on a restricted entity whose reliance on power remains, for the most part, unfathomed. Regardless of the diligent attempts by psychoanalysis to renovate its concepts, even of the most recent forms it has assumed in France by calling upon the highly sophisticated scientific apparatus ranging from linguistics to topology, psychoanalysis nevertheless remains dependent on its familialist, sexist, and capitalist premises.

The dismantling of the family structures at the end of the 19th century under the irresistible weight of Capital summoned forth an immediate reaction, whose driving force was analysis. Libidinal energy, freed by Freud from its reproductive function, thereby found itself checked in its substitutive formations—Oedipus and castration—which do nothing more than represent the unconscious and desire, rather than multiply the productive capacity. To go with Jacques Lacan from the father to the *Name-of-the-Father*, from the penis to the phallus, or from the imaginary to the symbolic, doesn't change a thing—the analysis blindly taking as its object the individual that has been shaped, fabricated, and subjugated by the great penal body, intensifying this subjugation by splitting the subject through the imposition of language—this did not free the individual, much as it professed to, from human and humanistic bondage.

However split, the individual remains the intangible framework of analysis. To reform psychoanalysis within the very form it adopted, therefore seems to be of no avail. What is necessary, on the contrary, is to displace its reference points and envision libidinal economy, at once to this side of, and beyond, the person. We must substitute for the neurotic model secreted by the conjugal enclosure and the difference between the sexes, a transpersonal and transsexual process where desire could be directly coupled to the socius. In short, we should on the one hand free psychoanalysis from its individualist premises—but, would there be anything left?—and on the other hand, connect it to the problems of power, whose economy psychoanalysis claims to provide.

Rather than merely question the analytical pyramid, the verticality of its organization, the hierarchization of its concepts, it would be fitting, in sum, to attack psychoanalysis transversally by producing a nomadic entity, an irreducible multiplicity, foreign both to the individualizing penal apparatus, while probing the political status of psychoanalysis. Nothing, therefore, is ever just one thing. Psychoanalysis has to do with politics, politics has to do with madness, madness has to do with creation, creation with drugs, drugs with prisons, prisons with asylums, asylums with the university, the university with Capital, and Capital with desire. A local struggle can therefore, at its peak, affect by degrees all of the social fabric. That is why the problem of French students at Nanterre University was able to produce during May '68 a revolutionary situation where power vacillated. As far as the situation here, of Columbia students during the '60s for instance, the complicity between knowledge and power inherent to the juridical and institutional framework, overcoding the transmission of knowledge, was brought into the open by the economic intervention of that big landlord that is Columbia University.

It so happens that periodically an institution starts in motion its own dissolution, and opens the door onto society at large. I have in mind the experience of what is called here "community mental health," such as those that are only just now being established in France. The dissemination of therapeutic services in the community assuredly broke with the isolation of the asylum, but, doesn't this amount, through more supple and diversified channels, to simultaneously providing psychiatric authority, which remains in control with a virtually limitless capacity for intervention, rather than requestioning, as it should, the social and moral division between the norm and abnormality that encodes all the other institutional divisions—the division of good and evil, of innocence and guilt? The opening of the asylum to the outside world ran the risk, on the contrary, of carrying mental repression outside of the asylum walls by bringing about a true psychiatrization of daily life. The loosening up of the institutions is an integral part of this process of subjugation, by means of which power, by making itself ever more invisible and anonymous, roots itself very deeply, by leaps and bounds, in the texture of the social field.

We should not then expect such an arrangement to shake up the system of normalization that denounces as "mad" the victims of asylum segregation, and as "delinquent" the very products of the penal institution. The fact that punishment stems not from some moral law, but from the social law, is precisely what makes of every crime a violent way to challenge the functioning of a society which takes great pains to fit crime within the category of anomaly, and therefore to call upon a psychiatric form of knowledge produced by confinement, so as to render the repression exercised in its name somewhat more acceptable. The struggles of prisoners must, then, simultaneously fight for concessions from the penal authorities, and explore the organization that rendered necessary the formation of these coercetive devices that prisons are. To quote Foucault's book on prisons: "If there is indeed an entire political stake in the prison, it is not one of knowing if it will be corrective or not, if the judges, the psychoanalysts, or the sociologists will exercise more power there than the administrators and the guards." At the limits there is not even an alternative, consisting in a choice between prison and something other than prison. The point currently made is rather that the rise of these devices of normalization, and the entire scope of the effects of power that these devices carry with them, through the setting up of new objectives.

What we must attempt to do, faced with the incredible adaptability of these repressive devices, whose strategy consists in making its way everywhere, and moving in all directions, is to subvert the constraints and rid ourselves step-by-step of the very prohibitions by means of which the normative individuality is maintained, prohibitions lowered on sex, on drugs, etc. The division moral/social, the judgement given on all forms of deviance, must all be attacked from all sides in a concrete and specific way in each case, without getting caught in a theoretical ghetto that would only respect the frameworks established by the organizations of power. It is at just this point that the forms of French thought stemming from May '68 are able to meet with the radical movement in America. It is not by chance that Gilles Deleuze and Félix Guattari's *Anti-Oedipus* resolutely turns its back on French theoreticism, to rejoin with an Anglo-Saxon pragmatism steeped in Jerry Rubin's cry, "Do it!"

Experimenting thereby constitutes a political act; it is the affirmative refusal to get bogged down in speculation or piety; put Freud or Marx to work, don't worship them. Experimenting does not consist in fixing the result in advance, nor in asking "What does it mean?" but "How does it work?"[and] "What relationship is there between what you are doing and your desires?" Don't, for instance, ask me what this colloquium means, but rather, what do *you* want to do with it? Do you want to be taught something and be subjected one more time? Do you want to get credits in *Schizo-Culture*? Do you want this colloquium to be deadly, oppressive, academic, meaningful, or do you want to step in and make it your thing, make it productive, open up in all directions, let it mushroom, let it loose, connect, analyze, and change; change the university, change your life, change everything?

It is always possible to interpret what I say or what I do, to associate this or that and organize the pieces in such a way that it makes sense, that is, even the whole strategy of meaning. It would, by the way, be utopian to think one is able to situate oneself outside of these machines of meaning, these machines of science. It all depends on what you want to do with them, if you want to submit to them, or if you want to use them in a perverse way, catching them off guard, quickly snatching them up in order to plug them into something else, onto the socius, or the cosmos.

Meaning always has the effect of averting the real phenomena of break and rupture. It need only return to a totally unforeseeable event, such as May '68 in France, and make it fit within a series of causal relations—no job for sociology students of Nanterre, for the satisfaction of the workers, you name it. Historical continuity is re-established at the price of a break between the public field of struggles of interest, and the supposedly private exercise of desire; between political economy and desiring economy. The event then loses its substance, its destructive energy, and disappears as such.

Psychoanalysis—which also exists on the basis of this division, since it privatizes desire—makes similar use of anamnesis in order to restore to the subject its "truth"; if there is something wrong with you, you had better look to the primal scene, etc. Every systematization renders secure and satisfies by the very fact that it emasculates the ruptures, engaging desire in an impasse. If the unconscious is structured like a language, as Jacques Lacan postulates, this opens it wide to the field of linguistic formalization, but immediately closes it to the social formations. Desire caught in the structure is bound to miss the Real, which would then only appear through its signifying representation on the screen of fantasy, whence we have a split subject, a castrated desire, since it cannot join with its object, and a univocal reality.

Psychoanalysis reduces rather than complexifies, and generalizes rather than singularizes. The purely logical matrix which it runs up against nevertheless doesn't stem from a science; it remains the indispensible instrument of a particular formation of power. In order to dissolve this formation we must produce a logic that will not give in to the instrumental role assigned to it, and this is what Jean-François Lyotard is presently trying to achieve.

The power of signs makes psychoanalysis into a technology of importization, but what is the status of these *sign-machines* themselves, insofar as they overcode the entire constellation of formations of power within the social field? Capital, having taken the sign-machines under its control, and having pushed them to their highest degree of abstraction, we must then attack the sign-machines themselves, the very metrics of power. For it is, in the last instance, the mode of formation of meaning that exercises, in each point of the disciplinary continuum, on each individual which it defines as such, the real power of normalization. One must therefore hit the repressive mechanism to its most fundamental, least perceptible level, since it shapes our mode of perception at the level of the functioning of signs, even before signs are caught in the paranoiac enclosure of a system, or lend themselves to a revolutionary eruption of desire in the social fabric.

One must not, consequently, abandon semiotics to the specialists. Since people are caught from the start in a powerful network of meaning, the semiotic operation reveals itself, through and through, as a political operation. Every revolutionary struggle must simultaneously, if it doesn't wish to fall into the old traps and recreate elsewhere the same setup it wishes to explode (I mean bureaucratism, dogmatism, phallocentrism, moralism, etc.), confront the power of signs. Capitalism always implied that one must pass by way of representation, since the sign stands for something else, by way of representatives—political representatives, institutional representatives—in order to have access to reality. But the real reality of Capital is to be found at the level of the manipulation of asignifying signs; see for instance the stock exchange.

The revolutionary takeover doesn't pass by way of the images proposed by capitalism. It must occur at the level of asignifying signs manipulated by capitalism. Revolution will take place where the conjunction of the semiotics of the power of the real forces, the semiotics of science, the semiotics of art and of revolutionary experience. One must take power over meanings, lose their repressive power, in order to obtain a force which changes our view of things.

John Rajchman

The Bodyguard

"The body," writes Foucault, "is directly plunged in the political field. The relations of power exercise an immediate hold on it. They invest it, mark it, train it, constrain it to work, oblige it to ceremonies, require signs from it." It was also in his body that Sigmund Freud suffered from his trip to the United States almost 67 years ago, in which he sought to introduce the new science of psychoanalysis with a series of impromptu lectures. "The free and easy manners of the Americans," reports Jones, "offended his good European sense of dignity and respect for learning." American cooking he held responsible for the lasting intestinal trouble the voyage incurred. His handwriting immediately deteriorated, and during his stay he suffered from appendicular pain, and worst of all from prostate discomfort, considerably aggravated by the facilities offered for solitary relief. "They escort you along long miles of corridor," he explained to Jones, "and ultimately you are taken to the very basement, where a marble palace awaits you, only just in time."

The French writers who have come to introduce their theories and to engage in discussion are not so likely to be put off and on guard as perhaps Freud was. America will have a different effect on their bodies and the corpus of their words; in fact, a 1975 *Schizo-Culture* colloquium is quite unlike a 1908 Clark University lecture series in several respects, which I would like to suggest, by offering as a reply to Freud's difficulties with marble palaces, this 1911 journal note of Kafka about a minor literature: "What in great literature goes on down below, constituting a not-indispensable cellar of the structure, here takes place in the full light of day. What there is a matter of passing interest for a few, here absorbs everyone no less than as a matter of life and death."

Like the body, the psychoanalytic institution has had its history; it has changed since 1908. To some extent, the *Schizo-Culture* colloquium is part of this history. Its speakers include four men from three countries who underwent analytic training; all, at the same time, have been involved in political struggles, although of different kinds. Félix Guattari, member of Lacan's psychoanalytic school, wrote in 1972 in collaboration with Gilles Deleuze, a philosopher, an extremely important theoretical and political work called the *Anti-Oedipus*. It is deeply and repeatedly critical of psychoanalysis, both as a theory and as a practice. Joel Kovel, a psychoanalyst in New York who has written an analysis of white racism, is to speak on the issue of the role of therapy and psychoanalysis in late capitalism. François Peraldi, an analyst also affiliated with Lacan's school but working in Canada, has been influenced by the critique of Deleuze and Guattari, the politicization of psychiatry they urge under the title of *schizoanalysis*. He will consider the issues involved in a particular case. Ronald Laing needs no introduction to an American audience.

The institution of psychoanalysis will also be considered in the light of its possible internal reversal, through which Deleuze and Guattari propose to establish a schizoanalysis; psychoanalytic theory in relation to politics will be discussed in another workshop where special attention will be given to the writings of the Frankfurt School; the issue of psychoanalysis and feminism will be discussed in a workshop considering the theoretical bases of feminism; and Arthur Danto will discuss psychoanalytic explanation.

It is important to know, however, that Deleuze, Guattari, and Lyotard are opposed to psychoanalysis, for this opposition is central to what they are proposing. Their opposition, which is presented as more than ideological critique, grows out of a deep interest in psychoanalysis on the part of the French left. All three are opposed to Marxist-Leninism. Foucault has been less outspoken on both scores. All four have written extensively on the philosopher Friedrich Nietzsche; the importance of Nietzsche for radical analysis emerges from their work. Finally, all have been concerned with what might be called the politics of deviance; the politics of madness and of psychiatry; the politics of madness and of prisons. If a single difference were to separate their positions on these struggles from certain ideologies developed by Anglo-Americans, I would say it is this: their rejection of humanism and moralism in politics; their radical critique of the human or social sciences; and finally, the importance given to the body.

Let us look at this more closely. Criminality, madness, perversion, deviance: their phantasmatic and disciplinary use is the object of an enormous media industry. But in their material reality, in their bodies, how are they related to the so-called normal person who is submitted to their media effects? This "normal person," in whom psychoanalysis has recorded—perhaps recoded—a suffering, the suffering called neurosis, with its main types: obsession; hysteria. "Neurosis," says Freud, "the negative of perversion, the fear of madness, the failed crimes of parricide and incest, the individual religion." The deviant is the object of exclusion, rejection, enclosure, marginalization, and repression; but in what way, through what paths, to what material procedures have these mechanisms been used to produce what Lacan has called "the modern figure of man": "an immense morbidity and its psychogenetic consequences, character neurosis, the mechanisms of failure, sexual impotence, *der gehemmte Mensch*." And finally, how are these mechanisms first produced by segregating the deviant population, linked to the bureaucracy, the workplaces, the symbolic communities, the universities, which Freud began to analyze, starting notably with a military and religious organization? Is it not possible to discern from the deviant and his body, to the normal person and his, a whole network of procedures, techniques, strategies, through which modern man, the disciplined, surveyed, examined man, is produced?

Let us recall with Lacan that the entire evolution of humanist law is strictly correlative in time and space to the abandonment of torture as a penal practice. How did this correlative evolution occur, and in virtue of what process was a correlation produced? Should we not, for example, cast a suspicious eye in the direction of the great technologies of knowledge called the human or social sciences, which also originate in the 17th century? It is well known that the metaphysical isolation by Descartes of what Lacan called *the subject of signs*, seeing in it the precondition for the emergence of psychoanalysis and the object of its practice, had as its correlative the mechanical body. But is not this mechanical, and therefore trainable body to be placed in the perspective of a whole set of hospital, military, and school regimentations, and the reflected empirical procedures to control and operate upon the body, as Foucault has suggested?

James Fessenden

Transversality and Style (Groups, Packs and Bands)

Now, this paper, it's a bit fragmentary. It's not as fragmentary as I'd have liked it to be however, so I apologize. There are rather large sections divided by occasional quotations from Friedrich Nietzsche, and these quotations are to be understood as bees, wasps, or butterflies, fertilising the blossoms. I thought that I'd better make that clear, you might not have quite gotten the point if I hadn't.

"A physician who treated me for some time, as if my nerves were sick, finally said: 'It's not your nerves, it is rather I that am nervous.'" (*Ecce Homo* Book III, 4)

I'd like to recall the context in which the notion of transversality was first introduced by Guattari in 1964, in part because I will then show how it has been detached from that context, but in part also to introduce through this example the whole notion of detachment itself. Guattari introduces transversality in the context of a distinction between what he calls *groupe-sujet* and *groupe-assujetti*—this terminology is somewhat confusing, or at least, it was somewhat confusing to me—*group assujetti* is one which has organized or centralized itself around a subject or one which has posited itself as subject to a subject, one might translate "subject*ed* group," as opposed to *groupe-sujet*, "subject group," which is its own subject or, if you like, is coextensive with its subject, or, best of all, *lacks* a subject. Subjected groups, those that are organized around a subject are organized vertically and horizontally; levels are distinguished; communication between the parts of the group can take place only along certain prescribed paths. Such groups tend to posit gods or presidents, but it must be emphasized that these leaders are not the cause of the group's self-perception as subjected, rather they are the effect of this self perception and are just as much subject to it as everyone else. Subjected groups strive for self-preservation and exclusion of other groups.

Subject groups, in opposition to subjected groups, are characterised not by vertical or by horizontal, but by transversal organization. Ideally there is a maximum of communication possible between all of the parts. The aim of subject groups is increase, and what might be called "openness to the real." This distinction in the later productions of Deleuze-Guattari seems to transform itself into a distinction between crowds and packs for, respectively, subjected groups and subject groups. I mention this both because the crowd/pack distinction originates with the relatively accessible, at least more accessible in the Anglo-Saxon world than *Anti-Oedipe* perhaps, a book called *Crowds and Power* by Elias Canetti, which is quoted in some of the recent works of Deleuze-Guattari, and also because later I will be discussing wolves, wasps, bees and also hummingbirds if there's time.

"The pack," Canetti writes, "is surrounded by emptiness. Its fiercest wish is to be more." This is also quoted by Deleuze-Guattari in one of their most recent papers, the paper on The Wolf Man that's been published in the journal *Minuit*. To continue with Canetti: "In the pack, the individual may be the centre, and then immediately afterwards at the edge again. When the pack forms a ring around the fire, each man will have neighbours to his right and left, but no one behind him. His back is naked and exposed to the wilderness." (Canetti, *Crowds and Power*, p. 93)

The opposition in aim between the two kinds of groups is basic, and connects the distinction with Nietzsche's objections to Darwinism. The crowd, or the subjected group, is fascinated or obsessed with its own identity, and wishes to preserve itself at all costs. This is also the aim of each of its members. But the pack does not desire preservation as it is, but rather, increase. Thus, Nietzsche as against Darwin: "A living thing wants, above all, to discharge its force. Preservation is only a consequence of this." (*Will to Power*, 650)

Now, Freud represents a step backward from Nietzsche, at least in one stage of his theory of instincts, for he posits as basic two instincts, one of which aims at preservation of the species—that's libido—the other aims at preservation of the individual—those are the ego instincts—for example, in the *New Introductory Lectures* this distinction is replaced by Eros and Thanatos. The instincts Freud posits aiming at self-preservation are thus typical of subjected groups, of crowds. And Guattari's position is that the explanatory devices used by Freud, such as the Oedipus complex, formation of the ego, castration complex, and so on, are modes of self-preservative organization on the part of a crowd of the subjected kind. The anxiety such formations as the Oedipus complex and the superego produce being continued as neurotic anxiety even after the real external dangers originally producing the anxiety have vanished. The subjected group as a whole preserves these descriptions—by "descriptions" I mean the descriptions of individuals that are found in the Oedipus complex, castration complex and so on—and imposes them on itself and its subjects, forcing the latter to repress desires incompatible with these descriptions, and causing the energy which supplies these desires to appear elsewhere in the form of symptoms.

Thus, the possibility arises that the whole group might be subjected to institutional therapy, in the same way that an individual is subjected to therapy. What is needed will be some agency comparable to the analyst upon which agency the group could transfer its reified self-description. What is required is not obviously an individual or group who would literally analyze the rest of the group but rather an agency that would allow the group as a whole to undertake such analysis of itself, that is, "to constitute in the group the conditions of an analysis of desires." (Deleuze, in his preface to Guattari's *Psychanalyse et transversalité.*)

Now, I'd like to limit myself to one immediate circumstance of this more general program, and that is the possibility that this function of constituting in the group the conditions of an analysis of desires could be undertaken by works of art. And therefore, the next step is to examine the role of transversality in artworks, which is just what Deleuze does in his analysis of Proust. What is involved here is a study of the causal efficacy of artworks upon societies. The theory that works of art could be deployed in order to break down distorted social categories, and make possible their replacement received perhaps its most developed expression in Schiller's *Letters on the Aesthetic Education of Man*, in 1796, and found its most influential modern representative in Nietzsche's *Birth of Tragedy*. I think there's a clear line of development between these works and the Deleuze-Guattari enterprise, but will attempt here to detach the latter from this series—much to your relief, no doubt.

This is one of two keys to understanding what will be presented here—

"The greater the impulse towards unity, the more one may conclude that weakness is present. The greater the impulse towards variety, differentiation, internal disintegration, the more force is present." (*Will to Power*, 655)

The sexual instinct as it is recognised by Freud is not a single, simple entity, but is made up of, as he puts it, "a great number of component instincts arising from different areas and regions of the body" (*New Introductory Lectures*, p. 98).

The sexual instinct goes through a number of stages, in which now one, now another of its components predominates. Furthermore, these various component instincts with their sources in the various erogenous zones are not all included in the final genital organization. This gives rise to a problem which is outlined in the paper called "Transformation of Instincts with Special Reference to Anal Eroticism" of 1916. Since, as he says there, "the organic sources of anal eroticism cannot be exhausted by the establishment of the genital organisation," the question arises, once the primacy of the genitals has been established, what happens to the energy which originally cathected the previous anal stage? That is, the anal erotic impulses do not simply go away after the genital stage has been established, but they're in an anomalous position. Time has passed them by, so to speak. With the establishment of genitality they have become *de trop*. There is, that is to say, a certain excess of energy within the system.

I shall relate Freud's resolution of this problem in a moment, but must call attention to the fact that it is not self-evidently a problem at all. Why does excess energy need really to be done away with? It produces tension, to be sure, and the key notion at work in making it a problem for Freud is, of course, his definition of pleasure as absence of tension. Nietzsche's definition of pleasure is more tolerant of excess, to say the least: "What is pleasure but an excitation of the feeling of power by an obstacle? Thus all pleasure includes pain. If the pleasure is to be very great, the pains must be protracted, and the tension of the bow tremendous." (*Will to Power*, 658)

So Freud is, once again I think, a step backward, and the step forward is taken by Deleuze-Guattari, perhaps surpassing Nietzsche in this, one doesn't know. The tension provided by the excess anal erotic energy is drained off, for Freud, in virtue of the fact that in the unconscious certain elements—"the conceptions faeces, money, gift, child, and penis, are seldom distinguished and are easily interchangeable. That is, these elements in the unconscious are often treated as if they were equivalent and could replace one another."

It's at this point that I should mention the third title for this paper that I just came up with last night, "The Extensionality of Desire." Now, I'm afraid that I won't go into it; I don't know if it will make too much sense, it's kind of a technical term in philosophy. By extensionality I mean literally "extendedness," and we'll see the importance of that. In philosophy the notion of extensionality arises … a desire is said to be extensional, with respect to all of those objects of it, which can be substituted for each other and still produce, as a result, that that particular object is desired. Another way of putting it is to say that the desire, the anal erotic desire, is referentially transparent with regard to these particular terms. That's also, I'm afraid, a philosophical term.

Now because of this substitutability ... you see the point is, it seems to me, that it might be a good idea to take as primitive, *not* something like a desire, and then ask, "What are the various objects that can all equally well stand as satisfactions of that desire, or that can be used as vehicles for the satisfactions of this desire?" You should begin by forgetting about the desire, just noticing that there are certain objects that seem to align themselves up in certain pathways. Perhaps it is not even necessary to posit any additional subject, such as desire, over and above this simple surface phenomenon—but let that pass.

Freud's point is then that the anal erotic interest in feces can, because of the similarity of the objects, easily become an interest in or desire for a penis, or a child, that is a desire for something which is also an object of desire of the genital impulses. I remember that the original question that we were asking was, what happens to the "ghost-town" of anal eroticism after *Westward Ho!* and all that sort of thing. Now, Freud's answer to this is that, by a certain transference of energy, the same objects which originally were satisfying to the anal erotic interests can become satisfying to the genital interests, so that genital interests may then be said to have co-opted the former.

This is because all of the objects in question—feces, child, and penis—can be seen as instances of the more general concept "detachable object." So, Freud writes—this is a stunning quotation, actually—"When a child unwillingly enough comes to realise that there are human creatures that do not possess a penis, that organ appears to him as something detachable from the body, and becomes unmistakably analogous to excrement, which was the first piece of bodily material that had to be renounced." (*New Introductory Lectures*, p. 101)

I must say, I am disappointed in you; I expected to hear gasps of shock and dismay. Look, forget about the *unwillingly enough*: when a child comes to realize that there are human creatures that do not possess a penis—well there are *some* children, namely females, who really don't come to realize this in the same sense that Freud is talking about here—let me just mention that in passing, I'll leave it to Ti-Grace to straighten it all out.

I'd better read the quotation again: "When a child unwillingly enough comes to realise that there are human creatures that do not possess a penis, that organ appears to him as something detachable from the body, and becomes unmistakably analogous to excrement, which was the first piece of bodily material that had to be renounced." Now, there are a good many remarks here crying out to be made, but I shall renounce some of them and proceed at once to the question most crucial for the present purposes. Namely, how does it come to pass that these objects are all represented by the child under the same description?

Freud points to the quite obvious fact that there is a certain similarity between the objects, but in the very quotation just mentioned he in fact describes this similarity under two aspects: detachable object, and object that has to be renounced. That is, these are two more general concepts which serve to bind together the instances, and in virtue of these instances having been bound together, allow the transformation of the energy, the transference of the energy from one to another.

So the first question is, Is it possible to regulate which of these alternative ways of describing what the similarity consists in will be operative? It has already been mentioned that the predicate having to be renounced possesses a certain social utility, and the question naturally arises, Can the similarity of these objects be represented in some other way that would have some other utility? And this of course leads to a second and more general question: Are the objects really all that similar? The objects are certainly not all detachable in the same sense, when looked at more microscopically, as it were.

Well, Freud would reply that there are after all some undeniable anatomical facts at the bottom of all this. He speaks indeed of an organic analogy, saying in the 1916 paper that some children develop in their phantasies "an organisation analogous to the genital one, in which the penis and vagina were represented by the fecal mass and the rectum." And that "normally, when the interest in faeces recedes, the organic analogy we have described here effects a transference of the interest onto the penis." This is from the *Collected Papers Vol. II*, p. 169, and I must mention that for some unaccountable reason, in both of its occurrences in this paper the German phrase "organischer Analogie" is translated "structural analogy."

Well, anyhow, Freud will reply, mistranslated or not, that it is just not a matter of chance, anatomy is destiny, etc. Well, excepting this for the sake of the argument, we may proceed to wonder whether it is not possible to grant the contiguity both anatomical and conceptual of penis and feces, and yet not allow us to be seduce into similarity. Whether, that is, we cannot succeed in introducing some distance into the system.

Now it's time for the second key quotation—

"Principal viewpoint: establish distances but create no antitheses. Dissolve the intermediate forms, and reduce their influence. This is the chief means of preserving distances." (*Will to Power*, 891)

It's all a question of respecting the partiality of partial objects. I'll just explain partial objects *very* schematically. According to Melanie Klein, the infant passes through two stages of development, in the first of which it is aware not of whole persons but only of parts of the body, paradigmatically the mother's breast. This first position she calls "the paranoid-schizoid position," and in it the ego—which is compounded from the beginning, for her, of libido and death instinct—experiences itself and its objects as split, because to defend itself from the anxiety resulting from the death instinct, it projects the latter outwards in the form of bad objects, often not onto a single object—although of course single objects can also be divided into good and bad—often not onto a single object, but divided into a multitude or swarm of persecutors. This is a very rough statement of the theory, obviously, but it does give a sense of one, at least, of the implications of the term *schizo*.

A psychoanalysis of the famous dream in which the Wolf Man looks out of his window and sees a number of wolves perched on the tree outside, a psychoanalysis of this dream will, by various means, reduce the wolves in number to one, the castrating father. A schizoanalysis accepts the indeterminate number of wolves as essential to the dream, which then has as its central component the notion of a pack, in which wolves have been known to travel. This schizoanalysis of the Wolfman case is to be found in the paper of Deleuze-Guattari, I think it was in *Minuit*, 1974. Occurrence, as elsewhere in the Wolfman's case history, of wasps and butterflies confirms this.

Now the pack, as you will recall, is not a unity in the same sense as the crowd. In the crowd each part has one determinate position in the whole, and its place relative to the other parts is defined. Communication between the parts can take place but only in certain directions along certain predetermined paths. This of course has something to do with what I was saying before about referential transparency, that is to say, a given desire is transparent with reference to a certain number of its objects, any number of which will satisfy it, so long as they are described properly. In the case of the pack, each part is where it is only by chance, and might just as well be somewhere else. Now in the center, a moment later on the periphery. So for packs, so far as communication is concerned, contiguity is meaningless. Two parts immediately adjacent to each other may be quite unable to communicate, and may have to be brought into connection by a third party. Two parts at a great distance from each other may yet nonetheless be in perfect communicative accord. Thus, in such a group, the pack, communication cannot take place along given vertical and horizontal axes as it can in a crowd: it will be transversal. And the fact of contiguity or distance will have nothing to do with the ease with which energy flows from one to the other. So in the pack, desire has become referentially opaque.

Now a quote from Deleuze on Proust, *Proust and Signs*, the English translation, p. 116: "In the universe thus fragmented there is no logos"—I'm still talking about the fragmented universe of the pack—"there is no logos which gathers up all the pieces. Hence, no law which attaches them to a whole to be regained. Yet there is a law but with a changed nature … The law becomes a primary power. The law no longer says what is good, but good is what the law says. There are no longer laws specified in such-and-such a manner, but there is *the* law, without any other specification. This formidable unity, *the* law, is absolutely empty, uniquely formal, since it causes us to know no totality, no Good of reference, no referring Logos. Far from conjoining and adapting parts, it separates and partitions them, sets noncommunication in the contiguous, incommensurability in the container. Not causing us to know anything, the law teaches us what it is only by marking our flesh, by already applying punishment to us, and thus the fantastic paradox: we do not know what the law intended before receiving punishment, hence we can obey the law only by being guilty, we can be answerable to it only by our guilt, because the law is applied to parts only as disjunct, and by disjoining them still further, by dismembering bodies, by tearing their members from them. Strictly speaking unknowable, the law makes itself known only by applying the harshest punishments to our agonized body."

Arthur Danto

Freudian Explanations and the Language of the Unconscious

I looked at Lyotard's outline this evening, and it does seem to me that there is the possibility here of a genuine sort of confrontation on a theory of language. And I daresay that the two views of language that will be presented this evening are at the antipodes of one another.

Let me very briefly state the polemical context in which my discussion this evening is to be located: I'm concerned with the logical possibility of irrationality, that is to say, how is irrationality possible? The thought behind it is a kind of theory, according to which the difference between the mad and the normal is that they have merely different beliefs than we do, but that the pattern of explanation of their conduct is exactly the same. That makes it very difficult then to see how there can be any difference except a difference in belief, and one of the things I want to try and argue this evening, based upon an examination of certain Freudian texts is that the pattern of explanation governing normal behavior is very different indeed from the pattern of explanation involved in abnormal or even schizophrenic behavior.

I'd like to begin the talk with a kind of text from Plato, from the dialogue of the *Philebus*, in which Plato is talking about pleasure and pain, and at a certain point Socrates raises the question whether there can be such things as true and false pleasures, as there are true and false beliefs, supposing that there is to begin with an analogy between pleasure and belief. And he speaks as follows, he says to Protarchus:

> SOCRATES: Well, now, I wonder whether you would agree in my explanation of this phenomenon.
> PROTARCHUS: What is your explanation?

> SOCRATES: I think that the soul at such times is like a book.
>
> PROTARCHUS: How so?
>
> SOCRATES: Memory and perception meet, and they and their attendant feelings seem to me almost to write down words in the soul, and when the inscribing feeling writes truly, then true opinion[s] ... come into our souls—but when the scribe within us writes falsely, the result is false.

The bearing of the text upon the structure of my paper will, I hope, become clear.

Freudian theory is sometimes treated as though it licenses a hermeneutical overlay on all our thought and conduct, none of which really and deeply means what we would suppose it does without benefit of that theory, and none of which is properly explained in the ways we would spontaneously explain it. It is as though Freud had discovered a system of "signatures" on the basis of which we decipher conduct, read through to its final, ulterior signification, decode its surface meaning. Whatever we do, and however fantastically various the modes of our behavior, the final meaning is everywhere and barrenly the same—so much so that one need hardly unriddle the signatures anymore, knowing in advance that the same dismal, fatal note sounds throughout, like the echo in the Marabar Caves.

Freud himself implied nothing quite so leveling or mechanical, and although certain everyday occurrences—slipups and errors, lapses of memory, and pre-eminently dreams—proved, according to his theory, to have a purpose in the economies of mental life scarcely appreciated before him, and even to be intentional enough to be explained through reasons rather than (mere) causes, Freud resisted treating all conduct as only symptomatic, as he resisted the dissolutive explanatory temptations of what he disparagingly spoke of as pansexuality. I believe that if we examine the structures of psychoanalytic explanation, we shall find a deep argument less against Freud himself than against the insensitive generalization of his theories that aims at absorbing the whole of thought and conduct to a simple explanatory principle. It is an argument peculiarly against wholesale Freudianism itself, and not against absorbing the whole of conduct to some single explanatory principle, whatever may be the arguments available against that sort of reductionism.

Philosophers have sometimes resisted such reductions by mounting one or another version of what are termed paradigm case arguments: If one learns the meaning of a term *T* with reference to certain instances, then of those instances we cannot coherently with the meaning rules of our language deny that these instances are *T*. Freudianism, then, is accused of traducing these meaning rules and collapsing into nonsense, entailing the inapplicability of just those terms we know best how to employ and through which we describe what is closest to us as humans. But, the argument continues, we cannot intelligibly sacrifice these uses without in effect sacrificing the forms of human life we live. Or, it has been argued to whatever effect, Freud expanded immensely the denotation of such a term as "sexual" while holding its connotation constant, a simultaneous dilation and contraction in meaning under which the concept suffers semantical fracture, so much so that it no longer can be clear what the theory comes to. I have no great sympathy with this style of argument, or with the conceptual conservatism its use enfranchises, but I have no interest in pausing to harass the tattered regiments of common-usage philosophy.

My argument turns, rather, on certain features of *representation* that figure prominently in Freud's striking explanation of dreams and neurotic symptomologies. What I want to maintain is that representations could not have those features if they did not have those other features through which they cause thought and conduct in normally explainable ways. Roughly, my thesis has this form: It is impossible, much as it is impossible for every description to be metaphorical, for every term to be a pun. And Freudian explanations involve, typically, a punning transformation of terms, dreams, and symptoms having as their roots, plays on words.

Let us consider a somewhat strange example of "mental causation" offered by G. E. M. Anscombe as preliminary to our discussion, from her book on intention: "A child saw a bit of red stuff on a turn in a stairway and asked what it was. He thought his nurse told him it was a bit of Satan and felt a dreadful fear of it. (No doubt she said it was a bit of satin.) What he was frightened of was the bit of stuff: the cause of his fright was his nurse's remark." The child was afraid of something (ribbon, say) that does not ordinarily elicit fear, and the etiology of the phobia enlists a factor that, as we shall see, plays a considerable role in Freud's theory: an unwitting play on words. The child is (rightly, in view of his religious education) afraid of Satan. The nurse says what is on the stair is some satin; so the child is afraid of what is on the stair—I assume a parity of phonetic values between the two words that does not quite carry over into Middle American speech. I can imagine a child growing to adulthood with a curious, mysterious fear of red satin, which his therapist will be able to explain (and perhaps cure) only to the extent that he can archeologize this early, forgotten episode—like someone who finds himself unable to see Greece because as a child he had a fastidious mother.

Using now a Saussurian distinction between the signifier (*signifiant*) and the signified (*signifié*)—between sign (sound image) and meaning—we have, as it were, two phonetically indiscriminable signs with quite discriminable meanings; and what has happened is that the child has effected an interchange of signifieds, in consequence of which his subsequent behavior is manifestly weird. This sort of interchange presupposes properties of representations—in this instance, associated phonetic values—distinct from their meanings, inseparable from their representational properties. Then what I want to claim is that signs (representations) can be causal through both sorts of properties, so that there are two distinct ways in which they may enter explanations, much as there are two distinct ways in which they enter communication. In Freudian explanations they are, as in Anscombe's example, causal through confusions of meaning of the sorts exemplified in puns. And confusions of meaning of this order are not possible unless signs have fixed meanings to confuse. But the distinction is crucial, and there is a difference in logic that we are constrained to mark depending upon which of the two ways a sign in fact occurs. Let me illustrate this commenting on a famous pun.

Paul Grice, to bring out a point in his discussions of conversational implicature, cites the dispatch sent by a British general upon his conquest of Sind: "*Peccavi.*" This, as Latinists appreciate, translates into the English sentence "I have sinned," which then admits the punning "I have Sind"—a turn of wit that would have been impossible with the latter-day name of approximately the same territory, Pakistan. The general, as it happens, was Sir Charles Napier, and he was not just announcing his victory in a remarkably arch way; he also was saying that he had, *literally*, sinned in winning, that his means were morally reprobate—and indeed they were, as anyone who reads those pages in the British conquest of India recognizes. There was, in fact, a major debate in England over the lightness of his conduct of his campaign. My concerns here remain logical rather than moral, however; I wish to comment on the overdetermination of his message as a linguistic specimen.

For one thing, we lose the overdetermination if we translate the message into any language but English—for example, *ho peccato, ich habe gesündigt, j'ai peché* all lose the *sounds* that make the pun possible. And it is the sounds in particular that I am thinking of as properties of the signifier in abstraction of the signified.

Translation is a particularly good test of whether such features of signifiers play a significant role in the content of any given message. Thus, it is a fair assumption that translations must be truth-preserving: that *S'* cannot be a good translation of *S* if *S* and *S'* differ in truth-value. For example, "Paris has five letters" obviously refers to the word rather than to the city. If we translate the statement into Italian this way, "Parigi ha cinque lettere," we get something obviously false. So it would only be a matter of luck that "Paris hat fünf Buchstaben" comes out right. Phrases whose semantics involve reference to signs as *significant* are made true or false on the basis of properties of these as entities—not on the basis of properties of their *significations* or their normal referenda. And it is these language-locked features of signs that play the central role in much of psychoanalytical explanation. These are, as it were, textual features that are lost or sacrificed when the texts are translated, and which, because they are *entities* as much as cities or stones, are untranslatable in this dimension of their being; it is only in their status as significant that we can translate them by finding equivalent signs having the same meaning.

Let me, before proceeding to our structures, cite two examples, both from French psychoanalysts who are especially sensitive to these factors, which turn on essentially untranslatable features of signs that nevertheless play an important part in the analysis of conduct. These examples, if they are sound, imply something crucial about psychoanalysis as well as about us: our conduct is deeply involved in these features of our own language, so much so that it would not be possible, one feels, to psychoanalyze a person whose language one did not know—say, by using a translator. The wider implications of this I shall defer until later in the paper.

The first example comes from Jacques Lacan. It is always difficult to know when he is being serious, as he is a profoundly frivolous writer, but he draws the example itself from a study by Freud of fetishism, which gives it a measure of validity. Nevertheless, Lacan's own sensibilities make him alive to features in the example that might have been utterly lost to someone who thought merely in the explanatory frameworks of street-corner psychotherapy. Here, then, is a man who can achieve sexual satisfaction only when something is shining on his partner's nose—a *Glanz auf der Nase*. Let me quote Lacan's gloss:

> Analysis showed that his early English-speaking years had seen the displacement of the burning curiosity which he felt for the phallus of his mother, that is, for

that eminent failure-to-be the privileged signification of which Freud revealed to us, into a *glance at the nose* in the forgotten language of his childhood, rather than *a shine on the nose.*

Here the transformation from glance at the nose to *Glanz auf der Nase* contains two elements it is important to distinguish. The nose may indeed be a visual metaphor for the penis. It is explicitly so treated in one of Goya's *Caprichos, El Vergonzoso*, and Goya writes in his sardonic accompanying commentary: "It would be a good thing if those with such obscene faces were to hide them in their pants." And perhaps "the nose" is an infantile usage for what certainly at the time could not have been designated by its right name with propriety. But, and this is the point, the nose has the appropriate shape to function in almost a universal lexicon as a substitute symbol for the penis.

Freud at times in *The Interpretation of Dreams* supposes that there might almost be a universal lexicon of such symbolic equivalents: "All elongated objects ... sticks, tree trunks and umbrellas ... all sharp weapons, such as knives, daggers, and pikes," represent the male member. "Boxes, cases, chests, cupboards and ovens" correspond to the female organ, also cavities, "ships, and vessels of all kinds." "Small animals and vermin represent small children." Freud is perhaps insufficiently sensitive to cultural parochialisms, which in some measure restrict the universal obviousness of some of these symbols, but in any case, the connection between the English *glance* and the German *Glanz* (and note that the English word has to be spoken in a British accent to get the phonetic equivalence) is not at all of this order of equivalence: it is a substitution that goes through only at the level of sound, and is so bound up with the physical qualities of spoken language that to destroy Freud's explanation it would suffice to show that the person involved had never known English, even if he indeed had had the more typical Freudian curiosity alluded to.

Let me bring the difference out this way: There is a painting by Titian titled *Venus with the Lute Player*. Venus is holding a flute, and it is disgustingly easy to give this a "Freudian interpretation." It could be given, moreover, by anyone who knows the game of "elongated objects." In the corner lies a *viol d'amore*. The term *viol* carries implications, at the phonetic level, of rape. (Think of the condensation in *Finnegans Wake*, where Joyce writes, almost at the beginning, of "Sir Tristram, violer d'amores.") Did Titian intend this connotation of sexual violation? I have absolutely no idea, but my point is less one in iconography than psycholinguistics:

unlike the flute, the viol can be read as *that* sort of symbol only by someone in whose language there is a phonetic parity between the two pertinent senses of *viol.*

My second illustration comes from a well-known paper on the unconscious by Jean Laplanche and Serge Leclaire. Much of it turns on the analysis of a dream, in which a girl, Liliane, appears. The dreamer and the girl are in a forest; at a certain point a unicorn crosses their path, and "we walk, all three of us, toward a clearing that we suppose is below." With the substance of the dream analysis I shall not be concerned, but I want to remark on this: The French word for unicorn is *licorne,* and as the analysis proceeds, the first syllable, which is morphemically indiscernible from the French word for bed (*lit*), becomes important. It also appears in the name Lili, which echoes also the infantine word for milk (*lolo*). A complex content is thus gradually found in the dream through these echoes. I have no idea whether their analysis is in fact sound. All I wish to say is that it is based not upon any properties of unicorns as such, but on the *word*—in French—for "unicorn"; and furthermore, that an American, having just the same dream, could not have it represent what it does in French: there is no phonetic echo from *uni-* to *bed*, much less *Lili* to *milk.*

To be sure, the single protruding horn can have, in virtue of Freud's glossary, a phallic significance transcending language: it is not an accidental application of a theory of sympathetic resemblances that the Chinese should have regarded pulverized rhinoceros horn as an aphrodisiac. The point, however, is that if we translate the dream, we lose its meaning utterly. Part of the meaning of the dream is given by features of the description of it, in which words are mentioned rather than used. It is the *word* "licorne" as a *word* that carries the symbolic charge; and it is just these sounds that do not carry over, here or elsewhere, into a translation. The same bedeviling properties haunt the psychoanalyst that haunt the translator of a poem, the meaning of which resides in part in the acoustic or graphic identity of the words it is composed of, and not merely in what these words might mean—which can, in principle, simply enough be transferred to verbal equivalents in another language. The translation of a poem has to be more than a translation: it has to be a reconstruction preserving the music of the sounds, so far as this is possible. We dream in our own languages in such a way that only someone who knows the language can unriddle the dream. And this, I think, goes a certain distance toward illuminating the claim I want to base upon the Socratic text that I mentioned before—that we are built as a text is built. "We are such stuff as dreams are made on," if we see Shakespeare's line through Freudian lenses.

II

I want now to discuss for a moment some questions about the unconscious—the Ucs. system, as Freud designates it. I think a good beginning in the philosophical analysis of unconscious beliefs has been made by Arthur Collins in his 1969 paper "Unconscious Beliefs," though I think it does not go as far as it ought in explaining how unconscious beliefs are possible.

Begin by considering a well-known asymmetry between the avowal and the ascription of belief: I cannot say that I believe that *p*, but *p* is false; but I can without tension say that *you* believe that *p*, but *p* is false. Imagine that a therapist ascribes to me the belief that competition is dangerous; *he* need not believe that competition is dangerous in order to say that *I* do. Suppose he ascribes this belief to me on the basis of a great deal of evidence—namely, my avoidance of competitive situations, or my failure whenever I am in them, though it is plain enough that I could have succeeded instead. This might be the case, for instance, if I went to a therapist with a complaint of impotence and there was no physiological basis for my failure to secure erection. But I could also fail examinations of all sorts, including ordinary tests of life—getting a decent job, finding a romantic partner, and so forth. The therapist acquaints me with this evidence. I accept his explanation: it makes sense of a great deal of my conduct. To be sure, I do not consciously believe that competition is dangerous *as such*. But I do—I may say—believe it unconsciously. There is no contradiction here of the sort that affects "I believe that *p*, but *p* is false, a contradiction (of whatever sort) that we now see implies a presumption of consciousness. So "I believe that *p* (unconsciously), but *p* is false" is a possible utterance. The upshot, then, is this: A belief of mine is unconscious if (1) I can believe it is false while knowing it to be mine and (2) I come to know it is my belief on the basis of the same sort of evidence by which I know what your beliefs are.

In Collins' view, the Ucs. system is, in effect, an Other Mind. Needless to say, none of this has to imply, even if true, that the knowledge of the truth will set me free: knowledge need not entail cure. But I would like to shelve therapeutic considerations completely and just stick to the philosophical points. And admirable as Collins' analysis is, I think one point in it that is overlooked is the *peculiarity* of unconscious beliefs. He has addressed himself only to certain epistemological disparities and parities; he maintains that none of our ordinary beliefs can be unconsciously held and has overlooked the possibility that "Competition is dangerous" could be a perfectly ordinary belief. And is the difference between conscious beliefs and unconscious beliefs merely the difference between conscious and unconscious? Note that this would make the patient's conduct altogether rational in the sense that doing what he does would be exactly right *if he held the belief to be true*: it would be paradigmatic of rational conduct. Of course, he may fail to satisfy a test of rationality in that he believes *p* and also does not believe it; but as I indicated, this inconsistency is exactly muted if we qualify the belief ascriptions as conscious and unconscious, just as there is no incoherence in "I believe that *p*, and you don't."

A degree of progress has been made on the matter by Peter Alexander, who has argued brilliantly that a condition for a belief as an unconscious reason for conduct is that it would not be a reason if it were conscious. This suggests a stronger criterion than any we have so far encountered, for after all, it is wholly reasonable to assume that the beliefs of Other Minds at least are conscious to them—they must believe them true if they believe them at all; and all Collins has furnished us with in distinguishing consciousness from unconsciousness is this difference between self-knowledge and other-knowledge. It is only complicating psychology to say that our unconscious is an Other Mind to us.

As indicated above, Collins says that none of our ordinary beliefs can be unconsciously held. But what is the criterion of ordinariness or normality? At least a beginning is made in saying that a belief is *unordinary* if it would not be given as a reason for the action *it in fact would explain* if it were conscious: it is not a reason that the agent would, or perhaps could, sensibly give for what he does. And the difficulty, in a way, with Collins' example is that one could very easily cite as a reason for one's conduct that one believed competition was dangerous.

Let us consider, then, Alexander's example of a man lunging at lampposts with his umbrella. Perhaps, like Collins' imaginary example, this is not intended to be taken with clinical exactitude as a routine symptom. Seeing someone behaving that way, we might rationalize his conduct by supposing him to be practicing fencing moves, or trying to unstick his umbrella, or, ineffectually, trying to impale fireflies. These would all be rational enough, but the truth is that it is to be explained through his Oedipus complex: I want to kill my father, who is my rival for my mother's love, but since I cannot admit to myself either the incestuous wish nor the parricidal one—indeed, am not conscious of it—I find some substitute way of gratifying my wish, in this instance lunging away at lampposts. And "I want to kill my father" could not be offered as a reason for lunging at lampposts unless I espoused some special magical theory and believed my behavior was a means to that, which is unlikely. The normal pattern of explanation in the case of action is this: I do *a* because I want *b* to happen, from which it is plausible to suppose that I also believe *a* to be a good means to *b*, or at least not inconsistent with the production of *b*.

Imagine I see a man posting a letter. The very use of the word *posting* implies that he intends the letter to arrive at a destination and regards putting it in a mailbox as a good way to ensure that that happens. If I see a man putting a letter deliberately in a trash can, so deliberately as to rule out the possibility that he is throwing it away, it is reasonable, especially if the letter has an unfranked stamp, to ascribe an error to him: Quixote-like, he has mistaken a trash can for a mailbox, or he's just absentminded. But suppose he says no, he has no confidence in the postal system, or he has more confidence in the department of sanitation than in the postal service and believes that his action is a means to having his letter arrive at its intended destination. Then, apart from my wondering why he has bothered to put a stamp on the letter, I can regard his behavior as rational; it is just his beliefs that are devious or false. But in any case, *R* counts as a reason for *b* only if the bridging beliefs can be attributed to a person. The question is, can they be so attributed in Alexander's case?

I think that what Alexander brings out is that we do not suppose the lunger *unconsciously* to hold the bridging belief that is required to rationalize his conduct. Or we do so only if we adhere to the universal applicability of the model just sketched, and resort to the unconscious system, in order to assure that it applies in every instance, whereas it is not plain that this is the case here. If it were, the behavior would be rational enough. As is more plausible, the bridging belief is not even unconsciously held. "The behavior," writes Alexander, "does not seem to be related to the alleged reasons in the way in which ordinary behavior is related to ordinary good reasons for it." But then he does not tell us how it is related to its reasons, only suggesting, in the manner of paradigm case argumentation, that we cannot call neurotic behavior rational without changing the meaning of either "good reason" or "rational" in some unhelpful way.

Nevertheless, Alexander does, through his examples, suggest a partial analysis of irrational behavior, which after all is what we are after: *b* is an irrational piece of conduct if *R* is *m*'s reason for *b* but *m* does not hold the necessary bridging beliefs. The question then to be asked is this: If he does not hold the requisite beliefs, in what sense does he have a reason for this conduct? In what way can *R* be a reason and yet not connect in any way through his own system of beliefs with what it is allegedly to explain? Unless we have an answer to this, we still have no very clear picture of irrational behavior. My claim is that Freud gives us such an answer, and indeed, we have already established the way in which this answer works. To this I now turn.

III

It is widely appreciated that Freud believed that dreams, as well as symptoms, were fulfillments of unconscious wishes, wishes that, though active enough to continue to cause conduct of a highly symbolic order, were not available to the person whose wishes they were. They were not so much forgotten as repressed, the wishes themselves being so forbidden or threatening that their owner could not admit to having them. In dreams especially, it is important to distinguish the *manifest dream content*, which is in some measure epiphenomenal, from the *latent dream thought*, itself housed in the unconscious, which stands to it in a causal relation and also in one further, more semantical relationship, which I would like to spell out.

Let the unconscious element be *W*(*p*)—the wish-that-*p*-be-the-case. Let the manifest element be *W*(*p**)—the wish-that-*p*-be-represented-as-fulfilled. But matters are not so simple as, say, wanting a glass of water and dreaming that one in fact has a glass of water: *p* itself undergoes a transformation as it passes the barrier from unconscious to conscious. This transformation is all that concerns me now. In some way, it is a very heavily disguised form of *p*, since there is no direct way that *p* can come to consciousness: Freud supposes it would be too painful and, indeed, that one would wake up, one function of dreams being to preserve sleep while allowing the repressed wish to rise transfigured to consciousness. Let the transfiguration of *p* be *p**. Freud at one point thought *p** might plausibly be a translation of *p*, the unconscious and conscious systems standing to one another as two languages do. He then abandoned this theory in *The Interpretation of Dreams* in favor of another one, which retains just the sorts of properties of representations I have been discussing. In the following excerpt, he now supposes that *p** is a rebus on *p*:

The dream-thoughts and the dream-content are presented to us like two versions of the same subject-matter in two different languages. Or, more properly, the dream-content seems like another transcript of the dream-thoughts into another mode of expression, whose characters and syntactic laws it is our business to discover. ... The dream-content ... is expressed as it were in a pictographic script, the characters of which have to be transposed individually into the language of the dream-thoughts. If we attempted to read these characters according to their pictorial value instead of according to their symbolic relation, we should clearly be led into error. … A dream is a picture-puzzle of this sort and our predecessors in the field of dream-interpretation have made the mistake of treating the rebus as a pictorial composition: and as such it has seemed to them nonsensical and worthless.

A rebus is a very elementary sort of puzzle, in which the "solution" is a sentence, the words of which are sounded in such a way as to generate homonyms that can be given pictorial representation—as "pick" in "take your pick" has as a homonym the "pick" of "pick and shovel" and can thus be represented via a picture of one. We solve the rebus by pronouncing the words that go with the individual pictures, replacing these with homonyms, and getting a spoken sentence that makes sense—the solution of the rebus. Usually, the pictures have nothing to do with one another; indeed, the row of pictograms in the typical rebus is nonsense.

Let me give some examples of rebuses. On the cornice of the house of Jacques Coeur in Bourges are alternate cockleshells and hearts. The French word for heart is *coeur*, his last name; the shell symbolizes the *coquille de St. Jacques*, the emblem of the pilgrims, so: Jacques Coeur. In the tympanum of St. Domenic's in Rome is a spotted dog where some prominent religious figure might be expected. This is one of the *domini cani*, the "dogs of God"—which, of course, is a rebus for *Dominicani*, the Dominican Order, for whose leader the church is named. An Italian printer celebrates his fiancée, Caterina, by showing a broken chain on which is superimposed a king. The chain is *catena*, king is *re*: hence *cate-re-na*. The two pieces of the chain correspond to the broken word. The fish is a symbol of Christ, but again, through a rebus: the word *ichthos*—Greek for fish—in fact is an acronym for Jesus Christ the Son of God, Savior (Ieusous Christos Theou Hyios, Soter). And so on. Duchamp's *L.H.O.O.Q.* is a good French rebus, yielding a mild obscenity when the letters are pronounced in French (but not in English). What is important to notice is that none of the *Bilderrätstel* show anything that tells us very much about what the phonetically equivalent solution describes. What have dogs to do with Dominicans or fish with Christ?

Freud wrote:

> Suppose I have a picture-puzzle [*Bilderrätstel*], a rebus, in front of me. It depicts a house with a boat on its roof, a single letter of the alphabet, the figure of a running man whose head has been conjured away, and so on. Now I might

> be misled into raising objections and declaring that the picture as a whole and its component parts are nonsensical. A boat has no business to be on the roof of a house, and a headless man cannot run. Moreover, the man is bigger than the house; and if the whole picture is intended to represent a landscape, letters ... are out of place in it. ... But obviously we can only form a proper judgement of the rebus if we put aside criticisms such as these ... [and] try to replace each separate element by a syllable or a word.

It is crucial that the solution of a rebus does not translate. A French rebus shows a man holding in his hand a large green letter *I—un grand I vert*—which gives as part of the solution *un grand hiver*, "a long winter," to which the English description "a big green I" has no phonetic tie whatever. Lose the language and you lose the possibility of resolving a puzzle of this sort. Think of the invitation alleged to have been sent to Voltaire by Frederick the Great: $\frac{p}{20}$ à $\frac{6}{100}$. It is indecipherable save in French.

Whatever the case, the dream-content stands to the dream-thought as a rebus stands to its solution. And much the same is true of symptoms, though with this difference: the symptom is an action whose description must be found, for we will see that the description, again, stands to the unconscious wish in this rebuslike relationship. I want now to illustrate this with some examples from the literature.

First, we begin with the famous case of the Rat Man (a Holmesian title), a profoundly disturbed and unfortunate man whom Freud analyzed. At one point the Rat Man began a peculiar regime. It occurred to him that he was too fat, and he began to get up from meals and engage in quite strenuous exercises. This was obsessional behavior, though he was able to give a perfectly good reason for doing it (and his own description of his behavior is critical): he was too thick (dick), and it was this being "thick" that he described himself as trying to change. The tact, I suppose, is that he was not all that "dick"—that is, not so thick as to merit that much exercise. Some line had been crossed, as in the case of the compulsive hand-washer for whom the ordinarily perfectly good reason "in order to be clean" seems no longer to be commensurate with the conduct.

In any case, there was something neurotic about the Rat Man's behavior, and what analysis brought out is the following: his beloved had an English suitor, the Rat Man's rival, whose name was Dick. So in getting rid of dick (thickness), he was in some way getting rid of Dick. It is plain that he had not selected a very efficient way of doing this, and also that he did not consciously believe that that was what he was doing; indeed, it would be absurd to attribute to him even the unconscious belief that in ridding himself of a thick waistline, he was doing his rival in—or the practical syllogism, "I want to get rid of my rival, and reducing my waistline is a good means of doing that. Jogging is said to reduce waistlines: so, I'll jog." Were the matter as simple as that, we would have only a wayward premise to rectify, and instruction in the technology of rival-riddance would take care of the Rat Man's therapeutic needs: what he would be lacking would be common sense or practical intelligence. (Of course, the matter would be different had his ladylove told him that the reason she preferred Dick to him was that he, the Rat Man, was too fat. Then, indeed, his conduct would be rational and even reasonable. But that is not the lethal sense of "getting rid of Dick" that festered in the Rat Man's unconscious.) The point is that he had no such belief as the practical syllogism requires. Nevertheless, getting rid of Dick (the rival) was his (real) reason for running. It is not even a bad reason for that, being too insane. And this, I think, is what Alexander has sensed. Speaking of one of the lapses Freud discusses, he writes:

> The woman who read "storks" for "stocks" does not appear, by so doing, to have furthered either the end of obtaining children or of concealing from herself her own unhappiness, and it is doubtful that she or others could have seen the behavior as achieving anything except with the help of Freud's theory. … In general, similar things can be said about Freud's explanations of neurotic symptoms. If I am said to *x* for unconscious reason *y*, it is nearly always the case that *y* is not the sort of thing which we would normally consider a good reason for *x*.

What is missing in this somewhat grudging account, which I believe is true as far as it goes, is the connection between the unconscious reason and the given one: they are related homonymically, as rebus to resolution. Second, Merleau-Ponty (whose wife was a psychoanalyst) gives this case en passant. A young girl was forbidden by her mother to see her lover anymore. The girl stopped eating not long afterward and settled into anorexia nervosa, a quite distressing eating disorder. Crude analysis suggests something like this: by ceasing to eat, she was trying to put pressure on her mother, or even to punish her mother, in a situation in which she herself had almost no other form of control over her life. The fact is, no one wants anyone to stop eating, certainly not one's daughter, and by doing what she (the girl) knew no one wanted her to do, she was asserting her autonomy and bringing her mother to her knees. So considered, her conduct was rational enough, though extreme—what R. D. Laing would call, I suppose, "a rational response to an irrational situation"—and therapy ought then to consist in finding some substitute way of achieving the same ends, or at least in showing her the suicidal consequences of protracted anorexia. Those with any experience in such disorders appreciate how ineffective such "therapy" is: the patients in some way cannot help themselves. In this instance what analysis evidently revealed was the following: the girl obviously resented her mother's interdiction and said to herself that she would not accept it. The actual form of the thought was "I won't swallow that." *Avaler*, like "swallow" in English, has this sense. And not swallowing is what she proceeded to do, though her reason was to resist her mother's demand. Once more we find this trivial phonetic connection between unconscious and conscious reasons.

On the basis then of these examples, and many more which could be cited, let us briefly sketch the structure of psychoanalytical explanations. Let R be m's reason for a piece of conduct (or any appropriate explanandum) that we call a; R is in the unconscious system, and the fact is that m has no bridging belief of the sort logically required by a practical syllogism, according to which R would be a good reason for a. And R^* is a good reason for a, but in fact it is not the explanation of m's doing a at all. The explanation is through R. But R^* has replaced R, and is able to do so through the fact that the phonetic values of R and R^* are close if not perfect (as "stork" is merely close to "stock").

Of course there is also the fact that the person in question is typically disturbed by the conduct, wishes he or she could stop, and so forth: something brings him or her to the therapist. As before, I am not concerned with the therapy; all I am saying is that if Freud is right, we must find a reason in the unconscious, a reason that in fact is never and can never be recognized as satisfying the conduct it explains, since that conduct is understood merely as satisfying the rebus-related but wholly irrelevant reason the patient might spontaneously accept or offer. The symptom is like a puzzle that has to be solved. It expresses a thought the patient cannot admit he or she has. More important for our purposes, the case of the anorexic offers a paradigm of irrational conduct, since it exactly satisfies the conditions we have specified. Obviously, I am in no position at all to offer any general account of anorexia.

Third, the Rat Man and the anorexic are victims of a truth that is hidden from them, which explains the therapeutic optimism that when the truth is revealed the symptoms will dissipate. Neither of these neurotics is deluded or deceived as such; they are only mistaken as to the real reasons for their conduct. And this stems from a mistake of a more philosophical order, because each applies to irrational conduct a structure of explanation that applies to rational action. The plausible reasons they give for what they do amount to rationalizations of their behavior—in the instance of the Rat Man, for example, that he is "too fat." Thus they regiment to the structures of practical reason behavior that answers to another sort of model. And so long as they persist in misapplying this model, their conduct will never, because it *can* never, if Freud is right, receive a correct account.

Symptoms, as we have seen, have something in common with at least that order of dream that disguises unfulfilled and repressed wishes, with perhaps this difference: The neurotic is right about what he is doing, at least under *some* description—for example, the Rat Man knows that he is running. He is mistaken only in the description of his conduct under which it can truly be explained. But dreamers are deceived into believing that something is happening which is not, and so are deceived about its causes and explanations. My dog, when he dreams, as apparently he does, of chasing squirrels in Riverside Park, believes not only that he is chasing squirrels but that their presence explains his conduct, if I may be permitted to assign him this degree of ratiocination. And as there are neither squirrels nor chase, nothing of what he believes he is explaining is there to be explained at all. What requires explanation is why he is dreaming and what; and caught up as he is in the dream, he is not aware that what he is caught up in is a dream, and misses the explanandum completely. So he is twice deceived, first in believing in the ultimate reality of his experience, and then in its explanation—like someone who believes that the presence of the palm trees in what he does not know is a mirage is to be accounted for by the presence of water.

Dreams are not, of course, disorders calling for cure, but there are cases intermediate between neurosis and dream, where the symptoms arise from the unconscious but the victim is also deluded, as we all may be said to be in dreams: and this, to a degree, must characterize psychosis. I want to mention as a concluding illustration a case of schizophrenia cited by Freud toward the end of his great paper on the unconscious. Here he cites some findings brought to his attention by his brilliant, ill-starred disciple, Victor Tausk. A girl, after a quarrel with her lover, came to him with this complaint: "*Her eyes were not right, they were twisted.*" As it happens, the German word for deceiver is *Augenverdreher*—eye-twister—and the girl went on to say "he had twisted her eyes; now … they were not her eyes any more." Freud cites this in illustration of "the meaning and the genesis of schizophrenic word-formation." Again, the girl complained that her lover had "*given a false impression of his position*" (the German *sich verstellen* means to feign or disguise oneself); and now she herself had changed her position (verstellen = to change the place of)—she claimed that in church she had felt a strange jerk and had to *change her position.*

A *hysteric*, Freud explains, instead of claiming his eyes were twisted, would have rolled them, and wondered why; instead of claiming his position had changed because of a jerk, he would actually have *manifested jerky behavior.* "In schizophrenia," Freud writes, "*words* are subjected to the same process as that which makes the dream-images out of latent dream-thoughts—to what we have called the primary psychical process. They undergo condensation, and by means of displacement transfer their cathexes to one another in their entirety." And finally, in explaining the strangeness of the symptom in schizophrenia, he says it derives from "the predominance of what has to do with words over what has to do with things. ... What has dictated the substitution is not the resemblance between the things denoted but the sameness of the words used to express them." Schizophrenics "find themselves obliged to be content with words instead of things."

IV

"To interpret the unconscious as Freud did," Lacan writes, "one would have to be as he was, an encyclopedia of the arts and muses, as well as an assiduous reader of *Fliegende Blätter.* And the task is made no easier by the fact that we are at the mercy of a thread woven with allusions, quotations, puns and equivocations. And is that our profession; to be antidotes to trifles? ... And yet," Lacan concludes, "that is what we psychoanalysts must resign ourselves to. The unconscious is neither primordial nor instinctual; what it knows about the elementary is no more than the elements of the signifier."

Just here, I think, we can perceive a curious blindness in Freud himself, as the very use of the expression "primary process" connotes—as though he were blocked from appreciating the import of his discoveries by a kind of romanticism, as though the unconscious itself were somehow primitive and savage. In fact the primary process involves conduct on the surfaces of language of an almost exquisitely, ultracivilized order—the sort of conduct that goes into the most mannered of literary productions, anagrams and acrostics, and self-referentiality, where letter becomes substance, and the enterprises pursued merely virtuoso, like elaborate palindromes. Even in his late writings, with a lifetime of accumulated evidence behind him, Freud was unable to perceive this.

The Ego and the Id—the "last of Freud's major theoretical works" (editor's preface)—appeared in 1923. Here Freud writes: "The real difference between a Ucs. and a Pes. idea (thought) consists in this: that the former is carried out on some material which remains unknown, whereas the latter (the Pes.) is in addition brought into connection with word-presentations." He then asks the question of how something goes from the unconscious to the preconscious (or for that matter, the conscious)—"How does a thing become conscious?"—and answers, "Through becoming connected with the word-presentations corresponding to it." A "material which remains unknown," indeed: when it has to be an almost logical truth that if the connection between dream-content and dream-thought, symptom and wish, is to be as I have described it, the unconscious itself must be made of the same stuff consciousness is—namely, words. After all, what is in the dynamically repressed is there by repression, and what is repressed today was once conscious, and connected then with "word-presentations," if that indeed is the criterion of consciousness. The dynamically repressed, whatever its relation to the id, is not the id. "How could a psychoanalyst of today not realize," Lacan asks rhetorically near the beginning of his essay, "that his realm of truth in fact is the word, when his whole experience must find in the word alone its instrument, its framework, its material, and even the static of its uncertainties?"

I am in no position, of course, to vouch for the accuracy of Freud's accounts. I am only interested in drawing attention to what must be the fabric of the mind if these accounts are in fact true—namely, that it is a fabric woven of language, and must be so in the normal case if Freud's characterization of the abnormal cases has the slightest basis in fact. For the *abnormal* cases all enshrine a fallacy, broadly speaking, of *quaternio terminorum*, and a consequent substitution of words for things—and, indeed, it is in exactly these terms that we may characterize irrational thought and conduct. But then, as I have argued, there can be confusion of meaning only if there can be clarity of meaning, and only if the vehicles of confusion exchange their identities like twins in an ancient dramatic form and appear henceforward *en travestie*. Not every phenomenon can be a Freudian one, not every explanation a Freudian explanation. But to the degree that it admits *those sorts of vagaries*, we get a glimpse of what the structure of mind and thought must in the normal case be. We are all of us, in our normal conduct, words made flesh.

Jean-François Lyotard

Sur la force des faibles / On the Strength of the Weak (Group Translation)

JEAN-FRANÇOIS LYOTARD: Je commencerai aujourd'hui par une histoire qui se trouve dans Aristote, selon lequel il y avait un rhéteur, un avocat qui s'appelait Corax et qui avait une certaine technè, un certain art, un certain tour, qu'Aristote décrit de la façon suivante : quelqu'un, qui est le client de Corax, est accusé d'avoir brutalisé une victime. Il y a deux cas, dit Aristote : premier cas, le client est quelqu'un de très fort ; deuxième cas, le client est quelqu'un de faible. Si le client n'est pas fort, c'est-à-dire s'il est faible, Corax va plaider en disant : "Il n'est pas vraisemblable que mon client, qui est faible, ait pu brutaliser quelqu'un". Très bien dit Aristote, Corax utilise la vraisemblance ; il est en effet invraisemblable que quelqu'un de faible brutalise quelqu'un d'autre. Mais dans l'autre cas, si le client est fort, la plaidoirie de Corax consiste à dire : "mon client savait justement que sa force rendait vraisemblable son inculpation ; connaissant cette vraisemblance, il s'est abstenu de toute brutalité et c'est pourquoi il est innocent".

Aristote proteste en disant : "c'est là un mauvais usage de la vraisemblance". C'est un mauvais usage de la vraisemblance, car on n'utilise pas ici la vraisemblance en elle même, pure et simple, mais on fait un usage vraisemblable de la vraisemblance. Autrement dit, le supposé inculpé prévoit la vraisemblance et se conduit en fonction de ce qu'il sera vraisemblable qu'on lui dise. Dans ce cas précis, la vraisemblance n'est pas pure parce qu'elle est rapportée à elle-même, elle n'est pas prise absolument ; il faut distinguer des vraisemblances absolues et des vraisemblances qui ne le sont pas, et Aristote conclut en disant : "voilà en quoi consistait toute la technè, tout l'art de Corax, à savoir de faire que le discours le plus faible devienne le discours le plus fort".

ROGER MCKEON: Is it necessary to translate? It is? Okay. So Lyotard started by telling a story which apparently inspired the title of his communication tonight.

He takes the story from Aristotle of a lawyer, Corax, and Aristotle tells us he has a *techne*, in other words an art, a technique. Corax's client has brutalized a victim and Aristotle says Corax, mastering this technique, has two possibilities: If the client is a weakling, he'll say it isn't likely that Corax did in fact brutalize the victim; if on the contrary the client is a hefty man, it isn't likely either because, knowing likelihood was against him, he wouldn't have brutalized the man in the first place.

Now, the first form of verisimilitude or likelihood is a good one, is acceptable to Aristotle. The second one isn't, inasmuch as it is a second-degree form of likelihood; Corax knows what the likelihood is, and plays on it. Is that clear?

MARK SEEM: You forgot one thing that would make the story clearer: You forgot to say that the client was accused of having brutalized the victim; you said the client had brutalized the victim.

MCKEON: I was forgetting the conclusion—Aristotle concludes the art of Corax consists in making the weakest discourse the strongest one.

LYOTARD: Je voudrais montrer très rapidement que ce qui est important, c'est de fabriquer des ruses à l'intérieur même du discours des maîtres, du discours magistral, et je m'en tiendrai ce soir à des problèmes de discours, mais ce qui m'intéresse, c'est, en dégageant ces petits opérateurs de ruse, de voir plus tard, la semaine prochaine, si ces opérateurs peuvent fonctionner dans d'autres champs que le discours et, évidemment, dans le champ de ce qu'on appelle le politique. Autrement dit, mon intention, s'il faut faire des déclarations d'intention, mon intention est une intention politique.

MCKEON: Now, what Lyotard intends to prove is that as far as we are concerned, what is important is to make up ruses or cunning, inside the discourse of the masters, the masterly or authoritative discourse. In French, *maître* has a double meaning: it is both the master and the schoolmaster, and his position in this particular case is not very comfortable. But that's another problem …

[Audience laughs]

Now, what he would like to try and find out tonight is whether the operators of ruse or cunning, which he mentioned earlier, can function in other fields than the discourse. Can they function, for instance, in the political field (which is the field he's mainly interested in)?

LYOTARD: Le discours du maître, le discours magistral, consiste essentiellement, je crois, dans une injonction portant sur la fonction même du discours, si l'on s'en tient, bien sûr, aux problèmes de discours, qui veut que cette fonction soit de dire le vrai. Quel rapport entre cela et la maîtrise ? Tout discours a fonction de vérité, tout discours de savoir doit découvrir, doit produire les conditions dans lesquelles les énoncés peuvent être affectés d'une valeur de vérité positive ou négative, doit, si vous voulez, pour le dire plus simplement, déterminer ses conditions de vérité. La détermination des conditions de vérité implique une sorte de métadiscours à l'intérieur du discours du maître ; ce métadiscours, c'est le discours philosophique lui même dans la tradition, c'est le discours logique dans les temps modernes. Autrement dit, il y a premièrement ce qui est dit et deuxièmement ce qui permet de le dire, le discours sur ce qui autorise à dire ce qu'on dit. Ce clivage est évidemment indispensable comme injonction, comme intention, comme projet du discours magistral.

MCKEON: So, the discourse of the masters consists mainly in injunctions concerning the discourse itself. The function of that discourse is … well, no …

SEEM: The function of the discourse is to say the truth, the true.

MCKEON: The function of the masterly discourse should be to say the truth, in order that we are compelled to say the truth. All truthful discourses must determine the conditions of truth, which implies a meta-discourse; the conditions of truth of a discourse imply a second-degree discourse defining its very conditions of truth. And this goes up to the discourse of logic in modern times. Now, this has two aspects—what is said and what authorizes one to say what he is saying—and this split is indispensable to the master's discourse.

LYOTARD: Il y a donc une sorte d'intimidation du discours du maître, qui consiste à nous imposer un certain nombre de principes, à savoir : vous devez, votre tâche est, de dire la vérité, de dire le vrai. Vous devez supposer que les conditions de cette vérité ne sont pas données, qu'elles sont cachées, c'est-à-dire qu'elles doivent être élaborées, découvertes ou construites ; qu'en somme les énoncés ordinaires ne sont pas nécessairement vrais. Que, par conséquent, il y a un manque de vérité dans les énoncés ordinaires, dans les énoncés de tous les jours. L'histoire n'est rien d'autre—telle est par exemple la position d'Augustin—l'histoire n'est rien d'autre qu'une lutte pour l'avènement du vrai ; la fonction politique n'est rien d'autre qu'une fonction pédagogique : elle consiste précisément à susciter la prise de conscience qui permettra de distinguer dans l'ensemble des énoncés dont nous sommes bombardés ceux qui sont vrais et ceux qui sont faux. L'efficacité du langage, dans cette perspective, c'est toujours l'efficacité par la vérité, c'est-à-dire par la conviction, qui consiste à réveiller chez l'auditeur une sorte de remémoration de la vérité perdue. Voilà, si vous voulez, un certain nombre de ces injonctions ; je ne prétends pas les épuiser, mais je voudrais souligner que toutes ces injonctions sont congruentes, qu'elles vont toutes dans le même sens, finalement, que ce soit sur le plan proprement discursif ou au niveau politique, ou à celui de la pratique historique ; c'est-à-dire qu'elles font du vrai à la fois l'objet et le moyen des discours.

MCKEON: There is a form of intimidation in the master's discourse, which imposes upon us a number of principles, you have them under your eyes, some of these principles are the following: you must seek to tell the truth; you must suppose the conditions of truth are hidden; you must also suppose they have to be elaborated, which implies that ordinary statements lack truth, their conditions not having been elaborated. History—and Lyotard refers here mainly to St. Augustine—is a struggle for the advent of truth. The political function in this direction is nothing more than a pedagogical function, it functions on the basis of persuasion. The efficiency of language is conviction, which completes the first part of the statement. All these injunctions go in the same direction. They all relate—whatever the level for discourse—to the fact that truth is both an object and a means of the very discourse we were talking about.

LYOTARD: Je n'ajouterai qu'une seule chose sur ce point, c'est que toute la position du discours marxiste relève de cette position magistrale, lui appartient entièrement.

MCKEON: Marxism in its entirety belongs to this masterly, authoritative position.

LYOTARD: Alors... la tendance schizo-culture, par exemple, cherche à éviter ces injonctions, en se plaçant en extériorité. Si l'on considère non seulement les discours eux-mêmes, mais aussi les pratiques des années '60, on peut très brièvement dire que la tentative générale a été de se placer en dehors de cette injonction magistrale et de produire, donc, une sorte d'extériorité sous des noms très différents : spontanéité, libido, pulsion, énergie, sauvagerie, folie et peut-être schizo.

MCKEON: The tendency in schizo-culture is to try and avoid the injunctions Lyotard was telling us about. By placing oneself outside, in the exteriority of the master's injunctions and discourse, not only at the level of discourse, but also if one looks at the practices since the '60s, the general attempt was to stay outside of the masterly injunctions in the name of spontaneity, libido, drive, instinct, call it as you like ... schizo—what did you call it?—savagery, madness, unsociability ...

LYOTARD: Or c'est justement cela que demandent la position et le discours magistraux. Je veux dire qu'il y a une ruse du discours magistral, du discours de l'Occident si vous voulez, il y a une ruse de ce discours qui consiste précisément à demander que pour l'éviter on se place à l'extérieur de lui. Cette ruse, elle est très simple, elle consiste à faire de l'extériorité le complément nécessaire de ce discours. Et j'ajouterai, un complément à conquérir, une zone opaque dans laquelle il faut que ce discours pénètre à son tour.

MCKEON: Now this position, the exteriority, is exactly what the masterly position asks for, that is exactly what it wants, what it is looking for. There is its ruse: he calls it "the ruse of the masterly discourse, the ruse of the Western world itself." Exteriority is the necessary complement of that discourse; it could not function without that exteriority. It is a complement the masterly discourse must and intends to conquer, a zone in which it must penetrate, an opaque zone which it must and intends to penetrate one day.

LYOTARD: Quand on se place en extériorité pour éviter la position magistrale, on continue cette position, on la nourrit. Je crois que cela est vrai pour toute critique, qui implique toujours la mise en extériorité de la position critiquante par rapport à la position critiquée, ce qui permettra à la position critiquée d'inclure la position critiquante comme son complément nécessaire. On peut faire toutes les transpositions, vous les faites facilement sur le plan politique.

MCKEON: So, if one places himself in the exteriority of the discourse of the masters, or outside that discourse, to avoid that position in order to criticize it, one is just continuing the discourse itself, nourishing it. And Lyotard just said—and I'd like him to explain it—that this is true of any form of criticism or critique, and among other things political criticism. I don't see this very clearly, and I'd like him to elaborate for us.

LYOTARD: Si on regarde par exemple ce qui s'est passé dans le mouvement ouvrier à la fin du XIXe siècle et au début du XXe, dans la première moitié, pour aller vite, du XXe, on assiste exactement à l'inclusion, à l'intérieur du fonctionnement de la société capitaliste, d'un mouvement qui se présentait d'abord et qui se présentait même théoriquement comme localisé à l'extérieur de ce système. Or il me semble qu'une grande partie du désarroi, de l'inquiétude qui règne dans les mouvements radicaux critiques, provient précisément de ce que cette extériorité a pratiquement, a de fait, disparu.

MCKEON: He gives as an example of this political inclusion of criticism inside the system: at roughly the beginning of the 20th century, a movement which gave itself as being outside the system, the working class movement, thought it could not express itself inside the system. It has proved since that it can: to put it briefly, a movement which theorized itself as being localized outside capitalist society was precisely being sucked into that system.

LYOTARD: Il faudrait donc imaginer une stratégie sans extériorité qui, en ce qui concerne le langage, se placerait non pas au dehors des règles du discours de la vérité, c'est-à-dire du discours du pouvoir, mais à l'intérieur de ces règles et qui, au lieu de s'en exclure sous le nom de délire ou de folie ou de je ne sais quoi, ou de cri, ou de pathos en général, jouerait au contraire ces règles, ou plutôt la règle de toutes ces règles contre elle-même en incluant les prétendus méta-énoncés dans ses propres énoncés. Et l'on verrait à ce moment là que la faiblesse qui est la nôtre (je ne sais pas très bien qui est nous), que cette faiblesse peut se servir de la force du pouvoir pour la neutraliser.

MCKEON: One should imagine a strategy without exteriority, which as far as language is concerned would not be outside the discourse of truth, the discourse of power, but which, instead of excluding itself, would use the rule of that discourse against itself by including meta-statements inside its own statements. One would then see our "weakness" can use the discourse of the strong against itself. So, the main thing is not to try and get out of it; on the contrary, to stay inside of it and use its rules against itself.

LYOTARD: Cette opération de contre-ruse qui éviterait la mise en extériorité porterait nécessairement contre l'élément essentiel dont je parlais tout à l'heure, à savoir l'exclusion des méta-énoncés, l'exclusion du discours sur les conditions du vrai. Elle porterait contre cette exclusion, c'est-à-dire qu'elle consisterait tout simplement à faire qu'il n'y ait pas de méta-énoncés ; et cela de la façon la plus immédiate, non pas en dénonçant le fait que les méta-énoncés sont supportés par tel ou tel intérêt, telle ou telle passion—à vouloir montrer cela on reste en effet dans le discours de la vérité, on pense qu'en le montrant on va convaincre, on suppose que l'action du discours critique est une action de conviction—cette opération consisterait donc, non pas à montrer les présupposés cachés des méta-énoncés des maîtres, mais à utiliser de petits opérateurs de ruse à l'intérieur même du discours magistral.

MCKEON: That operation, which is an operation of "counter-ruse," necessarily goes against exclusion of meta-statements as part of the masterly discourse, meta-statements on the conditions of truth. That operation would consist not in showing, because that is not sufficient, but in doing, that literally there are no meta-statements. Not by showing that the meta-statements are upheld by interests or passions—that would still be positioning oneself inside the discourse of truth, the masterly discourse—but instead by using small "ruse-operators"—what did you call them Mark?—operating agents inside the discourse criticism is deciding to destroy. And Lyotard is going to give some examples of this.

LYOTARD: J'entends maintenant illustrer ce point en revenant sur la technè de Corax dénoncée par Aristote. Aristote proteste contre un usage second de la vraisemblance (il est en train de décrire les opérations possibles à l'intérieur du discours de vraisemblance en général, et en particulier dans la rhétorique) et il dénonce la technè de Corax sur un point très précis, qui est : il y a une vraisemblance en soi ; par exemple, il est en soi vraisemblable que quelqu'un de fort ait brutalisé une victime. C'est vraisemblable en soi, mais lorsque je dis, moi, Corax, que mon client, justement parce qu'il est fort, sait que la vraisemblance joue contre lui, qu'elle l'accuse, et que pour cette raison même, il renonce à toute brutalité, on n'est plus dans la vraisemblance en soi, on est dans une vraisemblance relative. Relative à quoi ? Relative à la vraisemblance. C'est à dire que le client de Corax est quelqu'un qui produit un énoncé du genre : "il est vraisemblable que l'on m'accusera d'être l'auteur du méfait". Sa conduite inclut donc à l'avance les effets de la loi de la vraisemblance et, pour cette raison là, détourne cette loi. La vraisemblance à laquelle recourt le client est une vraisemblance au deuxième degré, qui implique que la première, c'est à dire en fait la vraisemblance tout court, n'est jamais non relative, qu'elle n'est jamais absolue, puisque tout absolu, tout non relatif peut toujours au moins être mis en rapport avec lui-même et que la mise en rapport du vraisemblable avec lui-même, c'est exactement l'opération sur laquelle repose la technè de Corax.

Vous voyez, par conséquent, que dans cette défense de Corax se trouve impliqué un enjeu logique, et sûrement politique aussi, très important, à savoir qu'il n'y a pas de position non relative, qu'on ne peut pas dire : voilà ce qu'est absolument parlant la vraisemblance, puisque la vraisemblance absolue peut être mise en rapport avec elle-même et à ce moment là produire l'effet inverse de ce qui est attendu. Car la vraisemblance absolue accuse le client, mais lorsqu'elle est rapportée à elle-même, elle le disculpe. C'est pourquoi Aristote proteste, car il comprend très bien—il était très intelligent—que là, sous cette petite affaire de rien du tout, se joue une très grosse partie. En effet, dans la mesure où le discours du maître, celui du juge, en l'occurrence, va juger d'après la vraisemblance, sur l'existence de vraisemblances plus vraies que les autres, pour affirmer qu'il est plus vraiment vraisemblable que quelqu'un de fort brutalise une victime, je peux faire jouer la vraisemblance avec elle-même pour en faire disparaître l'absolu. Et les effets sont retournés. Très grosse affaire, par conséquent, très grave affaire.

MCKEON: Corax's *techne*, his art, is denounced by Aristotle, who protects at what he thinks is a second-degree use of verisimilitude. There is a verisimilitude in itself, a primary verisimilitude; the example Lyotard gives is that a strong man can have brutalized a victim, it is likely. But when Corax says the verisimilitude in fact confuses the client, in the example of the strong man. But in the second degree the verisimilitude, the likelihood—"likelihood" is simpler—instead of accusing him, exculpates him. Corax's art includes in advance the effects of the law of likelihood. Second-degree verisimilitude implies that there is no unrelative or absolute likelihood. Relating the absolute in this case, the absolute likelihood to itself destroys its character of absoluteness. The consequence: there is no unrelative, absolute position. Absolute likelihood can be related to itself even though it accuses the client, in the end it innocents him. The discourse of the master is the discourse of the judge, but if I can relate it to itself this is the same thing; it automatically destroys its pretention to absoluteness.

[Some discussion—an audience member offers to interpret line by line.]

LYOTARD: Vous avez tous compris que dans cet exemple, le client qui est fort, c'est précisément le faible ; je veux dire que sa position est faible justement parce qu'il est fort. Une chose qui va tout à fait dans le même sens—

AUDIENCE: *Something that goes in the same sense, in the same way—*

LYOTARD: —c'est le paradoxe du menteur.

AUDIENCE: —is the paradox of the liar.

AUDIENCE: You should speak louder if you're going to do that.

LYOTARD: Ce paradoxe consiste à dire—

AUDIENCE: This paradox consists of saying—

LYOTARD: —"Si tu dis que tu mens—

AUDIENCE: —"If you lie—

LYOTARD: —et si tu dis vrai—

AUDIENCE: —and if you said truth—

LYOTARD: —alors tu mens."—

AUDIENCE: —then you lie."—

LYOTARD: —À prendre cette conclusion—

AUDIENCE: —And then you take his conclusion—

LYOTARD: —et à la reporter—

AUDIENCE: —and report it—

LYOTARD: —dans le raisonnement, qui devient:—

AUDIENCE: —in the reasonment it becomes:—

LYOTARD: "Mais si tu dis que tu mens et que tu mentes, c'est donc que tu dis vrai, etc."

AUDIENCE: "If you lie, and if you lie, then you say the truth."
AUDIENCE: You've made it worse; we can't follow the French or the English now.
AUDIENCE: That's true.

[Some animated discussion]

LYOTARD: Il y a eu beaucoup de tentatives de réfutation de ce paradoxe—
AUDIENCE: T—there have been many refutations of the paradox of the liar—
LYOTARD: Celle de Russell consiste, par exemple, à dire qu'il faut distinguer deux sortes, deux types d'énoncés—
AUDIENCE: Russell said you have to distinguish two types of statements—
LYOTARD: —des énoncés qui portent sur un domaine de référence quelconque et des énoncés qui portent sur les premiers énoncés—
AUDIENCE: —some which refer to a set of statements, and others which refer to the statement itself. On the first statement—
LYOTARD: —c'est-à-dire précisément la distinction que je faisais tout à l'heure en ce qui concerne énoncés et méta-énoncés.
AUDIENCE: —exactly the distinction I was referring to before between the statement and the meta-statement—
LYOTARD: Et Russell prétend résoudre le paradoxe en interdisant de mêler, de mélanger les énoncés du premier type et les énoncés du deuxième type—
AUDIENCE: And Russell's solution is, Don't mix statements of the first set with statements of the second one—
LYOTARD: Il y a un métadiscours et les effets du discours ne peuvent pas être reportés sur le métadiscours.
AUDIENCE: It means there is a meta-language and it cannot be reported to the language itself.
AUDIENCE: No, referred back to it.
AUDIENCE: Referred back to the language itself.
LYOTARD: Mais pourquoi est ce qu'il ne faut pas faire cela ? La réponse de Russell est simplement : si vous le faites, alors il n'y a plus de discours de vérité possible.
AUDIENCE: Why not? The answer of Russell is because if you do that, there is no possibility of speaking the truth.
LYOTARD: Autrement dit, la réfutation de Russell ne peut pas être une réfutation, elle est simplement la décision magistrale elle-même. À savoir, mes méta-énoncés ne sont pas du même ordre que les énoncés ordinaires.
AUDIENCE: In other words, the conclusion of Russell is that it's a matter of decision that my statements cannot be the same as the ordinary statements.

LYOTARD: Donc le paradoxe du menteur, qui est irréfutable, puisque pour le réfuter, il faut précisément sortir de ce paradoxe, implique qu'il n'y a pas de métadiscours de vérité et par conséquent détourne complètement la fonction du discours—

AUDIENCE: Therefore, the paradox of the liar, which cannot be refuted, changed completely the function of the speech—

LYOTARD: —parce qu'on ne pourra jamais décider si un énoncé est vrai ou faux.

AUDIENCE: —because one can never decide if one statement is right or wrong, true or false.

LYOTARD: Une autre histoire concerne un sophiste nommé Protagoras.

AUDIENCE: There is an anecdote about a sophist called Protagoras.

LYOTARD: Protagoras demande ses honoraires à son élève Euathlus.

AUDIENCE: He asked for his fees from his pupil, Euathlus.

LYOTARD: Celui-ci lui répond : tu ne m'as fait gagner aucune cause, tu ne m'as fait remporter aucune victoire dans les discours—

AUDIENCE: His student answered him, You made me win no case with my speech—

LYOTARD: —par conséquent je ne te dois rien.

AUDIENCE: —therefore, I owe you nothing.

LYOTARD: Et Protagoras rétorque : de toute façon tu me dois quelque chose, tu me dois l'argent, car si c'est moi qui l'emporte, tu devras me payer, et si c'est toi qui l'emportes, tu devras encore me payer.

AUDIENCE: And Protagoras answers him: Anyway, you owe me my fees because in our case, between you and I, if I win you will owe me the money, if I lose you will have won the case and you will owe me the money anyway.

[Heated exchange … "Oh well, that's alright"]

AUDIENCE: How many people don't understand French, Lyotard's French?

AUDIENCE: Two, three … many of you.

AUDIENCE: Be brave! How many of you don't understand the French?

AUDIENCE: The translation would be useful but it's distracting when it comes so quickly.

AUDIENCE: Yeah, well what do you suggest? You know, there's no professionals, everyone's volunteering … My suggestion would be to have—

AUDIENCE: *[Shouted]* Let Lyotard give his talk and then have an English translation which someone's writing in the meantime, instead of interrupting all the time!

AUDIENCE: There are a number of possibilities, but that's not all that easy. I understand the fact that … hey, fuck it! Knock off the shit! Okay. Now look, get the fuck up here and do it! Don't be such assholes. You too, ya fuck! Don't talk shit, come on! These guys have volunteered their time, okay, they're not paid, they're doing what they can do. Now my suggestion is that all the rest of you, that can speak French and English, sit next to somebody who can't understand French and translate for them!

AUDIENCE: Let's go back to this, okay.

AUDIENCE: Now what I suggest is that we stop for five minutes, and you ask questions if there are questions to be asked …

LYOTARD: No questions *[laughs]*

AUDIENCE: Can't you just write it down, and give us a translation at the end?

MCKEON: Well, it makes it very difficult to write it down, to stay in pace with Lyotard, and to give you the whole translation at the end … Look, we'll try to speed it up, we'll cut it more often if Lyotard agrees to that …

LYOTARD: Le débat dont parle Protagoras n'est pas celui auquel pense son élève. Euathlus pense en effet aux débats dans lesquels il s'est produit et où il a perdu.

MCKEON: Okay, let's start with Protagoras …

AUDIENCE: I could translate that—

[Audience laughs]

LYOTARD: Marvelous.

MCKEON: No, let's be serious, we can't do this.

AUDIENCE: This is a very old paradox, there's a teacher and a student: he teaches his student legal rhetoric, and he says, "If you win your first case, then you pay me; if you lose your first case, then I pay you."

[Audience laughter]

AUDIENCE: What, it's not? C'est pas ça?

AUDIENCE: Go back to the person we had before. You're an excellent translator; you got everything correct so far … These things are always very good, if not the first time then the second time!

[Audience laughter, applause]

MCKEON: Whoever wins in this case, Protagoras is making the money, that's the point …

[Audience laughs]

MCKEON: No, I'm serious about this!

LYOTARD: You are right … and me too *[laughs]*.

MCKEON: We're both right, obviously.

LYOTARD: Protagoras se réfère pour sa part au débat actuel entre son élève et lui-même et il dit : dans ce débat, forcément il va y avoir une issue, ou toi tu gagnes, ou c'est moi ; au cas où tu gagnerais, tu devrais me payer puisque notre contrat veut que l'élève de l'orateur paie son maître quand il a remporté une victoire. Et si c'est moi qui gagne, c'est-àdire, si c'est toi, mon élève qui perds, alors, c'est encore toi qui paies, puisque dans un débat judiciaire celui qui perd paie. Tout cela est parfaitement correct…

MCKEON: So, the same story …

LYOTARD: He was my student.

MCKEON: Yes, I *was* his student, that's right *[laughs]*. The student and Protagoras are not in fact speaking of the same debate: the debate the student is talking about is the one he is actually having with Protagoras; the one Protagoras is talking about is the one at the end of which, whatever happens, he gets paid. He doesn't care whether he wins or loses, the only thing he is interested in is making the money—I was serious earlier—and this was Lyotard's point.

LYOTARD: À l'intérieur de la relation magistrale, Protagoras considère son rapport à son élève une fois comme un rapport magistral, une fois comme un rapport d'adversaire, ce qui implique une chose importante, à savoir qu'il ne peut pas y avoir d'école, parce que le propre d'une école, et j'espère qu'il n'y aura pas d'école schizo, le propre d'une école, c'est au contraire qu'il y a un certain type de discours que je dirai protégé. Autrement dit, si l'élève, le disciple, tient ce discours à l'extérieur et si ce discours échoue, si donc il ne remporte pas de victoire extérieure, on dira, dans un rapport magistral, qu'il n'est pas assez formé, qu'il faut qu'il suive d'autres cours, qu'il poursuive ses études, qu'on doit le recycler, etc., mais l'adversité rencontrée par l'élève ne sera pas reportée à l'intérieur de la relation avec le maître ; au contraire, ce que dit Protagoras, c'est : de toute manière, cette relation d'adversité, elle traverse notre relation magistrale, et tu es aussi mon ennemi.

MCKEON: I'll summarize: The problem here is that the master is always the person who determines what the rules of the game are; the student doesn't have a word to say about it, so the master is always in the position of power. Whatever the strength of the student can be, he cannot overcome the teacher, because he is at the very beginning in a position of inferiority, and Protagoras makes this relation between teacher and student a relation of aggression, of conflict, which underlines their relation.

LYOTARD: Un autre aspect important de cette affaire qui mérite d'être relevé, c'est que le paradoxe de Protagoras consiste dans la même opération d'inclusion que le paradoxe du menteur. Lorsqu'Euathlus dit : je n'ai jamais gagné une cause donc je ne te dois rien, de quoi parle t il ? Il parle des débats extérieurs à son rapport à son maître. Que fait Protagoras ? Il inclut le débat actuel qu'il a avec son élève dans ces débats extérieurs. Donc, là encore, refus de considérer le débat à l'intérieur de l'école comme une sorte de méta-débat ; ce débat fait partie de la classe des débats.

MCKEON: Now the paradox in this case consists in the same operation as in the paradox of the liar. When Euathlus tells Protagoras, "I don't owe you anything, I've never won anything anyway," Protagoras doesn't accept the difference between the debate they are having as a scholarly debate in itself and real debates outside of the scholarly relation. He refuses to acknowledge the existence of a meta-debate. In other words, there is no place in which the meta-debate can exist as such, there are no meta-debates, they are all on the same level.

LYOTARD: La position du discours magistral exige la protection contre les débats extérieurs, elle implique donc que l'on s'enferme à l'intérieur d'une région de discours qui est en même temps une région sociale telle que les débats extérieurs ne pourront pas y entrer. Ce qui entrera ce seront seulement des débats sur les débats extérieurs. C'est ce qui fonde l'école, c'est-àdire, finalement, l'un des aspects de la relation magistrale.

MCKEON: The position of the masters' discourse has to be protected; school has to keep external debates from invading its own space for it to function normally. It has to reduce the discourse of the exteriority. It will never accept the ordinary speech; as such it will always try to include it and reduce it into a meta-discourse. It has—and I insist on this—to be protected against these intrusions and tends to neutralize them.

LYOTARD: Dans ce paradoxe, Protagoras considère Euathlus comme son adversaire s'il perd et comme son élève s'il gagne.

MCKEON: Protagoras considers Euathlus as his student if he wins, as his opponent if he loses.

LYOTARD: Il n'y a pas d'identité d'Euathlus, Euathlus n'est pas identifiable soit comme adversaire soit comme élève, ce qui implique qu'il y a déjà chez Protagoras le refus de toute une logique de l'attribution ou de la définition substantielle. Il n'y a pas de propriétés d'Euathlus.

MCKEON: That means there is no identity of Euathlus since Protagoras himself is going to define what Euathlus is according to the circumstances, and his identity is not fixed, it changes. Protagoras refuses the logic of predication.

LYOTARD: Encore une remarque : il y a dans le paradoxe de Protagoras l'inclusion du futur dans l'actuel. C'est-à-dire que Protagoras argumente contre son élève en incluant dans le débat actuel les résultats de ce débat et en disant : si tu perds—si c'est toi qui perdras comme on dit en turc—alors tu paieras, et si c'est toi qui gagneras, alors tu paieras aussi.

MCKEON: In the paradox of Protagoras there is an inclusion of the future into the current situation. Protagoras says, "If you are going to win, you are going to pay; if you lose, you're going to pay anyway."

LYOTARD: Et cette inclusion du futur se fait sur le mode d'une parodie, car ce discours de Protagoras par rapport à son élève, c'est exactement la parodie du discours magistral, puisque le maître sait déjà ce qui se passera. Autrement dit, le futur est inclus non pas comme contingent, mais comme identique à lui même. Le maître détient ce futur.

MCKEON: Protagoras' discourse is a parody of the masters' discourse. Protagoras determines beforehand what his student's future is going to be; he eliminates contingency. And Lyotard just said that is exactly the way capital functions, and I'd like him to elaborate. But what he means is, whatever happens, you're going to pay!

[Laughter]

LYOTARD: C'est une parodie du discours magistral dans la mesure même où ce que dit Protagoras, au fond, c'est qu'Euathlus n'a pas de futur contingent, il n'a pas de futur, c'est-à-dire que de toute manière il paiera, ce qui est exactement la position du capital par rapport à n'importe qui : l'absence de futur—que l'on perde ou que l'on gagne, il faut payer. Cela ne signifie pas pour autant que Protagoras soit en position de force et si j'ai dit tout à l'heure que dans le cas de Corax c'est l'inculpé qui est fort qui est justement très faible, parce que la vraisemblance est contre lui, dans le cas de Protagoras c'est Protagoras qui est faible, car il risque de ne pas être payé, or, pour un sophiste, c'est très grave, car les sophistes n'ont pas de revenus fonciers comme les philosophes, ce ne sont pas des fonctionnaires, ce sont des artistes, ils doivent être payés au coup par coup, à chaque prestation, à chaque performance…

MCKEON: In the paradox the strong man is finally the weak one, since the likelihood is against him: being strong, he is quite capable of brutalizing the victim. In Protagoras' own case, in the story, Protagoras is the strong man, but he is also finally the weak man because he depends on the weak one, the student, to make his living. He is an artist, he's not a civil servant or an employee, he doesn't make money on his land.

LYOTARD: Il y a beaucoup d'histoires comme ça et je crois qu'il faut les analyser avec soin car il n'est pas certain du tout qu'elles renvoient toutes aux mêmes opérateurs de ruse ; il est tout à fait possible que certaines s'appuient sur d'autres opérateurs, mais il me semble qu'il suffit de trois ou quatre exemples de ce genre pour dessiner une position de discours assez curieuse par rapport à la position magistrale ; cette position de discours peut très bien occuper la position magistrale, c'est pourquoi j'ai pris l'exemple de Protagoras qui en principe est le maître de l'élève, mais ce qui me frappe, c'est que Protagoras, occupant la position magistrale, utilise un raisonnement qui ne peut pas être celui d'un maître, qui pointe vers un autre type de discours que le discours platonicien, ou le discours magistral en général, de Platon à Marx, dont la position est en fait toujours la même. Il me semble qu'autre chose se dessine là, en ce qui concerne au moins le métier d'intellectuel, qui est un métier comme un autre, que d'autres armes apparaissent, qui sont de toutes petites armes mais qui sont très importantes, je crois, et très sérieuses. Ces armes, qui sont très faibles, ont néanmoins comme effet d'ébranler, serait ce pour un instant (cela n'a aucune importance, il ne s'agit pas d'obtenir des effets cumulatifs), d'ébranler la position magistrale et ce qui la soutient, c'est-à-dire la croyance qu'il y a un métadiscours, qu'il y a un ordre dans lequel effectivement les discours et aussi les pratiques, bien sûr, peuvent être fondés et bien fondés.

Il faudrait donc continuer à explorer ces paradoxes qu'on a appelés des paradoxes parce qu'on ne savait pas quoi en faire, parce qu'ils ont été rayés, détruits, comme les oeuvres de Protagoras lui même. On a affaire là à toute une position de discours possible, qui a réellement été effacée, dans laquelle nous pouvons retrouver des armes. Je crois qu'il serait intéressant de voir ce que ces armes peuvent produire comme effets dans l'ordre politique, voila à peu près ce que je voulais dire, pas plus.

MCKEON: Protagoras is a funny teacher because in his position he uses devices which in fact destroy his own discourse as the discourse of the master. And perhaps that is the function of a modern critical intellectual, the problem being not to try and fight outside of the discourse we are talking about, but fighting it from the inside, with the instruments that very discourse gives us, and they exist. Lyotard had planned to talk about Russell—he isn't doing it, and that's regrettable I think—but it is impossible to establish the masters' discourse as an absolute truth-making discourse. What Lyotard is interested in, of course, is research in the political field, and trying to find out what the incidences of these devices can be in the political field. That means, is there a possibility of using these devices in a practical way; instead of staying inside the discourse, it is about time one started using it against itself.

LYOTARD: Une dernière chose : cela veut dire en particulier, je crois qu'il faudrait imaginer des pratiques et notamment pratiques de discours, des pratiques politiques, donc, qui ne seraient pas construites autour de l'idée d'un renforcement par organisation et d'une efficacité par conviction. L'idée que l'efficacité politique radicale ne repose pas sur le fait qu'elle dit la vérité mérite d'être examinée.

Il faut se demander si l'on peut produire de l'efficacité politique non pas en la raccrochant à la croyance au vrai, mais au contraire en la développant dans le sens d'un relativisme au sens fort, général, c'est-à-dire en accélérant la décadence de l'idée de vérité, en renforçant cette décadence ; or, on ne peut pas la renforcer en lui opposant une autre vérité, ce qui n'a aucun intérêt, quelque nom qu'elle porte. Il serait beaucoup plus intéressant d'imaginer, me semble t il, une efficacité politique qui ne viserait pas la conviction, qui viserait des effets discontinus, locaux, qui pourraient disparaître, et qui n'entraîneraient pas chez ceux qui constatent ces effets une adhésion, mais plutôt autre chose, qui ne serait ni méfiance ni confiance, quelque chose que l'on peut appeler tragique, etc., mais je crois qu'il s'agirait plutôt d'humour, c'est très proche, du reste. Je crois qu'il se passe quelque chose de cet ordre maintenant : c'est certainement vrai, en tout cas, pour certains événements qui arrivent en France, bien que je ne sache pas encore très bien élaborer ça. Je peux du reste en donner un exemple, mais sous toutes réserves : il y a eu en France cette année un mouvement des prostituées.

Ce mouvement apparaît à première vue comme un mouvement revendicatif, c'est-à-dire que l'énoncé de ce mouvement était en première lecture : nous sommes des travailleuses, nous voulons avoir des conditions de travail correctes, etc., mais en même temps ce discours impliquait autre chose, qui a en fait ébranlé le rapport de cette société au corps féminin et même au désir en général. Il disait la chose suivante : si vous acceptez qu'il y ait plusieurs sortes de métiers et si vous considérez que les motivations pour faire ces métiers sont bonnes, sont recevables, acceptez aussi notre motivation, c'est-à-dire le désir de la prostitution. Or, ce problème est très, très grave, je crois qu'il s'agit là d'une action typiquement politique moderne : elle est ponctuelle, elle porte effectivement sur l'inclusion du désir de la prostitution dans la classe de tous les désirs… et elle travaille, me semble t il, dans le sens non pas d'une méfiance, mais d'une destruction de la confiance dans le fait qu'il y a les bons désirs et les mauvais. Des pratiques de ce type sont opératoires non pas parce qu'elles font apparaître une nouvelle vérité, mais parce qu'elles détruisent les métadiscours, dans des endroits précis, ponctuellement. Et cela veut dire qu'au fond une telle politique n'est plus centrée sur la question de la pédagogie, ce qui a toujours été le cas, car toute politique a toujours été pédagogique ; il ne faut plus dire : nous remporterons la victoire, nous nous renforcerons si nous arrivons à réveiller la vérité qui est aliénée, cachée, réprimée, etc., je ne sais quoi … Protagoras se fiche complètement de la conviction d'Euathlus, ce n'est pas en ces termes que se mesure l'efficace de son action.

MCKEON: To summarize: The problem at this point is not to try and reinforce a political efficiency by organizing—be it the masses, the unions, etc.—this is not what we are looking for. The problem is not to create a new truth either, it is not to convince anyone that we are being truthful in our criticism. What should be accelerated to start with is the de-cadence of truth; truth should no longer be used as a convincing factor, who cares about truth, and Protagoras doesn't give a damn. That's not what he's interested in, he's interested in being efficient, and his efficiency is not based on truth. What are the possibilities Lyotard sees as far as that's concerned? Humor, for one thing, and I think he should be pushed on that point too, and I think you are responsible for pushing him. So the problem is not to create a new truth but to destroy meta-languages one by one in a discontinuous way. Who cares whether people are convinced or not? That isn't the problem. Our activity should be punctual actions. And I guess that's all. No questions.

LYOTARD: No, no dialogue!

AUDIENCE: How do we address what you mean by "punctual actions" with respect to discourses—for example those of reportage, television—in relation to which the receiver of the discourse has no assault on power? One cannot interrupt the flow of television or the discourse of the *New York Times* …

[Translators confer with Lyotard]

SEEM: Your question is too long, and he would like to answer in a workshop.

MCKEON: Any quicker questions?

AUDIENCE: Could you give some examples of what kinds of actions could be used in a practical way, to turn the discourse against itself?

[Translators confer with Lyotard]

MCKEON: He cannot answer that question because he does not yet know what devices can be used in that field: that's what he's looking for! Such actions which have happened in the past, they happened in France and they happened here too, and you know that very well. And he thinks what should be done now is analyzing all these actions to see what we can get out of them. He has no answer, and I don't know if he should have an answer, I think that goes against the very principle of what he is saying: There is no truth, there are no pre-established answers, and the very efficiency of the devices he is talking about is that they cannot be foreseen.

LYOTARD: Un exemple …

ONTOLOGICAL-HYSTERIC THEATER WORKSHOP

Richard Foreman (director)
Francoise Kourilsky
Frantisek Deak
Stephen Koch

Others (including members of the cast of RHODA IN POTATOLAND: (HER FALL-STARTS) which opens in December, rehersals of which are open to schizo-culture participants).

The theater...as a totally corrupt form, in which a certain dream of "expressiveness" has joined with a second dream of "doing it well" to produce, almost without expeption, a universe of kitch.

The question (to all artists working today) should be "Can you do it 'wrong'?"
BUT
so frame the "wrongness", the "not well-done", so that its necessity & truthfullness & power and PLACE in the scheme of things (plus its wonderful, inevitable productivity) clearly emerge.

That framing, that creation of context in which act, gesture, word, are dropped, must be completely re-thought,
--for what is accepted now as frame, and/or context are simply allusions to a variety of institutionalized psychological-philosophical-political world views.

But the small micro-unit of gesture (or perhaps mental gesture) must become both the examined and the frame of the examined. Both at once. Which is to say the on-stage act must no longer be placed in an imaginary context (some aspect of the real world imagined, "evoked) but in the real context of its own self-destructiveness, its own burning-itself-out, as it performs itself and then, inevitably is swallowed but by a transience that ALSO belongs to it. Because THAT'S the context of the act-- the space and time that it creates, and into which it then vanishes.

The not-well-done is, really, everything that is done.
The context is the imaginary "well done" that the real not-well-done generates. The subject then must be... the stylistics of error. Compounded. Intensified, Spread out on a canvas (the stage) wide enough so that within the terms of that error, new spaces, gaps, appear, in which life flickers. Rest assured, if the art work produces anything MORE than a flicker of recognition (life echoing life) then there's been a misrepresentation.

610 Schermerhorn 9:30 A.M.
Friday Nov. 14

Cinegrams <——> Cinegraphs

All approaches to the study of film have considered the photograms as the operative unit, which is in keeping with the theories of signification (semiology but also a certain psychoanalysis), with the photogram's match to be found in the so-called impression of reality.

A specific operation of the type continuous/discontinuous that is infra-semantic can be separated out as the organizing process of intermittant images (cinema, video), from the most radical productions of the independent cinema (video art) as well as from current research on perception, both on the diachronic and the synchronic levels: cinegrams and cinegraphs do not narrate, nor do they represent.

After having displayed this infrasemantic level cinegrams and cinegraphs both produce their own temporality. One can then restore sight as opposed to the recognizable reference, the processes against narration, active present time against differed causal time, the media against the mediator, auto-production against mediations.

The infrasemantic does not lead to the ineffable. Beyond perception, energetics must encompass the functioning of the psychic apparatus engaged in the socius. It then becomes possible, not only to interrogate the established human sciences in their complicity with industrial narration - representation, but also to situate the first signs of a strategy of mutation.

--Claudine Eizykman
--Guy Fishman

Friday 9:30AM

516 HAMILTON

Fri Friday 9:30 AM 509 Butler

Capital Punishment: The people have always been punished by capital

Political sado-masichism. Our bondage to the State, Love, Property, Money, War, Death.

Organizing in Pittsburgh. Radical street theater in Pittsburgh. In the community and in front of the steel mills and in front of our house and in front of ourselves. The dialectics of the revolutionary, the how are we going to stay open in the 70's cookbook?

--steve benisrael

Friday 9:30 a.m. - Room 413A Butler

SCHIZO - CITY

The Schizo-City Workshop will focus its presentations and discussions on the following areas:

1) Identification and Classification of marginal urban groups and communities which are forced, for one reason or another, to engage in artifactual or unintended uses of the built-environment.

2) The problems of developing cognitive life styles outside of the conformities idealized and mandated by and in the existing structures of urban order.

3) The processes by which fixated meanings in intended objects and facilities in the urban environment are erased. How new meanings are produced and validated.

4) The role of brinkmanship, camouflage, the poetization of catastrophic existing conditions, transformations of the human self into human art object, body-politics, etc.

5) The problems of power, with special emphasis on power relations and religious residuals, e.g., sacred-profane dichotomy.

6) The pornographization of problematic situations, viz-a-viz, having to live lives on the brink of catastrophy.

7) The semiology of the visual culture of marginal communities and groups.

The workshop will take the form of visual presentations, commentaries, analyses, open discussions, etc. It is open to all participants and hopes to achieve a high degree of interaction.

--Glen Chase, architect, sociologist

PORTUGAL: the beginning of the beginning

Why is all this happening? "Logically" it shouldn't be. 2,000 years of Catholic punishment, 48 years of absolute/obsolete dictatorship, then all of a sudden an "anti-fascist military coup d'Etat". The unthinkable. An unheard of avalanche process of change in social relationships, in feodal economy structures, in political/libido control systems touched off by a bunch of "liberal" career officers who disobeyed the rule and whose aim was only to modernize not to completely transform. Upserge/inserge/breakthrough of those unexplainable social and sexual energies which "normally" stay caged up under disciplinarian "democracies" or dictatorships (i.e. Spain or U.S.S.R.). Class war between desire and castration, extasy and boredom as all oppressed groups/sexes/species COME OUT FROM UNDER THE PATRIARCAL ("Best Pizza") BLITZ, experiencing the explosion of the capitalist and/or Stalinist shithouse. First step: loosening up; second step: re-birth; third step: ? Should we/they confront or ignore State/Church/Party/Union/Army/School/Family institutionalized non-life? An armed mass movement can be REAL. It's there. It works. Massive creativity upsetting centralized and bureaucratic power, evacuating capitalist cash-flow constipation, have your psychic biolers been re-tubed lately? The slaves are burning their chairs, women are producing non authoritarian politics, children and taking over some schools burning down some others, revolutionnary workers councils are growing, agrarian reform exists, neighborhood associations are taking over their turfs— direct democracy, direct action, direct desire, direct change. . . What becomes of State/Party/Church/Family male-owned Centralized Power as the ancient slave/master relationships begin to slip crumble dissolve? How to deal with C.I.A./Pentagon/I.T.T./panic master plan to destroy the revolutionnary process and restore old world Order? What to do with remaining forms of male fascism masochistic work ethics, profit orientated repressive rituals, submissive behavior patterns? How/why do some castration habits still re-occur within the "new" politics of change and how to rid our lives of the Power junkies who always try to confiscate revolutionnary movements and sit on them? Portugal/New York, what? Default, crisis, paranoia, isn't the Bird of Paradise overdue? What do you plan to do when the shit hits the fan? Maybe some socio-cultural detoxification would be helpful in any case.

What this workshop is about is: SOCIAL REVOLUTION FEELS GOOD AND YOU OUGHT TO TRY IT SOME DAY.

(tight assed know-all bounty graduates please stay home or go to your usual race tracks, this workshop is for people who find revolution desirable. Modest proposals about direct information circuitry from Portual to U.S.A. -- video tapes, photos, etc. . . and possibilities of actions here in connection with Portugal. Bring your bodies too).

Jesus sucks, so do I,

Jean-Jacques Lebel

MAISON FRANCAISE 3rd floor

Anti-Psychiatry workshop

—… drugs, while that's if you sorta eke out a minimal existence from day to day and don't know where you're going to sleep the next night, well then if you don't have any other desires to be anything else or be anything else or enjoy anything else then you could be *happy*. Look, you're an actor, do you like being an actor, do you think it's a good life?

—Well yeah, but …

—Yeah, well there are lots of blacks in Harlem who'd like to be actors too, just like you, and enjoy this kind of life, and come here and talk about what makes the good life, you know? But they can't do it!

—I didn't say that, you said that!

—They're unhappy!

—You said that, you said, I'm not saying they want to be an actor …

—I'm saying there are individuals in Harlem who would like to be an actor. You know, it's a good life, it's an interesting life, it's a—

—It isn't good.

—Yeah.

—There are a lot of blacks who think that it is … you know.

—Well, what's your point?

—They can't do it, they can't do it because they're discriminated against, they don't have the same opportunities that other people do, who don't live in Harlem.

—It's all this idealism based around middle class morality, I mean, Jesus, any notion that the people here are operating with the idea that the middle class is somehow the offerer of human protection is so bizarre.

—It *is* offering them that, I'm sorry, I mean it is—I don't see many eccentrics here, I don't see many blacks, I don't see many working-class people here, I'm sorry, I just don't see it; it is offering them that …

[Uproar, laughter, shouts, and raised voices]

—Okay, there does seem to be two direct irreconcilable arguments going on here: that he is saying that there are people who are happy in Harlem, which cannot be true …

—It's true!

—… and you were all saying there are people who are unhappy, and that's also not true.

—Bullshit! / But that's not an argument!

—… Well, what he is saying is let people do their thing, whilst you're saying we need to work to reach out to society …

—But who's saying *we* know better?

—… Yes, yes, right.

—We're not just saying things for other people, people are telling us …

[Indistinct shouting]

—Who are you talking about?

—You're trying to tell them that they're unhappy.

—I'm not telling anyone anything! They're telling me, we're listening. If you're listening to a group of black middle class people, then work with them—I'm listening to other black people, we've had this conversation.

—Sure, to some extent if you operate with a model of how a whole human being should be, if you operate with the assumption that this society allows people to have the propensity to make improvements, then you idealize the bits and pieces of happiness that come out of all this put together, and complain that that's all of it, but it's not. Which is what the system does.

—But on the other hand, if you operate with a model of what a whole human being ought to be, that becomes just as much a social control as a model of performance in society as a bourgeois healthy human subject.

—Can I ask one question? I'm coming to this discussion of happiness, working with people who have just come out of hospital, and the situation is the opposite: it results in a situation where you're at a poverty level, and when you have to think about whether you're going to go on the subway, rather than eat, so you go on fasts at the end of the month before the welfare check. And so a lot of what they say might seem unformed or confused and they might not seem very functional, so go ahead and talk about happiness, but the misery's real …

—But your point in there just reinforces what we were trying to say, which is that in a society which is based on a classism, racism, and sexism, there isn't any liberation, people aren't liberated by somebody "outside," and these institutions, they just have to deal with the forces of oppression and repression.
—The woman who owns this place, upstairs, the woman with the power, wants us to leave. She wants "You kids to pack out!" It's crazy they didn't make better arrangements.
—We're going to have to wrap up.

[Recording cuts off.]

—I have a question. It seems to me that all this can be reduced to the following points. You don't like the idea of people being put in asylums, prisons, or being incarcerated under the current institutional ways in which these general institutions are established. On the other hand, you feel it's romantic to merely throw these people out into the community as you believe it's only a problem for certain people, and that ultimately the problem is really related to social organization, rather than anything else. Now, we all know that social organization is not going to change. What do you see as the function of the psychiatric and sociological community in the interim, to deal with these people?
—I'd like to say that in Jersey, for some reason the hospitals are empty. I think that, again, institutions are set up by the society, not for the purpose of revolution or social change but to smooth out inefficiently operating intellectual capitalist society. You can't expect the state to fund mental hygiene products for the purpose of revolution, nor can you expect psychiatrists to have a definition of human wholeness or health that is very different from the prevailing values of the social order. However, there obviously are people that lots and lots of people go to, the allied psychotherapy profession that the social workers and psychologists or "renegade psychiatrists" who have a real concern with, say, helping someone get food stamps or helping someone get a—we're talking about people who *can't make it from day to day*, because they are so crippled that every step they take in some way is an action designed to destroy themselves. We work in clinics and we try to help people, in spite of the intentions of the societies that set these things up, we try to help people survive, in whatever way we know how, using goodwill, good knowledge, or whatever, but it's hard, you know. To your question, the answer is kind of—we work with victims, and to expect that society is going to pay you to do anything but eliminate problems, the problematic aspects of people's behaviors, is romantic. Rockefeller did not

set up drugs treatment programs because he was interested in eliminating poverty—on the other hand, because those programs existed, the possibility of doing something for addicts, other than throwing them into jail for ten years, exists. And so you have to use *that* situation, because their decision to cut the cost of incarceration contains within it the possibility of doing something for the people who generally suffer from it.

—Now, I agree with you, I don't see society changing soon or radically at all in this country, and I asked you what you see there for the radical therapist or sociologist or psychiatrist. You just see yourself as having this very small role of working in a rather fixed position, within a system which is quite rigid, and you're trying to act as the strongest kind of buffer you can between someone who is a victim and this highly oppressive society; you see no other purpose. That's what I'm asking. It seems to me that you're saying that since you've just argued that society will not fund revolution, what is the—

—No, I did not say that!

[General uproar]

—I mean for me, if you ask that question, the point is what will most sociologists or most psychiatrists do? That's the way knowledge is made—the response of the rest of us to some extent has been controlled, but that is one thing that we can sometimes try to alleviate, but the state is not interested in the addict or the prisoner or the mental patient, and that is not why this is happening, despite what one reads in the news ...

—I mean, first of all, this notion of therapy is something more than adjustment ...

—The thing about the meaning of this is, there's radical politics, and then there's psychotherapy, and the project of radical politics and the project of psychotherapy are really quite different, and to confuse them is to do some terrible damage to the people you're working with both for the sake of what can and can't be done. And it's a very good distinction, because a lot of radical therapy is crap—you may, but in all likelihood you will *not,* help someone who's been really messed up by reading to them from Marx, Lenin, or Mao.

—Yeah, but I'd like to ask some people maybe who've been involved in organizing, what are the material conditions that make the difference for some people becoming engaged in political organizing in the most oppressive circumstances? In other words, what I'm suggesting is, I don't think all prisoners are political prisoners, I don't believe that deviants are by definition revolutionaries, I don't believe that schizophrenics are poets, and there's a difference in peoples' consciousness. Even in the conditions of the lowest oppression, you still have to be able to explain Attica, you know, under those conditions. It's through the worst conditions that some of the most oppressed also become conscious and organized, and I believe, become less miserable through revolutionary activity. And, I don't know how to explain it, but that happens.

—In fact the working classes and such in this country are not apparently nearly as oppressed in their way of seeing and not as oppressed as someone who is well versed in radical politics, or has an ideal in mind for America. We're not in a revolutionary position, anyone in this room, anyone who has organized, you've seen them out on the streets—we're not in this state where we can just decide that people are oppressed, this whole lie, I don't believe they feel are. What that means is that some of these working people aren't as angry at America as some of the intellectuals who are assigning this anger to them—enough!

—When you think of these extreme emotional reactions, people who have come in to us, we found they had not paid their rent, they had not eaten for a number of days, they had not slept, and so on. And so we found the people to pay the rent, we got them some food, gave them a chance to sleep, and in about three days they were out of there, and it just shows I think what can happen if you take them to the hospital.

—And that's another thing: a patient can't be a patient until he is shown to a doctor; this is a social relation, and the doctor then diagnoses the person.

—It's clear that there are still people who feel the function of radical therapy is first and foremost to politicize and unmask the social bases of their personal situation, and although that might be a goal, I'm not sure it's accomplished. But there's another element, you know, it has to do with meeting immediate needs. I would guess that a substantial proportion of people who have been in some form of therapy or another during their lives living in this city—and although I presume that many of us have suffered from some kind of economic crisis or real need at some moment, if you're honest about what goes on in your therapy, you know that obviously goes beyond that—that at the top, the problems that we each try to deal with in our own therapies are much more elusive in some way. Somehow not being able to cope with things, not being able to break out of what we begin to understand as self-imposed, and I think in a way it really does cause people tremendous disturbance to say the only problem they face when trying to get therapy is how to get food stamps, etc.

—I have doubts in my own mind about the strategy of meeting the needs of whatever kind through alternative forms of therapist. The need for those kind of services are so large, it seems to me, and the resources that would be required to meet that need are so out of reach that I don't see how it could ever help more than a handful. Even if it is effective, I wonder whether it is the best way to invest the limited energies available. I've done some work with the prisoners' union and our policy in general has been not to try to meet the social needs of prisoners in general, but to put the emphasis on organizing. For example, we respond with lawyers only to cases of oppression that arise out of political activity, because otherwise we could never get enough lawyers to handle all those cases. And if we see in particular that many of these needs stem from social processes, we might well decide in the long run we're better off concentrating on building movements directly to change the society, and not on helping prisoners individually. It might seem cruel, but ...
—It does! *[Laughter]* I guess if people felt that it really was a possibility for radical transformation in some approximate future, then that kind of strategy would seem less cruel than in a situation that was in many ways taking a direction of reaction to current sorts of crisis, where the possibility of radical transformation seems almost a fantasy. You know, it's easy to say that what we really need is major surgery, I know how to say that and believe it too, but you see people need bandages; you don't see operating.
—I think you brought up a really interesting point earlier on. It seems to me that historically men are seen to be stronger than women, in some cases weaker; but ultimately do you consider them weaker or stronger?
—Well, they have been considered more animal rather than whole human beings. For example in the 1880s it was this idea that women are closer to nature, dictated to by nature, that you don't have that capacity for a thoughtful act.
—I mean, doctors in the 1880s to '90s track the commiserating husbands in bouts of hysterics, the terrible implications for the individual: "This is a burden you'll have for the rest of your life," etc. If you look at a person who has no means of power, as a way of securing power it's the old "passive-aggressive," and maybe it is a political statement: The only way I can have power, the only way I can control my life is to be sick.
—Well, what are the connotations of that, is that good? I mean, if a person had that, would they think it was good or bad?

—And in other words you develop a certain kind of symptom; yeah, it assuages certain problems that you have, but at great cost. You know, you no longer feel anxiety, but you never leave your room either. There's certainly a certain amount of manipulation going in which she does achieve a certain amount of power, but it's at such cost that you could call it—I mean, I don't even think you have to make the claim that it's revolutionary; I think you could just make the claim that it's compensatory.

[Recording cuts off.]

—Are the papers gonna be available anywhere; are you gonna publish?

[Recording cuts off. Tape ends with ten minutes of Lyotard's session.]

Joel Kovel

Therapy in Late Capitalism

I'm going to be talking about what I would call "normal neurotic structures"—this is not to, say, differentiate them from those things we call psychotic, which can be discussed later—but what I mean is behavior that is marked by compulsivity owing to partially repressed destructive fantasies. The term *normal* here implies (1) that all of us are predisposed to neurosis by virtue of the peculiarities of the human self and (2) that neurosis is only made actual in societies in every case of which it plays a definite historical role.

The social conditions in which neurotic development can flourish are those of domination, of a social fabric composed of conflicting groups organized along lines of class, sex, race, etc., and where the division of labor reflects the power of one group over others. In such a setting, insofar as the production of a surplus allows a passage beyond brute necessity, the contradictions between what the social order is and what it can be will devolve downward, passing through the various fissures which comprise the geology of the society, and will eventually settle within the self as one form of neurotic distortion or another. The description just given can, of course, fit nearly every form of social order, and if capitalism is only one among all other social orders so far as generating madness goes. And some of the questions to previous speakers took that into account.

All known groups contain certain forms of behavior—I'll accept Robert Fine's conception of deviance as peculiar to ours—but in any event they contain forms of behavior which are askew in some way with the world. But each society does so in its own way. If capitalism is only one of the crowd of societies so far as imposing madness goes, its individual claim to distinction lies in taking what had been an individually present but discrete feature of other societies and universalizing it within its own boundaries.

A most striking feature of neurosis within capitalism is its ubiquity. The reason for this lies in the particular form of reality principle developed by capital—the fetishism of commodities. The commodity relation is, of course, predicated on the creation of objects of exchange, and of a universal standard, money, by means of which their value may be compared. As Marx consistently pointed out, to place something into a system of exchange means that it has to be abstracted and objectified—i.e. placed within a rationalized and calculable context. But this necessarily implies that the commodity relation must also include the creation and sustenance of a subject who performs the exchanging—a subject who, first, possesses a universal standard of objective rationality by means of which he can attend to the existence and exchange of objective commodities; and second, who is unable to perceive that these commodities are other than what they seem to be—i.e. who is prepared to accept their fetishization within the dominant system of value and exchange.

A social order, like capitalism, that imposes a universal imperative of rationalization will therefore universalize neurosis, for the simple reason that desire cannot go its own way to work out idiosyncratic solutions, but must be forever hurled against rationalization. In precapitalist society, people were amply crazy—the degree of brutal traumatization and privation that characterizes history saw to that. But there was no category of neurosis in which they all had to be inserted, precisely because there was no universal standard of reason in terms of which their madness appeared as negativity.

Once such a standard appears, courtesy of capital, it is only a short while until human relations experts pull up with their calipers, to determine the most exquisite distinctions within disturbed subjectivity. It would, however, greatly flatten out the historical process to confine capital's role in neurosis to the mere imposition of instrumental rationality. *For one thing, we must always bear in mind that what capital has imposed in the way of reason contains the severest contradictions even on an objective level. And for another*, we would miss much of what capitalism is about if we overlook its role in restructuring and marketing desire and impulse themselves. The contradictions within reason as well as the new forms of desire each enter into the history of neurosis. More, they become elements in the development of capitalist society.

AUDIENCE: Could you speak a little slower?

KOVEL: I'm sorry. I guess I picked up the need to get through this talk *[laughs]*. You haven't missed anything; the real talk begins here.

In order to grasp this flux, however, it is necessary to consider two moments within capitalist development which represent the early and contemporary phases of its trajectory and which reveal themselves in developments in personal life having to do with the altered nature of work and consumption.

In the early phase of capitalism, most of its energy went into the production and accumulation of commodities. This process required the transformation of productive activity into abstractable labor power. The alienation which resulted cost the individual control of his vital activity and made his productive capacity into a commodity that could not only be bought and sold, but was also subject to an inexorable process of domination by capital. Yet, alienation stopped short of the subjective world itself, except insofar as this became stunted through separation from the means of existence. And this was not due to any grace on capital's part, but simply to the fact that the inner sphere had only been partially developed as an organ of capitalist relations. It mattered little what subjective variations obtained within the time of labor's activity. From the standpoint of capital, what counted was the simple reproduction of the work force and its controlled delivery, like so many draft animals, to the workplace. Around this need there arose a religion and culture of asceticism, submission, and a crude, severe rationalization.

To assist the reproduction of labor, a family structure was emphasized that would generate an ample supply of fresh children to take up the slack of increased commodity production and which would moreover keep these children under control. For this latter function a line had to be maintained between the patriarchal dominators at the top of the social pyramid and their symbolic representative, the father within the family; this line passed through the individual conscience and bound each man and woman of society to church, state, and ultimately, capital.

The basic work relation of early capitalism, the abstraction and expropriation of labor-time, becomes even more expansive within the social world of late capitalist relations. Its forms become greatly complicated by subsequent developments in the relations of production. As capital proceeds down the self-ordained path of growth for its own sake and not for humanity's, it necessarily expands its productive power past the point at which simple accumulation serves its purposes. We may summarize these developments as the addition of a moment of disaccumulation—i.e. of the liquidation of surplus—occurring *pari passu* with the continuing expansion of the productive process.

This occurs at a point of transition, developing in an uneven manner across the Western world towards the close of the nineteenth century and the beginning of the twentieth, a phase during which machinery and the technical apparatus in general—fixed capital—outstrips the productive role of human labor—living capital. And as the machine takes over, writes Marx, "Labour no longer appears so much to be included within the production process, rather the human being comes to relate more as watchman and regulator to the production process itself. (*What holds for machinery holds likewise for the combination of human activities and the development of human intercourse.*)" *[My emphasis]*. And again, "In this transformation, it is ... the appropriation of his own general productive power ... in a word, *the development of the social individual* which appears as the great foundation-stone of production and of wealth. The *theft of alien labor-time, on which the present wealth is based*, appears a miserable foundation in face of this new one, created by large scale industry itself." *[My emphasis]*

This is Marx predicting—in 1858, I guess—what would happen later.

From the side of production, the social individual is a creature whose work becomes increasingly differentiated and remote from any comprehensible productive process. These trends are manifest in the rise of technocracy, the bureaucratization of work, and, of particular concern for our analysis, the immense development of service occupations. Increasingly, work becomes the cultivation and delivery of human relations themselves. And from these qualities it follows that human relations become technical, swaddled in instrumental logic and prepared for commodification. Rather than being freed by the development of science and productivity, labor becomes degraded, owing to the entrapment of productive reason within capitalist imperatives. The "watchman and regulator" of the production process becomes just another instrument within it: the human becomes mechanical and accordingly assumes a machinelike form of reason to the terms of which all living relations become subsumed.

Meanwhile the pace of production and the hunger for profit impose equally far-reaching alterations in consumption. What could be assumed automatically in an age of scarcity and accumulation becomes both more problematic and more compelling in light of disaccumulation. Now there is a surplus to be sold, though it is not to be simply disposed of but simultaneously wasted and revalued so that capital keeps moving. The consumerist imperative in late capital demands the cultivation of new forms of desire, and this desire is to develop intertwined with the equally contradictory moment of rationality.

However, the twin moments of rationalization and desire, as ill-suited to each other as they may seem to be from so many angles, share in common an immanent capacity to demolish the ground of authority. Since the system within which they are developed is neither rational nor gratifying, it is in constant danger of being exposed by the very forces it has to develop in order to keep going. Again, from the *Grundrisse*, Marx writes:

> Forces of production and social relations—two different sides of the development of the social individual—appear to capital as mere means, and are merely means for it to produce on its limited foundation. In fact, however, they are the material conditions to blow this foundation sky-high.

Of course Capital has long since gotten the point. No longer does it regard the social individual as a *mere* means, but rather as a means to be actively controlled with all the forces at its disposal. Indeed the contestation for the soul of the social individual has become a principal political struggle of advanced industrial society, and moreover defines the structure of our neuroses. Now these change[s?] do not take place through the abstract unfolding of ideal categories, nor by deliberate plots by capitalists in boardrooms, but rather take place within the historical development of the institutions of everyday life, the most critical of which is the family. The family becomes crucial because, in its attempt to fulfill its assigned function of reproducing the individual demanded by the social order, it succeeds mainly by transmitting the contradictions developed within that order into the spheres of personal life. The need of capital for a "social individual" is another way of saying that capital must intensify and enter into the terms of family life. The space for this was cleared out by the productive surge of late capitalism. As the moment of disaccumulation was reached, the demand for labor-time began to drop below the level at which child labor was needed. Meanwhile, the practice had come to seem odious, owing to the progressive development of the reformist impulse during the 19th century. The combination of these factors led to the abolition of child labor in late capitalism and the freeing up of childhood as a separate period. This was essential, for only a child can develop differentiated desire, and only a child can be trained for rationality, an enterprise which was undertaken by general public education.

Alongside of this occurred a rapid decline in infant mortality as the result of advances in sanitation and public health. Thus, children came to stay around long enough to be valued and cultivated; and, as their labor was no longer necessary as it was in peasant or early industrial society, they emerged into the disaccumulation phase as a whole new class of consumers, the satisfaction of whom became a new task for the family. A related development was the dissociation of sexuality from reproduction, which freed the former as a source of pleasure and desire. Meanwhile, family life was being buffeted about as a result of the increasing erosion of traditional sources of legitimacy. With the advance of alienation, the family became a personal refuge for great masses of people who could otherwise find neither meaning, gratification, nor power within community life. Yet, the cultural ties between the individual family and the larger community were becoming ever more attenuated, thus depriving personal relations of a coherent social framework. Authority itself became more and more impersonal and decreasingly mediated by kinship or community.

As a result, people looked for something within the family only to be frustrated. For the father, promised authority by virtue of his cultural heritage, yet denied it everywhere, family life became not the simple dream of a paterfamilias, but a hoax. He is on his way to becoming deadwood. For the mother, denied authority by phallic culture, she now unwittingly acquired the burden of becoming Mom—inculcating the categories of childhood, assuaging the hurts of her increasingly impotent husband and passively transmitting the values of consumerism as though they were instilled into her very milk. At the same time, the split of sex from reproduction opened up for her—even more than for the male—the possibility for gratification that had long been concealed beneath the triple burdens of domestic toil, childbearing and the ascetic sexist ideology. With the masculine monopoly of sexual power becoming seriously eroded from one side, and feminine masochistic submission cracking from the other, the result could only be the release of hostility and guilt into the matrix of the "social individual." And it is the incoming children who inherit this cauldron of emergent hope, pent-up rage, confused longing, and incoherent values.

In this context we can appreciate the achievement of Freud, who did no more than map out a subjective terrain that history had brought into view. And it is quite significant that the most prominent features of this landscape were the neuroses—no less significant than Freud's brilliant insight that neurotic development was entirely continuous with the normal.

Neurosis is the self-alienation of a subject who has been readied for freedom but runs afoul of personal history—a personal history whose particular terms from childhood on are both individually unique and determined by the general historical process. Neurosis therefore is an auxiliary form of inner domination which reproduces external domination on the realm of the unconscious. It was on this territory that Freud made his authentic achievement: the discovery of the lost infantile body revealed in the qualities of deep subjectivity itself—an infinitely fluid yet irreconcilable language of desire, terror, and hatred which peels the boundary of consciousness away from the registration of the material object and drapes it over phantoms of objects lost. To account for repression, Freud needed the hypothesis of instinctual drive, or *Trieb*—the dialectical nonidentity between unconscious fantasy and official waking thought. And to sustain his realization that repression was a radical process, Freud had to ground the concept of *Trieb* materially—i.e. the body had to be granted a real and disjunctive input with respect to the demands of culture. While he largely succeeded, Freud remained to some extent trapped in the terminology of the positivist neuropsychiatry whose assumptions he was demolishing. As a result, he left a legacy of difficulty in mediating psychoanalytic concepts with a genuinely historical social theory.

Every system of domination ensures that potential subjective conflict becomes actual —and maddening—through the class imposition of real suffering and deprivation. Capital's distinctive contribution to this schema was the binding of time through the regimentation of labor-power into an exchangeable commodity. The binding of real time and its eventual translation into the mediating categories of infantile life set forth the principal dichotomy within modern subjectivity: time bound vs. Promethean desire. Add domination and the patriarchal family, and we have the forms of the Oedipus complex under capitalism, which Freud read in his consulting room.

Thus capital ensured the universalization of a normal neurotic structure. Quantitative variations—too much infantile trauma, biological variations in race, and so forth—would suffice, as had always been the case, to bring out one or another clinical variety of "mental illness." To the extent that such afflicted individuals became unsuited for the social process, they would have to be dealt with in one way or another; and although we know that for centuries the fate of the mad had concerned society, it was also the case that only in the early phases of capital and the Enlightenment, as Foucault pointed out, was there any general differentiation between the "mentally disturbed" and the other assorted misfits who had eternally collected around the base of society.

Early capital may have set the stage for neurosis as a category through its industrial binding of time and universalization of reason, but otherwise it had little use for the problem. And this was because its control of the human world was mainly applied at the point of the quantification of labor itself. With the development of the "social individual," however, the essentially qualitative subjective world becomes necessarily an additional object of control, and neurosis finds itself increasingly at the center of culture. In the new order, dominated by technology, service work, and the commodification of the human relationship, the *way* a person behaves on and off the job becomes an essential aspect of the economic process. Thus the presence of neurosis takes on a significance unthinkable in the days of yore, when sturdy backs, sobriety, faith, and thrift would fit the bill. But of deeper interest yet is the fact that the structure of the neurotic experience itself is decisively affected by the ways of advanced capital.

In the early phase of capital, neurotic discord can be ideal—typically regarded as between an external, directly dominative force that attempts to bind time and an impulse which resists such binding. Since neurotic conflict is never simply between objective and subjective forces but involves subjective representations of what is real, there must be an inner registration, or internalization, of the external, directly dominative force. Put simply, the individual has to believe that father is there, backed up by God and State, to ward off impulse; and it is his belief in the image of such authority that enters into the neurotic conflict by becoming linked with infantile representations of the same. To continue the model, then, we would say that the suppressing force in early capitalist normal neurosis consists of a more or less direct representation of an actual authority.

In late capitalist neurosis this picture becomes altered by the diminution of direct, immediate authority, whether religious or secular, and its replacement by an internalized administration of one's own reason and desire. It is essential, however, that the reason which performs this function be of the kind that is instrumental and that fetishizes desire. Otherwise these agencies would go over to the side of impulse and freedom—i.e. they would lose their legitimating tie to the external administration of capitalist relations.

When one factors out the invariant or trivial elements and arrives at the ultimate historical basis of conflict, it may be seen as the struggle between the inviolable space within the subject and the intrusions of administered necessity. These terms can be mapped into Freud's formulation of the clash between the sexual instincts and civilization, since it is infantile sexuality, viewed in its fullest sense as Eros, timeless and uncommodifiable, which constitutes the core of subjectivity left over after all the taming measures have had their due. Nonetheless, the conflict is still experienced by the subject in terms of the actual people—lovers, bosses, coworkers, teachers, and toll-takers—who have come to play the crucial mediating roles between Eros and the administration. Without the concrete mediations of everyday life, there can be no symbolic scaffolding upon which the structures of consciousness, whether fake or true, can be built.

The nonreducibility of self-experience to either social demands or biological need is the precondition of neurotic conflict. The conflict itself, then, is always conducted through mental representations of real people which become split and tossed hither and yon as the subject vainly tries to synthesize the opposed trends within him. But for this to be so, the social world has to provide fundamental contradictions of its own such that an inner synthesis cannot be achieved. Thus from the standpoint of whether neurotic development occurs, it is all the same if the father exists as an actual suppressing authority or whether he is functionally absent and his power usurped. The *form* that the neurosis takes may be different of course—in the first instance we might, for example, expect a hysterical flight while in the second the picture is more likely to be some kind of narcissistic or schizoid disturbance—but neurosis will take root in both cases because real objects see to it that desire is both unfulfillable and dangerous.

A person growing up under late capitalism will be materially cared for and educated into instrumental reason regardless of whether he be working or middle class. Prolonged and nurtured childhood will have succeeded in stimulating desire well beyond the possibilities of any controlling structure to discharge or bind. Indeed, the very weakness of immediate parental authority, its steady usurpation by remoter expertise, guarantees that desire is both unchecked and ungratifiable. The parent can neither stop children nor be adequate to their yearning. And, the nonprovision of a worthy object becomes just as potent a repressing force as the actual threat of castration. In both instances the subject is left helplessly suffused with hate, at the mercy of desire, and driven to falsify consciousness.

In late capitalism, as throughout the history of the human species, the deeper body of alienated infantile feeling is relegated to the unconscious. However, certain auxiliary measures have been added to channel the highly developed surplus desire which flows into contemporary culture via the social individual. The principal structure which accommodates this process is instrumental reason itself. For all the circumstances which tend to stimulate desire do so under the sign of the reasonable imperative. The little children who learn to be creative in their progressive school learn too that the school is an administered entity in which one gets ahead by being creative (within limits, of course). And if the child is not privileged enough to get the point in such a setting, he will when he goes home and is told by some television ad to "feel free" in the interests of a soft drink.

Advanced capital has worked diligently at colonizing the new subjective territory its advance unearthed. The very usurpation of parental authority, which plays so large a role in introducing alienation within the subject, is itself a measure of this colonial administration. The parent either joins up—becoming, so to speak, a civil servant in the regime of mass culture—or he is swept aside to be left screaming in impotent rage, an object of scorn no less than covert yearning.

And like any proper colony, instrumentalized subjectivity provides raw material for the metropolitan region: commodifiable desire. The inchoate longing of childhood bubbles up out of the primary region of self-experience. From earliest infancy it passes through the refinery of instrumental logic as it enters the human world. And there it is named, sorted out, categorized, told—in the fundamental operation of instrumental reason—that it is not part of the subject, that it exists "out there" in abstractable, quantifiable, ultimately commodifiable terms. If, by definition, we term the forms of experience that have been instrumentally severed from subjectivity the secondary symbolic values, and correlatively we term that from which they have been severed primary symbolic values, then it may be that secondary symbolic value becomes valued over the primary. Otherwise the figure will become drawn back into the subjective world and out of the clutches of commodity relations—for *only secondary symbolic values can be exchanged.* It may be that this kind of operation is at the heart of what Marxist critics have called reification.

The simplest notion of the secondary objectification of fantasy in everyday life is the daydream: a controlled exercise in wish fulfillment whose energy derives from unfulfillable unconscious desire and the objects of which are given by the dominant culture. In this sense capital entails the commodification of daydreams. Such conceptions develop a truth if they are believed in; at least they remain stable enough to enter the marketplace where they acquire a more material grounding. And the developing person comes to believe in them because repression of infantile terror is made the easier thereby; and because, simply, to reify desire makes fulfillment seem nearer, since that which is materializable is also possessable, even on the installment plan.

The same configuration that serves the neurotic character structure becomes increasingly essential for the disposition of the surplus under late capitalism. From this standpoint it would seem that neurotic alienation is necessary in order to develop a primary subjective core which turns out fantasies suitable for skimming by the instruments of capital. The neurosis is the irritant, like the grain of sand to the oyster, that keeps a natural process in a state of chronic disequilibrium and so sustains another dislocation at a different point. Similarly, the sludge of secondary symbols accumulated as a result of the endless reification of mass culture obscures the basic disequilibrium even as it irritates it and keeps it going. Thus the various rationalizations which have come to surround neurotic experience in the post-Freudian era have only served to secure the basic neurotic disposition of the times. Were it otherwise, were people either happy or clear about what they wanted, then capital's ceaseless expansion would be endangered.

In addition to churning out saleable desire for the age of consumerism, neurosis has a number of other basic functions under late capitalism. Neurosis is perhaps the only way one can develop a rationalized subject suitable for doing the work of the social individual, who at the same time does not know what he or she wants, i.e., whose capacities to resist are compromised. The simultaneous efflorescence of infantile impulse and fear of a noninstrumental expression of the same makes it that much harder for the neurotic to experience outrage over oppression without lapsing into crippling self-doubt. Similarly, though the parricidal nucleus of the Oedipus complex persists as a spur to rebellion, so long as it remains under the aegis of a preponderantly neurotic organization the rebellion will almost surely be self-destructive and lead to a new round of submission. All in all, normal-neurotic character structures are one of the best ways for an oppressive order to maintain its domination without an embarrassing and economically stultifying overt authoritarianism. Further, designating the normal neurosis as one or another category of clinical neurosis both serves the labeling process so dear to instrumental reason and preoccupies people with reified or individualistic explanations for their unhappiness. And when one adds to this highly abbreviated presentation the reflection of how ruinous neurotic bickering and subjectivism have been to Left politics, it will not be hard to see how loyal a servant neurosis has been to its master, capital.

But slaves have been known to turn on their masters. The labeling of "psychopathology" represents, to be sure, one way of forestalling awareness of a fuller truth. But the opportunity to do so only exists because of the actual presence of a colossal burden of neurotic misery in the population, a weight that continually and palpably betrays the capitalist ideology, which maintains that commodity civilization promotes human happiness. If, given all this rationalization, comfort, fun, and choice, people are still wretched, unable to love, believe or feel some integrity to their lives, they might also begin to draw the conclusion that something was seriously wrong with their social order. Moreover, the threat posed by neurosis is not limited to the betrayal of capitalist ideology. For impulse

[Tape cuts off]

is antithetical to administration, while neurosis represents a kind of synthesis between the two. But it is a false and uneasy synthesis, owing to the partial breakthrough of impulse and its inherently sluggish educability. Thus the hidden unconscious forms of impulse become ever more threatening, not just to the individual in neurotic distress, but to the social order whose fundamental irrationality has to be cloaked in a film of rationalization. Neurosis is not only unfreedom; it also contains within itself a thrust toward freedom. Clinical neurosis should be regarded as a twisted effort at cure, yet one which still contains somewhere more hope for freedom than the normal neurosis it replaces.

Consequently, the various forms of therapy have arisen as new forms of mediation—re-mediations or *remedies*—to be inserted into the increasingly uneasy neurotic syntheses. The therapies are in this sense like a kind of mental Keynesianism resorted to by capital to iron out another type of endemic crisis; and like the economic analog, they suffer from a tendency to inflation, now manifest in the running riot of a whole Babel of schools.

The concept of what psychotherapy can be has come a long way from Freud's initial insight that making the unconscious conscious may relieve neurotic suffering. It has both retrieved its pre-Freudian roots in suggestion, religious healing, and, indeed, shamanism, and branched forward in countless novel directions. In all of these methods, however, one common condition obtains: the individual whose personal distress has been defined as neurosis undergoes an experience in which certain elements of his neurotic structure are reproduced, and as a result he becomes reunited with some portion of his existence that had been denied to him by neurotic splitting. Thus disequilibrium proceeds to re-equilibration; disunity to unification, always under the sign of self-appropriation. The therapies speak then of developing "insight," or of learning "appropriate behavior," of discovering one's "true self," or, as in family therapy, of re-establishing broken and chaotic family communications. The modes under which self-appropriation may occur are exceptionally varied but always involve some element of subjective belief or goal that the therapeutic method validates, as well as some objectification of this in the person of the therapist.

The therapy, then, is the dialogue within which these elements are related to each other. The belief or value system of the therapy establishes the vector of self-appropriation, while the actual therapist offers a concrete model for incorporation, a framework around which the self-appropriation can take place. Thus in Freud's method the analyst imposes the value of reflective truth-telling and offers his accepting yet disengaged attention to break the neurotic cycle; while in Jung's version, belief in a transcendent unconscious force is held out and the analyst becomes an active guide promoting symbolic reunification; or in Gestalt therapy, immediate contact with current awareness becomes the goal; or in behavioral treatment, altering learned, objectifiable behavior; in transactional analysis, appropriation of a reasonable standard of self-esteem in a group setting; and so forth.

Note that anything can work, at least for a while, in the therapy of a neurosis, so long as it is believed in and backed up with a real therapeutic presence that succeeds in objectively establishing some kind of dialogue with the inner structure of neurosis. The objective factor makes it impossible to airily dismiss the value of some supposed cures as bubbles destined to burst upon disillusionment. Illusions they might be, but no more so than the false consciousness imposed by class domination. While it is true that neurotic contradictions will not be ushered out of existence by therapeutic mumbo jumbo, this is not the same as claiming that a person will not be *convinced* that they have subsided.

Of course the two dialectics—the therapeutic and the societal—run together. Indeed it is just the social dimension which provides an essential framework of objectification around which therapeutic goals can crystallize (e.g., Jungian treatment works best for those whose life has prepared them to a religious worldview). Because of the nonidentity between individual and society, however, no absolute fit between personal telos and an objectified social framework can be obtained, and a great range of partial solutions, each with its own ideology, is possible.

We are thus in a position to attempt a critique of the differing possibilities for therapy according to two criteria: (1) the degree to which they objectively address themselves to the neurosis, as against blurring the realities or indulging in illusions; and (2) the values inherent in the kind of change they offer, both with respect to their respective methods and goals. Are the resistant powers within the subject employed for this end, or does the therapy attempt its unification on terrain that has already been colonized by capital? In other words, does the therapy become an immanent critique or a new form of fetish? Let us turn to a few examples for clarification.

Critiques of inner and outer worlds have to be made in the language of each sphere. Thus therapies which attempt to apply advanced political insights to emotional disturbances are only imposing another form of false consciousness. This is precisely the problem with so-called radical therapy, with its naive illusion that neurosis and oppression are directly connected so that, for example, a woman becoming conscious of her actual oppression as a woman would also be adequately dealing with neurotic distortions of her sexuality. The spontaneous activity of the subject generates a consciousness that is false by the standards of class consciousness. Yet it is also anchored in definite unconscious fantasies, which, though they may stem from a real childhood generated out of late capitalist contradictions, have been cut off by repression from political categories. Thus there is a false consciousness of both the objective and subjective dimensions, and it is deceptive to blend them together.

This is a dangerous question to overlook. It is not a mere intellectual failure to apply political categories to a therapeutic situation. For therapy mobilizes the neurosis in order to resolve it; but while mobilized, neurotic thinking, with its transference wishes of submission to therapeutic authority, will drag the most advanced political ideology back into domination and compulsivity. Similarly, though mental patients are blatantly abused by society, they do not cease thereby to be troubled on their own. The labeling which defines a career for them as psychotic has a real and deleterious effect on their inner subjective life, but does not occupy the whole ground of subjectivity. To regard people as defined by their oppression flattens the humanity—and the ultimate powers of resistance—out of them, and is no better than the crude categorization that passes for a medical model.

In this regard it should be pointed out that the subjectivity of psychotic people is radically isolated; both world and self are petrified into an objectification of far greater extent than the prevailing degree of capitalist reification. Thus they are lost even to the given state of unfreedom and correspondingly objective measures, such as drugs and restraint, may at times (although far less often than prevailing medical orthodoxy would have it) be necessary as a humane expedient. Here we may be able to appreciate the weakness of Laing's synthesis of the '60s, which fell short on both criteria. By minimizing the crippling objectification of the psychotic, Laing imposed a deep subjective therapy on them that they could ill tolerate, much less use. At the same time, as Russell Jacoby has observed, Laing tended to flatten the social dialectic by subsuming the alienation of labor into that of the subject. Thus a politically advanced position—one mediated through objective societal categories—is therapeutically backward; while a therapeutically advanced position—one that seeks to reclaim alienated subjective territory—is in itself politically inert. And yet given the historical relationship between neurosis and capitalism, therapy cannot be ignored as a possible element in any overall political strategy. Our analysis tells us, however, that therapeutic practice should be bracketed from objective political goals. Concretely put, a person should be free to unburden him- or herself in a therapeutic setting without regard for the objective consequences.

In a practical sense, for a therapy to flourish in the world of capitalist relations, it has to generate exchange value. This can be done in two ways (which may be combined in the real setting): the therapy can offer something that is perceived to be of genuine value because it is rare and in danger of being extinguished, like fine handicraft; or it can promise power by promoting unification with the main dynamic of capitalist expansion. With respect to the first type, we have therapy which offers the chance for deep subjective reflectivity and/or an intense, caring personal relationship. Time bought for these purposes will continue to have a premium value in a culture that works to obliterate both of them. To be sure, it is a value reserved for the privileged class. For the rest, therapeutic help will have to come either through a cut-rate compromise or via the second pathway—an already fetishized route. By being fetishized, therapy is able to help the subject defend against his deeper anxieties, thus feel less neurotic, indeed, full of "mental health."

In today's world the therapist has become a technologist of behavior and value. Everything there is to know about sex is known. The dialectic of ineffability is abolished by behavioral technology. Masters and Johnson, fresh from their conquest of the orgasm, dance on Reich's grave as the reigning experts on the ways of Eros. Spread out around them are a host of behavioral and cognitive therapists dedicated to the Skinnerian dogma that behavior is determined by its consequences—i.e., purely objectively, undialectically, positivistically, and instrumentally. Systems analysts abound with a somewhat more subtle but equally instrumental vision of people caught hopelessly in a net of communication. And of course the tide of drug treatment continues unabated. Indeed the ultimate is already with us: therapy by computer—and anybody who doubts that subjects have been found who like getting treated by a machine is out of touch with the pace of reification.

Similarly, commodifiable desire—the same that sells deodorants—has been amply mobilized in the interests of therapy. Here a glimmer of the hope set going by capital's democratization—that everyone is entitled to happiness—has become fused with the equation, happiness equals stimulation, into a powerful instrument upon which the neurotically troubled and alienated can seize. The basic thesis of this dimension of therapy is that the neurotic impulse should not be tinged with the hatefulness which is in fact its distinguishing feature. In order to promote this illusion, repression of the hateful side of impulse—the side which wants to possess, devour, castrate, and so forth—is necessary; and this is secured by magnifying the image of the nonhateful side—that which just wants to enjoy—out of proportion. Here consumer culture stands at the ready with its cornucopia to back up therapeutic ideology. The Human Potential Movement, with its joy therapy and maximization of encountering, spontaneity and impulse, bears witness to the fetishization of this dimension. In place of an authentic desire which might emerge through overcoming the historically induced split, Human Potential or post-Freudian psychology dredges up an internalized Manifest Destiny: nothing should be too much for these Americans who compulsively gobble up experience as though it were choice mineral rights. Instead of genuine freedom, then, which would mean an honest confrontation of hatred, evil, and madness, fetishized therapy offers us a Disneyland of the mind. And it should be noted that the therapy of an unreflective spontaneity bears more than a haphazard resemblance to the politics of spontaneity. The infantilism that afflicted Left politics of the 1960s—the "gimme now" variety—becomes swiftly retooled into the therapist of instant breakthrough (viz., Jerry Rubin).

All of the strands of bourgeois reification get rewoven in fetishized therapy. Its mystification returns through the adoration of the latest guru or in the cultivation of "pure" consciousness through meditation. Its idealistic naiveté crops up cloaked in the preachings of a Carl Rogers or an Erik Erikson. And its latent puritanical authoritarianism marches again dressed up, coyly enough, as the reality (sic) therapy of William Glasser. In sum, any ideological stance which preserves the split in bourgeois culture can be used to promote unification between the neurotically split subject and the alienated world. Thus it can be inserted into the neurotic disequilibrium where it will serve repression and reconvert a clinical into a normal neurosis.

Given the increasing alienation of bourgeois culture and its steady commodification of the subjective world, even this tenuous balance is hard to sustain; and the half-life of therapies now comes to resemble that of schools of art or rock groups. With progress in alienation, therapies have had to shout louder and promise more to get a rise out of their increasingly jaded subjects. As a result of these trends—which match on the cultural scale the development in the individual of forms of neurosis which lack clear lines of internal repression and hence lack classical symptoms—there has come to be a gradual coalescence of therapy with other forms of mass culture. Consider the case of transactional analysis, one of the most successful of the new therapies, and the first to be clearly modeled on the soap opera or situation comedy, with its apparatus of games, scripts, and so on. TA is unabashed about its congruity with consumerist culture—neurotic patterns, for example, are said to earn "trading stamps." This not only helps to account for its success as a therapy but also for its lead in the assimilation of the categories of therapy to those of social control on other levels—namely, its widespread use, along with other group therapies, in corporations, the military, and other arms of the bureaucracy as an instrument to help people get along with each other and the order of things. Thus, work, therapy, and everyday life each become suffused with the ethos of "human relations"—the model of a "social individual" suitable as a means of production and consumption and disinclined to resist the order of capital.

It should be emphasized that in actual practice, especially as it evolves over time, no therapy fits any category of fetishization in a neat fashion. Nor, except in rare instances, can any practice be assigned wholly to the camp of domination. A brief glance at the tangled path of psychoanalysis may show why. The main theme of the history of psychoanalysis—a history, it should be added, not yet adequately written —is that of the absorption of critique by the dominant culture. The heart of psychoanalytic therapy is restoration of integrity through the appropriation of reflective powers lost by neurotic splitting. But this is an attack at one of the points where neurosis buttresses the reification demanded by capitalist culture. Self-reflection counters the instrumentalization of reason so essential to capital. A reflective subject is a critical, resistant subject. Moreover, psychoanalysis in its critical form reveals both the existence of Eros and the actual shambles made of erotic prospects for human liberation by the bourgeois world. To be sure, it also plunges into the twisted hate which is the subjective tracing of outer domination, and so tends to discourage ready-made solutions to the human dilemma. But at its heart is a search for the truth, which necessarily serves the quest for freedom, as Marxists from Reich and Trotsky to Adorno, Marcuse and Jacoby have observed.

Consequently, in its initial phase (up to 1920), psychoanalysis was a fundamentally revolutionary doctrine, although Freud's ambivalence towards the critical potential of what he had discovered left the way open for a number of courses. After 1920 the battle for the future of psychoanalysis began, with Marxists, surrealists, etc., on the one side and bourgeois culture on the other. We cannot recount these struggles except to note that they took a decisive turn towards the bourgeois side when Stalinism forced anything critical out of Marxism and Nazism uprooted the psychoanalytic movement en masse and brought most of it to America. Before the emigration, the way had been cleared for the bourgeoisification of psychoanalysis with the realization by culture that in the new science a weapon had been handed to them for the exploitation of their new subjective domain. Significantly enough, it was Edward Bernays, Freud's nephew and the founder of public relations, who spearheaded the appropriation of psychodynamies by advertising and the mass media in general. Meanwhile, the first among neo-Freudians, Alfred Adler, was disseminating his consciousness-bound version of psychoanalysis among the educational and social-work establishments.

In general, in order to catch hold in American culture, a psychoanalytic idea had to be stripped of its dialectical thrust, as with the neo-Freudian de-emphasis on the unconscious. By the same token, orthodox Freudianism held onto the unconscious but grounded it in an unmediated id-psychology safe for bourgeois culture. In this guise psychoanalysis portrayed people as Hobbesian animals needing to be trained, an ideology compatible with historical formulations such as "Capitalism exists because of anal-sadistic instincts" or "The police exist because of the masochism of the masses."

Then in the 1930s the ego-psychology of Heinz Hartmann began to hold sway. As Adorno pointed out, Hartmann's work was in a basically correct theoretical direction insofar as it restored the principle of nonidentity within the subject (ego reflecting reality and id reflecting desire) and so tended to rescue psychoanalysis from the undialectical morass into which it had fallen. But the same deadly biologistic flaw inhered in Hartmann's ego, which was handed the job of "deinstinctualizing psychic energy." Given the class position of psychoanalysts and the need of World War II and postwar culture to justify the ways of the bourgeois god to man, it was an inevitable path to yet another flattening of the critical dialectic, this time the enshrinement of ego-reality over id-desire. Coordinated with this was the absorption of psychoanalysis into medical orthodoxy and psychiatric education as an avatar of truth about mental illness. The result was its transformation into an adjustment psychology that found itself trussed up in conformist thinking and upper middle class mores when the crises of the 1960s reopened the question of Marxist liberation.

Psychoanalytic practice—a term which embraces a goodly variety of pursuits—reflects the history of the doctrine. Thus psychoanalysis may be used as a mode of therapy in which the instrumental reasoning of ego psychology can be imposed as an ethos of intellectualized self-administration; or the conformism inherent in any undialectical psychology can appear as moralization, with all unconventional and protest activity being dismissed as "neurotic acting-out;" or a caricature of its original, unmediated depth psychology can persist as rampant subjectivism, the old idealist myth that passive contemplation is praxis enough for life's problems. All of these forms may be expected to crop up in one guise or another, simply because the therapy has been rooted in bourgeois culture as long as it has.

But just as that culture continually creates possibilities for its own overcoming, so can psychoanalytic practice touch from time to time its critical origins. Several conditions remain indispensable for this. One is the eschewing of any liberatory, radically curative, or transcendent goal which is to emerge from the therapy itself—i.e., there should be no superordinate value to what is going on, no pretense that a short cut through history has been found, nor that a "true self" will emerge at the end of the treatment. Another, related condition is the bracketing out of objective and political considerations during sessions, in the interest of permitting the emergence of even the most violent and forbidden thoughts (since, as in a dream, there would then be no realistic consequences). Yet another is the recognition that, under the sway of neurotic subjectivity, political thinking will degenerate towards domination, since it is the child-mind which is mobilized by the therapeutic situation. And finally, a certain respect for the integrity and worth of the person is necessary, no matter how far short of universality this may be along, however, with the insistence that this individual be truthful concerning his or her warps and blemishes.

Therapy so construed—be it psychoanalytic or otherwise—retains the possibility of critique by refusing to present itself as more than what it is. Its very modesty is its strength. Its refusal to provide the Big Answer opens for the subject the possibility of looking outward. And by moving negatively, refusing to give answers and drawing in the limits of its judgment, a critical therapy draws a line against the colonization of the subjective world which defines late capitalism, and thereby works toward the restoration of the dialectical mode of resistance. In concrete terms, the person who emerges from therapy conducted as critique is no True Self, nor even free of normal neurosis. But he or she has widened the scope of the choices that can be made, while a certain part of locked-in subjectivity has been freed to make real demands upon the world. In sum, they are more ready for love and the politics of liberation.

Whether these choices will be actualized depends ultimately on the nature of their objects. Here the future poses a whole new conjuncture of possibilities. For if capital is moving into a new phase of scarcity, with a heightened legitimation crisis and the real possibilities of an intensified authoritarianism, then the conditions under which subjectivity both grew and became neurotic will be drastically altered. The terms of our subjectivity were forged within a capitalism undergoing more or less incessant expansion. Our child-mind is a creature of the age of surplus: commodified desire is part of consumerist society; and instrumental reason requires delay, leisure, and an elaborate educational process. Clearly, all these conditions may become upset in the years to come. But if so, then the resistive powers immanent within the therapies will need all the more to be rescued and drawn into new forms of praxis for the struggles ahead.

Robert Fine

Psychiatry and Materialism and Q&A with François Peraldi et al.

At the beginning of *Capital*, Marx states, "Within the bourgeois world commodities appear as if they are a universal phenomenon. However, this appearance is a deceptive appearance. It is generated by the stability of the commodity form under capital." In fact, he says, commodity production is one highly specific form of production, and the commodity is one specific form of product. When political economy posits the universality of the commodity, it is taken in by the appearances generated by commodity production itself. The first task of a critical theory then is the recovery of this sense of historical specificity. It is only, furthermore, if the specificity of the commodity form can be grasped that the possibility of a transcendence, that is, the possibility of a world without commodities, can be theoretically grounded.

With regard to the phenomenon of deviance, Michel Foucault has pointed to the same issue. Namely, that contemporary thought has lost contact with its history. A brief survey of the dominant theories about deviance bears this out: almost without exception, theories of deviance affirm its universality. Positivism, for instance, conceives of deviance as a natural phenomenon, and thus not subject to a history at all. What they search for is the notion of a natural offense that exists independently of the circumstances of any particular period.

The discovery of culture and historical relativity did nothing to undermine the sense of the omnipresence of deviance, strangely enough. The forms of deviance might change—in one society, hysteria, in another, witchcraft, and so on—but the existence of deviance everywhere was not doubted. Relativity was incorporated by defining deviance in terms of a violation of the *conscience collective* or normative order of any society, whatever the particular content of this normative order. The specificity of the very notion of normative order or collective conscience was not addressed. Then this normative definition was reinforced by a functionalism which declared that deviance serves an indispensible function for any society; namely, that of reinforcing the moral order by means of the exclusion of the outsider. As Durkheim put it, wrongly, "The collective conscience is nourished at the scaffold."

Since this function was socially indispensable, it followed that deviance was present in all societies of all types: even the land of saints would have its nose-pickers. Phenomenological sociologists saw the sense of deviance as a necessary outgrowth of the imposition of a grid of meaning or of a symbolic universe on a world inherently disorderly, in constant movement and ungraspable in its fluidity. This imposition of order on the chaos of the Real, generates by necessity the anomalous. So in the words of one phenomenological sociologist, "All social reality is precarious. All societies are constructed in the face of chaos. The constant possibility of a gnomic terror is actualized whenever the legitimations that obscure their precariousness are threatened or collapse."

The labeling of such anomalies in terms of categories of deviance is a necessary defensive move on the part of any society, it is argued. It is seen as a required universe-maintaining mechanism for the protection of the social order against its gravest threat, the basic chaos of human existence.

AUDIENCE: *Why don't you tell us in language we can understand!*

ROBERT FINE: The kinship of phenomenology to functionalism is quite visible in this case. This brief travelogue through these theories exemplifies the systematic denial of historical specificity that we find in bourgeois thought. We literally cannot imagine a world without deviance, in which case it follows that a politics aimed at realizing such a world would make no sense. Under such circumstances many seek to decipher not the conditions for the emergence of deviance as a social form, but its historical character ... not its historical character, but its meaning.

It is to Foucault's credit, following Marx, that power as a universal phenomenon can be distinguished from the particular forms that it takes, and in particular the deviance form. A question then emerges as to what shape did critical thinking, critical theory, assume in the absence of any sense of history and the absence of the sense of the possibility of a world without deviance? It criticized not the fact that deviancy existed, not its determinate character, but its sense of objectivity. The problem was that its externality, exteriority, as we heard last night, became its scandal. However required it was in society that the sense of the externality of deviance be generated, this sense of objectivity was fundamentally an illusion, this form of theorizing that I've argued. The task of a critical theory was conceived of as making possible, for some at least, not the construction of a world in which deviance did not exist, but an escape from the illusions of externality.

This critique of objectivity has been so central to critical deviance theory that it becomes of central importance to tease out the nature of this argument. It has its roots, I believe, in the dialectical method, originating perhaps in Hegel, a method which recent work of Lucio Colletti has done much to elucidate. A few words about this method, because I think it has been one of the fundamental methods used in the critique of deviance. It is the method of the dialectic, essentially. What the dialectic sought to achieve in Hegel's terms was "the disappearance of all that is objective, all that is held to be true, all that is definite, all that is affirmative." The truth, in other words, of the material world lay in its being essentially an appearance, an illusion. The essence of the objective, by contrast, lay in the thought that constituted it. It is only in thought that the object truly is *in and for itself*, in that Hegelian language.

So a critical consciousness had to liberate itself from the truth of objective being, to do away with the objective was to do away with servitude. Now, although the appearance of objectivity was an illusion, it was still necessary, for it was only through this transparent appearance that the essence-thought would allow itself to be seen. The appearance of externality was the medium through which the absolute thought was reflected. It is at this point that what is called the dialectic of matter emerges. Since empirical things exist in some sense, but their existence disappears as their essence-thought is revealed, things both are and are not. They exist but their essence is that which is other than themselves, that is, thought. Hegel called this the identity of identity and nonidentity: the dialectic. The form of thought that could appreciate and eventually realize this dialectic was reason. The intellect, by contrast, consisting of common sense and science, was committed to the illusory principle of noncontradiction, according to which a thing cannot both exist and not exist. It was committed in other words to a belief in the objective world. By contrast, what Hegel thought was the absolute annihilation of this common sense world, objectivity, was akin to alienation. This is the tradition, I believe, that much of critical deviancy theory is derived from.

This critique of objectification emerges clearly when we contrast it with Marx. Marx assumed the existence of a real world, a nature transformed by man.

Criticism, then, should not be directed at the fact of objectivity itself, but at the determinate forms that the objective world takes. For Hegel, in contrast to Marx, it was the objective character of the object for self-consciousness, not its determinateness, that was the scandal of alienation. Similarly, the dialectical quality of deviance was said to lie in the illusoriness of the appearance of externality and objectivity, and in the truth of that which is other than itself, the thought and practice which gave it its sense of objectivity.

The theoretical goal was then to demonstrate this absence of real objectivity. Labeling theory, for example, says the object tended to dissolve the objectivity of madness by arguing that any man subjected to the methods of selective and exhaustive interpretation employed by psychiatry would appear mad. How, within this dialectical reasoning, is escape from or transcendence over the world of deviance possible? Only by withdrawing from the world of objects as such. Deviance, since it has not been analyzed in its determinateness, remains a phenomenon wherever that form of alienation, based on the separation of subject and object, persists. The problem for the theorist, in a nutshell, becomes this: What would a world without objects look like?

The dominant answer of modern theory is that society itself requires the illusion of objectivity. To escape from objectivity, and thus from deviance, requires an escape from society. The unchangeable requirement to practice itself; "the tragic fate," to use Simmel's terms, of the common sense actor, ahistorically caught within the confines of his natural attitude, have as their outcome the impossibility of transcending the world of objectivity, and thus of deviance.

Within the form of the dialectic, we find text after text insisting that it is a commonsense premise, as such, that deviance is an inherent feature of certain acts and persons. Transcendence then, of the world of deviance, requires, according to this kind of theorizing, a withdrawal from society and objectivity. Either through the development of a reflective theoretic attitude—the theorist then is postulated by the theorist as the one who can escape from this alienation, as Marx puts it, "The abstract thinker always puts himself at the centre of the world"—or perhaps through the development of a madness, which in its *schizo-culture*ness breaks down the world of objects.

So, antipsychiatry can find the theoretical grounding for the link between madness and truth. Left-Hegelianism—Hegelian Marxism—does such for the history of inert things. I had a discussion of that, which, for the sake of time, I shall leave out. If you want to discuss Hegelian Marxism we can do that in discussion.

I think I will just mention though, that Marxist Hegelianism also works within the problematic of the object. Alienation consists in objectivity, and I believe the basic stance of Hegelian Marxism is to look for the conditions under which objectivity in this sense will be constructed. Marcuse and Horkheimer and so on basically offer the position that scarcity, the demands of production itself on the one hand, and positivism on the other hand, force men into a domination of nature. It's through the end of scarcity, or through the abolition of positivism, that objectivity—"thing-ness," as such—can be overcome. And you get the beginnings there of a utopianism, but let's discuss that later if we want to.

So the critique of objectivity, the problem with the critique of objectivity, is that objectivity as such seems to be an inescapable feature of this world. However, there is a second thread to the critique of objectivity, which is often confused with this first thread that I've already discussed. In this thread, the critique of objectification is not a critique of objectivity as such, as if that is akin to alienation, but of a particular form of social relation.

One of the clearest statements of this latter position is found in Sartre's analysis of objectification and "the look" in *Being and Nothingness*, and I shall very briefly look at his argument. Now, Sartre's argument goes roughly like this: "The possibility of shame," Sartre says, "is predicated on the look of the other. I have just made an awkward gesture; the gesture clings to me, I neither judge it nor blame it. I simply live it. I realize it in the mode of for-itself. But now suddenly I raise my head. Somebody was there and has seen me. Suddenly I realize the vulgarity of my gesture, and I am ashamed." If you look through a keyhole, you simply do it. As Sartre puts it, "I am my acts." But from the moment when a creak in the floorboard reveals the presence of another looking at you, from that moment the possibility of shame is generated. You become the object of another's look. "Shame is," he says, "by nature, recognition. I recognize that I am as the Other sees me."

"The look," says Sartre, "negates the eye." To see the Other's eye is to see him as an object. To feel the Other's look is to feel the Other has you as his object. The eye may be the support for the look, but they are not the same. For the look to exist, the Other does not have to be physically present in the form of an observable eye. Say, for example, the creak represents a false alarm, and no one is actually present. "Far from disappearing," Sartre says, "with my first alarm, the other is present everywhere—below me, above me, in my neighboring rooms—

and I continued to feel profoundly my being-for-others. What then is it that has falsely appeared? It is not the Other-as-subject, nor is it his presence to me. It is the Other's facticity, that is, the contingent connection between the Other and an object-being in my world."

The look is the intermediary through which I become an object. My acts become objects for another, subject to another's assessment and evaluation. They now become a source of shame and pride to me. I become a kind of slave to another, dependent on his look and appraisal for my identity.

AUDIENCE: *Many of us have read this already; could you skip over it?*

FINE: Okay, I'd like to just remind you of certain parts because there's some analogies drawn later. Shame, in the first instance then, is the product of being such an object. The Other—I want to remind you of certain points because it ties in with what is coming later—the Other, as subject to the look, is essentially free. In experiencing the look and experiencing myself as an unrevealed object-ness, I experience the inapprehensible subjectivity of the other directly, and so on. I experience the Other's infinite freedom.

How then does one who is subject of another's look transcend that objectivity? He does it by making the Other an object. The objectification of the Other is a defense on the part of my being, which, precisely by conferring on the other being-for-me, frees me from my being-for-the-Other. And so on.

Now in this analysis, which I'll cut short because I think most of you do know it, Sartre sees objectification as a social relation, right, of a master-slave variety. But he, like his contemporaries, cannot conceive of this relation as a historical one.

1. This relation between self and Other, subject and object, master and slave, is posited as a historically universal one. It coincides with the existence of society itself.
2. Within the social world there is no escape. Either you are a slave, the object, or you transform the Other into slave objects, and only thus recover your subjectivity. Within society there's no exit. Since this is in the nature of society as such, the Other always represents the threat of objectification; "Hell is other people," and so on.
3. Escape from this enslavement of self or Other is only possible by means of escape from society. The original existential act of a spontaneous ego, when "I am my acts," represents both an original freedom and an emancipative possibility.

Now Sartre I think can be criticized on two grounds. Either his description of objectification has no reality, except in his own mind, or, what his description of objectification captures is the essence of the look, as it exists. His mistake then would be, to paraphrase Marx, that he passes off what exists for the essence of the look itself. It is the latter that I believe he does.

The subject-object dialectic that Sartre describes is, I believe, a reality. But it is a specific historical reality with a comparatively recent genesis. The social and historical reality of this dialectic can be exemplified by returning to the beginning of the 19th century and the emergence of the modern prison and the asylum. Consider, for instance, the plan devised by Jeremy Bentham, discussed by John Rajchman briefly yesterday, called the Panopticon; the plan for a model prison. This prison constituted a world almost exactly akin to that described by Sartre. It is a realization of the Sartrean world, or rather, Sartre represents the hypothesization of this world.

How was this world constructed? First it was constructed through architecture. The building was to be a circular one with cells around the circumference, and an inspector located in the center. By this means, the prisoner could be kept under maximum possible observation. The prisoner was not only to be under observation, but to feel under constant observation. This could be achieved if the prisoner did not know when he was actually under observation; if through technical devices, he were prevented from seeing the eye of the inspector. Then, to paraphrase Sartre, the inspector would be everywhere, below, above, and so on. The gaze then was to be one-way; the prisoner as object, the guard as subject; the prisoner prevented from returning the inspector's look. He was to be looked at, but not himself to look.

If the prisoner was to be no more than object to the inspector's look, then two further measures had to be taken. First, the prisoner had to be prevented from having any reciprocal effect on the nature of this gaze. In Sartre's language, he needed to be made into a "defenseless being in the face of a freedom that was not his own." So the organization of the prison was orientated to negate any form of reciprocal action on the part of the prisoner. Here's one example: in a sexually mixed prison, the female offender might be able to influence a male inspector by a display of nudeness in the course of dressing and undressing. Prevention of this was an organizational achievement. Firstly, the design of the building would make it difficult for a woman to show herself to a male inspector. Second, the female prisoner would also be under constant observation from a female guard who would punish her for any such lewdness. Thirdly, the male inspector would himself be under the ever-present watch of a female inspector. In this way, sexuality would as a source of subjectivity be negated.

I'll give you a quote from Bentham so you can get the feel for this: "Female rulers might want firmness. In male ones, probity and partiality might be warped by the attraction of female eyes. The Panopticon principle dispels this difficulty. The weakness of the matron would find support in the masculine firmness of the governor and his subordinates. A weakness of a different kind on the male side of the establishment would find its proper check and corrective in the vigilance of matronly severity." And so on.

So too the possibility of affecting the guard through violence, or the threat of violence, could be overcome by a combination of constant surveillance and the isolation of the prisoners from each other. The ideal was that the prisoner could only vent his rage by beating his head against the brick wall of his cell. The design was such that "a single female might bid defiance against the whole throng of prisoners." Even the prisoners' power of contamination through plague, that contagion that was so much the fear of the 18th century, would—by cleanliness, by the separation of the prisoners from each other, and by eliminating the need for physical contact between the prisoner and the guard—be overcome.

So, to give you another short quote from Bentham: "Another advantage of the Panopticon is the great load of trouble and disgust that it takes off the shoulders of those occasional inspectors of a higher order, such as judges and other magistrates, who call down to this irksome task from the superior ranks of life, cannot but feel a proportional repugnance to the discharge of it. To do their business they must approach near to and come almost in contact with each inhabitant. Among the other courses of reluctance, none at present are so forceful, none so happily well grounded … as the danger of infection." And this danger, this threat of infection that the prisoner had, was to be negated.

The suppression then of any force of reciprocity—visual, violent, sexual, contaminative—was the first condition for making the prisoner a pure object of the inspector's gaze. The second condition lay in the suppression of a dialogue among the conflicts themselves, for such dialogue would be a source of subjectivity. The elimination of dialogue could be achieved physically by solitary confinement. If this was not possible, then at least interaction between prisoners was never to escape the inspector's surveillance. Crowds, for example then, were to be altogether avoided. For example: "Crowds, among men whose characters have undergone any form of stain, are unfavorable to good morals. They exclude reflection and they fortify men against shame. Shame is the fear of the disapprobation of those with whom we live, but how should this disapprobation of criminality display itself among a throng of criminals?" And so on. In other words, dialogue had to be controlled, and checked.

So this relation between prisoner and inspector was to become an exact replica of the subject-object, master-slave relation. By punishing prisoners for offenses committed by their companions, they were to be encouraged to become inspectors over each other. Failure to inform would brand the offender as an accomplice. Bentham called this the principle of mutual responsibility: "Here if anywhere is the place for the law of mutual responsibility to show itself to advantage. Confined within the boundary of each cell, it can never transgress the limits of its strictest justice. Either inform, or suffer as an accomplice. What artifice can elude, what conspiracy withstand, so just yet inexorable a law?"

On this principle, Bentham said: "This is a principle that has stood for ages as an object of admiration, and it is the highest principle of the Panopticon." Among the inspectors, the same principle again: subordinate keepers would be under the same inspection by their superiors as the prisoners were by them. This was a world in which there was to be no escape from the tyranny of objectification. The organization of the prison was to establish once and for all that the convict was no more than guilty object, and that his experience could only be an inward one of shame.

The Panopticon, then, represents the reality that Sartre was later to describe. Two features, I believe, we can note immediately about this reality: first, that it had a particular historical genesis; secondly that its construction was predicated on a total repression. If the Panopticon represented the end of struggle between two wills, two desires, between two subjects, if its symbol lies in the bourgeois aspiration of a universal state which encapsulates all the particular wills within it in a moment of reconciliation, this could only be done at the cost of a systematic and absolute repression. Bentham was well aware of the repressive nature of this reconciliation between the individual and the state: "Allow for dialogue, allow for reciprocity, and the language of guilt will immediately submit to the language of resistance and opposition."

The analysis of an institution like the Panopticon establishes two things: first, that deviance as we know it, in its objectivity, is a historical phenomenon of recent vintage. Secondly, that the existence of deviance is based on the existence of institutionally embedded and repressively organized social relations. From which it follows that overcoming deviance is a historical possibility, and that this possibility requires not just a new way of thinking, antipositivism, or a new discourse, but the practical overthrow of the real existing social relations.

But still, there are two related questions: what kind of practice is required? A reformist one, that seeks only the abolition of certain forms of institutions, or a revolutionary one, that seeks the overthrow of a whole mode of production? An answer to this question hangs on an answer to a prior theoretical question: What accounts for the emergence of Panoptism? Is it the necessary product of, say, the capitalist mode of production, or is it, as it were, a mere byproduct of a particular moment, say, in capitalist development? The emergence of the deviance form of power can and should be tied I believe to the emergence of commodity production as such.

The specificity of commodity production then, very briefly, consists in this—and here we shall see the relation—the product that the producer produces is produced not for his own personal use, nor for the use of the collectivity of which he is directly a part, but for exchange in the marketplace. But what allows one product to be exchanged for another? They must have something in common, but what does a machine and twenty coats have in common? Not their use, not even the fact that labor went into their production, for how can the labor of a tailor be compared to the labor of a machine builder? Their comparability lies in the fact that each required a certain amount of labor time, abstract labor time, divorced from the particular skill required for their production. The product as a commodity is not then a particular use value, but it is what Marx calls value: the embodiment of purely abstract labor time.

So both the product and labor under such conditions are two-fold phenomena. The commodity is a combination of use values and exchange value. Labor is the combination of particular labor for use and abstract labor for exchange. To view the coat and the machine as values requires an abstraction from their different uses. The value form extracts from the material composition and use of the product; turn and examine the commodity, and insofar as it is an object of value, it's impossible to grasp it. It is only when one commodity is compared or exchanged with another that value appears. The machine took ten times as much abstract labor time as the coat to make; its value is therefore ten times as great. When these forms of exchange become sufficiently stabilized, it appears falsely as if the value exists intrinsically in the material product itself. So it is that there is definite relations among men, that allow their labor to become abstract labor, appear as a relation between things, the value of one commodity compared to the value of another.

The crux of the matter lies, I believe, in the privatized nature of labor itself. It is only when private individuals or groups carry on their work independently of each other that their products assume the form of commodities. The relation between the individual producer and society becomes indirect. It is also through exchange that the social relation comes into existence; that exchange requires the abstraction of the product from its particularity. Plus the denial of the real social relations between men, for the value assumes a life of its own inside the product. In other words, it is when labor is privatized, when labor is not collective, when there is no overall plan, and the relations between men become indirect ones, mediated by exchange, that the moment of sociation, exchange, assumes the form of a relation between things. The material product and the body of the producer are necessarily abstracted away.

In this sense, commodity production is the dialectic in practice. The ideal, the abstract, becomes the real, that is, the value. The material world, real things, become no more than the manifestations of value. It is for this reason that the commodity is described by Marx as a very queer thing abounding in metaphysical subtleties. Fetishism then does not lie in a spurious objectification—this argument is taken basically from Colletti's recent work—quite the opposite, it lies in the triumph of the dialectic, the abstract becomes the real, the material becomes the illusion. When we turn to power, and to deviance, we find the following: it is precisely when the direct relations of man to society are shattered—the collectivity, the law, the father telling his subjects what to do—that direct relation is broken. And indirect relations are set up through the privatization of labor. The power no longer appears as a social relation at all. The exchange of will, the will or desire, the desire of the individual and the desire of the state requires an abstraction from the particularity of that will, of that desire, from the materiality of the act from the body of the doer. The social relation of power assumes the form, first of an abstraction, and second as a value inherent in the person or act itself. In short, it assumes the form of deviance.

If I am right, then the crucial connection is between commodity production and deviance, and the overcoming of the mystification of the latter—which is also at the same time the overcoming of the mystification of the dialectic—is predicated on the revolution of the former.

AUDIENCE: *I'd like to come up and speak.*

ROBERT FINE: Sure.

AUDIENCE: *I'd like to speak second.*

FINE: You shall be second.

AUDIENCE: *I'm nervous about speaking, but I'd like to speak anyway. I'm angry—perhaps I've misunderstood the nature of this conference—I heard you say the basic question was, at one point, "What would a world without objects look like?" And if this is the only question worth asking, I feel like this conference is not worth a concerned human being's time. I may have misunderstood the nature of this conference but I am sincerely missing words such as* human beings, people, man, woman, feelings, love, joy, sexuality, *etc.*

Robert Fine, I'm mad at you. I think that obscure language, in the third person, whose end result is to further distance from the reality of trying to stay sane in a mad world, is irrelevant. Instead of intellectual posturings which we are to applaud in one way or another, which co-opt our energy, our focus, and our time, I would like to see a focus on the alienations which are within the reach of two hands, and two eyes, and two ears, on our own streets of New York City. I wish there had been some attention to the crimes of sexism and its psychological effects, some concern for the devastations on the mind of racism and ageism, the rape of human beings on the streets that you walk right here in New York, the oppressions of the struggle of the capitalist system to right itself on the shoulders of the masses, the oppressive quality of an educational system that segregates mind from body from feelings and makes us feel mindless, unless we can play the kind of acrobatic games that I just heard right here.

I think these are the things that should be our concerns, and I think that other intellectual posturings are a co-option of radical energy. I feel that this talk is an experience in the tyranny of intellectualism that prevents a clear focus on the need for change, rather than helping set up a climate in which radical change can take place, and I'm really indeed impressed with the ability of this audience, that are hopefully radical thinkers, to not rise up in protest against this kind of a speech. To this co-option of revolutionary energy I am indeed very mad.

[Loud applause, cheers]

I'm thinking of alienation, and I feel sympathetic because I've written articles in which I've felt that I've had to speak in the language of this kind, and it's sheer hell to write, so I feel sympathetic to you for writing it and for wanting to deliver it. But it was an ordeal to listen to it, and I'm not an anti-intellectual, I believe, I'm very interested in Sartre for instance, and I'm very interested in therapy and antipsychiatry;

I'm a therapist, I live this every day. I'm really interested, but it was an ordeal for me to listen to this kind of thing. And I just wanted to call attention to one linguistic usage, that speaking of alienation, what was alienated about your way of speaking to us—I've just jotted down some very alienated examples of how you set yourself up as an objective authority, even though your subject matter is to criticize the notion of objectivity and objectification. Listen to the language: "the problem for the theorist in a nutshell becomes this"; "the crux of the matter I believe lies in the privatized nature of labor itself"; "two features I believe we can note immediately about this." Now that kind of language takes away from me my space to think; I find that language alienating, I find it oppressive and it takes away my energy, and I wonder if you could listen to your own language a little bit.

[Some applause]

FINE: Does anyone else want to come up?

[Some laughter, then murmuring]

FINE: Come up!

[More audience noise, someone shouts, "Schizo!"]

FRANÇOIS PERALDI: I think Guattari had a very good point when he said that we should not be subjected to read papers, which are largely quotations, which we all know in the original. And I think this was irresponsible, and the glosses you put over were feeble and empty. I think it was a complete travesty.

[Hisses, scattered applause]

I would very much like to see Guattari get the thing in hand so that we use the time we have at our disposal, and that the people who have something to say, say what you have to say, and not give us an anthology of Bentham or Sartre or others' summary.

FINE: Go ahead, it's a free forum.

AUDIENCE: *I would like to ask a question addressed to you, okay. Because I disagree with the central point of your paper, but nonetheless I think that it was an important paper. And I disagree that it's useless to repeat those quotations of Marx and of Sartre because I think they were useful. But with respect to the problem of the liberation of women or the domination of women: women have been dominated for a long time, before what I would consider to be commodity production came into existence, and women have been victims of the master-slave relationship for a very long time. So I would like to ask you, in terms of this objectification relationship, how you would confront the problem of the domination of women, either in terms of current commodity relationship or in terms of another relationship, because I don't see how your explanation fits.*

FINE: Well my basic—I mean, I don't have anything very profound that I want to say now, that I can say about domination of women. The relation between domination and the paper I just gave is that deviance represents, I believe—and we usually use words like *madness* or *criminality*—represents one particular form of domination, and it's a peculiarly mystified form of domination. Domination pre-existed deviance; in fact deviance, I'm arguing, only emerged with commodity production and with capitalism. And so the domination of women, and other forms of domination too, certainly pre-existed this particular form of domination, which I was trying to analyze. That's all I've really got to say.

AUDIENCE: *Define what you mean by 'deviance' then.*

FINE: Well the whole paper in a sense—I mean, one of the troubles is that offering a definition of deviance doesn't get anywhere, I mean, a definition's not going to help you. In a sense the whole paper is an attempt to bring out—and especially through looking at Sartre and through looking at the institution—what we mean when we talk about deviance, and especially what we mean when we talk about its objectified character. So I don't think I could say in a single definition what I was trying to get out through the paper.

AUDIENCE: *Yeah, she said what I had in mind too, but that I didn't think of women, I thought in more general terms, and I think there are other forms of dominance. I think your answer was too easy, because your paper was sort of confused, but one of the things I understood is that the objectification of the individual, and a certain way of looking at these problems of deviance, is strictly related with a society based on the use of commodities. Is that right?*

FINE: That's right.

AUDIENCE: *But since deviance has always existed before, especially in primitive societies and societies in which you do not think of commodities at all, I mean if this is the point of your paper, it's so weak, and you should explain why.*

FINE: No, you've missed the whole point of the paper. The whole point of the paper is to argue that the belief that we usually have, and that we are accustomed to make, you and me and all of us, that deviance does exist in every society, is a mystification generated by this society, that it's not true. Can I give an example?

AUDIENCE: *Can I answer?*

FINE: Yeah.

AUDIENCE: *I think that your language and your academic presentation, of texts which a lot of people were familiar with too, tended to obscure your point, as is my understanding. Now, let me see if I can re-present it briefly: you seem to be saying that* *the very character of commodity form is the condition of an impersonal domination, that since relations between human beings are created into things—thing-ified so to speak—that it is the character of relations in general to present themselves as objects. Now there may be differences between ways people behave, that is, differences between normal ways of behavior and abnormal or anormal ways of behavior, physically speaking, in other societies, even egalitarian societies, primitive societies, but there are other ways of dealing with their behavior other than taking them as objects.*

In other words, domination, if it appears, even—Marx made this point about feudalism, that domination is a personal relationship in feudal societies—domination in our society is an objective relationship, an impersonal relationship, it involves objectification. So the notion of objective form itself turns out to be an artifact of the bourgeois period, because the very nature of the dominance relations, which come of commodity relationships which take relationships between people as a sort of objectively defined by some abstract quantity. Now if I understand your point …

FINE: So far, perfect.

AUDIENCE: … *if I understand your point, it might have been much easier to state it, to pull it out away from the façade of exegesis. You know, an exegetical way getting at this was not the way to do it, and incidentally, this covers the objection to me—of course we could have taken a very different form in previous societies, I mean that would be the only reply you could have had; domination took a very different historical form. Women were not seen as objects, because in a certain sense no human beings were seen wholly as objects, previously. You see, this is the argument you have to make, clearly.*

FINE: Yeah, why don't you, you've expressed exactly what I was just saying, yes.

AUDIENCE: *You see, at best, the way we look at a dominated person would be as something fairly problematic. In other words your way would be a mixture of objective and personal things. These things can be extremely confused, and the categorical element of present domination and present social relations is lacking.*

PERALDI: Excuse me, may I have this back? I am going to make a remark that is going to be at the same time my own conference that I am not ready to make. And it was going to be a nonconference, so if it doesn't work it doesn't matter now. What I am to say, is to make a correlation between what is happening here now and the title of this, whatever this is. But in that case, what I would like to point out is that we are supposed to deal with something that is schizo, and which is a problem of power, where we are going to choose to analyze it. And in my conference I was willing to talk about the fact that a schizo is someone who is always in the position of being affirmative against all forms of institutional power. And the strange thing is that I was going to talk about that in a situation which is exactly the image of what power is in an institution, in a bourgeois institution, where you exchange only ideas on a kind of ideal level without at all analyzing what could be the mechanism of power here. When you sent Félix Guattari away at the beginning of the conference, that was a gesture of power. And then you are going to talk about power somewhere in the prisons, somewhere in the psychiatric hospital, and you won't be able to analyze what's happening *here!*

[Audience applause]

AUDIENCE: *Excuse me, I don't know your name and I'd like to address something to you. I think it's presumptuous and wrong to assume that schizophrenics are not confused and I think this whole conversation is absurd, I mean ...*

PERALDI: Absurd perhaps to you.

AUDIENCE: *But it doesn't attribute anything to having any kind of confusion or distortion of emphasis of mind, and I think that's erroneous and actually I think you guys are, um, are—*

PERALDI: —nuts.

[Audience laughs]

AUDIENCE: *No! Um...*

SYLVÈRE LOTRINGER: Maybe we could ask François Peraldi to elaborate on it, since he was about to talk about the institution and the schizo. Maybe you can make the correlation clearer by talking also about your experience in the institution and against the institution?

PERALDI: Well, this is very simple: the things that we tried to do when we were working with schizos was to shape them into some kind of a different structure, because it's well known that they haven't got any, if you have ever heard of that. Well anyhow, they are not supposed to be in contact with reality and if they have to be made in contact with reality you have to beat the whole symbolic process into them, and the usual way to do that in an institution is to go through a certain pattern of power, which is the Oedipal structuration of the schizo, which is supposed not to be recognized, or something like that.

Well, when we tried to do so in this institution we failed completely, and the main point was that—in the example I was going to bring to you that was a kind of story of schizos and institutions—was that they react in a very strong way to that kind of structuration, powerful structuration that we were trying to shape them into. And the fact that they reacted strongly, that they did in a very, in a way that we should do perhaps here, they just put fire into the furnace, and half of the chateau in which they were living exploded.

So instead of trying to understand what do they have, what is their problem, what happens with them, are they curable, are they incurable, what's happening with them, we just began to interrogate ourselves in the institution and see what we were doing, what kind of discourse in the institution where we were holding, you know, what kind of a discourse we were … we were not even subjects of these discourses, we were just bringing discourses from one place to another one. And then, when we began to analyze that, first of all there had been a kind of dissolution of the machinery of power of which we were the agents while trying to re-Oedipalize the schizophrenic.

So what I would like to say to make the link with here, is that this situation, why I'm here, standing in front of you, not over there, because really one cannot do it anymore, but that's exactly the same—if I'm standing there or I continue doing that *[he walks away from the microphone]* or anything we are in the same relationship of some kind, we are bringing you ideas, bringing you theories and so on, where we feed whatever it is working on that pattern in institutions, you know.

AUDIENCE: *I have an objection to that.*

PERALDI: So, what I wanted to say is that perhaps we have the opportunity here, now, which may be exceptional, to … rather than to say what happens somewhere else in terms of analyzing machinery of powers in an institution, just to assess here what is happening in these terms, now. You know, because there has been that small incident at the beginning when we tried to introduce another function in this kind of colloquium or whatever this may be, when we tried to introduce a new shape, there has been immediately that reaction, "No, we have to read our papers, and you, you have to listen to it," which is exactly the usual shape, you know, through which university and power is working …

[General uproar and disagreement.]

AUDIENCE: *I don't really accept it's a matter of power, we want it that way. It was you, you were committed to give an opinion or thought, but we said we wanted …*

Michel Foucault

We Are Not Repressed

I have taken on a piece of work that is a sort of sequel to my book on the history of madness. I once had the idea of writing something like a history of sexual repression, a history of the sexual anomaly, the mechanisms that both designate and repress it. I failed to go through with this piece of work for a number of reasons: I have been trying for a long time to figure out what these reasons are.

The first reason I gave myself was this: that I couldn't find the necessary documents. But in fact if I couldn't find the documents, it was probably simply because such documents didn't exist—that is, that what I was looking for was not there to be deciphered in terms of the body of mechanisms that we call repression.

It seems to me that a number of people before me, and I too, followed a definite schema of analysis which was elaborated from 1920 to 1930 around the person and the work of Wilhelm Reich. Now I have the feeling that this schema, whose validity I admit, and though it has given rise to a certain number of works, researches, analyses, and, to a certain point, to very interesting discoveries, still will not lead our historical research toward success. Van Ussel has written a recent book in a rather Reichian style on the history of sexual repression. It is an interesting book, but it strikes me as rather limited in its results, and above all it fails to take account of the whole of a historical reality. I am going to try only to indicate a few of the principal characteristics of this reality.

I now see the Reichian schema as an obstacle rather than an instrument. What does this schema consist of? Caricaturing it a bit, I would say that according to this schema we are now living, in fact we have been living since the 18th century at least, under a sexual regime that could be called Victorian. The Queen's scowl, the pout of the imperial prude, could serve as the emblem of our unhappy, hypocritical, and silent sexuality.

In general, for this Reichian schema, for the style of analysis that I will call anti-repressive, up until the beginning of the 17th century sexuality was the beneficiary of a sort of franchise, a franchise in both senses of the word, since it involved both a nonrepressed sexual practice, an open and above-board sexual practice, and a free and joyful prattle, a kind of discourse free of reticences and disguises, about this sexuality. Reference is usually made (especially by Van Hussel) to Erasmus' famous dialogue, in which he instructs a young man on how to get on in life, how one should make love to a prostitute, etc. This golden age of loquacious and sunny sexuality gave way to a twilight that took us into the heart of the 19th century, the Victorian night (the Victorian night in which all cats are gray), when love could be made only in the shadows, out of the hay, behind life's cellar stairs; when love could only be spoken through veiled words, in words carefully coded according to a well-established rhetoric.

In brief, from the beginning of the 17th century a sexuality of shadows would have begun to spread itself over the Western world, a sexuality trapped in the spatial metonymy of the brothel and in the obligatory metaphors of discourse, from which Freud would have finally rescued us. This schema, which I am caricaturing, is based on a methodological principle and an explanatory hypothesis. The methodological principle is this: it is the possibility that is established in these "anti-repressive" analyses, at any rate in this style of writing the history of sexual repression, the possibility of making use of a whole set of notions like those of interdiction, of censorship, of suppression (*refoulement*), of repression, to decode this great repressive process. Consequently this anti-repression holds that in studying processes without a subject—in a society, the exercise and discourse of sexuality—it is valid to use categories worked out by Freud or his followers for the analysis of the speaking subject or the subject of desire.

I believe that this vast myth of Victorianism, this vast fresco of Victorianism, little by little taking over our sexuality and plunging it into darkness, carries with it the burdensome methodological hypothesis that the processes of history and the mechanisms of the subject are continuous with each other. And, moreover, it was Reich himself who said that the main Freudian categories, or at least those categories by which Freud analyzed the mechanisms of the superego, were social categories.

There, I think, lies the methodological hypothesis that can be found throughout this analysis of repression, or of the history of repression. To this methodological hypothesis is linked an explanatory hypothesis: that the great censorship we can see developing in the course of the 16th, 17th, and 18th centuries, to triumph at last in the 19th, can best be seen as an effect caused by the development of capitalism.

Capitalism, at least in its early period, could not afford the luxury of a sexuality that was both visible and verbal. Several reasons have been given for this. The most simpleminded ones, advanced, for example, by Van Hussel, are that capitalism requires a certain number of well-defined mechanisms to assure the reproduction of the labor power it needs to feed perpetually into the labor market. This called for the organization and rigorous coding of a conjugal family oriented entirely around the production of children, i.e. the reproduction of labor power. Get married and have a lot of children to help boost production.

This explanation runs up against a number of blatant historical difficulties—the fact, for instance, that birth control got started in Europe at exactly the same time as the great development of capitalism at the end of the 18th century. To this rather simplistic explanation one could oppose the one given by Reich a long time ago, when he explained that sexual repression was necessary for capitalism because the latter had to mobilize individuals' psychic forces for the job of the suppression of sexuality. Once occupied with internal tasks, the individual's psychological forces would no longer be available for external political and social tasks like rebellions, political struggle, etc.

The disciplining of individuals during the capitalist period would have taken place, according to Reich, because of this need to mobilize psychological energy for the suppression of sexuality. It makes little difference whether you accept Reich's explanation or Van Hussel's: in general we can say that according to this schema there was a period from the end of the 18th century to the beginning of the 20th, during which we lived under Capitalism the Repressor. Thus there would have been a sort of propensity toward Victorianism essential to capitalist society, at least during its first phase. The only love that capitalism can stand is love for Queen Victoria or a love within the boundaries of her modesty.

These are considerable themes, they have had a very great political importance for the last fifty years, and I do not plan to discuss them here. There can be no question of dismissing them with a few pirouettes. For fifty years Sex-Politik has been sustained by this analysis; for fifty years the struggle for sexual liberation has been animated by these themes.

All of this should be taken into consideration, even if it is easy to denounce a sort of facile, barely disguised Hegelianism behind it: capitalism, the negative moment, bound for a proximate *Aufhebung*. All right, at the risk of passing for a pessimist, I will say that capitalism is a great deal more than this, that it is not just a negative moment. It is this notion of repression that I would like to try to analyze, because it seems to run through all the historical analyses that have been attempted according to the Reichian schema. It is the demolition or at any rate the putting into question of this notion that I would like to sketch out now.

Under the notion of repression I think we can group a number of important postulates, namely:

First postulate (which is, I believe, necessarily at work in the entire repressive discourse I've been talking about): there is a necessary parallelism, a simultaneity, an interlocking between, on the one hand, the rejection of desire or the drive *(la pulsion)* from reality, and, on the other hand, their exclusion outside discourse and discursive practices.

When the Reichians (which I mean in a very general sense) speak of repression, they always assume that to silence and to forbid, to exclude from discourse and to exclude from reality, are, on the whole, in the end, the same thing. They suppose that what is involved is all kinds of ways of barring sexuality access to manifestation, whether this is manifestation in reality or manifestation in discourse.

It seems to me that the analysis of repression within this schema always more or less assumes the use of this somewhat confused notion of manifestation. Repression would be whatever keeps sexuality from manifesting itself either in discourse or in reality.

And it seems to me that in the same way they fit the analysis of historical processes, they fit the analysis of what happened to sexuality and its repression at the end of the 18th century, into a sort of "hysterical" model; that is, they suppose that in this period a sort of mechanism of hysterical suppression got started, for which we can to some extent find the law and the scale model among real people who are hysterics.

We can also understand why in this analysis it is absolutely necessary to find a sort of point of articulation between, on the one hand, that which allows exclusion from the order of reality, and, on the other, that which allows exclusion from the order of discourse. Whence the need to find a support either in the symbolic field or in the signifying chain, a symbolic field and a signifying chain that are at once linguistic structures and supports for reality. The notion of the signifying chain makes it possible to think in a single thought both the rejection of the drive outside reality and its exclusion from the field of discourse.

What I would like to show is that mechanisms of rejection are without a doubt all the more powerful for the very fact that they operate through more widely deployed discursive practices; in other words, we can suppose that discourse—the discourse that names, that describes, that designates, that analyzes, that recounts, that metaphorizes, etc.—constitutes the field of the object and at the same time creates power effects that make it possible for subjugation to take place. In a word, it would be a question of disconnecting barriers in the order of reality from exclusions in the order of discourse; and we would have to look in the direction of the deployment of discourse, in the direction of its very abundance, for the barrier-mechanisms that are at work in reality. And at the same time we would have to abandon the hysterical model and we would also have to replace exclusion outside the signifying chain (as an analytical category) by the deployment of discourses and of their power effects.

Consequently, it would be necessary to envisage a history of sexuality that would take for its basic model not a simultaneous blocking both in the order of discourse and in the order of reality, but, on the contrary, that would take as its point of attack the newer effects that come into being through the very deployment and overabundance of discourse. In other words: the more talking goes on, the more power there is; and it is not power that reduces speech to silence.

A second postulate which I think is linked to the notion of repression, and is equally present throughout the analyses made in the name of anti-repressive discourse:

In all the analyses that I have been talking about and from which I want to differentiate myself, *power* is always analyzed in a reduced, schematic—I was going to say pejorative—at any rate, a *negative* form. Which is to say that these analyses assume that power exerts itself basically in the form of an interdiction and an exclusion: thou shalt not say, thou shalt not do. In this we are supposed to have the essential aspect of the mechanism of power; in a word, penal law would be the very essence of power in its exercise and it is precisely the importance given to the law that allows all the mechanisms of power to be absorbed into the thin, schematic, empty form of the interdiction, the ban. Repression would then be power acting as the law of interdiction, pursuing and prosecuting all those who violate the ban.

In the first postulate we immediately noticed the use of a hysterical model to make an analysis of historical processes. And indeed it seems to me that here, by reducing power to the law and the law to a taboo, the Reichian approach has fit the analysis of historical processes into the model that psychoanalysis developed to analyze obsessional neurosis and the legalistic niceties of its mechanism.

Now it seems to me that power does something very different from just *forbidding*. And this is precisely what makes it so formidable, what makes it so difficult to defend oneself from it and triumph over it. Things would be very nice and political work would be very easy if the essential role and function of power was just to say no, if the only role and function of power was to prevent and exclude.

But what gives power its force, what makes it so hard to get around and master, is that power is positive in its effects. Power invents, power creates, power produces. It produces more than a law that forbids desire—it produces desire itself, power induces and produces desire, power gives desire its objects, power, indeed, is desirable. Power not only produces desire; to an equal degree, and this goes much farther, beyond the law that is imposed on the subject, power produces the very form of the subject, it produces what makes up the subject. The form the subject takes is, precisely, determined by power. Power produces desire and the subject.

Power must not be seen simply as law and interdiction. Power relations point out the lines of desire, positions for the subject, places of enunciation, fields of objectification, etc. Rather than reducing the exercise of power to the single juridical and legalistic form of the interdiction, I think we must try to analyze it in military rather than juridical terms, in terms of strategy and tactics. Whence, if you will, a second imperative, a second methodological prescription that I would propose: to study the strategies of power rather than the interdictions of the law.

A third postulate linked to the notion of repression and assumed when one does an anti-repressive analysis:

This postulate is that power, especially repressive power, would always and essentially produce effects of misrecognition (*meconnaissance*). In acting as a ban, in barring access to manifestation, the major effect of repressive power would be to prevent the formation of knowledge: to prevent it in the strongest sense, by producing the unconscious; or to prevent it in a weaker and more superficial sense, by bringing about a whole series of effects on the order of denial of reality, ignorance, blindness, or false consciousness.

In brief, the major effect of power would be *not knowing*, or at any rate the impossibility of access to the truth. Power would be that which bars access to the truth. And it strikes me that here, just as we noted in the use of the hysterical model and the model of obsessional neurosis, the Reichians apply a model to historical material which was constructed to deal with the mechanisms of denial and misrecognition among paranoiacs.

So, I think that the hysterical model, the obsessional model, the paranoiac model are what we find behind the three great postulates that are linked to the use of the notion of repression:

The first postulate, the symbolic chain which allows both exclusion outside of reality and exclusion outside of discourse.

The second postulate, which confounds or merges the exercise of power and the application of taboos.

Finally, the third postulate, which supposes that wherever there is power the green grass of knowledge cannot grow.

Now, I wonder if it wouldn't be possible, just as we reversed the first two postulates, to also reverse the last one and say that power, with the discursive practices that bear it and pronounce its effects, is the producer of knowledge. Power not only creates true discourses, but what is much more important, it creates the constraints that allow us to separate true discourse from false discourse.

And, consequently, instead of denouncing the misrecognitions that we would like to blame on the interdiction, we should try to reconstitute and study the ties that might exist among strategies of power, discursive practices, and the production of knowledge. This is the third methodological prescription that I would propose.

Thus the history of sexuality would not be the analysis of the mechanisms that have repressed it and buried it in darkness since the 17th century, that have sworn it to silence, to interdiction and misrecognition. The historical study of sexuality would be the analysis of the discursive practices and the knowledge that allowed the strategies of power to invade (*investir*) this sexuality.

It would therefore mean the abandonment of the whole set of notions that are necessarily at work in an analysis in the negative terms of repression, the symbolic and manifestation, the law and the interdiction, the unconscious and misrecognition, to get rid of all this and try to begin an analysis of discourses, strategies, and knowledge.

One more word before turning to how this sort of analysis can be done. A word on how it is that analysis in terms of repression could have received such privileges for such a long time—why these privileges were granted to the law, interdiction, misrecognition, in the deciphering of the historical process.

There are good reasons for this. I could mention several, but there is one that I want to insist on: this is what I will call the payoff (*le bénéfice*) of the enunciator. A payoff that must be taken into consideration is the critique of a discourse, but which must not be understood as the personal interest of the individual who is speaking.

To situate the enunciator's payoff within anti-repressive discourse I will say this: the first postulate linked to the notion of repression (the postulate of parallelism between exclusion from discourse and exclusion from reality) allows whoever is making the analysis of repression, whoever is discoursing on anti-repressive themes, to think and make others think is real whatever he can observe as an event in discourse; or, again, it lets him think and makes others think that what appears, what reappears, what returns in his own discourse at the moment he speaks also returns in reality, precisely because it is working inside a symbolic chain in which the effects of discourse are at the same time effects of reality.

At one blow the enunciator, he who is speaking the anti-repressive discourse, gives his discourse a sort of fundamental justification and a kind of immediate access to reality: *What I say in my discourse is at the same time inscribed in reality.* Quite a payoff.

The second postulate (the postulate that reduces the effects of power to the form of an interdiction) allows the analyst who is speaking an anti-repressive discourse to think and make others think that the lifting of the interdiction is an attack on the fundamental mechanisms of power. This postulate lets him valorize all transgressions of the law, those he formulates in his discourse and eventually those that he practices, as an immediate subversion of power.

Finally, the third and last postulate (the postulate of a link between power effects and misrecognitions) lets him valorize his own discourse about truth as being liberating and disalienating, that is, that analyses of repression in the style I have been talking about permit whoever performs them to define for himself, immediately and therefore in a utopian way, a subversive position: I am speaking, so they'd better watch out.

This is the position of him who only speaks, and whose discourse alone is supposed to produce truth beyond all power, to leap the ban at a single bound, attain a new law, and bring about real effects.

This position, as you have no doubt recognized, is held every day in well-known institutions, by both the professor and the psychoanalyst. Basically, in using the notion of repression, one puts oneself in relation to history, in relation to society, in relation to reality, in the position of what I might call the professorial analyst, at the same time in the professor's armchair and behind the analyst's couch. One becomes the professorial analyst of culture, condemned to do nothing else, and enraptured by having nothing to do but to speak in place of, or to make speak, the silence of hysterics, of undergraduates, and all of history's speechless oppressed, speak.

It lets one do nothing else, and be enraptured by having nothing else to do than to alleviate the legalistic scruples of obsessive neurotics (if you're a psychoanalyst), the zeal of graduate students (if you're a professor), or the obsequiousness of loquacious moralists (if you're a historian), by presenting the example of one's own verbal dance.

Finally, this allows the denunciation by a critique in terms of truth of denials of the paranoiac (if you're a psychiatrist), the misrecognitions of faculty colleagues who are always fooling themselves (if you're a professor), ideology (if you're a historian)—all of these provide ways to bring power effects back into one's own discourse.

So this is what I would call, in general, the "enunciator's payoffs," payoffs assured to whoever speaks by means of "anti-repressive" theory, which he himself is helping to develop. These conditions explain the fact that "anti-repressive" discourse would be a genre that circulates so obstinately between university auditorium and analytic couch.

Let us try now to look at how to begin the analysis of these enigmatic historical processes that involve the status, the functioning, the "repression" of sexuality.

If I have been led to try (without, of course, any guarantee of the outcome) to get rid of this notion of repression, it is because I actually found myself faced with a very simple empirical difficulty: repression, silencing, the whole mechanism by which sexuality is supposed to have been banished both from discourse and from reality since the 17th century—I looked for it, and I didn't find it. Certainly when rummaging through juridical works one can find plenty of strict, severe, cruel, barbaric laws on adultery, rape, the corruption of minors, homosexuality, etc. But when one tries to see what their juridical effects have been, it is very surprising to find that although these famous laws on adultery, dating from the end of the Middle Ages, have produced a certain number of condemnations per year, a certain number of confessions, a considerable number of commitments to convents—still all of this is not very serious, and you could hardly say that we have pinned down the mechanism of repression. Everyone knows that homosexuals were burned at the stake until Cambacérès (for his own personal reasons) had the law against homosexuality removed from the French penal code in 1810—it looks like you, too, are going to benefit from this in the next few days. Now, up until 1789, homosexuals were supposed to end up at the stake; in fact, how many homosexuals were actually condemned to the stake in a country like France in the 15th century? A few individuals—not a few individuals a year, but a few individuals a century. Which doesn't say much for the honor of the sect, even if "a few individuals" are quite enough for it to stand.

Thus, at this level it is very difficult to grasp the mechanism of repression itself; and, on the other hand, while the mechanism of repression and the way it really works escape us (above all from the 17th century on, the beginning of the period of Victorianism), we can observe a number of other, remarkable things. This one first of all: birth control, destined for such great import both in history and in the very biology of the human species, was empirically a popular practice, which developed among the peasants of England and the south of France during the second half of the 18th century. Consequently, the knowledge of birth control, the exchange of instruction, information, techniques, all were developing at a time that is supposed to be the period of absolute interdiction.

This same epoch saw the development of illegitimate birth as an institution, and the development of infanticide, and above all this was a period that witnessed the growth of a mass of discourse about sexuality. From the 18th century on, we are dealing with a veritable explosion of sexual discourse. Of course, this didn't appear out of a situation of total silence; and one can say, or at least one can suppose, that literature became a bit more prudish at this time, but after all, literature is only one infinitely limited part of the immense field of discursive practices.

While literature may have been more modest, sexuality was bursting into a whole series of other kinds of discourses, including scientific discourse. It was at this moment that demography appeared. Sexuality made an equally important entry into medicine in the 18th century; it entered into biology in the 17th and 18th centuries. And not only do we see it taking its place in a whole series of new discourses, but we also see it appearing on the horizon of a whole series of preoccupations: the texts of urban planners and architects, for example, at the end of the 18th century, are haunted by the problem of sexuality; and philanthropists, who were the first social workers, were haunted by sexuality. They thought about nothing else; they talked about nothing else. The 18th century is also the period when we see the sexuality of the child and the adolescent become a problem.

I certainly don't intend to make this explosion of discourse, of knowledge, of information, of controls, of preoccupations about sexuality, into a proof for some kind of liberation. We are dealing with something else—but what we are dealing with is not a simple repression, and the notion of a simple repression that is also a silencing and the beginning of an age of prudery is out of the question. I believe, if you will, that it is time to put an end to this kind of dualism, of Manichaeism, which puts discourse, freedom, truth, broad daylight on one side, and on the other silence, repression, ignorance, night.

Instead of making this division we must try to reunite all these elements and describe what I would call a technological constellation (*ensemble*), which would be a three-dimensional constellation including discourse, knowledge, and power, within which modern sexuality would have been caught (I was going to say "produced"), that is, both invaded and controlled, constituted as an object, formulated in "truth" and defined as an object, as the target of a possible knowledge. Sexuality was not "repressed"—I would say rather that it was "expressed," not in the sense that it finally got translated into words, but in the sense that at that moment a discourse on sexuality came into being: a discourse on sexuality that was at once a power relationship and an object relation. The theme, the general form of this piece of work would consequently be not the repression of sexuality as a fundamental mechanism that we must start from to understand all the others; the theme of this research should be the ensemble of the technology of sexuality or the ensemble of explicit sexual systems.

Two remarks preliminary to this study:

1. Interdiction, barriers, silences, definitely had their place in this technological ensemble, but instead of being its kernel, instead of constituting the very center of the mechanism, it seems to me that this ensemble (barring, exclusion, etc.) is only one part of the mechanism. For example, the mere fact of sexual repression in literary discourse does not mean that the contemporary growth of discourse on sexuality in the sciences, medicine, etc., was a derivation from, or a compensation for literature.

What we have to try to consider is the ensemble constituted both by the discourses in which sexuality does not appear and by the other simultaneous discourses in which, on the contrary, sexuality does appear under a certain form. It is this relationship among discourses, this inter-discursive framework or web, that we should try to analyze, without determining the point where or the moment when sexuality is not given the privilege of being the root cause of everything else. In the same way, it is not a question of explaining brothels by Queen Victoria and saying that, of course, sexuality had to pop up in brothels since it had been marked by repression and prudery; instead, we should begin to see brothels and Queen Victoria as twin brothers.

2. Certainly this technology of sexuality was not first invented in the 18th century in European society.

Every society has its own sexual technology, its forms of discourse, knowledge, and power concerning sexuality.

In this third and final section of my talk, I am going to try and show you how I see the general form of this sexual technology, whose reality I would like to put in place of the rather dull and dismal notion of repression.

What is the sexual technology within which we are living? I will mention only four of its essential traits. The first trait did not begin in the 18th century; it is far older than that …

The first trait is already found in the Middle Ages; it is the fact that in the Western world sexuality is not something that isn't talked about. On the contrary it is something that is talked about a great deal, even something that *has to be talked about*. That is, one must talk about one's sexuality and talk about it in a specific way: within a very precise discursive operation, that of *confession* (*l'aveu*). In the West sexuality has not been something that you hide but something that you confess. And it is to the degree that sexuality has been caught within the techniques of confession that it must consequently become silent at a particular moment or in a particular situation.

Thus, we would have to do a whole history of confession since the Middle Ages:

—the judicial confession, of fairly recent importance (the Inquisition)

—the penitential confession, also recent

—the confession of sins against the sixth and ninth commandments. These led to a whole series of very intricate and precise elaborations of technique to find out how, in what conditions, why this confession should be made …

In any case, confession was certainly one of the parts of the apparatus into which sexuality penetrated. Even in theology and in the priesthood, this sexual confession worked its way in, in more and more subtle forms, and it is the obligation to make this confession that we will find prolonged and displaced, from the 18th century on, in a completely different context—that of medical power and familial power.

A very clear example of this is provided by masturbation. Between 1720 and 1760, masturbation became one of the great European problems, one could say the major problem of medical psychology. One of the themes that immediately appeared was that in order to cure someone of this new disease, it was absolutely necessary that he confess it. You could find out whether he masturbated, you could find out the remedies to cure him, you could learn the techniques to keep him from doing it, but in the end he could never be cured if he didn't confess. And throughout the huge mass of literature put out by the anti-masturbation crusade for a century, you can find advice to parents on how to drag a confession out of their children, how to creep into junior's bedroom at night or in the morning on tiptoe; there were even handbooks to describe the color of the stain according to types of sheet … A technique for the confession of sexuality by child to parents doubled, controlled by the confession to the doctor—for the doctor too had to get a confession. In fact one very interesting book written at the beginning of the 19th century says that it's not enough to make a confession to the family, nor even enough to make one to the family doctor—in order to cure, confession must be made to a doctor specializing in sexuality.

This same confessional technique appears in general medicine at the end of the 18th century. This same technique of confession, transposed into the Christian technique, will be taken up again and put in control of psychiatry, with a far wider scope and greater rigor. In 19th-century psychiatry, the sexual confession became one of the cornerstones of the "curative" operation. It is this same confessional practice that Freud brought back in the technique of psychoanalysis.

So you see that, for the last six or seven centuries, sexuality has been less something that you do than something that you confess, by which and through which are established a whole set of obligatory procedures of elocution, enunciation, and confession; the obligations of silence are doubtless the counterpart of these. So that is what the first trait of this technology of sexuality is: sexuality is something that must be talked about inside a ritual discourse organized around a power relationship.

The second trait, more recent in the technology of sexuality, is what I will call the tendency toward somatization.

What I mean is this: if you take the legislation, the constraints and obligations of discourse about sexuality that appear in confessional manuals up to about the middle of the 16th century, you will see that the only thing that was considered, the only thing that had to be confessed, the only thing that had to be controlled, the only thing that was pertinent in any way for discourse on sexuality and its power over sexuality, was what had to do with the relationship between individuals. People were supposed to confess to adultery, to rape, to incest, sodomy, bestiality; the question was who you had sexual relations with and what kind of relations they were, how you got an orgasm, etc. ...

Now, starting in the 16th century, we can see the appearance and the growing importance of a sin which was certainly part of the traditional list, but in the midst of others. This was the sin of *la mollitiesse*, i.e. of masturbation, of caressing oneself. And if this was a sin in the priesthood and the moral theology of the Middle Ages and the Renaissance, it was because it too was a relational sin. You were supposed to have a sexual relationship with someone, yet you reached the "effusio seminis" outside such a relationship. It is a sin against the relationship by default.

Starting in the 16th century, this sin takes on a completely different position, related to a completely different function. *Mollitiesse*, no longer masturbation itself as much as the caress of oneself, relations with one's own body, bodily complicity in one's own desire, is on its way to becoming the definitive sin of lust. The violation of the sixth and ninth commandments was no longer having a wicked relationship with a married woman or a forbidden woman, the first sin was to have directed hand or gaze to oneself. In moral theology, the relationship with one's own body became the heart and root of all the sins of lust; this is what becomes the pertinent element of any confession, and in 16th- and 17th-century confessional manuals, the confessor is told to always ask the penitent first of all about sins against the sixth commandment: *Did you happen to stroke yourself? Did your hand end up somewhere it shouldn't?*

So the body becomes present, the relationship with one's own body, and at the same time the entire body becomes the object of sexual observation and sexual control. Sexuality is not what links you with someone else by a carnal relationship, but something that implicates the entire body; and, parallel to this, a whole new kind of analysis is coming into being, in which desire, concupiscence, complicity, consent, imagination, will all be put through an extraordinarily fine analysis, an extremely precise grid that will constitute, if you will, the global organization of the desiring body. It is this desiring body and no longer the forbidden relationship that will be the object of the new sexual technology that is getting established in the 17th century.

Desire and the body, desire in the body, the body as the place of desire, as the surface and volume of the deployment of desire—it is this, and no longer the relation to another and the law, that prescribes or forbids that relation, which I think is the target of this technology.

This transformation takes place at the same time as the increase in control over individuals by the mechanisms of sermons, confessions, direction of the conscience. It corresponds to the establishment of a widespread, subtle, analytical power that defines individuals as individuals and constitutes them as individuals on the level of their bodies. From the 17th century on, it is the body as a whole that is to be accounted for in sexuality, in the knowledge of sexuality, in the power exercised over sexuality.

The third trait: the "pedocentrism" that dates from the 18th century. From this time on, the privileged point of control, of discourse, and of knowledge of sexuality, will be the child. The 18th century literally invented childhood sexuality. It was the 18th century that constituted it both as an object of knowledge and as the target for power relations, for control.

The first form of this technology of infantile sexuality was a campaign against masturbation beginning around 1710–20 in England, 1740 in Germany, and 1760 in France. Its interest lies in the fact that there we see joined, on the one hand, the old practice of the examination of conscience and, on the other hand, the obligation of confession, and, thirdly, the disciplinary technique of surveillance, particularly in schools and high schools. The consequences of this episode were capital for three reasons. First, the colonization of sexuality by medicine: for the first time sexuality becomes a medical object and the doctor obtains the privileged right of observation vis-à-vis sexuality. The second major consequence is that the sexuality of the child receives a causal power that is, in a sense, limitless since infantile masturbation is thought to lead to and entail innumerable pathologies up until one's last days. The third consequence, finally, the family in the restricted sense, i.e. the mother and the father, are made responsible for the life and for the health of their child through their sexuality. Watching over this childhood sexuality, observing it, diagnosing it, discovering it when it is hidden, has now become a fundamental obligation of the parents. Parents, in their children, don't merely have an heir, they have before them and within their group a sexual object. Through the intermediary of the controls that weigh on the child's body, the familial space has become, from the 18th century on, a sexually saturated space. The prohibition against masturbation, which is a fundamental ethnological fact in our society—doubtless more important than the prohibition against incest—has as a correlative the obligation of incestuous intention on the part of the parents towards their child. In our society, the prohibition against masturbation as a relation of pleasure is doubled by an obligation of incest as a relation of power.

The fourth trait that joins all the others is the fact that the sexual technology is constituted at the beginning of the 19th century as a *scientia sexualis*. Doubtless every society has constituted for itself a knowledge of sexuality, but one can distinguish two major types of sexual knowledge: the first type which would be an *ars erotica*, and whose example is to be found in ancient China. Here I am referring to Von Gulick's book. In this case, the knowledge of sexuality has as its basic function the intensification of pleasure. This knowledge is in a relation with medicine, but this medicine is understood as a technique of medicines and drugs, as an art of intensifying sensations by prolonging life. This knowledge is also linked to pedagogy, but the latter is understood as an initiation and a transmission of the secret. In the West, on the contrary, the *scientia sexualis* does not have the function of intensifying pleasure, but rather that of causing relations of power to function in the finest and most intricate elements of the body and its conduct. Sexuality is linked to truth, not because it would be an access to truth, but because truth permits access to sexuality and permits its subjugation as an object.

We can now trace some consequences of all this:

First, in relation to Freud, we can point out the sexual etiology of behavior problems, infantile sexuality, a libido and a desire that are not fixed to a procreative, heterosexual relationship, and a practice of sexual discursivity in the form of a confession. These things existed before Freud, not as a theory but as constituent elements of this particular technology of this specific arrangement of discourse, knowledge, and power, which took over sexuality in our society in the 18th century.

Secondly, this sketch of the history of sexual technology shows that what has happened since the 18th century is an immense explosion, a continuing explosion, on the question of sexuality, and that it is impossible to reduce this event to a simple silencing, to the mechanisms of the law, to interdictions and censorship.

We are dealing with a complex strategy that connects the exercise of power and the constitution of knowledge, that connects relations of subjugation and object relations. Consequently, anti-repressive discourse seems inadequate to account for the history of sexuality.

William Burroughs Q&A

What is a schizo-culture according to you?

WILLIAM BURROUGHS: Well, I think the "schizo-culture" here is being used in rather a special sense. Not referring rather to clinical schizophrenia but to the fact that the culture is divided up into all sorts of classes and groups, etc., and that some of the old lines are breaking down, and that this is a healthy sign.

Do you think that too much concentration is being placed in our culture on identifying, describing, you know, saying "This is this," and this kind of a description of what exactly our culture is, "What are we?" like, you know, as opposed to past cultures that maybe were more preoccupied with basic arts and, you know, cultural uh…

BURROUGHS: Well yes, this defining, etc., is a luxury that the affluent society permits itself. I mean, poor people in Morocco and Spain and places like that are just too busy keeping alive to think about what they are, who they are …

Can I ask one thing? What do you think of all this fascism? [audience laughter]

BURROUGHS: Ah, well … *[chuckles]*

And if… we have been told that we are, and how they interpret the fact that they are fascist if they are.

BURROUGHS: Well, every question is different, and poses a different problem.

Just because it would be stupid to call in the army, that's no reassurance that they won't call in the army. All the examples seem like cases where they were least likely to before.

BURROUGHS: Every time they have done so they have regretted it. I don't say that they won't. I say they'll regret it if they do. Because some of these people have read history, after all. They know what happened in the Roman Republic, they know what happened in Germany, and to a lesser extent what happened in Spain, all those places ...

It seems your analysis is based on one good thing, and that is hoping for enlightened self-interest amongst leaders. Seems that one hitch in what you said, that you need to work out is, if we get an insane leader ...

BURROUGHS: Yes. Which has happened, a number of times.

Well, I mean, I don't really know if this cultural revolution you talked about has helped things along ... [indistinct] and I don't understand what the content of what you've said has to do with the rest of this lecture, this series. And I mean, I don't understand what this lack of censorship is trying to do. I mean, this is what we've been talking about all day, that these things, I mean, all these cultural revolutions, we are fooling ourselves, that's the whole joke.

BURROUGHS: Well, are we fooling ourselves? These are very serious concessions that are being made. Remember that all censorship is political, and when they start removing censorship they have made a concession, and that's important. Don't expect to get everything all at once, because you won't—yeah?

A lot of your analysis was in terms of the limits of the use of control—what about, which you mentioned in passing when answering his question, what about the demand for control, in the sense of the demand to be controlled? Don't you think that in some sense if fascism is to develop it has to develop either through a growth in the demand to be controlled or, more subtly you might say, in the growth of the control of the demand to be controlled?

BURROUGHS: I ... don't quite follow you. *[audience laughter]*

No, but that's what I'm saying, is that, I mean, as you get a greater and greater amount of co-operation, it's quite obvious that a lot of people get freaked out by it, and people have a great problem dealing with change, so I mean obviously they're going to want something to control that change and slow it down. Now, if the impasses that you've described are correct, the leadership has to control that demand to slow down change, and 'cause that could always get out of hand, and from your analysis it would seem that if it did get out of hand that would create exactly the kind of situations where they would have to exercise the sorts of repression that would be suicidal for them to exercise. You see, and that's how even giving them the assumptions of rationality you are forgetting about insane leaders, and things still could get out of hand.

BURROUGHS: Well, of course, I said that. They're never more dangerous than when embarking on a self-defeating course. That's what happens. It's unlikely that it would happen unless we got in some kind of war, I mean a serious war.

Do you think that it's happening now is what I really want to ask you …

BURROUGHS: No, I don't think so.

I have a related question. You said that you were optimistic, that is, we have every reason to believe this change will continue in its present direction. You also said that "they," I guess you were referring to the leaders, are not in fact to take back any of their concessions. Are we to then assume that this is to culminate in a complete lack of control, at some point in the future, or rather, I think more pragmatically, is that there is going to be a trade-off point?

BURROUGHS: Trade-off point. I think there will be continued modifications of control. They can't very well take everything back at this point.

What do you mean by "continued modifications"?

BURROUGHS: Well, what we have seen in the last thirty years. Now even ten or twenty years ago there was no right to protest, even the right to protest is a very important concession. A minority group thirty years ago had absolutely no recourse against police brutality or anything else. Now they can protest and that undoubtedly has had an effect.

So are we to assume that there will be a culmination of this general direction, resulting in a total lack of control?

BURROUGHS: Ah well, I wouldn't … I mean, I'm not a prophet; I wouldn't speculate about the future. I'm talking about what has happened up until now.

This seems to be a sort of big boom theory of history, with sort of a continual diffusion of power, and theoretically I mean it would seem to come down to this area of total noncontrol or … But it seems clear also that what we know until now is that societies can reconstitute themselves at high levels of control, and I think that's what some of the earlier questions were about—you've defined some of the techniques by which governments or those in power maintain their control but … And you also defined a situation where one group would want to re-establish or establish control, but what you don't seem to have spoken to as far of the question was, what the specific techniques of this re-establishing or establishing controls would be when there is a low level of control.

BURROUGHS: Well, it depends on what you mean by "low level of control"—if you have complete anarchy, such as we might have if we got in a war with China, and this country was subject to atom bombing, the control reverts to almost a mediaeval or warlord state, where anyone with a small army is in a pretty good position. If that's what you mean by when control reaches a state when it doesn't exist, well then you do get warlords and city states in that kind of a situation.

Yeah, but we're not in the Middle Ages any more, I mean, that might've been, we may be able to explain how power was reconstituted in the Middle Ages, but how would you see that happening now, I mean, do you see it happening in the very same way?

BURROUGHS: *[Interrupting]* It isn't happening now. It isn't happening now. We're not anywhere near that, we're not in a state of anarchy.

But you don't see that point coming?

BURROUGHS: Well, I could see it coming under certain circumstances. I could see it coming if we got in a war; I could see it coming with a complete economic collapse. But none of these things are right here now, or even around the corner.

Can you envision a complex social organization where control doesn't exist?

BURROUGHS: Uhm, no, not with regard to a heterogeneous city population. I mean, there is, a certain control is absolutely necessary. Where's all the food come from here—it's brought in, right? There's a whole unseen bureaucracy that is bringing that food in, and putting it in the shops, it's providing power, etc. If those people didn't work, millions of people would be starving overnight. So any system must find a way to keep those people on their jobs, whether economically or giving them food coupons, or whatever.

But your presentation was from the standpoint of controllers and exploitation, and are those necessarily connected?

BURROUGHS: No, I mean, I wouldn't say that you would say that the necessity of maintaining power and food in a big city was necessarily a part of exploitation …

[Shouted] Down with Foucault!

[Audience laughter]

BURROUGHS: *[Chuckling]* Hear hear … well, okay …

SYLVÈRE LOTRINGER: I would like to thank very much Mr. William Burroughs, and I'd like to make an announcement. I'm sure you're all well aware that Michel Foucault won't speak tonight as planned, I'm sorry to say so. Michel Foucault wanted to avoid having to go through a heavy translation session, and he had his paper read this afternoon, late this afternoon, and I'm sorry for people who were not aware of this fact.

[Audience noise]

LOTRINGER: Okay. Michel Foucault will be part of the panel tomorrow morning and I would like you, if possible, to be right on time—we will start on time tomorrow morning because R. D. Laing will be coming for just a few hours from Boston, and we will start as planned at 9:30, so be on time. Thank you.

Where?

LOTRINGER: Here, right here, 9:30 tomorrow. Thank you.

[Applause]

FEMALE VOICE: Can I have your attention?

Schizo-Culture

Feminist Theory, Feminist Practice

Christine Maurice, Angeline Goreau and others

. . . .

We propose, first of all, to situate our workshop on feminism within the structure of this colloquium and to discuss the ways in which it corresponds to the position of women intellectuals within the univesity and, more broadly, knowledge, culture and discourse itself. We will compare the different directions that femin ism as an intellectual movement has taken in Franee and America. We will elaborate their respective positions toward the problematice of developing an analysis that provides an alternative to the "objective," scientific production of knowledge. Since women have been virtually excluded from intellectual tradition, how can we have access to a structure which has denied us a role in its history; how can we develop our own language, our own voice, our own theoretical stance without reproducing the ideology and analytical terms of the dominant discourse.

What are the theoretical bases, either explicit or unstated, of the texts most important to feminism in America: Kate Millet's Sexual Politics, Shulamith Firestone's Dialectic of Sex, Simone de Beavoir's Second Sex , and others. For example, we will discuss different views of the problem of reproduction(biological), of women's role in production (work), and the conditions of material life. This will tie together out theories of theory and practice of theory.

SAT. 6:00 PM 136 THOMPSON

R.D. Laing, Howie Harp, Judy Clark, Michel Foucault

Roundtable on Prisons and Psychiatry

RONALD D. LAING: We are talking about what we do to people who lose whatever protection they can get in our society. When that protection is lost, we see how unbridled the attack on people is.

Supposing someone is mentally ill, then all the more reason not to be treated in that way. All the more reason not to attack people with terror and add more of the same. The most prevailing anxiety, terror, fear that I find going around the world is another thing that has got no name for it. What most people are frightened of is other people. We are frightened of each other. And we have got good reason to be frightened of each other because we can see what happens to any of us when other people have got the chance to do us in. They do us in. If one is in a position of not being able to defend oneself (l suppose you could call that being mentally ill, in our society) then there is all the more chance that one will be done in.

People come to London from all over the world in the hope of finding some place where they can just get into, where the heat will be off, where they are not going to be walked over. No one is going to do anything to them and there is no hassle. It is a place where it is not against the law to be terrified, or to feel. A lack of feeling of and for each other is what is cultured in our society. When I was last over in this country, I met a lot of students and was asked a lot of questions on everything from Transcendental Meditation to Behavior Modification. The single most frequent question I was asked though was: "How do we get in touch with our feelings?" People feel their feelings have become numb.

What we call tranquilizers were originally employed on rats and laboratory animals. You first try these things out on some remote population, say Kashmir East, then you try them out on prisoners, especially black prisoners; then you try them out on mental patients, then you try them out on ourselves, on our own children. These drugs were employed, and are still employed as a chemical variable to enhance conditionability. In other words, they are drugs that were introduced into the human population because they were found to make rats more amenable to be conditioned. And of course you have to have a nice term, which has got nothing to do with their reality: you call them "tranquilizers." They are not tranquilizers, they are drugs of conditionability.

In England, there was only one chair of psychiatry before World War I. A psychiatrist then wrote a paper called "The Economic Use of Manpower in the British Army." We ought, he said, to treat soldiers in the same way we treat tanks and the rest of our equipment. A doctor once told me, when my wife wasn't very well: you should take better care of your wife, she is your most important single piece of equipment... We instrumentize ourselves, we mechanize ourselves. We are not, however, just analogues of machines, we are machines, but rather poorly constructed machines, all that gristle and flesh and so on, we are not nearly as functionally effective as a real, proper machine, we are a rather inadequate machine. But we've got to be aware of the ideological warfare, we've got to be aware of the whole nexus. It's not just a matter of winning one victory: although this is very important. As soon as they have got to stop hacking up people in one domain, then it goes on in another way. Every time it gets a bit more subtle, every time it gets a bit more technicalized and, from their point of view, effective.

To keep one's feelings going and still act upon them and challenge the system in whatever skilful means it presents itself through a comprehensive awareness of the nature of our society as a whole, is very largely a function of the intellectual. This isn't a trivial function, it does cut ice, it does make a difference. It is an endless task but this doesn't mean that we are going to let the bastards get away with it.

HOWIE HARP: I would like to add that if there is such a thing as "mental illness" I believe that it is a reaction to present social and economic conditions. A normal reaction to abnormal conditions.

In this society, showing emotions is considered a weakness or a sign of instability. In order to be considered "normal", you have to go to work, to school, you have to become some sort of a machine or a robot. Many people in society, as a result, never get a chance to express themselves, to express their creativity.

There is such a thing as problems in living and sometimes it manifests itself in people being "incoherent" and "psychotic", and all these kinds of things. As

R.D. Laing said, it all depends how you treat this, and my opinion is that when someone goes through a psychotic break or a schizophrenic reaction, I think it's a *learning experience*. I don't think it should be called mental illness, it should be called just that: a learning experience, a change in a person's head. There is no such thing as an emotional disturbance that has no relationship at all to the outside environment. I personally believe that everything we think, everything we feel is directly caused by our environment. We live in a very repressive society, and in this society it's very easy to freak out, or rather it is very hard to freak out because you end up in a hospital... But a lot of people want to freak out. Very often I ask people, as I would ask people in this audience, how many of you have at one time or another wanted to get up and start yelling and screaming? I'm sure that everyone here has wanted to do that. But how many people have actually done it?

LAING: It's an extraordinary society where yelling and screaming are regarded as freaking out! It's a perfectly natural thing to do. It's one of the things that anyone normally adjusted to the world should do: to raise one's voice to full volume at least once or twice a day. But that's called freaking out...

HARP: That's called freaking out in our society and when you do it, you're locked up, you're given Thorazine, shock treatment, seclusion, restraint, psychosurgery, alienation, etc. People have problems, people have emotional crises and inasmuch as psychology has any value, it brings about some understanding of the workings of the human mind. It is one thing, though, to understand what's going on in the mind and it is another to place value judgements on it, such as: this is abnormal-sick, this is normal-healthy. In doing this, the practice of psychology becomes oppressive and a knowledge that psychology holds becomes abused. Institutional psychiatry is the total abuse of that knowledge, since it coercively enforces those value judgements on the individuals. I believe, from my own experiences as well as those of hundreds of people I have known, that no one freaks out without any relationship at all to what has been going on in their lives. We should not put the blame on the individual and say: there is something wrong with you. We at Project Release start out by saying: O.K., if you're upset, what's going on in your life that's causing you to be upset. In this society, institutional psychiatry lays the blame and lays the emphasis on the individual and not on the environment, on society as a whole. If somebody's upset, we ask: where are you not being treated the way you should be, or where are you being prevented from doing something you want to do? I've worked in crisis centers and I have found that it is a better way to deal with people's problems.

As far as the genetic root of illness, I've heard a lot about that. As a matter of fact, I was put in an institution for a few months to try to prove that my mental illness was genetic because a lot of my relatives had been in mental hospitals: I was sort of following a family tradition… I don't know of anybody in this room who doesn't have some kind of chemical imbalance because of the processed food we eat, with all its chemicals and the pollution in the air. If vitamins can help solve this chemical imbalance, if they work, fine. When someone is upset, it has been shown that there is a *change* in his chemical make-up. But whether this is an imbalance is quite another thing…

I just resent anybody telling me that I'm mentally ill because my mother's mentally ill. I think it's a lot of bullshit. I think my mother was reacting to very oppressive conditions, and so was I.

JUDY CLARK: I want to follow up on some of the things Howie Harp was saying. People look for some abstract situation when the basic realities of society are taken away. They wonder if there is a chemical imbalance, if there is something that is genetic because they don't look at the basic realities.

The lives of the people I work with in the prison movement were determined from the time they were born. It was determined that they would end up in a series of institutions. It usually started out at youth homes, oftentimes with a stopover in a mental institution, and ended up in the prison. The basic conditions that will determine you ending up there have to do with poverty.

People who are trained to work in those institutions are part of them. They are taught to hate the patients, to hate the inmates, to hate the kids who are in those institutions. Professionals are made to be antisocial beings. We are all social animals but, what you are taught to do in colleges like this is to separate yourself out and hate those you are treating or those you are housing, or those you are guarding. The main thing professionals do is to not separate themselves out. There are basic social movements going on from the bottom up in every one of those institutions. They can begin to identify with those base-up movements of resistance instead of going through a lot of intellectual trauma about "Is there a use for me in this society?" Well, the use is to resocialize ourselves, resocialize people who have become professionals by embedding ourselves more in the realities, and in that reality of existence that people from the base up are involved in. In this city, in every institution, in every hospital, there is a mounting pressure and a mounting resistance and professionals are needed to be a part of it, not separated from it.

One way you are trained in this university is to hate the environment around you. When I used to live in New York City, Columbia University was a very political institution. When I came back from jail, I was shocked to find there was a student rally on this campus asking for more police to protect them from the community around them. This is what students in these institutions are being taught to do, to feel that they need to be protected from communities around them that are pretty angry because of what has been done in their lives by these institutions.

LAING: I would like to make two brief responses to the question of heredity and mental illness. My last book is a detailed analysis of some of the work done on so-called genetics. I don't think a single piece of scientific work ever established anywhere that the so-called schizophrenia is a genetic condition. All these studies beg the very questions we are challenging, and I don't think it stands up to a detailed critique.

My second response is that we certainly are social beings and our chemistry is social. The idea that our chemistry somehow happens in some arcane, in some environmental isolated place, that it has nothing to do with other people and with our social environment is absolutely ridiculous.

Just as much as our thinking is always in relationship to the world, so is our chemistry, our minds, our emotions. There is nothing that changes the chemistry of my body so much as going into a safe room, an easy welcoming situation. If it is a tight, anxious, hostile environment, then I am sure that a needle in my veins would record the fluctuations of my chemistry, it would also be changing. Studies of chemistry should be studies of *social* chemistry. Chemists haven't gotten around to that and sociologists haven't got around to that. This is a purely artificial development: we section ourselves up, we institutionalize these sections, we study bits and pieces and then we try to put it all together! When so-called tranquilizers first came into a mental hospital in the fifties, I remember a staff meeting in which one of the patients, a so-called manic woman, was discussed. She had been put on a lot of tranquilizers. A woman in the staff asked: "Do these new drugs have any effect on height?" She was asked what she exactly meant. Well, she said, I am sure this woman shrunk at least three inches since she was on tranquilizers. This is a very interesting observation in a social system. You put a chemical in the body of one person and through a mediating link this actually affects the perception of someone else on a quantitative as well as a qualitative way. When you put chemistry into the skin of a person, not only is that person's chemistry social but this is a social act because it's affecting the whole social system. Until we get such an awareness, until it leads to some decent research on this subject, we haven't got anywhere to go.

MICHEL FOUCAULT: I completely agree with what Ronald Laing said about the power of the medical profession, and the extension of it at the present time. On the basis of these two authorities, therefore, Howie Harp and Ronald Laing, I would like to introduce a problem which is perhaps still alien, too alien, to many occupations.

A few days ago I was in Latin America, in Brazil, where, as you know, there are a large number of political prisoners. Several hundred journalists, students, professors, intellectuals and lawyers have been arrested there during these last few weeks. And in Brazil, of course, arrested also means tortured. But one thing is quite remarkable. It seemed that recently, techniques of torture have been developed and perfected to a considerable extent with the help of American technicians. One of the characteristics of the new techniques of torture is this: the person who does the torturing is not the same as the one who poses the questions. Someone sits in one room with just a computer in front of him, and, on the basis of the computer, determines what questions he should put to the victim. He then writes the question down and transmits it to another person, his subordinate, who applies the torture in another room until the answer is obtained. Once he gets an answer, it is fed back into the computer to verify whether it is consistent with information already obtained.

Forgive this digression which appears to be speaking only incidentally about mental hospitals and not about medicine at all. Except that a new character has been introduced in this new technique, which is now constantly present in the ritual of torture: the doctor. A doctor is now present at practically all the important tortures. His role is first of all to say what torture will be most effective, and, secondly, to give medical examinations to make sure that the patient is not a heart case, for example, and in risk of dying. Thirdly, the doctor administers various kinds of injections to revive the patient so that he can physically withstand the tortures and, at the same time, suffer them psychologically in the harshest manner.

This is certainly just one example of what happens in many other countries of the world besides Latin America. So, on this basis, I would like to make a few remarks. I am completely astonished—well, not astonished in fact, but apparently, rhetorically, astonished—to see how fiercely the different medical associations of the world, be they in the United States, France, Europe, South America—how carefully they claim the right to determine themselves, for the doctor, the rights of life and death. Look what happened in France with abortion. The doctors said: our profession consists in preserving life and must never decide in favor of death. Look what happened in the United States in the case that was judged four or five days ago, the Quinlin case, where the doctors said: "we are committed to preserving life and to not causing death in any event." Do you ever see these medical associations which get so aroused about abortion denounce the political role of medicine in the prisons, the police stations, the torture chambers? Is there a group or association of doctors that demands the exclusion of doctors who serve this kind of function, from the medical profession?

I should add that in these torture sessions not just general doctors serve as technical advisers, but also sometimes psychiatrists, and even psychoanalysts. In Rio there is a psychoanalyst who belongs to, shall we say, the most sophisticated school of psychoanalysis and who is an official adviser to the police on torture. I do not think that this Freudian school has ever denounced this person.

Since we have before us the example of a group which defends former mental patients, do you not think one could create an association of people, tied to medicine in one way or another, either as doctors, nurses, students, etc., whose function and role it would be to denounce, wherever it might occur, this explicit, effective, nominal, individual collaboration of doctors with police practices?

The other thing I would like to add is this. It seems to me that the participation of doctors in politics and judicial affairs poses a whole series of serious questions in a more general way than in the examples I have just said. I think that the role of psychiatrist-experts in law courts is not a medical activity at all. It is impossible to give a medical meaning to the diagnosis, judgement, description or clinical picture given by an expert in a criminal law court. The medical-legal discourse is not medical at all, but completely legal. Since, at the moment, we are talking about a critique of medical power, don't you think right now would be the time to begin a specific action against the presence and functioning of the medical person in legal and police practices?

I will end simply with a question: what, in your opinion, is the best method to use, the best kind of organization to choose to begin this action at a local level as well as a national or international one?

CLARK: I want to talk about the prison movement in the United States. I work on a paper called "Midnight Special." It is written by prisoners and sent back into the prisons all over the country. The movement is very developed. It involves widely different activities, from study groups to breaking down the class divisions and racist usages inside prisons, up to the events that hit the headlines when rebellions occur. I could talk about the whole spectrum of reality within the prisons. I will choose, within the context of this conference, to talk about oppression inside the prison system: behavior modification.

Behavior modification is the use of physical and psychological terror against people who are organizing inside and rebelling against the conditions inside. It began as a reform under the basic assumption that prisoners are in prison not because they can't survive on the streets, but because of some maladjustments. So they should be readjusted. This is a very new trend that has taken over a lot of the prisons inside. It happens in many women's prisons, in the State prisons and it's most highly developed in the Federal prison system—first in Springfield, Missouri, and then in Marion, Illinois under the Start Program and the Care Program. A new prison in Butler, North Carolina was set up as an institute where prisoners will be sent from all over the country. They will experiment on them, try various methods against them.

When we first got letters in "Midnight Special" about behavior modification, they came from places like Vacaville in California. They were using shock treatment and drugs as well as certain kinds of "therapeutic means" against prisoners. Nerve-deadening drugs administered would create a deathlike state. They have permanent effects on people. I have worked with people who have been administered these drugs over the years, and it affects their central nervous system, it affects their capability of operating, it creates paranoia, and that was at the first onslaught what they began to use. A lot of that was exposed in California a few years ago. A number of psychiatrists who were involved in these programs finally freaked out, they were using torture methods against prisoners. They attended a big psychological conference in California and exposed it, and a movement started to be built against the use of these kinds of drugs.

Then we started to get letters that informed us that this program had a lot more to it than just the use of drugs, that it was a more subtle kind of development. The best example was the Start Program in Marion, Illinois, and what they do is exactly what they say they are trying to do: they are trying to modify the behavior of prisoners. First of all, who was sent to those programs? The people who have been actively organizing inside. Many prisoners who were involved in the Attica rebellion or in political work inside, or detained on political charges, were sent to a behavior modification program they tried to start in New York State. This is a step-by-step program. You're first thrown into a strip cell where you have nothing. You have no clothes, no recreation, no reading materials. You are not allowed to receive letters from the outside. You're not allowed to talk to anyone else. You have no privileges. Then they give you certain ways to show that you will be cooperative. If you're not cooperative, you're kept in step one. You never leave it. If you are cooperative, you get to step two.

What cooperation usually means is that you will involve yourself in therapy groups. What they do in these therapy groups, the main tactic they use is *attack* therapy. People in a group will be informed of your own history, on your childhood, on various realities in your life. The group will focus on one person, and you are supposed to scream at him about these things in his past, about these practices that are terrible, that are "anti-social," or against the prison administration. If you don't accept this role you are thrown back into the strip cell. If you do accept it, you are allowed into step two of a program.

In step two, you get a few more privileges. You get your clothes back, or a better diet. You will be able to see a doctor if there is anything wrong with your medical care. Maybe you will be able to get letters from your family. You have more privileges, but also more responsibilities. Behavior modification is just that: if you modify your behavior, if you do exactly what they tell you to do and attack new people coming into the programs, you can get to the next step. You can't go before a parole board and get out of prison until you get to the last step of this program.

The program is designed to break down the will of people inside; it forces them to see each other, and to maintain unity with each other, as their only means of survival. This is exactly what it means to modify your behavior. It means to cooperate with the administration against other prisoners. The end result is to produce someone who will follow the rules of a prison and therefore, when let out, follow the rules of society no matter what the rules are in the prison and when you get out. Someone who will turn against those who are in your same situation. What it teaches you, in other words, is pure capitalist ethic: the way you get ahead is to stamp on someone below you.

That system is being used in many places now. Most people who go into those programs, though, will not accept the system. So they are put in "control units." Control units are what they always had inside prisons, that is, segregation. You are kept in there; you are in isolation and you never get out of that isolation. There are rules in prisons according to which people should not be put into permanent isolation. Isolation is a punishment; they have to give you a hearing to prove that there is a reason to punish you before they can put you in these kinds of units. But since these are behavior modification programs, they say that it is not for punishment, it is for your own treatment that they are putting you into them! Whatever due process exists inside the prisons is eliminated in the name of therapy. They actually keep people in isolation for years and years.

There is a lawsuit in Marion Penitentiary against the use of long-term segregation and the control unit. Two years ago the struggle against the Start Program culminated. It began when they sent six prisoners into the Start Program, including a prisoner named Eddy Sanchez, who is a guy who had been in jail most of his life, who started out when he was a kid. When Eddy got inside he knew that this was a hook-up and he was not going to accept it. He organized six other people, three black men, two Puerto Ricans and one white man, who refused to have anything to do with the program. Three years ago they went on a 42-day hunger strike. They got the word to the outside and people started writing letters to Norman Carlson, who was at that time the head of the Federal Bureau of Prisons. They began to develop momentum against the program by taking the kind of stand they did, which is a pretty extreme stand, of refusing to eat for 42 days. They felt it was the only way they could dramatize the situation. And they were successful. It began to develop into a movement. As a result, they were chained to their beds and beaten, then thrown back into their cells. They set fire to their cells. Each time they did something, the administration would respond, and they would counter-respond while word would be going to the outside so that the pressure would mount both from the inside and from outside. Their example disrupted the entire situation because the whole program is based on setting up the kind of coercive situation that will force everyone to go along with the game. These people wouldn't go along with the game, no matter what they did to them, and it mounted into a movement inside the Start Program as well as outside. Eddy is a fantastic writer, and a great strategist. He just sent out word all over the country and Carlson found himself with letters mounting up by the hundreds to his office, and with psychiatrists calling him up and with law students calling him up and lawyers filing suits. People inside were able to successfully mount that kind of campaign but with great risk to their own lives.

Eventually a suit was put into court that broke open and allowed liberal psychologists and also church groups to come inside the prisons to check out what were the conditions of these therapeutic programs. What they found was that they were horror shows! There is no way that you could define them as "treatment." Evidence started to come out in court and the prison system had to close down the Start Program. That was a major victory, and it was won by a lot of blood and struggle.

When they closed down Start, they tried to say, "Well, we found out that a few things were wrong with this kind of program, so we closed this one down." So now everyone can go home and forget about it. But in fact what they did was to decentralize these programs and put them all over the different prisons instead of keeping them in one. They also kept all the people who were in the control unit in Marion in the control unit. Some people have been in isolation cells in Marion, Illinois for over three years… There's a suit fighting the use of the control unit as a mere continuation of the behavior modification technique meant to isolate the most political elements inside from the rest of the population. Hearings on that suit took place all summer long. Some of it hit the press, but most of it didn't. And we're still waiting for a decision.

Behavior modification is called a reform because instead of "hacks", guards (we call them "hacks" inside, that is, going up through the ranks and becoming wardens of prisons) now psychologists are becoming wardens of prisons. That is true in Marion and it is true in Butler, North Carolina. It amounts to show that, "We're bringing in real professionals who really know, they're not just going to use brute force, they are professionals!" It throws some strange light on the use of professionals or what professionals will allow themselves to be used to do inside the prisons.

The other reason for developing the Butler Center in North Carolina is that the personnel used in these experimental programs come from the three universities in the area, including Duke University. Students who learn psychological means and methods are actually being used to develop terror campaigns inside Butler, North Carolina. Butler really is the crystallization of all these various techniques. They will use drugs, they will use the most outright kind of psychological means, and they will also use the whole step-by-step program. In Butler you start out in cold isolation and if you graduate all the way through you end up on the part of the prison grounds that looks like a college campus. If you go along with the game, you end up being rehabilitated, you end up in the true

American dream of being on a college campus. What you have to do is simply to go along with the technique of putting down people who are with you. This is why they make it like a college campus. They say they want to help people learn how to survive on the outside, get them used to the kind of lives they could live if they became normal citizens in the United States of America. So they take people who were first inside prisons because they are black, Third World and poor, and they say they are helping them get used to life on the outside by ending up being on this college campus. Now you know, and I know, that it is not the type of life on the outside that people who are in prison, or most people who aren't in prison, have to learn to survive with when they get outside. They may graduate to this college campus inside, but when they get outside they are going to graduate to welfare, the unemployment lines, to methadone centers, and to the streets. They have learned very little about survival on the outside. What they have learned is that what the Man says is: "You play my game or you get your ass kicked!" This is a big movement inside right now and one of the reasons we are trying to develop it as a movement is the fact that the ultimate tool of these kinds of reforms is to set people up against each other. We see this as just one dimension of what they use on the outside all the time. Prisoners think that it is important for them to resist inside these behavior modification programs if these can be instituted inside, they will be instituted on the outside.

It is actually just one step from utilizing them in schools. A prisoner once wrote to us that he was in a behavior modification program being given drugs inside. His son was defined as a hyperactive child on the outside and was being given Ritalin. He said, "What's the difference? The reason I have got to resist inside is that they just practice inside what they are going to use on the population on the outside..."

Another area where behavior modification comes down very sharply is in women's prisons. There is definitely something wrong with everyone who goes as far as the administration is concerned, but particularly so for a woman. It means that she is anti-social, she is not playing her role. As a result, they often don't use the same kind of physical terror against women inside. Rather psychological terror. The use of drugs inside of women's prisons is enormous. When I was at Cook County Jail, the doctor came in to see us once a week. If there was anything wrong with you on a Monday, that was your problem. He wasn't going to come until Thursday anyway. When you did finally get to see him, there were two drugs he gave out. One was aspirin. They did give you aspirin. And the other was Thorazine.

Many people are inside because they are drug addicts. They kick heroin when they are inside, but they get addicted to drugs like Thorazine. Thorazine is used on a massive scale because it slows people down, it slows their reactions down so it keeps them quiet, keeps them muted. When people are rebellious, especially when they get into fights they will give them intravenous Thorazine. They call it "drug assaults." These are used massively in women's prisons. In many women's jails, you can't ever come before the Parole board unless you are first willing to see a psychiatrist for a certain amount of time.

In Bedford Hills, which is the State Women's penitentiary in New York, there was a mounting resistance around a whole lot of conditions inside. They said: "What is wrong with these women who are complaining about bad medical care is that they have psychological problems." They took six of the ringleaders and they sent them to Mattawan State Hospital, which is a mental hospital. One of them was a woman named Carol Crux. She is a small woman but very powerful, and she beat up a couple of guards. They then assaulted her. They sent eleven male guards into her cell one night and they beat the shit out of her. The other women on her wing heard that she was being beaten up so the next day, when they were in the yard, they refused to go back into the cells. They said, "We won't go until we can go to the warden and see what happened to Carol Crux. Why did they do what they did to Carol Crux?" That was what precipitated them sending six of those sisters to Mattawan. Most of those women had no one on the outside to fight for them, so they did it without any kind of legal redress. They were sent to Mattawan and immediately put on high doses of drugs. The only thing that stopped it is that these women just were not going to take them.

Bronx Legal Services, which is a community organization in the Bronx, took up the case of these women and managed to get it into Federal Court. The courts are not going to institute a great ruling for these women, but they have become a way of exposing what is happening inside. Women were able to come on the stand to testify about what had been going on against them, the drugs that were being used against them and the long-term segregation that was inflicted on them without due process. This is something prisons don't like, when word about it gets outside because pressure from the outside starts to mount up. Eventually they won that suit and the women were sent back to Bedford. What you find inside, therefore, is the development of a very terrifying institution of behavior modification.

It has many different manifestations besides the step-by-step programs I described and use of drugs. We learned a lot from prisoners. People who developed these programs studied the use of brainwashing techniques during warfare on prisoners of war in different countries. They wrote up all the various techniques they found successful in breaking people's will to survive, to resist, to act as individuals. They listed, I think, 22 techniques. For instance, prisoners would never receive their mail. Then the guards would tell the prisoners, "Oh, your people on the outside are abandoning you." Or simply the use of deprivation, perceptual deprivation—being kept inside a strip cell. Not only are you isolated from other people but you hear no voices. Sometimes a light will be kept on 24 hours a day. Sometimes the light will be off for a week, so that you lose your sense of time and space. These techniques have only one goal: to break down people's own individual capacities and spirits.

On the one hand, it is very terrifying. On the other hand, what you learn from the prison system is that they can set up the most monolithic and terrifying kinds of systems of oppression; people will continue to resist them. The human spirit does not get broken. It maintains itself by building a unity among each other. People define the problem and understand it. They analyze the conditions used against them and realize that their major weapon is their own unity. They realize that their unity is in fact greater than the technology used against them and that, in the protracted struggle, the prisoners will win. This is a lesson that we could put to use on the outside. The more you learn about this lesson, the more you can respond to it both by looking at our own lives and the way our behavior is modified in this society. Whether people's resistance inside will survive technology developed to break our spirits as human beings is thus a key question to us.

When I get letters from Eddy Sanchez, I feel I have a large stake in his capability of resisting. It is a mirror image; it reflects my own sense of my capability of resisting. The fact that Eddy has almost singlehandedly been able to mount the kind of campaign he has, gather the kind of support he has, been able to disrupt even his being kept in isolation in a State prison in Washington state is a victory to people's ability to resist.

The reason I wanted to focus on behavior modificiation is that it is liberals who are instituting that technique, and it's professionals who are utilizing it in the name of developing a more humane kind of system. It teaches us what professionalism and the sciences mean in this society, how they get distorted, the way they are utilized and what we can do to resist. They know now whatever they use will be found out by people and that pressure on the outside will mount against it.

FOUCAULT: The problem for the generation which turned twenty in the 1930s was how to fight fascism, how to fight the fascists, how to fight the different forms, the different milieux in which fascism appeared. Depending on the balance of powers, depending on the global political and economic situation, forms of struggle, the struggle against fascism between the years 1930 and 1945 was a specific kind of struggle. I think that what has happened since 1960 is characterized by the appearance of new forms of fascism, new forms of fascist consciousness, new forms of description of fascism, and new forms of the fight against fascism. And the role of the intellectual, since the sixties, has been precisely to situate, in terms of his or her own experiences, competence, personal choices, desire—situate him or herself in such a way as to both make apparent forms of fascism which are unfortunately not recognized, or too easily tolerated, to describe them, to try to render them intolerable, and to define the specific form of struggle that can be undertaken against fascism.

Look, for example, at what has been happening concerning psychiatry and mental hospitals. You have a whole series of works which were essentially concerned, ostensibly, with either the actual functioning of hospitals, their origin, or their psychiatric effects, yet at the same time these works have all been tied to forms of contestation, of struggle, of transformation of medical practice. The same thing can be said about the work that has been done on prisons. If you compare, for example, the reform projects that emerged during the last hundred years with what has been happening during the last ten years, you see considerable differences. For the last ten years the problem of prisons has been posed in terms which are theoretical and practical at the same time, descriptive and organizational terms, if you will, and to that extent I think the question "Are you a writer or a militant?" is passé today. And in any case, the specificity of what has been undertaken recently precludes theoretical or historical analysis being separate from concrete struggle.

The problem I posed a little while ago concerning Brazil is not a question about what I, as an individual, can do about the current situation in Brazil. Medicine functions in some kind of police or judicial capacity in all countries. What would be interesting, I think, would be to determine just what kinds of struggle could be undertaken in each country against the medical participation in repressive legal institutions.

Félix Guattari

Notes on Power and Meaning

There is an entire technology of power. Even the syntactic, relational, and other meanings proceed from there. The primacy of the micropolitical pragmatics over the phonological, syntactic, and semantic components of language. The primacy of the formations of power over the unconscious:

—Starting always from the subject and the object
—Imposing a reference point
—Squashing the multiplicities
—Making the flows translatable
—Paradigmatizing expression
—Policing speech, bringing order to writing
—Matching up the words, the phonemes, disciplining them, making them shape up and toe the line
—Guaranteeing the hegemony of a language—and especially a national language—as a machine of power, as the locale for a conjunction, and making translatable all of the local formations of power

Semiotic subjugation on all levels: body—socius—gestures—mimicry—speech—attitudes—glances—dance—tears—organs—a license to drive—a license to fuck—watch what you're saying—don't talk to me in that tone of voice.

The unconscious is structured like a language to the extent, and only to the extent, that it falls into the clutches of a formation of power. The unconscious is structured by the formations of power. Unless, that is, it escapes language to work on the same level as the asignifying semiotic flows and the material flows of all sorts. Power does not, it no longer exists outside the meaningful, significant secretions. This does not mean that one then falls into nonsense, anarchy, guilty and incestuous indifference.

It's the opposite of any and everything!

—Connections that cover all directions
—A highly accurate diagrammatism
—A way out from empty redundancies
—Sign-cosmos-socius connections

Along with meanings, all of the powers that exist over the body, the other, the sexual partner, the brother, the militant, and the citizen entertained relations of genealogical filiation.

It is impossible to break the chain of power-hierarchy-impotization-castration without assembling a concrete machine of another type: diagrammatic conjunction of the material, semiotic and social flows according to a nonmeaningful, nonsignificant, noninterpretative, nonsubjectifying relationship.

Refrain, wherever possible, from the desire to lower oneself into the structures of the dominant unconscious. Produce the unconscious. Refuse to induce or deduce it. Against the dominant meanings, even the slightest escape from meaning, the rupture of a block of childhood, a weird desire, something funny like that for no reason ...

No simple oppositions: schizo/parano, revolution/fascism. Give foolishness its place. Buddhists, Maoists-masochists, Stalino-vegetarians, anarcho-Catholics ... the same battle! Help the bureaucrats out—"Can we be of help to you old buddy!" Microfascism is a lot less hard to come by than macrofascism. "Keep cool, take it easy!"

Keep in mind the micro, first in yourself and all around you. Otherwise you run the risk of losing sight of the macro.

Félix Guattari

Molecular Revolutions and Q&A

There are a number of things I would like to share and discuss with you now, but I get the feeling that I could talk about absolutely anything—my private life, how I vote—except desire or revolution. They would seem truly obscene here at Columbia University.

It has reached the point where I wonder if one wouldn't really have to be a member of the CIA in order to undertake such a thing. There is something like a CIA virus here that seems to have contaminated many people and that keeps recurring at different times, and I cant help asking myself whether I haven't caught the bug.

If one could get beyond these walls or through this muffling that constitutes a sort of wall of sound within the university, I think one might begin to recognize that the world crisis is accelerating at a considerable pace. Am I simply caught up in an accelerating schizo-process? For some years now we have been experiencing a process comparable to that of 1929—a full range of regional conflicts, of local political confrontations, of economic crises. There are no extreme, salient characters of a Hitler or Mussolini magnitude on the political scene right now, yet extermination camps do exist. The entire country of Bangladesh is such a camp; thousands, tens of thousands of people are dying there, or on the verge of it, because they are locked in a particular economic situation, which results from a specific governmental policy, and no alternatives exist except being exterminated. I do believe that a whole series of factors are leading to an absolute crisis at all levels of social organization throughout the world. This situation should call for revolutionary solutions, but nothing, no one, no organization is prepared to deal with it and its imperatives. The obscene thesis I wish to defend before you now is this: all these organizations—Bolshevik, Marxist-Leninist, communist,

Spontaneist (in one form or another), Social Democratic—are missing an essential aspect of this revolutionary struggle and its development.

There are two ways of rejecting the revolution. The first is to refuse to see it where it exists; the second is to see it where it manifestly will not occur. These are, in a nutshell, the reformist and the dogmatic pathways. Indeed, a revolution of great amplitude is developing today, but at the molecular or microscopic level.

I believe that this molecular revolution can only develop in a parallel way with the general political crisis. Some people say that the social turmoil in the United States during the 1960s, or in France in '68, was a spontaneist event—transitory, marginal—and that such a utopian revolution leads nowhere. But in my opinion, important things began happening only after that revolution, which perhaps was the last revolution in the old style. Molecular revolution develops in relatively unknown areas. Gilles Deleuze was just telling us there isn't much to try to understand. We see students rebelling, playing at the barricades. We see teenagers changing life in the high schools. We see prisoners setting half the French prisons on fire. We see the President of the French Republic shaking hands with the prisoners. Women's revolts are moving in all sorts of directions, at many levels: against inherited politics, on the problem of abortion, on the question of prostitution. We see the struggles of immigrants or ethnic minorities, the struggle of homosexuals, of drug users, of mental patients. We even find previously unimaginable social categories being mobilized in France, for example some judges …

When we put this all together on the table, side by side, we may ask: What does all this have in common? Can we use all this to start a revolution? Does this have anything to do, for example, with what is going on right now in Portugal, where officers of the colonial army are playing the Cohn-Bendits? We can certainly dismiss these phenomena as marginal, try to recoup them as excess force, which is precisely the attitude most of the groupuscules have; or—and this is my hypothesis—we can assume that the molecular revolution of which I spoke is located and developing here in an irreversible manner and that each time these movements fail because the old forms and structures of organization take power, holding the rhizomatic element of desire in a system of arborescent power. Therefore, the main question for me is a radical change of attitude with regard to political problems. On the one hand, there are the "serious" things one sees in the papers, on television—the questions of power in the parties, the unions, the groupuscules. On the other hand, there are the little things, the things of private life: the militant's wife who stays at home to look after the children, the petty bureaucrat making deals in the corridors of Congress—these are at the root of most political schisms and assume a programmatic aspect, but are invariably linked to the phenomena of bureaucratic investment and the special caste that runs these organizations.

I believe that revolutionary movements, whatever they may be, do not change their orientation because of ideology. Ideology does not weigh very heavily compared to the libidinal trafficking that effectively goes on among all these organizations. It all comes to the same thing: either political objectives are the echo of all kinds of struggles, and are associated with an analysis of the phenomena of desire and of the social unconscious within the present organization, or else the bureaucratic impasses and recuperations will necessarily recur, the desire of the masses and of interest groups will go through representatives, and result from a representation.

We all have experienced these kinds of militant initiatives. We should be able to understand why things work that way, why desire is being delegated to representatives and bureaucrats of all kinds, why revolutionary desire is turned into organizational microfascism.

Certainly there must be a more powerful investment that comes to replace revolutionary desire. My explanation, provisionally, arises from the fact that capitalist power is not only exercised in the economic domain and through the subjugation of class, nor is it exercised only through police, foremen, teachers, and professors, but also on another front which I would call the *semiotic subjugation* of all individuals. Children begin learning about capitalism in the cradle, before they have access to speech. They learn to perceive capitalist objects and relations on television, through the family, in the nursery. If they somehow manage to escape semiotic subjugation, then specialized institutions are there to take care of them: psychology, psychoanalysis, to name but two.

Capitalism cannot successfully put together its work force unless it proceeds through a series of semiotic subjugations. The difficult thing—and one that raises a basic theoretical problem—is how to conceive the articulation and unification of struggles on all these fronts: the front of traditional political and social struggle; the liberation of oppressed ethnic groups and regions; linguistic struggles; struggles for a better neighborhood, for a more communal way of life; struggles to change family life or whatever takes the place of it; struggles to change modes of subjugation that recur in couples, whether heterosexual or homosexual. I put all these struggles under the term "microfascist," although I don't particularly like it.

I use it simply because it startles and annoys people. There is a microfascism of one's own body, of one's organs, the kind of bulimia that leads to anorexia, a perceptual bulimia that blinds one to the value of things, except for their exchange value, their use value, to the expense of the values of desire.

This raises an important theoretical question, a question that, for me, Deleuze, and several others, has changed somewhat, lately. We thought the most formidable enemy was psychoanalysis because it reduced all forms of desire to a particular formation, the family. But there is another danger, of which psychoanalysis is but one point of application: it is the reduction of all modes of semiotization. What I call *semiotization* is what happens with perception, with movement in space, with singing, dancing, mimicry, caressing, contact, everything that concerns the body. All these modes of semiotization are being reduced to the dominant language, the language of power, which coordinates its syntactic regulation with speech production in its totality. What one learns at school or in the university is not essentially a content or data, but a behavioral model adapted to certain social castes.

What you require of your students before all else when you make them take an exam is a certain style of semiotic molding, a certain initiation to the given castes. This initiation is all the more brutal in the context of manual formation, with the training of workers. Exams, or the movement from position to position in factory work, always depend on whether one is black, Puerto Rican, or raised in a well-to-do neighborhood, whether one has the right accent, is a man or woman. There are signs of recognition, signs of power that operate during instructional formation, and they are veritable rites of initiation. I have taken the example of the university, but I could easily have taken examples from many other formations of power.

Dominant power extends the semiotic subjugation of individuals unless the struggle is pursued on every front, particularly those of power formations. Most people don't even notice this semiotic subjugation; it's as though they do not want to believe it exists, yet this is what political organizations with all their bureaucrats are about; this is what contributes to create, engender, and maintain all forms of recuperation.

There is something that interests me very much in the United States. It has been happening for a number of years, notably with the beat generation, and is probably due to the very acuteness of the problems concerning the semiotics of the body, of perception. This is much less true in Europe where one is tied down to a certain intellectualist conception of relations and of the unconscious. The various rationalizations or justifications that are given here for reintroducing a semiotics of the body interest me less. Some involve Zen Buddhism, or various forms of technology, like the tai chi that was being done just now on the stage … It seems to me that something is being sought there in some sort of blind way. Blindness takes multiple forms. In France, for example, we have networks of gurus in psycho-analytic societies; we even have a personality like Reverend Moon heading an important psychoanalytic organization. But psychoanalysis only involves a particular set of people. In the United States, apparently, the virus of psychoanalysis has been more or less averted, but I sometimes wonder if its hierarchical systems aren't reproduced in the systems of gurus, the systems for representing desire.

The problem is this: One cannot strive toward a political objective without identifying as well all the microfascisms, all the modes of semiotic subjugation of power that reproduce themselves through that struggle, and no myth of a return to spontaneity or to nature will change anything. However naïvely one assumes to be innocent in this regard, whether in relation to our children, our partner, or our students (for professors), I believe this innocence is equivalent to guilt and engenders guilt. The question is neither of innocence or guilt but of finding the microfascism one harbors in oneself, particularly when one does not see it. The last thing I would want to bring up here, of course, is that it can receive an individual solution. It can only be dealt with a new type of *arrangement of enunciation.* One example of these arrangements of enunciation—an impossible, truly awful arrangement from the vantage point of desire—is that of this room itself, with some individual raised above everyone else, with a prepared discussion which would make it impossible for anyone really to start a discussion. Yesterday I proposed changing the whole format, the whole type of work we are doing here, and to my great surprise, I realized that everyone wanted the conference to remain as it was. Some people even asked for their money back, although no one here was being paid to speak.

At various times there were attempts to produce this kind of dialogue. The only people who came forward to try and start a dialogue—completely phony, but full of real desire—were those who falsely accused us of being CIA agents.

As one invests in the libidinal economy of the micropolitics of desire, of microfascism, so must one precisely identify the alliances and possibilities that exist concretely at the level of political struggles and which are completely different in nature. I once told Jean-Jacques Lebel, regarding his workshop on Portugal, that the judgment one makes concerning the attitude of the Portuguese Communist Party is necessarily different from Spinola's and his own, and yet the mechanisms of bureaucratization and the ignorance about the desire of the masses are comparable in both cases.

Another example: in France we have some groups, gangs, or people who wear swastikas on their backs and who walk around covered with all sorts of fascist insignia. Yet one should not confuse their microfascism with the fascism of political groups like Occident, etc. To the extent that one fights microfascism at the molecular level, one can also prevent it from happening at the level of large political groups. If one believes that each one of us is immunized against microfascist contamination, against semiotic contamination by capitalism, then we can surely expect to see unbridled forms of macrofascism well up.

Q&A[1]

After a systematic attack (at least I think so) on psychoanalysis, Gilles Deleuze and I began asking ourselves about the linguistic and semiotic conceptions underlying formations of power in psychoanalysis, in the university, and in general.

A sort of generalized suppression of what I call the *semiotic components of expression* takes place in a certain type of writing, such that even when people speak, they speak as if they were writing. At the same time, the rules of their speech not only depend on a certain syntax, but on a certain *law of writing.*

Unlike primitive societies, our society doesn't think much of speech—only writing, writing that is signed, attested. Subjugation in capitalist societies is basically a semiotic subjugation linked to writing. Those who escape writing give up any hope of survival. They end up in specialized institutions. Whether at work or in any other area of life, one must always make sure that the semiotic modes one uses relate to a phenomenon of the law of writing. If I make a gesture, it must relate to a text that says: "Is it appropriate to make this gesture at this point?" If my gesture is incoherent, there will be, as in a computer, some written or digitalized device that will say: "This person may be mad or drugged, perhaps

1. On the second day of the conference Guattari broke up the scheduled panel and half the crowd followed him to a smaller room for discussion—the Q&A included here is taken from that session. Foucault also chose to give his paper at the same session..

we should call the police, or maybe he is a poet: that individual belongs to a certain society and should be referred to a written text." I think, therefore, that the problem posed in this colloquium—whether to read certain texts or not—is basically a problem of the formation of power that goes beyond the university.

Doesn't this relate to what Antonin Artaud said about the written text?

Absolutely. Artaud understood theater and cinema in their multiplicity of semiotic components. Most of the time a film is based on a written text, a script, and the plastic and aural elements are referred to, and alienated from, the text.

Isn't it more a question here of linearity rather than of writing, strictly speaking?

Certainly, or what could be called digitalization, putting everything into digits.

Is the problem of linearity specific to capitalism, or is there a form of writing specific to capital?

Yes, I believe so. The whole evolution of systems of enunciation tends toward the individuation of enunciation and toward the degeneration of collective arrangements of enunciation. In other words, one moves toward a situation where the entirety of complex systems of expression—as in dance, tattoo, mime, etc.—is abandoned for an individuation that implies the position of a speaker and an auditor, such that the only thing that remains of a communication is the transmission of information quantified in "bits." Yet, in another arrangement, the essence of communication is a communication of *desire*. A child who plays, or a lover who courts someone, does not transmit information, he creates a richly expressive situation in which a whole series of semiotic components are involved.

Capitalism refuses to take these components into consideration; what it wants is: (1) people to express themselves in a way that confirms the division of labor; (2) desire to be expressed only in a way that the system can recoup, or only if it is linearized, quantified in systems of production. A number of people here have remarked that linearization is the best way of transmitting data for a given purpose, even in genetic systems. For example, consider what happens in a primitive society when a purchase is made. The purchase is often a body linked to interminable discussions; it is more often like a donation, even though it is presented as an exchange. Today, shopping ideally demands that the salesperson behaves like a computer. Even if the salesperson is someone affable and displays all the iconic components of seduction, she nonetheless seduces according to a precise code. Her skirt must be a certain length, her smile artificial, etc. The best way for capitalism to ensure semiotic subjugation is to encode desire in a linear way. Whether in a factory or a bank, capitalism does not want people who bring the totality of what they are, with their desire and their problems. One doesn't ask them to desire, to be in love, or to be depressed; one asks them to do the work. They must suppress what they feel, what they are, their entire perceptive semiotics, all their problems. To work in capitalist society implies isolating the usable quantity of semiotization which has a precise relation to a law of writing.

That's questioning capitalism in an extremely broad sense.

Clearly, one must also include bureaucratic socialism.

To take up the question of linearity again, what consequence follows, according to you, from the critique and rejection of the Oedipal triangle in Lacan? What is the impact of such a critique in terms of revolutionary action; not just as critical exegesis, but as intellectual praxis?

To me, the Lacanian definition of the unconscious seems particularly pertinent if one remembers that it forgets the unconscious of the capitalist socialist bureaucratic social field. What, in fact, does Lacan say? He says that the unconscious is structured like a language and that a signifier represents the subject for another signifier. One gains access to the unconscious through representation, the symbolic order, the articulation of persons in the symbolic order, through the triangle and castration. In fact, and this is really what it's all about, desire can only exist insofar as it is represented, as it passes through representatives. Otherwise, one falls into the black night of incestuous indifferentiation of drives, etc. For the whole question lies here; if one follows Lacan closely to the end, what does he ultimately say? You accede to desire by the signifier and by castration, and the desire to which you accede is an impossible desire.

I think that Lacan is completely right in terms of the unconscious of the capitalist social field, for as soon as someone represents our desire, as soon as the mother represents the desire of the child, as soon as the teacher represents the desire of the students, as soon as the orator represents the desire of the audience, or the leader, the desire of the followers, or ourselves in our ambition to be something for someone who represents our desire ("I've got to be 'macho,' or else what will she think of me?"), then there is no more desire. I think the position of the subject and the object in the unconscious is one that continually implies not a metaphysical, general subject, but a particular subject, a type of particular object in a definite socioeconomic field. Desire as such escapes the subject as well as the object, and in particular the series of so-called partial objects. Partial objects of psychoanalysis only appear in a repressive field. For those who remember Freud's monograph *Little Hans*, the anal partial object appears when all the other objects have been forbidden, the little girl next door or crossing the street, going for a walk, sleeping with the mother, or masturbating—then, when everything has become impossible, the phobic object appears, the phobic subject appears.

Systems of signification are always linked with formations of power and each time the formations of power intervene in order to provide the significations and the significative behaviors, the goal is always to hierarchize them, to organize and make them compatible with a central formation of power, which is that of the state, of capitalist power mediated by the existence of a national language, the national language being the machine of a system of general law that is differentiated into as many particular languages as will specify the particular positions of each one. The national language is the instrument of translatability which specifies each person's way of speaking. An immigrant does not speak the same way as a teacher, as a woman, as a manager, etc., but in any case each is profiled against a system of general translatability. I do not believe one should separate functions of transmission, of communication, of language, or the functions of the power of law. It is the same type of instrument that institutes a law of syntax, that institutes an economic law, a law of exchange, a law of labor division and alienation, of extortion, of surplus value.

And yet I am so talkative myself that I don't see how one could accuse me of denying language and power. It would be absurd to go to war against power in general. On the contrary, certain types of politics of power, certain types of arrangements of power, certain uses of language, notably national languages, are normalized in the context of a historical situation, which implies the seizure of power by a certain linguistic caste, the destruction of dialects, the rejection of special languages of all kinds—professional as well as infantile or feminine (see Robin Lakoff's study)—I think that is what happens. It would be absurd to oppose desire and power. Desire is power; power is desire. What is at issue is what type of politics is pursued with regard to different linguistic arrangements that exist. Because—and this seems essential to me—capitalist and socialist-bureaucratic power infiltrate and intervene in all modes of individual semiotization today, they proceed more through semiotic subjugation than through direct subjugation by the police or by explicit use of physical pressure. Capitalist power injects a microfascism into all the attitudes of the individuals, into their relation to perception, to the body, to children, to sexual partners, etc. If a struggle can be led against the capitalist system, it can only be done, in my opinion, through combining a struggle—with visible, external objectives—against the power of the bourgeoisie, against its institutions and systems of exploitation, with a thorough understanding of all the semiotic infiltrations on which capital is based. Consequently, each time one detects an area of struggle against bureaucracy in the organizations against reformist politics, etc., one must also see just how much we ourselves are contaminated by, are carriers of, this microfascism. Everything is done, everything organized in what I will call the *individuation of the enunciation*, so that one is prevented from taking up such work, so that an individual is always coiled up in himself, his family, his sexuality, so that such work of liberation is made impossible. Thus, this process of fusing a revolutionary political struggle with analysis is only conceivable on condition that another instrument be forged. In our terminology (i.e., with Gilles Deleuze) this instrument is called a *collective arrangement of enunciation*. This doesn't mean it's necessarily a group: a collective arrangement of enunciation can bring both people and individuals into play—but also machines, organs. This can be a microscopic endeavor, like that of certain characters we find in novels (I am thinking of Beckett's *Molloy*); it can be Transcendental Meditation or a group work. But the collective arrangement of enunciation is not a solution by the group; it is simply an attempt to create opportunities of conjunction between different semiotic components in order that they not be systematically broken, linearized, separated.

In the previous talk, the person who was "discoursing" came to me and said: "If I spoke a long time, all at once, it was because I felt inhibited, because I could not speak." We did not function as a collective arrangement of enunciation; I didn't manage to relate my own inhibition about hearing him with his inhibition about speaking. It always comes back to the idea that if you abandon the discourse of reason, you fall into the black night of passions, of murder, and the dissolution of all social life. But I think the discourse of reason is the pathology, the morbid discourse par excellence. Simply look at what happens in the world, because it is the discourse of reason that is in power everywhere.

In your collective arrangement of enunciation, how do you prevent the reimposition of linearity and syntax?

It would also be absurd to want to suppress the information, the redundancies, the suggestions, the images all the powers-that-be want to suppress. The question, then, is not semiotic, or linguistic, or psychoanalytic—it is political. It consists in asking oneself where the emphasis is put—on the politics of significative redundancy or on the multiple connections of an entirely different nature.

You have to be more precise. You speak of semiotics, of information, of collective arrangements of enunciation, i.e., of linguistics, and then you displace your argumentation from the linguistic or psychological system to that of politics. I no longer follow you.

Each time it is the same thing. Let's take a concrete example: teaching writing in school. The question is often posed in a different, global method. Society being made as it is, even in a completely liberated school, one can hardly imagine refusing to teach children how to write or to recognize linguistic traffic signs. What matters is whether one uses this semiotic apprenticeship to bring together Power and the semiotic subjugation of the individual or if one does something else. What school does is not to transmit information, but to impose a semiotic modeling on the body. And that is political. One must start modeling people in a way that ensures their semiotic receptiveness to the system if one wants them to accept the alienations of the bureaucratic capitalist-socialist system. Otherwise they would not be able to work in factories or offices; they would have to be sent away to asylums, or universities.

Do you completely reject the system of knowledge elaborated by Lacan through linguistics and psychoanalysis?

Completely. I believe Lacan described the unconscious in a capitalist system, in the socialist-bureaucratic system. This constitutes the very ideal of psychoanalysis.

But is it valid as a system for describing this system?

Certainly. Psychoanalytic societies (and this is why we pay them dearly) represent an ideal, a certain model that can have great importance for the other domains of power—in the university and elsewhere—because they represent a way of making sure desire is invested in the signifier and only the signifier, in pure listening, even the silent listening of the analyst. It is the ideal of semiotic subjugation pushed to its highest expression.

According to Nietzsche, one assumes or goes beyond one's own weaknesses in adjusting oneself to them, in refining them. Yet Nietzsche is a reactionary. Is it possible for someone who is a radical to propose going further into psychoanalytic discourse and industrial discourse?

First of all, I am no Nietzschean. Second, I do not think of going beyond my weaknesses. Third, I am soaked to my neck in psychoanalysis and in the university, and I do not see what I could bring to this domain. All the more so since I do not believe that anything can be changed by a transmission of information between speaker and listener. This is not, then, even a problem of ideological striving or of striving for truth, as one could have understood it here. It is simply this: either there will be other types of arrangement of enunciation in which the person will be a small element juxtaposed to something else (beginning with me) or there will be nothing. And worse than nothing: the development of fascism in continuous linear fashion is taking place in many countries, and there you have it.

Ti-Grace Atkinson

The Psyche of Social Movements

The following are long fragments from Ti-Grace Atkinson's lecture preserved in the transcription of the tape. It seemed important to add her voice to the chorus of the conference.

Revolution—I was very interested to hear how often that word was used, tossed about. But I would suggest instead that the struggle between the Psyche and the Mind is a struggle against our past as well as our present. Shall we indeed form a Psyche, that of Greek and Roman mythology, which struggled for a long time with that abstraction, Venus? Both represented beauty and the objectification of women. Will the women's movement continue on its present path until it too falls into the delirium of love, that is, of Cupid? Shall we too choose the ultimate escape—immortality—but through the gains made against (…) Jupiter; the ultimate power of man; the state? I did not choose my words lightly for this evening, but I define my topic as the Psyche of Political Movements.

I left the National Organization for Women in 1968 over an essentially linguistic clarification. It seemed that the leadership as well as the membership of the organization were clashing over every issue, pulling in two different directions. Naturally this brought the organization to a stand still. After some long months of this, some of the key people, who were also struggling with each other, were ready to resort to practically any amount of resolution (…) It occurred to me to inquire about each one's definition of the word revolution since it was over strategy that we seemed to be at odds the most. "Oh God, there goes Grace with her petty academic distinctions again." I almost wished I'd never asked. The definitions of this word were such in their contrarity that it was as if no such referent existed at all. Little did I realize then that that was in fact the case, and the problem. Some women said that revolution meant getting women up into positions of power; this theory assumes it would be possible to sneak 51% of the population past 49%, and ignore the problem of class identification in oppressed classes. Others claimed revolution would end up destroying both the positions and later the very concept itself of power. This linguistic clarification explained why women committed to liberating themselves were pulling in two different directions, although I realized that our analysis (…) was also reflective of the separation. But we were left then with the problem of what to do with our radically different interpretation of the word, if not to mention the reality. Our positions appeared so diametrically opposed that it would seem clear to me that the only solution was to separate. Thus began the new distinction within the women's movement between feminism and radical feminism. But what does revolution really mean? The dictionaries are of remarkably little help, perhaps because above all it is a concept defined by properties. Still, to its extensive meaning, the English Revolution, the American Revolution, the French Revolution, the Chinese Revolution, the Russian Revolution, etc., one component remains constant—the use of violence.

You might wonder why bother to make such an obvious and simple point. The government obviously knows that revolution means violence. [And while feminists for the most part would fight each other to the death for the] right to use the word revolution as a proper description of their aim, scarcely one today would accept as relevant to themselves the verbal concept of violence. There has been much discussion of this subject since 1971 at least. Can you imagine a public debate held with several hundred people discussing whether or not indeed we should use violence as a tactic. This event speaks for itself. An oppressed people depends much upon surprise as a weapon. In fact any revolutionary tactic has this essential feature. And feminists are not fools. Looking back, in view of many such instances in that period it is about this time when the movement chose [the Psyche]. As the seventies have approached, our present day, the mid-'70s, deeply tragic consequences have caught up with the women's movement, even in the midst of its full flight from reality. But then the present situation is so tragic just because of its existence in a vacuum from reality. Somehow it seems most appropriate for me to discuss my last points here at Columbia University; my own political history began while I was studying here, and I have recently been readmitted to the philosophy department to finish the PhD program I started several years ago. In the late '60s one could not be a student here and remain unconversant with the Vietnam War and its issues. (…) I was certainly on the side of the anti-war rally group.

Sometimes I dread coming up here to this campus. I feel as if I'm walking on people's graves. And if I look around it's as if I've been in a time machine; it's hard to believe, given the pastoral attitude of the student that 1969 and 1970 ever really happened. Most unfortunately, even those who were quite active in the anti-war movement seem to have short memories. We used to shout, "Bring the war home," and so it finally came. But instead of meeting that war head-on, on our own territory, most people retreated to their original homes. The war was over. Its end was even celebrated in Sheep Meadow park early this year.[1]

Of course there were still a few odds and ends. People couldn't make the pony. People who had acted in accordance with their words were eventually driven underground. I suppose they have to be afraid in the underground's ranks eventually. I regret it turned out to have to be a woman. But that too was predictable. Jane Abbott surrendered formally to the government in November of last year and cooperated fully. Jane surrendered to Jupiter and was made one with the state. And then the shake-up. The FBI, the grand juries, the arrests of fugitives who remained safely underground for over 4 years. Jane Abbott announced that revolution was specifically violent for feminism—a questionable acquisition for the women's movement at best. (…) When the government hit this movement, terror and panic has prevailed. It is quickly established that the state was the enemy of women, of men, and is not relevant to women.

It obviously followed that the state's [actions] were unreal as well. I quote from a friend of mine, Jill Johnston, in "Bonnies Without Clydes": "cooperation is to believe in the FBI."[2] I kid you not. Please don't misunderstand me. I appreciate the sentiments behind denying the reality of the unpleasant. But a problem remains. What do you do when the FBI knocks on your door and wants to know

1. Sheep Meadow in Central Park, was the site for Vietnam protests involving hundreds of thousands of people.
2. Jill Johnston, "The Myth of Bonnies Without Clydes: Lesbian Feminism and the Male Left." *The Village Voice*, April 28, 1975

any information you might possess concerning known fugitives, and can jam you before a grand jury, give you immunity, put you away for along time if you don't talk. There are obviously several possibilities, but the primary one chosen by the hundreds that I know of is full. I suppose it eases the conscience to know that after all you're only talking to headlights. And then a few of your friends start getting picked up. Like Susan Saxe. These are some of the issues that I've been [occupied with]; this clean-up job is something that I've been working very hard on. I don't know how many of you have seen, how many people here are familiar with who Susan Saxe is? Well, in '69–'70 she is alleged to have participated in a bank [heist in Boston.[3] She was brought to a] political trial, I was on the defence committee. A couple of people in the audience too, we were on it. We had to work very very hard for 6 months. She got [a twelve year sentence].

I was part of the anti-war movement. I don't know whether they lived, but these people need them because the court's very susceptible to public pressure. And certainly people in the academic community in Boston should be accessible to the support of someone like [Susan Saxe] unless when it comes down to it, it's revolution, revolution, revolution, but hey, no guns. Allende tried the trick of making the cultural revolution first. Later on it came up. As I said before, she is not getting support. In the jury project, what they have done [is publicize the case]; she has the highest recognition rate of any person brought to trial in some time. It's 91% recognition rate in Boston. The same as Ford's.[4]

There's nothing that people were doing that seemed to be having any effect on the government. There were massive marches, there was escalation of the resistance. There has been gradually an escalation from a draft resistance, to going to Canada to destruction of property. Now, control yourself. Going to a bank is something we all do. It's simply a question of methods that you use. It is a very standard thing, political act.

(Interruption)

3. Thee FBI arrested the three male participants within days, but they tracked Susan for four and a half years, put her on the FBI's most wanted list. They flooded the communities, interrogated hundreds of women, took them to court. She was picked up in Philadelphia in March and brought to a political trial.
4. Gerald Ford was President of the United States from 1974 to 1977.

Sunday, 9:30 a.m.- Maison Française

FEMINISM AND THERAPY

The only real therapy for women is social revolution. The only force that will change the psychic structure of the female, relieve her suffering and her own role in her own subordination will be the revolutionary transformation of society. Only a revolutionary culture in which women have equal power with men will allow for the development of a concept of self that will permit women to develop her strengths and self worth. The psychology of the female is determined by the needs of the society in which she lives. The internalization of powerlessness, dependency and the need for females to repress their desires for self actualization are the expressions of the ideology and practice of bourgeois patriarchal culture.

The mass struggle for women's liberation since the late 1960's in the USA has had many effects on the psychological experience of women. For the first time in nearly a century american women were affirmed in their unity and struggle to be human to be full people. Feminist therapy comes out of this movement - not out of psychoanalysis and psychotherapy. The late 1960's saw the involvement of thousands and thousands of women in consciousness-raising groups and self-conscious political activity of women. For the first time women located collectively the source of their own powerlessness and craziness - the male dominated societies in which they lived. Every female attitude, action and non-action could then be seen as a response to an oppressive culture not some internal, personal problem. As women grew more united in their struggles against the state, so they also found themselves to be hindered and deprived in their own development. Consciousness-raising named the enemy without, feminist therapy arose to sort out how the enemy got inside.

* * * * *

We plan to present a case which will illustrate some of the themes we see in feminist therapy.

--Susie Orbach
--Lela Zaphiropoulos

MARXISM AND PSYCHOANALYSIS

The workshop proposes to discuss the crucial relation between the theoreis of Marx and Freud an attempts to relate them, xxxx as they concern radical political struggles today.

Xxxxxx theorists Deleuze, Guattari, Goux, Schneider, Baufillard Horkeimer Marcuse will be used to consider such issues as the materialist categories in Freud, the problem of desire for historical materialism, the relation between desie and labor in the _Anti-Oedipus_.
Three short position statements will open discussion.

Sunday Maison francaise 2:30 560 West 113

Sunday, November 16

2:30 to 6:00 P.M. -- 136 Thompson, Teachers College, 120 and Broadway
"Workshop on the Quality of Life in the South Bronx"

***** "WE DON'T FLY COLORS NO MORE" *****

Presents a look inside the people and their conditions of life in the South Bronx.

A series of 96 hours was made with the active help of the young people and Mrs. Arine Alvarez, mother of 8 children and other mothers.

The South Bronx portrays the energy and strength of people trying to make changes in a society which tries to keep them imprisoned in their environment. Dope, gangs, Criminal Justice and urban decay are systems and symptoms of a decaying city inside in which the people struggle to overcome those systems and create alternatives of possibility and joy.

The clarity and honesty of their portraits demonstrate how they survive and live.

The desire of both the children and the adults to make change challenges the society to respond.

Producer Director ....Martine Barrat
Assistant Director ....Charles Shaw
Video Assistants..................Clement Can-
Debby Colman
Stephan Barrat

Artistic Co-Producer ....Wilma Moses

Thanks to the C.E.R.F.I. and especially Felix Guattari for funding to do this project.

David Morris

Schizo-Culture in Its Own Voice

In 1974 Sylvère Lotringer and John Rajchman left New York and the early Semiotext(e) collective—then a semiotics discussion group at Columbia University—to spend a year in France. Rajchman recalls: "I was a graduate student. Semiotext(e) started as this structuralist, Russian formalist group, with different tendencies … I was on a slightly different wavelength to that, so when Sylvère decided to push in this other direction I was a natural ally.… The seventies in the two places, New York and Paris, was a very interesting time, and we were sort of connecting the wires between these two things."[1] As Sylvère has explained, his general idea was to stage a Semiotext(e) event and to introduce some then-unknown French thinkers to the United States, but really they had no idea what they were doing, or what was to come.

"So we devised a cast of characters, and the idea of having this kind of 'encounter' structure, and we went back to New York."[2] It was a fine opportunity to put some post-'68 ideas into practice: inviting speakers from diverse disciplinary and ideological perspectives, encouraging dialogue and disagreement; combining spectacle and philosophy, grassroots activism and radical theory; and utilizing fluid and disparate modes of exchange, from public conversations and roundtables to a proliferation of small-scale workshops. "I mean, we had R.D. Laing and the people involved in political movements dealing with asylums and prisons, and anti-psychiatry and all of that, which now seems kind of this lost radical moment, but then was very present."[3]

1. Personal interview, 2011. This reconstruction is drawn from interviews conducted between 2011–13 by David Morris and Sylvère Lotringer. Unless noted all other quotations and documents are taken from the recordings and materials available in the archive at Fales library, NYU.
2. Rajchman, 2011.
3. Rajchman, 2011.

The press release promised "an unprecedented international exchange/confrontation … From France are coming the major representatives of a movement which since May '68 has produced a breakthrough more far-reaching than the existentialism of the fifties or the structuralism of the sixties. Called a 'revolution of desire' the movement, on the intellectual side, has introduced a strategy for dissolving and questioning systems which support them. On the pragmatic side, through its new analysis of capitalism, the movement has joined forces with the political challenge to psychiatric, penal, and patriarchal oppression as well as radical artistic innovation."

Hyped as a "slugfest" and selected as a "pick of the week" by *The Village Voice*, the weekend saw a mob of over two thousand descend on the venue, a group including radicals, ex-cons, students, psychiatrists, Black Panthers, experimental theater troupes, Marxists, and extremist quasi-Marxist provocateurs. Naturally, things got completely out of hand. Fights erupted in the audience, schedules broke down, talks were heckled and booed, and the speakers themselves argued constantly, changed the conference format, and upstaged and chased one another from the podium. "We invited people that were interested in these issues politically, but frequently, intellectually speaking were like Frankfurt school people or had different kinds of critical vocabularies. The fact that they were involved in those political and social movements was more important than their ideology, so retrospectively that's of course what produced lots of very odd tensions, that's maybe one way of thinking how we got into so much trouble."[4]

But it is only now that this event has come into view. It disappeared almost as soon as it happened: only a handful of academic publications give it more than a passing mention, none published before 2003. When I contacted Sylvère to ask about Schizo-Culture, he complimented my good timing: some of the original recordings had just been recovered and he was working on a comprehensive document of the event. Unlike comparable conferences from that era (and against the grain of academia) it was never documented in any significant way—the Schizo-Culture publication arrived three years late, with few of the papers and little indication that the event had ever happened. "It was an 'untimely' event, more powerful for what it still had in store than by its immediate impact," as Sylvère told me. "I was aware that it would take time for it to resurface. And I also realized that it shouldn't be resurrected historically, or explicitly, i.e.

4. Rajchman, 2011.

academically, that it would be better to hint at it discreetly here and there (mostly in footnotes and bibliographies in Semiotext(e) books) in order to raise people's attention—and desires to know more. The growing interest in Foucault, Deleuze and Guattari was bound to do it anyway, but I was weary of the way theory was being quickly co-opted and flattened out mediatically. I didn't want Schizo-Culture to become fashionable, and forgotten like everything else. I am still not sure that it will be a good thing to bring it out in the open now, but at least it could now be appreciated for what it was, and what it is."[5]

The 1966 John Hopkins conference "Languages of Criticism and the Sciences of Man" is sometimes suggested as a point of comparison (or at least an alternative entry-point for "French theory"), but Schizo-Culture was something quite different. "Languages of Criticism…" was a conference that quickly served its purpose, introducing figures from French intellectual life, such as Derrida, Lacan and Barthes, to American academia. It came with a "controversy" built in, but in announcing the arrival of structuralism—like so many translations into "theory"—it simultaneously announced its death as a living body of thought. Never really a cohesive intellectual movement to begin with, "structuralism" in France was hitting a dead end, just as its various mutations were taking off in the States.

By 1975 the sixties counterculture was also looking very different, and the long postwar economic boom was in free fall, a crisis that reached its peak during the years 1974–76. New York itself was a paradigm of hyper-congestion and deep irrationality: "It was a broken down city, very psychotic. So the conference was pretty well adapted to it. It really brought out the best and the worst of New York at the time."[6] Betty Kronsky, a therapist and conference attendee, observed at the time that "more has to be understood about the despair of living in the United States in 1975. We have given up on lucidity; our socioeconomic situation seems too murky to lend itself to analysis. We are too confused by the facts of our oppression—by the real facts, such as no jobs, a city about to default, news media reduced to the point where information becomes unavailable. Our French visitors came to us with an optimism which to us seemed glib and bizarre. …"[7]

As William Burroughs remarked: "I think that 'schizo culture' is being used here in a special sense, not referring so much to clinical schizophrenia but to the

5. Lotringer, 2011.
6. Lotringer, 2011.
7. Betty Kronsky (response letter, 1975).

fact that the culture is divided up into all sorts of classes and groups, et cetera, and some of the old lines are breaking down, and this is a healthy sign." Rajchman notes, "The thing was a little bit out of control ... for everybody. It was kind of a free space. It all sounds very nice and liberal but it opened up the possibilities for these incredible divisions and tensions."[8]

The conference began with introductions by Lotringer and Rajchman who made explicit some of the main concerns of the conference: to connect the French visitors with the New York avant-garde, and to break with "theoretical ghettos of all kinds" towards pragmatism and activism. Although much of Rajchman's talk "The Bodyguard" is lost, he recalls: "[in France] *Surveiller et punir* had just come out, and [Deleuze-Guattari's] 'bodies without organs', and the body is also rather important in art of the '70s. But what I said about it, I'm not sure." Whatever was said, Foucault was impressed: they stayed in contact, which (as well as the encounter with Deleuze) would be a strong influence on Rajchman's subsequent work.

The introductions were followed by James Fessenden's "Transversality and Style: Groups, Packs and Bands." Fessenden is described by philosopher Gillian Rose in her 1995 memoir *Love's Work*: "a philosopher, musician and aesthete, a 'dandy of thought' as he referred wryly to himself"[9] and she credits him with introducing her to continental philosophy, modern art and music, as well as the '70s New York scene. Fessenden was invited to Schizo-Culture by Rajchman, a friend and former colleague at Bennington College; by 1975 Fessenden had moved back to live on 111th Street and Broadway (Rose describes this tiny, cluttered, dusty apartment as "the emblem of the postmodern city"). At the time he was also working on a PhD on Nietzsche with Arthur Danto, and improbably later became Senior Commissioner investigating corruption and cocaine dealing in the New York City Police Dept., before his death as a result of AIDS in the early 1990s.

Fessenden's paper at Schizo-Culture was, as he affirms, "a bit fragmentary." The concept of transversality is taken from two early Guattari essays "Transversality" and "The Group and the Individual," concerning the problem of conducting psychoanalysis in group situations, specifically at La Borde, the experimental Lacanian clinic where he worked. Fessenden connected it in turn with Deleuze-Guattari's later work on packs, Proust and (anti-)Freudian theory. "Transversality" is a geometric, spatial term—a single line intersected by several other lines—and a mode

8. Rajchman, 2011.
9. Gillian Rose, *Love's Work*, p.101.

of organization: "Transversality is a dimension that tries to overcome both the impasse of pure verticality and that of mere horizontality: it tends to be achieved when there is maximum communication amongst different levels and, above all, in different meanings. It is this that an independent group is working towards."[10] Rather than a horizontal organization of multiple networked "centers," or a vertical, centralized "pyramid," Guattari's transversality requires a necessarily shifting, non-reproducible and a-centric model of organization, a model which he would attempt to put into practice the following day. Guattari's work in this area was also influential on psychiatric practice (see François Peraldi's "A Schizo and the Institution") as well as Semiotext(e)'s future formations.

A very different group interaction amongst different meanings would occur later that first day. The session paired Arthur Danto with Jean-François Lyotard—Danto spoke on the language of the unconscious and Lyotard gave an improvised lecture entitled "On the Strength of the Weak." Danto recalls Schizo-Culture as "about as close as real life offers to a Richard Foreman-like situation. Sylvère, for some reason, put me in the same slot that first evening as Lyotard, a man who has what I think of as the true gift of incoherence. The rest of the French have been trying to achieve it, but he was born with it, like perfect pitch. Lyotard spoke in French, and there was a table with three people whose purpose was to translate what Lyotard was saying. Here was Lyotard in front of the microphone, here were three graduate students. And they couldn't agree! Finally, they would say, 'Well, we think this is what he means …'"[11]

Roger McKeon remembers slightly differently: "I was Lyotard's designated consecutive 'interpreter'. At some point in the delivery of his talk, an unknown dude in the audience started hollering that the translation was not to his liking, so I invited him to step up and replace me. He did so and did not last very long, thank god. He had no idea what he was taking on and very quickly got on everyone's nerves, except for Lyotard's, who was most amused."[12] And had Danto stayed to listen, he would have seen the translation develop into a more complex process. On the tape recording, audience members interject their own versions of Lyotard's points; they argue, discuss, agree, and argue some more as the talk

---

10. See Guattari's "Transversality, " in *Molecular Revolution: Psychiatry and Politics*.

11. Arthur Danto, from roundtable discussion "Beyond Sense and Nonsense: Perspectives on the Ontological at 30" in *Theater*, Fall 1997 28(1): 22–34.

12. Roger McKeon, 2011.

goes on. The situation became increasingly confrontational, but after some confusion the translation was negotiated collectively and dispersed throughout the assembled group. As one participant, Claudine Eizykman, recalls: "Jean-François Lyotard's talk took place in great tension with the public as the subject required intense concentration, and the author's struggle with his demonstration of the paradox of the liar was brought to fruition by sharing the anxiety and intensity of a thought in the making."[13]

On the second day of the conference a panel discussion was scheduled with Joel Kovel, François Peraldi, Robert Fine, and chaired by Félix Guattari. Kovel was known as a radical psychiatrist for his psychoanalytic study, *White Racism* (1972), and had recently joined the *Telos* collective. A revised version of his paper can be found in *Telos*, Winter 1976–77, and reflects Kovel's intellectual concerns at the time, attempting to apply this newfound Marxism to his own psychoanalytic practice: "trying to become a Marxist-Freudian, or a Freudo-Marxian." The panel marks the first of Guattari's structural interventions, as Kovel remembers, "I felt that I didn't belong at this conference from the beginning, and then of course the next day was very chaotic … Félix was to chair, and he came and explicitly said 'I am the chair of this panel and I abolish this panel!' And that really infuriated me… he asked people to follow him, so a considerable number of people got up and left the audience and I just said 'listen, I worked hard on this and I don't care what you guys do, but I'm here to read my paper'…and I just read my paper. And a lot of people stayed, and then the other two guys read their papers…and it wasn't the end of the world but it certainly was a shocking experience."[14]

Another observer noted that "The American audience might have been more friendly to Guattari if they had better understood from him how much he had learned from us. … Guattari should have understood that given the tension and paranoias with which we all now live, his efforts to tamper with the format would have been interpreted as an act of demagoguery."[15] Yet even those who chose not to follow seemed to agree. Robert Fine remembers a theater group "who were very taken by Guattari's critique of rationality, his sense of poetry, and lived it out,

13. Claudine Eizykman, 2011.
14. Kovel, 2011.
15. Kronsky, 1975.

played it out, acted it out, and he got quite cross at the way they were acting it out."[16] On the recordings you also hear Fine facing a barrage of criticism, from "Robert Fine, I'm mad at you!" to "This is an exercise in the tyranny of intellectualism, co-opting revolutionary energy!" (to much applause). François Peraldi compared the situation to the problematic group formations of his experimental clinic, and the struggle of the staff to improve their situation: "When you sent Félix Guattari away at the beginning of the conference, that was a gesture of power. And then you are going to talk about power somewhere in the prisons, somewhere in the psychiatric hospital, and you won't be able to analyze what's happening here!"[17]

As Peraldi would explain in his paper, "Power does not function through the substance of the contents, of the ideologies, but rather, on the level of the form of the contents… those forms specific to communication."[18] Peraldi (1938–1993) completed his analytic training in Paris and earned his doctorate in linguistics under Roland Barthes and would later edit *Polysexuality* (Semiotext(e), 1981) and teach at the University of Montreal. He died as a result of AIDS in 1993 but still has a following for his seminars and theoretical work. Like other speakers, Peraldi continually returned to a spatial analysis of the institution, and the actors within it, describing schizophrenia's "fantastic use of space," and the importance of displacement: not to force things to fit the world but to open a breach, to produce new spaces within that world.

Robert Fine, then a young Marxist sociologist, was invited to the conference by Rajchman: "I didn't know much about it when he invited me, but I was working in England and I thought 'what the heck?' I'll go along, it'll be a trip down to New York. … I had no idea what I was coming to." Fine's paper was on prisons by way of a discussion of deviance and Bentham's Panopticon (see also Rajchman's "The Bodyguard"). 1975 was the year of *Surveiller et punir*, but Fine came to the Panopticon independently and in a classical Marxist framework. The talk is notable for the audience's hostility towards Fine's high-academic reading (as fellow panel member François Peraldi puts it: "Don't just read the paper! This was an absolute travesty!"). Fine, for his part, was unfazed: "There were attacks from various left-wingers, and from Black groups, and from women, you know, so it was a bit of a

16. NB. Fine remembers it as the Living Theater, but most likely it was Richard Foreman's group as the Living Theater were in Europe at the time.
17. Peraldi (at Schizo-Culture, 1975).
18. See Peraldi's "A Schizo and the institution" from Schizo-Culture Issue.

humdinger of different leftwing orientations, as it were, having a go at the main speakers. I was in a Trotskyist group at the time in England, there were a couple of groups in England who would do that kind of thing… so I was used to it."[19]

So as it turned out, Schizo-Culture was more about confrontation than connection. As one attendee asked "Have you forgotten the suspicions and hostilities many Americans have against Frenchmen, against intellectuals, against academicians, against leftists, and against French intellectual academician leftists overwhelmingly?"[20] Another wrote that "'all forms of madness' were not, in fact, being treated equally. At one point I heard Sylvère Lotringer scream at a spectator 'That's what it comes down to, doesn't it: anti-intellectual, anti-French.'"[21] But it is possible to sketch out several distinct but related schisms that these arguments reveal—looking back, it is clear that the event's many confrontations identify deeper ruptures that would take years or even decades to surface.

"For the most part, Marxist language was out of favor at the conference, even though most of the speakers saw themselves as political people, and shared assumptions that were basically Marxist ones. There seemed to be a constant anxiety about this problem."[22] Foucault and Lyotard are paradigmatic of a whole generation that tried to move beyond the Marxism they grew up with—Deleuze would later remark, "Félix Guattari and I have remained Marxists, in our two different ways," but each of the French thinkers' "different ways" would alienate Anglophone ideologues new and old. Michel Rosenfeld—who chaired the panel with Laing and Foucault—remembers that "they all talked about pragmatism, but it meant different things for different sides."[23] Lyotard was in America at the invitation of the Frankfurt-Marxist journal *Telos*, but his thinking was now far removed from his younger "intellectual militancy." In particular his experience of the Algerian Revolution led him to reject the grand narratives of classical Marxism, sensing that Algeria would require a new articulation of interests from within Algerian society, on the basis of individuals or small collectivities.[24] As he wrote of Marx in 1974, "We will rather treat him as a 'work of art.'"[25]

---

19. Fine, 2011.
20. Kronsky, *ibid.*
21. Barbara Damrosch, unpublished article, 1975.
22. Damrosch, *ibid.*
23. Rosenfeld, 2013.
24. See Lyotard 'Algeria' http://www.marxists.org/history/etol/newspape/isj/1963/no013/lyotard.htm
25. *Economie Libidinale* (1974; published as *Libidinal Economy*, 1993).

And if "Marx, Freud and Saussure make up a strange, three-headed Repressor, a dominant major language,"[26] the crowd's antipathy towards dominant language is palpable in the conference recordings—as someone shouts at Robert Fine, "Tell us in language we can understand!" At the same time, the post-Marxist colonization of old Marxist concerns like prisons and institutional politics left many others baffled and bemused. Kovel recalls the pre-conference reception at the French consulate:

> I received this letter saying such-and-such number on Fifth Avenue—Wow—and I lived on the other side of the park, so I walked over and this is the government of France, you know, it was in a building of extreme elegance, 79th St. and Fifth Ave … it was crazy, it was an official French government reception. Now in my later years I always feel I have a lot to learn about this world, and I certainly felt I had a lot to learn back then, but one thing I know for sure is that France is a capitalist country and the French state was a capitalist state, and the capitalist state was my enemy![27]

In the early 1970s an explosion of political activism aligned itself across race, sex and sexuality, in countless formations. "Without placing the upsurges of 1968–73 in the Black, Chicano, Asian American, Puerto Rican and American Indian communities, as well as among women and lesbians and gays, at the centre of analysis; and without grasping the links between those movements and the upheavals in the armed forces, the prisons, among welfare recipients, on many shop floors and among urban youth—it is simply impossible to grasp those years' political dynamics and the reasons that revolutionary ideas gained such a following."[28] "Most definitely there was a connection [with late sixties radicalism] I mean, it was different, late sixties radicalism was directly activist, and it was always about doing, you could never say anything without doing it, afterwards or at the same time. Whereas by '75 the activism in New York had pretty much come to an end and the Vietnam war was over so instead of the sort of activism that was true of the sixties, early seventies, you know, things had gone a bit crazy."[29]

---

26. Deleuze Dialogues, p.11.
27. Kovel, 2011.
28. Max Elbaum, *Revolution in the Air*, p.25.
29. Fine, 2011.

Mark Poster, who led a Frankfurt School workshop at Schizo-Culture and is also a member of the *Telos* collective remembers that "There was a feeling of things falling apart in '75, it seemed like the movement could not be sustained much longer and was losing a sense of direction and community."[30] And alongside internal divisions there were increasing attacks from governmental and miscellaneous other forces, such as Lyndon LaRouche's Labor Committee (who accused Foucault of being paid by the CIA)—"The Larouchites were just nightmares. I used to see them again and again ... They had techniques of kind of like induced madness. They would go and break up meetings, so their job was sort of to destroy the New Left, and destroy solidarity. And it played not a huge role but a very definite role in the fractionating of the US left into a lot of small [groups]."[31]

As Guattari reflected towards the end of the conference, "There is something like a CIA virus here. I can't help asking myself whether I haven't caught the bug."[32] Still, it remains unclear who was, and was not, CIA. Besides the Larouchites there was Richard Foreman's Ontological-Hysteric Theater choreographing stunts in the crowd— "It was hilarious. Doubtless, at least some of the disruptions were staged"[33]—as well as other more foreboding figures: "In the later session, the one I was involved with, they occupied the room before we got there, Doug Kellner and I, and once we tried to kick them out, claiming it was our room scheduled for the panel, they started taking pictures of us as if they were CIA agents, you know, to intimidate us."[34] "There were rumors they were connected to the Russians, there were rumors they were connected to Rockefeller, big capital, and so on."[35]

Following Guattari to the "schizo-discussion" Foucault chose to deliver his paper, much earlier than scheduled, to the assembled group (it was read out by his translator Mark Seem whilst Foucault looked on). Schizo-Culture was one of his first major speaking appearances in the United States, and this paper marks the beginning of the final period of Foucault's work—the "period of crisis," as Deleuze later characterized it—in which he would go on to develop his accounts of governmentality, neoliberal politics and biopower. Foucault took this opportunity

30. Poster, 2011.
31. Kovel, 2011.
32. Guattari (at Schizo-Culture, 1975).
33. John Bell Young, 2011.
34. Poster, 2011.
35. Fine, 2011.

to introduce his projected five-part History of Sexuality, and his paper is an early draft of part of the opening volume, *La volonté de savoir* (1976).

Foucault's paper had two further targets: the first is the Freudian concept of repression as developed by Wilhelm Reich, later taken up by Frankfurt Marxists and the '60s 'sexual revolution'. His second target is the 'enunciators' of the repressive concept: i.e. Frankfurt School Marxism. Foucault attacks those who 'only speak', mistaking their discourse for political interventions 'at the same time inscribed in reality'—a provocation for armchair radicals old and new. This also anticipated a much broader collision, between French and German traditions of critical thought (see, for example, the Foucault-Habermas debate), whose commitments led them to theorize very close to one another, but from completely opposite positions; a confrontation on competing demands of rationality, politics, and modernity.

Foucault's lecture kicked off his 'crisis period', and similarly Lyotard's talk marks a transition in the development of his ideas, a move away from economies of desire and towards 'the postmodern'. Formerly a natural ally of Deleuze-Guattari, in his lecture Lyotard criticized 'the schizo-culture trend' for taking an 'outside' position. But his solution is another linguistic turn, to turn the 'master dialogue' against itself' and accelerate the decline of truth. This later linguistic phase—seen in texts such as *La Condition postmoderne: Rapport sur le savoir* (1979) and the agonistic demands of *Le Différend* (1983)—is what would subsequently estrange Lyotard from his theoretical allies. Even at the conference itself the French visitors were reportedly unimpressed by Lyotard's talk, a suggestion of the break that was to come.[36]

Elsewhere, "Foucault managed to rather indimidate Guattari—Guattari was in full flow at one of his talks when Foucault entered the room, and Guattari just couldn't carry on speaking, he lost his whole thread."[37] "I remember walking in a subway with Foucault and Guattari where there was lots of tension between the two I didn't quite understand. … the two figures were already involved in their separate groups, they came [to Schizo-Culture] with that energy, and then they divided or split up."[38] And these crises coincided with the most fertile and frantic period of postwar French thought: "I was surprised first of all how many

36. See Sylvère's introduction.

37. Fine, 2011.

38. Rajchman, 2011. See also Deleuze's letter to Foucault published under the title "Desire and Pleasure."

disagreements and tensions the whole thing generated. But, you know, tensions are not necessarily bad, and divisions and problems are not necessarily negative. When you open things up a little bit you necessarily have this clash of forces." [39]

"On the evening of the second day William Burroughs, crotchety and abrupt, talked about how the powerful grow weak in protecting themselves against the people they have hired to protect them; how trying to kill a story makes it news; how controllers of colonies become more stupid and shortsighted than those they control; and how dangerous governments can be when they are in the process of defeating themselves."[40] The CIA interruptions led Foucault to denounce Schizo-Culture as the end of the sixties counterculture, but at that time William Burroughs was still very much an emblem of that era. Lotringer, with James Grauerholz and John Giorno, would later organize 1978's Nova convention, again placing Burroughs in dialogue with a dizzying array of figures from the New Wave, No Wave and avant-gardes, "to put him back on the map in his home country." The Burroughs event makes an interesting comparison:

> At the time New York artists were mostly anti-intellectual, including William Burroughs who had a healthy distrust of "intellectuals" (which he himself was in his own way). [The Nova convention] was easier to put on the map since it assembled around him, for the last time, the entire American artistic "avant-garde." The event had a huge coverage, a dozen pages in the Village Voice and in the Soho News. It was retrospective, not untimely, and fulfilled everybody's acknowledged wishes. It was an important, but recognizable event. The last gasp of a vitality that went back to the '60s. The potential of Schizo-Culture could only have been grasped much later on. What shows this very clearly is that in spite of the huge crowd that attended, there was no media coverage, except the leftist WBAI. Not one article in English, or one photo were ever published in the press, nothing in the media to recognize the unusual nature of the event. It wasn't easily identifiable, because it was bringing strains of the culture(s) that were not usually woven together. That it exploded in many different ways underlines the fact that there were different fault lines that were activated on this occasion.[41]

---

39. Rajchman, 2011.
40. Damrosch, *ibid.*
41. Lotringer, 2011.

Burroughs' understanding of Schizo-Culture is impeccably Deleuzian, and in turn Deleuze would frequently refer to Burroughs in his own work. Burroughs had an inbuilt French connection from the Paris Beat Hotel, where he and Brion Gysin discovered the cut-up, a strategy both aesthetic, literary, to "establish new connections between images, [so] one's range of vision consequently expands"[42] but more importantly, political: to reveal subliminal codes, break down the linguistic sequence (see Louis Wolfson, or Cage's *Empty Words*), and produce new propaganda, new forces. "Everything had meaning. The danger and the fear were real enough. When somebody is trying to kill you, you know it. Better get up off your tail and fight."[43]

The conference also hosted a wide range of small-scale workshops for attendees to participate in, on a diverse range of subjects, from experimental theater and filmmaking to psychoanalysis and local drug rehabilitation clinics: scheduled sessions included "When a Poet is Accused of Murder" (with The Last Poets), "Psychiatry and Social Control," "Schizo-City," "Cinema: Representation and Energetics," "Network Intervention in Schizophrenia," "Feminism and Therapy," "Mental Patients' Liberation," "Gay Liberation" and "Politics of Psycho-Surgery."

"Some of the best discussion took place in small workshops, where people involved with social problems talked about their work without egotism, sexism and mystification, and really tried to look on the other side of the obvious. Two feminist therapists, Susie Orbach and Lela Zaphiropoulos, talked about the problem of mothers and daughters in a way I'd never heard before Ron Bayer noted that the recent decline in the population of mental institutions shouldn't give us reason to rejoice: it is simply the result of de-funding, and an increasing reliance on drugs. Irene Javors, in a brief history of women, madness and patriarchy, showed how middle class women have been considered weaker than men, hence more prone to madness, and how lower class ones have been seen as closer to nature, hence stronger than men and able to withstand harsher forms of 'cure.'"[44]

Irene Javors has written extensively on cultural and mental health issues, as well as being a practicing psychotherapist. She agrees that much of the real work

42. Burroughs interview in *Burroughs Live*, also cut up into Burroughs and Gysin's *The Third Mind*, p.4.
43. Burroughs, *The Western Lands*, p.252 on his discovery of the cut-up technique.
44. Damrosch, *ibid.*

of the conference took place away from the "organized chaos and overblown male egos competing with each other" that characterized the main part of the conference.[45] In light of her continued work in the field, Javors reflects "I participated on a panel whose topic was the de-institutionalization of the mentally ill. … Unfortunately, the US absorbed these de-constructionist ideas and closed the asylums claiming that the needs of the mentally ill could be served in assisted living facilities. As expected, this didn't work well, no oversight as to medication and care, and many ended up on the street." But "despite the '70s outré overlay to the conference, the organizers were making a heartfelt attempt to deal with psychiatric abuses—I wish that there would be such an attempt today given the current over-medicating and over-diagnosing."[46] Javors was also involved in setting up a feminist therapy center in Manhattan at the time, and anti-psychiatry was closely related to the Women's Movement, seen in institutions like the Association for Women in Psychology (co-founded by Phyllis Chesler). There is a darker side to this connection—in her 1970 essay "Woman and Her Mind: The Story of Everyday Life," Meredith Tax presents "female schizophrenia" as a description of women's everyday experience, and the condition recurs both as metaphor and, in some cases, clinical reality in histories of second wave feminism.

In the 1960s and 1970s, a diverse collection of social and political forces coalesced around the politics of madness (as a clinical entity) and madness as a process (à la Artaud). The movement drew its impetus from thinkers on both sides of the Atlantic: Thomas Szasz's *The Myth of Mental Illness* (1960) and R.D. Laing's *The Divided Self* (1960) were extremely influential, and in France Foucault had just completed his study on the history of madness, translated in abridged form as *Madness and Civilization* (1964), and *The Birth of the Clinic* (1973). There was a very different form of anti-psychiatry in France, with groups such as "Psych et Pol" (associated with Antoinette Fouque and Héléne Cixous), Jacques Lacan's psychoanalysis as subversion, experimental institutions like La Borde, Deleuze-Guattari's *Anti-Oedipe* (1972), and countless post-'68 institutional and political struggles. (Sherry Turkle, who apparently was at Schizo-Culture, has written in detail on French anti-psychiatry.)[47]

45. Javors, 2012.

46. Javors, 2012.

47. See Turkle's paper "French Anti-Psychiatry" (1980). Robert D'Amico: "If I recall correctly the writer Sherry Turkle attended, but did not give a talk … I remember us sitting together at the back of an auditorium waiting for something to start."

At the final day's roundtable session Foucault and Laing were paired with activists Judy Clark and Howie Harp; Laing barefoot, feet dangling from the stage. The subsequent Q&A is lost, but Lynne Tillman recalls one of Laing's remarks, that "graduate students [are] the most depressed population in any society."[48] Howie Harp was a founding member of numerous activist groups and support centers including the Psychiatric Survivors, Project Release, Mental Patients Liberation Front, and the Oakland Independence Support Center. The anti-psychiatry movement was also driven in large part by ground level organizing such as Harp's. A former psychiatric patient himself, he has said about his work: "I don't really believe in those labels, but there have been times in my life when I went into what can be called a manic episode, and when I went into severe depressions. What I'm doing with my life right now is trying to learn how to control what I call manic energy. If it can be controlled and directed and channeled, it could be really valuable and real powerful. I'd rather learn how to control it, rather than be cured of it."[49] At the time Judy Clark was working with the National Lawyers Guild to edit "The Midnight Special," a newspaper written by prisoners, comparable to the newsletters of the GIP (Group de l'information sur les prisons—of which Foucault was a founding member—which gathered and published prisoner's accounts of their situation). Clark would become involved with the Black Liberation Army, and was jailed in 1983 for her role as getaway driver in a Brinks truck holdup (see Sylvère's introduction). The Black Panther movement seems also to have inspired many of Foucault and the GIP's own ideas about political incarceration and "war by other means."[50]

On the afternoon of the final day Gilles Deleuze was paired with John Cage. Deleuze spoke first, and his talk was one of the earliest presentations of their "rhizome"; long before the concept ever appeared in print and certainly the first time it had ever been presented to an English-speaking audience. Asked afterwards by *Le Monde* whether it was necessary to speak differently to an American audience, he explained: "I had the same experience in Italy, when people could not understand the language. Basically, it doesn't much matter. Take John Cage for instance, he invented a language. We are all equal, ahead of being French, American, or

48. Tillman, 2012.
49. *New York Times* obituary, 14th February 1995.
50. See Brady Thomas Heiner 'Foucault and the Black Panthers' City: Analysis of Urban Trends, *Culture, Theory, Policy, Action* 11.3 (December 2007): 313–56.

anything else."[51] Deleuze's performance "took place in a very good mood" and (despite his refusal of translation) even held up as an example of conceptual clarity: "It might have helped if some of the papers had been delivered in a prose that even non-semiologists might have understood. I am not a philistine, but I know there must be a simple way of summarizing some of the message, to cut through the paragraphs with a metaphor as did Deleuze and Guattari."[52]

And the rhizome has had a wild and diverse influence, as well as an inbuilt American connection, as Deleuze-Guattari later wrote, "Everything important that has happened or is happening takes the route of the American rhizome: the beatniks, the underground, bands and gangs… Patti Smith sings the bible of the American dentist: Don't go for the root, follow the canal …"[53] The preview of Schizo-Culture in *The Village Voice* even promised that "The event will culminate with a Schizo Party on November 16 with Patti Smith"; although it's not clear she ever knew about it, and she didn't show up.

Cage presented his own 'new language' during the same afternoon session, performing part of his 'Empty Words'. Lynne Tillman remembers: 'He walked onto the stage and began to speak, without the microphone. He stood at the center of the small stage and addressed the crowd. He talked without amplification, and soon people in the audience shouted, "We can't hear you. Use the mike. We can't hear you." John Cage said, 'You can, if you listen.' Everyone stopped doing whatever he or she was doing, settled down, there was no more buzz or rustling, there was silence, and John Cage spoke again, without the microphone, and everyone listened and heard perfectly."[54]

Cage had been performing "Empty Words" since 1974. The piece uses text as a means of musical production, by applying I Ching chance operations to Thoreau's notebooks. An unidentified speaker on one of the recordings remarks: "There's a lot can act upon the state of flux. Take Cage's example, Cage's example, of a rhizomatic movement from music to sound. And music … and voids and spaces and silence." As Cage remarked in 1974 "what was interesting me was

51. Quoted in Bernard Merigot "La Schizo Culture a New York: Notes sur un colloque", *Le Monde* (undated copy held in Fales archive).
52. Eizkyman, 2011; Kronsky, 1975.
53. Deleuze and Guattari, *A Thousand Plateaus*, p.21. See also Michelle Koerner's "The Uses of Literature: Gilles Deleuze's American Rhizome," http://dukespace.lib.duke.edu/dspace/handle/10161/3033.
54. Tillman, 2012.

making English less understandable. Because when it's understandable, well, people control one another, and poetry disappears … I was talking with my friend Norman O. Brown, and he said, "Syntax (which is what makes things understandable) is the army, is the arrangement of the army."[55]

The final evening session of the conference paired Ti-Grace Atkinson with Félix Guattari. Atkinson asked to speak second, and so Guattari began to improvise from his notes, over the noise of a band setting up on the stage. He reflected on the events of the weekend, and his attempts to break up the conventions of political radicalism in order that something new and durable might emerge: "In our terminology (i.e. with Gilles Deleuze) this instrument is called a collective arrangement of enunciation. This doesn't mean it's necessarily a group: A collective arrangement of enunciation can bring both people and individuals into play—but also machines, organs. [It] is not a solution by the group. It is simply an attempt to create opportunities of conjunction between different semiotic components in order that they not be systematically broken, linearized, separated."

But in fact, Guattari's talk was cut short by his fellow speaker Ti-Grace Atkinson. Throughout Schizo-Culture Atkinson and her followers had been confronting the other speakers, and the situation was surely exacerbated by an angry exchange the previous day with Foucault: "They said 'you're not interested in women' or something like that, and he said 'you're right, I'm not—you're interested in women, you do it!"[56] Since the mid-1960s, radical currents within the Women's Movement would frequently find themselves at odds with the male-dominated New Left. With tension running high and the band looking set to drown out Atkinson's turn to speak, all hell broke loose—Guattari was heckled and booed until he left (or according to some accounts, was chased) from the stage.

In 1968 Atkinson had resigned as president of the New York chapter of the National Organization of Women—cutting ties with the chapter group she'd co-founded, she formed a new group, The Feminists, and began to pursue a more radical understanding of feminism. The two-part essay "Declaration of War/Metaphysical Cannibalism" (1969) provides something of a mission statement: towards, amongst other things, a nonbiological class-based analysis of gender, and tactical steps for its eventual destruction/transcendence.[57] (The essay

55. Cage interview, August 8th, 1974 (available on archive.org).
56. Fine, 2011.
57. *Amazon Odyssey*, p.47.

was written for a major Canadian news magazine, but rejected on the grounds that it was "too esoteric.") Her early influence on radical feminism is hard to overstate, but her work from this period was never published in an extended format (although a detailed sketch can be made from her public lectures and papers in the 1974 collection *Amazon Odyssey*).

At Schizo-Culture she asked "Can you imagine a public debate held with several hundred people discussing whether or not indeed we should use violence as a tactic? This event speaks for itself. An oppressed people depends much upon surprise as a weapon."[58] The second part of Atkinson's introduction of radical feminism, following her "Declaration of War," was "Metaphysical Cannibalism." As she explained, this means "to eat one's own kind, especially that aspect considered most potent to the victim whilst alive—its constructive imagination." This is the basis for Atkinson's theory of oppression, and her projected unpublished "dream book" *Women and Oppression*. Her account of the pathology of oppression is based on a "dilemma at the heart of being"; the oppressor attempts to resolve this dilemma at the expense of others, seeking power and venting frustration; whereas the oppressed attempts to resolve it via self-destruction, insanity, or other "mental escapes." [59]

Like many other important feminists of that time, and in stark contrast to many of the other speakers at Schizo-Culture, Atkinson disappeared from public intellectual life during the 1970s—as Kate Millett writes: "Recently a book inquired Who Stole Feminism? I sure didn't. Nor did Ti-Grace Atkinson. Nor Jill Johnston. We're all out of print. .... Some women in this generation disappeared to struggle alone in makeshift oblivion. Or vanished into asylums and have yet to return to tell the tale, as has Shula Firestone. There were despairs that could only end in death: Maria del Drago chose suicide, so did Ellen Frankfurt, and Elizabeth Fischer, founder of *Aphra*, the first feminist literary journal."[60]

A letter written "To the organizers of the Schizo-Culture conference" in 1975 concludes: "Finally, let me say that I am excited about this conference and

---

58. From "The Psyche of Social Movements," lecture given at Schizo-Culture, 1975.
59. See Ti-Grace Atkinson's *Amazon Odyssey* for a detailed account of this theory and http://www.glennhorowitz.com/dobkin/women_and_oppression for more details of the unfinished typescript
60. From *The Guardian* (London) Tuesday June 23, 1998—an excerpt titled "The Feminist Time Forgot" was circulated widely online, but not Millett's self-described "longer and funnier" version, "Out of the Loop," *On the Issues Magazine*, Summer 1998.

would like to attend its sequel, where the real issues might yet be joined. Meanwhile, I am encouraged by the knowledge that I have always felt comfortable with rhizomatic phenomena, perhaps because I am an American and a woman."[61] As well as the clashes there were other unexpected points of connection across Schizo-Culture; for instance, the general resistance to forms of institutionalized or financialized language (cf. also Ti-Grace Atkinson's resignation from N.O.W. over "an essentially linguistic clarification."). At another point Guattari is asked whether there is a form of writing specific to capitalism; he describes a process of 'degeneration of collective arrangements of enunciation ... the transmission of information quantified in 'bits.'" He rejects this process—"what could be called digitalization, putting everything into digits"—but also rejects the old forms of counterculture spectacle, with their "myth[s] of a return to nature and spontaneity."

Frequently—quite deliberately—Schizo Culture existed in a space between politics and pure theater. Richard Foreman was invited by Lotringer to run an experimental theater workshop, in which he proposed "the question to all artists working today should be 'Can you do it "wrong"?'" Apparently inspired by Guattari's interventions, Foreman's group also began to perform and disrupt during the conference itself. His invitation to the Ontological-Hysteric Theater workshop states: "The theater ... as a totally corrupt form, in which a certain dream of "expressiveness" has joined with a second dream of "doing it well" to produce, almost without exception, a universe of kitsch ..." Far from "transmissions of information," for better or worse Schizo-Culture was an event of encounters, live interventions, performance: "Compounded. Intensified. Spread out on a canvas (the stage) wide enough so that within the terms of that error, new spaces, gaps, appear..."

Jean-Jacques Lebel also ran a workshop during the weekend, based on the 1974 Carnation revolution, titled "Portugal: the beginning of the beginning." Lebel is a key figure in the post-war conversation between French and American avant-gardes: encouraged by Marcel Duchamp (Lebel's father was a friend) but expelled from the Surrealists by André Breton, he was responsible for importing American beat poetry to France, and conversely, with orchestrating the first American Happening in Europe ("L'enterrement de la chose" in Venice, 1960). Lebel was active in the street actions of '68, and a believer in the political promise of theater, as well the theatrical promise of politics: "the first stage of an

61. Betty Kronsky *ibid.*

uprising, the first stage of any revolution, is always theatrical… a gigantic fiesta, a revelatory and sensuous explosion outside of the 'normal' pattern of politics."[62]

As well as this, Schizo-Culture happened both within and without its institutional setting. It took place inside university buildings but Columbia wanted nothing to do with it, so Semiotext(e) had to pay for campus facilities—on one recording you even hear a workshop being ejected mid-session. As such, it opened up a space outside of academic "information exchanges." Rajchman notes that "[Deleuze] seemed to already have had a very interesting model for how philosophy participates in these other kinds of spaces, why it needs them, why it's addressed to this outside space, while yet still being academic in some ways."[63]

In his essay alluding to Burroughs' lecture at Schizo-Culture, Deleuze writes "We are in a generalized crisis in relation to all the environments of enclosure; prison, hospital, factory, school, family. But everyone knows that these institutions are finished, whatever the length of their expiration periods. It's only a matter of administering their last rites and of keeping people employed until the installation of the new forces knocking at the door."[64] And Schizo-Culture can be seen in just such terms—a process of breaking down, but also opening up. For Sylvère personally "Schizo-Culture just broke me apart. I went, for months I was totally isolated. I was this strange guy in town, and it was like, a little scary, so I went through all these periods where I was a bit crazy. … Schizo-Culture was a definite earthquake, it broke up in all directions, and it was a wonderful event for that. I don't think anyone could have wanted it that way, because it just exploded, but the explosion was good for me, I never regretted it. It was a definite new departure."[65]

The press release announced the conference as a tool for predicting the future, as well as a means of individual and social change. But as one attendee asked: "I am grateful to you for having organized the conference, which introduced me to an important current of thought previously unknown to me. However, I am also left with a feeling of discomfort and sadness related to the smoldering hostilities and lack of receptivity of the conference participants. How to understand the complex phenomena of the weekend?"[66]

---

62. Lebel, 'Notes on Political Street Theater, Paris: 1968, 1969' *The Drama Review*. 1969–06, nr. 44, p.112.
63. Rajchman, 2011.
64. Deleuze "Postscript on the Societies of Control"; see also "Control and Becoming."
65. Lotringer, 2011.
66. Betty Kronsky *ibid.*, emphasis mine.

In one barely-audible fragment from the conference recordings, an unknown speaker explains: "a book, how it speaks, or a lecture, is not something to be understood. It must not be interpreted: it must be experienced, it must be *used*." For Rajchman "it was good this was out of control in a certain sense. A lot of my memories of this period, and I think even of the conference itself, have to do with that formation of groups, the spaces in which the energies that come into those groups, how they produce things. ... And so if you like that kind of intellectual approach you retrospectively think 'my god!' ... at the time that seemed much less coherent, much less extraordinary.[67] Or in John Cage's words, it is perhaps best understood as an experiment, 'not ... to be later judged in terms of success and failure, but simply as of an act, the outcome of which is unknown."[68]

So the more pressing and difficult question is what Schizo-Culture means in the present; how its actions and schisms might be used in a different way, now. The event has been historicized in various ways, as a point of entry for "French theory" into the United States, as marking the end of the sixties or even announcing the start of the nineties. But really it makes little sense in terms of cause and effect: it arrived at the wrong time and fell apart. Roger McKeon suggests that "Schizo-Culture in itself is not all that important, and I'm not sure it can be considered to have had (and even less to still have) an impact or a legacy of its own. You cannot unleash liberty and expect it to stay the course. Maybe that is the true lesson to be learned from the circus: a tightrope walker should not expect to have followers."[69]

Or perhaps its followers arrived right on time. "Now that Semiotext(e) has a bit more visibility, and that more people understand the kind of politics we have pursued for all these years, Schizo-Culture will be viewed in an entirely different way than it would have been ten or twenty years ago, and will make it worth it retrospectively. Events don't have to be picked up when they happen, one can recognize them by the fact that they left many things incomplete and that one could still extend them differently in a different context and historical situation. Whether it will do that or not, we'll see."[70]

---

67. Rajchman, 2011.
68. Cage, "Experimental Music: Doctrine" (1955) in *Silence: Lectures and Writings* p.13 (also referenced by Deleuze-Guattari in *Anti-Oedipus* p. 371. See also their *What is Philosophy*, p.111: "experimentation is always that which is in the process of coming about—the new, remarkable and interesting that replace the appearance of truth and are more demanding than it is.... History is not about experimentation, it is only the set of almost negative conditions that make possible the experimentation of something that escapes history.")
69. McKeon, 2011.
70. Lotringer, 2011.